FINANCE, TRADE, AND POLITICS
IN BRITISH FOREIGN POLICY
1815-1914

Finance, Trade, and Politics
in British Foreign Policy
1815-1914

D. C. M. PLATT

CLARENDON PRESS · OXFORD

1968

Oxford University Press, Ely House, London W.1

GLASGOW NEW YORK TORONTO MELBOURNE WELLINGTON
CAPE TOWN SALISBURY IBADAN NAIROBI LUSAKA ADDIS ABABA
BOMBAY CALCUTTA MADRAS KARACHI LAHORE DACCA
KUALA LUMPUR HONG KONG TOKYO

PRINTED IN GREAT BRITAIN BY
HAZELL WATSON AND VINEY LTD
AYLESBURY, BUCKS

ACKNOWLEDGEMENTS

I AM indebted to the Editors of the *Economic History Review* and *Inter-American Economic Affairs* for permission to use material which originally appeared in those journals.

Transcripts of Crown-copyright records in the Public Record Office and the Foreign Office Library appear by permission of the Controller of Her Majesty's Stationery Office, and I must also express my gratitude to The Curator of Historical Records at the Scottish Record Office for permission to quote from material in his custody.

It is a pleasure to acknowledge the patience and endurance of my wife, Sarah Platt, over the many years of preparation, and her active assistance in the presentation of the final typescript.

CONTENTS

LIST OF MAPS   ix

ABBREVIATIONS   xi

INTRODUCTION   xiii

I. H.M. GOVERNMENT AND OVERSEAS FINANCE

    Introduction   3
    1. The London Money Market and the Banks   7
    2. H.M. Government and the Bondholders   34
    3. Contracts and Concessions   54
    Conclusion   73

II. H.M. GOVERNMENT AND OVERSEAS TRADE

    Introduction   81
    1. Overseas Trade Policy   85
    2. British Commercial Diplomacy   102
    Conclusion   141

III. FINANCE, TRADE, AND BRITISH FOREIGN POLICY

    Introduction   151
    1. Egypt   154
    2. Turkey   181
    3. Persia   219
    4. Africa   249
    5. China and the Far East   262
    6. Latin America   308
    Conclusion   353

APPENDIXES
    1. Government Machinery for Overseas Trade
        1. London   371
        2. Overseas   381

II. Lord Palmerston's Circular on Loans to
Foreign States, January 1848   398

III. Edmund Hammond to Hyde Clark, 26
April 1871   400

IV. Earl Granville's Circular on Letters of
Introduction, 8 March 1881   402

V. James Bryce's Memorandum on Diplomatic
and Consular Assistance to British Trade
Abroad, 17 July 1886   403

VI. Extract from the Report of Sir Eyre
Crowe's Foreign Office Committee,
10 August 1916   416

SELECT BIBLIOGRAPHY   418

INDEX   435

LIST OF MAPS

1. The Near East   183

2. Persia, 1914   221

3. Africa, 1914   251

4. The Far East   264

5. Mexico and Central America   311

6. South America   314

ABBREVIATIONS

B.&F.S.P.:	British and Foreign State Papers (London, 1841–)
B.D.O.W.:	British Documents on the Origins of the War, 1898–1914, edited by G. P. Gooch and Harold Temperley (11 vol., London, 1926–1938)
P.R.O.,B.T.:	Public Record Office, London; Board of Trade papers
P.R.O.,F.O.:	Public Record Office, London; Foreign Office papers
F.O.,C.P.:	Foreign Office Library; Confidential Print
P.P.:	Parliamentary Papers
Parl.Deb.:	Parliamentary Debates
H.C.Deb.:	House of Commons Debates, 1909–
H.L.Deb.:	House of Lords Debates, 1909–

INTRODUCTION

IT IS one of the more curious features of British historiography that for the century before 1914—the century of Britain's leadership in world trade and finance—no serious study exists of the relationship between finance, trade, and politics in the conduct of British foreign policy. Some progress has been made in defining this relationship at a local level and over limited periods of time. But the few essays in general analysis are superficial, inadequately documented and, as often as not, politically distorted, identifying themselves with one side or another in the debate over 'economic imperialism'. As it is, although a great deal is known about political problems in British diplomacy, and more is rapidly being discovered about the purely economic relationship of the United Kingdom with its overseas markets, it cannot be said that the interaction between the two is fully understood. The diplomatic historian by-passes trade and finance; the economic historian has no patience with diplomacy. But can it be doubted that politicians and officials faced political and economic problems often at one and the same time, and that the answers they reached had both a political and an economic rationale?

*   *   *

British statesmen, however aristocratic, however inexperienced in trade and finance, could not afford to ignore Britain's dependence on overseas trade. They may have been interested in the political power which wealth brought with it, they may have believed that trade meant peace, or they may simply have agreed that economic progress brought greater happiness and more of the good things of life; but, whatever their reasons, they appreciated that the answer lay with trade. The younger Pitt's remark that 'British policy is British trade' explained what lay behind so much of British diplomacy—not necessarily as the first consideration, since national security naturally took first place, but as an important element both in contributing to that security and in its own right.

When Foreign Secretaries laid stress on the need to promote and protect British trade, they were making more than a polite

gesture to the 'tradesman'. Palmerston told the Commons in
1834 that to accuse a British Secretary of State of indifference to
the commercial interests of the country was to accuse him of
being deficient in common sense. A few years later he claimed
(in answer to the criticism that he had neglected British commercial interests injured by the French blockade of Buenos
Aires and Mexico) that there had never existed an Administration which had paid more attention to commercial interests than
the Government in which he served—British Ministers 'looked
upon the interest of England as the interest which ought to be
the polar star and guiding principle of their conduct.'[1] Lord
Clarendon, Foreign Secretary from 1853–58, 1865–66, and
1868–70, was known for the interest he took in British commerce. An ardent Free Trader, he had had some early experience of commercial affairs as a Commissioner of Customs and
as the negotiator of a commercial treaty with France in 1831,
and he had served briefly as President of the Board of Trade
before promotion to the Foreign Office. In answer to a question
from the Select Committee on Trade with Foreign Nations
(1864) in which it had been suggested that diplomatists (in the
opinion of commercial men) were inclined to give preference to
politics over commerce, Clarendon retorted that speaking for
himself if he were in authority there would be nothing he
would treat more severely than any neglect of commercial
interests; he was sure in any case that much more attention
was now being paid to commercial questions at the Foreign
Office and by all heads of Missions than twenty or thirty
years ago—'the magnitude of our commercial relations has
created an interest that did not exist before'.[2] Walter Bagehot,
in his biographical sketch of Lord Clarendon, draws attention
to the zeal for commerce which made him peculiarly suited
to the transition age in which he lived, possessing both the
aristocratic graces of the past and the commercial tastes and
business knowledge of the future. Bagehot explains, however,
that though Clarendon used the agency of the Foreign Office to
forward commercial interests, he employed only 'legitimate
functions' for trade promotion, interesting himself above all

1. 23 *Parl.Deb.*3s.790 (9 May 1834); 46 *Parl.Deb.*3s.904 (19 March 1839).
2. Minutes of Evidence, *Report of the Select Committee on Trade with Foreign
Nations*, P.P.1864(493)VII, Q.3045.

in the provision of commercial intelligence; he was too much a man of his times to adopt an aggressive foreign policy in the interests of trade, since 'the old notion of fighting for foreign markets, or of intriguing for their exclusive use, had completely died out'.[3]

British Foreign Secretaries, when compelled to define the general overseas policy of H.M. Government, emphasized the importance of trade. Lord Granville, who replaced Palmerston on his dismissal in 1851, was asked by the Queen to prepare a general statement which might guide the Cabinet in future. He drafted a Memorandum which explained that, while the Cabinet was not prepared to sacrifice 'all considerations of a higher character' in pushing our manufactures by any means into every corner of the world, 'yet considering the great natural advantages of our Foreign Commerce, and the powerful means of civilization it affords, one of the first duties of a British Government must always be to obtain for our Foreign Trade that security which is essential to its success'.[4] Lord Malmesbury, on taking office a few years later, prepared a short Circular to acquaint British diplomatists (and the Governments to which they were accredited) with the principles of British foreign policy. He stressed the great importance H.M. Government attached to the preservation of international peace and amity. Its surest guarantee, he said, was 'the maintenance and extension of commercial and social intercourse between nations', an object which H.M. Government would always keep in view and for which it was always prepared to negotiate.[5]

Granville remained at the Foreign Office until as late as 1885, and his general attitude—shared by his contemporaries and formed during the height of British pre-eminence in world trade—was inherited by his successors. But the pressure of foreign competition in the last decades of the century gave an extra edge to the interest of British statesmen in the condition of overseas trade. There was a great deal of truth, despite the hyperbole, in Joseph Chamberlain's remarks to the Birmingham

3. Walter Bagehot, *Biographical Studies* (London, 1881), pp. 346, 349.
4. Harold Temperley, 'Lord Granville's Unpublished Memorandum on Foreign Policy, 1852', *Cambridge Historical Journal*, II (1928), 299–300.
5. W. G. Beasley, 'Lord Malmesbury's Foreign Office Circular of 8 March 1858', *Bulletin of the Institute of Historical Research*, 23 (1950), 227.

Chamber of Commerce in November 1896. All the great Offices of State, he explained, were occupied with commercial affairs.

The Foreign Office and the Colonial Office are chiefly engaged in finding new markets and in defending old ones. The War Office and Admiralty are mostly occupied in preparations for the defence of these markets, and for the protection of our commerce. The Boards of Agriculture and of Trade are entirely concerned with those two great branches of industry. Even the Education Department bases its claim upon public money on the necessity of keeping our people well to the front in commercial competition which they have to sustain; and the Home Office finds the largest scope for its activity in the protection of the life and health of manual labourers who are engaged in those industries. Therefore, it is not too much to say that commerce is the greatest of all political interests, and that that Government deserves most the popular approval which does the most to increase our trade and to settle it on a firm foundation.[6]

Indeed, in considering the attitude of British statesmen to overseas trade, it is not the importance which they attached to trade which is in doubt so much as the methods they felt appropriate to its promotion.

Officials, whose business it was to shape general expressions of goodwill into a concrete policy, often felt less enthusiastic. But, even in the early days, there were always some who remained fully alive to the importance of trade. Stratford Canning, in a paper on 'International Relations' written from his retirement, came to the conclusion that we were acting 'in obedience to the Creator' in promoting and protecting the salutary process of international trade; commerce was the 'source of blessings to our race, the bond of nations, and first-born of peace'.[7] Sir Henry Bulwer, Stratford's successor at Constantinople, described himself to the British community 'as a Liberal who had devoted himself to trade, commerce, and finance, who was not a mere diplomat but a littérateur, an economist, and a practical man of business'.[8] Robert Morier

6. Quoted in W. H. S. Gastrell, *Our Trade in relation to Foreign Competition* (London, 1897), p. 14.
7. Viscount Stratford de Redcliffe, *The Eastern Question* (London, 1881), pp. 155–6.
8. As reported in Sir Edmund Hornby, *An Autobiography* (London, 1938), p. 117.

'made rather a speciality of commercial work'; he was an ardent Cobdenite and a close friend of Sir Louis Mallet at the Board of Trade. Giving evidence (while still a junior official) before the Select Committee on Trade with Foreign Nations, he claimed that the feeling among the younger members of the diplomatic service, who wished to make a serious profession of diplomacy, was that it was necessary to devote a considerable amount of attention to trading matters.[9] Interest continued to develop, and by 1914 Sir Arthur Hardinge's attitude was not unrepresentative. Hardinge was questioned by the Royal Commission on the Civil Service on the common complaint that British diplomatists were relatively reluctant to push the interests of commerce abroad. He agreed that this might have been more true in the past, when Victorian ambassadors were inclined to look on commercial disputes as 'largely consular matters', but he claimed that he had never known it to be so in his own time; rather, it had always been impressed upon British diplomatists that commercial competition was most important and that they should 'back up British traders strongly'.[10] Sir Austin Lee, giving evidence shortly afterwards, confirmed Hardinge's point. When he first went to Paris in 1872, there had been practically no contact whatsoever between the Embassy and the Chamber of Commerce, and this had continued to be the case for many years. However, there had been an entire change both in the Diplomatic and Consular Services, and there was now no reason for complaint. On the contrary, Lee thought that men now rather vied with each other in their attempts to make themselves commercially useful.[11]

* * *

To this extent, statesmen and officials were conscious of the priority of British trade and prepared to give it their support: the nature and limits of this support will be described in the following chapters. But in the century before 1914 there were certain barriers to a full and enthusiastic promotion by the State both of finance and trade overseas.

The complaints which the Royal Commission was investi-

9. Minutes of Evidence, *Report of the Select Committee on Trade with Foreign Nations*, P.P.1864(493)VII, Q.3154.
10. Minutes of Evidence, *Fifth Report of the Royal Commission on the Civil Service*, P.P.1914–16(Cd.7749)XI, Q.38,362.
11. ibid. Q.41,790.

gating when it examined Sir Arthur Hardinge merely repeated
those taken in evidence before every relevant Select Committee
and Royal Commission over the previous century, and they
were expressed as vigorously and persistently in the press and in
Chambers of Commerce at home and abroad. Francis Hirst, the
Editor of *The Economist*, gave a violently critical account to the
1914 Commission of the social and commercial attitude of the
Foreign Service. The Foreign Office, he claimed, had not, as
late as 1914, formulated any principles or rules about foreign
loans, concessions, or the Open Door; its attitude to commerce
was much that of 'the Homeric heroes or the Samurai of Japan'.
The only commercial agents received at the Embassies abroad
were the agents—normally aristocrats, ex-officers, or officials—
of the great armament companies; 'as to the other commercial
travellers, if they travel in soap, if they travel in Lancashire
cotton or West Riding cloth, or Nottingham lace, or Dundee
sacking, or Leicester hosiery, or the tools and machinery of the
Midlands and the North, you do not meet those unfortunate
commercial travellers at dinner at the embassies'.[12] Hirst's
point was confirmed by the amusing experience of Sir Lawrence
Jones, who visited Romania after the War to negotiate the
contract for the 1922 External Loan. He was given some help
by the Commercial Attaché, but had little to do with the
Ambassador. When finally he received an invitation to lunch
at the Embassy, the Ambassador's wife, Lady Dering, 'playfully
betrayed the rather revealing fact that, before our arrival, the
Ambassador had been under the impression that bankers were
not people to be received socially'.[13] Harold Nicolson, it
seems, was under a similar impression. Contrasting his views on
the status of government service with those of J. P. Morgan and
Company, he explained that the whole standpoint was different:
'you see . . . I regard bankers and banking as rather low-class
fellows. They regard officials as stupid and corrupt'.[14]

Many of the criticisms, no doubt, were wide of the mark. It
was not that British officials necessarily despised trade or undervalued its contribution to the national welfare; their opinion of

12. ibid. Q.40,658.
13. L. E. Jones, *Georgian Afternoon* (London, 1958), p. 106.
14. Nigel Nicolson (ed.), *Harold Nicolson. Diaries and Letters 1930–1939* (London, 1966), p. 203.

the best means of promoting the general interest simply differed from that of the merchant or financier. When Mr. Horsfall asked in the Commons (1857) for a Select Committee to enquire into the operation and improvement of the Board of Trade, officials at the Board were most indignant. The Secretary (James Booth), in a long Memorandum in which he attempted to anticipate Horsfall's points, argued fiercely against the probable contention that the Board of Trade should be composed of businessmen. It was the duty of the Board of Trade, he said, to watch over the interests of the public no less than those of the traders. Experience had shown that traders were likely to take a narrow and short-sighted view of their interests, and were ever ready to sacrifice the public interest if they believed it to be in conflict with their own. The great benefits brought by Free Trade had been obtained by the Board of Trade in the teeth of fierce and interested commercial opposition; a Board which represented the views of traders as a class would be ill-adapted to the safeguarding of the public interest.[15]

Much the same applied to the Foreign Office. As Sir John Tilley pointed out many years later, the Foreign Office regarded itself as charged with obtaining the best terms it could for British trade *in general*; its critics wanted assistance for *individuals*, and were not satisfied when told that British consuls were actually more efficient than foreign consuls in performing those duties which the Foreign Office thought appropriate. Tilley added that he believed that the Foreign Office was right and the critics wrong, 'at least so long as British trade was in the ascendant'.[16]

Officials were ready enough to accept a limited responsibility for British trade overseas, but this fell far short of the assistance so often demanded. The problem was what to do about it, and what distinction was to be made between 'respectable' and suspect classes of traders and enterprises. If diplomatists listened to one group of critics and promoted their interests, they might injure equally respectable but competing British

15. Memorandum dated 2 June 1857:P.R.O.,B.T/1/543, file no. 908/57. Booth's attitude was typical of Board of Trade officials at the time; see, for example, Roger Prouty, *The Transformation of the Board of Trade, 1830–1855* (London, 1957), pp. 102–6.
16. Sir John Tilley and Stephen Gaselee, *The Foreign Office* (London, 1933), pp. 227–8.

interests; they might also, by identifying themselves with a particular interest, lose that status and respectability which was so vital for the efficient performance of their functions in the interest of H.M. Government and Britain as a whole. 'I have no doubt', said the Hon. Henry Elliot in his evidence before the Select Committee on the Diplomatic Service, 9 May 1861, 'that there may be occasions on which [British merchants] have not received all the attention to which they are entitled; but I think it is much more common that they have asked for a great deal more than they had a right to expect.'[17]

*   *   *

The traditions and social composition of the Foreign Office, the Diplomatic Service, and the Consular Service weighed against enthusiastic support for individual traders or financiers overseas. The Foreign Office before the First World War was a curious compound of snobberies and professional priorities. Far greater professional prestige and status were attached to duties connected with the politics of Europe than of America or the Far East. When Vansittart became Head of the American Department, as late as the 1920's, he found that he was seldom troubled by the upper levels of the Foreign Office; the Old World—to many like Austen Chamberlain—was still far more important, and it was 'better form to be pro-German or pro-Russian than pro-French or pro-American ... Britons seldom condescended to transatlantic politics'; as for China, the public had long regarded it as 'the concern of specialists, old traders, and motley missionaries who competed hotly for souls'.[18] Politics, in turn, were more respectable than trade. Layard described the Commercial Department as 'a kind of black hole'; and when in 1879 Lord Odo Russell suggested the need for a commercial expert on the staff of the Berlin Embassy, an Under-Secretary at the Foreign Office was discouraging— he was, Salisbury explained, 'severely orthodox and rather looks upon all traders as an old maid looks upon all men—as being in a conspiracy to surprise him into some illicit favour'.[19]

17. Minutes of Evidence, *Report of the Select Committee on the Diplomatic Service*, P.P.1861(459)VI, Q.1584.
18. Lord Vansittart, *The Mist Procession* (London, 1958), pp 317–18, 329.
19. Lady Gwendolen Cecil, *Life of Robert, Marquis of Salisbury* (London, 1931), III, 216.

The charms of *la haute politique*, complained *The Times* in 1886, were more attractive than the wants of commerce, and they were not only more attractive, they were more fashionable and more rewarding. Those parts of the world which lay outside the main stream of European politics, and which had only commercial problems to offer, were disdained by diplomatic careerists. To accept an appointment in a Latin American capital, Vansittart once said, was to choose a tombstone rather than a stepping-stone; and when Sir William White was wondering, at a key point in his career, whether he should take the offer of the Rio Legation, Sir Robert Morier strongly advised him against it. Morier argued that it would be madness to go to Rio, since it would undoubtedly deny White his chance *einzugreifen in die Weltgeschichte*,[20] and Lord Edmund Fitzmaurice added the warning that 'at Rio, away from his beloved Roumans, Poles, Croats, Turks, Serbs, Slovenes, and Bulgars, he would die of sheer *ennui* in three months'. Even in 1959, Sir Geoffrey Thompson, looking back over a diplomatic career which had begun and ended in Rio, could claim that 'Service in South America was looked at askance in the old Diplomatic Service, as it still is to a wide extent in the Foreign Service of today, because of the lack of "political work" '.[21]

The low status of commercial work was reflected in the position of the Consular Service. Disraeli had recommended the merging of the consular and diplomatic body as early as 1842, almost exactly a century before it actually took place. He argued that the division of duties between the Services 'originated in an assumed difference between political and commercial interests', and, where one Service was placed above the other, seemed to give commercial interests an inferior character. The distinction between political and commercial interests was arbitrary, fanciful, and without foundation—

A political interest, if it meant anything, was a public interest, and in a country where commerce was one of the principal sources of public wealth, and the avowed intention of the public revenue, a commercial interest was a public interest of the highest class.[22]

20. H. Sutherland Edwards, *Sir William White, his Life and Correspondence* (London, 1902), pp. 13, 217–18.
21. Sir Geoffrey Thompson, *Front-Line Diplomat* (London, 1959), p. 49.
22. 61 *Parl.Deb.3s.*220 (8 March 1842).

Disraeli, of course, lost sight of the problem, but it remained as a plague both on social relationships within the Foreign Office and on the status of commercial work throughout the Service—a plague which spread to the Commercial Department, the Commercial Attachés, the Commercial Agents, and, in 1919, to the new Commercial Diplomatic Service.

The Consular Service—described at one time or another as the 'Cinderella', 'poor relation', or 'step-child' among the overseas services—received no serious attention until the 1903 reforms. There was some truth in the criticism (in an anonymous but well-informed article in the *Quarterly Review* of April 1903) that the Service was 'a harbour of refuge for retired army officers and for failures whose only recommendation is aristocratic, official, or personal influence, or an easy source of reward for persons to whom the Government of the day is in some way indebted'. Consular appointments had included Beau Brummell, Charles Lever, and Richard Burton; and where businessmen were employed, it was often only when their own business had failed. One such trader, appointed in Latin America, felt that he should call on the Foreign Office while home on leave—'Why,' said one Foreign Officer to another, 'he does not even talk the Queen's English. What dreadful people are these Consuls. Dreadful. Dreadful.' And Sir Gerald Campbell, who told this anecdote, added a further one of how he himself, as a young consul in Brazil in 1907, had dined with the British Minister one evening at Petropolis—

I ventured a remark to the effect that I did not see why in time (mind you) members of the Consular Service might not be as acceptable to God and man as are Officers in the Navy and Army ... Delicately putting his monocle in place as though the place was sore, [the Minister] stared and ejaculated, 'My dear Campbell, is a Consul ever *any*body?'[23]

The Consuls, who were often, despite their haphazard recruitment, competent, well-meaning, and dedicated officials, were well aware of their humiliating position. J. A. Crowe, the first and most distinguished of British Commercial Attachés, felt compelled to write a bitter Memorandum for the Foreign Office during the 1886 review, in which he explained the social

23. Sir Gerald Campbell, *Of True Experience* (London, 1949), pp. 20, 22.

barrier which stood between diplomatists of all nationalities and knowledge of, or sympathy with, trade; he knew it, he said, from long experience, and no one knew better than he what suffering these social distinctions entailed.[24] Members of the Consular Service recognized the higher status of political work in the weighting they themselves gave to posts within the Service. A post such as Hamburg (which, as the most important of the Hanseatic towns, was semi-diplomatic in character) carried added prestige, as did some of the combined diplomatic and consular posts in Latin America. Where there was no chance of political responsibility, the more popular posts were those in important cities where no Legation existed to take priority. The Service itself was divided into the General Service, the Levant Service, and the China, Japan and Siam Services, and it was the General Service—because it carried least political responsibility—which stood lowest on the social scale.

The Times in 1886 had spoken of the 'condescending and even contemptuous attitude' which British diplomatists had only too often maintained towards commerce. Time and again the evidence confirmed it. That same year a businessman wrote to James Bryce at the Foreign Office, reporting his constant experience that British consuls in China and Japan regarded themselves as concerned solely with diplomatic matters; when conversation turned to commerce they were of no assistance whatsoever. There was the case, he said, of an English storekeeper at Bangkok who wished to recover a £600 debt; he had applied to the British consul for assistance, but his application had been 'contemptuously refused, the Consul alleging that he had "nothing to do with shopkeepers" '.[25] On another, perhaps apocryphal, occasion, a deputation of British merchants called on the British Ambassador at Constantinople with a request for his assistance. The Ambassador told them that British trade was no business of his, and advised them, if they were discontented, to take their trade elsewhere.[26] And there was that conversation between Sir Edward Law and a young attaché at one of the Embassies, in the course of which the

24. Memorandum dated 27 February 1886; P.R.O.,F.O./83/932.
25. Bentley M. Baumann to James Bryce, 11 March 1886: P.R.O.,F.O/83/932
26. William Miller, *Travels and Politics in the Near East* (London, 1898), p. 494.

attaché had exclaimed—'But, my dear Law, you are speaking of merchants; you don't seem to understand that we do not deal with such classes at Embassies!'[27]

By 1886, no doubt, most officials must have lost their contempt for trade. James Bryce, in his Memorandum, could find no evidence to support the accusation that British diplomatists tended to snub traders: whatever may have been the case in the past, 'when rich men often entered the Diplomatic Service as an excuse for fashionable idleness', the importance of our foreign trade for the well-being and political influence of the country was now fully appreciated by the Diplomatic and Consular Services.[28] Bryce had already told the Commons some months earlier that if any tendency to snub still existed at the Foreign Office, it was fast disappearing, while he added (1897) that he believed 'that the old reproach that the Foreign Office disdained commerce had long since ceased to be true'.[29] But he was too optimistic. A departmental committee of the Board of Trade reported in 1917 the belief among many British manufacturers that British diplomatists, until very recently, had considered trade to be beneath their notice.

This old and bad tradition is no doubt dying, but it appears to be dying hard. Several witnesses referred to cases in which members of British Legations have told them politely that they could not be bothered with trade concerns.[30]

The attitude was plainly absurd, but it was not uncommon in the Foreign Service for much of the period before 1914. Harold Nicolson has argued that it was a reaction from the old Venetian type of trading diplomacy. He pointed out that British diplomatists in the Levant and the Far East were originally agents of the Levant and East India Companies, performing the dual function of representing national and trading interests. Once it was established, in the first decades of the nineteenth century, that diplomatists represented only their national governments, British officials were so anxious to break

27. Theodore Morison and G. T. Hutchinson, *The Life of Sir Edward Fitz-Gerald Law* (Edinburgh, 1911), p. 166.
28. See Appendix V.
29. 304 *Parl.Deb.3s.*637 (2 April 1886); 50 *Parl.Deb.4s.*545 (24 June 1897).
30. *Report of the Departmental Committee appointed by the Board of Trade to consider the position of the Engineering Trades after the War*, P.P.1918(Cd.9073)XIII.

with the trading tradition (and the associations that went with it) that they reacted violently against commerce, assuming that any connexion with it 'implied a lowering of their own status from sovereign representatives to commercial travellers'.[31]

There is some truth in this, but it is not an explanation which will account for an attitude as strong, or almost as strong, throughout the Foreign Service, in London, and across the world. A more fundamental reason exists, surely, in the combination of the new policy of *laissez-faire* with the continued aristocratic tradition of the Service. Noblemen, bored, dispirited, and inexperienced in matters of commerce and finance, found in *laissez-faire* exactly the rationalization they were looking for; they could avoid a distasteful contact with the persons and problems of traders and financiers merely by referring, in perfect good faith, to the traditions of non-intervention, Free Trade, and open competition. And it was true that *haut politique*, at their level and in the society with which they mixed, *was* far more interesting.

The aristocratic composition of the Foreign Service (the Foreign Office and the Diplomatic Service) was no legend before 1914. John Bright complained, in a speech at Glasgow in December 1858, of a lord in Paris, another in Madrid, another in Berlin, another (until recently) in Vienna, another in Constantinople, and another in Washington; there was almost certain to be a British nobleman representing the Foreign Office abroad, 'particularly where the society is most pleasant and the climate most agreeable'. Lords and diplomatists—he wrote in his journal after the signature of Cobden's Commercial Treaty with France in 1860—had been in Paris, spending £15,000 a year, for the past half century, and had done nothing: 'Cobden, a simple citizen, unpaid, unofficial, but earnest and disinterested, has done all.'[32] Bright's complaints were fully justified, especially for the European appointments. When Sir William White was on the point (in 1879) of being transferred from the Consular to the Diplomatic Service with the future rank of Envoy-Extraordinary and Minister Pleni-

31. Harold Nicolson, *Diplomacy* (London, edn. 1950), pp. 162–3.
32. Quoted in G. M. Trevelyan, *The Life of John Bright* (London, 1913), p. 285.

potentiary, he wrote to Cadman Jones to pass on the news and wonder at his success in life. It was true, he said, that there were four other former Consuls at present occupying similar positions, but their appointments, unlike his, were out of Europe where it was almost unheard of for anyone who was not 'a scion of nobility or a Court favourite' to have reached such rank.[33] Robert Nightingale's analysis of aristocratic representation at the principal British Embassies and Legations between 1851 and 1929 (*The Realist*, December 1929) bears him out. At the great Embassies of Paris, Berlin, Vienna and St. Petersburg, the ratio of aristocrats to those of non-aristocratic birth, according to Nightingale, was 8 to 9, 10 to 12, 12 to 16, and 11 to 15 respectively.

The Foreign Service, from the Ministers down to the junior clerks and attachés, was traditionally aristocratic. The Foreign Secretary himself was almost always selected from one of the great noble families, and the same was true, with more exceptions, of the Parliamentary Under-Secretary. Henry Layard was one such exception; Sir Charles Dilke another. Dilke, appointed Under-Secretary in 1880, was regarded as decidedly middle-class, and Wilfred Blunt remembered 'the disgust with which Dilke's appointment was received at the Foreign Office, where aristocratic pretensions are traditional among the clerks'.[34] Layard had been brought into contact with the snobbery of British diplomatists long before he reached office. In 1842 he had undertaken, at the request of Colonel Taylor, the British Consul General at Baghdad, to deliver some despatches to Stratford Canning at Constantinople. This he did at considerable personal inconvenience, but when he arrived at the Embassy he was asked brusquely for the despatches by an Attaché. After telling him that the Ambassador was too busy to see him, the Attaché left the room before he had had a chance to say anything. Layard was bitterly offended. Looking back on the incident, he wrote in his autobiography that he had no doubt exaggerated the matter at the time, 'but I was young and impetuous, and the manner in which the members of an Embassy were in those days accustomed to treat British subjects

33. Edwards, *Sir William White*, p. 271.
34. Wilfrid Scawen Blunt, *Secret History of the English Occupation of Egypt* (London, 1907), p. 90.

who were not supposed to enjoy an equal position in society with themselves may have justified, to a certain extent, the warmth of my remonstrances'. He added, however, that great changes had since taken place, and public opinion had compelled diplomatists to discharge their duties to the public in a more becoming fashion.[35]

But the changes which Layard described were more in the attitude of diplomatists than in their rank in society. There was a certain logic in the appointment of aristocrats to the Foreign Service. Bagehot, normally no friend of the aristocratic tradition, admitted that the aristocracy was likely to retain its advantage in the conduct of diplomacy—'The old-world diplomacy of Europe', he wrote in the '60s, 'was largely carried on in drawing-rooms, and, to a great extent, of necessity still is so.' Since this was undeniably the case, it was important in the national interest to appoint men who could move easily and naturally in European Society. The personal friendships with members of the governing class which Lord Frederic Hamilton, for example, was able to form automatically in Berlin, Vienna, and St. Petersburg, would have been unthinkable for persons of lower rank. Hamilton, in his delightful reminiscences, wrote of the Austrian aristocracy in the last decades of the century—interrelated, charming, and unintellectual—that 'the degree of warmth of their reception of foreigners was largely dependent upon whether he, or she, could show the indispensable *sechzehn Ahnen* (the "sixteen quarterings")'. The caste regulations of the Habsburg Court, Hamilton added, were so inflexible that even the beautiful Countess Karolyi, wife of the Austrian Ambassador at Berlin, was never asked to Court in Vienna since she lacked the necessary quarterings.[36]

Whether for reasons of greater efficiency, or whether, in Bright's over-quoted phrase, as 'a gigantic system of out-door relief for the aristocracy of England', the aristocratic tradition in Foreign Service appointments, particularly to the Diplomatic Service, remained undiminished until after the First World War. The Macdonnell Commission (the Royal Commission on the Civil Service, 1912–14), when it studied the

35. Sir Henry Layard, *Autobiography and Letters* (London, 1903), p. 18.
36. Lord Frederic Hamilton, *The Vanished Pomps of Yesterday* (London, 7th edn. n.d.), pp. 50, 64.

educational background of successful competitors for attaché-
ships between 1908 and 1913, discovered that 25 out of the 37
were from Eton, and that only a very small fraction had been
educated outside the more expensive public schools; only one
candidate came from a university other than Oxford or Cambridge. The Commission concluded, after examining further
conditions for entry into the Diplomatic Service, that the Service
was effectively closed to all British subjects, however well-
qualified, unless they had private means; the minimum private
income officially required was £400 a year—'The effect is to
limit candidature to a narrow circle of society.'[37]

As a result of the Civil Service reforms, 'limited competition'
replaced pure patronage in 1857 as the normal means of
entry into the Diplomatic Service, but there was a property
qualification, and the candidates could be selected only from
those nominated by the Foreign Secretary. A competitive
examination was introduced in Granville's last term of office
(in the early '80s), but it was under the same conditions, and
what it meant, as Algernon Cecil was to point out many years
later, was that 'a selection was made from among, as a rule,
three or four men, possessed of incomes of not less than four
hundred a year, the knowledge of two or three foreign languages, some familiarity with the Graces, and a nodding acquaintance with the Muses.'[38] The nominations were transferred
from the Foreign Secretary to a Board of Selection in 1907, and
at the same time the examinations for Foreign Office Clerk-
ships, for which there was no property qualification, were
assimilated to those for the Home Civil Service. But the effect
was slight. The property qualification and the stringent language
requirements (which normally meant one or two years of study
on the Continent) preserved the Diplomatic Service for the
wealthier classes, if not necessarily for the aristocrats; while the
Board of Selection (which had an absolute veto, and which
judged candidates by means of an oral examination) made sure
that mere wealth did not admit the parvenu. The Foreign
Office, even with a strictly competitive examination and no

37. *Fifth Report of the Royal Commission on the Civil Service*, P.P.1914–16(Cd.
7748)XI, Pt.I, chs.I and II.
38. Algernon Cecil in A. W. Ward and G. P. Gooch (eds.), *The Cambridge
History of British Foreign Policy 1783–1919* (Cambridge, 1923), p. 612.

property qualification, was still—according to Cecil—'recruiting its Clerks mainly among Etonians' in the years immediately before the War.

The problem of the 'democratization' of the Foreign Office has yet to be solved. The property qualification for overseas service ended in 1919, and salaries and allowances were set at a level which was intended to cover all reasonable expenses. But the level has never been entirely realistic, and the Plowden Committee, recognizing that 'the overseas Services should be representative of the nation as a whole and not only of the wealthier segments of society', felt bound as recently as the end of 1963 to recommend substantial increases in overseas allowances. The 1943 Foreign Office reforms, the Committee argued, had been intended to open the Service to recruits from any social sphere; but though many men without private means had in fact joined the Service since 1945, they had since found themselves in financial difficulties.[39]

The social composition of recruits to the Service, as discovered by the Plowden Committee, was certainly an improvement on that existing before 1943. Kenneth Lindsay, in the debate on the '43 reforms, had reported that over the previous twenty years there had not been 'any democratization worth noticing'. Seventy per cent. of those entering the Service since 1919 had come from Eton or eight other public schools, and there was not a single man in the Service, with the exception of three or four who had come in 'almost by accident', who had been to an elementary school or a school outside the Headmasters' Conference.[40] But even the Plowden Committee found that, over a ten year period, only 28 per cent. of the successful applicants for the Senior Branch of the Foreign Service came from Direct Grant and State Schools, and that, from among the universities, Oxford contributed 59 per cent., Cambridge 35·2 per cent., and all the remaining universities only 5·3 per cent. between them. The Committee was aware that social class had had little to do with the actual selection and that the Civil Service Commissioners were only too anxious to expand the range of recruitment, but it could not feel satisfied either with

39. *Report of the Committee on Representational Services Overseas* (the Plowden Committee), P.P.1964(Cmnd.2276), para. 443.
40. 387 *H.C.Deb.5s.*1427 (18 March 1943).

the school or the university background of new entrants to the Service.[41]

* * *

Most politicians and officials were continually aware of the importance to Britain of a healthy trade overseas. But social convention, in a class-bound society, was certain to act as a barrier to unqualified trade promotion, while, in the century before 1914, a much more formidable barrier existed in the ideology both of *laissez-faire* and of what Keynes once called its 'most fervent expression', Free Trade.

As early as 1820 the Select Committee on Foreign Trade had argued that 'the skill, enterprise, and capital of British merchants and manufacturers require only an open and equal field for exertion', and that the most valuable boon which could be conferred was unlimited freedom from all interference.[42] There was always, of course, a measure of dissent with pure *laissez-faire*, which became more vocal as the century progressed, but 'hands-off business' remained a popular and influential attitude of mind until well into this century. The effect on officials was predictable. Government Departments seldom took the initiative in expanding their functions. Expansion followed outside pressure, and where that pressure—as in the case of the demand for greater state intervention on behalf of foreign trade and finance—was met by a strong countercurrent of *laissez-faire*, an outlet could be found through that favourite Departmental escape-valve: the argument that public demand was insufficiently unanimous as yet to justify action.

One of the most emphatic statements of *laissez-faire* in overseas trade was published in Lord Farrer's *The State in its Relation to Trade* (London, 1881). Farrer had been an official in the Board of Trade from 1848–86 (the last twenty years of which he served as its Permanent Secretary), and his book accurately reflects the Victorian official's distrust of the extension of state intervention. In his Conclusion, Farrer summarized the scope of the commercial functions undertaken by the State. They included the maintenance of order (without which trade would

41. *Report of the Committee on Representational Services Overseas*, P.P.1964(Cmnd. 2276), paras. 357–65.
42. *Report from the Select Committee appointed to consider the Means of Maintaining and Improving the Foreign Trade of the Country*, P.P.1820(300)II.

be impossible); the enforcement of contracts; the provision of a system of weights and measures and a medium of exchange; the repudiation of monopolies except where they existed to reward invention or where, as in the case of public utilities, they were inevitable (in which case the State was prepared to regulate prices and conditions and even to undertake the supply itself); a policy of non-intervention in price-fixing or in the play of the free market (but no hesitation in intervening where life and health were endangered); a readiness to raise part of the general revenue from trade in return for the security the State provided in peace and war. 'Under this system', Farrer claimed, 'the chief feature of which is as much individual freedom as is consistent with the welfare of an organized society, and the performance of self-imposed obligations, British trade has grown to be such as the world has never seen before. The State has given protection, and has established forms and modes of action. But its chief praise in relation to trade has been that it has left as much scope as possible to the free energy and self-interest of its people'.[43]

Lord Farrer's views were echoed by his successors. In 1897 W. H. S. Gastrell, a former Commercial Attaché at Berlin, Stockholm and Copenhagen, published a book on British overseas trade and foreign competition in which he concluded that the Government's function was limited to the collection of information; action in applying the results of modern research to manufacturing and improving the processes of production must come from the commercial community.[44] That same year the Board of Trade itself, when considering measures by which the supply of commercial information might be improved, was careful to stress how unwise it would be 'to take any step which might have the effect of weakening the power exercised by the enlightened self-interest of those who are directly engaged in home and foreign trade'.[45]

The improved condition of world trade in the first decade of this century naturally eased the pressure for state intervention, but even early in the decade, while conditions were still un-

43. T. H. Farrer, *The State in its Relation to Trade* (London, edn. 1902), pp. 207–8.
44. Gastrell, *Our Trade in relation to Foreign Competition*, p. 29.
45. Board of Trade to Treasury, 29 April 1897: P.R.O.,B.T/13/29, file no. 12804.

favourable, the evidence presented by officials to the Select Committee on Steamship Subsidies in 1902 was overwhelmingly *laissez-faire*.[46] Again, the effect of intense state intervention and control during the First World War was not, in many quarters, to emphasize the advantages of planning and direction, but rather to disgust both officials and businessmen with the whole process of state control. A Board of Trade departmental committee on Shipping and Shipbuilding—which included officials and industrialists—was fanatically *laissez-faire*. Its report of March 1918 observed the 'sound rule' that Government intervention should not be invoked 'save in exceptional circumstances or in cases where the matter cannot be settled by the industries'; the first measure of reconstruction after the War was to be the early removal of Government operation and control, which was not only 'alien to the British genius' but always tended to paralyse individual effort.[47]

The Committee, among the many similar Committees formed during 1917–18 to consider the position of British industry after the War, was exceptionally violent in its rejection of state intervention, but it soon became clear, by the early '20s, that *laissez-faire* was no answer to the recent transformation of Britain's relative position in world trade. But it would have been surprising if officials, brought up in a climate of *laissez-faire*, had been able to adapt themselves immediately to the new conditions. For the older officials, this was clearly impossible. Lord Bradbury, an eminent Civil Servant who had headed the Treasury between 1913 and 1919, could not bring himself to accept the interventionist bias of the Committee on Finance and Industry. The Committee, in response to the Depression, had felt bound to conclude in its 1931 Report that Britain might well have reached the state 'when an era of conscious and deliberate management must succeed the era of undirected national evolution'. Bradbury found it impossible to abandon orthodox economics, and, in his Memorandum of Dissent, continued to argue that the best contribution the State could make to industry and the maintenance of employment

46. See, for example, the evidence of Sir Robert Giffen, Sir Spencer Walpole, and Mr. Buxton Forman: Minutes of Evidence, *Report of the Select Committee on Steamship Subsidies*, P.P.1902(385)IX, QQ.157, 2535, 2776–9.
47. *Final Report of the Departmental Committee on Shipping and Shipbuilding*, P.P. 1918(Cd.9092)XIII.

was strict economy in public expenditure and prudent financial administration which would lighten the burden of debt. He felt that interference by the State with the natural channels of international trade would be more likely to retard than promote economic recovery.[48]

The *Chamber of Commerce Journal*, back in 1895, had hailed Mr. Chamberlain's Circular Despatch on competition in the Colonies as marking 'the official abandonment of the principle of *laissez-faire*'; it was at least twenty years ahead of its time. There is a great deal of truth, of course, in J. Bartlet Brebner's argument that *laissez-faire* had been abandoned from early in the last century over a wide sector of Victorian administration, particularly with respect to social legislation.[49] Adam Smith himself had made allowances for this when he included among the duties of the sovereign that of 'creating and maintaining those public institutions and those public works, which, though they may be in the highest degree advantageous to a great society, are, however, of such a nature, that the profit could never repay the expense to any individual or small number of individuals, and which it therefore cannot be expected that any individual or small number of individuals should erect or maintain'. Applying a similar line of argument to foreign trade, Adam Smith had been prepared to concede that a limited monopoly might be given by the State to mercantile companies which undertook, at their own risk and expense, to 'establish a new trade with some remote and barbarous nation'; in this case, a monopoly was the price of persuading private citizens (in the public interest) to undertake the business. But to interfere with the free play of the market, with the ordinary processes of supply and demand, was to strike at the very basis of classical political economy. 'The protection of trade in general', said Adam Smith, 'has always been considered as essential to the defence of the commonwealth, and, upon that account, a necessary part of the duty of the executive power.'[50]

48. Annex to the *Report of the Committee on Finance and Industry*, P.P.1930–31 (Cmd.3897)XIII.
49. J. Bartlet Brebner, 'Laissez Faire and State Intervention in Nineteenth-Century Britain', *Journal of Economic History*, Supplement VIII (1948), 59–73.
50. Adam Smith, *An Inquiry into the nature and causes of the Wealth of Nations* (London, 1776), Bk. V, ch. 1.

There it stopped. Interference with the market (other than simply for the protection of trade and the maintenance of free and open competition) represented a break with classical economic theory far sharper than any which might have been created by Victorian social legislation, with the result that even if officials abandoned pure *laissez-faire* in home administration, foreign trade and finance remained as its last stronghold. Under pressure in the 1880's, 'the protection of trade in general' compelled the British Government to make some concessions on state intervention, but concessions were limited in scope and by circumstances, and confined to those particular parts of the world where foreign diplomatic pressure made British intervention inevitable. *Laissez-faire* remained as the usual official attitude of mind—to be modified only under exceptional circumstances—until at least the First World War (and probably as late as the Depression).

Laissez-faire was able to keep its popularity with officials in part because it had the support of a majority of business and parliamentary opinion. In relation to overseas trade, serious criticism began as early as the 1870's, but it is doubtful whether public opinion in general had turned against *laissez-faire* until the beginning of the 1930's. Keynes's sardonic remark that 'to suggest social action for the public good to the City of London is like discussing the *Origin of Species* with a Bishop sixty years ago' was still almost as universally true of the year in which he wrote (1926) as it had been half a century earlier.[51] Economists, businessmen, statesmen had rallied to *laissez-faire* as doubts increased in the last decades of the century. Leone Levi argued in 1872 that Britain had reached her present position 'not by restricting and entangling trade and industry, not by thwarting the laws of nature, but by removing every barrier, and by opening every avenue to the legitimate exercise of personal energies'.[52] The essence of George Baden-Powell's *State Aid and State Interference* (London, 1882) was contained in the emphatic claim that 'in order to secure the highest and most lasting prosperity for commerce and industry, *State Aid should be invoked or utilised for the sole purpose of disestablishing State Inter-*

51. J. M. Keynes, *The End of Laissez-Faire* (London, 1926), p. 38.
52. Leone Levi, *History of British Commerce and of the Economic Progress of he British Nation 1763–1870* (London, 1872), viii.

ference'. Armitage-Smith felt that the problem of foreign competition at the turn of the century could be met not by Government interference or regulation, but by the skill and adaptability of British merchants and manufacturers.[53] J. W. Root, a few years later, could see no practicable direction in which imperial trade could be promoted by government action; in the future as in the past the solution lay with individual effort, and 'the less governments interfere as a rule the better'.[54]

The arguments of *laissez-faire* economists were echoed in the Chambers of Commerce and by the politicians. When the Foreign Office was canvassing Chamber of Commerce opinion in 1886 on the measures which the Government might be expected to take to increase diplomatic and consular assistance to commerce, the reaction even after a decade of commercial depression was guarded. Hamilton Dunlop, the Chairman of the Southampton Chamber of Commerce, told Mr. Kennedy that the most practical suggestion to British traders—though he did not wish to be quoted on it—was 'Do your own business'. A great deal of Chamber of Commerce agitation, he added, was mere idle talk, the result of having to find something to agitate.[55] The Chambers of Commerce were approached again on the same subject in 1897, and opinion if anything had hardened against state intervention. Commercial conditions had improved and businessmen saw little advantage in increased action by the State. The Blackburn Chamber felt that the Government should not interfere in the business of merchants or pioneers of trade, and that its functions should properly be limited to providing adequate protection. Glasgow agreed, urging that 'merchants should be left to conduct their own business at their individual cost and risk, in their own way, and for their own advantage'. Manchester emphasized the inefficiency of disinterested officials even in obtaining commercial information; private enterprise, in which the rewards depended entirely on individual energy and watchfulness, could cope

53. G. Armitage-Smith, *The Free-Trade Movement and its Results* (London, 1898), p. 223.
54. J. W. Root, *The Trade Relations of the British Empire* (Liverpool, 1903), pp. 402, 407.
55. Hamilton Dunlop to C. M. Kennedy, 14 March 1886: P.R.O.,F.O/83/932.

much more flexibly with the constant and rapid change of world trading conditions.[56] Identical arguments recurred in what became one of the most important forums (if also the most partial) for the discussion of the proper relationship between government and business—the evidence taken by the Select Committee on Steamship Subsidies in 1901 and 1902. Time and again steamship-owners rejected government assistance and claimed that they could do business better on their own. When the Committee came to report, it concluded that free competition, without British Government subsidies or control of freights, was 'more healthy and likely to be more beneficial to the nation and Empire' than a system under which the ship-owner would be dependent less on his individual skill and energy and more on the favour and support of the State.[57]

The commercial prosperity of the early years of this century convinced businessmen of the virtues of independence. Mr. Langdon (Manchester Chamber of Commerce), speaking at the Sixth Congress of the Chamber of Commerce of the Empire, July 1906, in opposition to any transformation of British Consuls into Imperial salesmen and debt collectors, was enthusiastically received. Individuals, he maintained, had built up and carried on the trade of Great Britain as they had the trade of the Empire, and 'if the day ever came when they had to rely on the assistance of paid State officials for that trade, he should be deeply sorry'. (Cheers.)[58] Even just before the War, when severe, government-promoted foreign competition for contracts and concessions was shaking the confidence of the strongest supporters of individual initiative, the President of the Association of Chambers of Commerce of the United Kingdom—questioned by the Royal Commission on the Civil Service as to his opinion on the proper degree of consular assistance to trade—denied that consuls should act as commercial travellers for British manufacturers; consuls should serve only the general interest of British trade, and the best guide to

56. Appendix No. 6, *Report of the Commercial Intelligence Committee*, P.P.1898 (c.8963) XXXIII.
57. *Report from the Select Committee on Steamship Subsidies*, P.P.1902(385)IX, para. 50.
58. *Official Report of the Proceedings at the Sixth Congress of Chambers of Commerce of the Empire*, 10–12 July 1906 (London, 1906), p. 57.

action, so long as a British firm was doing business, was to leave it alone.[59]

It is difficult, with experience of the 1930's, to appreciate the strength and inflexibility of commercial opposition to Government intervention, or the bitterness of feeling against the State created by enforced war-time controls. No businessman has ever worked in closer harness with the British Government than Lord Inchcape. Yet no man could have been more bitterly opposed to bureaucracy and government control. Speaking in the Lords in August 1918, Inchcape declared his distaste for Government interference:

We don't want the business side of the country to be carried on by the Government. Make no mistake—if any attempt is made by any Government to interfere with the liberties of the people, or to dragoon them after the German fashion, that Government will be ignominiously hounded from power. This country has made its way by individual effort and organisation; it would be fatal to smother them.[60]

The most important economic manifestation of *laissez-faire* was Free Trade. The sequence is simple enough. Although all Free Traders did not necessarily believe in complete *laissez-faire*, anyone who accepted *laissez-faire* had no alternative to accepting Free Trade; Free Trade was 'hands-off business' applied to tariff policy. In a fulsome account of the blessings of Free Trade prepared by E. A. Bowring for publication in the *Moniteur* in 1855, Bowring claimed that the difficulty was to make any selection from the mass of evidence which could be used to demonstrate the benefits brought, in a mere fifteen or sixteen years, by the adoption of the principles of Free Trade—'or, to speak more accurately, from the reversion to the simple precepts of Nature, which have been so well epitomized by a great Frenchman in five short words: *"Laissez-faire et laissez aller"* '.[61]

The Board of Trade, in which Bowring served at the time, was closely identified with the policy and promotion of Free

59. Minutes of Evidence, *Fifth Report of the Royal Commission on the Civil Service*, P.P.1914–16(Cd.7749)XI, QQ.42,056–60.
60. Quoted in Hector Bolitho, *Lord Inchcape* (London, 1936), pp. 134–5.
61. 'Effects of the Free Trade Policy recently inaugurated in England, as indicated by its Practical Results'; P.R.O.,B.T/1/553A, file no. 1277/60.

Trade. The tradition dated at least from William Huskisson, who was already known as an advanced free trader when he joined the Board in 1822. His tariff consolidations, carried out in the 1825 Acts, began a series of rationalizations and reforms which, by 1860, had abolished protective tariffs altogether. Huskisson's assistant with the 1825 tariff reforms, James Deacon Hume, became Joint Secretary to the Board of Trade in 1828; he was a founding member of the Political Economy Club in 1821, and spoke repeatedly at its meetings on the subject of Free Trade; he himself was one of the most prominent free traders of his age. Poulett Thomson, who became Vice-President of the Board of Trade in the Whig Government of 1830, rising to President in 1834, had spoken frequently in support of Free Trade since his entrance into the Commons in 1826, and was responsible for a series of reductions in Customs duties and the negotiation of a number of commercial treaties. Others at the Board of Trade, such as George Richardson Porter (author of *The Progress of the Nation* and head of the Statistical Department), John MacGregor (the statistician, and Hume's successor as Joint Secretary in 1840), Henry Labouchere (Vice-President from 1835–9, President 1839–41, 1847–52), Sir John Shaw-Lefevre (Joint Assistant-Secretary 1841–7), and later Farrer, Rawson, Mallet, and Giffen, were strong and partisan supporters of Free Trade and often members of the Cobden Club (the motto of which, formulated by Goldwin Smith, was 'Free Trade, Peace, and Good Will among Nations'). Farrer's *Free Trade versus Fair Trade* (published by the Cobden Club in 1882) was praised by Francis Hirst as handling every Protectionist argument 'with unsparing vigour and invariable lucidity, stat[ing] the case for Free Trade in a manner that has seldom been equalled' and Hirst, writing of the '80s, reported that at that time the Civil Service, 'nurtured in the traditions of Peel and Gladstone, provided an atmosphere which was highly unfavourable to Protection'. It was Farrer, Hirst explained, who had briefed Joseph Chamberlain (as President of the Board of Trade, 1880–5) in his vigorous rejection of Fair Trade.[62]

The Board of Trade remained the traditional home of Free

62. F. W. Hirst, *From Adam Smith to Philip Snowden: a history of Free Trade in Great Britain* (London, 1925), p. 46.

Trade until well into this century, and R. W. Rawson and other old officials of the Board—according to Hirst, himself an ardent Free Trader—were fond of describing 'the official interferences with commerce, the petitions from merchants, the wire-pulling of rival interests, the endless litigation that arose from the intricacies and absurdities of the Customs'.[63] Memories such as these acted as a healthy disincentive to revived Protectionism, and reinforced official preference, already pronounced, for the simplicity of *laissez-faire*. Prejudices were never, in fact, put to the test; Protection was defeated decisively in the election of 1905, and the Liberal Government which returned, pledged to maintain Free Trade, remained in office until 1916. Hancock, writing at the beginning of the Second World War, described how British commercial policy over the previous half-century might almost be dramatized as a struggle between the individualist City and free trade Manchester on the one hand and protectionist Birmingham on the other; 'in the years before the Great War the old Manchester and the old City still governed British commercial policy, and beat back Birmingham's attacks upon the constituencies'.[64]

* * *

There can be no doubt of the importance which British statesmen and officials were accustomed to attach to the security and maintenance of overseas trade. But the action they were prepared to take was limited both by their aristocratic tastes and prejudices and by the *laissez-faire*, Free Trade

63. F. W. Hirst, *Gladstone as Financier and Economist* (London, 1931), p. 44. Dr. Lucy Brown has described the partisan Free Trade attitude of Board of Trade officials in the 1830's and 1840's in *The Board of Trade and the Free-Trade Movement 1830–42* (Oxford, 1958).
64. W. K. Hancock, *Survey of British Commonwealth Affairs, II* (London, 1940), p. 92. The division of opinion was much the same fifteen years later. Commenting on the evidence it had received on tariff policy, the Committee on Trade and Industry reported that 'the trend of evidence from the cotton trade was strongly against, while that from the iron and steel and engineering trades was on the whole, and with some exceptions, favourable to tariff protection. The wool trade was described as divided on the subject, and the chemical industries as fairly satisfied with the present position, which in the case of certain of their products includes an element of protection'. The Committee concluded that there was 'no strong and general trend of organised commercial opinion in favour of any material change of national tariff policy'. *Final Report of the Committee on Industry and Trade*, P.P.1928–29 (Cmd.3282)VII, Section VIII(1).

tradition of classical political economy. The chapters which follow will indicate first (in Parts I and II) the extent to which H.M. Government was prepared to promote British finance and trade overseas, and then (in Part III) the actual impact of British financial and trading interests on the formulation of British foreign policy.

PART I

H.M. GOVERNMENT AND OVERSEAS FINANCE

PART I

H.M. GOVERNMENT AND
OVERSEAS FINANCE

INTRODUCTION

ONE OF the most remarkable phenomena in British economic history has been the immense outflow of capital overseas in the half-century before 1914. Albert H. Imlah calculated recently that the balance of credit abroad rose in our favour from about £10 million in 1815 to £208·7 million in 1850, £692·3 million in 1870, £1,189·4 million in 1880, £1,935·1 million in 1890, £2,396·9 million in 1900, £3,371·3 million in 1910, and £3,989·6 million in 1913.[1] It was this investment, and what Winston Churchill once spoke of as 'the great force of capital, the great, subtle, omnipresent influence of capital', which has attracted so much unfavourable comment in the debate over the relationship of business and government; capital exports, indeed, rather than commodity exports lay at the basis of the Lenin/Bukharin theory of imperialism.

There is little point in restating the general argument for and against the economic interpretation of imperialism. The ground is covered well enough already.[2] But it may, all the same, be worth suggesting some of the problems which tend to recur, such as the means by which business was said to influence government, the interrelationship of government and business in the

1. Albert H. Imlah, *Economic Elements in the Pax Britannica* (Cambridge, Mass., 1958), Table 4, pp. 70–75.
2. The classic economic interpretation, of course, is J. A. Hobson's *Imperialism, a Study* (1902), more particularly as reinforced by V. I. Lenin, *Imperialism, the Highest Stage of Capitalism* (1917) and Nikolai Bukharin, *Imperialism and World Economy* (1917). The most competent of the many contrary arguments are those put by William A. Langer, 'A Critique of Imperialism', *Foreign Affairs*, 24 (1935); Mark Blaug, 'Economic Imperialism Revisited', *Yale Review*, L (1961); David Landes, 'Some Thoughts on the Nature of Economic Imperialism', *Journal of Economic History*, XXI (1961); and D. K. Fieldhouse, ' "Imperialism": An Historiographical Revision', *Economic History Review*, 2nd ser. XIV (1961).

'governing class', the individual cases of statesmen or officials accused of a direct subordination of public to private interest.

It can be argued that in a country like Britain at the turn of the century, with its commercial wealth and its position at the hub of world finance, an almost unlimited opportunity existed for business to bring influence to bear on government. Retired officials or statesmen out of office might be offered commercial directorships, not simply for whatever direct influence they might still have, but in return for their knowledge of the inner workings of the government machine. Private shareholdings at Westminster or Whitehall might influence a decision to assist or intervene. Individual interests could disguise themselves under the cloak of nationalism; an emotional appeal to the flag could find a direct response among officials, or create such a climate of opinion among the voting public that no statesman could withstand popular pressure to intervene. The newspapers were often the mouthpiece of individual financial or commercial interests; trained civil service minds, no doubt, could discount much of the interested material, but could they always be sure of distinguishing the particular from the general interest? Business interests might form themselves into powerful 'lobbies' or associations and bring unremitting pressure to bear on behalf of certain specific causes, calling on organized economic and political support from all parts of the country and from British business communities abroad. These lobbies, and the larger individual businesses themselves, were generally well informed, often had private sources of information on developments abroad more complete than those available to the Government, and could match and master any public servant on technical detail; no government could afford to ignore the information services they provided, and that information, if not necessarily maliciously distorted, was taken from only one point of view. Officials abroad, however impartial in intention, could not escape contact with, and generally influence from, local communities of their own nationals; over time, impartiality tended to be replaced either by strong and partisan support for local British interests or by its opposite, complete identification with the aspirations of the nation to which they were accredited. Finally there was the crude mechanism of the bribe, seldom direct but rather in the form of contributions to party campaign funds, offers of employment when the Party was out of office, lavish hospitality.

The need for direct pressure—so the argument runs—seldom existed. Businessmen, politicians, and officials shared their beliefs, social status, and general interests to such an extent that they acted together automatically. Lenin wrote of 'the "interlocking" of bankers, ministers, big industrialists and rentiers'; Hobson noted the 'natural alliance' of all vested interests threatened by movements of social reform; Leonard Woolf described the invisible wires linking boardrooms, the Church, officials, the aristocracy, and statesmen. Others have emphasized the ready interchange between officials, statesmen, and businessmen at a certain level of public life; their common social and educational background; their membership of the same clubs; intermarriage and mutual aid; friendships and the frequent exchange of hospitality, including the English country house 'week-end'.

These, of course, are forms of social or intellectual contact for which concrete evidence has probably never existed. What record is likely to survive of an informal contact over a club bar, or of a conversation at dinner in a country house? And it is rare, for these and other less attractive reasons, to find an argument conducted on this level which is prepared to descend from the general to the particular. But both Brailsford and Hallgarten have made much of Lord Rosebery's marriage link with the Rothschilds; Lambert and Staley have pointed to Evelyn Baring's family association with Baring Bros.; Rothstein has suggested the implications for Egyptian finance of Goschen's former partnership in the financial house of Messrs. Frühling and Goschen; Sweezy linked Joseph Chamberlain's imperialism with 'the family fortune and the interests of the Birmingham arms industry'; Hirst denounced the sinister and unexplained relationship between Chamberlain and Rhodes; Rhodes in turn—according to Hallgarten—was financed by the Rothschilds (who were probably responsible for the Boer War), while finance capital *Hochimperialismus* reached its peak under the personal patronage of Edward VII; George V, indeed, was described by Michel Pavlovitch as 'the crowned agent of the English banks'!

Absurd though some of these arguments may be when taken to extremes, it would be as absurd to deny them any substance whatever. Victorian officials have a deserved reputation for integrity, yet even these officials had their exceptions, and the same, of course, was true of the politicians. The difficulty is that the personal evidence for or against 'influence' and corruption simply does not exist. But it is a difficulty which can be overcome by the use of a different kind and quality of evidence. In the following chapters an attempt will be made to define H.M. Government's attitude to the issue and expenditure of foreign loans, to the protection of the bondholders, and to the promotion of contracts and concessions overseas. In the course of this definition a 'departmental view' will emerge which will suggest how officials and politicians were most likely to react. On the basis of this, and allowing for the occasional exception, it should be possible to decide the extent of the influence which financial factors—even on a very personal level —could exert on the conduct of British foreign policy.

CHAPTER I

THE LONDON MONEY MARKET AND THE BANKS

SCHOLARS HAVE long been interested in the problem of the degree of control exercised by the Powers over international money markets before the First World War.[1] French government control of the Bourse has been traced back as far as 1785, and it was certainly in active operation by the third decade of the nineteenth century. The refusal of a quotation on the Bourse was a weapon which the Government used with some frequency, and to this extent it was able to influence the nature and direction of French overseas investments, often along purely political lines. The German Government, though naturally later in developing a policy, treated foreign loans in much the same way as France. It was not prepared to take up a position on every foreign loan issued in Germany; but it regarded itself as at liberty to intervene where political reasons existed for doing so, and intervention was fairly common after the 1880's.

Though both the French and German Governments took an active part in overseas loans, in neither case was there a complete unity of interest between financiers and officials. Examples of government intervention, such as French intervention in Tunis and Russia or German in Morocco, tend almost always to take the form of finance capital acting on the initiative of Government, rather than the reverse; the stimulus to action

1. The most useful general survey is still Herbert Feis, *Europe: The World's Banker, 1870–1914* (New Haven, 1930); others of value are Jacob Viner, 'Political Aspects of International Finance, Parts I and II', *Journal of Business of the University of Chicago*, I (April and July, 1928), Eugene Staley, *War and the Private Investor* (New York, 1935), ch. IV. Specialized studies include, for France, Yves Guyot's 'The Amount, Direction and Nature of French Investments', *Annals of the American Academy of Political and Social Science*, LXVIII (1916), and Frederick L. Schuman, *War and Diplomacy in the French Republic* (New York, 1931), pp. 391–400; for Germany, Walter H. C. Laves, 'German Governmental Influence on Foreign Investments, 1871–1915', *Political Science Quarterly*, 43 (1928); for the United States, Benjamin H. Williams, *Economic Foreign Policy of the United States* (New York, 1929), and James W. Angell, *Financial Foreign Policy of the United States* (New York, 1933).

came from the politicians or officials, after which the capitalists had to be persuaded, often with great difficulty, to follow with their investments—'*Die deutschen Banken*', said the German Secretary for Foreign Affairs, '*streiken geradezu alle, sobald man von Marokko spricht.*' And government control over the money market was far from perfect. Early in 1910 M. Pichon had boasted to Sir Francis Bertie, the British Ambassador in Paris, that if the French financiers approved German terms for participation in the Baghdad Railway project which were unacceptable to the French Government, they could be brought to heel by an official refusal of a quotation on the Paris Bourse.[2] Eighteen months later, Bertie felt that the French Government had 'rather overrated' its power to exercise political control. The Ottoman Bank and the Deutsche Bank had come to an understanding for a mutual allocation of a 30 per cent option on all enterprises undertaken in Turkey. The Ottoman Bank, therefore, had an option on the Baghdad Railway, and although the shares were not quoted on the Bourse, they were widely circulated from hand to hand in Paris—Government or no Government. Shares could also be bought through Swiss or Belgian banks, and there was nothing to stop French investors putting money into German enterprises, which then in turn released German funds for investment in the Baghdad Railway.[3] The French Secretary of Legation subsequently admitted to the Foreign Office (in another context) that Turkey could always get French money in some way or another; wealthy people in Paris would be attracted by Turkish terms, 'and the French Government could not control the financial operations of individual Frenchmen, or even of some financial institutions'.[4]

While the French and German Governments at least attempted to keep a hand on overseas loans, the American Government on the whole avoided contact with loan issues until the end of the First World War—a self-denial made the less arduous, perhaps, by the fact that it was not until then that the United States became a really important overseas lender. Before the War, the Taft Administration had undertaken an active overseas investment policy in the Caribbean region and

2. Bertie to Grey, 11 January 1910: No. 319, *B.D.O.W.*,VI,424.
3. Bertie to Grey, 17 July 1911: No. 33, *B.D.O.W.*,X,Pt.II,44.
4. Minutes by Mr. Parker, 18 August 1913: No. 137, *B.D.O.W.*,X,Pt.II,210.

in China, but American capitalists, like French and German, had to be persuaded to take part. Staley reports a conversation with Huntington Wilson in 1913 in which Wilson, who had been Assistant Secretary of State during the Taft Administration, explained that he had had a great deal of trouble at times persuading U.S. bankers to invest money in certain Caribbean countries where the U.S. Government policy required capital backing—'He remembers', Staley wrote, 'phone calls to New York appealing to the patriotism of certain bankers there not to withdraw from placements already made or asking them to put new capital into loans to Central American governments, and conferences were held to the same end.'[5]

But the Taft policy was disowned by the Wilson Administration, and the United States retreated to non-intervention until 1918. In the early summer of that year the U.S. Government took the initiative in suggesting the formation of an American banking group as the nucleus of a four-Power Consortium for future Chinese loans; in doing so, the State Department recognized the risk that attached to the expansion of U.S. interests abroad, and undertook to aid U.S. enterprise 'in every proper way and to make prompt and vigorous representations, and to take every possible step to ensure the execution of equitable contracts made in good faith by its citizens in foreign lands'.[6] The relationship between the U.S. Government and overseas loan issues was put on a more formal basis by the State Department's declaration of 3 March 1922. The Secretary of State requested American firms considering a foreign loan to let the State Department know the facts of the case and to keep it informed of developments; the Department would be ready to reply to any enquiry for its views on a projected loan, and, while it accepted no responsibility for the loan transactions, it felt that, in view of the national interest which might be involved, it should have the opportunity to say whether or not there was any objection to a particular issue.[7]

* * *

5. Staley, *War and the Private Investor*, p. 272.
6. State Dept. to American bankers, 9 July 1918: printed as Enclosure 2 in No. 1, *Correspondence respecting the new Financial Consortium in China*, P.P.1921 (Cmd. 1214)XLII.
7. The full text is printed as Appendix III to W. S. Culbertson, *International Economic Policies; a survey of the economics of diplomacy* (New York, 1925), p. 499.

Characteristically, the British Government has never made so precise a statement of its position. But it is possible to reconstruct, from individual statements and incidents, a reasonably coherent picture of British official policy.

The tendency, in considering the relationship between government and finance, has been to defend unnecessarily extreme positions. Some writers, following Hobson and Lenin, have accepted a complete identity of interests and objectives between government and overseas lender. Others share the emphatically contrary position taken by Jacob Viner in his articles in the *Journal of Business of the University of Chicago* (April and July 1928), in which he slapped down 'second rate literature on international economic relations' with its unhesitating imputation, without a shadow of evidence, of the pursuit of questionable practices by foreign countries. Viner took his argument too far, but he was right in calling attention to the fact that all kinds of respectable authorities have accepted a control over loan issues which simply did not exist. He quotes, for example, C. K. Hobson's belief (in the introduction to his *Export of Capital*) that it was 'customary for financiers to seek the support of the Foreign Office when negotiating new loans'. And Hobson was not alone. Brailsford claimed that the understanding between the City and Downing Street was so 'admirably close' that the City never invested where such investment might hamper British foreign policy.[8] U.S. Secretary Knox believed, in 1912, that the Council of Foreign Bondholders could not consider any loan proposal unless 'submitted to and approved by the British Foreign Office'.[9] Viallate declared that English banking houses which specialized in foreign loan issues 'consult the Foreign Office before committing themselves, and follow its advice'.[10] Culbertson, though agreeing that H.M. Government had not aggressively directed its overseas investments to serve political ends (in this respect, more nearly resembling U.S. than French practice), explained that the Foreign Office expected nevertheless to be consulted on any loans which involved, or might involve, Imperial interests; moreover, 'the government

8. H. N. Brailsford, *The War of Steel and Gold* (London, 1914), p. 220.
9. Quoted by Clyde Eagleton, *The Responsibility of States in International Law* (New York, 1928), p. 180 fn. 57.
10. Achille Viallate, *Economic Imperialism and International Relations during the last fifty years* (New York, 1923), p. 58.

frequently cooperates with the Corporation of Foreign Bond-holders to protect foreign loans or investments once made'.[11]

While there is some truth in all this, the final emphasis is most misleading. Until the days of Exchange Control, H.M. Government never accepted responsibility for vetting all over-seas loan proposals. If the cases of official intervention are separated from the remaining proposals (the great majority put before the London capital market), it will be found that, with the exception of colonial development loans, they relate entirely to loans directly tied to international political interests. Palmerston had explained in 1840 (in answer to the request from some English bankers for a Government guarantee to a Turkish loan) that it was 'quite impossible for H.M.'s Govern-ment to take any part or to give any security direct or indirect'. He felt that there was no middle way; either the Government abstained altogether from saying anything which might sway individuals in lending their money to a foreign government, or it agreed to go the whole way with a Treaty of Guarantee.[12] And he knew very well that a Guarantee would be unaccept-able in Parliament without a strong political reason.

In a very general sense, this remained official policy until the end of the period. The Earl of Crawford, speaking for the Government, could still assure the Lords as late as 1922 that the government exercised no control over capital issues, and that it was government policy 'not to intervene between foreign governments and potential lenders in this market'.[13] The refusal to intervene applied equally to the *expenditure* of loans. 'Tied' loans (loans negotiated on condition that they were spent partially or in full on goods or services provided by the lender) were most uncommon before 1914, and the Committee on Industry and Trade, when considering the problem of directing and controlling the export of capital in British interests, concluded in its Final Report of 1929 that the practical difficulties were so great that, in its opinion, the balance of advantage was against intervention.[14]

11. Culbertson, *International Economic Policies*, p. 379.
12. Quoted by Olive Anderson, 'Great Britain and the Beginnings of the Ottoman Public Debt', *Historical Journal*, VII (1964), 47.
13. 49 *H.L.Deb.*5s.279–280(2 March 1922).
14. *Final Report of the Committee on Industry and Trade*, P.P.1929(Cmd.3282) VII, Section IV(3).

Exceptions, of course, exist. Palmerston found it difficult to stand aside when he saw British investors on the point of throwing their money away; he used the *Globe* and the *Morning Chronicle* as an unofficial means of putting his views before the public, and a draft exists in Palmerston's handwriting of a short leading article for the *Globe* warning the public against subscribing to a Uruguayan loan in 1835.[15] Later, in the case of the Tarapacá bondholder dispute with Chile (when Chile refused to consider a settlement so long as the London Stock Exchange obstructed the issue of a new Chilean loan), the Foreign Office went so far as to urge the Stock Exchange to withdraw its opposition; but the British Minister was warned that the Foreign Office had no control over the acceptance or rejection of loans.[16]

Such genuine intervention as did take place in loan issues during the period before 1914 was restricted to cases for which a real national political interest existed. In Greek finance, for example, H.M. Government had taken part, jointly with France and Russia, in guaranteeing a major loan in 1833 designed to give the new Kingdom of Greece a basis for financial stability and progress. Continual default brought the Foreign Office, much against its will, into close contact with Greek financial affairs for much of the last century. After a series of minor interventions which included the Anglo-French occupation of Piraeus in 1854 and the despatch of Major Law in 1892 to report on the state of Greek finances, Britain became party to an international financial Control (established in 1898 to supervise the payment of certain revenues assigned to the Guaranteed debt of 1833, the various loans of the '80s and the early '90s, and the new Guaranteed Loan). Like the Turkish Guaranteed Loan of 1855, the Greek Guaranteed Loans of 1833 and 1898 had nothing to do with the interests of British investors. The mechanism of a British Government guarantee was adopted to make it possible, for political reasons, to raise a loan on relatively easy terms in the European money markets on behalf of a country with no credit standing of its own.

15. Draft dated 24 October 1835: cited by Sir Charles Webster, *The Art and Practice of Diplomacy* (London, 1961), p. 195.
16. Foreign Office Memorandum, 26 February 1889: No. 38, *Further Correspondence respecting the Claims of Peruvian Bondholders, 1889,* F.O.,C.P.5878.

The guarantee system, by which H.M. Government agreed to make up interest payments should the debtor State find itself unable to service the loan, was the only form of intervention with the money market which a *laissez-faire* Government was prepared to consider: working within the framework of a free market, a guarantee meant, in effect, that British Government credit was substituted for that of the debtor State. But it was a system which was used as rarely as possible. A number of guarantees were given to promote the economic development of the Empire, among the earliest of which were those for Canadian and Indian loans. But unless there was an excellent political reason for doing so, no guarantees were accepted for economic development loans outside the Empire. For all the importance which Canning attached to Latin American markets, he completely refused to give guarantees for Latin American loans; he argued that such guarantees could lead to nothing except endless and tedious political complications. His attitude was reflected in H.M. Government's reaction to subsequent requests for financial assistance or guarantees for economic development abroad. Earl Percy, the Under-Secretary of State for Foreign Affairs, told the Commons in 1904 (in answer to Joseph Walton's pressure for increased government assistance) that H.M. Government had 'deliberately adopted an attitude of *laissez-faire*', and that it altogether declined to use State credit for the purpose of financing or assisting industrial or commercial undertakings overseas.[17]

Time and again over the last century requests were put to the government for guarantees for foreign railway projects, and they were always declined. In reply to Baron Reuter's suggestion of a government guarantee for a railway from the Mediterranean to the borders of India, the Treasury pointed out (1873) that 'it would be contrary to established rule for H.M. Government to guarantee interest on the cost of work undertaken in a foreign country'.[18] In spite of increasing political interest in the area, the Foreign Office felt unable to offer any guarantee for the projected Euphrates Valley Railway in 1883,[19] nor would

17. 129 *Parl.Deb.4s.*616(8 February 1904).
18. Quoted by L. E. Frechtling, 'The Reuter Concession in Persia', *Asiatic Review*, XXXIV (July 1938), 526.
19. 282 *Parl.Deb.3s.*510–11(26 July 1883).

the British Government or the Government of India consent to
the proposals put forward in the late '8os by Messrs. Mac-
Kinnon and MacKenzie for a Persian railway system, since the
proposals depended on a government guarantee.[20] The Anglo-
Russian Convention of 1907 gave Britain a strong interest in
retaining Russian favour in Persia, but the Foreign Office felt
it quite impossible to interest British capital in the proposed
Russian line from Tehran to Khanikin. Sir Arthur Nicolson
wrote to the British Ambassador at St. Petersburg early in 1911
to explain that British financiers could not be expected to
interest themselves in a scheme of this kind without a guarantee,
and that it was equally clear that H.M. Government would be
unable to furnish such a guarantee for railways in North
Persia—'As you know, it is very rare for the Government to give
guarantees for such enterprises, and we must reserve ourselves
for undertakings in which our trade is directly interested.'[21]
Much the same attitude was adopted in China, a further area
of political and financial tension during the first years of this
century. Salisbury had firmly resisted all mercantile pressure
for a Government guarantee for that Chamber of Commerce
panacea, the Burma/Yunnan Railway; he and his successors
resisted equally the many proposals which were put before
them for government guarantees for railway construction
within the British sphere of interest in China.[22]

The railway projects, substantial though some of them were,
did not offer sufficient political advantage to win the support of
Parliament. Though Salisbury on occasions and Sir Edward
Grey on others felt that a guarantee might be politically sound,
they both realized how difficult it would be to convert Parliament, and they normally refused even to try. A situation had to
have the emotional attraction of the rebirth of Greece, the
military urgency of buttressing Turkey, or the strategic importance of rebuilding Egypt, before Parliament would consent to a
guarantee. In a case like Morocco, where British political
interests existed but where those interests were not of prime

20. R. L. Greaves, *Persia and the Defence of India, 1884–1892* (London, 1959),
pp. 144 ff.
21. Nicolson to Buchanan, 28 February 1911: No. 702, *B.D.O.W.*,X,Pt.I,
680.
22. N. A. Pelcovits, *Old China Hands and the Foreign Office* (New York, 1948),
pp. 204, 229, 234–5.

importance, a guarantee was refused in the early '60s and again in 1902;[23] guarantees were refused to Turkey on all but the one occasion of the Crimean loan, and they were denied to China after H.M. Government had recovered from its fright of 1898. When Lansdowne rejected British participation in a proposed International Guaranteed Loan to China in 1901, he explained that it would be impossible to ask Parliament to pledge British credit—which stood higher than that of the other Powers—in raising a cheap loan on the international money market. Britain's share in such a loan simply did not make it worth while. But, he added, there was more to it than just that. He had been assured by those who had experience in these matters that former international guarantees had had the most inconvenient results; we had no desire to reproduce for China the complications of the Greek Loan of 1898.[24]

The opposition in Parliament even to the most obviously critical guarantees gives an idea both of the strength and of the rationale of feeling against them. In the case of the Crimean War Loan of 1855, the Cabinet was most reluctant to put forward a guarantee proposal. Clarendon told Stratford at Constantinople that the Cabinet would, he supposed, agree to a guarantee 'if it *must* be', but reminded him that H.M. Government, or rather the House of Commons, 'object to all guarantees and subsidies'.[25] When the proposal came up for debate, it was criticized most sternly by many of the leading politicians of the day. Gladstone felt that any guaranteed loan to a foreign Power, but especially to one placed in such equivocal circumstances as Turkey, was 'a bad and dangerous proceeding'; we should be prepared to give Turkey, if the need could be shown, whatever she required to carry on the war, but we should not allow ourselves to be inveigled into a guarantee which might give rise to the most formidable political difficulties, and which would certainly impose a heavy burden upon the people. Disraeli argued that the appointment of Allied Commissioners

23. F. R. Flournoy, *British Policy towards Morocco in the Age of Palmerston 1830–1865* (London, 1935), pp. 204–6: A. J. P. Taylor, 'British Policy in Morocco, 1886–1902', *English Historical Review*, 66 (1951), 372.
24. Lansdowne to Monson, 8 May 1901, and Lansdowne to Scott, 20 May 1901; Nos. 59 and 84, *Correspondence respecting the Affairs of China*, P.P.1902 (Cd.1005)CXXX.
25. Anderson, *Historical Journal*, VII, 54.

to control the expenditure of the Loan was 'an arrangement pregnant with political difficulties and dangers', and John Bright's strongest criticism of the loan was that it would be 'the first step in a direction which may ultimately lead to the partition of Turkey'. Mr. Ricardo could see no reason why the British taxpayer should be sacrificed so that Turkey might get her loan at a better price, and Cardwell added that, while he appreciated the need to secure the stability of the Turkish Government, 'he was not prepared to purchase that stability by voting for subsidies which he believed to be in themselves mischievous and certain to be followed by mischievous consequences'.[26] When a new Turkish Guaranteed Loan proposal was put forward in 1860, Palmerston, freed from the pressure of war, felt able to reject it vigorously on the grounds that Turkey should practice self-help and solve her own problems, that there was no point in pushing good money after bad, and that financial control would no doubt end in political control.[27]

The Turkish experience was certainly discouraging. When considering the prospect of a guaranteed loan to the Government of Egypt in 1884, Childers (the Chancellor of the Exchequer) reminded Mr. Alonzo Money that this was what we had done for Turkey in the Crimean Loan of 1855—'We set her on her legs with a vengeance, and she never stopped borrowing and wasting till she blew up'.[28] The following year Gladstone found himself with the unenviable task of persuading the Commons to accept the Egyptian guarantee. In the great debate of 26–27 March 1885, in which all the arguments against guaranteed loans were again put forward, Gladstone proved to his own satisfaction that such loans were not, in fact, invariably

26. 139 *Parl.Deb.3s.*1228–9, 1243, 1287, 1491, 1505 (20–27 July 1855). Olive Anderson argues that these July debates 'give a much exaggerated impression of the extent to which Parliament still entertained old prejudices against guaranteeing loans to British allies' [*A Liberal State at War* (London, 1967), p. 225]. This was certainly true of the particular case of the 1855 Loan, raised as it was at a desperate stage of the Crimean War. But it was not true of the attitude to subsequent guarantee proposals, as the examples given below will indicate. War finance is, after all, the special case *par excellence*.
27. Harold Temperley, 'British policy towards Parliamentary Rule and Constitutionalism in Turkey (1830–1914)', *Cambridge Historical Journal*, IV (1933), 164–5.
28. Childers to Money, 17 January 1884: quoted in Spencer Childers, *The Life and Correspondence of the Rt. Hon. Hugh C. E. Childers* (London, 1901), II, 199.

dangerous.[29] But the belief survived that an international guaranteed loan would give the Powers a stake in Egypt which would make our task of government that much more difficult, and which might lead, finally, to political disintegration.

The Egyptian Guaranteed Loan proved far less politically damaging, in actual fact, than the existing Control and Capitulations. But it was this experience, both of the Guarantee and of the Control, which weighed heavily against British acceptance of international Control in Portugal in 1899. Salisbury refused to join in the Franco-German pressure on Portugal; a Control over the Portuguese Customs in the interests of the Bondholders would, he said (with the partition of Portuguese Africa in mind), 'obviously be only the preliminary to demands of a much graver nature'.[30]

*   *   *

The Guaranteed Loans and the few 'political' loans to which H.M. Government's approval was attached (such as the Turkish Loans of 1854 and 1862 and the Moroccan Loan of 1861) were the only foreign loan flotations in which H.M. Government played a major part before the turn of the century. But other Powers were far less hesitant in making diplomatic use of their loans, and it proved impossible to remain entirely inflexible on non-intervention, especially in cases where political interests were likely to be damaged. The clash between the new and the old policies is neatly illustrated in the Chinese loan negotiations of the early '80s. Sir Julian Pauncefote was prepared to take the view that conditions in China (and more particularly the action of other Powers in pressing the interests of their own subjects) made it necessary to modify the old rule at least to the extent of making sure that British interests were properly protected. Granville seemed inclined to agree, but the Chancellor of the Exchequer, Mr. Childers, was strongly opposed to any government commitment towards British banking interests, and objected violently to the interference of British diplomatists in cases where British subjects were attempting to induce foreign governments to borrow money at exorbitant rates of interest. Mr. Childers' traditionalist view

29. 296 *Parl.Deb.*3s.690–4 (26 March 1885).
30. Salisbury to McDonnell, 7 June 1899: No. 21, *Correspondence relative to the Claims of the Portuguese Bondholders, 1893–1901*, F.O.,C.P.7537.

proved more acceptable at the time, and when Mr. McLaren suggested in the Commons, 22 January 1886, that H.M. Government might persuade the Chinese to raise their loans for public works in the London Money Market, he received the sharp answer from the Conservative Under-Secretary (Mr. Bourke) that 'it would be altogether contrary to the usual practice of the British Government to interfere with the manner in which the Government of China may see fit to raise loans'.[31]

But no Government could ignore indefinitely the increasing political importance of loans in areas such as the Levant and the Far East. The situation in Turkey, Persia, and China will be described in more detail below—for each of these countries British diplomatists were obliged to keep a sharp eye on the relative position of British finance, and in London the Foreign Office kept in contact with the City over all major financial questions. Negotiations were conducted with some delicacy, but H.M. Government's 'approval' or 'disapproval' of politically important projects such as British participation in the Trans-Persian Railway were enough to control the response of British financiers. Sometimes—as with the Crisp Loan to the Chinese Government—a British financier would refuse to follow the Foreign Office line, and since there was no machinery similar to French official control over the Bourse, he might be able to get away with it. But investors, as well as financiers, were sensitive to Foreign Office reactions to their loans, especially in disturbed parts of the world where they might have to call, at some point or another, for diplomatic protection. The Foreign Office itself was aware of this long before the peak period of diplomatic intervention. Salisbury, discussing three alternative Russian proposals for railway construction in Persia in 1890, felt that there was not much that could or need be done about the line through Khorassan to Herat or that from the Russian frontier to Tehran. But the third proposal, a line through Bunder Abbas, would involve a Russian approach to the money market, and in that case 'we should have them at our mercy'.

By announcing that we should look upon the construction of the line as a hostile act, and that we would not undertake, in the case of any

31. Pelcovits, *Old China Hands*, pp. 137–8; 303 *Parl.Deb.3s.*1802 (25 March 1886); 302 *Parl.Deb.3s.*191 (22 January 1886).

future disturbance, to respect the property of any shareholder or other person in the line, or any obligation upon it, we should effectually prevent money being raised on any Bourse in Europe.[32]

So blunt a weapon was seldom, if ever, used; the market was ready to take account of the Foreign Secretary's wishes, in part at least because it knew that those wishes would be expressed only in cases of real political importance to the Empire.

A clear explanation of the official attitude was given in the summer of 1914. During his examination by the Royal Commission on the Civil Service, Sir William Tyrrell (principal private secretary to the Secretary of State for Foreign Affairs) was asked about the relationship of the Foreign Office with such matters as the raising of foreign loans. He answered that the Secretary of State had, he knew, called in expert advice on occasion in questions such as an Austrian, Chinese or Turkish loan; but, he added, 'they are rare occasions, because we do not have the same intimate relations, say, with the financial world as foreign offices have abroad'.[33] The point was expanded a fortnight later by Sir Edward Grey himself. The Brazilian Government was proposing a new loan issue, and information had been received that the French and German Governments had told the Brazilians that no further loan would be authorized for issue and subscription in either country until the existing French and German creditors had been provided for. The question was whether the British Government would do the same, and prevent the issue of the new loan by British financiers in London. Grey pointed out, in reply to a Question in the House on 25 June, that some foreign governments had much more control over loan issues than we had; H.M. Government had 'no real control over British financiers as to whether they will subscribe or not'.[34] The subject was again raised during the debate on the Foreign Office Vote on 10 July. Sir J. D. Rees asked the British Government to make representations to the Brazilian Government on behalf of certain British claimants. Grey replied that H.M. Government, unlike the French

32. Salisbury to Sir Henry Drummond Wolff, 19 May 1890; quoted in full as Appendix VI by Greaves, *Persia and the Defence of India*, p. 270.
33. Minutes of Evidence, *Fifth Report of the Royal Commission on the Civil Service*, P.P.1914–16(Cd.7749)XI, QQ.40,933–5.
34. 63 *H.C.Deb*.5s.1960–1 (25 June 1914).

Government, could not use the question of the new Brazilian Loan to bring pressure on Brazil. The French Government could deny the Loan a quotation on the Bourse until claims had been settled, but in London the British Government had 'nothing to do with bringing out the loan'; and, Grey added, 'I think it is a good thing that the Government have not'. It was up to British financiers, he continued, to make their own arrangements with the Brazilian Government, and the British Government could not ask them to sacrifice their interests by withholding the loan merely so that some claims, with which they had no connexion, should be settled first. British financiers ran their business independently of politics, and if the British Government interfered, for example, with the granting or withholding of a loan, they would naturally expect the Government to come under some obligation to them. Grey felt that this kind of interference was not desirable, and that it was much better to leave British financiers to deal with such matters on their own. He concluded with a remark which might serve as the key to the H.M. Government's attitude to loan flotations overseas:

I do not say there are no cases in which loans have a political character and in which financiers come to the Foreign Office and ask if there is any objection to them. But generally speaking, and especially in South America, these are things in which the Foreign Office do not interfere.[35]

The outbreak of war made it necessary, for obvious economic reasons, to broaden the scope of state control. After 18 January 1915 Treasury sanction had to be obtained before any prospectus could be issued; the Treasury was careful, however, to make it clear that in considering whether or not it had any objections to new issues it took no account of, nor was it responsible for, the financial soundness of the schemes or the correctness of any statements made about them.[36] Borchard explains that control continued to be exercised by 'requests' from the Treasury or the Bank of England rather than by statute, but that the relations between issuing bankers and the officials were such that 'requests' had all the force of statute; the control was extended,

35. 64 *H.C.Deb.*5s.1448–9 (10 July 1914).
36. Max Winkler, *Foreign Bonds, an Autopsy* (Philadelphia, 1933), p. 149.

during the Depression, from new foreign issues to large purchases of foreign securities by British subjects, and controls became progressively tighter thereafter.[37]

A further effect of the Great War had been to create a more positive attitude towards the 'tying' of loans. 'Tied loans', though rare before 1914, had begun to make their appearance in areas of particularly sharp international rivalry. In the Shantung Agreement between the German and Chinese Governments of 6 March 1898, the Chinese Government accepted that if Chinese schemes requiring foreign capital were to be proposed for the development of Shantung, first application would be made to German capitalists; similarly, German manufacturers were to be approached first for the necessary machinery and materials, and only if they declined would the Chinese be at liberty to go elsewhere. International railway agreements with China early in this century normally contained the undertaking that the issuing house would act as the agent for purchasing all plant and materials, and the effect of this (when combined with the filling of the highest managerial and engineering posts by Europeans) was often, and for some nationalities always, to place orders with the creditor Power. But the first specifically *tied* loan undertaken by the British and Chinese Corporation was not negotiated until 1907, when Article 9 of the Canton/ Kowloon Railway Loan Agreement insisted that 'at equal rates and qualities, goods of British manufacture shall be given preference over other goods of foreign origin'.[38] This practice, which was never positively directed by the British Government, was not widely followed. In fact in the case of the Hukuang Railway Agreement of 1911, H.M. Government accepted the arguments put forward for *open* public tenders for Chinese railway material (at least as among the recognized Consortium Group); a policy of restricting orders to certain nationalities would, it was said, deprive China of the advantage of obtaining materials at the lowest competitive prices and lay her open to collusive action among the lenders in fixing price levels. The existing preference given to the Consortium was felt adequate

37. Edwin Borchard, *State Insolvency and Foreign Bondholders* (New Haven, 1951), I, 220–1.
38. The Chinese Railway Agreements are printed as Appendices A–F of P. H. Kent, *Railway Enterprise in China* (London, 1907), pp. 203–98.

to protect it against unfair competition from outsiders, and the advantage of open competition within the Consortium was that British manufacturers would have an opportunity to tender for any supply contracts without being limited to amounts proportionate to the British share in the Consortium's loan.[39]

Even in China, then, no clear position was taken on tied loans before 1914. But the argument was revived in the evidence given before the various war-time Committees, appointed to consider the competitive position of British industry once peace was restored. After weighing the evidence the Committees felt, on the whole, that Britain could no longer afford to resist the continental practice of insisting that money lent abroad should return, in large part, in the form of export orders. The 1916 Sub-Committee recommended that British financial houses should be urged to negotiate preferential treatment for British contractors and manufacturers, and the Departmental Committee on the Iron and Steel Trades advised that H.M. Government's permission for the issue of foreign railway and public works loans should be conditional on the purchase, so far as possible, of British plant and material.[40] But the old objections still appeared in Sir Hugh Bell's minority report, when he claimed that the limitations which the practice of tying loans would impose on lenders were 'eminently inadvisable', amounting, in fact, to a policy of protection from which he entirely dissented.

In the years immediately after the War, Government restrictions on the export of capital meant that the Treasury was unlikely to give permission for any overseas loan contract unless it was satisfied that the capital expended would return in the form of orders.[41] But in general, tied loans again went out of fashion during the 1920's, and the Committee on Finance and

39. Quoted in Hong Kong & Shanghai Bank to Foreign Office, 3 June 1919: No. 14, *Correspondence respecting the new Financial Consortium in China*, P.P.1921 (Cmd.1214)XLII.

40. *Report of a Sub-Committee of the Commercial Intelligence Committee with respect to measures for securing the position, after the War, of certain branches of British Industry*, P.P.1916(Cd.8181)XV; *Report of the Departmental Committee appointed to consider the position of the Iron and Steel Trades after the War*, P.P.1918(Cd. 9071)XIII.

41. Foreign Office to Hong Kong and Shanghai Bank, 20 May 1919: No. 10, *Correspondence respecting the new Financial Consortium in China*, P.P.1921(Cmd. 1214)XLII.

Industry felt it necessary in 1931 to draw attention once more to the need for some action in meeting the dangers of 'tied' enterprises developed by other Powers.[42]

*　　*　　*

The relationship of the British Government with the banks— the 'finance capitalists' themselves—was very much part-and-parcel of its attitude towards foreign loan issues and expenditure. In explaining how little control he had over London loan issues, Grey had pointed in 1914 to the lack of contact between the Foreign Office and the financial houses except in circumstances of political importance to the Empire. Similarly, in accounting for the lack of 'tying' conditions in British overseas finance, the war-time Committees had emphasized the differences which existed between British and Continental banking practices.

Lenin's belief that the 'monopoly' stage of capitalism had been reached in the early years of this century and his interpretation of the workings of 'finance capital' were based on what he understood to be the case in Germany; building on this, he constructed a model for the inter-relationship of government and finance which he assumed to apply equally to the United Kingdom. Since the publication of Lenin's booklet on Imperialism in 1917, it has, of course, been pointed out many times that the Lenin model does not fit the situation in Britain before the First World War, in part because of the relative scarcity of monopolistic combinations in Britain at the time, in part because of the differences in the banking system, and in part because of the quality of the British overseas investor.

The financial organization of London had developed in answer to the needs of commerce and trade, rather than of industry. When British industry began its nineteenth-century expansion, its financial requirements were modest. The units were small scale, and their needs were generally met by capital obtained privately within families or by reinvested profits; it was rare to make calls on the London capital market. Moreover, British capital was concentrated in relatively fewer hands than French or German. British investors tended to fall within a higher social and intellectual category than the peasant and

42. *Report of the Committee on Finance and Industry*, P.P.1930–31(Cmd.3897), para. 384.

petit bourgeois investors of the Continent; they were more
inclined to exercise their own independent judgement, and less
obliged to depend on the judgement of the bankers. British
industry—the Committee on Finance and Industry concluded
in 1931—'though making full use of the ordinary banking
facilities offered by the joint stock banks, maintained its
independence of any financial control'.[43] German industry, in
contrast, because of the scarcity of capital and of independent
investors, had been forced to associate itself much more closely
with the bankers. Dr. Goldschmidt claimed, in his evidence
before the 1931 Committee, that 'scarcely a single important
company in Germany has been founded without the collaboration of a bank'. Investment capital was more plentiful in
France, but the typical investor was a cautious, very small
capitalist, interested in low fixed-interest-yielding government
securities or debentures, and unwilling or unable to exercise
judgement independently of the large banks.

'Finance capital', then, in the Leninist sense of bank capital
on loan to industry, was a relatively insignificant element in the
economic structure of Britain before 1914, and a cheap victory
may always be gained over the Leninist theory of Imperialism
by accepting Lenin's own claim that it depended on the
emergence of finance capital at the beginning of the twentieth
century. But this, in a sense, is a verbal quibble, and it is more
to the point to decide how the different conditions in Britain
affected the relationship between London financial houses,
overseas enterprise and the British Government.

Industry in Britain, having made its own way without appeals
for outside aid, was naturally reinforced in that spirit of *laissez-
faire* and individualism which was so influential in determining
the extent of Government intervention in British enterprise
overseas. Moreover, as the Committee on Finance and Industry
pointed out, British industry, 'having grown up on strongly
individualistic lines, has been anxious to steer clear of anything
which might savour of banking control or even interference, this
attitude coinciding with the views which prevail in this country
as to the province of sound banking'.[44] There was slight
pressure from either side, therefore, to build up those vast,
interlocking, financial and industrial combines which, on the

43. ibid. para. 377.   44. ibid. para. 397.

Continent, were able understandably to exercise so powerful an influence on government.

In some areas of the world, where British political or general trading interests were very closely involved with financial and industrial success, the British Government would, indeed, have welcomed a closer collaboration on Continental lines between British financiers, contractors and industrialists. In China, for example, Sir John Jordan pressed anxiously for the formation of syndicates and combines which would prove more competitive with the organized groups of French, Belgian, German and Japanese capitalists. Reporting the formation of a gigantic Japanese syndicate designed to achieve a leading place in the industrial development of China, Jordan told Grey in March 1914 that it was 'manifestly futile to trust to individual efforts to compete with the organized machinery of these Franco-Chinese and Japanese-Chinese companies, and unless we are prepared to organize some combination of the same kind we must expect to be outdistanced by our rivals in the scramble for concessions'.[45] The history of Chinese loan negotiations in the years immediately before the First World War proved how genuine was the competition between individual capitalists in London for Chinese business, and how embarrassing this competition could be for the British Government. There was every incentive, where there were no political or general interests at stake, for the British Government to leave British capitalists to fight it out between themselves.

A further point is that the independence of the British investor—whether as an individual, a concessionaire, a contractor, or a partner in a financial house—made it difficult indeed for the British Government, short of a guarantee, to make sure that British investments followed its lead even on those comparatively rare occasions when it chose to take one. The French and German Governments had their own troubles with investors, and it is a mistake to believe that even Continental financiers were prepared to run unnecessary risks merely for patriotic reasons. But their troubles, with their relatively docile peasant investors and their *banques d'affaires*, were as nothing compared with those experienced by H.M. Government.

Lord Cranborne's remark (in the context of the failure of British capitalists to develop the large number of Chinese con-

45. Jordan to Grey, 15 March 1914: P.R.O.,F.O./405/216.

cessions secured by Sir Claude Macdonald in 1898) that 'you may take a horse to the water, but you cannot make him drink', applied equally to the reaction of British capitalists to 'political' concessions elsewhere in the world. Consul Wood's efforts in Tunisia in the '60s and '70s to promote political stability by foreign investment met with the problem that the London capital market was not prepared to take up and exploit the concessions he had been able to obtain.[46] The same was true of British enterprise in Turkey. The War Office told Salisbury in April 1888 that railway building in Asiatic Turkey was of great political and commercial importance to Britain, and that he should give any such enterprise 'a very considerable amount of support'. Dr. Smith notes that Salisbury's comment on this 'neatly summed up Great Britain's major difficulty'—'What is the use of all this', Salisbury asked, 'unless we know where the money is coming from?'[47] Twenty years later, Sir Nicholas O'Conor, in a covering despatch to Mr. Block's Memorandum on Franco-German economic penetration in Turkey, told Grey that the reluctance of British capitalists to invest in any form of enterprise in Turkey was a fact that had been evident for many years past, though he thought that the French public might yet have cause to regret their eager purchase of Ottoman funds.[48] The Young Turk Revolution improved things for a while, but right to the end of the period the Foreign Office had the greatest difficulty in persuading British capitalists to follow up political gains with investment.

Nor was it possible to interest British capital in Persia without political and financial guarantees, or without such artificial stimulants as the Royal Charter granted to the Imperial Bank on its formation in 1889. British capital—Whigham reported in 1903—would not flow into Persia without the guarantee of the British and Indian Governments, and we might just as well abandon any hope of doing anything in Persian railway development, and any hope of maintaining our prestige, unless we were prepared to give that guarantee.[49] In 1911, Sir Edward

46. A. Raymond, 'Les tentatives anglaises de pénétration économique en Tunisie (1856–1877)', *Revue Historique*, CCXIV (1955), 64–65.
47. Colin L. Smith, *The Embassy of Sir William White at Constantinople, 1886–1891* (London, 1957), p. 118.
48. O'Conor to Grey, 3 July 1906: No. 147, *B.D.O.W.*,V,174–5.
49. H. J. Whigham, *The Persian Problem* (London, 1903), pp. 423–4.

Grey still found it necessary to tell the Russians that he could not hold out any prospect of British capital being willing to go into Persian railways without some guarantee, and that he doubted whether French capital would do so either. Why should it, Mr. Parker had asked within the Department, when it could be invested at 5 per cent. in the South Manchurian Railway with a full guarantee from the Japanese Government?[50]

The fact was that the British Government, faced with a large but independent investing public, had no means of persuading more than a fraction of those investors to follow its lead, short of accepting responsibility itself for overseas loans. Continental investors were no more anxious to lose their money, but their decisions might often be taken for them by the directors of the *banques d'affaires* who, as individuals, were much more open to government influence, persuasion and even corruption. These points can be exaggerated—British investors made a number of foolish decisions, and many had not the least idea how to handle their money—but it is the proportion of investment ready to follow a political lead that is important, as well as the willingness of politicians or officials to give that lead.

A third point which develops from the individualistic nature of British finance and industry is one which goes further in explaining the shortage of 'tied' loans before 1914. It is clear that if issue houses in the City of London and manufacturers in the provinces had no contact with each other and no common financial interest, City financiers were unlikely to limit the scope and competitiveness of their overseas loan business by insisting on tying clauses in the loan contract. The acceptance by a foreign borrower of a 'tied' loan implied the counter-concession of easier terms—it implied a sacrifice by the lender. Since the lender and the manufacturer (who might expect to gain from a 'tied' loan) were seldom the same person, there was no obvious gain to the lender, and normally a clear loss, in imposing tying conditions in loan contracts. The popularity of London as the world centre for the issue of central, provincial, municipal government and public utility loans depended at least to some extent on the freedom from restrictive loan con-

50. Grey to Buchanan, 17 February 1911, and Alwyn Parker's minute on Buchanan to Grey, 16 February 1911: Nos. 692, 690, *B.D.O.W.*,X,Pt.I, 668–9, 667.

tracts, and the London Money Market was unprepared to sacrifice the advantage it gained from this liberal tradition in the interests of British manufacturers. The British and Chinese Corporation had accepted a 'tying' clause in 1907 as an acknowledgement, no doubt, of diplomatic assistance in obtaining the loan contract in the first place. But the attitude of the Hong Kong and Shanghai Bank towards a similar clause in the Hukuang Railway Agreement of 1911 showed the conflict of interest which was certain to exist between financiers, contractors and manufacturers, unless organised into a combination which crossed all these lines. Such combinations existed on the Continent, especially in Germany, and it was natural enough for the great German banks to make sure that their overseas loans brought orders for the industrial enterprises in which they themselves were so deeply interested. The British Government, though not prepared to direct the expenditure of overseas loans, would clearly have welcomed a closer tie-up between British overseas investment and export orders for British industry, and to some extent this came automatically through the British-operated enterprises abroad. But the Foreign Office tradition of non-intervention was too strong to permit any radical change of policy before 1914 (effectively, before the 1930's). Inhibited by *laissez-faire*, British politicians and officials refused to intervene in the free play of the capital market, and without positive government direction it proved impossible to obtain the same level of co-operation between British finance, commerce, and industry as existed so naturally on the Continent.

Although there were occasional complaints from British manufacturers and economists, it is doubtful whether this refusal to 'tie' loans to the purchase of British products did much real damage to British industry before the First World War. Germany in particular negotiated a number of tied loans, and France did the same; but restrictive loan contracts were open to much the same objections in Berlin and Paris as they were in London. Staley reports that not more than ten per cent of long-term international capital investments were in fact 'tied' in the early years of this century.[51]

In any case, the tendency was for much of the money lent abroad to come back in the form of orders irrespective of the

51. Staley, *War and the Private Investor*, p. 103.

existence of tying conditions in loan contracts. This was particularly the case with railway and public utility loans, which
had become the most popular form of foreign investment after
the early '70s. Railways, docks, gas works, telephone systems,
power stations, for which capital was raised in London, were
often built by British contractors and operated, once completed,
under British management. There was a natural inclination
(quite apart from patriotism) for British contractors, consulting
engineers and managers to use equipment with which they were
already familiar. Culbertson, for example, quotes the complaints
of a witness before the U.S. Federal Trade Commission on the
difficulty of selling American railway materials to the British-
controlled railways in Argentina: the witness claimed that
managements gave every possible preference to British products
even where a substantial saving might have been made by the
use of competitive American construction methods and
materials; in one case, in spite of urgent recommendations from
the chief and assistant engineers in Buenos Aires, the consulting
engineers and directors in London had adopted a 'very expensive and antiquated construction' in place of an American
design which would have produced a saving of 'upward of
$100,000'.[52] There was obviously much exaggeration in such
stories, and any number of cases existed of the adoption by
British-controlled railways of Belgian or American locomotives
and equipment on a simple cost and performance calculation.
But, whatever the reasons, orders *did* tend to follow capital.
Earl Winterton (the Under-Secretary of State for India)
explained as late as 1923, even after the war-time revival of
interest in tied loans, that all but five per cent. of Indian railway
contracts over the previous year had been placed in Britain
without any form of compulsion: what better answer could
there be—he asked—to the argument for a 75 per cent. 'tying'
condition in the new East India Loan?[53]

*   *   *

These factors were bound to affect the relationship of H.M.
Government and the bankers and to emphasize its difference

52. W. S. Culbertson, *Commercial Policy in War Time and After* (New York,
1919), pp. 323–4.
53. 166 *H.C.Deb.5s.*2080–1 (17 July 1923).

in character from that existing on the Continent, even if British officials and politicians had not themselves been so firmly in the grip of individualism, non-intervention, and *laissez-faire*. The Lenin model clearly does not apply, but neither, in fact, does the opposite condition described by Jacob Viner in his two articles of 1928. Viner, discussing such institutions as the Crédit Foncier, the Deutsche Asiatische Bank, the Prussian State Bank, and the Russian State Bank (state or quasi-state banks under the control of officials, which undertook loans to foreign governments), concluded that 'neither Great Britain nor the United States have banking instrumentalities which can be readily used in this way in the furtherance of their foreign policy'. In the same article, he considered French and German examples of government pressure on bankers to undertake loans to foreign governments, but claimed that he could find 'no evidence that the British government has ever exerted pressure on, or even requested, British bankers to make loans to any foreign government'.[54] The history of the Imperial Bank of Persia, the Hong Kong and Shanghai Bank, the negotiations with British financiers in Turkey and the National Bank of Turkey itself, make nonsense of so extreme a claim; it is impossible to ignore the close contacts which existed between certain of the overseas banks and H.M. Government. But at the same time the whole tradition of non-intervention in normal overseas financial transactions suggests that there must have been special conditions which made this departure from the rule necessary, and perhaps that there were even special limitations on the extent of the collaboration once it had been agreed to.

There can be no doubt that the Imperial Bank of Persia acted as the direct agent of the British Government. Its Royal Charter had been granted in 1889 in face of a persistent refusal to give such Charters over the previous quarter century. But the

54. Professor Viner, however, seems himself to have become aware, very soon after the publication of these articles, of a number of cases which did not fit his argument. For instance, he discusses the 1908 incident (when Grey attempted to persuade British banking houses to interest themselves in a Turkish loan) in his later article, written presumably after he had seen the recently-published Vol. V of *B.D.O.W.*: 'International Finance and Balance of Power Diplomacy. 1880–1914', *South Western Political and Social Science Quarterly*, IX(1929),432.

motives for agreeing to a Charter were political; the Bank was intended to rebuild Persian prosperity as a barrier to a Russian take-over. Though unsuccessful in its first aims, the Imperial Bank of Persia acted in and after the late '90s as the barely-disguised medium through which the Governments of Britain and India could forestall the Russians in the competition for 'political' loans. The Hong Kong and Shanghai Bank, in contrast, was far more independent of the British Government, primarily because of its powerful position in Far Eastern finance, which owed virtually nothing to British Government assistance. However, it became in 1898, together with the British and Chinese Corporation and the Peking Syndicate, the 'chosen instrument' of British financial diplomacy in China, and remained as such until the end of the period. The National Bank of Turkey, founded in 1909, was the direct brain-child of the Foreign Office. It was intended to restore the British position by creating—in emulation of the French-dominated Imperial Ottoman Bank and the Deutsche Bank—a single centre of British financial enterprise and influence at Constantinople; its first Governor was a seconded civil servant, Sir Henry Babington-Smith.

These banks and their associates enjoyed preferential treatment in the conduct of their business to a degree unheard-of elsewhere. The Imperial Bank of Persia was the only British institution of its kind at Tehran, and there was no question, therefore, of frequent calls for preferential treatment from the British Government. But in 1910, when Messrs. Seligman and the Bank were in rivalry over a Persian loan, the British Government was inclined to favour the latter.[55] There was much greater rivalry in Chinese finance and railway construction, but the British Government pledged itself to the British and Chinese Corporation and the Peking Syndicate for railway and mining concessions until late in the first decade of this century, and then bound itself to the exclusive support of the Hong Kong and Shanghai Bank in the International Consortium; official encouragements were printed in loan prospectuses, and contracts and concessions were formally registered at the Peking Legation. In Turkey the tradition of individual pre-

55. Noted in Sir G. Buchanan's Annual Report for Russia, 1910: No. 747 *B.D.O.W.*,X,Pt.I, 745.

ference was as old as Lord Stratford's assistance to the Ottoman
Bank in the '50s and as Lord Hobart's decision in 1862 to back
the Ottoman Bank against its British competitor, the Imperial
National Bank of Turkey.[56]

But if all this seems, on the face of it, to build up to a fairly
considerable degree of association between H.M. Government,
the City, and the overseas banks, it does so only if taken in
isolation and out of context with points already made. Everything so far has tended to indicate the distaste which British
politicians were likely to feel for a diplomacy governed by the
wishes of financiers. Lord Salisbury, writing to Sir Henry Elliot
at the end of 1879 on the situation at Cairo, remarked that it
was 'an unpleasant reflection that—as regards Egypt, France,
Austria, and Germany have all shaped their diplomatic action,
and that with great perseverance, purely to satisfy the interests
of certain bankers who were able to put pressure on their
foreign offices'; this, he complained, was 'a new feature in
diplomacy'.[57] Salisbury remained at the head of British
foreign policy for another twenty years, and his successors were
as little inclined as he was to mould their policy around
the wishes of the bankers. Lansdowne told the Lords in 1903
that it was a 'rare occurrence' for H.M. Government to be in
confidential communication with the City—'probably much
rarer in this country than in any other country in the world'.[58]

Two reasons alone were sufficiently powerful to overcome the
traditional reluctance of politicians and officials to interest
themselves in financial enterprise overseas: a serious political
danger (usually in some form or another connected with the
security of India and our routes to the East), or an alarming
threat to our existing relative position in world trade created by
the 'unfair' commercial and financial diplomacy of competitive
trading Powers. Where these reasons existed, as they did in
Turkey, Persia, and China, the Government was compelled to
take action. In the circumstances, the only action it could take
was to support those British financial interests which were of
sufficient resources and respectability to stand up to fierce

56. The details are in A. S. J. Baster, *The International Banks* (London, 1935),
pp. 80–93.
57. Salisbury to Elliot, 30 December 1879: quoted in Cecil, *Life of Salisbury*,
II, 359.
58. 121 *Parl.Deb.*4*s*.1344 (5 May 1903).

foreign competition; and this meant, if the policy were to be realistic, abandoning the rule of equal treatment and fair opportunities for all, putting pressure on British interests to combine and to adopt just those monopoly positions against which the Government fought so hard elsewhere, and putting the whole weight of British power and prestige behind individual groups of capitalists. It was a policy to which the British Government was never fully converted before 1914, or to which it was converted too late to make really effective. In China, from at least 1907 Sir Edward Grey and Sir John Jordan were in grave doubt as to how much longer they could justify a policy of preferential treatment, either to themselves or to the nation; the position in 1914 was that, officially at least, full competition was on the point of being restored. In Turkey, Baster points out, the fact that the National Bank was late in arrival and that its power and influence were 'decidedly less' than that of its French and German rivals, was 'in harmony with the general hesitant attitude of the British Government on the question of political interference in foreign investment'.[59] As for the British overseas banks in less critical parts of the world—in Latin America, in India, and in many parts of the East—no favours were asked or received from the British Government; they were 'typically the product of unrestricted private enterprise'.[60]

59. Baster, *International Banks*, p. 112.   60. ibid, p. 236.

CHAPTER 2

H.M. GOVERNMENT AND THE BONDHOLDERS

THE BRITISH Government, with rare exceptions, took no part in the negotiation, issue or expenditure of foreign government loans before 1914. But could it be true, nevertheless, that the investors in those loans—the bondholders —were able to mobilize official support for their claims? The Foreign Office had always been prepared to protect British interests, if not so ready to promote them. In claiming official protection, were the bondholders in fact in the position to exercise a substantial influence over British foreign policy? 'History shows,' said Hobson, 'in the cases of Egypt, Turkey, China, the hand of the bondholder, and of the potential bond-holder, in politics', and the trail set by Hobson has been followed eagerly, and often uncritically, by generations of historians. The bondholder was, and is still, described as an influential factor in British policy, and it is certainly time that some attempt was made to define the attitude of the British Government towards him and the lengths to which it would go on his behalf.

The defaults of the early 1820's first brought the problem of bondholder claims to the attention of the Foreign Office. Canning refused diplomatic intervention in the case of the Colombian default of 1823, and argued that that Loan, like all other such transactions in South America, had been entered into on the understanding that the responsibility of H.M. Government was in no way engaged.[1] Speaking in a debate the following year on the recognition of the new Latin American Republics, Canning pointed out that although he did not mean to throw the slightest blame on British subjects who employed their capital in loans to those States he felt that such people 'ought not to carry with them the force and influence of the British government, in order to compel foreign states to fulfil their contracts'.[2] He made his attitude unmistakably clear a

1. L. H. Jenks, *The Migration of British Capital to 1875* (London, 1938), p. 117.
2. 11 *Parl.Deb.2s.*1404 (15 June 1824).

few months later in reply to a request for intervention in Spain. He told Mr. Cairncross that he did not consider it as 'any part of the duty of the Government to interfere in any way to procure the repayment of loans made by British subjects to Foreign Powers, States, or individuals'.[3]

Canning had set the pattern for Foreign Office policy towards the bondholders, and it was a pattern which was to be followed well into this century. Aberdeen, while sympathizing with the hardships suffered by the South American and Mexican bond- holders to the extent of authorizing (in 1829) the good offices of British diplomatists on their behalf, observed that their griev- ances arose out of purely private transactions for which H.M. Government was not responsible and upon which it could not claim to interfere as a matter of right with foreign States.[4] The Chancellor of the Exchequer, Henry Goulburn, explained to the Commons a few days later that the Spanish bondholders stood on an entirely different footing from those British claimants against Spain whose property had been seized by Spanish war- ships. The bondholders, he said, had invested their money relying on the good faith of the Spanish government, and they themselves must be prepared to bear the misfortune if that government failed to meet its engagements; it would be a dangerous principle to admit that H.M. Government should interfere in such cases.[5]

Palmerston was no more anxious than his predecessors to intervene authoritatively on behalf of the bondholders. Within a year of taking office as Foreign Secretary he had refused official intervention against Colombia and Argentina,[6] and the position he then adopted was maintained throughout his long years of control over British foreign policy.[7] Speaking in reply

3. No. 1, *Correspondence relating to Loans to Foreign States*, P.P.1847(839.)LXIX.
4. Backhouse to Ewing, 8 April 1829: No. 83, ibid. The same position was taken with respect to the Spanish Loans in 1842 and 1846 (Nos. 21, 25, ibid.).
5. 21 *Parl.Deb.2s.*885–6 (16 April 1829).
6. No. 165, *Correspondence relating to Loans to Foreign States*, P.P.1847(839) LXIX (for Colombia); H. S. Ferns, *Britain and Argentina in the Nineteenth Century* (Oxford, 1960), pp. 222–3.
7. This can be confirmed by the following references: No. 29, *Correspondence relating to Loans to Foreign States*, P.P.1847(839)LXIX (for Spain, 1847); Nos. 7, 19, *Correspondence relating to Loans to Foreign States*, P.P.1854(53)LXIX (for Spain, 1849); No. 125, ibid. (for Ecuador, 1850); No. 17, ibid. (for Spain 1851); 143 *Parl.Deb.3s.*1237 (for Spain, 1856); 167 *Parl.Deb.3s.*526–7 (for Mexico and generally, 1862).

to Lord George Bentinck's motion on the Spanish bondholders, 6 July 1847, Palmerston refused active intervention against Spain. It was doubtful, he said, whether it was to the advantage of Britain to encourage her subjects to invest their capital in loans to foreign states, but, in any case, if the principle were established that the British Government was prepared to enforce payment in the event of default, Britain would be placed in the position of being liable at any point to become involved in serious international disputes without official control or influence over their origins. Palmerston felt that it would be unwise to intervene in the Spanish grievance, but added (for the benefit of hardened defaulters) that he was not disposed to question the doctrine that as a matter of strict right the British Government was entitled to demand redress and to enforce such redress if denied. He ended with the warning that, unless steps were taken by the debtor states to repay the £150 million (and interest) due to British subjects, the British Government might be compelled by the force of public opinion and the votes of Parliament to depart from the traditional policy of non-intervention in such cases.[8]

The 1848 Circular, addressed to British diplomatic representatives in the debtor States, confirmed and strengthened the views which Palmerston had already expressed in the Commons. Palmerston argued that it was a question of discretion and not of international right whether or not H.M. Government should accept bondholder grievances as the subject of diplomatic negotiations. Every Government, he said, had an undoubted right to use diplomacy in support of the well-founded complaints of its subjects against another Government, and redress might be demanded for the unsatisfied pecuniary claims of individuals; the right to demand redress could not, in the case of the bondholders, be decreased merely because of the great number of individuals and the very large sums of money involved. The British Government had hitherto abstained from official intervention on the grounds that the losses of imprudent British subjects would deter others from employing their capital in loans to foreign governments rather than in profitable undertakings at home, but the losses 'might become so great that it would be too high a price for the nation to pay for such warnings

8. 93 *Parl.Deb.3s.*1298–1306.

as to the future, and in such a state of things it might become the duty of the British Government to make these matters the subject of diplomatic negotiations'.[9]

Palmerston had intended the warnings in his speech and Circular to have a psychological effect which would make an actual change of policy unnecessary, and when it came to the point he had no cause to accept a change in following years. In spite of his threats, British policy continued to be governed by international right, and the discretion which he claimed was never exercised. Bondholder disputes were referred to the Law Officers, and their opinions on the rights and wrongs of intervention were based first on international law and only then on expediency—and expediency could act *against* bondholder interests as often as in their favour. Harding, for example, in his report of September 1856 on the legality of forcible intervention on behalf of the Venezuelan bondholders, decided that intervention would in this case be justified in law on grounds of flagrant violation of laws and of contract and of the fraudulent diversion of funds legally due and specially appropriated and assigned under severe penalties to the bondholders. But, he added, the expediency of a resort to force should be considered, as should the effect it would have in encouraging unwise speculations, and the break it would represent with the former tradition of H.M. Government in refusing to use force to collect bondholder debts.[10]

The Foreign Office continued (along the lines suggested in Harding's report) to distinguish between the right to intervene for claims originating in actual wrongs (for which redress was due, bondholder or not, under international law), and the general claims of the bondholders, whose misfortunes originated in voluntary speculations for the success or failure of which H.M. Government was in no degree responsible and in the advantage of which H.M. Government would not have shared.[11] At the end of April 1871 the Permanent Under-

9. The Circular is printed in full as Appendix II.
10. Bound in P.R.O.,F.O./83/2401.
11. It seems unnecessary to spell this out in detail, but the evidence for it exists in Lord Stanley's important despatch to Mr. Fagan, 15 September 1858, on British claims against Venezuela: P.R.O.,F.O./80/192; the evidence of the Rt. Hon. Edmund Hammond, Permanent Under-Secretary, on bondholder claims and Foreign Office policy in South America: Minutes of

Secretary (Edmund Hammond) sent a letter to the Council of
Foreign Bondholders which reaffirmed the Foreign Office
position and emphasized that Lord Granville was prepared to
depart in no respect from the views and principles frequently
laid down by his predecessors. H.M. Government, Hammond
continued, were in no way party to private loan transactions
with foreign states. Contracts of this kind concerned solely the
debtor Powers and the speculating capitalists (who were content to take extraordinary risks in the hope of large contingent
profits). Endless trouble would certainly arise from active intervention on behalf of the bondholders, and for these and other
obvious reasons the British Government had abstained 'as a
matter of wise policy' from intervention on behalf of the bondholders. H.M. Government would always be prepared to give its
unofficial support to bondholder claims and to exert its moral
influence on their behalf, but forcible measures such as reprisals,
and still less of a more warlike character, must never be
expected.[12]

Granville's policy was inherited by his successor, Lord Rosebery, and Bryce's Memorandum (prepared under Rosebery's
direction) explained the difficulties of permitting diplomatic
assistance to British subjects seeking contracts or concessions in
the 'more remote and less developed countries', adding that
these dangers of corruption and damage to the dignity and
usefulness of diplomatists were 'especially visible in the case of
loans at high rates of interest which the subjects of civilized
States sometimes seek to press on Eastern Governments':

Besides the political mischief which is apt to flow from such usurious
transactions (of which there has been ample evidence in recent
years), they confer no benefit on either the commerce or manufacturers of the country to which the lender belongs, and are there-

Evidence, *Report of the Select Committee on the Diplomatic and Consular Services*,
P.P.1870(382)VII, QQ.591–2; Lord Stanley's statement, as Earl of Derby
and Foreign Secretary 1874, that the remedy of the Spanish bondholders lay
not with the British government but with the exclusion of the debtor State
from the London money market: 221 *Parl.Deb.*3s.388–9 (21 July 1874); also
the Foreign Office's replies to the requests of the Peruvian bondholders for
intervention: Nos. 7, 9, 15, *Correspondence respecting the Complaints of the Peruvian
Bondholders*, P.P.1877(c.1835)LXXXVIII; and the reply of Derby's Under-
Secretary, Mr. Bourke, to the request for intervention on behalf of the Turkish bondholders: 225 *Parl.Deb.*3s.214 (18 June 1875).
12. Hammond to Hyde Clarke, 26 April 1871: printed as Appendix III.

fore no proper objects of the benevolent intervention of his Government.[13]

In contrast, Lord Salisbury's sympathy with bondholder claims has been interpreted as marking a change in Foreign Office policy towards a less inhibited approach to intervention. In a minute on a group of papers (including a copy of Lord Granville's letter of 1871) which had been prepared to guide him in his policy towards the Peruvian bondholders, Lord Salisbury complained that he did not 'quite understand the principle of absolute abstinence from interference in such cases'. We always interfered, he added, when a foreign Government committed a wrong towards a single British subject; why should we not interfere when that wrong was done to hundreds?[14] But this was in October 1878, and Salisbury had only recently succeeded Derby at the Foreign Office. He was soon put right. A couple of years later he was telling the British Minister at Caracas that the 1848 Circular still expressed the policy of H.M. Government on intervention,[15] and the instances of permissible intervention which he quoted to a deputation of Turkish bondholders earlier that year were only those which had always been acceptable to the Foreign Office. Salisbury told the Turkish bondholders that he had seen it occasionally said that H.M. Government should never interfere on behalf of injured bondholders. He himself felt unable to accept this, since the bondholders were British subjects and their legitimate interests were the concern of their Government as much as those of any other subjects. The Foreign Office judged each case on its particular circumstance. In cases of simple default due to misfortune or necessity, it would be improper for H.M. Government to exact payment; but where unfair discrimination had been exercised between equal creditors, or where the preferential rights and securities of British subjects were unjustly denied, grounds

13. The Memorandum is printed as Appendix V.
14. Annexed to a Foreign Office minute on the Peruvian bondholders, 1 October 1878: **P.R.O.,F.O.**/61/323.
15. No. 53, *Further Correspondence respecting the Claims of British Subjects on Venezuela 1879–1880*, F.O.,C.P.4394. The 1848 Circular again formed the basis of Foreign Office policy during the 90's under both Rosebery and Salisbury: for example, H.M. Government's attitude to the Argentine bondholders as observed in Ferns, *Britain and Argentina*, pp. 476, 478n.

would exist for special sympathy from the Foreign Office.[16]

H.M. Government grew more receptive to bondholder complaints as increased foreign competition in the '80s and '90s compelled a general relaxation of the traditional policy of non-intervention in trade and finance overseas. But Salisbury's reaction to the renewed complaints of the Turkish bondholders in 1887 was to offer them no more than 'a tender, but perfectly platonic, expression of sympathy', and when Balfour, as Prime Minister, was accused of subordinating British policy to the Venezuelan bondholders in 1902, he had a sharp reply. International action, he admitted, might occasionally be justified on their behalf, but he looked on such action 'with the gravest doubt and suspicion', doubted whether we had ever in the past gone to war for the bondholders, and would be very sorry to see that made a national practice.[17]

The Great War and its aftermath made no noticeable impression on the official attitude towards bondholder claims. International Law remained the basis for determining policy, and in 1928 the British official Reply to a League of Nations' enquiry on government interpretations of international law set out in full the conditions on which the British Government felt able to intervene. The Reply pointed out that repudiation of debts by a Legislature necessarily by-passed recourse to local tribunals, and in the case not of an inability to pay but of a determination not to implement a contract, the responsibility of the State would be engaged. Each case, however, would have to be examined on its merits. If the repudiated debt were guaranteed by another State which was called upon to implement the guarantee, the debtor State would, of course, be directly responsible to the guarantor. But a mere failure of the State to fulfil the terms of a bondholder contract did not amount to a violation of international law, since the obligation of the State was merely to a private person. Unless—the Reply concluded—the failure to fulfil the contract with a private person

16. Interview reported in *The Times*, 7 January 1889, 7e, f. Salisbury made the same point in his comment on the Delagoa Bay Railway claim; he noted that intervention could be justified if the pecuniary injury to British subjects resulted from deliberate wrong, but not in cases merely of failure, mistake, or misfortune on the part of a foreign Government: 337 *Parl.Deb.3s.*1810 (9 July 1889).

17. 116 *Parl.Deb.4s.*1273 (15 December 1902).

was accompanied by some circumstances rendering it a violation of the State's duty to that person's own State, the *international* responsibility of the State was not engaged.[18]

*   *   *

It is perfectly clear, then, that official intervention was
denied to the bondholders unless their loans were under British
Government guarantee, or unless some incident had transformed their claims from the level of private debt-collecting to
that of an international obligation. Bondholders, as far as the
British Government was concerned, were individuals choosing
to invest abroad for their own profit; in doing so, they were acting independently of the interests of their nation and gambling
merely on a higher rate of return on their capital. The British
Government had never concerned itself with the business
affairs and decisions of individuals, and claims for sympathy
were greatly diminished by the official prejudice against the
diversion of useful investment to the unilateral benefit of foreign
States. The bondholders were particularly unfortunate in three
respects: a clear policy of non-intervention had been laid down
from the beginning; their claims were always readily distinguish-
able from the general interest; and, by the end of the century,
even the term 'bondholder' itself tended to evoke an automatically hostile response from officials and the public alike.

But although the general policy of H.M. Government towards the bondholders was clear enough, it is still very necessary—if misunderstandings are to be avoided—to explain how
this general policy worked out in practice. The rule was no
official or 'authoritative' intervention. But the 'good offices' of
British diplomatists were often extended to the bondholders,
and 'good offices'—when exercised by such men as Consul-
General Chatfield in Central America or Consul-General
Wilson in Chile—must have been difficult indeed to distinguish from unqualified diplomatic intervention. Chatfield
was finally disowned by the Foreign Office (as were all those
who imitated his methods), but it was far from easy to lay down
the law for behaviour in distant and politically unstable
countries, especially before the days of telegraph. And the
distinction between the types and degrees of intervention

18. *League of Nations Publication V,* Legal 1929, V.3, 202–3.

available to the bondholders is further confused by practices such as the supply of letters of introduction to bondholder agents, the use of British diplomatists as a channel of communication between the bondholders and foreign governments, and the occasional employment of British diplomatists and consuls as salaried or unsalaried agents of the bondholders.

Letters of introduction to British diplomatic representatives overseas were given, if requested, to the appointed agents of the bondholders, but they were always qualified by the instruction that the British representative should avoid any action which might be interpreted as official intervention.[19] When diplomatists actually introduced bondholder agents to debtor Governments they were equally careful to dissociate themselves from more than a mere recommendation to favourable consideration.[20] From the days of the first defaults British diplomatic agents were prepared also to transmit bondholder Memorials and letters to defaulting Governments, even where the bondholders had their own agents on the spot, and the effect was to appear to give official sanction to the bondholder complaints. But such action could be taken only on instructions from the Foreign Office, and the Foreign Office (which was aware of the implied responsibility) often refused its permission. Palmerston, when approached by the Rothschilds in the '40s to present a memorial through the Washington legation on behalf of the State bondholders, declined to have anything to do with it on the grounds that 'British subjects who buy foreign securities do so at their own risk and must abide the consequences of any speculation of this kind which they may enter into'.[21] Examples exist both for the Egyptian and the Turkish bondholders of official refusals to transmit bondholder Memori-

19. For example, Mr. Bourke's answer to a Question in the House on the letter of introduction supplied to Mr. Clark, agent for Mr. Croyle's Committee of Peruvian bondholders: 235 *Parl.Deb.*3s.1391–2 (17 July 1877); also Foreign Office letter to Mr. Brogden, M.P., on the letter of introduction given to Mr. C. L. Smiles (21 May 1884): No. 168, *Further Correspondence respecting the Foreign Creditors of Peru 1881–1884*, F.O.,C.P.5046.
20. The standard qualification is made in Mr. Turner's Note to the New Granadian Foreign Minister, 20 November 1832: No. 174, *Correspondence relating to Loans to Foreign States*, P.P.1847(839)LXIX.
21. Quoted by Reginald C. McGrane, 'Some Aspects of American State Debts in the Forties', *American Historical Review*, XXXVIII (July 1933), 682.

als.[22] But a firm policy could not be laid down for every occasion and circumstance. In some cases there was no danger of incurring official responsibility; in others, foreign diplomatists were the only agency through which foreigners could communicate with the central government. As Granville explained in 1884 to the outraged Childers (Chancellor of the Exchequer), Sir Harry Parkes had had no choice in acting as he did in the case of the Chinese Telegraph Loan, because foreigners had no access to the Chinese Government except through diplomatic channels and 'on that account Foreign Ministers in China have necessarily become the medium of communication with the Supreme Government in matters of this kind'.[23]

The practice of permitting the employment of consuls and diplomatists as agents of the bondholders was even more ambiguous. British consular agents in Central America during the '30s and '40s of the last century acted virtually as official agents of the bondholders not only in the transmission of correspondence with the local governments, but also in arranging for the division of the Federal Debt on the dissolution of the Central American Federation in 1838, and in taking charge of the sale of tobacco consigned to the servicing of the foreign debt. Consul-General Chatfield described himself, indeed, to the Government of Costa Rica as 'acting under the instructions of Her Britannic Majesty's Government for the benefit of the bondholders, invested with full authority to represent their interests in Central America, and to treat thereon with the local Government'.[24] A Parliamentary return in 1872 showed the Chargé d'Affaires, the Consul at Cartagena, the Vice-Consul at Bogotá and the Acting Vice-Consul at Santa Martha all acting as Agents for the Colombian External Debt with a commission of 1 per cent. on sums remitted, while the Chargé d'Affaires for Central America was Agent for the Custom House duties mortgaged to British bondholders at San José

22. Lord Tenterden to the Turkish bondholders, 12 April 1876: No. 17, *Correspondence respecting the Ottoman Loans*, P.P.1877(c.1744)XCII; Tenterden to the Egyptian bondholders, 29 May 1876: No. 88, *Correspondence respecting the Finances of Egypt*, P.P.1876(c.1484)LXXXIII.
23. Quoted by Chung-sien Chen, 'British Loans to China from 1860 to 1913, with special reference to the period 1894–1913', London thesis, 1940, p. 60.
24. Nos. 144, 146, 153, *Correspondence relating to Loans to Foreign States*, P.P. 1847(839)LXIX.

(Costa Rica) at a commission of $1\frac{1}{4}$ per cent. on receipts.[25]

The existence of these agencies gave some protection—sometimes accidentally, sometimes by design—to bondholder interests. In the case of the Moroccan Loan of 1861, Earl Russell would not consent to a guarantee. But he was so anxious, for political reasons, to make the loan a success that he agreed to the assignment of the interest and the sinking fund to an Agent appointed by the Foreign Office on the express understanding that, although it would not bind the British Government to make good any deficiencies in the revenue set apart for servicing the loan, it would at least guarantee to the contractors that the money would be faithfully appropriated to the purposes of the loan.[26]

But the Foreign Office attempted, so far as possible, to limit government responsibility. In 1830, when Lord Aberdeen, at the urgent request of the Mexican bondholders, authorized the British Vice-Consuls at Vera Cruz and Tampico to receive and transmit the money due to the bondholders from the Mexican authorities, the Foreign Office was careful to explain that this was to be the full extent of their functions and that they were not to be permitted to act as the general agents of the bondholders; the Vice-Consuls were told, furthermore, that they were at perfect liberty to accept or decline the bondholders' proposal and that they would be undertaking the agency entirely on their own responsibility.[27] Similar restrictions were imposed on agencies accepted later in the century. Mr. Corbett, the Chargé d'Affaires in Central America, was permitted to receive the duties hypothecated to the bondholders by the Government of Costa Rica only on the understanding that he acted in the matter without official responsibility or inter-

25. *Return of Consuls restricted from Trading and of Appointments other than Consular held by any such Consuls*, P.P.1872(c.472)LXI. The British Minister at Tangier also acted as Commissioner for the Moorish Loan, but he received no remuneration for his services either from the Loan contractors or from the Moroccan Government: information on this is in P.R.O.,F.O/83/381.
26. No. 6, *Papers relating to the loan raised by the Emperor of Morocco in London*, P.P.1862(2916)LXIV.
27. No. 86, *Correspondence relating to Loans to Foreign States*, P.P.1847(839) LXIX. Other contemporary examples can be found in Palmerston's authorization of an agency for the Peruvian bondholders (1832) and Aberdeen's for similar agencies in New Granada (1842): Nos. 252, 202, ibid.

ference;[28] and when, towards the end of the century, the Chilean Government offered a settlement of the nitrate certificate holders' claims which included the transmission of the amounts awarded (less a 5 per cent. commission) through H.M. Government, the Foreign Office reluctantly agreed, but only on the express condition that this should not imply any undertaking to enforce the claims of the certificate holders or to be responsible for the failure of the Arrangement.[29]

However hedged with conditions, the mere existence of agencies created complications and misunderstandings. The bondholders of the Venezuelan 1826 Loan, for whom the Chargé d'Affaires at Caracas had been allowed at one point to act, attempted to use this permission as giving them a special claim for Foreign Office intervention, in spite of the fact—as Lord Stanley reminded the Law Officers—that the agency had been accepted (in deference to the repeated requests of the bondholders) only on the 'express and recorded' understanding that H.M. Government incurred no liability and that the Chargé d'Affaires was acting merely by permission, not by direction of, the Foreign Office.[30] Equally in the case of the Corbett agency for the Costa Rican Loan, the fact of the agency was used by the loan contractors to improve the appearance of the prospectus for a Second Issue of £500,000; the agency in turn led to angry denunciations by the Costa Rican Finance Minister who accused Mr. Corbett of acting in his official capacity to press the purely private interests of the Costa Rican bondholders.[31]

* * *

The furnishing of letters of introduction, the transmission of memorials, and the acceptance of agencies were matters entirely at the discretion of the Foreign Office and its agents overseas; they were undertaken *ex gratia* in consideration of 'the great respectability of the parties represented', 'the importance

28. Appendix No. 3, *Return of Consuls restricted from Trading*, P.P.1872(c.472) LXI.
29. Nos. 58, 59, *Further Correspondence respecting the claims of the Peruvian Bondholders 1887*, F.O.,C.P.5630.
30. Stanley to Law Officers, 23 May 1867: P.R.O.,F.O/80/188.
31. Appendices 21 and 23, *Report from the Select Committee on Loans to Foreign States*, P.P.1875(367)XI.

of the interests at stake', or 'the disappointments and hardships to which a large body of Her Majesty's subjects are exposed'. They were acts of mercy, sometimes readily agreed to but as often harshly denied. The general rule remained to avoid intervention if at all possible.

But there were certain circumstances in which the Foreign Office felt a duty to intervene on behalf of the bondholders. It would have been illogical, for instance, to have denied bondholders that protection against discriminatory treatment which was given to every other British interest overseas. J. D. Harding advised the Foreign Office that it might support the claims of two British bondholders against the Venezuelan Government, 'inasmuch as even a South American Government cannot be permitted to pay the French holders of its Bonds, and at the same time to withhold payment from English holders of other Bonds of the very same description'.[32] The same view was taken of any international settlement of bondholder claims, and the Foreign Office invariably felt obliged at least to make sure that British bondholders received treatment parallel to that obtained by other nationalities.[33]

Moreover, while H.M. Government felt that it had no right to protest against such legitimate acts of sovereignty as an emergency decision to pay a lower rate of interest on an External Debt,[34] the Conversion of a Debt,[35] or the reduction in the value of a Debt by government-authorized depreciation of the currency,[36] the Foreign Office considered itself through-

32. Opinion dated 19 May 1854: P.R.O.,F.O/83/2400.
33. For example, in the Dominican Republic at the beginning of the twentieth century, when a protest was delivered and redress officially demanded on behalf of the British bondholders as against the favoured French and Belgians: William H. Wynne, *State Insolvency and Foreign Bondholders* (New Haven, 1951), II, 255–7 and ns.
34. Elliot to Derby, 7 October 1875: No. 14, *Correspondence respecting the various Ottoman Loans*, P.P.1876(c.1424)LXXXIV. The Turks were sensible enough not to reduce the rate of interest on the Guaranteed Loan of 1855, in which case H.M. Government would have been obliged to pay up or intervene.
35. Aberdeen's refusal to support the Portuguese bondholders against the Conversion of 1842: No. 62, *Correspondence relating to Loans to Foreign States*, P.P.1847(839)LXIX; refusal by the Foreign Office to intervene in an Argentine Conversion in 1882: Ferns, *Britain and Argentina*, p. 386.
36. When the French Government refused after the 1914–18 War to compensate British holders of the French Loans for losses resulting from the depreciation of the franc, the Foreign Office could only protest unofficially on grounds of equity.

out the period entitled to secure the inalienability of securities already hypothecated to British bondholders. During the first half of the century, protests were delivered by British diplomatic representatives in Chile, Peru, Ecuador, and Nicaragua against the diversion of hypothecated funds.[37] In the second half, Salisbury was able to secure the priority of previous hypothecations over the Russian Indemnity at the Congress of Berlin in 1878;[38] the British Chargé d'Affaires at Lima officially protested (1884) against the sale or lease of the Pisco/Yca Railway without any reservation of the prior lien of the bondholders;[39] the Law Officers agreed (1895) that Britain would be entitled to protest against any diversion of the Nicaraguan export duties secured to the bondholders of the railway loan;[40] and, in 1898, Greece was compelled to accept an International Financial Control designed to secure the rapid payment of the Turkish indemnity without damage to the rights of the old creditors of the Public Debt. As late as 1913 a British warship was sent to Guatemala to assist Lionel Carden in his efforts to obtain the return of the alienated coffee duties to the payment of the coupons on the British loan.[41]

The transfer of territory from one State to another might also result in government intervention on behalf of the bondholders, although the British Government never developed a completely consistent policy either for a simple transfer or for the distribution of a debt following the subdivision of a State into two or more independent States. Britain maintained, on the division of the State of Colombia into New Granada, Venezuela and Ecuador (1829–31), that each of the new states was responsible for a proportion of the debt contracted by the original Republic.[42] Similarly, when the Central American Federation

37. Nos. 337, 273, *Correspondence relating to Loans to Foreign States*, P.P.1847 (839)LXIX.
38. H. M. Government continued to keep a watchful eye on these hypothecated duties after the Congress: Layard to the Porte, 23 October 1879, and Salisbury to Layard, 28 February 1880: Inclosure in No. 83, No. 102, *Correspondence respecting the Ottoman Loans*, P.P.1880(c.2709)LXXXII.
39. Inclosure 2 in No. 5, *Further Correspondence respecting the claims of Peruvian Bondholders 1885*, F.O.,C.P.5245.
40. No. 38, *Reports by the Law Officers of the Crown 1895*, F.O.,C.P.6796.
41. Borchard, *State Insolvency and Foreign Bondholders*, I, 258.
42. Phillimore's Reports on Ecuador, 13 April and 4 November 1863, cited in Lord McNair, *International Law Opinions* (Cambridge, 1956), I, 174–5: also J. D. Harding's Report on Buenos Aires, 10 June 1854, in which he insisted

dissolved, the individual States were again held responsible for the Federal Debt,[43] and the same applied to the new Balkan States created at the Congress of Berlin. But no positive steps were taken by the British Government to insist that Panama should take over any proportion of the Colombian Debt when she declared herself independent in 1903, in spite of the bondholders' request that recognition should be withheld until Panama's share of the Debt was acknowledged. Where territory was transferred, the position was even less clear. The Law Officers admitted, in their Report on the cession of the Peruvian Province of Tarapacá to Chile, 2 February 1884, that it would be more equitable if a State were to assume a proportion of the debt of another State when it annexed some part of the other's territory, but they denied that there was any fixed rule of international law to that effect. Treaties of Peace had frequently, but not invariably, provided for the equitable apportionment of the debt, and the Law Officers felt that if there had not been some special circumstances in the Tarapacá claim which justified intervention it might have been doubted whether H.M. Government would have had any grounds for official action.[44]

Where, of course, there was any question of an international obligation between States, H.M. Government was bound to intervene. Palmerston admitted during the 1847 debate on the Spanish bondholders that the British Government would be obliged by custom to intervene where the transaction in dispute had been founded on previous compacts between two governments or had had the sanction of the British Government. He went on to explain that, in the case of the British holders of the French *rentes*, Castlereagh had distinctly made it known that compensation had been exacted from them in the 1814 Treaty

that it was a 'well-known principle of international Law that neither a revolution in the Government, nor even a division of territory of one of the contracting powers, cancels Treaty obligations or affects the rights of the other contracting power': ibid., 176.
43. For example in Chatfield's Note to the Nicaraguan Government, 14 February 1848, in which he remarked (with characteristic exaggeration) that 'it is one of the commonest principles of law and justice that each joint debtor should be responsible for the whole of a joint debt, and this principle Her Majesty's Government will, if necessary, be prepared to uphold': No. 96, *Correspondence relating to Loans to Foreign States*, P.P.1854(53)LXIX.
44. McNair, *International Law Opinions*, I, 170–1.

merely because, by prior treaty, the French Government had been bound not to confiscate British property; Castlereagh had warned the British public that if in future they invested their money in French funds without the sanction of the British Government, they must not look for similar support in the event of further confiscation.[45] When Palmerston was again requested some years later to intervene on behalf of the Spanish bondholders, he claimed that the British Government had not been a party to the original transaction and could not therefore claim such an international right as that currently urged by the Spanish Government on the Government of Mexico (where the Spanish demands were founded on an engagement entered into between the two Governments).[46] But such intervention as took place on behalf of the Egyptian bondholders between July 1880 and the summer of 1882 was founded on the international arrangements sanctioned by international law and forming an international obligation on Egypt.[47] And if a loan were 'guaranteed' by the British Government, there was obviously no room for manoeuvre; an international obligation existed which no British statesman could ignore.

As a general rule, the Foreign Office refused altogether to take any part in negotiating an Agreement, or to sanction provisions in Agreements which, if accepted, would have created an international responsibility. The Honduras bond-holders, for example, wanted to make it a condition of settlement that the British and French Governments should 'take note' of the Arrangement of the Loan with the Honduras Government. The Foreign Office refused to accept this condition, since it was felt that it meant nothing and that the discovery that it was meaningless would make the position worse than before; the Foreign Office itself was not inclined to accept any responsibility.[48] When the Peruvian bondholders came to an arrangement with the competing interests of Messrs. Dreyfus, the Foreign Office declined to accept the suggestion that the British Government should join the French Govern-

45. 93 *Parl.Deb.3s.*1298,1305 (6 July 1847).
46. 143 *Parl.Deb.3s.*1237 (22 July 1856).
47. 273 *Parl.Deb.3s.*1942–3 (16 August 1882).
48. Undated memorandum by Arthur Larcom (attached to the preliminary contract between the bondholders and the Venezuelan Government, 11 January 1905): P.R.O.,F.O/80/476.

ment in acceding to Article IV of the Agreement, since it
imposed on the two Governments 'obligations of a very extensive and undefined character'. The Earl of Iddesleigh added
that H.M. Government were not aware of any precedent for
such a course, and 'must decline altogether entering into any
compact with the claimants such as would be involved in
accepting the obligation "to take charge of their interests" in
accordance with the provisions of the Agreement in question'.[49]

But where little prospect of responsibility seemed to arise, or
where political reasons made it seem sensible to keep in step
with the other creditor Powers, the Foreign Office occasionally
accepted a diplomatic article in an Agreement. Lord Lansdowne reluctantly agreed to Article VI of the draft Covenant
of 1901 between the bondholders and Guatemala, by which the
Government of Guatemala was to 'notify' the arrangement to
the interested Governments as a binding engagement on the
part of Guatemala, and by which a memorandum was to be
endorsed on the bonds to the effect that one or more of the
creditor Governments had taken note of the undertaking;[50]
and he came very close to accepting a similar clause in the
Bases of Arrangement (1902) of the Portuguese External Debt
(where good political reasons existed for an active interest in
Portuguese affairs).[51] But in a parallel apolitical case a few
years later, when the bondholders attempted to write an international obligation into their provisional contract with Venezuela, Lansdowne rejected the clause outright.[52]

*   *   *

The part played by the bondholders in determining British
foreign policy is often, perhaps even normally, misunderstood.
Since the beginning of this century the bondholders have
served as scapegoats in interpretations of economic imperialism

49. No. 64, *Further Correspondence respecting the Claims of Peruvian Bondholders
1886*, F.O.,C.P.5426.
50. Memorandum forwarded to Lansdowne by Lord Avebury, 1 November
1902, and the attached memorandum by Villiers, 5 November 1902: P.R.O.,
F.O/80/476. The clause was based (with far less justice) on the formula used
in the Chinese Imperial Railway 5 per cent. Loan of 1898.
51. Inclosure 2 in No. 43, Nos. 47–54, *Further Correspondence respecting the
Claims of the Portuguese Bondholders 1901–1903, Pt. II*, F.O.,C.P.8535.
52. Foreign Office to Council of Foreign Bondholders, 22 March 1905;
P.R.O.,F.O/80/476.

which turn increasingly on finance rather than trade. Indeed, only a few years ago John Strachey, experienced politician as he was, felt no hesitation in including the bondholders among the agents of British imperialism. And historians themselves have found difficulty in reaching a reliable conclusion. Much of the explanation for isolated examples of government intervention on behalf of the bondholders is to be found in the official interpretation of a Government's obligations under international law. But an historian cannot have a Law Officer at his elbow; he is understandably shy of invading the territory of the international lawyers, and those invaluable guides to British policy in the protection of British subjects abroad—the Law Officers' Reports—have remained, for some reason, largely unexplored. The result has been that many examples are quoted of 'successful pressure' by the bondholders on Whitehall which, if examined, turn out to be no more than the limited response which was available to any British subject under the current interpretation of international law. The British Government was bound to provide a degree of protection in certain well-defined circumstances, and, except that officials tended to be prejudiced *against* the bondholders, it mattered little to the Foreign Office whether this protection was claimed by a bondholder, a merchant, a traveller, or someone's wandering maiden aunt.

It is not even clear that in the majority of cases where bondholders came into conflict with debtor Governments, they actually wanted or expected diplomatic assistance. Victorian bondholders, after all, were as schooled in *laissez-faire* as other members of the middle and upper classes. They had their own means of exerting pressure on foreign governments which were often more effective than calls for dilatory diplomatic assistance. From the first decades of the nineteenth century they had organized themselves into committees for each Debt in default, and in February 1869 the Corporation of Foreign Bondholders was established to provide a focus for their activities. London was still the principal market for foreign Government Loans, and pressure could always be brought to bear on any Government simply by threatening to withhold quotations on the London Stock Exchange or to publicize defaults. As for diplomatic assistance, Goschen had warned the bondholders in the earliest

days of his connexion with their Council that the reward for
risk was the high rate of interest obtainable abroad, and that it
would be dangerous to foster the impression that when Englishmen lent money to foreign Governments they were creating a
national obligation guaranteed by the full power of the British
State.[53] A quarter of a century later Lord Farrer chaired a
meeting of the Rosario, Cordoba, and Santa Fé bondholders
at which he told his suffering audience that 'it was idle to
suggest the interference of our Government', and explained that
the bondholders' committee had not asked the Government to
do anything, not thinking it either their business to do so, or
the business of the Government to interfere on their behalf.[54]

It is easy enough to lose one's way in that maze of distinctions
—so happily navigated by the Victorian diplomatist—between
'unofficial' or 'official' action, 'good offices' and 'authoritative'
intervention. It is as simple to miss the important distinction
between Convention and ordinary bondholders—a distinction
which is most relevant, for example, to the British decision to
participate in the international coercion of Mexico in 1861–2.[55]
Convention bondholders, of course, were those British subjects
who, as a result of a Diplomatic Convention, had accepted
bonds from foreign governments in settlement of their legitimate
claims (for personal injury or damage to property). In contrast
to ordinary investors or speculators in the External Debt, they
were entitled to demand diplomatic intervention until their
bonds were paid off. Mr. Bunch, the British Minister at Caracas, made the distinction in his despatch to Salisbury of 28
April 1879. Listing his objections to the Venezuelan proposal for
the amalgamation of the 'Diplomatic' [Convention] Debt and the
ordinary External Debt, Bunch explained that the ordinary
bondholders had lent their money voluntarily, whereas the
holders of bonds in the 'Diplomatic' Debt had been 'despoiled
of their property in violation of distinct treaty stipulations':

53. Quoted by Jenks, *Migration of British Capital*, pp. 290–1.
54. Meeting reported in *The Times*, 10 July 1895, 14a.
55. Victor Dahl writes of the influence of the 'creditors' on British policy
towards Mexico ['Business Influence in the Anglo-Mexican Reconciliation
of 1884', *Inter-American Economic Affairs*, 15 (1961–2), 33–51]. But his conclusions are invalidated by his failure to distinguish between the varieties of
'creditor'. Support of the Convention bondholder was obviously a very
different matter from official promotion of the claims of British bondholders
in the ordinary External Debt.

The first have no right to expect anything beyond the usual treatment of contributors to foreign loans, viz., reasonable honesty and such payments as the circumstances of the debtor may warrant; the second have a distinct right to be paid in cash, with proper interest and within a given time. It would scarcely be fair to put them into the same category as their fellow-sufferers. The one may be entitled to good offices, the others have a right to efficient protection.[56]

This, indeed, was the essence of the Foreign Office attitude to the protection of bondholder interests overseas before the First World War. 'Good offices' were the full extent of diplomatic support available to the bondholders, and a sharp distinction was drawn between the ordinary claimant legitimately aggrieved by damage to his person or property overseas, and the home-based bondholder drawing interest on a loan for which he himself was responsible and by which British investment was diverted abroad to the benefit of a foreign State.

56. No. 8, *Correspondence relating to Venezuela*, F.O.,C.P.4055.

CHAPTER 3
CONTRACTS AND CONCESSIONS

THE SHEER size of international loans, the number of financiers interested in their promotion and flotation, and the wide range of individual investors, have tended to focus attention on international capital issues. But the activities of the 'concession-monger' have often been at least as influential in creating international tension and in contributing to what has become known as 'economic imperialism'.

It will come as no surprise to learn that the British Government before the 1880's did not regard the promotion of contracts and concessions as included within its legitimate functions. Contracts and concessions, it argued, were the concern of individual entrepreneurs, and it was up to them to negotiate direct with foreign governments, on their own and without diplomatic intervention; any interference by the British Government would run against the tradition of *laissez-faire*, involve British diplomatic representatives in transactions which would injure their prestige and their ability to serve Britain's general interest, and identify British diplomatic support, against existing practice, with an individual interest (in conflict, perhaps, with competing British interests of equal respectability). The Government, of course, was prepared to give concessionaires such protection as it was bound to provide by its interpretation of international law, but this would be no more nor less than the protection available to any British subject overseas.

Sir Edmund Hornby, looking back on a judicial career at Constantinople and Shanghai which had covered most of the third quarter of the last century, asked whether the Foreign Offices of civilized countries would ever learn that it was 'no part of their business to sanction the use of their diplomatic agents to promote the interests of reckless gamblers'. Legitimate business enterprise, he claimed, made its own way without diplomatic assistance and there was nothing to be said against it; 'but turning Ambassadors and Ministers into the agents and humble servants of speculators and concession hunters is quite another thing'.[1] Hornby's views were echoed in the replies to Mr. Bryce's request, early in 1886, for Service opinions on the proper degree of diplomatic assistance to British interests overseas. Edmund Monson, from Copenhagen, pointed to the danger (and probable damage) to diplomatic usefulness and integrity in becoming entangled in speculative contracts and concessions in areas such as East Europe and South America, where it was 'but too notorious that the standard of morality, alike political and commercial, is regulated by considerations repudiated as discreditable by the professors of an older and higher civilization'. Sir Robert Morier, British Ambassador at St. Petersburg, reminded Bryce that 'no rule had been more absolutely insisted upon in the dealings of Her Majesty's Missions abroad' than that unless there had been a denial of justice or a breach of Treaty obligations 'no assistance shall be rendered to further private interests'. Mr. J. A. Crowe, the British Commercial Attaché at Paris, felt that a Diplomatic or Consular Agent might just find it feasible to promote the interests of concession-hunters in remote countries, but he quoted the recent case of a British Minister in Eastern Europe whose interference in a railway concession had led to the request for his recall and to a rebuke from the Foreign Office for his ill-advised intervention in matters of foreign trade. Consul Stanley of San Francisco claimed himself entirely against diplomatic pressure for concessions from foreign Governments, Municipalities and Corporations, and felt that the customary non-intervention had materially strengthened British diplomatic influence when it had had legitimately to be exerted for British interests generally. Consul-General Thomas Michell (Norway) noted that it was certainly undesirable for British consular officers to be mixed up in 'concession-mongering'. There were few such cases, he said, in which negotiations were not conducted in a spirit inconsistent with the character of a British official, and which, should he participate, would not consequently vitiate his position and paralyze his general utility. Moreover, contracts and concessions were open to competition; suspicion, reproaches and complaints would result from the favouring of one firm over another. Michell's brother, Consul

1. Hornby, *Autobiography*, pp. 114–15.

John Michell of St. Petersburg, argued that British promoters
should depend for their success on their own enterprise, the
merit of their undertakings and the activity of their agents,
rather than on British official co-operation (a co-operation
which would compromise the independence of position hitherto
enjoyed by British consuls abroad). He added that 'all efforts
on the part of British consular officers to assist their countrymen
in obtaining concessions, contracts, etc., by the exercise of undue
influence and pressure on official and private persons, are for
many reasons to be highly deprecated'. Consul George Brackenbury reported from Lisbon that, while he could not speak for
uncivilized countries, the objections to a policy of promoting
concessions in European countries and those of like civilization
were 'obvious, and some of them insuperable'. A Consular
Agent, he explained, would be brought into close contact with
intrigue and backstairs influence which, however much he
himself stood aside, would 'lower his character, and *pro tanto*
his usefulness, not only with the foreign authorities, but also
with those of our own people with whom he has to deal'.[2]

The strong distaste shown by British officials for pressure for
contracts and concessions overseas was shared by the politicians.
In the case of the notorious Reuter concession for the development of Persia, Earl Granville had entirely refused Government
protection and assistance, moral or material: although H.M.
Government would be happy to see Persian resources developed
—he told the Lords in 1873—it would be 'altogether out of our
usual course' to act otherwise.[3] The debate twenty years later
over a further Persian concession—the Talbot Tobacco Concession—gives an interesting indication of the strength of
popular feeling against Government assistance to the 'concession-monger'. James Bryce, now in Opposition, pointed out
that it had been well-established in Granville's 1881 Circular
and in his own 1886 Blue Books that the British Government
and its overseas representatives should deal with attempts to
obtain concessions with the greatest caution and tact, 'not only
because it is desirable not to waste our influence, which should

2. Nos. 37, 44, 32, 75, Inclosure in No. 67, Inclosure in No. 77, No. 71,
Correspondence respecting Diplomatic Assistance to British Trade Abroad, P.P.1886
(c.4779)LX.
3. 217 *Parl.Deb.3s.296–7* (14 July 1873).

be reserved for political purposes, upon mere pecuniary matters, but also because a great deal of suspicion is likely to attach to the Foreign Office and its Representatives if they endeavour to press the claims of their own subjects'. In spite of Government denials, he felt that these principles had been transgressed, and his view was shared by Mr. Labouchere, Sir G. Trevelyan, Mr. Seymour Keay, Mr. Winterbotham, Mr. Morton, and Mr. Hunter—in fact, by all the speakers in the debate other than the Government spokesman, Mr. Lowther.[4] Lowther did not defend a change of policy, but claimed merely that the British Government had had nothing to do with the negotiation of the Talbot concession; he had in fact already declared himself, in a letter to *The Times* only six weeks before, as opposed to pressure for concessions.[5]

*   *   *

Official distrust of 'concession-mongering' was soundly based, and it continued to determine British official policy until 1914. But the same factors of rising foreign competition and 'unfair' foreign diplomatic pressure which were affecting traditional policies everywhere during and after the '80s, forced the Foreign Office to consider whether there were not exceptional cases in which the official policy might have to be waived. In the mid-'80s a vigorous campaign had been conducted in the press and in the Chambers of Commerce to bring British diplomacy more into line with the kind of pressure for contracts and concessions accepted and exercised by foreign diplomatists in the East. *The Times*'s Far Eastern Correspondent, writing at the beginning of 1886, reminded his readers of the long and honourable tradition by which British officials kept strictly aloof from the commercial dealings of British subjects with native officials. With some notorious exceptions, this tradition had been observed equally by other diplomatists, but recently there had been some bitter complaints about a wholly new policy of 'touting' for orders adopted by German officials. It might be time, therefore, to consider whether British officials might not go a bit further in giving assistance, especially in a place like

4. The debate on the Talbot Concession, which forms part of the Supply debate of 26 May 1892, is printed in : 4 *Parl.Deb.4s.*1944–62.
5. *The Times*, 9 April 1892, 6c.

China where competition was no longer 'fair' and where foreign officials formed a necessary bridge between Chinese officialdom and despised commerce.[6] In a leading article a couple of months later, *The Times* returned to the subject, pointing out that the British practice of non-intervention implied, if it were to work fairly, 'that trade should be perfectly free, and neither trammelled nor favoured by Government and law'; this, alas, was no longer the case, and though only 'Socialistic dreamers' would expect the Government to supply British businessmen with trade or find them customers, the Government might fairly be expected to help British trade (especially with information). In semi-civilized Powers such as China, which were just beginning to modernize themselves, officials might well second the efforts of British merchants and manufacturers to prove that British rails and ships were better and cheaper than German—'To abstain from so doing, in the face of the desperate efforts of Germany and France, is magnificent, but it is not business.'[7]

Meanwhile, the Chambers of Commerce and individual businessmen were arguing along similar lines. Both the London and the Glasgow Chambers of Commerce drew the attention of H.M. Government to the kind of support which foreign diplomatists were now giving. They were aware of the long tradition of non-intervention at the Foreign Office, but, as the Glasgow Directors suggested, where there was any doubt in future about the proper degree of diplomatic assistance, action might be determined 'by reference to the nature and extent of the support which our foreign competitors received from the Representatives of their Governments'.[8] Others took up the point of the peculiar appropriateness of diplomatic pressure at a time when China seemed on the verge of substantial railway and defence development. The Secretary of the British Iron Trade Association felt that the Chinese Government could not hold out much longer on railway concessions, and he reported the Association's view that British diplomatists might suitably be employed in attempting at least to ensure that British houses

6. ibid. 2 January 1886, 12a, b.
7. ibid, 1 March 1886, 9b, c.
8. Glasgow Chamber of Commerce to Rosebery, 19 March 1886: No. 24, *Correspondence respecting Diplomatic Assistance to British Trade Abroad*, P.P.1886 (c.4779)LX (the views of the London Chamber of Commerce are printed as No. 1, ibid.).

should have the same facilities as their foreign rivals when the concessions became available.[9] Sir Robert Jardine, in a private letter to Lord Rosebery at about the same time, argued that just now, when great changes were taking place in the attitude of the Chinese Government, it was particularly important that British traders should get support to the extent of a guarantee of fair play in the international competition for railway and war material contracts.[10] These views, of course, were impressed on the Foreign Office time and again over the next few months.

The only really substantial development in Foreign Office policy had in fact already taken place, and the result of the agitation was merely to put this in black and white. In August 1885 Lord Salisbury, anxious at the reports of German diplomatic activity in Japan, had instructed the British Minister at Tokyo to support British commercial interests where foreign diplomatists were interfering to their detriment; and six months later, identical instructions were sent to the Minister at Peking.[11] But James Bryce (Under-Secretary of State to Salisbury's successor, Lord Rosebery) was obviously impressed by the unanimous disapproval of 'touting' for trade and 'concession-mongering' which he had received in answer to his Foreign Service Circular of March 1886. He had also been warned by Plunkett in Japan and O'Conor in China of the damage which was likely to be done to the position and dignity of British diplomatic representatives in the East by any direct imitation of German methods. Rosebery, in fact, had instructed O'Conor in April that the wisest course for the moment in China (where the German and American Ministers were said to be scrambling for railway contracts and concessions) was to stand aloof, while at the same time keeping a sharp eye on the contracts and concessions obtained by the subjects of other Governments.[12] It was unlikely, therefore, that Bryce's Memo-

---

9. British Iron Trade Association to Foreign Office, 18 March 1886: No. 22, ibid.
10. Jardine to Rosebery, 8 March 1886: P.R.O.,F.O/83/932.
11. Nos. 36, 38, *Correspondence respecting Diplomatic Assistance*, P.P.1886(c.4779) LX.
12. Rosebery to O'Conor, Secret, 9 April 1886: No. 43, *Correspondence respecting British Trade and Commerce in China and other Foreign Countries 1885–1886*, F.O.,C.P.5471.

randum (prepared very largely in answer to the diplomatic threat to our commercial and financial position in the Far East) would—for contracts and concessions, at least—show any advance on the permission given by Salisbury the previous year. Nor did it. Mr. Bryce pointed out that the question of contracts and concessions presented special difficulties both because of the danger of converting diplomatists into trade agents and because of the problem of discriminating between different British interests. But it would be the duty of British diplomatists to make sure that British subjects obtained 'a fair hearing and full consideration' and that 'competitors belonging to other countries gain[ed] no advantage by the influence of their Envoys'. When foreign envoys were using exceptional pressure, Bryce continued, British diplomatists might find it necessary to do the same, reminding the local government simultaneously that H.M. Government would regard exceptional favour to the subjects of other Powers as 'a departure, amounting to a mark of unfriendliness to itself, from the safe rule of equal favour and open competition'. But such pressure, if justified by local and particular circumstances, was only to be exerted under the following four conditions: that no preference was shown among British competitors; that no questionable means, such as bribes, should be connived at; that no guarantee should be given to a British contractor without special instructions from London; and that without such instructions, no action should be taken in support of a British subject which would entail an obligation on H.M. Government.[13]

* * *

In parts of the world where foreign diplomatic pressure was a real problem, the effect of Salisbury's 1885 instructions and Bryce's Memorandum of the following year was perceptible, if in no sense revolutionary. Mr. Bourne, who was Acting-Consul at Tamsui (Northern Formosa) told the Royal Commission on Civil Establishments only a few years later that he himself had negotiated some concessions on behalf of British merchants and had received the approval of the Foreign Office for doing so, although ten years before this would have been 'out of the ordinary routine of consular work'; he added that the younger

13. Bryce's Memorandum is printed as Appendix V.

generation of consuls were doing all that they could for trade, certainly more than the older consuls who had been 'brought up under another system'.[14] But Bryce, giving evidence before the same Royal Commission, explained that the general view taken in 1886 was that a British representative abroad should not allow himself to become a mere trading agent, and that if he imitated the practices of some other foreign powers this would damage both his own dignity and that of his country; he might, it was true, legitimately counter foreign diplomatic pressure, but only so long as he did not directly identify himself with a British merchant, or give any ground for the impression that his diplomatic post was 'sinking into a mere trading agency'.[15]

The storm in the Commons over the Talbot Tobacco Concession showed the continued strength of the opposition to any direct link between officials and the individual concession-monger, and there is no doubt that only the strongest reasons could have persuaded the Foreign Office to change its mind. Two forms of concessions alone carried sufficient weight— concessions of the category discussed in 1886, to be pressed for in counteraction of the pressure of foreign governments and of the 'unfair' treatment of British trade, and a second category of 'political concessions', demanded not for the benefits they would provide for British contractors or investors but for their importance as part of a British political interest. Within the first category came some of the concessions negotiated by Sir Claude MacDonald in China during the 1898 'Battle of Concessions', and such contracts and concessions as the Embassy at Constantinople was able to obtain before the Young Turk Revolutions. Sir Edward Grey, who had been Lord Rosebery's Under-Secretary in the last Gladstone Administration, remembered how impossible it was in the Turkey of the early '90s to get a concession of any kind without the aid of diplomacy. 'Where diplomatic pressure was the rule,' he said, 'commercial interest could not succeed without it', and the Embassy, with the approval of the Foreign Office, did what it

14. Minutes of Evidence, *Report of the Royal Commission on Civil Establishments,* P.P.1890(c.6172)XXVII, QQ.29,973–7.
15. ibid. QQ.28,009–10. See also the evidence of Sir Philip Currie, Permanent Under-Secretary, ibid. QQ.26,983–6.

could to help British firms in their applications for railway concessions in Asia Minor.[16]

But in commercial concessions generally, the limit set to Foreign Office support stopped short of the sacrifice of political interests or the use of force. In 1898, Lord Salisbury warned concessionaires who applied for British Government support that although H.M. Government might make forceful representations on their behalf to counteract German diplomatic pressure in Turkey, it did not intend to 'proceed from words to blows';[17] and his warning applied equally to Persia and the Far East. There was a certain amount of feeling in the Commons that the Government had gone too far in taking so active a part in the 1898 scramble in China. Mr. Buchanan, who was later to be a junior Minister in the Liberal Government of 1906, pointed out in the debate on 'British Commercial and Political interests in China' (March 1900) that nine-tenths of the recent Blue Book on China (China No. 1, 1900) had consisted of negotiations between the Foreign Office and the Peking Legation as the result of which the claims of various British concessionaires were forced on the Tsungli-Yamen. It was not pleasant, he said, to read of this constant pressure for concessions, and he reminded the Commons of Mr. Brodrick's declaration of 8 February 1899 in which the Under-Secretary had explained that the Foreign Office could not go to China and insist 'as an act of pure piracy' that every mine, railway, and other concession over a large part of China should be handed to British concessionaires. Mr. Brodrick, speaking at the same debate, observed that it could not be said that the Foreign Office had been backward in obtaining concessions for British subjects in China; but he repeated that we could hardly force such concessions on the Chinese Government where they were demanded by British subjects, often without any serious financial backing, who felt, for example, that they would like a concession for the mining rights over an entire Chinese province; nor could we disagree with the Chinese Government's decision to call a halt to further grants of concessions

16. Viscount Grey of Falloden, *Twenty-five Years, 1892–1916* (London, 1925), I, 9.
17. Salisbury to Currie, 24 March 1898, quoted by Harold S. W. Corrigan, 'British, French and German Interests in Asiatic Turkey, 1881–1914', London thesis, 1954, p. 174.

until the existing grants had been worked.[18] Some months later, in the context of Turkish concessions, Mr. Brodrick argued that the Government could not go beyond 'friendly representations'—'We are not the custodians of any concession which may be given by foreign Powers all over the world, but we desire to do the best we can for our own interests'.[19]

The 'best we can' was limited to ensuring, as far as possible, a fair field and no favour; pressure could be applied only in answer to foreign diplomatic pressure. On the whole, the four pre-conditions to diplomatic support set out by Mr. Bryce in 1886 continued to guide the Government in the assistance it was prepared to give to commercial concessions, although it did not prove entirely possible to hold to the position that no preference should be shown among British competitors. In China, for example, and even in Turkey, the alternative to pressing the interests of one particular British firm was often the loss of the contract or concession altogether, and in these circumstances the 'no preference' rule had to be abandoned.

However, the second category of concessions—the 'strategic' or 'political' concessions—demanded a different quality of diplomatic pressure. The decision on the extent to which they were to be supported depended on a political rather than a commercial or financial calculation, and if political interests required the use of force, then force was used. The distinction between a 'political' concession and a 'commercial' concession —like that between 'unofficial', 'officious', and 'official' inter-vention—was clear to the old-style diplomatist, but less so to the Government of the 'semi-civilized' country with which he dealt. In Persia, for example, British officials were not interested in excluding 'legitimate commerce' by other Powers, or even certain categories of concessions. The concessions restricted to Britain and Russia were those which, in whatever form, gave opportunities for the exercise of political influence. An exchange of opinions between Sir Arthur Nicolson (British Ambassador at St. Petersburg) and Sir Charles Hardinge (the Permanent Under-Secretary) illustrates the distinction. Nicolson reported a conversation with M. Isvolsky, the Russian Foreign Minister, in which he had argued that because railway and other con-

18. 81 *Parl.Deb.4s.*872, 883–4 (30 March 1900).
19. 87 *Parl.Deb.4s.*482–3 (2 August 1900).

cessions in countries such as Persia 'carried more with them than appeared on the surface', we could not admit other Powers to concessions within our sphere; but even in our own spheres we had no wish to close the door to legitimate commerce, while throughout the rest of Persia there would be room enough for any concessions which other Powers might wish to promote. Hardinge's comment was that it might distinctly be stated in the preamble to the Convention that 'the door will be open in the spheres of influence to the trade of all countries and the concessions to be reserved might be limited to roads, railways, telegraphs, harbours and irrigation'.[20] Exactly the same problems were faced in China, where Jordan in 1914 was careful to distinguish between industrial interests 'of a political complexion' (railway, territorial or perhaps mining concessions, loans involving control over Government undertakings), and non-political industrial interests such as '*bona fide* participation in shipping, mines, or mills'. The first group alone were to be restricted to British subjects within the British sphere of interest; the others, since they threatened no political interest, would be open to the world.[21]

The general rules which governed the degree of pressure to be exercised on behalf of British contractors or concessionaires abroad did not, of course, apply to 'political' concessions, and the failure to grasp this distinction between 'political' and 'commercial' concessions lies at the root of much of the criticism of economic imperialism. No doubt the methods used in pressing 'political' concessions on semi-civilized powers were often indefensible, but they had nothing directly to do with the interests of British financiers.

This, then, was the position in 1914. Contracts and concessions did not normally, as far as H.M. Government was concerned, form the subject of diplomatic negotiations. There was a general permission (subject to certain fairly stringent conditions) to apply diplomatic pressure where foreign Powers were themselves using diplomatic influence to our detriment, and there were classes of concessions which were supported, at

20. Nicolson to Grey, 4 November 1906, and Hardinge's minute on this despatch and enclosure: No. 367, *B.D.O.W.*,IV,409,411. The final position is described in the chapter on Persia in Pt. III below.
21. Jordan to Grey, 27 February 1914: P.R.O.,F.O/405/216.

crisis points in British overseas diplomatic relations, as political weapons and for purely political purposes. The increase of foreign competition, and the tendency to use concessions ever more frequently as political weapons, made it difficult to hold back. Grey especially found this to be the case, but when he defended the record of his Government in obtaining concessions in Turkey, Persia, and China, he pointed out that the laurels to be gained from pressing for commercial concessions were the kind one preferred to keep in one's pocket rather than wear on one's brow, and that he personally would have much preferred to see concessions given out of good will than obtained by diplomatic pressure.[22] The Royal Commission on the Civil Service, in fact, advised against identifying either the Diplomatic Service or the Consular Service with the interests of individual concessionaires.[23] And even Sir Eyre Crowe's Foreign Office Committee of 1916 (which, under pressure of war, favoured a less negative approach to commercial and financial diplomacy) agreed that some restriction must be placed on the Government's freedom to promote and negotiate commercial and industrial concessions abroad.[24]

* * *

It has been suggested already that one of the reasons why Government support for contracts and concessions has attracted so much criticism has been the failure to distinguish between the policy adopted towards 'political' concessions and towards 'commercial' or 'financial' concessions. There is, however, another source of confusion. The argument, as far as the British Government was concerned, was over the *promotion* and *negotiation* of contracts and concessions, not over their *protection* once negotiated; the question of the appropriate degree of protection to be given by British diplomatists was decided according to the British interpretation of international law. But critics have seldom been careful to distinguish between promotion and protection. Legitimate acts of protection have been confused with a supposed Government pressure for contracts and concessions, with the result that promotion and

22. 64 *Parl.Deb.5s.*1442 (10 July 1914).
23. *Fifth Report of the Royal Commission on the Civil Service*, P.P.1914–16(Cd. 7748)XI,Pt.II,ch.V,para.13.
24. An extract from the Report is printed as Appendix VI.

protection are united into a general condemnation of H.M. Government, apparently under the thumb of London financiers, ruthlessly pressing the City's interests on the peoples of the under-developed world.

Even the most reputable authorities on international diplomatic protection have assumed too much on far too little evidence. Professor Borchard, for example, citing only the very doubtful authority of the rupture of British diplomatic relations with Bolivia in 1853 (which was by no means simply a contract case), claimed that the general belief that Britain did not interfere in claims arising out of contracts was 'erroneously based' on Palmerston's 1848 Circular, to which he added, in a footnote, that 'in fact, Great Britain has often interposed to redress breaches of contract'.[25] The error was Borchard's. The Foreign Office consistently refused (with certain exceptions recognized in international law) to support a contract claim unless there had been a denial of justice before the local tribunals. The rule, formulated by Borchard himself, that 'diplomatic interposition will not lie for the nature or anticipated consequences of the contractual relation, but only for arbitrary incidents or results, such as a denial of justice or flagrant violation of local or international law',[26] remained broadly true for British diplomatic policy throughout the period. Intervention could be justified internationally if British subjects were denied free access to local tribunals,[27] or fair treatment before the tribunals;[28] if a settlement had been reached with regard to

25. E. M. Borchard, *The Diplomatic Protection of Citizens Abroad or the Law of International Claims* (New York, 1928), pp. 290–1 and ns.
26. Borchard, *Diplomatic Protection*, p. 284.
27. Aberdeen's intervention in the Montgomery, Nicod & Co. case against the Mexican Government (1843): particularly No. 124, *Correspondence relating to loans made by British subjects*, P.P.1847(839)LXIX; H.M. Government's insistence on the constitution of the Arbitration Tribunal contemplated in the contract in the case of the cancellation of the concession of Messrs. Punchard and Co. in Colombia (the Antioquia Railway Case, 1895–1896): No. 13, *Reports by the Law Officers of the Crown 1895*, F.O.,C.P. 6796; the parallel case of *Military Equipment Stores and Tortoise Tents Co.* v. *Argentine Government*: No. 11, *Reports by the Law Officers of the Crown 1899*, F.O.,C.P.7356.
28. J. Dodson's report, 28 April 1840, on the contract claims of Mr. Wright against the Kingdom of the Two Sicilies: McNair, *International Law Opinions*, II, 306; *Cotesworth and Powell* v. *Colombia*: Research in International Law of the Harvard Law School, 'Draft Convention and Comments on Responsibility of States for Injuries to Aliens', *American Journal of International Law*, 23 (Special Supplement, April 1929), 178, 184, 186–7.

the cancellation of a contract, and the settlement were not carried out;[29] and if a Government arbitrarily and unjustly cancelled a contract without permitting reference to legal tribunals or observing the due processes of law. With these exceptions, the remedy in contract cases was by Petition of Right, or by a provision in municipal law permitting the State to be sued before the ordinary tribunals.

H.M. Government's prejudice against intervention in contract cases was long-standing. Herbert Jenner, in a Report on a Brazilian claim in July 1831, explained that:

It has been the constant practice of Her Majesty's Government to decline to interfere in the transactions between British Subjects settled and carrying on trade in foreign countries and the Government of those countries. Such transactions are entered into by the individuals upon their own responsibility, and without any reference or sanction of Her Majesty's Government, whose interference for the purpose of enforcing the fulfilment of such contracts on the part of foreign Governments, they have therefore no right to expect, and which might and in many cases probably would involve the two Governments in discussions of an unpleasant nature and eventually lead to serious misunderstandings between them.[30]

Sir J. Dodson, a decade later, reported that the British Government was not in the habit of intervening to enforce contracts voluntarily entered into by British subjects with foreign governments,[31] and Sir Robert Phillimore, while disagreeing (21 March 1867) with the policy of total abstention, maintained that H.M. Government should not interfere unless a clear injustice had been done.[32] The normal official attitude

29. Messrs. Waring Bros., railway contractors, against the Government of Brazil: *Correspondence respecting the Claim of Messrs. Waring Brothers on the Brazilian Government 1886–87*, F.O.,C.P.5678.
30. McNair, *International Law Opinions*, II, 201. Also Jenner's Report of 27 January 1830 on Mr. O'Shea's contract claim against the Spanish Government, ibid.
31. *Wright v. the Kingdom of the Two Sicilies*, 28 April 1840: ibid. II, 306; *Mackintosh v. the Government of Venezuela*, 14 May 1842: P.R.O.,F.O./83/2400.
32. Contract claims against the Government of Brazil: No. 2, *Reports from the Law Officers of the Crown 1867*, F.O.,C.P.1745. The apparent approval of unconditional Government intervention in contract claims, expressed in Phillimore's Report, 18 June 1867 (on the claim of *Mr. Mangles v. the Portuguese Government*) and in Travers Twiss's Report of 28 December 1867 (on British contract claims on the Government of Colombia) must, in the light of No. 2, be considered subject to the same condition: Nos. 75, 45, ibid.

to contract claims was explained by Lord Tenterden in his letter to the Ceará Water Company of Brazil, 23 May 1876. Lord Tenterden told the Company that 'in a case of the alleged violation of a contract entered into by a British Company, or by British subjects, for an undertaking in a foreign country, redress must always, in the first instance, be sought from the legal tribunals of the country in which the undertaking is intended to be carried out, and Her Majesty's Government can only interfere diplomatically when there has been a manifest failure of justice'.[33]

Claims for the cancellation of contracts or concessions could serve as grounds for diplomatic intervention only in circumstances of manifest injustice. As with most claims, first recourse was to the local tribunals, and it was only on the refusal of such recourse, or in the absence of any effective remedy thereby, that diplomatic intervention could be justified in international law. Cancellation following a failure to complete a part of the contract, in the absence of injustice, could not, of course, justify intervention.[34] The Foreign Office refused to intervene, for example, on behalf of the cancelled concessions of the Venezuela-Panama Gold Mine Co. Ltd. (1887) or of the Orinoco Railway Co. (1889), on the grounds that the concessions had been cancelled for a failure to fulfil the terms of the contract and that a remedy must be sought, if at all, before the

---

33. Annex to No. 15, *Reports by the Law Officers of the Crown 1876*, F.O.,C.P. 4028. Further examples of refusal to intervene before the exhaustion of local remedies can be found in J. D. Harding's Report (13 July 1855) on an alleged injustice to Messrs. Samuel Phillips and Co. in the Brazilian Courts of Law: McNair, *International Law Opinions*, II, 308; the Earl of Malmesbury's opinion that British subjects confined by their contracts to Paraguay during the great Paraguayan War should seek redress by civil process: 191 *Parl.Deb.3s.* 456 (30 March 1868); the British Government's refusal to make a personal representation to the Sultan of Turkey on the question of the Haidan Pasha/ Ismid railway: 331 *Parl.Deb.3s.*314 (27 November 1888); and Sir Edward Grey's answer to the request for intervention on behalf of the British contractors of the Piraeus and Larissa Railway: 23 *Parl.Deb.4s.*1431 (26 April 1894).
34. See, for example, the Law Officers' Report (4 July 1873) on the cancellation of Mr. Greenhill's contract for the construction of two iron piers at San José and Tulate, Guatemala. The Law Officers agreed that the Guatemalan Government had a perfect right to cancel the concession on Greenhill's failure to complete his part of the contract, and felt that H.M. Government could take no steps in the matter: P.R.O.,F.O/83/2243.

local tribunals.[35] But patent injustice, and the lack of any means of obtaining justice, legitimized intervention in such cases as the cancellation of the Delagoa Bay Railway in 1889[36] and of the Dom Pedro I Railway concessions in 1887.[37]

'Good offices' were frequently offered to British companies suffering cancellation of concessions on grounds of non-fulfilment if it appeared that there were any extenuating circumstances. On the suggestion of the U.S. Government, the British Government even entered into an unusual agreement with the United States and the Netherlands in 1914 to withhold diplomatic support from any citizen or subject assuming rights to any Mexican contracts or concessions forfeited by other subjects or citizens on grounds of non-fulfilment, provided that the forfeiture resulted directly from the current political unrest.[38] But this attempt to limit indirectly the sovereignty of the Mexican Republic was part of the price H.M. Government paid for coming into line with President Wilson's policy for the regeneration of Mexico, and the 1914 agreement was not permitted to serve as a precedent. The British Reply of 1928 admitted the right of the State, as sovereign, to cancel a concession or contract on grounds of public policy, provided that compensation was paid. Circumstances other than non-compliance with the terms might justify cancellation when public policy considerations were not operative (such as the usual legal grounds of fraud or impossibility of execution), but these should properly be dealt with by national law before the national legal tribunals.[39]

35. Law Officers' Report, 28 November 1887: P.R.O.,F.O/80/459; Sanderson to Mr. G. P. Harding, 15 May 1889 (printed in a pamphlet attached to Harris's letter to Davidson, 3 March 1896): P.R.O.,F.O./80/459. Also Salisbury's reply to the Minas Central Railway Co.'s claim for diplomatic support against the Brazilian Government: Printed Memoranda No. 884, F.O.,C.P. 5711.
36. J. B. Moore, *A Digest of International Law* (Washington, 1906), VI, 727–8.
37. *Memorandum on Questions in Dispute between Great Britain and Brazil,* F.O.,C.P.5711.
38. *Notes exchanged between H.M. Government and the U.S. Government on the Subject of Oil Properties and Mining Rights in Mexico,* P.P.1914(Cd.7463)CI; *Notes exchanged with the Netherlands Minister on the Subject of Oil Properties in Mexico,* P.P.1914(Cd.7468)CI.
39. *League of Nations Publication V,* Legal 1929, V.3, 205–6. Note, however, that the British Government did not accept the unilateral cancellation of the Anglo-Persian Oil Contract of 1932, which it described as a 'confiscatory measure and a breach of international law': S. Friedman, *Expropriation in*

Major confiscations and expropriations of the property of foreigners were phenomena rather of the twentieth century than of the nineteenth.[40] The British Government never admitted the right of expropriation, except in cases of civil necessity, *force majeure*, and, more recently, nationalization—and compensation even in these exceptional cases was always demanded. But minor cases of confiscation and expropriation were, of course, common throughout the nineteenth century, and wherever confiscation by act of State threatened the interests of British subjects, the Foreign Office was ready to protest. The Sulphur Monopoly in Sicily (1838),[41] the State Monopoly of Insurance in Uruguay (1911),[42] and the Italian State Life Insurance Monopoly (also in 1911)[43] were, in effect, confiscatory measures (without compensation) against substantial existing foreign interests. Since these measures were established by law, redress could only be had through diplomatic action, and the British Government was successful in obtaining either a complete repeal or substantial modifications. British diplomatic protests against the Chilean Law of Expropriation of the Nitrate Railways (1891),[44] against the expropriation of property belonging to the Antioquia Railway Co. (Colombia, 1895),[45] and against the Portuguese confiscation of the property

International Law (London, 1953), p. 154. The explanation for this inconsistency seems to have been (1) the controlling interest of the British Government in the Anglo-Iranian Oil Co., and (2) the fact that the concession was, in effect, an international agreement between States, the abrogation of which necessarily gave the right (in international law) of diplomatic intervention. The British Protest of 14 October 1952 against the revocation of the 1933 concession (*The Times*, 16 October 1952, 5a) was more securely based on the principles accepted in the Reply of 1928. H.M. Government did not, this time, demand the revival of the concessions agreement, and merely indicated its intention to press for compensation for the cancelled concession.

40. For a complete and admirable study of this problem, see B. A. Wortley, *Expropriation in Public International Law* (Cambridge, 1959); also Georg Schwarzenberger, 'The Protection of British Property Abroad', *Current Legal Problems*, V (1952), 295–323.

41. A. P. Fachiri, 'Expropriation and International Law', *British Year Book of International Law*, VI (1925), 163–4.

42. Sir John Fischer Williams, 'International Law and the Property of Aliens', *British Year Book of International Law*, IX (1928), 4.

43. Fachiri, *British Year Book of International Law*, VI, 166–7.

44. Salisbury to Kennedy, 25 July 1891: No. 265, *Correspondence respecting the Revolution in Chile*, P.P.1892(c.6636)XCV.

45. Foreign Office to Law Officers, 11 March 1895: No. 13, *Reports by the Law Officers of the Crown 1895*, F.O.,C.P.6796.

of British shareholders in the Delagoa Bay Railway Co.,[46] give some indication of the attitude generally adopted towards arbitrary and unilateral acts of confiscation.

When, in 1918, the Soviet Government published a series of confiscatory decrees, the British Government joined in the international Note reserving the right to claim damages for all losses suffered thereby,[47] and the confiscations which have been a characteristic feature of the post-war world have always provoked protests from the Foreign Office. Mexico's oil expropriations of 1938 brought prolonged diplomatic intervention, resulting in compensatory measures in 1946. The British Government argued that, though 'the right to expropriate on *bona fide* grounds of public interest and on payment of adequate compensation' was admitted, it was evident that Mexico could advance neither of these grounds in justification of her action.[48] And the Labour Government after 1945 necessarily acknowledged the right of nationalization, limited, however, by the inevitable proviso of adequate compensation.[49]

*   *   *

The proper limits of diplomatic protection have always been arguable, and it is easy enough to lose the wood for the trees. But one point needs to be made very firmly, and that is that

46. Fachiri, *British Year Book of International Law*, VI, 165–6; also British protests against the Portuguese confiscation of religious properties, 1910: ibid., 168.
47. Andreas H. Roth, *The Minimum Standard of International Law Applied to Aliens* (Leiden, 1949), p. 176.
48. The Earl of Plymouth's statement in the Lords, 23 May 1938: 109 *H.L. Deb.*5s.330–1; also No. 1, *Correspondence with the Mexican Government regarding the Expropriation of Oil Properties in Mexico*, P.P.1937–8(Cmd.5758)XXXI [the British Government actually demanded *restoration*, not merely compensation]. Note also H.M. Government's insistence on 'prompt, adequate and effective' compensation as required by international law in the case of the Greek Land Reforms of the early 1950's, where only a third of the value of foreign property was offered in compensation for seizure: Wortley, *Expropriation*, p. 98; the British Memorial on the Anglo-Iranian Oil Co. case, together with the precedents cited, in which the rule of 'prompt, adequate, and effective compensation' was firmly stated: ibid., pp. 33–34.
49. For example, H.M. Government's attitude to the Czech nationalizations of 1945: 417 *H.C.Deb.*5s.1691 (20 December 1945); to the Burmese nationalizations of 1948: 452 *H.C.Deb.*5s.657 (17 June 1948); to the Persian nationalization of 1951: 487 *H.C.Deb.*5s.1008–12 (1 May 1951), and 488 *H.C.Deb.*5s.42 (29 May 1951); and to the Egyptian nationalization of 1956: Wortley, *Expropriation*, p. 71.

for contracts and concessions, as for the bondholders or any
other aspect of diplomatic protection, H.M. Government was
guided not by pressure from the City but by the standards of
international law accepted at the time. Positive action depended,
time and time again, on the opinion of the Law Officers. If the
Law Officers decided that the British claimants had no case,
the Foreign Office took no action; but where there *was* a case,
H.M. Government prosecuted it as vigorously as it could, since
it was bound to protect the persons and property of British
subjects.

Inevitably, diplomatic protection, however legitimate, has
been confused with pressure for contracts and concessions. In
the first section of this chapter it was shown that government
pressure for contracts and concessions was limited to 'political'
concessions or to cases where foreign diplomatic pressure
threatened the ideal condition of 'a fair field and no favour'. In
the second section, an attempt has been made to explain the
conditions under which H.M. Government felt obliged to
intervene in protecting British contractors and concessionaires,
once their business was under way.[50] Neither in promotion nor in
protection can it be claimed that the decisive factor was
pressure from British finance. Such pressure, of course, existed,
but the decision to intervene in any particular case depended
first on the non-interventionist tradition which had determined
British financial policy since the 1820's, and then on its rele-
vance to the two dominant strains in Victorian foreign policy—
the national political interest, and the fair and equal treatment
of British trade and finance overseas.

50. The distinction was recognized to the end of the period. Replying (15
May 1914) to a question from Lord Macdonnell, Mr. Musgrove, Secretary
of the London Chamber of Commerce, argued that the Diplomatic Service
could be most useful to trade in supporting British contractors and concession holders overseas, 'but hitherto that support has usually been given
after the concession has been obtained'. Pressed on the point, he agreed
that little, if any, assistance was given in obtaining concessions: Minutes
of evidence, *Report of the Royal Commission on the Civil Service*, P.P.1914-16
(Cd.7749)XI,QQ.38,841-2.

CONCLUSION

IN GENERAL, the Foreign Office was bound by certain traditional rules of conduct which applied to overseas finance, wherever it was and whatever its size. The interests of the bondholders were never promoted, and the extent of the protection they received was limited by what today might seem too rigid and narrow an interpretation of Government responsibility. In overseas finance, H.M. Government avoided, so far as it could, any contact with the promotion, issue, and expenditure of loans, and it restricted its intervention on behalf of contracts and concessions to those which were political in character, to cases where foreign diplomatic pressure was creating unfair competition, and to genuine claims for diplomatic protection based on our rights in international law. 'It was', Sir Rennell Rodd once wrote, 'certainly not the Foreign Office of the "nation of shopkeepers" which first initiated the practice of using political influence as a lever to procure commercial concessions'.[1]

But as foreign pressure increased, more inevitably was heard of securing 'fair shares' for British capital, or of protecting that capital against 'undue risks'; and there had obviously been a very substantial development in the Foreign Office attitude which permitted Sir Edward Grey to claim, just before the First World War, that H.M. Government was prepared to give 'the utmost support we can' to *bona fide* British capital applying for concessions in any part of the world for which there were no valid political objections.[2] Grey had in mind propaganda and persuasion rather than physical pressure, but his attitude was a startling advance on the *laissez-faire* of his predecessors.

* * *

An answer, however, has yet to be attempted to the argument on the subtle, personal pressures on politicians and officials, summarized in the Introduction to Part 1. It is true that there

1. Sir Rennell Rodd, *Diplomacy* (London, 1929), p. 47.
2. 64 *H.C.Deb.*5s.1446 (10 July 1914).

were close, sometimes personal, contacts between certain levels of politicians, officials and financiers. Mr. Gladstone was a close friend of Bertram Wodehouse Currie, the leading partner in Glyn's; he often stayed at Coombe (where he once held a meeting of his Ministers), and frequently turned to Currie for advice on matters of finance. Sir Henry Drummond Wolff and Sir Henry Layard were party politicians, international financiers, and diplomatists at one point or another during their careers. And even that most distinguished example of the British aristocratic tradition in diplomacy—the Marquis of Dufferin and Ava—accepted a chairmanship from Whitaker Wright at the close of his career and was ruined for his pains. But it is one thing to cite these connexions, and quite another to prove that they had any influence on each other. 'The idea of Mr. Gladstone as the agent of Rothschilds and Barings', wrote Lionel Robbins in *The Economic Causes of War*, 'can only be regarded as comic'; and Robbins wondered whether those who constructed theories of economic imperialism had 'ever as much as seen an animal of the species, banker':

The picture drawn seems so different, the psychological attitude assumed so unlike anything that can normally be witnessed in the circles of high finance, that one feels that one has walked through the looking-glass into a world in which all one's usual estimates of men and the way they move have gone completely topsy-turvy.

Businessmen frequently came into contact with officials; and, no doubt, a financier could sometimes persuade an official of the justice of his cause over lunch at the club. But it is naïve to believe that the Victorian class system was all that flexible; that top businessmen automatically moved in the highest social circles; that the members of the Travellers' Club (a favourite with the Foreign Service) were one and the same as the members of the City. The question that must be asked of an official or of a politician is not merely whose cousin he was, what directorships he might hold in the future, what friends he had in the present, but what traditions and precedents existed to guide him? What reply was he likely to give, in an unrecorded conversation at Brooks, to a request for government pressure behind a particular commercial or financial interest overseas?

The answer lies with that 'departmental view' described in

the previous chapters. The official was not a free agent—he had broadly to follow the lines of policy already established. His views were likely to be *laissez-faire* and Free Trade. He distrusted the bondholders, whom he believed to be damaging the national interest by sending their money abroad. He was particularly careful about contractors and 'concession-mongers', support of whom was likely to wreck his reputation and destroy his general usefulness to the nation. He was probably, like Layard over the Raikes charges in 1869,[3] supremely sensitive to any conflict between public and private interests. He believed that his duty was to serve the interests of the nation as a whole and not a sectional interest, and he knew that if he supported a sectional interest he would have to meet the bitter criticism of excluded competitors. He was a patriot, but he was also a Victorian, trained according to the strict morality of the time. If he served in the Diplomatic Service, he was an aristocrat with, as likely as not, a share of the aristocratic contempt for 'trade'. If he worked in the Foreign Office, he was bound by precedent and red tape—his reaction to a new situation was to call for a Library Memorandum which would guide him safely along the paths followed in the past. If he was in the Board of Trade, he was a member of the Cobden Club, disinclined to any intervention if intervention could be avoided, a Free Trader to the core. The reply which he was most likely to give to the financier, as they talked over the problems of a Central American loan, a harbour contract in the Mediterranean, a railway from Burma to Yunnan, hopes for opening textile mills in central China, was in the negative, or, if not, at the very least carefully qualified by considerations which depended on the action of other Powers or on the general political interest of the Empire.

By trade, the politician was more inclined to listen to a 'lobby'. But if he held office in the Foreign Office before 1914 he was even more aristocratic than his Ambassadors, and even less knowledgeable about trade and finance. The fact that the commercial side of the Foreign Office was under the supervision of the Under-Secretary of State—a political position of low prestige and little power within the Department—meant that Junior Ministers at the Foreign Office came almost immediately

3. Layard's position is described by Gordon Waterfield, *Layard of Nineveh* (London, 1963), pp. 312–13.

under the influence of the 'departmental view'. When Curzon accepted the Parliamentary Under-Secretaryship in 1895 there were great hopes of change, but even he was able to achieve no basic development in the Government's policy towards trade and finance; traditional attitudes were too strong for him. Politicians in any case had better things to do (once in office) than follow the popular mood. 'Music halls', said Curzon himself in 1908, 'are not the council chambers of statesmen, and Cabinet Ministers are not or are not supposed to be comedians.'[4]

*   *   *

Small indeed is the part played by common sense in evaluating the evidence for successful financial pressure on foreign policy; political passions, whether on the Right or on the Left, are too easily aroused. 'Economic imperialism' is a political rather than an historical label; and political polemicists know what they want to say long before they find the evidence to support it. When the earliest and most convincing attacks were made on the influence of finance capital—Hobson, Hilferding, Brailsford, Lenin, and Bukharin—the archives of the Powers were not available for inspection. Much could have been learnt from the published Blue Books, but there was always the understandable suspicion that the more controversial evidence had been subtracted. Hobson and his successors were in fact looking at financial diplomacy from the point of view of the journalist or of the gleaner of casual information. When they read in the popular press—as they must often have done—of an interview between the Foreign Secretary and a delegation of bond-holders, financiers or concession-mongers, they had no means of discovering what attitude was taken, and they assumed the worst. But records of these interviews are now available, as are the minutes and memoranda in which officials discussed financial policy. Although there is no disputing the facts—that such and such a concession was obtained, that this bank was given official support while that bank was not, that the bondholders of the 1855 Ottoman Guaranteed Loan received the full diplomatic support of H.M. Government—the reasons *why* the Foreign Office should have behaved as it did can now be given

4. Lord Curzon, 'The True Imperialism', *Nineteenth Century*, LXIII (1908), 160.

with some approach to accuracy; and these reasons, while they had little to do with the narrow interests of City financiers, turned increasingly on the growing threat to Britain's political, financial, and commercial position in and after the last quarter of the nineteenth century.

Hobson, of course, was perfectly aware of this threat, and the deterioration of Britain's economic position relative to that of the other Powers forms a major point in his argument. But his analysis of its effect fails because of the unreal picture he draws of the pressure exerted by surplus capital and its exporters on H.M. Government's policy overseas. Hobson's detractors, however, in their efforts to cut the ground from under his feet, have undervalued or denied altogether the influence that the threat to Britain's economic position after the late '70s must inevitably have had on the formulation of British policy. It should be possible to strike a more realistic balance between the two when the general shape of British government policy towards overseas finance—the subject of Part I—is taken in conjunction with the evidence of that policy in action provided in Part III.

PART II
H.M. GOVERNMENT AND
OVERSEAS TRADE

PART II
H.M. GOVERNMENT AND
OVERSEAS TRADE

INTRODUCTION

THE CENTRAL fact in the relationship of H.M. Government to overseas trade was the continued popularity of Free Trade. *Laissez-faire* and Free Trade remained the instinctive official attitude towards trade until as recently as the early '30s. But within the general framework of *laissez-faire*, there was always a certain freedom of manoeuvre. British preeminence in overseas markets remained substantially unchallenged until the last quarter of the nineteenth century, and in the circumstances there was no pressure for change in government policy towards trade. But new problems needing a whole new set of answers were created both by rising foreign competition and by a new code of foreign diplomatic behaviour after the mid-'80s, and these problems focused more particularly on the industrialization of Germany.

German unification had created the conditions under which rapid industrial development could take place, while at the same time releasing the energies which this development required. Germany early in the '80s was only just beginning her industrial transformation, but the development was astonishingly rapid. The Royal Commission on the Depression of Trade and Industry, in its final report of December 1886, quoted evidence to show that German perseverance and enterprise were making themselves felt in every quarter of the world, and that it was German trade which was most dangerously competitive in both home and neutral markets; we no longer had any advantages over the Germans in production, and their ability to adapt themselves to markets and to find a footing for their trade was giving them the lead. In neutral markets, the Commission concluded, such as those within the Empire and especially in the East, Britain was 'beginning to feel the effects of competition in quarters where our trade formerly enjoyed a practical monopoly'.[1]

The alarm had already been sounded. The Earl of Harrowby had complained in July 1884 of the great anxiety which the commercial depression was causing among men of the greatest experience; he urged H.M. Government to hurry forward any negotiations it might have in hand for commercial treaties so that fresh outlets might be opened for British commerce.[2] A few days later, Mr. Whitley in the Commons warned the Under-Secretary of State of the 'great amount of commercial depression' in existence, and of the strong feeling among the commercial men of Liverpool that the Government should do everything in its power to protect British trading interests overseas.[3] Under pressure from the Chambers of Commerce, in Parliament, from individuals and from the press, Lord Rosebery and his Parliamentary Under-Secretary (James Bryce) decided that the time had come to redefine the scope of diplomatic assistance to commerce. Winding up his speech at the important debate of 2 April 1886 on competition in foreign trade, Bryce assured the House that the Foreign Office was now fully alive to the situation and could be trusted to attend to it. They were 'well aware that commerce was the life-blood of Britain', and that the unavoidable depression in British agriculture made it even more important that British commerce should be maintained; it 'could only be maintained, in the face of the fierce competition of today, by turning to account every resource which the government possessed'.[4] Bryce's remedy was published three months later in his Memorandum, the burden of which was to authorize exceptional intervention on behalf of British interests in places where their position was being threatened by the diplomatic action of foreign Powers. But at the same time Bryce defined a general policy for government action on behalf of trade which was still distinctly *laissez-faire*.[5]

The argument in Part I has shown that the permission to use diplomatic pressure where it was necessary to counteract that of

1. *Final Report of the Royal Commission on Depression of Trade and Industry*, P.P. 1886(c.4893)XXIII.
2. 291 *Parl.Deb.*3s.1147 (31 July 1884).
3. ibid. 1702 (4 August 1884).
4. 304 *Parl.Deb.*3s.641 (2 April 1886).
5. The Memorandum is printed as Appendix V.

other Powers, though of slight immediate impact, was to be of some consequence ultimately in the conduct of British diplomacy in the Levant and the Far East. But the blow to the principle of *laissez-faire* was less damaging than it might seem. H.M. Government had always recognized an obligation to secure fair and equal treatment for British trade overseas; the instruction to meet 'unfair' pressure by foreign diplomatists was merely a realistic extension of this obligation. Moreover, the spirit of *laissez-faire* was not abandoned as the basis of general policy, even if it was found necessary to intervene in some individual cases. Curzon agreed with Sir Albert Rollit in August 1895 when Rollit expressed the hope that the era of *laissez-faire* in commercial diplomacy was over; but he warned the Commons that

At the same time there was a consideration on the other side which they ought to bear in mind. If they contemplated that commercial conquest of the world which they claimed to have made, it had been made not by the protection or activity of Governments, but by the intrepidity and enterprise of their individual traders. ['Hear, hear!'] It was the duty, and should be the pleasure of a Government to sustain and stimulate the efforts of their traders to hold their own, but more depended upon maintaining the features of their national character, which had made them what they were, than upon any artificial support that Government, Consuls, or diplomats could give. ['Hear, hear!'][6]

Laissez-faire was under pressure, but it was under pressure not to transform itself altogether into an active policy of official promotion and intervention on behalf of British trade and capital, but to adapt itself to the obligation to secure 'fair' treatment, equal favour and open competition overseas.

Free Trade in turn came under attack from 'Fair' Trade, just as its intellectual parent, *laissez-faire*, suffered from the demand for 'fair' competition. The point that needs emphasis is that the renewal of the demand for Protection after the 1870's was not intended, as in the past, to secure a *special* position for British manufacturers but to ensure *equality* of treatment. Fair Trade was not a complete return to Protection; its supporters were in the main happy to see the continuance of Free Trade wherever it was observed by both parties. It was only where one

6. 36 *Parl.Deb.*4s.1274 (30 August 1895).

party imposed protective tariffs or gave bounties that corresponding duties were demanded to counteract the protection enjoyed by foreign producers. As Professor Fuchs explained at the end of the last century, home and foreign producers were to be placed 'on an equal footing, with regard to the *artificial* conditions of production, caused by such things as export bounties, protective duties and indirect taxation; while in regard to the *natural* differences in the conditions of production, nothing was to be altered'. It was this, Fuchs concluded, which distinguished Fair Trade from Protection, 'for the policy of Protection is precisely to level down these natural differences'.[7] Fair Trade, as it began in the '70s and as it continued for many, or most, of its supporters until after the First World War, was no more than a realistic assessment of what was necessary to secure *equality* of treatment for British trade in an increasingly Protectionist world; its misfortune was that it became popularly identified— falsely as it happened—with a return to the discredited Protectionism which had ended effectively with the repeal of the Corn Laws.[8] Genuine Protectionism in the Continental tradition was uncommon in Britain before 1914.

*   *   *

The tradition of *laissez-faire*, modified after the mid-'80s by the need to maintain fair and equal treatment, determined H.M. Government's attitude to trade overseas. The economic manifestation of *laissez-faire* was Free Trade, and the following chapters will discuss first the overseas trade policy which developed within the *laissez-faire*, Free Trade tradition, and then the range of commercial diplomacy which that tradition permitted.

7. C. J. Fuchs, *The Trade Policy of Great Britain and her Colonies since 1860* (London edn., 1905), p. 191.
8. Useful analyses of the 'tariff reform' movement are available in Sydney H. Zebel, 'Fair Trade: an English Reaction to the Breakdown of the Cobden Treaty System', *Journal of Modern History*, XII (1940), 161–85; and Benjamin H. Brown, *The Tariff Reform Movement in Great Britain, 1881–1895* (New York, 1943).

CHAPTER 1

OVERSEAS TRADE POLICY

'IT IS the business of Government', Palmerston told Auckland on 22 January 1841, 'to open and to secure the roads for the merchant'; and security, the Open Door, free competition, and equality of opportunity and of treatment in the markets of the world, together formed the guiding principles of British official policy towards overseas trade before the First World War.

All Victorians were agreed, politicians, traders, and officials, that the opening of the world to trade was an objective which the Government might be expected to pursue. They may well have differed about the means, but they shared a belief in the ends; material and even moral progress, they felt, might be expected automatically from the expansion of trade. Richard Cobden, for example, fiercely opposed as he was to the Anglo-Chinese Wars, welcomed their outcome—the opening of China to world trade. It was morally wrong, he argued, to open markets at the point of a bayonet, but access to those markets was in practice of mutual benefit and would, in the end, bring that expansion of trade which was the best guarantee of world peace. Most London-based officials shared the Cobdenite view. They resented the use of force and gave strict and frequent instructions against it, but they felt certain that the opening of markets to trade was an operation which none could have cause to regret, even if, as in China, the natives themselves—blinded by prejudice and suspicion—fought to preserve their isolation.

Force was, indeed, the exception. The favourite instrument of official policy was the Commercial Treaty—normally the beginning and the end of positive commercial diplomacy until the First World War. Once a Treaty had been negotiated it was up to the British trader to look after his own interests in fair and equal competition with rival foreign traders, and the Foreign Office would intervene only to protect him against injustice or against evasion of the terms of the Treaty itself.

*   *   *

British Commercial Treaties in the nineteenth century were entirely different in character from those of the eighteenth. Under Mercantilism the function of a commercial treaty had been to secure mutual advantages by means of differential duties as *against* other trading nations. The Free Trade commercial treaty, in contrast, rejected any form of differential duty; it consisted ideally of only one clause—'the most-favoured-nation' clause. The object of the Mercantilist Treaty was to create and sustain monopolies; the object of a Free Trade Treaty was to throw open world trade for the benefit of all.

The Commercial Treaties which H.M. Government negotiated after Huskisson's Reciprocity of Duties Act of 1823 were intended to reduce barriers to trade: there was no attempt, as in the old-style treaties, to exclude other nations from the advantages gained. H.M. Government, Lord Malmesbury assured foreign governments in 1858, 'looked for no commercial advantages in any quarter which they would not be prepared to share with every other nation in the world'.[1] And this was no empty claim. The very substantial commercial privileges gained by Britain in the Anglo-Turkish Commercial Convention of 16 August 1838—the Balta Liman Convention—were freely available to any trading nation which cared to conclude a parallel Convention. The opening-up of China by the Treaties of Nanking (1842) and Tientsin (1858) was never intended to apply simply to British trade, and foreign trade shared in all the advantages and privileges gained by British coercion.

Three categories of Commercial Treaty were negotiated by the British Government during the last century: reciprocity treaties, such as those concluded with many European Governments; Open-Door treaties, such as the treaties with Turkey, Morocco, China, Japan; and pure, Free Trade treaties (consisting simply of the most-favoured-nation clause), such as the Anglo-Persian Treaty of Commerce of October 1841 and the treaties with the Latin American Republics.

The classic reciprocity treaty was the Anglo-French Commercial Treaty of 1860. In a sense it was unexpected, since the principle of reciprocity had seemed abandoned (together with Protection) in 1846, when—*The Times* explained—Britain 'being no longer a child had put away childish things'. The

1. Quoted by Beasley, *Bulletin of the Institute of Historical Research*, 23, 227.

interest of the Anglo-French Commercial Treaty lies not so much in the substantial material gains it brought to British trade during the '6os as in the permanent effect on British treaty policy left by the reaction *against* that treaty in and after the 1870's.

In the heyday of mid-Victorian Free Trade, any negotiation of tariff levels between nations was regarded as heresy. The initiative for the Anglo-French Commercial Treaty had come, in fact, from a French Free Trader, M. Michel Chevalier, and Cobden's first reaction, when approached by Chevalier in 1859, was to reject the idea as opposed to the sound principles which had guided British policy since the tariff reforms of 1846. Cobden still shared the view that all nations should be left to adjust their fiscal policy to their own interest unhampered by treaty arrangements with other countries, and that Britain in particular, having adopted Free Trade, should avoid any tariff arrangement with another country, and especially an arrangement such as that suggested by Chevalier which was not equally applicable to any other country. Cobden's second point was overcome in part by an agreement to make any British treaty concessions to France open equally to all other trading nations, but the first remained in force and was one of the objections listed by Gladstone in his retrospective Memorandum on the 1860 Treaty (prepared for the guidance of the Foreign Office in October 1871). Gladstone pointed out that there had been many arguments against the Treaty in 1860, of which the principal had been the unfortunate experience of such treaties in the past, the need to preserve liberty of action with respect to *revenue* duties, and the undesirability of interfering with a purely internal struggle within France between protectionists and free traders. These, he felt, had been overruled at the time by the expectation that the Treaty might form the model for tariff reductions throughout Europe and by its effect in maintaining and promoting European peace.[2]

At the time, indeed, the promotion of peace had first priority. Cobden told Chevalier in September 1859 that his motives were centred on the need to remove impediments to an improvement in the *political* relationships between France and England;

2. A. L. Dunham, *The Anglo-French Treaty of Commerce of 1860 and the Progress of the Industrial Revolution in France* (Ann Arbor, 1930), pp. 302-3.

mutual trading dependence was the only way of achieving this.[3] In a letter to M. Arles Dufour a couple of months later, Cobden described how he had used a similar line of argument in conversation with Napoleon III. 'Free Trade', he had said, 'is God's diplomacy, and there is no other certain way of uniting people in bonds of peace'; he had added that it did not matter if the Treaty took one or two years to come into effect, since all he wanted was the moral effect which the adoption of the new commercial policy would bring; and he had explained emphatically that England, with existing markets greater than our capacity to supply, had no need for the extra custom which an Anglo-French Commercial Treaty might be expected to bring.[4] When Gladstone looked back on the Treaty many years later, he still felt that it had averted a real risk of a war against France, and possibly Italy also.[5] And there is every reason to suppose that Napoleon's own motives were, as Cobden told Sumner, 'nine-tenths political, rather than politico-economical, with a view to cement the alliance with this country'.[6]

Whether originally political or commercial in intention, the Anglo-French Treaty met both needs admirably over the next decade. Political tension declined, and a series of similar treaties was negotiated both by Britain and France with the principal European states. By the end of the '60s there seemed a real possibility of general Free Trade on the Continent. The onset of the Depression in the early '70s put an end to such hopes, but even before the Depression the Anglo-French Treaty itself had run into trouble. During the last years of the Second Empire pressure had been increasing (particularly from the French textile industry) to modify the Treaty, and the replacement of Napoleon in 1870 by the protectionist Thiers not only killed genuine Free Trade in France—if it had ever existed—but gave the Gladstone Administration the opportunity to withdraw from a position which it had never regarded as completely satisfactory. As Lord Lyons (the British Ambassador in Paris)

3. Quoted in J. A. Hobson, *Richard Cobden, the International Man* (London, 1918), pp. 224–5.
4. Cobden to Dufour, 26 December 1859: ibid., pp. 246–7.
5. W. E. Gladstone, 'The History of 1852–1860, and Greville's Latest Journals', *English Historical Review*, II (1887), 302.
6. Cobden to Charles Sumner, 3 December 1861: Hobson, *Richard Cobden*, p. 384.

had predicted, in February 1872 Thiers gave notice of the termination of the 1860 Treaty, and a new, much more limited Treaty was signed on 5 November that year.

H.M. Government protested at the time against the termination of the treaty, but only on grounds of expediency. Gladstone had argued in his 1871 Memorandum that if the French really intended to raise their duties it might be better to fall back on the old policy (by which the cause of Free Trade was believed served best by leaving each nation to decide its tariff levels solely in the light of its own interests). Lord Lyons was inclined to agree, and would have preferred to see the Treaty reduced simply to a most-favoured-nation clause.[7] When a new French Administration proposed to return to the 1860 conditions in 1873, it was surprised to find itself coldly received by the British. Lord Lyons told the Duc de Broglie that Britain had had enough of commercial treaties, and that she believed in the freedom of each country to set its own tariffs subject only to security for British trade and navigation against any special disfavour.[8]

The Cobdenites (or 'positive' Free Traders) were, of course, furious at Gladstone's relapse. Sir Louis Mallet, who had taken so large a part in negotiating Cobdenite Commercial Treaties throughout the '60s, complained to a Berlin official in 1871 that he was now completely helpless, since Mr. Lowe, the Chancellor of the Exchequer, was bitterly opposed to the reciprocity treaties. Recalling, some years later, the orthodox Free Trade policy of the first Gladstone Administration (1868–1874), Mallet observed that he had never served under a Government so unsympathetic and even hostile to 'the free trade policy in the largest sense'; they had effectually demolished all his work at the Board of Trade.[9]

The 1872 Treaty was denounced, in turn, by the French Government in 1879, and the Treaty of 1882 which replaced it took the form merely of a most-favoured-nation agreement. Subsequent commercial treaties negotiated abroad by H.M.

7. Lord Newton, *Lord Lyons, a Record of British Diplomacy* (London, 1913), II, 4; this work contains a valuable description of the British attitude to the renegotiation of the Treaty between 1871 and 1882.
8. Lyons to Granville, 15 July 1873: summarized in Dunham, *Anglo-French Treaty of Commerce*, pp. 317–18.
9. Bernard Mallet, *Sir Louis Mallet* (London, 1905), pp. 91, 102.

Government followed this example, and continued to do so until after the First World War. Gladstone, who as President of the Board of Trade under Peel claimed ample personal experience of 'the difficulties, nay, the mischiefs' of reciprocal trade negotiations, summed up reciprocity negotiations ironically as the argument that 'I will not, or at least I wish you to believe that I will not, secure for myself certain changes of commercial law, which I know to be beneficial, unless you will add to that benefit another benefit, in its nature perfectly separate, by making certain other changes in your law'.[10] While the English voters continued to believe, with Gladstone, in the benefits of Free Trade even if adopted unilaterally, and while continued prosperity enabled British tariff policy to be determined by the interests of the consumer rather than the producer, the reciprocity treaty gave place to the simple, most-favoured-nation treaty of orthodox Free Trade.

However, the Open Door Treaty still remains to be discussed, and it is the Open Door Treaty which has, in fact, attracted the most criticism. Open Door treaties, negotiated normally in unsettled, semi-civilized or entirely new markets, shared the common characteristic of all Victorian commercial treaties in that they were intended to provide equal opportunities for the trade of all nations. Canning's declaration of 1824 that Britain sought 'no exclusive privileges of trade, no invidious preference, but equal freedom of commerce for all' applied not only to Spanish America but to all parts of the world, civilized or uncivilized, in new markets or old. But an Open Door Treaty, fair though it was in its treatment of rival trading nations, was far less so with respect to the nation which was being opened to world trade. The Anglo-Turkish Commercial Treaty of 1838, while throwing open trade on generous terms to the nations of the world, imposed severe restrictions on the tariff autonomy of the Porte. Import duties were limited to 3 per cent. with an *ad valorem* interior duty of 9 per cent; export duties for foreign traders were set at 3 per cent. plus 2 per cent. interior duty. Even when the Turkish Commercial Treaties expired in 1883–1884, Turkey was precluded by the Capitulations from imposing new duties on imports from the Capitulatory Powers without their consent, and duties were fixed at 8 per cent. *ad valorem*.

10. Gladstone, *English Historical Review*, II, 299.

With a country like Turkey, constantly in need of money, the discretionary power to withhold consent to a rise in the tariffs was a political weapon of very great influence indeed, and it was a weapon which all the Powers, Britain included, frequently employed.

Commercial Treaties on this pattern—which set limits to the freedom to raise or lower tariff levels—were comparatively rare. But even a most-favoured-nation treaty might become almost as annoying to a developing economy if it were negotiated in perpetuity. This was the case with a number of the earlier Commercial Treaties. Gladstone had the grace to wonder, in the Memorandum which he prepared in February 1845 for his successor at the Board of Trade, whether we were entirely justified in insisting on preserving our most-favoured-nation rights indefinitely. But he was unable to make up his mind on the particular issue of New Granada's wish to make its Treaty terminable; there was, he pointed out, the contrary argument that unsophisticated Latin American governments might use the opportunity to adopt unrestrained Protection under the misguided impression, derived from European experience, that it would provide the key to national wealth.[11] H.M. Government tended, therefore, to hold to the strict letter of the treaties, and the position of Britain as the principal exporter of manufactured goods set severe limits on the local tariff policy of Latin American governments so long as Britain continued to enjoy most-favoured-nation treatment.

The history of the Anglo-Venezuelan Commercial Treaty of 1825 is a case in point. As early as 1841 the Venezuelan Government was attempting to obtain the agreement of the Foreign Office to a fixed time-limit to the Treaties of 1825 and 1834. Palmerston's answer was utterly uncompromising. If the negotiators of the 1825 Treaty, he argued, had felt it expedient to limit the duration of the Treaty, they would have inserted an Article to that effect; as it was, H.M. Government could see no reason to consent to a limitation where no limitation existed or was intended to exist.[12] Palmerston's answer served as the model

11. Memorandum on the business of the Board of Trade, dated 2 February 1845: printed as Appendix V to Sir Hubert Llewellyn Smith, *The Board of Trade* (London, 1928).

12. Quoted in No. 3, *Correspondence respecting the Commercial Treaty between Great Britain and Venezuela 1825–1886*, P.P.1886(c.4911) LXXIII.

for the following decades. When, for example, President Guzman Blanco proposed in 1897 to bring the Treaty to an end, Mr. Robert Bunch (the British Minister at Caracas), suspecting that the President's motives were spite against Great Britain and the desire to denounce the most-favoured-nation clause in favour of commercial advantages for France and Spain, concluded that the Treaty suited us very well and that we were unlikely to get another so favourable to our interests. A Foreign Office minute on his despatch agreed that 'we have only to go on insisting upon the maintenance of the present treaty'.[13]

The Open Door Treaties, valuable though they were in the general interests of world trade, contained elements—such as the political exploitation of the Turkish fixed tariffs, or the opposition to the termination of the Anglo-Venezuelan Treaty of 1825—which were frankly deplorable. But it should at least be said that genuine reciprocity between States, even between the most civilized of states, is chimerical, and it can hardly be wondered at if a treaty exemption from forced loans or from interference in the practice of religion meant more to a British subject, say, in nineteenth century Caracas, than it did to a Venezuelan in contemporary London or Manchester. A precondition for the investment of capital and the expansion of foreign trade was the security guaranteed to foreigners and their property by Treaty. In the less civilized areas, or in those with widely different customs and modes of life, British commercial treaties in the last century were necessarily broader in their application; if, in becoming so, they became less reciprocal, there was nothing much anybody could do about it except—if he could afford to do so—refuse a Treaty altogether. The early Latin American Treaties were negotiated in return for the invaluable political benefit of British recognition and the protection of the Royal Navy, and their security brought an investment of £1,000 million of British capital by 1914. There was some gain and some loss, but who indeed can—or should—draw up the final balance sheet?

* * *

Commercial Treaties, of one form or another, formed the basis of active commercial diplomacy until 1914, and the heart

13. Bunch to Salisbury, 21 July 1879: P.R.O.,F.O/80/260.

of each treaty was the most-favoured-nation clause. Useful though that clause was, and compatible though it seemed with contemporary ideas of *laissez-faire* and Free Trade, it was no panacea. It aimed, after all, only at *equality* of opportunity, and it did not always achieve even that. There were many ways in which an existing most-favoured-nation agreement might be evaded. If tariffs were minutely subdivided—as they were by many European governments—then a tariff reduction could be introduced which would have no effect on one country while greatly influencing the trade of another. The classic example is the German tariff of 1902 where a special rate was given to 'large dappled mountain cattle or brown cattle, reared at a spot at least 300 meters above sea level, and which have at least one month's grazing each year at a spot at least 800 meters above sea level'.

The Foreign Office felt itself obliged only to preserve a position of *equality* for British trade; it saw no need to negotiate preferential treatment. But even this limited obligation implied constant vigilance against monopolies, differentials, bounties and any form of national discrimination. One of the main objectives of the Balta Liman Convention of 1838 was to put an end to Turkish and Egyptian monopolies which were damaging British trade. Palmerston had always taken an active interest in the Turkish monopolies, and he was as active in counteracting that other threat to the British competitive position in the Ottoman Empire—Russian trading privileges. Balta Liman solved most of these problems in a manner eminently satisfactory to British trade, but six years later Aberdeen was still instructing Stratford Canning to require from the Porte that 'British commerce in Turkey be placed precisely upon the same footing as Russian commerce'.[14]

Throughout the century the same problems recurred, whether in Latin America, Egypt, China, Persia, or any other area where foreign trade was likely to seek advantage in some form of special position. H.M. Government normally felt itself

14. Aberdeen to Canning, 7 October 1844: quoted by Vernon J. Puryear, *International Economics and Diplomacy in the Near East: a Study of British Commercial Policy in the Levant 1834–1853* (Stanford, 1935), p. 194. H.M. Government's attitude towards the Turkish monopolies is also described by Frank E. Bailey, 'The Economics of British Foreign Policy, 1825–50', *Journal of Modern History*, XII (1940), 478–82.

entitled to protest only where treaty rights had been infringed, but it was difficult to withhold government pressure on behalf of British interests if another government had, however illegitimately, successfully pressed the claims of its own subjects. When the French Government in the 1860's secured compensation from the Egyptian Khedive Ismail for the French shareholders in the *Société Agricole et Industrielle d'Egypte*, the British Foreign Office, having preserved up to that moment an attitude of scrupulous fairness, insisted that the British shareholders should be indemnified on the same terms as the French —in spite of the obvious imperfections in their claim.[15] The rule was to limit intervention to maintaining treaty rights, but the rule could be waived if the action of another Power went beyond the terms of the treaty. The proposal of the Argentine Government in 1891 to tax foreign insurance companies did not, Sir Ernest Hertslet thought, infringe the 1825 Commercial Treaty, and the British Government had never protested against similar action by the French and Greek Governments; but if the United States were to protest successfully, Britain might claim like treatment from the Argentine Government under the most-favoured-nation clause.[16]

H.M. Government in similar cases was always watchful to ensure that any gains obtained by foreign governments for their trade or finance were shared by competing British interests. But if asked by British interests to initiate action, the Foreign Office normally retreated behind the shelter of the limited rights given by the conventional most-favoured-nation treaty. The Under Secretary of State, replying to a request to interfere with the Venezuelan tariff in 1886, explained that H.M. Government was only entitled by Treaty to claim most-favoured-nation treatment, and that unless it could be shown that British goods were being less favourably treated than those of other nationalities, there was no ground for diplomatic intervention.[17]

The rapid growth of foreign competition towards the end of the century tended, of course, to multiply these problems of differential treatment, whether in the form of diplomatic pressure abroad or in that of bounties, subsidies and special

15. David S. Landes, *Bankers and Pashas* (London, 1958), p. 303.
16. Ferns, *Britain and Argentina*, p. 466.
17. 308 *Parl.Deb.3s.*790 (30 August 1886).

railway rates at home. Much of the anxiety felt by the British Government about the progress of the Baghdad Railway derived from the fear that differential rates would be imposed to the advantage of German trade in Mesopotamia and to the detriment of our own. It could be argued, too, that the international crisis in China began when the French Government rejected the British policy of opening China equally to world trade and, by the Treaties of Saigon (1874) and Tientsin (1885), imposed preferential treatment for French merchants and financiers. Once one Government had adopted this line, it was difficult for the others to hold back and watch their national interests damaged or destroyed. But the traditional British policy was explained by Sir Claude MacDonald at the height of the international battle for Chinese concessions (July 1898); he had, he told Salisbury, 'consistently informed the Chinese Government that, as to differential rates and privileges, we want none ourselves, and cannot admit that other nationalities have a claim to them'.[18]

*   *   *

Free Trade, free competition, and equality of opportunity governed British policy. It has been argued, of course, that the British belief in equality was insincere and that, in any case, it survived only so long as Britain enjoyed that natural superiority created by her industrial pre-eminence and by her existing network of trading and financial agencies across the face of the world. While there is much truth in the second point, there is little in the first. Once Britain had lost her natural advantages —which was not, however, decisively to be the case until the early 1930's—she became as protectionist and interventionist as the majority of her trading rivals. But it is carrying cynicism too far to maintain that the Victorian belief in *laissez-faire* and equality of opportunity was anything but genuine. The conclusive evidence lies in the attitude of British statesmen and officials to equality of opportunity and free competition even *within* British overseas trade. Genuine competition must exist, they argued, not merely between British traders and the rest (in the knowledge that British trade in any case had the natural

18. MacDonald to Salisbury, 23 July 1898: No. 245, *Correspondence respecting the Affairs of China*, P.P.1899(c.9131)CIX.

advantage and could only gain from free competition), but equally among British traders themselves. No monopolies or preferential treatment could be tolerated, nor could assistance be extended to individuals: the Government must act for the community as a whole and never in support of a private interest.

The function of government, to a nineteenth-century British statesman, was to uphold the general interest. Austen Henry Layard, as Under Secretary of State, reminded the Commons in 1864 that, although it was not unnatural for Chambers of Commerce to consider their interests paramount to almost everything else in importance, 'it should be remembered that the duty of the Government was not to watch over one interest to the exclusion of all others, but that its aim should be the promotion of the general welfare of the community'.[19] Half a century later—in spite of all the changes that had taken place, and all the compromises that foreign competition had forced on *laissez-faire*—the Royal Commission on the Civil Service felt it natural to inform the commercial community that the Consular Service, like the Diplomatic Service, existed for the benefit of the community as a whole, and that the influence and efficiency of either service would be impaired if it allowed itself to become identified with the interests of individual traders or concessionaires.[20] The 1914–18 War cast doubt on the expediency of a continued policy of non-intervention on behalf of individuals overseas, and Lord Robert Cecil, introducing some relatively mild Foreign Service reforms during the Supply debate of July 1918, spoke confidently of a new and self-evident link between commercial and political interests overseas. He was surprised to hear cries of 'No!' and 'That is the German doctrine', and when he sat down, Mr. Holt (who had been a member of the Royal Commission on the Civil Service) disagreed profoundly. It was not the State's duty, Holt said, to represent 'the separate private interests of every individual in the country':

Do let us make a complete severance between this idea of pushing trade and of representing the interests of the country as a whole. I really believe that this German idea, that it is the duty of the Government of the country to push the private interests of individ-

19. 174 *Parl.Deb.3s.*1093 (15 April 1864).
20. *Fifth Report of the Royal Commission on the Civil Service*, P.P.1914–16(Cd. 7748)XI, Pt.II, ch.V, para.13.

uals as individuals in a foreign country has quite as much to do with wars as most other things. I would earnestly impress on the Foreign Office that they should allow traders to mind their own business and confine themselves to minding those affairs which are the interests of the country as a whole.[21]

The distinction is not yet obsolete. D. G. Stewart-Smith, in a Monday Club pamphlet 'The Handmaidens of Diplomacy' (1964), argued that the commercial functions of the Foreign Service should be transferred to the Federation of British Industries; if this could not be done, the Commercial Department must be at least doubled in size and the unpalatable fact be accepted that public funds would inevitably be used to promote the interests of individual British companies. This, he concluded, must surely be wrong!

* * *

The prejudice against diplomatic pressure on behalf of individual commercial or financial interests was one of the most deep-rooted of Victorian reservations in the conduct of commercial diplomacy. It emerges very strongly in Lord Granville's 1881 Circular on Letters of Introduction,[22] in the replies to Lord Rosebery's Circular of March 1886 and in the 1886 Memorandum,[23] in the final report of the Royal Commission on the Depression of Trade and Industry (December 1886),[24] and in the report of the Royal Commission on Civil Establishments (July 1890).[25] In the twentieth century, it reappears in the Report of the Royal Commission on the Civil Service, and, in a more moderate form, in the report of Sir Eyre Crowe's Departmental Committee of 1916.[26]

The prejudice was not without a reasoned foundation. Its background, of course, was the general belief that the State existed to promote the interests of the nation as a whole—the belief which made Mr. Asquith, as Prime Minister, praise Free

21. 109 *H.C.Deb.*5s.568–71 (31 July 1918).
22. Granville's 1881 Circular is printed as Appendix IV.
23. Bryce's Memorandum is printed as Appendix V.
24. *Final Report of the Royal Commission on Depression of Trade and Industry*, P.P. 1886(c.4893)XXIII, para. 99.
25. *Report of the Royal Commission on Civil Establishments (Foreign Office, Diplomatic and Consular Services)*, P.P.1890(c.6172)XXVII, para. 45.
26. See above, and extract from Sir Eyre Crowe's Report printed as Appendix VI.

Trade as being 'on the side of the public and of the community, as against special interests and particular classes'.[27] But there were practical reasons against the identification of officials with individual interests. Lord Rosebery, addressing the Leeds Chamber of Commerce on 11 October 1888, explained his doubts as to the expediency of British consuls making representations to foreign governments on behalf of particular firms. There might well be several British firms, he said, competing for the same business—how was the Consul to discriminate between them or to escape charges of forwarding some commercial interest of his own, and how were consuls and diplomatists to maintain 'the high, independent, and unsullied position which they possess' if they were to be given instructions to promote individual trading interests?[28]

The pressure of foreign competition, as in every aspect of British commercial and financial diplomacy, made it impossible after the mid '80s to maintain unqualified non-intervention. German diplomatic pressure, in particular, was creating a situation which made it increasingly difficult for the Foreign Office to stand aside. And German diplomatists, of course, had excellent reasons for adopting a more forward policy—their firms were breaking into markets in which Britain had enjoyed a virtual monopoly, they had little assistance from any existing trade agencies or overseas banks (while their British competitors enjoyed a world-wide system built up since the early years of the century), and, since they were new to the markets, the problem of German firms competing with each other for diplomatic assistance was far less likely to arise.

Whatever the reasons, it was obvious that something would have to be done, and in the letter to Bryce (the Under-Secretary of State) which began the 1886 re-evaluation, Lord Rosebery suggested an enquiry into how much further it was possible for British consuls and diplomatists to go in developing and assisting commerce (without, however, 'running the risk of possible connexion with private firms or enterprise, and the consequent

27. In his speech at the Cobden Club's dinner to the First International Free Trade Congress, 4 August 1908, printed in the *Report of the Proceedings* (London, 1908), p. 46.
28. Address printed in *Lord Rosebery's Speeches (1874–1896)*, (London, 1896), pp. 48–49.

lowering of the standard and repute of those services').[29]
Bryce's conclusion on this point—after listing the various
reasons which made it unwise for a diplomatist to identify himself with any particular enterprise—was that if British diplomatists had erred by abstention in such cases, they had erred on
the safer side. But he confirmed the discretion of British diplomatists to intervene on behalf of individual British interests
where foreign diplomatists were acting to their disadvantage.[30]

Bryce's exception to the rule of non-intervention, though an
important factor, for example, in British policy during the
'Battle for Concessions' in China in 1898, was a reaction to
special circumstances and not an abandonment of the traditional overseas trade policy. When Mr. Lawson, a member of the
Royal Commission on Civil Establishments, asked Bryce a few
years later whether British diplomacy should be assimilated to
'the German system' ('assistance to a particular firm by getting
them contracts for all kinds of business'), Bryce replied that it
would never do for a British consul to associate himself with the
interests of a particular British firm; he had, he explained,
encouraged British consuls in 1886 to go a little further in
assisting British trade overseas by gaining information, sending
home reports and so on, but 'not of course in the way of pushing
the business of particular British firms'.[31] Sir Percy Anderson,
senior clerk of the African and Consular Department (and,
incidentally, the *eminence grise* of British policy in the Partition
of Africa), gave evidence before the same Royal Commission.
Mr. Lawson asked him whether it was true that he objected to
consuls acting for particular firms in any way and thereby
giving them a kind of official recommendation. Sir Percy replied
that it was certainly the case that the Foreign Office did not
allow that, and that whatever was said about Germany in this
respect applied almost exclusively to the East.[32] When the
Commission came to report, it observed that it had not been the
practice, nor was it desirable, for consuls to be encouraged to
push the interests of particular traders to the extent that was
done, for example, by Germany; the principal object of their

29. Rosebery to Bryce, 27 February 1886: P.R.O.,F.O/83/932.
30. See Appendix V.
31. Minutes of Evidence, *Report of the Royal Commission on Civil Establishments,*
P.P.1890(c.6172)XXVII, QQ.28,122–4.
32. ibid., QQ.27,421–2.

attention should be the provision of information on the conditions of trade in their districts and on fresh openings for
British enterprise.

When Sir Percy Anderson called attention to the behaviour
of Germany in the East, he had put his finger on the point which
continued to upset calculations at the Foreign Office as to the
precise degree of support which might legitimately be given to
British commerce and finance overseas. The history of British
official support for the Hong Kong and Shanghai Banking
Corporation illustrates how impossible it was to avoid supporting a particular interest in regions where parallel foreign
interests were receiving the enthusiastic support of their own
Governments—diplomatic pressure, spread between a number
of competing British interests, would have been worse than useless. But it also reveals the reluctance which H.M. Government
continued to feel right to the end of the period to commit itself
to the promotion of particular interests to the exclusion of other
interests of equal respectability. Sir Edward Grey told Sir
Charles Addis, manager of the Hong Kong Bank, that although
his firm was entitled to the exclusive support of H.M. Government for the Hankow-Canton and Hankow-Szechuan Railways, he could not commit the Government to support one
particular firm for all time with respect to any future Chinese
railway business, thus debarring from official good offices other
British firms of good standing which wished to compete.[33] The
compromise rule which came to be adopted by the Foreign Office
in areas of exceptional diplomatic pressure (such as the Levant
and the Far East) was to accept that official assistance might
have to be given to particular British interests in face of strong
foreign competition, but that it must be assistance which would
not prejudice similar applications which might be made by
other competing British firms.[34] Equality of treatment between
British traders, if at all possible, was still the aim, but in competition with foreign traders overseas, genuine equality, unfortunately, was now often inseparable from diplomatic pressure.

33. Sir Edward Grey to Sir J. Jordan, 12 May 1909: P.R.O.,F.O/405/197.
34. This point is made, on the question of the degree of assistance which the
Foreign Office should give to individual firms, by Mr. Algernon Law, Controller of Commercial and Consular Affairs at the Foreign Office, 2 July
1914: Minutes of Evidence, *Fifth Report of the Royal Commission on the Civil
Service*, P.P.1914–16(Cd.7749)XI, Q.43,049.

British overseas trade policy before 1914 began and ended with the principle of equality. To a Victorian or Edwardian official the function of the State went no further than the creation and safeguarding of conditions under which British traders competed fairly and equally between themselves and with the traders of other nations. In order even to secure this much, it became necessary after the mid '80s increasingly to consider the use of diplomatic pressure to counteract the pressure applied by other Governments. But H.M. Government was satisfied if it was able to recreate free competition. With the occasional exception in areas like the Persian Gulf where British interests were political rather than commercial, the Foreign Office never attempted to compete with foreign Governments in applying new forms of pressure on behalf of national trading interests.

There was nothing particularly moral about non-intervention. Britain had little to fear from genuine competition before the First World War and could easily afford to stand aloof. But a policy of non-intervention, clearly, is politically less inflammatory than its opposite, and, this being so, the interests of British trade overseas might be expected to have had—and did have— a very different impact on foreign policy than parallel interests in Germany, France, or even the United States.

CHAPTER 2
BRITISH COMMERCIAL DIPLOMACY

LAISSEZ-FAIRE and an active tradition of commercial diplomacy can scarcely coexist. The President of the Board of Trade, the Rt. Hon. Gerald Balfour, told the Commons in June 1904 that he himself undoubtedly favoured the view that 'the commercial and industrial prosperity of this country must in the main rest with individual effort, and that all that a Government Department could do was to some extent to remove difficulties and to supply information'; apart from this, he thought, and apart from communication with foreign governments over their tariffs—which was the work of the Foreign Office and not of the Board of Trade—there was not much else that could be done.[1] By and large, British business agreed. Many of the leading British merchants and manufacturers in the North and the Midlands, as well as in the traditionally Free Trade London, would never have dreamt of asking for further government assistance: they shared Sir Charles Dilke's opinion that it was better to 'trust to the laws of supply and demand, and to the energy of our own people'.

It was perfectly true that political and economic pressure was making it increasingly difficult after the mid-'80s to sustain an undiluted *laissez-faire*, Free Trade position. Sir Robert Giffen, head progressively of the Statistical, Commercial, and Labour Department of the Board of Trade from 1876 until his retirement in 1897, is described by the *Dictionary of National Biography* as a 'sturdy individualist' and a strong Free Trader, who 'viewed with suspicion any infraction of the maxim *laissez-faire*'. He had helped Farrer, the Permanent Secretary, to torpedo the proposal to protect the British sugar refining industry and the West Indian producers against foreign, bounty-fed sugar imports, on the orthodox grounds that Britain could have no objection to bounties which were actually lowering the price of sugar to the British consumer at the expense of the foreign

1. 136 *Parl.Deb.*4s.325–6 (16 June 1904).

tax-payer: it was up to the British producer whether he sank or swam. But in 1902 Giffen was compelled to admit that the State owed 'something to individuals whose living is threatened by the action of powerful governments'.[2] And international politics were interfering in matters which, two or three decades before, had been of purely commercial interest. Giffen (in his introduction to the new, 1902 edition of Lord Farrer's *The State in its Relation to Trade*) pointed to the question of colonial preference, for which the self-governing colonies had been pressing for a number of years. This would mean the reintroduction of Protection, but the decision as to whether or not to agree to a preferential tariff was political, not commercial. Would British statesmen find it possible, he asked, to deny the colonies their wishes and risk causing serious affront, however much we might dislike arrangements of this kind? As for shipping subsidies:

Half a century ago, and even later, such subsidies would have been laughed at by earnest and convinced free traders. The feeling would have been that if foreign powers gave money to carry English goods and passengers cheaply we should let them.

But very recently Britain had seen substantial portions of her merchant fleet bought up by foreign syndicates. For political reasons, and in order to maintain imperial communications within our hands, we could not allow this to go too far, or permit foreign shipping subsidies to force British shipowners out of business; 'protection or no protection, a feeling is growing up that foreign subsidies, and similar hostile attacks on our shipping, must be met by adequate measures of retaliation'. In Giffen's evidence before the Select Committee on Steamship Subsidies, he had told the Committee that what we were facing, in the question of foreign shipping subsidies, was 'a hostile attack on a vital industry of the country in time of peace carried on directly or indirectly, not by ordinary competitors but by foreign governments'. The question was political rather than economic because, as Adam Smith had pointed out in connexion with the Navigation Laws, there were some things

2. Minutes of Evidence, *Report of the Select Committee on Steamship Subsidies*, P.P.1902(385)IX, Q.180.

which were more important to a community than opulence, and the first thing to be considered was the security of the State.[3]

If Giffen, a prominent member of the Cobden Club and one of the most distinguished of a long line of Free Trade officials, could concede so much, the retreat from *laissez-faire* was certainly under way in Whitehall. And a retreat in Whitehall could become a rout in the East. The British Minister at Peking told Rosebery in 1886 that the British consuls in China found themselves in a very different position from their colleagues in Europe both with respect to British commerce and to foreign diplomatists. He had himself always gone on the principle that 'to be efficient and render the best service within their power to British commerce, [consuls] ought not only to report commercial matters to the Foreign Office and to Her Majesty's Legation, but also be on the look out to show British merchants and traders when and how to take advantage of commercial openings, and, if necessary, to introduce British Agents willingly, yet with just discrimination, to the local authorities'.[4]

Within the limit of 'just discrimination' suggested by O'Conor, British diplomatists might in practice be prepared to go well beyond their strict duty in countries where conditions for the conduct of trade were not ideal. But in general they worked in an official climate which continued favourable to *laissez-faire* and Free Trade. A number of reasons have been, and will be, suggested for this official conservatism, but there is one which needs particular emphasis—the peculiar and sustained optimism of officials, of Liberal politicians, and even of businessmen as to the competitive condition of British trade overseas.

Board of Trade officials and such members of the Foreign Office as concerned themselves with matters of trade were ardent Free Traders during the 1880's. Assault by Fair Traders on their cherished opinions made them anxious to prove the futility of intervention and the extravagance of the tales of

3. ibid., QQ.180–1.
4. O'Conor to Rosebery, 6 March 1886: No. 50, *Correspondence respecting British Trade and Commerce in China and other Foreign Countries 1885–86*, F.O., C.P. 5471.

increased foreign competition.[5] Joseph Chamberlain, in his early days as President of the Board of Trade, argued that the effects and extent of foreign competition were almost always exaggerated and that he was confident, from his own experience in the hardware and iron trades, that there had never been any serious and sustained foreign competition with Britain's standard industries.[6] By 1886 he had become alarmed by the effects of unemployment and the loss of Britain's supremacy in world trade; and he presented the Foreign Office with an embarrassing Memorandum urging the creation of demand by loans totalling £500,000,000 spread over twenty years for the development of Chinese railways.[7] But business revived towards the end of the decade, and Chamberlain himself, with a background of business individualism, was never a convinced interventionist. Only a year after the Chinese Memorandum, he replied discouragingly to Law's suggestion that a Commercial Intelligence Department should be established as the core of the proposed Imperial Institute. Chamberlain explained that his experience as a manufacturer with world-wide commercial connexions had persuaded him that the private enterprise of individuals yielded far better results than Government enquiries; as a rule, only those who were inexperienced or unsuccessful in trade demanded Government assistance.[8]

The effect of Chamberlain's famous Circular despatch of 28 November 1895 was to strengthen official belief in British ability to meet foreign competition. The despatch—to all Colonial Governors—was intended (as Alexander Harris explained in his Introductory Memorandum to the Blue Book) to discover 'the extent to which the *generally alleged* displacement of British by foreign goods was *really* taking place in Colonial markets'.[9] The replies showed that the faults lay rather with the inefficiency

5. A good analysis of the growing competitiveness of German trade, separating the myth from the reality, is given by Ross J. S. Hoffman, *Great Britain and the German Trade Rivalry, 1875–1914* (Philadelphia, 1933); also, though less valuable in this context because more political, Raymond J. Sontag, *Germany and England 1848–1894* (New York, 1938).
6. 264 *Parl.Deb.*3s.1799 (12 August 1881).
7. J. L. Garvin, *The Life of Joseph Chamberlain* (London, 1933), II, 448–9.
8. Quoted in Morison and Hutchinson, *Life of Sir Edward Law*, p. 63.
9. (My italics): *Trade of the British Empire and Foreign Competition*, P.P.1897 (c.8449)LX.

of British selling methods, delivery, and packaging than with any irremediable commercial superiority among our foreign competitors. Its conclusions had been powerfully anticipated by Sir Courtenay Boyle's Memorandum to the President of the Board of Trade of 16 January 1897. Sir Courtenay compiled a number of tables for the exports of the main trading rivals, which he summarized in the following five year averages for the beginning and end of the period with which he was dealing (1880–1895):

	Average 1880–4 Million £	Average 1891–5 Million £
United Kingdom	234	227
France	138	134
Germany	156	155
United States	166	183

Arguing from these figures, he concluded that in no country at all had there been a conspicuous advance in the export trade, and that there was nothing in the general figures to suggest that English exports were diminishing or those of our European rivals increasing. The United States had made some progress, but even this was not so considerable when allowances were made for her increase in population, and it took the form mainly of increased exports of agricultural products. Measuring per head of population, Britain was far ahead of Germany or of any other competitor as an exporting nation, and the gains of Germany and the United States had had no very serious effect upon British trade; it was just that 'beginning from a lower level each country is travelling upwards more rapidly than we are who occupy a much higher eminence'. Sir Courtenay admitted that competition in neutral markets and even in home markets would probably become increasingly serious unless Britain became more active, and that we should be prepared to recognize that, in changing conditions, we could hardly expect to maintain our past pre-eminence. But the State, he concluded, could only give limited assistance in developing and increasing our competitive power. Britain's commercial position had been attained, and must be preserved, by individual effort; what the

State could properly do was limited to the supply of accurate commercial information, in the provision of which, Sir Courtenay thought, we were 'somewhat behindhand'.[10]

The Board of Trade's optimism continued, so much so that it was commented on specifically in the *Report of the Select Committee on Steamship Subsidies*: the Board's belief, 'stated with the greatest confidence', was that British shipping was maintaining its flourishing position as against foreign competition, and that the more rapid proportionate increase of foreign tonnage derived from the fact that it started at a lower figure.[11] But Liberal politicians were just as optimistic, and the booming conditions of world trade in the first decade of this century did nothing to discourage them. No doubt their optimism was in part a political response to Chamberlain's tariff proposals, in much the same way as officials reacted against Fair Trade in the '80s. Mr. Asquith argued in the autumn of 1903 that Chamberlain's proposals started from the assumption that 'British trade is in a parlous state' whereas it was, in fact, 'not otherwise than healthy and steadily progressing both in volume and in value'. It was 'manifestly untrue' that our export trade was stagnant; between 1877 and 1902 the net produce of British labour and capital exported had risen from £140,000,000 to £224,000,000.[12] The election campaign of 1905 was fought on the same optimistic assumptions, and in 1908 Winston Churchill, as President of the Board of Trade and British Government representative at the International Free Trade Congress, could claim that British experience served as a substantial object lesson in international affairs on the possibility of combining Free Trade with power and prosperity:

10. *Memorandum on the Comparative Statistics of Population, Industry and Commerce in the United Kingdom and some Leading Foreign Countries*, P.P.1897(c.8322) LXXXIII. Board of Trade surveys of a similar kind had managed to produce as encouraging results over the previous decade. Sir Robert Giffen's reports both of January 1888 and April 1894 concluded that there was no evidence to indicate any weakening in the United Kingdom's hold upon the export trade of the world in comparison with its chief competitors: *Statistical Tables relating to the Progress of the Foreign Trade of the United Kingdom, and of other Countries, in recent years*, P.P.1888(c.5297)XCIII; ibid., P.P.1894 (c.7349)LXXX.
11. *Report of the Select Committee on Steamship Subsidies*, P.P.1902(385)IX, para.32.
12. H. H. Asquith, *Trade and the Empire* (London, 1903), pp. 54–56.

We levy no discriminatory duties, nor do we seek artificially to stimulate our exports; and yet we find ourselves with a rich and fertile home market, and able, man for man, to export to foreign countries, in spite of all their tariffs, more than twice as much man for man, as has yet been achieved by any country in the world.[13]

Laissez-faire and official optimism between them made certain that the emphasis in Whitehall continued to be placed on improvements in commercial intelligence as the sole useful and legitimate outlet for increased government assistance to trade. This had certainly been Sir Courtenay Boyle's conclusion in his 1897 Memorandum; and when he wrote to the Treasury three months later to ask for its assent to the appointment of a Committee to investigate further means of government assistance to overseas trade, he pointed out that, although the State could do more than it was doing at present to facilitate the supply and publication of commercial information, 'it would be unwise to take any step which might have the effect of weakening the power exercised by the enlightened self-interest of those who are directly engaged in home and foreign trade'.[14]

*   *   *

Commercial intelligence was H.M. Government's main contribution to the progress of British trade overseas before the First World War. British consuls had always been expected to produce an Annual Report on the trade and navigation of their particular districts, and they were also instructed to report any new developments or matters of immediate commercial interest as they arose. The growing interest in accurate information, which had been reflected in the formation of the Statistical Department at the Board of Trade in 1832, meant that information from Consuls was systematized from a comparatively early date; Board of Trade enquiries attempted to pose questions which would be of real value to British trade. A questionnaire circulated to Consuls as early as August 1832 asked, for example, for information on the state of commerce (whether it was stationary, thriving or declining), together with an indication of what intelligent individuals on the spot thought

13. *Report of the Proceedings of the International Free Trade Congress* (London, 1908), p. 2.
14. Board of Trade to Treasury, 29 April 1897: P.R.O.,B.T/13/29, file no. 12804.

to be the reasons for advance or decline. It asked, too, for Consular opinions on the measures which both Governments might take which would be most likely to promote and extend mutual trade, and for information of any kind which might enable the Board of Trade to form an accurate estimate of the trade and navigation of each country overseas, of the means by which they were conducted, and of the prospects for increase.[15] But the problem, as the Vice-President of the Board of Trade (Charles Poulett Thomson) told the Select Committee on Public Documents six months later, was that the foreign statistics were generally so imperfect that it was impossible to say as yet whether information would arrive in a form suitable for tabulation.[16]

Whatever the obstacles, H.M. Government continued to attach a great deal of importance to the collection of commercial intelligence. In 1857 Lord Clarendon, whom Bagehot had described as having 'an exceptional interest in commerce and statistics', extended the duty of collecting information to the diplomatic service. The purpose of the extension, admittedly, was less to improve the quantity and quality of commercial information than to increase the general knowledge of Secretaries of Embassy and Legation on the commercial affairs with which they would have to deal as heads of mission, and to give the Foreign Office a means of gauging the quality of diplomatists overseas. But Clarendon made the important point that while consuls provided ample reports on their own areas, these were necessarily limited and local in their knowledge and scope; on the other hand:

Her Majesty's diplomatic servants, residing at the capitals, have opportunities for arriving at a more general appreciation of the commercial progress of the several countries, and of ascertaining the grounds on which legislative interference with the course of trade is resorted to, and the effect which such interference is calculated to have, not only on local or general interests in the countries themselves, but also on the commercial relations of those countries with foreign nations.

Clarendon encouraged Secretaries to visit commercial centres

15. Printed as Appendix No. 1, *Report from the Select Committee on Consular Establishment*, P.P.1835(499)VI.
16. Minutes of Evidence, *First Report from the Select Committee on Public Documents*, P.P.1833(44)XII, QQ.152–4.

and ports and to suggest means by which British trade 'might obtain facilities, or be relieved from burdens and obstructions'.[17]

Clarendon's initiative was extended by Lord Russell. In addition to the half-yearly reports called for by Clarendon, Russell's Circular of 24 January 1860 instructed Secretaries to prepare an annual report on the 'finances, public credit, shipping, commerce, manufactures, and agriculture of the several countries in which they have resided during the past year'.[18] A couple of months later, Lord Russell sent out a further Circular emphasizing the need for punctuality in reports, and explaining again that the object of the reports was not so much to obtain the latest statistical information as to 'impose upon the secretaries the duty of keeping their attention constantly alive to all matters connected with the industry, commerce, and resources of the country in which they resided, and of reporting either generally upon the whole, or specifically upon any branch of them'.[19] A fourth Circular, despatched by Russell in 1863, called on all H.M. Ministers abroad to forward home as a matter of urgency any official announcements with respect to tariffs, commerce, navigation, and currency, so that the information could be communicated immediately to British trading interests via the *London Gazette*.[20] And in a Circular of the following year Lord Russell required that junior members of Chancery should also draw up reports on commerce, industry, and politics for the information of the Head of Mission—though these reports were not to be sent home.[21]

The policy expressed by these Circulars was continued, though the actual number of reports required was reduced (by 1885) to one commercial and one financial report a year. A Circular of 6 April 1872 called for reports from H.M. diplomatic representatives on general questions of British trade and on means for its further development; and another (of 8 May

17. Minutes of Evidence, *Report of the Select Committee on Consular Service and Appointments*, P.P.1857–1858(482)VIII, Q.708 (copy of Clarendon's Circular of 24 February 1857 handed in by Hammond in the course of his evidence).
18. No. 11 in Appendix No. 2, *Report from the Select Committee on the Diplomatic Service*, P.P.1861(459)VI.
19. Circular dated 31 March 1860: No. 15 in Appendix No. 2, ibid.
20. Appendix No. 4, *Report of the Select Committee on Trade with Foreign Nations*, P.P.1864(493)VII.
21. No. 5, *Circulars addressed to Her Majesty's Ministers Abroad, 1862–66*, P.P.1867–1868(4005)XL.

1878) instructed Missions to forward 'Précis of Parliamentary debates or proceedings, or the proceedings of public bodies, on matters affecting British commercial interests'.[22]

Unfortunately, the presentation of the mass of information provided by this elaborate system of commercial reports did not keep pace with the quantity. Poor editing and the absence of any kind of index—Mr. Watherston complained to the British Association in 1881—made the mountain of miscellaneous commercial information published by the Government virtually useless to those merchants whom it was primarily intended to serve.[23] The Controller of H.M. Stationery Office had already called attention to the under-use of Government statistical services. In a letter to the Board of Trade ten years before, he had suggested economies in the volume of statistics prepared and published for that Department. The *Monthly Statement of Trade and Navigation of the United Kingdom* and the corresponding *Statement for certain Foreign Countries* were 'absolutely useless' for commercial purposes. Between 1750 and 2000 copies of each were printed, but it was difficult to believe that, besides those issued to Government Departments, more than a hundred copies were ever opened—'Statesmen, Statisticians, Journalists, often use them; members of Parliament very rarely; merchants almost never'.[24]

However, the 1886 review of government assistance to trade resulted in an important reform in the system of commercial intelligence. Lord Rosebery announced the monthly publication of the new *Board of Trade Journal* which was intended, without superseding the reports from H.M. Representatives abroad published by the Foreign Office, to present summaries of the more important items of information rather sooner than had previously been possible. Moreover, the *Journal* was to include any useful information gathered by the Board of Trade on shipping, railways and commercial affairs generally, and particular attention was to be paid to the publication of early intelligence on actual and proposed changes in Customs tariffs

22. Appendix (A), *Correspondence respecting Diplomatic Assistance to British Trade Abroad*, P.P.1886(c.4779)LX.
23. Printed as Appendix E, *Final Report of the Royal Commission on the Depression of Trade and Industry*, P.P.1886(c.4893)XXIII.
24. H.M. Stationery Office to the Board of Trade, 18 January 1870: P.R.O., B.T/13/4, file no. 1394.

and regulations. The commercial reaction to the new publication was universally favourable, though there were some requests for an even more rapid means of distributing urgent information. In response to public demand, the *Board of Trade Journal* was converted into a weekly, but its value was not entirely unquestioned, and *The Economist*—always a stern critic of government intervention—described it (in 1895) as of extremely limited use for practical trading purposes and as certainly not diminishing the need for more prompt and effective information from consuls overseas.[25] The practice had also developed of publishing information in the national press on any likely openings for British enterprise abroad, and, by the last decade of the nineteenth century, the Foreign Office was in the habit of corresponding directly with trade associations on the subject of desirable contracts for which tenders were invited. The *Board of Trade Journal* itself had a special section on 'Openings for British Trade' in which information on possible openings and contracts abroad was brought before the commercial community.

While the existing machinery was extended, the Manchester Chamber of Commerce was actively canvassing the appointment of a new institution—a permanent advisory committee on commercial intelligence, to consist of officials of the Foreign Office and the Board of Trade and representatives of commerce. Rosebery rejected the suggestion when it was put to him in February 1893, but the Chamber re-submitted it to the Departmental Committee on Commercial Intelligence of 1898. The 1898 Committee recommended the formation of such a Committee in its report, and the Advisory Committee on Commercial Intelligence was appointed by the President of the Board of Trade in May 1900.

The Advisory Committee on Commercial Intelligence, together with the new Intelligence Branch of the Commercial, Labour, and Statistical Department of the Board of Trade, went a long way towards rationalizing the entire system of commercial intelligence. Mr. Worthington's commercial mission to Latin America in 1898 (with the object of discovering the reason for any decline in British trade and of suggesting a remedy) set the pattern for the following years, and the

25. *The Economist*, 7 December 1895, 1585.

Commercial Intelligence Committee was responsible for sending Commercial Missions to Persia, Siberia, and South Africa in 1903, Australia and New Zealand in 1905, Canada and Newfoundland in 1906, Mesopotamia in 1907, Syria and Palestine in 1909, and Central America, Venezuela and Colombia in 1911. The Commercial Intelligence Branch, judging by the scale of its correspondence, was at least in part a success. In a letter to the Treasury appealing for an increase in staff, the Board of Trade pointed out that written inquiries received by the Branch had increased from 938 in 1900 to 4,547 in the first ten months of 1907; personal inquiries had risen from 299 to 2,899; letters and circulars despatched, from 2,123 to 34,514.[26]

Yet in spite of the very considerable improvements in the supply of commercial intelligence since 1886, and in spite of the new sources of information created by the appointment of Commercial Attachés after 1880 and Commercial Agents for an experimental period after 1899, criticism of quantity, quality and presentation continued. Lucie Duff Gordon's scornful description for 1866 of 'old Colquhoun (the British Consul-General) going in his cocked hat to ask the Fellaheen what wages they got' may have been unjust for a later period, but there was a general impression among the commercial community well into this century that Britain was poorly served in its Consular reports by comparison with the United States, Germany, France, and even Belgium. Elijah Helm of the Manchester Chamber of Commerce, rising to second Joseph Walton's motion on the Consular Service at the Montreal Congress of Chambers of Commerce of the Empire, August 1903, claimed that the consular reports, with some exceptions, were almost useless. His remark was greeted by 'Hear, hear!' from the audience, and he went on to emphasize that the reports were of 'little or no use whatever to manufacturers and merchants and all who are interested in trade and commerce'.[27]

No businessman, of course, is ever quite satisfied with his relationship with the State—it either interferes too much or too little. But the criticism of the commercial intelligence services at the turn of the century is worth investigating for the

26. Board of Trade to Treasury, 30 December 1907: P.R.O.,B.T/13/42, file no. 19443.
27. *Official Report of the Fifth Congress* (Montreal, 1903), p. 38.

light it throws on commercial and official attitudes to the
legitimate scope of government assistance to trade.

Generally speaking, the larger manufacturers and traders
attached little importance to consular reports. They had their
own sources of information through their branches, their
agencies, or through the extensive network of British banking,
insurance, and cable companies overseas; they stood to lose,
in fact, rather than to gain by official broadcasting of commercial or financial information. The Glasgow Chamber of
Commerce, which spoke for the larger interests, was prepared
even to suggest that there were good reasons to oppose official
publicity for public tenders invited by foreign governments;
official reports, it claimed, should be limited to 'doing for
traders at large what, individually, or in combination, traders
cannot do for themselves'.[28] But, in contrast, the smaller
businesses, or those just beginning to consider new export
markets or overseas contracts, clamoured for increased supplies
of up-to-date information which they themselves were in no
position to obtain. The difficulty was to strike some balance
between them, and to tread that narrow line between assistance
to one interest and damage to another. Consular Instructions
for 1914 warned Consuls to decline requests for information
from British firms which manifestly related to the business of
their British competitors, while if information were to be
provided on foreign manufactures, care should be taken that
this was unlikely to damage the competitive position of British
manufacturing industries.

28. A Glasgow Chamber of Commerce Memorandum explaining, in reply
to Sir Courtenay Boyle's Circular of 27 August 1897, the Chamber's objections to unlimited, government-supplied, commercial intelligence services,
is printed as Appendix 6, *Report of the Commercial Intelligence Committee*, P.P.
1898(c.8963)XXXIII. It is interesting to find the same arguments being put
forward by a Merchants' Association during the 1920's, in the evidence it
gave before the Committee on Industry and Trade. The Committee observed in reply that this was a criticism against the whole principle of
Government assistance in disseminating commercial intelligence, and that
the Committee itself felt that 'in these days of keen world competition, more
especially in a country whose very existence depends on the development and
maintenance of its export trade, the action of the State in assisting exporters
by the organization of commercial intelligence is abundantly justified, and
in any case the principle has been accepted in this country for many years.':
Final Report of the Committee on Industry and Trade, P.P.1928–29(Cmd.3282)
VII, Section VI(1).

In commercial intelligence, as in so many other aspects of British commercial diplomacy, there was a limit to the degree of assistance which the Foreign Office was prepared to give, a limit which was relaxed as foreign competition increased. In the 1860's, Layard had felt indignant that he should be asked the current price of Bohemian glass and Dresden china, and had told the Commons that it was no part of the duty of the Foreign Office to supply information on details of this kind which people should be able to obtain by their own efforts or through proper agents.[29] By the end of the century similar requests were handled without question by the Commercial Intelligence Branch of the Board of Trade. But there were, in fact, good reasons, both practical and traditional, for limiting the supply of commercial intelligence by public agencies to the needs of British commerce in general, rather than attempting to extend it to meet those of the individual.

The attitude of the Foreign Office towards commercial intelligence was explained in Consul-General W. L. Booker's despatch to Lord Rosebery of 26 April 1886. British traders, he felt, had a right to look to Consuls for such information as would give them a good idea of the character of trade in unfamiliar markets. But:

They ought not to expect to be more than generally made acquainted with what class of goods they are likely to find customers for; specific information should be sought for through unofficial sources.[30]

The limits which Booker had set might occasionally be interpreted rather inflexibly. A Lancashire M.P. told the story of a capable businessman, the representative of a large commercial house in Bradford, who had gone out to the Far East to open up a trade. In the course of his travels he had asked one of the British consuls in China to provide him with a list of traders in a particular line of business. The consul had handed him a general list of traders and, when asked specifically for the names of houses dealing in textiles, had replied: 'Oh, if you think I am here for the purpose of making business easy for commercial

29. 177 *Parl.Deb.3s.*1879(17 March 1865).
30. No. 70, *Correspondence respecting Diplomatic Assistance to British Trade Abroad*, P.P.1886(c.4779)LX.

travellers, I am not your man; if you want anything in a general way I shall be glad to help, but if you want anything with reference to a particular business, you will have to go over the way to the German consul, who, I believe, has assorted lists of traders.'[31]

This was obviously an absurd position to take, but the objections to direct and specialized commercial intelligence were less easily answered. In the first place, it was not impossible that a merchant might be persuaded to take up business on the strength of a particular recommendation in a consular report, blaming the Government when it failed. Then, a consul could not be expected to have the technical knowledge which alone could make his report of value to specialists—a general report was as much as he was genuinely qualified to provide. Mr. Bryce, in his 1886 Memorandum, explained very distinctly that:

... the most we can expect from a Consul preparing a Report is that he should understand the laws, the social system, the commercial and industrial conditions of the country where he is placed, and that he should be careful to refer to the best sources, written or oral, for information on those matters which lie outside his own range of knowledge. He may thus produce Reports which will be useful to the merchant or manufacturer at home, not, perhaps, as a maker of or dealer in any special class of goods, but as a mercantile man, who wishes to know the prospects of British trade generally in a given district.[32]

Consuls were quick to notice the difficulty of gathering accurate commercial information, and the disadvantage of supplying it once obtained. Consul Crawfurd of Oporto pointed out (1886) that even if a consul were able to provide useful information on detailed points for particular trades, 'his Report could only be valuable if it were addressed confidentially to one particular individual, and if it were so addressed without the smallest loss of time'.[33] The British consul at Samoa reported that the Consular Service was ready and able to search for markets and to provide the most elementary trade information:

31. 97 *Parl.Deb.*4s.1011 (19 July 1901).
32. Appendix V.
33. No. 69, *Correspondence respecting Diplomatic Assistance to British Trade Abroad*, P.P.1886(c.4779)LX.

but it is obvious that in pointing out these markets and in giving this information the markets in question are really spoilt and rendered useless, for whereas one firm finding out the market for itself might make good profits, those profits dwindle to zero if they are to be shared by a hundred other British firms.[34]

And there were always the interests of British merchants on the spot to be considered. Not only did State-supplied commercial information assist the smaller British manufacturers as against the larger; it threatened vested interests abroad. Messrs. Law and Llewellyn-Smith (of the Commercial Departments of the Foreign Office and Board of Trade respectively) told the Walrond Committee on the Consular Service (1903) that firms abroad were not willing to provide information which might injure their own monopolies or endanger their competitive position; consuls had some difficulty in obtaining accurate commercial information. To some extent information provided to foreign firms for the purpose of encouraging them to buy from British manufacturers was injuring the interest of British merchants abroad (by allowing foreigners to trade directly with British manufacturers)—though on this point the Board of Trade did not feel that it was desirable 'to establish any hard and fast rule which would recognise that those old-established houses should have a monopoly'; and a consul, by putting a foreign manufacturer in touch with British buyers, might be injuring the interests of English and Colonial competitors, and by-passing local British middlemen into the bargain. Finally, there was the not inconsiderable risk that information provided by British consuls might be used competitively by foreign merchants and manufacturers.[35]

The last point, in fact, became increasingly important as foreign competition reached serious proportions at the turn of the century. Lord Rosebery explained the problem in a speech to the Leeds Chamber of Commerce in October 1888. He told the Chamber how glad he was that the new and more substantial reports issued since the 1886 reforms had met with commer-

34. Report dated March 1898, printed as Appendix, *Opinions of H.M. Diplomatic and Consular Officers on British Trade Methods*, P.P.1899(c.9078) XCVI.
35. Minutes of Evidence, *Report of the Departmental Committee on the Consular Service* (the Walrond Committee), F.O.,C.P.7973.

cial approval, but confessed that he himself had been a little disappointed by the fact that foreign competitors were able to make so much better use of these reports than we were ourselves; what we were doing was to provide hints to foreign competitors as to how best they might compete with us. Rosebery's conclusion—many years before the policy was actually adopted—was that copies of the reports might be passed out confidentially to the Chambers of Commerce before general publication, so that British traders might at least have some advantage in using them.[36]

While most of the information provided in consular reports was, of course, of a general nature and of interest to British trade as a whole (and could therefore hardly be considered as confidential), the kind of points which Rosebery raised, and which many Chambers of Commerce raised after him, were so obviously sensible that there was an increasing tendency at the turn of the century to keep back news of particular trading opportunities which might be of value to British commerce. Until the end of 1906, the Commercial Intelligence Branch forwarded this information confidentially to Chambers of Commerce, and it was not published (if at all) until after British traders had had the advantage of a start on their foreign competitors. Moreover, unpublished lists of possible buyers of British goods were kept by the Commercial Intelligence Branch specifically for use by *British* business. The system proved satisfactory, but it was realized that something more would have to be done to reach all British manufacturers or traders, whether or not they were members of local Chambers of Commerce. It was decided, therefore, to establish a special list at the Commercial Intelligence Branch of British firms interested in particular branches of commerce, and to forward direct to them any information which might be of value; the only condition imposed in return for this service was that the firms on the list should become subscribers to the *Board of Trade Journal*. The new scheme was successful in attracting a large number of firms, and was able, within reasonable limits, to prevent the leakage of confidential information overseas.

36. Speech given on 11 October 1888, and printed in *Rosebery's Speeches*, pp. 47–49.

But there were two difficult problems of detail which a *laissez-faire* State had to meet in deciding how far it should go in providing information—first, the recommendation of agents and lawyers abroad, and then the more controversial point of credit information.

The Foreign Office, while feeling a certain reluctance to accept the implied responsibility, recognized its duty to be prepared to recommend agents abroad for the products of British manufacturers. The nature of the problem appears from a letter written by a British firm to Lord Rosebery in 1886. The firm explained the difficulty it experienced in obtaining suitable representation abroad, and suggested the opening of a Registry at British consulates of local firms willing to take up agencies for British houses. This in itself was an innocent enough suggestion, but the letter continued to explain that 'all members of such Consular Commercial Registers were to have the moral guarantee of the British Consul as to their *bona fides* and sound position'.[37] The suggestion was not taken up, and the attitude of the Foreign Office continued to be one of intense suspicion of anything which might involve H.M. Government in an implied or stated guarantee. But an incident in 1900 shows the extent to which the Foreign Office eventually committed itself. Mr. Milligan, the British Commercial Agent at Zurich, was proposing to conduct the preliminary negotiations with prospective agents for the goods of a Liverpool firm. Sir Henry Bergne felt that this would imply the acceptance of a dangerous degree of responsibility, and argued that the proper limit of the Agent's function as an official was the indication of the best local agents (without any responsibility for the selection). St. John Brodrick, the Parliamentary Under-Secretary, agreed in the main with Sir Henry's minute but could see no objection to Mr. Milligan taking any steps which would not actually involve him in the responsibility of selection.[38] When the subject was again raised by Mr. Milligan, the consensus of opinion at the Foreign Office seems to have been that the finding of agents and the *preliminary* negotiations for their

37. No. 15, *Correspondence respecting Diplomatic Assistance to British Trade Abroad*, P.P.1886(c.4779)LX.
38. St. John to Salisbury, 14 October 1900, and minutes: P.R.O.,F.O/83/1784.

selection were proper functions of a Commercial Agent.[39]

The recommendation of lawyers presented further problems. In common with the recommendation of agents, there was the danger of an implied responsibility. A Foreign Office minute of March 1886 pointed out that:

Our Consuls constantly help private firms by advice and by recommendations of lawyers, agents, etc.—The result frequently is that the other lawyers, agents, etc., complain of the Consul's favouritism or accuse him of corrupt motives and that the private firms try to make H.M.G. responsible for the consul's advice.[40]

The position, however, was clearly defined by Mr. Bryce, both in his Memorandum of the following July and in his letters to the Chambers of Commerce a few days later. Mr. Bryce remarked on the difficulties experienced by traders in knowing and interpreting the law in countries in which they were not established or with which they did business through the post or by local agents. He agreed that it should be the function of H.M. representatives to recommend competent and trustworthy lawyers and accountants, and to give British litigants 'such advice and help as their own experience may show to be useful'.[41] But he refused to accept the suggestion that H.M. Consuls should act as quasi-Public Prosecutors in cases of trade mark infringement or violation of mercantile agreements. This, he argued, was the work of a specialist lawyer, and 'consular officers could not be expected to execute the function with satisfaction either to themselves, or to them whose interests they might be attempting to represent'.[42]

Implied government responsibility was again the main obstacle to the provision of information on the credit-standing of foreign firms. There could be no question of the value of this information to British subjects trading overseas. A deputation consisting of the President and the Secretary of the Association of Chambers of Commerce called on the Foreign Office in

39. Conyngham Greene to Lansdowne, 23 August 1901, and minutes: P.R.O.,F.O/83/1881.
40. Sir V. Lister's minute on Sir Jacob Behrens' letter of 4 March 1886: P.R.O.,F.O/83/932.
41. Memorandum printed as Appendix V.
42. No. 4, *Correspondence respecting Diplomatic Assistance to British Trade Abroad, Part II*, P.P.1886(c.4779)LX.

October 1899 to express the anxious wish of British merchants for Foreign Office assistance in obtaining information on the standing of foreign firms—a task which was particularly difficult in North and South America, and in East Europe. The Secretary (Mr. Fithian) explained that this information was the one thing for which commercial men were always asking. Sir M. Gosselin, who received the deputation, put forward the traditional Foreign Office view that incorrect information would cause the British enquirer to suffer (and would probably bring an accusation of responsibility), while if it were known that a British representative had been reporting unfavourably on certain houses of business within his locality, his position might be made intolerable.[43] Admittedly, Mr. Bryce's Memorandum had expressed the opinion that H.M. representatives should, 'where they are in a position and feel at liberty to do so', be prepared to provide the best information they had on the respectability of foreign commercial houses.[44] But this was hastily qualified in Bryce's letter to the Chambers of Commerce. He told the Chambers that Lord Rosebery saw great difficulty in directing consuls to report on the solvency of business firms, and that 'such a course might open a door to all kinds of misapprehension, complaint, and possibly even litigation . . .'.[45]

The obstinacy of the Foreign Office on this point was complicated by the readiness, for instance, of Belgian consuls and of the Handels Museum in Vienna to provide credit information (though without guarantees). Yet the United States Government adopted the same attitude as the Foreign Office. Mr. Porter, Acting Secretary of State, replying to the suggestion of Messrs. Stearns and Co. (19 January 1886) that instructions should be given to consuls to make inquiries on the financial standing of foreign individuals and firms, explained that 'such a matter does not come within the proper functions of the Department', and added that consuls did not have time or opportunity to arrive at a just conclusion on matters of such

43. Memorandum dated 11 October 1899: P.R.O.,F.O/83/1784.
44. See Appendix V, but Bryce added that if H.M. Representatives were to give any information on credit 'they will have to speak guardedly, warning the questioner that they give no guarantee'.
45. No. 4, *Correspondence respecting Diplomatic Assistance to British Trade Abroad, Pt. II*, P.P.1886(c.4779)LX.

difficulty and delicacy.[46] The point continued to be pressed by British commerce, especially in the evidence taken before the Departmental Committee on Commercial Intelligence (1898), but the Committee's Report reaffirmed the Government's opposition to an alteration of established policy.[47]

As a result of prolonged commercial pressure, a slight relaxation was permitted when Commercial Agents were first appointed. The instructions provided for the use of Agents contained a section on credit information, inserted on the advice of Sir J. H. Sanderson and based on the formula used by bankers in a similar situation:

The commercial agent is not bound to answer inquiries as to the standing of commercial firms.

He may, however, at his discretion reply:

1. That the firm is held in high repute, or is generally considered one of high standing.

2. That according to the information that the agent has been able to obtain the firm is respectable, though not in a large way of business.

3. That the agent regrets that he is unable to furnish information on the subject.[48]

But even this was questioned. When Mr. Cooke (the Commercial Agent in Moscow) wrote to inquire what his position was to be on credit information, Sir Henry Bergne advised that he should not feel bound to provide such information at all; if he did, he would certainly be held responsible for it.[49] The Board of Trade felt much the same. It cautioned Mr. Melville, the new Commercial Agent for Central America, against giving credit information in his official capacity on commercial firms in the Central American Republics.[50] And Commercial Agents were officially warned by the Foreign Office in 1905 that whenever they gave the names of firms they must make it

46. Quoted by Francis Wharton, *A Digest of the International Law of the United States* (Washington, 1886), pp. 794–5.
47. *Report of the Commercial Intelligence Committee*, P.P.1898(c.8962)XXXIII.
48. Memorandum of Instructions for British Commercial Agents, attached to a minute by Lord Salisbury, 20 March 1900: P.R.O.,F.O/83/1784.
49. Minute on Sir Charles Scott's despatch, 5 January 1900: P.R.O.,F.O/83/1784.
50. Board of Trade to Foreign Office, 10 June 1903: P.R.O.,F.O/83/2100.

clear that they accepted no responsibility for financial standing. A similar instruction had been inserted in a Foreign Office Circular to consular officers the previous year.[51]

The compromise which was finally reached (and which still applies today) was that whereas credit or financial reports on firms overseas could not be given and should be obtained from specialized sources such as banks and credit reporting agencies, H.M. Government was prepared at its own discretion and without accepting any responsibility to give information on general status (the local standing of the firm, the scope of its business activities, the size of its organization).[52]

The extent to which commercial intelligence could be provided by H.M. Government before the First World War was limited both by the jealousies of the commercial community and by the caution and rigidity of officials. But it is unquestionably the case that, even within these limitations, much more might have been achieved. One of the chief obstacles was shortage of funds. The Departmental Committee of 1916 which, under the chairmanship of Sir Eyre Crowe, considered the reform of the overseas services, complained very reasonably that while the Consular Service must be considered the basis of any sound system of commercial intelligence, its staff and pay were quite inadequate for this purpose; consuls were overwhelmed with routine duties which, with consular staff reduced to a minimum, left no time for the collection of commercial intelligence.[53]

But money alone was no solution. There was not enough interest among the commercial community to make the whole system really worthwhile. Nine years after the establishment of the Commercial Intelligence Branch of the Board of Trade, a good many of the businessmen spoken to by Mr. Gastrell (the British Commercial Attaché at Berlin) on his tour of British commercial centres in 1908–9, were not even aware of its existence, nor had they heard of Government Blue Books, of the fact that these could generally be consulted at their own

51. Memorandum dated 8 June 1905: P.R.O.,F.O/83/2100.
52. See *Handbook to the Commercial Intelligence Branch of the Board of Trade* (H.M.S.O., London, 1906), pp. 12–13, and the handbook prepared by the modern Export Services Branch of the Board of Trade, *British Government Services to Exporters* (H.M.S.O.), p. 3.
53. Report printed as Appendix VI.

Chambers of Commerce, or even of the possibility of writing direct to consuls abroad on commercial matters.[54]

The fault was not entirely theirs. The Foreign Office itself took the minimum interest in the flood of commercial reports received from British consuls, commercial attachés and commercial agents overseas. One of the most constant of consular complaints was the complete indifference with which the Service's efforts were met at the Foreign Office, and the lack of any relation between consular performance and promotions. The Steamship Subsidies Committee closely questioned Sir Henry Bergne (head of the Commercial Department) on precisely this point. Sir Henry was obliged to admit that there was no one at the Foreign Office who was specifically instructed to bring points of importance to the notice of the commercial community; he felt that the circulation of the printed reports to all the Chambers of Commerce and the Public Libraries was enough indication that they contained material worth looking at. The Committee was not satisfied with this answer, and Mr. Norman asked whether there was anybody who was responsible for studying the reports before they were filed in the Foreign Office Library. Sir Henry answered that this would be a very laborious job for which the Department was not properly staffed; he himself, he added, sometimes skimmed through the reports before they were sent on to the Board of Trade, but he could not say that he read them all through. When he was recalled to give further evidence a few days later, the Committee again raised the point, and Sir Henry repeated that there was no machinery at the Foreign Office for bringing points to the notice of individual traders or manufacturers; he had, very occasionally, sent copies of reports with marked passages to particular people, but that was 'only by way of exceptional favour'.[55]

The anonymous writer of a *Quarterly Review* article of April 1903 ('The Consular Service and its Wrongs') seized on Bergne's evidence and pointed out how little influence efficient performance of commercial intelligence duties was likely to

---

54. *Report on the Results of Mr. Gastrell's Visits to Chambers of Commerce, 1908–1909*, F.O.,C.P.9519.
55. Minutes of Evidence, *Report of the Select Committee on Steamship Subsidies*, P.P.1901(300)VIII, QQ.323–4; 346–51; 390–9; 433–4.

have in a Department which regarded its function merely as a post office for the transmission of reports to the Board of Trade and the Chambers of Commerce. He asked whether continued zeal or efficiency might be expected from even the most energetic and intelligent consul when the task of estimating the comparative value of the reports was left entirely to the Board of Trade (which had no voice in the consular appointments or promotions). The answer was given in a Memorandum privately prepared for the Foreign Office by Mr. Cockerell of the Consular Department in September 1904. Out of the 188 Consular officers from whom Annual Trade Reports were expected, only 17 had sent in their reports, as instructed, by March 31, while at the date of writing 76 reports were still awaited, and only eight consuls had written to explain the cause of delay.[56]

Some attempt was made to improve the position. The editing of the reports by the Board of Trade before publication was a useful reform, and the Foreign Office, after the Great War, made it clear in the Consular Instructions that promotion prospects depended henceforward on the quality of commercial intelligence. But the pace of progress was incredibly slow. It was clear, for example, from the evidence presented to the Walrond Committee in 1903 and to the Royal Commission on the Civil Service in 1914, that the Foreign Office itself regarded the relatively new institution of frequent special consular reports on immediate developments (tariff changes, new Customs regulations, changes in the proportion of duties payable in gold, etc.) as of far greater value to British commerce than the regular Annual Reports. Annual Reports were described as useful rather for general statistical purposes, for comparison with previous years, and as reviews of past conditions (which might conceivably be of value to a trader in need of a general picture of a possible new market overseas). Yet fifty years later the Plowden Committee made precisely the same points, and suggested the same remedy. British industry, it said, set comparatively little store by the type of periodic economic report hitherto circulated; it preferred to receive *ad hoc* reports heralding new trends or containing information on

56. Memorandum dated 14 September 1904, bound under subheading 'Various' in P.R.O.,F.O/83/2152.

new developments relevant to particular interests; there was scope for 'targeting' export information, even if this led to complaints from firms outside the target area.[57]

* * *

While commercial intelligence was the most important of the direct services offered to British trade before 1914, there were clearly a number of other services, such as fishery agreements, arbitration agreements, waterway treaties, telegraph and communications agreements, conventions covering industrial property, patents, copyrights and trade marks, international exhibitions, commercial museums, and the promotion of overseas Chambers of Commerce, which occupied the Commercial, Consular and Treaty Departments from time to time. These services did not, on the whole, create problems or raise issues concerning the relationship of State to Trade, and it would be out of context to discuss them here. But there were certain further diplomatic services, such as the introduction of British traders to foreign governments, the 'touting' of their trade, and pressure for the repayment of debts, which involved points of principle of some importance, and which act, therefore, as a useful illustration of the precise degree of assistance which H.M. Government was prepared to give to British traders overseas.

On the face of it, there is nothing either unusual or objectionable about an official letter of introduction for a British traveller overseas. But it will be remembered that the Foreign Office was completely opposed, save in the most exceptional circumstances, to the promotion of individual trading or financial interests. It was obvious early in the last century— and it was to become increasingly obvious—that a letter of introduction could have a value altogether apart from its social convenience. Such letters were normally directed to British diplomatic representatives, and the implication, carefully avoided by the Foreign Office, could well have been that H.M. Government favoured the particular enterprise of the bearer. The value of the letters, especially in underdeveloped countries, was obvious enough to the applicants. Mr. W. J.

57. *Report of the Committee on Representational Services Overseas*, P.P.1964(Cmnd. 2276), paras. 237, 239.

Henwood, recently appointed by the directors of the Imperial Brazilian Mining Corporation to inspect and report on their extensive mining properties in the 'remote and ill civilized province of Minas Geraes', wrote to ask Aberdeen (26 June 1843) for 'such distinguished countenance and such additional safety' as would be provided by a letter of introduction to the British Minister in Brazil. A few months later, an application was received for a letter of introduction for Mr. Thomas Lloyd, connected with a highly respectable banking establishment in Birmingham, who wanted to do business in the West Indies and Mexico. The application noted that 'with such powerful credentials the object of his journey will be greatly facilitated'. Mr. Bathurst's application for letters of introduction, 17 August 1863, made the point that 'undoubtedly, it is something more than a mere social advantage, in such a semi-barbarous country as China, to be known at Her Majesty's Legation'; and the Memorial of Theodore Souvazoglu, a naturalized British subject and a businessman of some prominence in Manchester, claimed that he was exposed to 'inconvenience and probable loss' in his business in Persia for lack of an introduction to the British Legation.[58]

In all these cases letters of introduction were in fact given, but only because the applicants were well-backed, or already known to the Foreign Office. The attitude of the Foreign Office to letters of introduction had been established by Lord Palmerston at least as early as 1834. J. Backhouse explained (in a Memorandum prepared for the use of Palmerston's successor) that much inconvenience had resulted from the prevalent belief that letters of introduction were to be had for the asking, and from the offence felt by those to whom such introductions were refused:

The plan which Lord Palmerston tried was, to declare such Letters to be, not common official forms—but the personal Introductions of the Individual Secretary of State; and therefore to be asked for according to the same Rules which Gentlemen would observe in the intercourse of Private Life, and by application (whether verbal or in writing) to the Secretary of State himself. . . . This plan did not prevent L.P. from granting Letters even to parties who were not

58. The first two applications and correspondence are in P.R.O.,F.O/83/91, the last two in P.R.O.,F.O/83/494.

personally known to him; provided there was anything in their
Rank, Station, personal character, or connections, which merited
attention—but it enabled him to evade a vast number of applications from strangers and others, which could otherwise hardly have
been refused without giving rise to complaints and disagreeable
discussions as to the comparative respectability of the parties who
succeeded, and of those who failed, in their applications.[59]

Provided that the necessary conditions were fulfilled, the
Foreign Office had no particular objection to supplying introductions to British businessmen. But it was always made clear
that the introductions implied no responsibility for, or even
approbation of, the business itself. In the case of Mr. Schutze,
who was on his way to Shanghai, Mr. Hammond noted that:

as Mr. Schutze is about to engage in business at that place, Lord
Clarendon would not think it right to recommend him specifically
to H.M. Consul—He will however receive from the British Consul,
if Partner in a British House, such protection in case of need as the
Members of a British Mercantile Firm are entitled to receive from,
and as can properly be given by, a British Consul.[60]

Where a letter of introduction was likely to give an unfair
competitive advantage to one British firm over another, it was
refused. Mr. E. Salis Schwabe applied for an introduction,
through the British Ambassador at St. Petersburg, to the
Governor General at Xhaborovsk, explaining that he proposed
to set up an import-export business at Vladivostock. A Foreign
Office minute commented that 'to ask Sir C. Scott to obtain
such special facilities would I think almost amount to a
differential treatment in favour of a particular trader which
would be unusual',[61] and Mr. Schwabe was merely given the
standard form of introduction. But in new areas of trade, or
in places where British diplomatic representation did not as
yet exist, the Foreign Office would occasionally give a direct
introduction. Mr. Hughes, in his attempt (1841) to open up
Paraguay to British trade, was provided with a letter of
introduction from Palmerston to the Paraguayan dictator, Dr.

59. Memorandum dated 25 December 1834: P.R.O.,FO/83/89.
60. E. Hammond to Mr. Schaeffer, 30 January 1869: P.R.O.,F.O/83/494.
61. Mr. Salis Schwabe to the Under-Secretary of State, 23 August 1898:
P.R.O.,F.O/83/1784.

Francia, requesting his admission to Paraguayan territory and soliciting His Excellency's good offices.[62]

The Foreign Office records suggest that letters of introduction were rarely exploited. The few cases which did occur set the Foreign Office on its guard. Mr. E. Bathurst, formerly Vice-Consul at Copenhagen and Cape Haytien, applied to the Foreign Office for introductions to assist his travels in China, Japan, Australia, and America. As a vice-consul he was, of course, known to the Foreign Office and the introductions were provided. Unfortunately, it emerged that he had been guilty of 'very disreputable transactions in different parts of Australia'; in fact, shortly after receiving the letters of introduction, Mr. Bathurst had been convicted and imprisoned for various acts of swindling. Out on ticket-of-leave from prison, he had forwarded his introductions to the various consuls and requested them to put him into business relations with good mercantile houses in their areas. The Foreign Office, when it caught up with what had been happening, immediately cancelled his introductions, but not before they had been the cause of some agitated correspondence from the consuls.[63] Letters of introduction were similarly refused to a Mr. Clarence Shepard, who had had such letters for many years but who had become suspected of promoting fraudulent companies. The Colonial Office covered itself against these situations by refusing categorically for most of the century to give official introductions to those who were going out on business, but its attitude became less rigid in later years.

The final position of the Foreign Office was clearly established in a Circular dated 8 March 1881. Earl Granville noted that it had been the general rule of the Foreign Office that letters of introduction or recommendation should be refused to promoters of specific commercial or industrial undertakings or to concession hunters. The Secretary of State, he said, could not be expected to form a judgement of the soundness or practicability of such undertakings, or to be acquainted with the nature or merits of rival enterprises. An embarrassing position might arise if discrimination were practised between British subjects

62. John Macgregor's *Report on the Spanish American Republics*, P.P.1847(769) LXIV.
63. The papers for the incident are in P.R.O.,F.O/83/494.

of equal respectability; but it was not always possible to deny letters of introduction to British subjects of standing and respectability, which would show that they were persons worthy of consideration and which would gain them access to the authorities before whom their proposals were to be laid. It might also happen that (as in the case of Mr. Bathurst) letters granted for social purposes might be turned to account for the promotion of private business affairs. In order, therefore, to guard against any possibility of a misunderstanding, Earl Granville ended by warning all British representatives that

letters of introduction must not under any circumstances be construed as committing the Home Government to the promoting of any particular enterprise, but only as intended to insure for the bearer that he should meet with such a reception as a traveller of respectability is entitled to.[64]

The position taken by Lord Granville was confirmed by the General Instructions to British Consular Officers, which included, even after the First World War, an identical warning, with the additional explanation that 'particular enterprise' included specific commercial or industrial undertakings, or applications for concessions.

Introductions from the Foreign Office to British representatives created one problem; yet another arose from the introduction of British commercial interests to foreign governments or industry by British diplomatists on the spot. Thomas Michell, H.M. Consul-General in Norway, argued (1886) that even by introducing any particular firm or syndicate to the local authorities, 'the Consular officer would be assumed to give a tacit, if not open, guarantee, both of respectability and of capacity to fulfil the conditions of a concession or contract'. And the failures which occasionally occurred in such undertakings made it all the more advisable that the consul's local influence should not be prejudiced by intervention.[65] The general attitude of the Foreign Office was not quite so fastidious. Consul John Michell (St. Petersburg) felt that no objection could possibly be raised to the introduction of 'British capital-

64. The Circular is printed as Appendix IV.
65. Inclosure in No. 67, *Correspondence respecting Diplomatic Assistance to British Trade Abroad*, P.P.1886(c.4779)LX.

ists, manufacturers, shipowners, and men of commerce generally, to Government officials and other persons with whom such capitalists, &c., may desire to be brought into contact', provided that good offices were limited strictly to the formality of introduction and confined to those officially recommended by the Foreign Office.[66] Mr Bryce's 1886 Memorandum agreed that British representatives should be prepared to introduce properly-recommended British subjects to persons, firms, or Government officials in their districts, but added that there was much room for discretion in any question of *recommending* British merchants; diplomatists should normally avoid making themselves responsible for any person not travelling on an official mission.[67] The evidence taken before the Royal Commission on the Civil Service (1914) suggests that by the end of the period it was definitely considered to be part of the duty of British representatives to bring British merchants into touch with local commerce and officialdom, even if duty ceased precisely at this point.[68]

*   *   *

But if it seemed not unreasonable to expect British representatives, and more especially consuls, to act in the first instance as intermediaries between British commerce and its overseas markets, it was obviously quite another matter to demand that they should go further and perform the functions of agents or commercial travellers for individual British firms, or act as 'touts' for particular British goods. The objections were the familiar fear of responsibility, reluctance to compromise political functions, and distaste for any discrimination between rival British firms. Consul Lewis Joel wrote to Rosebery from Cadiz, 1886, enclosing a printed slip included in some circulars; the slip offered him a consideration if business resulted from his good offices. He argued, reasonably enough, that 'were Consuls permitted to advocate, or lend their influence to promote, the interests of particular firms, offers of a consideration for so doing would be indefinitely multiplied, and as this influence could only be used in favour of one firm in each particular

66. Inclosure in No. 77, ibid.   67. See Appendix V.
68. Particularly, Minutes of Evidence, *Fifth Report of the Royal Commission on the Civil Service*, P.P.1914–16(Cd.7749)XI, QQ.40,491; 42,578–80; 42,917–18.

trade, the disappointed firms who would complain to your Lordship of interested motives and undue preference would be legion'. Consul Joel was not alone in this criticism. Consul Ward of Bordeaux noted the 'well-established rule . . . that Her Majesty's Consuls cannot act as private agents for British firms or associations or for individuals', any deviation from which would prejudice both the interests of the public service and British commercial interests as a whole. And Sir Philip Currie told the London Chamber of Commerce, 22 February 1886, that British representatives could not be expected to act as agents for particular firms, nor was it desirable that they should.[69]

The attitude of the Foreign Office was firmly backed by the Royal Commissions of 1886 and 1914, and by the Commercial Intelligence Committee of 1898. The Royal Commission on the Depression of Trade and Industry explained that it was very important, having regard to their position and duties abroad, that H.M.'s diplomatic and consular officers should be neither directly nor indirectly engaged in commercial operations, and the Commission feared that 'inconvenience would be felt if they assumed in any degree the character of agents for mercantile houses'.[70] The Departmental Committee of 1898 considered it their duty to discourage any expectation that consuls should act as agents for the sale or advertisement of British goods.[71] The Royal Commission on the Civil Service repudiated the impression that Consular Officers should perform the duties of commercial travellers in securing the sale of particular products or the allocation of contracts or concessions to particular firms. Consuls were not qualified to perform services of this kind, and it was undesirable for the community that they should attempt to do so.[72]

The suggestion of 'touting' British goods was particularly unpopular. Lord Cranborne explained to the Commons in 1902 that it was not easy to expand the commercial duties of consuls.

69. Nos. 68, 58 and 3 resp., *Correspondence respecting Diplomatic Assistance to British Trade Abroad*, P.P.1886(c.4779)LX.
70. *Final Report of the Royal Commission on the Depression of Trade and Industry* P.P.1886(c.4893)XXIII, para.98.
71. *Report of the Commercial Intelligence Committee*, P.P.1898(c.8962)XXXIII, para.24.
72. *Fifth Report of the Royal Commission on the Civil Service*, P.P.1914–16(Cd. 7748)XI, Pt.II, ch.V, para.13.

Anything like using public servants as advertisers or touts for particular articles had to be avoided. Such a thing would be greatly resented in this country.[73]

Neither Sir Henry Austin Lee, British Commercial Attaché at Paris, nor Mr. John Broderick, British Consul at Amsterdam, felt (in their evidence before the Royal Commission of 1914) that it was consistent with their duty to visit particular foreign firms and ask whether they would take certain British goods.[74] And 'touting' in Eastern countries had peculiar disadvantages. Mr. Harold Satow, Consul at Trebizond, pointed out that there was perhaps an exaggerated idea of officials in the East. The ordinary Turk would be rather surprised to see a consul touting British goods round the bazaar. Mr Satow agreed that if Britain wanted a service of 'high and specialized touts', it would be better to have official commercial travellers entirely distinct from the consular service.[75]

But here in the question of agencies, as elsewhere, there were qualifications to the general rule. The Memorandum of Instructions sent to the Commercial Attachés at Paris, Vienna, Berlin, and Madrid, 1 April 1896, explained that 'although you are not expected and cannot be asked to act as agent or commercial traveller for private firms, or to push their particular business, it may still lie in your power to render them substantial assistance in the pursuance of legitimate enterprise, and you should endeavour to do so as far as possible'.[76] There were certain commercial agencies which even consuls restricted from trading were allowed to hold. A general permission had been given to H.M. Consuls to act as agents for the Post Office, for Lloyd's, and for shipping companies carrying H.M. mails. Under the revised Consular Instructions of 1868, no agencies were to be undertaken by non-trading consuls without the previous permission of the Secretary of State. The question was brought before the public again at the Select Committee on the Diplomatic and Consular Services (1870), and on 21 July 1871 Earl Granville addressed a definitive Circular to Consuls in

73. 111 *Parl.Deb.4s.*298–9 (15 July 1902).
74. Minutes of Evidence, *Fifth Report of the Royal Commission on the Civil Service*, P.P.1914–16(Cd.7749)XI, QQ.41,791–4; 40,493.
75. ibid., QQ.39,885–6.
76. No. 7, *Correspondence respecting Diplomatic Assistance to British Trade Abroad*, P.P.1897(c.8432)LXXXVIII.

which he remarked that it had come to his notice that some restricted consuls had acted as Agents for private vessels, and had derived pecuniary advantages from such agencies. He pointed out that restricted consuls were strictly forbidden to act as agents for ships—a term which included, besides the agency for ships themselves, 'agency for goods carried in ships, and for any shipping purpose or business whatever, whether such agency is carried on or conducted, directly or indirectly, as agent, correspondent, consignee, or broker, in any way on account of shippers, owners, charterers, insurers, repairers, or salvers'.[77] A further Circular, dated 11 August 1871, called for information on appointments and salaries other than consular, whether in the Public Service or connected with private speculation (railways, shipping companies, and so forth). The returns revealed for Latin America, for example, besides bond-holder agencies, three further agencies held for the Royal Mail line—Consul Hutchinson (Callao), Consul Cowper (Puerto Rico), and Vice-Consul Stacey (Santa Martha, Colombia); the chairmanship of the Local Committee of the Buenos Ayres Great Southern Railway Company (held by Consul Parish, Buenos Aires); and the post of Chief Cashier of the Anglo-Costa Rican Bank (Consul Meugens, San José).[78] Four Consular officers from other parts of the world were listed as having functions outside the accepted Lloyd's Agencies and Post Office/mail agencies. All four held agencies or local director-ships of English insurance companies, and were able to produce evidence of Foreign Office sanction when called upon to do so. Consul Parish was himself in the position to explain that his acceptance of the railway chairmanship had been sanctioned by the Foreign Office, at the representation of Sir Edward Thornton, British Minister in Argentina.[79]

By 1922 the Consular Instructions permitted consular officers restricted from trading to act in certain circumstances as agents for Lloyd's and for Steam Navigation Companies, provided that the agencies did not interfere with the performance of their official duties and provided that prior permission

77. For Circular and correspondence, see P.R.O.,F.O/83/380.
78. P.R.O.,F.O/83/381.
79. Appendix, *Second Return of Consuls restricted from Trading and of Appointments other than Consular held by any such Consuls*, P.P.1872(c.533)LXI.

had been obtained from the Secretary of State. But Consuls were to abstain from speculative investments in their areas, and were to take no part (without official sanction) in 'the promotion, direction or registration of public companies, banking institutions, loans, or mining transactions'.

'Touting' for trade was not a function recognized by the Foreign Office before the First World War. The extent to which British officials were prepared to depart from the rule depended entirely on their personalities; many stood on their dignity and refused to do anything, while others were prepared to go some way to help out British manufacturers and traders. Mr. Charles Clipperton, the British Consul at Rouen, was questioned closely on this point during his evidence before the Royal Commission on the Civil Service in May 1914. Lord Macdonnell (the Chairman) opened the examination by reporting the information received by the Commission that it was the tradition at English missions and consulates abroad *not* to push the trade of a particular individual or a particular firm. Clipperton, who was prepared to see consuls playing a more active role, agreed that consuls should not, perhaps, be prepared to push trade, but felt nevertheless that they should give traders all the information by which they could push trade for themselves. He was brought back to the point by Mr. Graham Wallas, who put the case of a British proprietor of a patented set of rubber heels. The proprietor had asked a Consul to help him in finding a market abroad: what, Mr. Wallas asked, would the ideal and enthusiastic consul do in such a case? Clipperton replied that he personally would tell the proprietor that there were a great many boot and shoe stores in Rouen and that he had no doubt that the article could be sold if a French-speaking commercial traveller were sent to promote it; he himself, he added, would not mind visiting one or two places to start with. Mr. Wallas took this up, and asked him whether he believed that the ideal consul should act as a commercial traveller and go with a sample into somebody's house? Clipperton would not go as far as that, but he pointed out that if one lived in a foreign city one generally had one's usual tradesmen; he would be prepared to go to his own, show them the product, and practically make his bootmaker buy some of them. Sir Henry Primrose then asked him whether he wanted to see British consuls made into commercial travellers for British firms, paid at the public expense; take, for example—he said—the case of the patented rubber heels. Clipperton admitted that he would not take a sample round to every bootmaker in Rouen, but there are many informal ways in which much might be done for British trade; it might not be the duty of Consuls to undertake work of this kind, but 'if you take an interest in your work, there are so many things you may do that I do not think you are called upon to do'.[80]

The position, no doubt, is much the same today. Commerce has become respectable, and activity on behalf of British trade is a factor which weighs much more heavily with the Foreign Office than it did even in the 1920's (when the Commercial Department, as Vansittart once said, was the place where Duff Cooper went to sleep off the excesses of the night before). But the old distinctions are not yet dead, even among commercial men. Some years ago the Federation of British Industries published a *Survey of Export Trade Facilities* in which the publicity services which the Government could appropriately provide overseas were discussed. The Survey observed that this publicity (news services, feature articles, photographs, publications, display materials and films) could only be of general application; the object was not to replace the sales publicity of individual firms, but to build up a general picture of a dynamic and export-conscious Britain—Government information officers could not replace advertising agents, any more than Government commercial officers should act as salesmen.[81]

*   *   *

If government officials were not prepared to promote individual sales, they were unlikely to accept responsibility for bad debts. The official debt-collector has always taken a prominent place in the rogues' gallery of economic imperialism, and, as always, there is an element of truth in it. In countries for which extra-territorial jurisdiction existed, it was unavoidable that the Powers should, in some form or another, find themselves involved in the collection of private debts. Of the many claims pressed on the Turkish Government at Constantinople, or

80. Minutes of Evidence, *Fifth Report of the Royal Commission on the Civil Service*, P.P.1914–16(Cd.7749)XI, QQ.39,012; 39,217–9; 39,238–41.
81. Federation of British Industries, *A Survey of Export Trade Facilities* (London, 1959), Appendix F.

tried in the Consular Courts, a large proportion were concerned with the collection of commercial debts. Disputes between foreigners were tried exclusively by the Consular Courts, but commercial cases involving Turks went before a Turkish Court at which two foreign assessors sat with the three Turkish judges; the assessors had equal votes with the judges, and the consent of the Embassy dragoman was necessary before sentence was passed.

To this extent, foreign government responsibility was engaged. But it would be a mistake to imagine that assistance— even where foreigners enjoyed extra-territorial rights—was unqualified. Sir Henry Lytton Bulwer, the most energetic of Victorian Ambassadors at Constantinople in pressing for the redress of British claims, praised the high tone adopted by American diplomatists in defence of the persons and property of their citizens, and indicated that the Americans were prepared to go further in this respect than British officials. Mr. Rylands, a member of the Select Committee on the Diplomatic and Consular Services (1870) to which Sir Henry was giving evidence at the time, asked him whether this meant that he felt it desirable to use diplomatists to bully foreign governments into paying their debts. He replied that he himself was against interfering in these private transactions; he thought that when a man was looking for great profits he took great risks, and that the Government should interfere only in exceptional circumstances.[82]

Sir Henry's attitude was shared by British officials for the century before 1914. Sir Henry Bergne, for example, as Superintendent of the Commercial Department from 1894 until his retirement in 1902, believed it to be 'no part of the duty of a consul to recover debts'.[83] His comment took the form of a departmental minute on a request for a ruling received from Mr. Cooke, the British Commercial Agent at St. Petersburg; and the point was argued out in the Foreign Office as to whether the same rule should apply to Commercial Agents. Lord Cranborne, the Parliamentary Under-Secretary, felt that the point could be left to Mr. Cooke's discretion, although he might be warned of the complications to which debt-collecting often

82. Minutes of Evidence, *Report of the Select Committee on Diplomatic and Consular Services*, P.P.1870(382)VII, Q.5197.
83. Marginal comment on Mr. Cooke's letter to Sir Charles Scott, enclosed in Scott's despatch of 5 January 1900: P.R.O.,F.O/83/1784.

gave rise. Lord Lansdowne, however, overruled him, and in a despatch to the British Ambassador of July 1901 observed, for the information of Mr. Cooke, that it did not appear advisable for a Commercial Agent, any more than for a Consul, to take action in the matter of recovering debts; Consuls were not permitted to do so, and he could see no reason why the same rule should not apply to Commercial Agents.[84]

The point was considered again in an exchange of letters between the Foreign Office and the Board of Trade a couple of years later. Mr. Melville, the British Commercial Agent in Central America, had reported his activities in collecting overdue accounts for British firms which had been unable to obtain payment in the ordinary manner through the banks. Mr. Cartwright minuted on the reverse—'Is it right that the Commercial Agent should collect debts?' Algernon Law, of the Commercial Department, thought that it was very doubtful, and the matter was referred to the Board of Trade for an opinion. The Board agreed with Lansdowne that debt-collecting should form no part of the duties of a British Commercial Agent, and an instruction to this effect was sent to Mr. Melville soon afterwards.[85]

But the question of debt-collecting was not one which lent itself to a rigid and inflexible ruling. There was a world of difference between a formal demand for the payment of a foreign Government debt and a word in the ear of a defaulting tradesman. The more sensible of British consuls and diplomatists recognized the distinction and did what they could, within reason, to help in the recovery of minor debts—there was often no-one else to whom a distant British manufacturer could turn. Although Lansdowne had taken so firm a stand in the early years of this century, and although as late as 1914 the British Consul at Amsterdam assured the Royal Commission on the Civil Service that the Consular Service would, generally speaking, refuse to collect debts for British firms,[86] some kind of a compromise had existed in the background since at least as

84. Minutes on Scott to Lansdowne, 13 June 1901, and Lansdowne's reply, 16 July 1901: P.R.O.,F.O/83/1881.
85. The correspondence, which begins with Thornton to Lansdowne, 29 April 1903, is in P.R.O.,F.O/83/2100.
86. Minutes of Evidence, *Fifth Report of the Royal Commission on the Civil Service*, P.P.1914–16(Cd.7749)XI, Q.40,492.

early as 1886. In Bryce's Memorandum the Foreign Office had taken the position that, while a Consul could not be expected to become a debt collector, 'he may sometimes be able to keep or to help a British merchant out of a peculiarly annoying source of loss'.[87] Bryce told the British Chambers of Commerce a few days later that consuls had frequently, in practice, given such assistance in recovering debts as their position permitted, but that the difficulties which were likely to arise from interference with litigation or from unjust and fictitious claims made it impossible to lay down a general instruction on the subject.[88] Modern Consular Instructions leave it to the discretion of individual consuls to decide whether or not they should assist in cases of debt recovery.

Much of the confusion which exists over debt-collecting overseas has arisen from the failure of commentators to distinguish between the collection of trading debts and claims based on breach of treaty. Ordinary debt-collecting, without the sanction of treaty, found little favour with the Foreign Office—'the failure of the debtor', the Law Officers advised in 1874, 'even though the debtor be the State, affords no reason for the intervention of Her Majesty's Government'.[89] But a breach of treaty in a case which involved the collection of a debt entitled (or even obliged) H.M. Government to intervene to exactly the same degree as for any other treaty infringement. The distinction is illustrated in the Law Officers' Report on Mr. Robert Littlejohn's claim for payment from the Uruguayan Government for some appropriated gunpowder. The Law Officers felt that the appropriation was a breach of Article IX of the Anglo-Uruguayan Treaty. On the assumption that it was a forcible appropriation for military purposes and without the consent of Mr. Littlejohn, and in the knowledge that the claim did not arise merely from Mr. Littlejohn's misguided trust in the Government of Uruguay (having its origin in the breach of an international obligation), H.M. Government was entitled to prefer the claim and to insist on full reparation.[90]

* * *

87. See Appendix V.
88. No. 3, *Correspondence respecting Diplomatic Assistance to British Trade Abroad*, Pt. II, P.P.1886(c.4779)LX.
89. No. 4, *Reports from the Law Officers of the Crown, 1874*, F.O.,C.P.4331.
90. No. 112, *Reports from the Law Officers of the Crown, 1881*, F.O.,C.P.4637.

When it came to the point, the cool attitude of British officials to introductions and to the recommendation of agents and lawyers, and their refusal to give credit information or collect debts, left them with little that they could do directly for British trade. Much depended on the individual, and some diplomatists were able to achieve a great deal informally and without instructions. But in general it would be fair to say that commercial diplomacy before 1914 amounted to little more than the compilation and transmission of commercial intelligence.

CONCLUSION

EVEN IN 1886, a year which, in many respects, marked a new and more positive phase in the relationship between finance, trade, and the conduct of British foreign policy, the line traditionally drawn between the functions appropriate to business and government was maintained. When Mr. Mundella, the President of the Board of Trade, announced the opening of the new phase to an enthusiastic audience at the annual dinner of the Associated Chambers of Commerce, he emphasized that what the national trading interests wanted was better information and a higher status in the eyes of the Foreign Office; they did not expect the Government to provide them with trade or find them customers. Mr. Bryce, replying to a toast that same evening, again drew attention to the efforts which were to be made to improve government intelligence services. But he warned the Chambers that British diplomatists and consuls could not be made agents for particular British firms; they could not be expected to push the interests of individuals. He believed, he said, that he would have the sympathy of everyone in declaring that it should be 'the constant aim of our policy to maintain the character of our representatives, and raise them above the suspicion of having any personal interests to serve in representing this country'.[1]

The pressure for change increased during the '90s. New markets in Africa, Persia, and China were threatened by foreign competition—competition which was 'unfairly' weighted by foreign diplomatic pressure and inclined to Protectionism. 'Is it not true', Mr. Sinclair asked the Commons in 1902, 'that the nation should awake to the fact that foreign competitors are ever increasing and encroaching on our preserves? Does not everyone know that our merchants have no facilities and that in every market foreign firms obtain contracts which are ours by right?'[2] The Government had already taken action. But the

1. Speeches given at the annual dinner of the Associated Chambers of Commerce, 24 February 1886, and reported in a special Supplement to the *Chamber of Commerce Journal*, 10 March 1886.
2. 107 *Parl.Deb.4s.*1056 (8 May 1902).

H.M. Government and Overseas Trade

action it had felt appropriate—and which Viscount Cranborne, the Under-Secretary of State, described as that 'new departure' and 'new era' in which British diplomacy would have to be employed to uphold Britain's competitive position in world markets—amounted to no more than a further improvement in commercial intelligence (the new Commercial Intelligence Branch of the Board of Trade). Cranborne explained that while the Foreign Office would do its best, this could never amount to very much. The success of British trade must depend on the energy, skill and enterprise of the British trader, and he (Cranborne) would be sorry to think that British traders would have nothing to rely upon except the assistance of public officials.[3]

Laissez-faire survived the Great War and it survived the 1920's; it lost its appeal only with the Depression. 'Of our nation pre-eminently it may be said', the Committee on Finance and Industry reported in June 1931, 'that it has attained its great position not by the pursuit of any preconceived plan, but by a process of almost haphazard evolution':

There has been little conscious direction of the national activities to definite ends. The policy compendiously known as 'laissez-faire' has prevailed. To this trust in the operation of natural causes we owe the development of our great political, financial and social institutions and the amazing growth of our industrial activities. But we also owe to it in part many of our deficiencies, such as our industrial instability, our social maladjustments, our slums.[4]

*   *   *

The continued popularity of *laissez-faire* set the level of permissible government intervention at its lowest. The duty of government ceased, it was believed, where equality of opportunity had been assured for British commercial enterprise overseas. But it is at least arguable that the economic expression of *laissez-faire*—Free Trade—made even this a duty which was difficult, and sometimes impossible, to fulfil. The devotion of Victorians in general to a literal interpretation of Free Trade left so little room for compromise that the direct interests of British trade overseas were often sacrificed to an ideal. This was excusable, perhaps, while there was still some hope of con-

3. 97 *Parl.Deb.4s.*1012–13,1023 (19 July 1901).
4. *Report of the Committee on Finance and Industry*, P.P.1930–31(Cmnd.3897) XIII, para.8.

vincing the world of the universal benefit to be derived from Free Trade; it became markedly less so once it was obvious that the world had no intention of following our example.

Soon after H.M. Government had itself been converted to the principles of Free Trade, British officials were instructed to canvass its virtues overseas. Palmerston's reaction to an Argentine decision in 1837 to raise tariffs yet again was to explain to the British Minister at Buenos Aires that, although he could not claim any right to remonstrate formally, the Minister should at least try to convince the Argentines of the merit of Free Trade and of the disaster that would inevitably follow from a policy of high tariffs.[5] Free Trade propaganda was published on a more formal level by a Circular sent to a selection of Heads of Mission in 1851, pointing to the advantages of Free Trade and instructing British representatives overseas to bring these advantages to the notice of the local government. A further Circular was despatched to all Heads of Mission in 1861, and yet another was being prepared in 1864 at the time of the Select Committee on Trade with Foreign Nations. Meanwhile, the Board of Trade was actively spreading the gospel. Sir Louis Mallet complained, in a letter to Mr. Mundella, that he had spent some of his best years drafting admirable papers of arguments and facts which were then addressed by Lord Clarendon to foreign governments; none of which, he added, 'produced the smallest result'.[6] And Mallet's experience, unfortunately, was the rule.

Cobden had spoken optimistically in the Commons (during the debate on Mr. Forster's motion of 15 April 1864) of the inevitability of foreign Governments reforming their tariffs in their own interest once we had convinced them of the happy results which had followed from our own adoption of Free Trade. He suggested that this might be achieved by the preparation of a manual on British Free Trade policy by the Board of Trade, which would be circulated to our diplomatists and translated into other languages for a wider impact on foreign courts.[7] Giving evidence at the Select Committee

5. Ferns, *Britain and Argentina*, pp. 251–2.
6. Mallet to Mundella, 5 December 1877: quoted by Bernard Mallet, *Sir Louis Mallet*, p. 59.
7. 174 *Parl.Deb.3s.*,1087, 1118 (15 April 1864).

appointed as a result of Forster's motion, Cobden even proposed that a 'Free Trade Department' should be established at
the Foreign Office on the lines of the existing Slave Trade
Department.[8] Indeed, it was during the '60s that Britain,
through the active medium of Cobdenite Commercial Treaties,
came nearest to achieving universal acceptance for Free Trade.
The Cobdenite Treaties, which offered mutual incentives to the
reduction of tariffs as a concrete addition to the theoretical
benefits of Free Trade, could bargain their way towards the
liberalizing of national tariff scales at least so long as world
economic conditions remained favourable. They were an improvement on what Sir Robert Morier called purely *negative*
Free Trade: 'the policy of letting things be until Providence and
common-sense (neither of which has yet shown much inclination
to stir in the matter) will be pleased to interfere and bring other
nations beside ourselves to acknowledge the saving truth of the
Gospel according to Free Trade'.[9] But Gladstone's abandonment, on purely theoretical grounds, of any tariff negotiations
based on reciprocal concessions—just at that point in time when
the world was experiencing strong pressure to return to full
Protection—meant that the stick was left again without the
carrot; and the stick alone, applied as always 'informally',
could not persuade developing industrial nations against their
obvious interest in Protection. Towards the end of the century,
Salisbury begged to be excused from any return to 'the somewhat antiquated policy of remonstrance'. He told the Associated
Chambers of Commerce that the whole object of raising tariffs
was to exclude foreign commodities, and when we reproached
other countries with the complaint that our trade was being kept
out by their Protective policies the only result was that they said:

'Thank you, I am very much obliged to you. That is just what I
intended.' And they give another turn of the screw to the tariff in
order that the effect may be quite unmistakable and leave you to
your reproaches.[10]

The result, inevitably, was that unilateral Free Trade

8. Minutes of Evidence, *Report of the Select Committee on Trade with Foreign
Nations*, P.P.1864(493)VII, Q.1844.
9. Morier to Mallet, 1869, quoted by Rosslyn Wemyss, *Memoirs and Letters
of the Rt. Hon. Sir Robert Morier* (London, 1911), II, 134.
10. Quoted by Fuchs, *Trade Policy of Great Britain*, p. 71.

limited the scope and effectiveness of British commercial diplomacy throughout the period; we entered keen world competition, as Curzon told the Commons in 1895, with one hand tied behind our backs, 'without anything to give, to promise, or to threaten'.[11] Bound as we were by Free Trade, we could not threaten retaliation, nor could we consider bounties or subsidies even in the interests of equality.

Gladstone had defined the Liberal attitude towards retaliation when, in a speech at Leeds in 1881, he had referred to the great Christian precept of turning the other cheek; the *Protectionist* precept, he claimed, was that 'if somebody smites you on the one cheek you should smite yourself on the other'. And it was this argument, forcefully presented by Lord Farrer and Sir Robert Giffen of the Board of Trade, which finally defeated (in 1889) the move to aid British sugar producers and refiners by imposing countervailing duties. Under extreme pressure, H.M. Government did in fact depart from its rule by becoming a signatory to the Brussels Sugar Convention of 1902 (which included a penal clause), but at the time there seemed little alternative. The Government of India, strongly opposed as it was in theory to the bounty system, had already been compelled to impose countervailing duties on foreign, bounty-fed sugar to safeguard its own industry. The German and Austrian cartel bounties on refined sugar had brought a glut on world sugar markets and reduced the price of sugar, it was said, to a price £2 below the cost of production in any other country in the world. The British West Indian colonies were facing ruin, and the home sugar-refining industry claimed itself to be in an equally dangerous condition. As Sir Robert Giffen argued in his evidence before the Select Committee on Steamship Subsidies, it might be shown theoretically that countries like Britain gained on the whole, as consumers, from foreign bounties, but, he added, the State could not ignore a threat to the very livelihood of a section of the Community.[12]

11. 36 *Parl.Deb.4s.*1272 (30 August 1895).
12. Minutes of Evidence, *Report of the Select Committee on Steamship Subsidies*, P.P.1902(385)IX, Q.180. The arguments for, and conditions of, Britain's adherence to the Brussels Sugar Convention are contained in the following Blue-Books: *Correspondence relating to the Sugar Conference at Brussels, 1901–1902*, P.P.1902(Cd.940)CIV; *Correspondence relating to the Brussels Sugar Bounty Conference*, P.P.1902(Cd.1013)CIV.

However, even in the case of sugar bounties Free Trade was too strong for the retaliationists. Mr. Asquith described the Sugar Bill in one of his Free Trade campaign speeches of the autumn of 1903 as the very first attempt in his time to persuade Parliament to consent to a course which would increase the price of one of the necessities of life; the Liberals had always opposed retaliation, he explained, because experience had shown how futile it was as a weapon of offence, bringing more harm to its users than to those against whom it was directed.[13] And a decade later, under Asquith's Premiership, Britain withdrew from the Brussels Convention.

The argument for Steamship Subsidies met with a similar response. In spite of strong pressure from some of the British shipowners (notably the sailing-ship owners), H.M. Government consistently refused, with only trivial exceptions, to consent to a system of subsidies intended to neutralize the effect of the very substantial assistance given by the French and German Governments to their shipping industries. Generous mail and Admiralty subsidies existed which, indirectly, may well have assisted some British shipowners against foreign competition. But the subsidy system was as much anathema to a Liberal Government before 1914 as were retaliation, countervailing duties, or bounties of any kind which might interfere with the purity of Free Trade, free contract and free competition. As late as 1929 the Committee on Industry and Trade believed national shipping subsidies or flag discrimination to be very undesirable, and its general conclusion on the whole issue of active retaliation was characteristic of British tariff policy before the '30s:

The foundation of healthy commercial intercourse is fair and considerate treatment on both sides, and by far the most potent method of ensuring that British commerce shall receive fair and considerate treatment in overseas markets is to maintain the confidence of other countries that their trade is on the whole fairly and considerately dealt with in Great Britain.[14]

It would be a mistake to believe that this opposition to the general principle of retaliation left Britain completely power-

13. Speech of 8 October 1903, printed in Asquith, *Trade and the Empire*, p. 12.
14. *Final Report of the Committee on Industry and Trade*, P.P.1928–29(Cmd.3282) VII, Sect.IV(4) and Sect.III(1).

less. An elaborate structure of 'revenue' duties still existed which must have looked much like protective duties to the foreigner; and it was by no means unknown for a British negotiator to use a tariff rate designed originally for revenue purposes as a bargaining counter in an international tariff agreement. Nor could foreign governments be certain of the exact point at which devotion to Free Trade principles might have to be surrendered, as in the case of the Brussels Convention of 1902, to expediency. Nor were they in a position to estimate the effect which Empire pressure for imperial preference might have at any moment on British tariff policy. Most-favoured-nation clauses, whatever their weaknesses as a method of control over determined Protectionists, were at least partially effective in preserving Britain's competitive position over much of the world.[15]

But the point is that active commercial diplomacy through tariff negotiation was denied to the Foreign Office; and there was really no peaceable means other than retaliation by which genuine equality of treatment could have been guaranteed for British overseas trade in a number of the more controversial markets. It might be argued, paradoxically, that Free Trade was at least one of the factors in British imperial expansion in and after the 1880's; the refusal to retaliate left no alternative to expansion if the new markets of the world were to be kept open equally to British trade.

In the circumstances it is not really so surprising to find that, under normal conditions, British overseas trade before 1914 owed very little to government assistance and promotion. Once world markets had been opened and signatures fixed to Commercial Treaties—and often before either, as in the opening of West Africa—British trade was very much on its own; it expanded at its own speed, fought its own battles, built up its own network of agencies, communications, banking and insurance facilities without further government intervention

15. The Committee on Industry and Trade took rather an optimistic view both of the power of the most-favoured-nation clause and of Britain's ability to hold her own against those nations which were able to offer tariff reductions in commercial negotiations. The Committee's *Final Report* was presented to Parliament in March 1929; it might not have felt so confident a couple of years later: *Final Report of the Committee on Industry and Trade*, P.P.1928–29(Cmnd.3282)VII, Sect.III(1).

save in defence of existing Treaty rights. As recently as 1943 Dr. Burgin could tell the Commons, during the debate on the Eden Reforms, that businessmen did not go for information on the conduct of their international affairs to the British Embassy or consulate, but to a cable office, a newspaper, one of the large international companies, the Associated Chambers of Commerce, or the Federation of British Industries.[16] The assistance available to British traders through government agencies was so hedged around with limitations and exceptions that there was little incentive to apply for assistance except in real emergencies. The English merchant, as a French journalist explained in the 1880's, unlike his foreign competitors:

> sent derrière lui la forte entité de la Grand-Bretagne industrielle, commerciale et maritime, et autour de lui, des compatriotes qui reproduisent un véritable abrégé de la mère patrie. Cette protection Consulaire, il la réclame seulement pour des difficultés nées, seulement en cas de déni de justice, d'abus de la part de l'autorité locale, et alors, nous le répétons, il la trouve énergique, infatigable.[17]

16. 387 *H.C.Deb.*5s.1415 (18 March 1943).
17. Quoted in No. 57, *Correspondence respecting Diplomatic Assistance to British Trade Abroad*, P.P.1886(c.4779)LX.

PART III

FINANCE, TRADE, AND BRITISH FOREIGN POLICY

PART III

FINANCE, TRADE, AND
BRITISH FOREIGN POLICY

INTRODUCTION

THE PREVAILING attitude at the Foreign Office throughout the century before 1914 was, quite clearly, non-
interventionist. Although international competition and
diplomatic pressure were creating the need for a more positive
policy in many parts of the world, and although the obligation
to increase the scope of government assistance to finance and
trade overseas was widely recognized after the mid-'80s, the
inherited tradition of *laissez-faire* still continued to govern
official policy unless and until formidable reasons developed for
rejecting it. The influence, therefore, of finance and trade on
British policy in the 'civilized' areas of the world—in Europe,
in the Russian dominions, and in North America—was minimal. Under normal conditions the limit of the functions
expected from H.M. Government in the promotion of finance
and trade was the provision of adequate commercial intelligence.
Foreign policy was formed by political conflict, independently of
commerce and along traditional lines.

Some of the problems discussed in previous chapters have
related to incidents in these 'civilized' areas—to 'touting' for
trade in France; to confiscations in Italy, Portugal, and the
U.S.S.R.; to sugar cartels in Germany and Austria; to contracts and concessions in Eastern Europe; to debt-collecting in
Russia; to the trials and tribulations of the bondholders in
Spain, France, and North America. But these were not the
occasion of any development in British foreign policy. H.M.
Government was simply under an obligation—which it had
always recognized—to protect British interests overseas, where-
ever they might be, and to ensure that those interests received
fair treatment in relation to the interests of other nations. And
in 'civilized' countries, this obligation meant no more than a
watchful insistence on British rights. However distasteful the

British Government might find the tariff policy of other European Powers, it never questioned their right to decide such policies for themselves. British officials would have regarded it as fanciful, and contrary to the traditions of the Foreign Service, to insist on a railway concession in Germany merely as compensation for a Belgian concession, or on an arms contract in Italy because Krupps had already submitted a successful tender. And apart from a certain give-and-take between Allies, this was an attitude shared by the great majority of officials at European capitals. The competitive diplomatic pressure which, in the Levant, Africa, and the Far East, had brought British officials reluctantly into the race in defence of British interests, scarcely existed. Economic weapons, of course, were as valuable to diplomacy in Europe as they were elsewhere. France and Germany made relatively free use of their hold over the Bourse and the *banques d'affaires*. Britain, in turn, had always been prepared to employ her financial and commercial resources—through subsidies, loans, and trade restriction—to promote her war aims. But if politics were able to make use of finance and trade to this degree, finance and trade received, and wanted, little from politics. The divorce between commerce and diplomacy reached the limit of absurdity in Europe, so much so, according to J. A. Crowe, that 'in diplomatic circles of all classes, the very mention of commerce, or an inkling that commercial questions are the sole questions which a diplomatic officer has to treat, is sufficient to place him outside the pale of communion with his fellows'. Political developments and increased commercial competition made this an attitude more difficult to maintain, and certainly the hardening of political alignments in Europe after the Entente Cordiale brought financiers to the Foreign Office for consultations on, say, a proposed Austrian Loan. But generally speaking, so Sir Edward Grey told the Commons in 1914, these were things in which the Foreign Office did not interfere.

The situation in the 'semi-civilized' or 'barbarous' nations was quite different, and it was here that the obligation to preserve a 'fair field and no favour' for financial and commercial interests created the need for something very much more positive in terms of British foreign policy. The argument will be taken further during the following studies of British policy in certain of the 'semi-civilized' and 'barbarous' areas—in Egypt, Turkey, Persia, Africa, China, and Latin America—for all of which the relationship between finance, trade and British foreign policy has always been at its most indistinct. The result will be summarized in the Conclusion. But it might be said at once that, while the influence of finance and trade on British policy in Europe and North America was slight throughout the period, and while, for the world in general and over most of the nineteenth century, it took the form simply of the urge to open the world to trade, the situation *outside* Europe was transformed in and after the 1880's. It is then that the evidence for finance and trade as determining factors in extra-European diplomacy and imperial expansion ('formal' and 'informal') becomes overwhelming.

In Parts I and II an attempt has been made to describe the general relationship between finance, trade, and the British Government overseas, the final effect of which is to suggest that whatever influence financiers and traders might have exerted, that influence was unlikely to fit the pattern described, for example, in Hobson's *Imperialism*. The function of the six studies in Part III is to apply this new category of information to a number of controversial situations, with a view to arriving, ultimately, at a more realistic assessment of the degree to which British financial and trading interests could actually influence the course of British foreign policy.

CHAPTER 1

EGYPT

JOHN STRACHEY'S recent attempt to explain the motives of
British imperialism took the occupation of Egypt in 1882
and the Boer War as its twin pillars. Strachey accepted the
economic interpretation of the 'new' imperialism as 'the best
guiding thread to an understanding of the imperialist policies
of the highly developed capitalisms of the recent past', and he
explained how Egypt and South Africa served as examples of
'how British domination followed what might be called British
rentier and British entrepreneurial investment, respectively,
exactly as Lenin's theory would have predicted'.[1]

Strachey was in good company. Wilfrid Scawen Blunt, who
had been one of Arabi Pasha's strongest supporters, published
in 1907 his *Secret History of the English Occupation of Egypt*, the
burden of which was to accuse Gladstone's government of
acting with and for the bondholders. The *Secret History* was
followed in 1910 by Theodore Rothstein's *Egypt's Ruin: a
Financial and Administrative Record*; based on a careful if selective
use of the Blue Books, it bore out the claim in Blunt's Introduction that it would serve to remind Sir Edward Grey and his
Liberal Cabinet colleagues 'of the initial wrong done to the
Egyptians by England as a money-lending nation backed by
military force'. A few years later Rosa Luxemburg chose
Egypt, among others, as showing 'militarism as the executor of
the accumulation of capital',[2] and Brailsford found Egypt the
'perfect epitome' of the tendencies he had been sketching in his
views on capital and imperialism, in which diplomatic rivalries
had their origin in the 'restless movements of capital to win
fresh fields for investment'.[3] Frederic C. Howe, a sharp critic of
all financial imperialism, described the occupation of Egypt in
1882 as the beginning of a process by which Great Britain,

1. John Strachey, *The End of Empire* (London, 1959), pp. 97, 118.
2. Rosa Luxemburg, *The Accumulation of Capital* (London, edn. 1963), p. 439.
3. Brailsford, *War of Steel and Gold*, pp. 95, 125.

France and Germany 'at the dictation of overseas concession holders and financiers' brought more than 100,000,000 people into subjection.[4] Culbertson, while less uncritical in his acceptance of the economic interpretation, nevertheless agreed that the chief reason for British Government intervention was to protect its Egyptian bondholders.[5] Bakeless, a disciple of Brailsford, felt that the British occupation of Egypt offered 'one of the clearest examples possible of the rôle played by economics and finance . . . in producing wars'; the Egyptian intervention was 'largely a matter of helping out European investors who had made a bad bargain'.[6] Moon described the events leading up to the British occupation of Egypt almost entirely in terms of the bondholders, although he accepted the Suez Canal as a factor in influencing British statesmen. The Rothschilds, he claimed, 'utilized their political influence to bring about the conquest of Egypt'.[7] N. D. Harris argued that France and Great Britain found the commercial and financial interests of their citizens overseas 'a good and sufficient reason for intervention', and entered Egypt to safeguard the interests of their creditors.[8] Harold Laski was confident that no one now (1933) denied that the British occupation of Egypt was undertaken 'in order to secure the investment of the British bondholders'.[9] Hallgarten—rather out of his depth away from Germany—took Egypt as the classic example of British finance capital intervention.[10] And Dr. Mustafa, in a capable study of the period, felt able to argue that 'so compelling was the power of money that bankers and capitalists such as the Goschens, the Oppenheims and the Rothschilds were able to induce the Governments of great states such as England and France to

---

4. Frederic C. Howe, 'Dollar Diplomacy and Financial Imperialism under the Wilson Administration', *Annals of the American Academy of Political and Social Science*, LXVIII (1916), 317.
5. Culbertson, *Commercial Policy*, p. 328, and ibid., *International Economic Policies*, p. 380.
6. John Bakeless, *The Economic Causes of Modern War* (New York, 1921), pp. 64, 209.
7. P. T. Moon, *Imperialism and World Politics* (New York, edn. 1937), pp. 223-9, 61.
8. N. D. Harris, *Europe and Africa* (Cambridge, Mass., 1927), p. 17.
9. In Leonard Woolf (ed.), *The Intelligent Man's Way to Prevent War* (London, 1933), p. 506.
10. G. W. F. Hallgarten, *Imperialismus vor 1914* (Munich, 1951), I, 71.

change their previous practice and afford their official aid in the collection of contractual debts'.[11]

In spite of the several careful studies of the Occupation which have since suggested the slight factual basis of the original Blunt/Rothstein interpretation,[12] the 'bondholder' thesis is now so firmly a part of the folk-lore of economic imperialism that scholarship is unlikely to shake it. Donald Southgate, for example, while well aware (in his recent biography) that Palmerston himself would never have considered forcible intervention on behalf of the bondholders, tranquilly accepts the popular belief that Gladstone occupied Egypt 'in the interest of British bondholders'.[13]

*   *   *

Clarendon, as far back as 1840, had anticipated the main heads of British interest in Egypt, as he had that shift in interest from Turkey to Egypt which was not finally to be acknowledged until the 1890's. In a Memorandum on the Eastern Question, which he communicated to Palmerston on 14 March 1840, he argued that:

Looking exclusively in our own interests, I cannot but think they lie more in the direction of Egypt than of Turkey. The overland communication with India is daily becoming more important. . . .

As regards the progress of civilization, too, and the development of the commercial and agricultural resources of the East, I think we have much more to expect from the Pacha than from the Sultan.[14]

With the development of the Indian Empire and of British interest in the Far East, the overland route came to play an increasingly important part in British political and strategic calculations. In trade, the route was less important than it might seem, since it was more economical until at least the late '70s to send bulk cargo round the Cape rather than overland or through the Suez Canal. But high class cargo (textiles on the

11. Ahmed Abdel-Rehim Mustafa, 'The Domestic and Foreign Affairs of Egypt from 1876 to 1882', London thesis, 1955, pp. 58–59.
12. Notably A. A. H. Knightbridge, 'Gladstone and the Invasion of Egypt in 1882', Oxford thesis, 1960; R. Robinson and J. Gallagher, *Africa and the Victorians: the Official Mind of Imperialism* (London, 1961), ch.IV.
13. Donald Southgate, *The Most English Minister: the Policies and Politics of Palmerston* (London, 1966), p. 144.
14. Quoted in Maxwell, *Life of Clarendon*, I, 190–1.

outward journey, tea and raw cotton on the return) shifted quickly to the Canal route; and Egypt itself was an interesting market, was developing into an important source of raw material (cotton) for Britain's major industry, and was attracting, under the spendthrift administration of the Khedive Ismail (1863–79), an astonishing inflow of foreign capital. When Ismail succeeded Said, he inherited a public debt of just over £3¼ million. By 1876 the funded debt had increased to £68,110,000, in addition to which there was a floating debt of about £26,000,000. Apart, unfortunately, from the £16,000,000 invested in the Suez Canal, there was very little to show for it.[15]

'The origin of the Egyptian Question in its present phase', Lord Cromer explained in the opening sentence of *Modern Egypt*, 'was financial', and this spares us, so Brailsford claims, any historical controversy; Strachey felt that 'no more terse statement of the economic motives for imperial expansion has ever been made'. But what Cromer had meant was that the financial embarrassments of the Khedive created the political situation in which, slowly and with intense reluctance, H.M. Government was compelled to take over political control of the area. The British Government needed stability; it needed it for reasons primarily of politics and strategy, but undoubtedly also in the interests of British trade The wild borrowing of the Khedive created a financial crisis which threatened stability, and H.M. Government was finally compelled to intervene. But it is a tortuous process of reasoning which can conclude from this that the *motives* of the British Government, except in the most indirect sense, were to secure prompt and punctual payment of the interest on the External Debt.

Even Wilfrid Blunt admits that the first two stages in the direct entanglement of H.M. Government in the affairs of Egypt—the Suez Canal purchase and Mr. Cave's mission— were without question 'Ismail's own foolish doing'.[16] The story of the Suez Canal purchase and of the motives behind it is too well-known to bear repetition, but Mr. Cave's mission, at the beginning of 1876, was the first occasion on which H.M. Government had taken a direct and active interest in Egyptian finance. It was, as Blunt suggested, in response to an initiative

15. Lord Cromer, *Modern Egypt* (London, 1908), I, 11.
16. Blunt, *Secret History*, pp. 20–21.

from the Khedive who was hoping for some form of public testimonial (in the form of a published report by British officials) which—by testifying to his continued solvency—would enable him to raise even more money from the increasingly suspicious European money-markets. Accordingly, in 1875 the Egyptian Government requested the assistance of two British officials in the Finance Department. The response of the Treasury, in the absence of sufficient information, was to suggest sending out an exploratory mission; and a mission led by the Right Hon. Stephen Cave, M.P., H.M. Paymaster General, left for Egypt at the end of the year. But the Foreign Secretary (the Earl of Derby) was careful to inform the British Agent and Consul-General in Egypt that:

> Her Majesty's Government especially wish that it should be understood that this special Mission must not be taken to imply any desire to interfere with the internal affairs of Egypt, but is of a purely friendly character, dictated by the interest which this country has always taken in the welfare and prosperity of Egypt.[17]

Mr. Cave reported early in 1876, but his scheme to effect the conversion of the Egyptian debt (which had by now reached some £91 million) came to nothing. In the meantime H.M. Government had indignantly rejected a half-hearted French proposal that the time had arrived for the establishment of some form of Anglo-French Control on the lines of the successful Tunis Joint Commission.[18] And the request of the British bond-holders for H.M. Government's intervention in the Egyptian Loans of 1862, 1864, and 1867, met with a refusal to give more than unofficial assistance of the usual restricted nature.[19]

The steady deterioration of the financial situation in Egypt persuaded the British bondholders to send out a representative later in 1876 to negotiate a settlement with the Khedive. They chose the Right Hon. George Goschen, a former Liberal Minister with family ties with the firm Frühling and Goschen, promoters of the 1862 and 1864 Loans; and their choice, naturally, has aroused furious suspicion among the later critics

17. No. 12, *Correspondence respecting Mr. Cave's Special Mission to Egypt*, P.P.1876(c.1396)LXXXIII.
18. Nos. 1, 2, *Correspondence respecting the finances of Egypt*, P.P.1876(c.1484) LXXXIII.
19. For example, Nos. 74, 84 & 88, ibid.

of British intervention. Rothstein, after observing the facts about Goschen's political and financial connexions, claimed that Goschen could therefore act 'officially in the interests of the bondholders and unofficially in the political interests of England, without committing the Government, and yet carrying out its wishes'. He dismissed H.M. Government's declaration that Messrs. Goschen and Joubert, the two bondholders' representatives, were conducting business entirely on their own account as 'one of those pious lies which Ministers often permit themselves *pro bono publico*'.[20] Others felt the same, and Goschen, a man of great integrity who had broken his links with the family firm many years before, was well aware of it. There was a note almost of desperation in his remarks to Wilfrid Blunt during an interview several years later (in 1882), when he took particular pains to impress on him that he was not taking a financial view of the Egyptian situation. As Blunt was leaving, Goschen's last words were: 'You may be sure at least of one thing, and that is, that whatever the Government may do in Egypt they will do on general grounds of policy, not in the interests of the Bond-holders.'[21]

Evidence was published shortly after the appearance of Rothstein's *Egypt's Ruin* which put the particular relationship between Goschen's mission and the British Government into perspective. Arthur D. Elliot, in his biography of Goschen (published in 1911), reported that Goschen had only accepted the bondholders' mission on condition that his position was to be entirely honorary and that his duties would interfere neither with his perfect freedom of political action nor with his right to reject steps which, even if in the interests of the bondholders, were politically inexpedient. Before he left for Egypt he had, of course, been in touch with H.M. Government, and the Chancellor of the Exchequer (Sir Stafford Northcote) could see no objection to Goschen's proposals—'they may succeed or fail; but at the worst they can do no harm. I shall be ready to certify through our Consul-General, if desired, that Mr. G. is a man who can be trusted, and who commands general respect in England'. And, as Elliot points out, 'these were, politically

20. Theodore Rothstein, *Egypt's Ruin. A Financial and Administrative Record* (London, 1910), pp. 27–29.
21. Blunt, *Secret History*, p. 224.

speaking, his only credentials'.[22] The British Government was naturally interested in a settlement between the Khedive and his bondholders as a factor in promoting increased stability in Egypt, and Goschen, as a former Cabinet Minister, was a public figure whose presence in Egypt could not be ignored by the Consul-General. But the Foreign Office took no direct part in negotiating the terms of the settlement. When Goschen was presented, with some pomp, to the Khedive, the Khedive asked the British Consul-General if he was to understand that the negotiations were to be considered as 'diplomatic'. Mr. Vivian replied that he was only authorized to give unofficial assistance to Mr. Goschen, as Her Majesty's Government had no desire to interfere in the internal affairs of Egypt, though it would gladly see Egypt freed from her current financial embarrassment.[23]

The Arrangement of the Debt, which Goschen finally negotiated, included the establishment of a Commission of the *Caisse de la Dette Publique*, to be presided over by two Commissioners nominated—the bondholders hoped—by the French and British Governments. The French Government could see no difficulty, and further Commissioners were nominated by the Austrian and Italian Governments. But the British Government resolutely refused to make a nomination on the grounds that such an appointment would involve an undesirable degree of Government responsibility for the success of the bondholder settlement. When Captain Evelyn Baring was appointed as the English Commissioner, he served as an appointee of the Egyptian Government and of the bondholders, but with no official status with H.M. Government.

The contrast between the attitude of the British and French Government towards the bondholders is described by Baring himself when, as Lord Cromer, he looked back on a long period of distinguished service in Egypt. Pointing out that he, unlike the French Commissioner (M. de Blignières), had not been appointed by his own Government, he observed that 'the tendencies and traditions of the British Government, moreover,

22. Hon. Arthur D. Elliot, *Life of Lord Goschen, 1831–1907* (London, 1911), I, 168, 174.
23. No. 20, *Further Correspondence respecting the Finances of Egypt*, P.P.1878–79 (c.2233)LXXVIII.

ran counter to any endeavour to enforce the claims of the foreign creditors at whatsoever cost to the population of Egypt', whereas 'the French Government were greatly under the influence of the bondholder interest'. Speaking as a former representative of the British bondholders, Baring remarked on the fact that the bondholders' influence in England was limited, for 'a strong body of public opinion existed which was hostile to their presumed interests, and which, in its anxiety to do justice to the people of Egypt, was inclined sometimes even to err on the side of doing less than justice to the foreign creditors'. In France, however, no body of public opinion apparently existed 'which could act as a check on the extreme views advanced by the foreign creditors of Egypt'.[24] M. de Freycinet (who had been French Foreign Minister from December 1879 to September 1880 and again during the crucial months of 1882) confirmed Cromer's opinion when he explained, in retrospect, that France had made two serious mistakes. One was to work hand-in-hand with the English, with whom French views and the French character were quite out of touch. The second was '*de trop subordonner notre politique à la question financière*'. It was right, he argued, for a government to defend the persons and property of its nationals abroad. But it was quite a different matter with bondholders, '*disséminés un peu partout, intéressants à coup sûr, mais qui n'ont pu se dissimuler le caractère aléatoire de leurs opérations.*' In such cases governments were not bound to intervene so urgently, and indeed France had not made war on Turkey, Portugal or other countries which had defaulted on their debts; why, then, had she been so exacting against Egypt and concentrated her diplomatic efforts, at the sacrifice of her freedom of action, on the collection of debts? De Freycinet pointed to the contrast with Britain:

Les Anglais ont été mieux avisés. Ils n'ont pas craint, en diverses circonstances, de demander des sacrifices aux créanciers et, quand ils s'adressaient au gouvernement égyptien en faveur de ces derniers, ils ont eu soin de parler aussi du sort des populations, des réformes utiles, du 'developpement prudent des institutions'; en un mot ils ont évité de paraître uniquement préoccupés d'intérêts particuliers, si respectables qu'ils pussent être à leurs yeux.[25]

24. Cromer, *Modern Egypt*, I, 40–42.
25. C. de Freycinet, *La Question d'Egypte* (Paris, 1905), pp. 168–9.

But H.M. Government was not, in fact, attempting to conceal bondholder interests behind a façade of benevolence: it genuinely regarded those interests as entirely subordinate to those of politics, strategy, and trade. As the financial situation in Egypt grew more desperate in the course of 1877, so did the tone of the British Consul-General's despatches. But when, for example, Vivian urged the Foreign Office, in a despatch dated 7 December 1877, to depart in some measure from H.M. Government's rule of non-interference by backing the principle of a full inquiry into the whole financial situation in Egypt, his argument was not that action was necessary in the interests of the British creditors but that 'unless something can be done, and that quickly, the Khedive and his government must inevitably drift into bankruptcy, with all the political complications that may result from it'.[26] Vivian's despatch of 23 February 1878, in which he expanded on these views, bears the mark of a Blue Book composition, but it is worth quoting in full because it summarizes the British official rationalization of intervention in 1878:

I can well understand [he told Derby] the disinclination and hesitation of Her Majesty's Government to depart from their long-established principle to refuse to interfere officially for the protection of persons who have chosen to invest their capital in foreign stocks with the hope of obtaining a high rate of interest. It is right to lay down as a general rule that speculators must accept the risks and perils together with the advantages of such enterprises, and that if things go wrong they must not expect the power and authority of England to be employed to extricate them from their difficulties.

But this sound rule does not quite apply to the case of Egypt. It is not only the bondholders and creditors whose interests are imperilled, but the whole Government of the country is thrown out of gear by financial mismanagement. Egypt pleads want of means as an excuse for failing to keep engagements sanctioned and protected by solemn Conventions with foreign Governments, such as the execution of the sentences of the Tribunals of the Reform. The resources of the country are becoming seriously exhausted, and its credit impaired, while affairs are becoming so entangled as to challenge the interference of foreign Governments for the protection of the interests of their subjects, although such interference could hardly be viewed with indifference by Her Majesty's Government.

26. No. 102, *Further Correspondence respecting the Finances of Egypt*, P.P.1878–79 (c.2233)LXXVIII.

I therefore think the case of Egypt is so exceptional as to justify Her Majesty's Government in departing in some measure from their sound rule of non-interference in similar cases.[27]

Meanwhile, both the French Government and the British Treasury were pressing for some measure of financial enquiry or control in Egypt. Lord Lyons reported from Paris on 5 February that M. Waddington had spoken to him about the urgency of France and England jointly insisting on the appointment of a proper and independent Commission, with powers enabling it to enquire closely not only into the revenue of Egypt but also into its expenditure. M. Waddington argued that unless England and France exerted themselves at once the matter would slip out of their hands. The British and French Governments should bestir themselves, he thought, to prevent the sacrifice of the interests of the numerous French and English holders of Egyptian bonds and to obtain something like a reasonable and honest administration of the Egyptian finances. Derby replied guardedly that H.M. Government would be happy to co-operate with the French Government in any useful manner 'which shall not be inconsistent with the Khedive's independent administration of Egypt'.[28] But Derby was being lobbied also by the Treasury. On 4 February the Treasury had urged pressure on the Khedive to obtain his consent to a broad investigation of Egyptian finances, and this suggestion was repeated in a further letter on 4 March. The Lords Commissioners added that the Foreign Office should bear in mind the immediate interest of the British Exchequer in Egyptian solvency. The Khedive owed H.M. Government £200,000 p.a. on account of the Suez Canal shares. He was further bound by Firman of the Porte to remit a certain portion of the Egyptian tribute to the Bank of England, £72,000 of which was appropriated to meet charges on the Turkish Guaranteed Loan of 1855; this was already a month in default.[29]

By the beginning of March, 1878, the Powers seem to have come to the conclusion that immediate intervention was necessary. The French Ambassador communicated a Pro-Memoria to Derby, dated 3 March, in which joint 'officious' assistance by the British and French Consuls-General was

27. No. 144, ibid.   28. Nos. 127, 128, ibid.   29. No. 147, ibid.

suggested to the propositions of the bondholders' representatives in Cairo.[30] The Pro-Memoria argued that the Governments would be seriously embarrassed if the Egyptian creditors took their case before the Mixed Tribunals in Egypt and if the judgement given by the Tribunals were then ignored by the Khedive. The Powers bore some responsibility for the constitution of these Tribunals, and their inefficacy would reflect on the Powers themselves; too many claimants were already complaining of the non-execution of favourable judgements against the Khedive.[31] The French Pro-Memoria was matched by an Austro-Hungarian Memorandum (communicated to Derby on 5 March) suggesting a *démarche* by the Powers, and on 9 March the German Ambassador, Count Munster, spoke to Derby on the desirability of united action by all the Powers 'if only to avoid the possibility of separate action on the part of some of them'.[32]

Derby, however, was by then already convinced that action was necessary, and in response to the French Pro-Memoria he took a step which put British diplomacy in Egypt on to an entirely new plane. On 8 March 1878, Derby instructed Vivian 'to lose no time in concerting with your French colleague the best means of giving effect to the proposals of the French government, in which Her Majesty's Government entirely concur. You are authorized to represent officiously, but in firm language, the extreme necessity of the Khedive assenting to a full and complete inquiry, in which the interests of the bondholders should be adequately represented'.[33] Under strong pressure, the Khedive agreed to a Commission of Inquiry, and the British Government appointed Mr. Rivers Wilson, a British official, to serve as its representative on the Commission.

On the face of it, this was an unprecedented degree of intervention on behalf of the bondholders, since the Inquiry was

30. This was to be '*un appui purement officieux . . . qui ne doit d'aucune façon avoir pour consequence de compromettre l'action officielle des Gouvernements*'. In the language of diplomacy, 'officious' in contrast to 'official' implies 'having an extraneous relation to official matters or duties: having the character of a friendly communication, or informal action, on the part of a government or its representatives' (*Shorter O.E.D.*, 3rd. edn.)

31. No. 149, *Further Correspondence respecting the Finances of Egypt*, P.P.1878–79 (c.2233)LXXVIII.

32. Nos. 148, 151, ibid.

33. No. 150, ibid.

intended to establish the real condition of Egypt with a view to a composition between the Khedive and his creditors. This was certainly the view of the Government's critics in the Commons. But, as the Chancellor of the Exchequer explained, the step had been taken 'with no desire to interfere merely for the sake o obtaining justice for the Khedive's creditors or anyone else, which would be a very inconvenient course to follow', but in order to anticipate that setting-aside of the judgements of the Mixed Tribunals which would provide a pretext for the Powers to intervene in the affairs of Egypt.[34]

Britain, with its problem of imperial communications and its growing trading interest in the area, was clearly the Power with most at stake in Egypt; what no British Government could afford to contemplate was the unilateral action of some other Power in Egypt, particularly France, if Britain herself remained unprepared to act. Whereas in March she had been forced to join the Powers in the demand for an Inquiry, in April she found herself compelled, under pressure from France, to call for full payment of the Debt coupon due on 1 May 1878, aligning herself, necessarily, with all the horrors and oppression which accompanied Egyptian tax collections. Lord Cromer discussed the point frankly in *Modern Egypt*. He asked why the British Government should thus have abandoned both its local policy of tempering its support for the creditors by consideration for the interests of the Egyptian people, and its general policy, long-established, of maintaining that British subjects who invested their money in foreign countries did so at their own risk. There must, he argued, have been some special reason for 'so brusque a departure from the principles heretofore adopted', and he found it in the fact that the Congress of Berlin was about to meet: 'Egyptian interests had to give way to broader diplomatic considerations. It was necessary to conciliate the French. The French initiative was, therefore, followed.'[35]

* * *

The story of the events which culminated in the bombardment of Alexandria, the battle of Tel el Kebir, and the occupation of Cairo by Sir Garnet Wolseley's army on the night of 14–15 September, 1882, is already familiar. But an outline of

34. 239 *Parl.Deb.3s.*226–8 (29 March 1878).
35. Cromer, *Modern Egypt*, I, 37–38.

the main events might help in placing the extent to which H.M. Government allowed itself to be influenced by the Egyptian creditors.

The Commission of Inquiry issued a preliminary report in August 1878, the substance of which was accepted by the Khedive. On the Khedive's initiative, Mr. Rivers Wilson was then persuaded to accept the office of Egyptian Minister of Finance with M. de Blignières at the Ministry of Public Works. Later that year, again under pressure from the French Government which attached very great importance—M. Waddington told Lord Lyons—to securing the co-operation of the Rothschilds in putting Egyptian finances in order, H.M. Government took yet another step towards linking its interests with those of international finance by consenting to nominate Mr. Rowsell, Director of Navy Contracts, as the British Commissioner on the Commission of Management of the Daïra lands (the security for a loan of £8,500,000 issued by the Rothschilds). But the Government was careful to declare that it accepted no liability, in any contingency, for the payment of the interest on this loan. When Messrs. Rothschild & Sons approached H.M. Government in December 1878 ('your Lordship having taken so much interest in the negotiations of the said loan, and having contributed so considerably to its success . . .') to request that permission be given to H.M. Consul-General in Egypt to act as the representative of the contractors of the Loan, Lord Salisbury refused to agree. The Foreign Office pointed out primly that 'in the opinion of Her Majesty's Government, were such an official authority as that proposed by you to be given to Mr. Vivian by them it might lead to misconceptions which possibly could result hereafter in inconveniences'.[36]

The political situation was again deteriorating in Egypt, and Nubar Pasha's Ministry, which had had the warm support of Britain and France, fell in February 1879. In the second week of April, the Khedive staged a *coup d'état* by which he resumed full control, dismissed his European Ministers, and replaced them by an entirely native Ministry under Chérif Pasha. A

36. Nos. 250, 254, 277, 282, *Further Correspondence respecting the Finances of Egypt*, P.P.1878–79(c.2233)LXXVIII; also *Correspondence respecting the Appointment of Commissioners for the Management of the Daïra Lands in Egypt*, P.P. 1878–79(c.2224)LXXVIII.

nationalistic Decree of 22 April defied the authority of the
Mixed Tribunals over Egyptian finances, and all efforts failed
to replace the European ministers. Both France and Britain
became anxious for the future of financial reform, but French
interests were still firmly linked with those of their bondholders
—an association which was becoming increasingly distasteful
to H.M. Government. Lord Salisbury complained to the British
Ambassador in Paris, 10 April 1879, that:

It may be quite tolerable and even agreeable to the French Government to go into partnership with the bondholders, or rather to act
as sheriff's officers for them. But to us it is a new and very embarrassing sensation. Egypt can never prosper so long as some 25 per cent.
of her revenue goes in paying interest on her debt. We have no wish
to part company with France, still less do we mean that France
should acquire in Egypt any special ascendancy; but subject to
these two considerations, I should be glad to be free of the com-
panionship of the bondholders.[37]

The Prime Minister shared Salisbury's feelings. In a letter to
Salisbury early in June which discussed French policy and the
deterioration of the Egyptian situation, Beaconsfield observed
that 'in France, finance, and even private finance, is politics';
as for British policy, he felt that if the Government spoke out and
declared that their policy involved not merely the abdication of
the Khedive but the liquidation of Egyptian finance, the House
and the country would support them—'It must not be, and it is
not, a mere bondholders' policy.'[38]

Whether or not, as Wilfrid Blunt claims, the deposition of the
Khedive in June 1879 was the work of the Rothschilds acting
through Bismarck—and the description of Bismarck as the
agent of the Rothschilds *does* seem a little unlikely—it is clear
that in the deposition of the Khedive, as in the intervention of
the previous year, H.M. Government was acting under pressure
from the other interested Powers. On 19 June, Britain and
France jointly requested Ismail to abdicate in favour of his son
Tewfik. The German and Austrian Consuls-General presented
a similar request a few days later, and, in response to an Im-

37. Quoted in Ward and Gooch, *Cambridge History of British Foreign Policy*,
p. 161 n.
38. W. F. Monypenny and G. E. Buckle, *The Life of Benjamin Disraeli, Earl
of Beaconsfield* (London, 1910–20), VI, 444–5.

perial Iradé, Ismail finally consented. Explaining the reasons
for this move by the Powers, Salisbury complained to Lascelles
(at Cairo) that in normal circumstances the wisest policy would
have been merely to have abandoned Egypt to her ruin. Unfortunately, Egypt's geographical position and England's part
in determining her existence as a State made it impossible for
the British Government to ignore her; 'they are bound, both by
duty and interest, to do all that lies in their power to arrest misgovernment, before it results in the material ruin and almost
incurable disorder to which, it is evident by other Oriental
examples, that such misgovernment will necessarily lead'.[39]

But it was not long before English critics had raised the point
of the extent to which the abdication was demanded in the
interests of the bondholders. The Chancellor of the Exchequer,
pressed to explain whether the abdication was purely the result
of misgovernment or whether it had something to do with the
Khedive's failure to meet his engagements with his creditors,
replied sensibly enough that it was impossible to deny that the
disastrous financial situation brought upon Egypt by the
Khedive's foreign loans, and the complications legal and
otherwise arising from this situation, had created the explosive
political environment in which intervention had become
necessary. But he argued that it would be incorrect to give the
failure of the Khedive to execute his engagements to his creditors
as the reason for the action of H.M. Government.[40] Six weeks
later, in the Egyptian debate of 11 August, Sir Stafford Northcote was again compelled to define H.M. Government's position.
We had not intervened, he claimed, for the sake of the creditors,
but for the sake of preventing anarchy and misrule in Egypt:

It has been a mere accident, and an incident of the position, that
we have been obliged to interfere with the measures taken by the
Khedive which were likely to be prejudicial to his creditors. . . . The
cardinal principle of the English policy in Egypt upon which we
acted was that Egypt ought to be maintained in a flourishing and,
as far as possible, independent position, and that English interests
should be, I will not say predominant, but that they should not be
overshadowed by the interests of any other Power.

39. No. 15, *Further Correspondence respecting the Affairs of Egypt*, P.P.1878–79
(c.2352)LXXVIII.
40. 247 *Parl.Deb.3s.*728–9 (26 June 1879).

Sir Stafford referred to the complications of the international tribunals in Egypt, the number of just claims pressed, and the cruel exactions imposed on the 'unfortunate fellaheen'. He denied that in all these matters the British Government itself had been acting for the bondholders, but 'the bondholders are a powerful force in various countries, and the action of this force is perfectly certain to bring about more and more complications, and possibly political complications, if we are to stand aside'.[41]

The deposition of the Khedive, of course, revived the problem of how Egypt was to be set on her feet again under the tutelage of the Powers. The French Government put forward a plan for a revived Control with new authority and with the Controllers appointed by the Powers, under their direction and irremoveable without their consent. Lord Salisbury was uneasy about the position of the English Controller, which he felt to be 'a considerable advance in the direction of *ingérence* over anything we did either in the case of Rivers Wilson or Romaine'. But, as he told Lord Lyons, it was not easy to retain the character of non-intervention just after having deposed a Khedive, and he supposed that 'any further prudery would be out of place'.[42] H.M. Government agreed, therefore, to appoint Evelyn Baring as Controller, while M. de Blignières was appointed by the Government of France. In addition, a Commission of Liquidation was established by the five interested Powers (Germany, Austria-Hungary, France, Great Britain and Italy) which was to report on the finances of Egypt and produce a draft Law for the Settlement of the Debt, binding both on Egypt and on the Powers. Sir Charles Rivers Wilson and Mr. Auckland Colvin served as British Government Commissioners, with Sir Charles acting as President. Salisbury, who considered that the details of the Liquidation lay outside the functions of diplomacy and who had no wish to interfere with the distribution of assets to individual creditors, seems to have regarded the Commission as the trustee of the interests of Egypt rather than of her creditors. He told Lord Lyons that he thought the liquidators should be instructed '*first* to determine how much is necessary in order to carry on the Government, and then

41. 249 *Parl.Deb.*3s.713–16 (11 August 1879).
42. Cecil, *Life of Salisbury*, II, 356–7.

apportion the residue as may seem to them just. But perhaps the last doctrine should not be talked of just yet.'[43]

But the significance of the Commission in international law—and this was to weigh heavily with Gladstone in 1882—was that, since it was established by Decree of the Khedive (31 March 1880) and agreed in the Declaration of the Powers signed the same day by their Representatives, there could be no doubt that the settlement effected by the Law of Liquidation constituted an international engagement for the Powers who accepted it. Breach of the Law and failure to settle with the creditors—whatever the previous policy towards intervention might have been—presented henceforward a prima facie case for immediate intervention by H.M. Government.

*   *   *

It was at this point, however, in 1880, that Disraeli was replaced by Gladstone, and a change of government provides the opportunity to take stock of Tory policy in Egypt. Looking back—in February 1884—on the actions of the Government in which he had served as Chancellor of the Exchequer, Sir Stafford Northcote asked rhetorically what our objective had been in Egypt. It had been, he said, to secure for Egypt a good and efficient Administration which would, on the one hand, maintain Egyptian credit and independence, and, on the other, safeguard our route to India while diminishing or doing away with all dangers of the interference of other Powers in that direction. 'Our policy', he concluded, 'was not a policy for the benefit of a number of creditors or bondholders, or whatever you call them, but it was a policy of an Imperial character, and with the minimum of interference to maintain the position of that important country, so important in the chain of our communications.'[44]

But, as the Government had realized at the time, it was unrealistic to take the policy of non-intervention too far. In his secret instructions to the new British Consul-General (Edward Malet) of 16 October 1879, Salisbury had stressed that the leading aim of British policy in Egypt was the maintenance of

43. Inclosure in No. 106, No. 125, *Correspondence respecting the Affairs of Egypt* P.P.1880(c.2549)LXXIX; Cecil, *Life of Salisbury*, II, 357.
44. 284 *Parl.Deb.3s.*1452(19 February 1884).

Egyptian neutrality (by which he meant a state of affairs where no Great Power was more powerful than Britain). We could secure this purpose by annexing Egypt, and if anarchy developed we would have to annex. But in the present circumstances annexation would confer no advantages other than opportunities for the employment of English people and English capital, and these were outweighed by the military and financial responsibilities which it would entail. The continuance of native rule remained, therefore, our obvious objective.[45]

The Tory Government was concerned primarily with stable government in Egypt—preferably native government—in the interests of Imperial commerce and strategy. Its policy had no relation, except incidentally, with the interests of the British bondholders. What was true of Disraeli's Government could only, in this case, have been more true of Gladstone's. If Disraeli's Cabinet were reluctant to annex, any Cabinet containing Gladstone, Granville, and Harcourt was likely to detest it. And among the politicians of the day it would be difficult to find one less suited to the part of bondholder agent than Mr. Gladstone.

Gladstone, in opposition, had already taken up a strong position on Egypt. In an article in *Nineteenth Century* in August 1877, he had protested against an intervention which could only lead us into further adventures in Africa—'Our first site in Egypt, be it by larceny or be it by emption, will be the almost certain egg of a North African Empire that will grow and grow till we finally join hands across the Equator with Natal and Cape Town.' We had, he claimed, quite enough imperial responsibility in the East, and he denounced further intervention for the reasons that empire could only be extended by immoral means, that the true British route to India lay round the Cape of Good Hope, that it would be the basis for further African expansion, and that it would cast a permanent blight

45. Quoted by Mustafa, 'Domestic and Foreign Affairs of Egypt,' pp. 260–1. Robert Blake has recently confirmed Disraeli's own determination to avoid annexation; Britain finally occupied Egypt 'but no such intention existed in Disraeli's mind at the time. Historians who have seen in his action a deeply matured plan which came to fruition later are in error . . . His objective [in purchasing the Suez Canal shares] was rather to forestall France and prevent a French occupation than to take any step towards seizing Egypt for Britain': Robert Blake, *Disraeli* (London, 1966), p. 587.

on Anglo-French relations. Gladstone's writings and speeches up to the point of taking office followed similar lines, and in a speech in Glasgow in December 1879 he ridiculed the idea that Britain, as a small island at one end of the world with enormous possessions at the other, was entitled to claim a preferential right to the possession or control of the intermediate territory in order to safeguard the road to India.[46]

But a politician in opposition must be prepared to eat his words in office. Gladstone, whose opinion that the Cape was our natural route to India was still (in 1877) just sustainable, was compelled to acknowledge by 1882 that the Canal was of immediate strategic importance to the Empire, with an enormous, though as yet only partially realized potential for the future of Imperial commerce and for the enhanced position of British shipping in the world's carrying trade. In the circumstances, he no more than Salisbury could afford to allow British interests to be subordinated in Egypt to those of another Great Power, nor could he accept anarchy. It is possible on the basis of subsequent information to throw doubt on the existence of a genuine state of anarchy in Egypt in 1882, but it is less easy to question the fact that Gladstone, most of his Cabinet, Sir Edward Malet in Cairo, and even the partisan Wilfrid Blunt, believed in the imminence of a Holy War which could end in the massacre of Europeans in the East. Blunt had written in his diary on 12 July 1882—at the time of the bombardment of the Alexandrian forts—that a religious war was inevitable. He admitted later that the allusions he had made in his diary to an expected Mohammedan rising in India might, in the light of subsequent events, seem somewhat exaggerated. But they were justified by the ideas prevalent at the time, and 'the dread of a general conflagration in the East is perhaps the best excuse that can be made for our Government's action in pressing on in July an immediate violent solution of its difficulty in Egypt'.[47]

For the present purposes, the details of the events which culminated in the Occupation are unimportant, but there were a number of revealing contemporary comments and incidents which throw light on the direction which British policy was being forced to take. Edward Malet, the new Consul-General,

46. *The Times*, 6 December 1879, 10f–11a.
47. Blunt, *Secret History*, pp. 368–9, 375n.

found that the course pursued by the Commission of Liquidation was increasingly in conflict with his instructions. He told his parents in a letter dated from Cairo, 17 May 1880, that British policy (and his instructions) had been to make the interests of the creditors subsidiary to the interests of Egypt, but that the Commission, or a part of it, wanted to take more money from the Revenues than the Government thought it could spare. It was a case, he said, of 'pull devil, pull baker', and he did not feel easy about it. Malet's relations with the British Controller-General, Sir Auckland Colvin (who had succeeded Evelyn Baring in 1880), were more harmonious. He observed that he and the Controller 'were frequently obliged to weigh very carefully the counterclaims of diplomacy and finance, which we represented respectively, for, of necessity, they now and then clashed, but I do not believe that there was, on any occasion, a needless subservience of either to the other'.[48] The Liberal Government, which had inherited the Control, was only too conscious of its political dangers, but Dilke's view was that the Control was working well from the Egyptian and economic point of view, and, since it was there, it should be maintained as the only thing between us and anarchy.[49]

Anarchy remained a constant nightmare to British politicians and officials. Sir Charles Dilke (Under Secretary of State) maintained as early as the spring of 1881 that the British and French Governments would be driven, sooner or later, to occupy Egypt with a joint force. But time and again H.M. Government expressed its preference for a prosperous, independent and stable Egypt. 'The only circumstance which could force us to depart from [this policy]', Granville told Malet on 4 November 1881, 'would be the occurrence in Egypt of a state of anarchy.'[50] Rightly or wrongly, the ascendancy of Arabi Pasha's military party seemed to H.M. Government to create just those conditions in which anarchy might be said to exist. By January 1882, Malet could see no way of getting out of our difficulties short of armed intervention; he was reluctant to intervene since, as he told Granville, he owned 'to having a

48. Sir Edward Malet, *Egypt 1879–1883* (London, 1909), p. 79.
49. Quoted in Stephen Gwynn and Gertrude M. Tuckwell, *The Life of the Rt. Hon. Sir Charles W. Dilke* (London, 1917), I, 455.
50. No. 122, *Correspondence respecting the Affairs of Egypt*, P.P.1882(c.3161) LXXXII.

repugnance to a war engaged on behalf of bondholders, and which would have for effect to repress the first attempt of a Mussulman country at Parliamentary Government'. His reluctance was, of course, shared by Granville himself; Granville asked him as late as 21 April how far he believed forcible intervention could be avoided, and added that he himself detested the very thought of it.[51]

But the Joint Anglo-French Note of 6 January 1882—which had been presented under pressure from Gambetta, and which pledged the governments to maintain the Khedive on his throne as the only guarantee of good order and the development of general prosperity in Egypt—had gone too far. It had finally antagonized the Egyptian Nationalists, threatened the armed intervention which all detested, and made foreign intervention, as Cromer later admitted, 'almost an unavoidable necessity'. By the end of May, Cromer described official business, except at the Ministry of War, as at a standstill, the whole country in a state of panic, and Malet threatening the Foreign Office with a collision between the Moslems and the Christians at any moment.[52] Cromer may have been exaggerating, but similar views were shared by the Europeans in Egypt at the time and formed the basis of H.M. Government's policy. Gladstone, when he justified himself to John Bright after the bombardment, claimed that 'sheer military violence' was the only governing factor in contemporary Egypt; every legitimate authority had been put down, and 'a situation of *force* had been created which could only be met by force'.[53] He had convinced himself of the 'seemingly wanton wickedness of Arabi'. Sir Charles Dilke tells, for example, the revealing story of an occasion, late at night on 20 July, when news had just reached the Foreign Office that Arabi had diverted the salt water from the Lake into the great, fresh-water canal. He had had to inform Gladstone and Childers at once:

Their replies [he reported] were full of character. Mr. Gladstone dramatically shivered, and said with a grimace: 'What a wicked wretch!' Childers said: 'How clever!'[54]

51. Malet, *Egypt*, pp. 246, 245, 282.
52. Cromer, *Modern Egypt*, I, 281-2.
53. Gladstone to John Bright, 14 July 1882: quoted in John Morley, *The Life of William Ewart Gladstone* (London, edn. 1911), II, 65.
54. Quoted in Gwynn and Tuckwell, *Life of Dilke*, I, 472.

Cromer was clearly right in his claim that by the end of May 'the question of protecting European financial interests in Egypt had fallen completely into the background'.[55] On 25 May the English and French Agents at Cairo presented a Note proposing the temporary retirement from Egypt of Arabi Pasha and the resignation of the Ministry, and affirmed their intention to insist on these conditions. The Ministry resigned at the request of the Khedive, but this led to open revolt among the military, and Arabi was maintained as Minister of War. At the end of May, Admiral Sir Beauchamp Seymour, in command of the English squadron which had arrived at Alexandria, reported that the military party seemed to be in control of the city and that earthworks were being built rapidly abreast H.M.S. *Invincible*. On 11 June a serious riot broke out in Alexandria in which at least fifty Europeans were killed and H.M. Consul severely injured. The military authorities at Alexandria continued their warlike preparations in spite of warnings from the British admiral, and on 10 July the admiral issued a 24-hour ultimatum. No satisfactory answer was received, and the forts were bombarded and destroyed.

The French Government had withdrawn its squadron a few days before, and de Freycinet claims that private information available to the French did not suggest a state of affairs sufficiently grave to justify a bombardment; he put the bombardment down to the persuasive powers of Admiral Seymour who, '*avec le tempérament habituel des marins anglais, avait hâte de "faire parler la poudre"* '.[56] Blunt seems in turn to have believed that Seymour bombarded Alexandria in order to revenge himself for the death of his body servant, Strackett, killed in the June riot.[57] But whatever the immediate reason—and the admiral's character is not an implausible suggestion as at least one of the contributory factors—armed intervention of some kind was by this time acceptable to most of the British Cabinet. Dilke, supported by Hartington and Chamberlain in the Cabinet, was putting strong pressure on the Government to intervene. In a memorandum which he presented to his colleagues early

55. The bondholders received barely a mention in the British diplomatic correspondence between Cairo and London, January to July 1882: P.R.O., F.O/78/3434–9.
56. de Freycinet, *La Question d'Egypte*, pp. 281, 284–5.
57. Blunt, *Secret History*, p. 317.

in July, he had pointed out that, because so many Liberals believed that intervention was contemplated only on account of the bondholders, the Government owed it to itself to explain that its motive was to secure settled government in Cairo in order to safeguard the Canal and keep open the route to India. But, as he explained afterwards, while he warmly supported intervention on these grounds, he had 'always opposed an intervention which made us in the least responsible for Egyptian finance, or an intervention followed by an occupation'.[58]

For Gladstone the turning point had been the Alexandrian massacres, up to which time he, in company with Granville and Bright, had formed the peace party in the Cabinet. The Cabinet was discussing the possibility of finding itself compelled to send British troops to Egypt four days after the June massacres, though it could not agree on the need to do more than simply to protect the Suez Canal; the decision to send an expeditionary force into Egypt was not taken until the Cabinet meeting of 20 July.[59] But by the time the bombardment took place, Gladstone himself was reconciled to the use of force in some form or another, and Dilke reports him in the Commons on the day after the bombardment as 'in a fighting humour':

I have the notes on which he made his speech, which give all the heads, and are interesting to compare with the speech as it stands in Hansard. He put our defence upon 'the safety of the fleet' and 'safety of Europeans throughout the East'. He was indignant, in reply to Gourley, about the bondholders, and, in reply to Lawson, about our 'drifting into war', and he certainly believed, as I believed at that moment, that the Alexandria massacres had been the work of Arabi, for one of his notes is: 'International atrocity. Wholesale massacre of the people, to overrule the people of that country.'[60]

At the same time, the Foreign Office was drafting a long despatch to Lord Dufferin (the British Ambassador at Constantinople) which was intended both for the information of the Sultan and for publication. The despatch summarized British objectives as maintaining the open and unrestricted navigation of the Suez Canal, securing good and quiet government in an

58. Gwynn and Tuckwell, *Life of Dilke*, I, 465.
59. Spencer Childers, *Life of Childers*, II, 88–96.
60. Gwynn and Tuckwell, *Life of Dilke*, I, 468–9.

Egypt freed from the predominant influence of any single Power, holding Egypt to her international engagements, and protecting Britain's extensive commercial and industrial interests in Egypt from injury and outrage (—'a principle which is not applicable only in Egypt, but is essential for our national interests in all parts of the world').[61]

The only reference to the bondholders in the entire despatch was that contained in the words 'international engagements'—a status which their claims had achieved by virtue of the adherence of the Powers to the Law of Liquidation. Gladstone, for all his dislike and distrust of the Stock Exchange, believed that once a bondholder claim had reached the status of an international engagement, it must be upheld. The Law of Liquidation, he maintained, had been established 'under the highest and widest international sanction, which we have no right, even if we had any disposition, to overlook; and even if we had any disposition to overlook it we have no power'.[62] But it is worth pointing out that even this position was more favourable to the bondholders than that considered expedient by some of his colleagues. When the Foreign Office's draft reached Chamberlain and Dilke, it was, so Dilke says, 'much knocked about'—'The chief alterations . . . which we made, or tried to make, in the despatch were in the direction of omitting all reference to the financial engagements of Egypt, which we were most unwilling to take upon ourselves in any manner.'[63]

The history of the next couple of months was one of abortive negotiations with the Porte to secure the landing of a Turkish force to restore order in Egypt, followed, when the Turks had prevaricated to the point of general exasperation, by the replacement of that force by a British army under Sir Garnet Wolseley. The army marched out of Alexandria on 18 August and, five days later, Arabi Pasha's army was routed and destroyed at Tel el Kebir. The overthrow of the Egyptian

61. *Copy of a Despatch from Earl Granville to the Earl of Dufferin respecting the Affairs of Egypt*, P.P.1882(c.3258)LXXXII.
62. 273 *Parl.Deb.3s.*1943(16 August 1882).
63. Gwynn and Tuckwell, *Life of Dilke*, I, 469. Dilke, though he makes a slight mistake in dating this despatch (which he claims to have been prepared on 13 July, whereas the Blue Book despatch is dated 11 July), is clearly referring to Granville's massive recapitulation of British policy in Egypt. An alteration to which he refers, for example, is incorporated in the text of the 11 July despatch.

Nationalists left a vacuum in the government of Egypt which H.M. Government, reluctant as it was to do so, was compelled to fill. Baring wrote to Salisbury several years later that the main reason why it had proved impossible to carry out an evacuation was not the danger from the dervishes in the South —though this was 'an excellent working argument'—but 'the utter incapacity of the Egyptian ruling classes'.[64] And there can be no doubt at all that the leaders of the Liberal Cabinet genuinely wanted evacuation. Lewis Harcourt noted in his Journal for 17 November 1884 that his father had told the Cabinet that the only thing we could do was to get out of Egypt as soon as possible, 'on which Selborne observed,"that is the opinion of one member of the Cabinet", to which Mr. Gladstone replied, "you had better say *two*" '.[65]

It is perfectly true that the British occupation of Egypt, and the remarkable improvement in Egyptian finance in the second half of the decade, proved the salvation of the bondholders, but this was an incidental consequence of sound government, not the reason for that government's existence. If H.M. Government had interfered in Egyptian finance, Lord Edmond Fitzmaurice told the Commons in 1884, it was not on behalf of the bondholders, but because it was 'impossible to separate the financial from the political condition of the country'.[66] Indeed, H.M. Government, in taking over the administration of Egypt, automatically put itself on the other side of the table from the bondholders. British interests in general, as distinct from the interests of the bondholders, lay in sound government, prosperity, and a reduction in the burden of the External Debt. The British taxpayer would suffer if the rate of interest were not reduced, and Evelyn Baring felt that 'in point of justice . . . the bondholders should certainly go to the wall'.[67] British officials charged with the administration of Egypt naturally identified themselves with the cause of Egyptian prosperity rather than with that of an anonymous group of

64. Quoted by C. J. Lowe, *Salisbury and the Mediterranean, 1886–1896* (London, 1965), p. 56.
65. Quoted in A. G. Gardiner, *The Life of Sir William Harcourt*, (London, 1923), I, 514.
66. 290 *Parl.Deb.*3s.904–5 (14 July 1884).
67. Baring to Childers, 26 February 1884: Spencer Childers, *Life of Childers*, II, 201.

bondholders; administrative expenses, they argued, must take precedence over the interests of the creditors. In the great debate of March 1885 on the projected £9,000,000 International Guaranteed Loan (designed to put Egypt on her feet again), there were frequent references to the British bondholders, none of which were sympathetic; the general opinion had turned against the bondholders, who were commonly described as Shylocks and usurers. In the months before the Guaranteed Loan, when the financial condition of Egypt was looking really desperate, there had even been a move in the Cabinet to repudiate the Debt. The division within the Cabinet was neatly expressed by Chamberlain in a conversation with Harcourt that January. Harcourt, in despair, had remarked that there were as many Egyptian policies as there were men in the Cabinet, to which Chamberlain had replied that there were only three that mattered—'Hartington's with his "Pay and stay", yours, which is "Pay and scuttle", and mine, which is "Scuttle and repudiate".'[68]

*   *   *

There is much for which H.M. Government can be blamed in the Occupation of Egypt—its misjudgement of Arabi Pasha and of Egyptian Nationalism (which it confused, unjustly as it happened, with militarism), its readiness to be frightened by cries of anarchy, its dependence on the viewpoint of expatriate European officials, its inability to stand up to pressure from France. But whatever the mistakes and failures, neither Disraeli's Administration nor Gladstone's based its policy on the payment of the coupons on the External Debt. Though British interests in Egypt were largely commercial, as Salisbury explained to Count Karolyi in November 1879, British action 'was dictated in the main by exclusively political considerations'.[69] 'Apart from the Canal', Gladstone wrote privately to Ripon after Tel el Kebir, 'we have no interest in Egypt itself which could warrant intervention'.[70]

Strachey's contrast between intervention in Egypt in 1882

68. Gardiner, *Life of Harcourt*, I, 515.
69. No. 167, *Correspondence respecting the Affairs of Egypt*, P.P.1880(c.2549) LXXIX.
70. Quoted by Knightbridge, 'Gladstone and the Invasion of Egypt,' p. 260.

and 1956—the one for the bondholders, the other for the Canal—is unreal: both were aimed at the Canal. But the intervention of 1882 was no planned operation; it was a forced progress along lines determined by the security of the Empire. Egypt joined the Empire in 1882 not because it offered a field for the investment of surplus capital, nor because existing British bondholdings were insecure, but because the trade and even existence of the Empire were threatened by anarchy within. Up to the last moment, Gladstone resisted armed intervention, and once it had taken place he aimed only at the restoration of order and at evacuation. Restoring order, Alfred Milner claimed, 'was not merely our professed, but our true and only object; yet we were very far at the time from realizing all that it implied'.[71]

Gladstone's policy was certainly inept and confused, but de Freycinet—who, after all, was in a good position to judge—was surely right in concluding that '*En toute cette affaire, il n'y eut, je le crois, chez nos voisins aucun plan préconçu, ni desseins machiavéliques. Les événements leur ont forcé la main; M. Gladstone a subi l'aventure égyptienne, bien plus qu'il ne l'a recherchée.*'[72]

71. Alfred Milner, *England in Egypt* (London, edn. 1894), p. 21.
72. de Freycinet, *La Question d'Égypte*, p. 231.

CHAPTER 2

TURKEY

'TURKEY'S FATE', Moravitz explained at the turn of the century, 'is that of Sancho Panza and his dinner: as soon as the minister of finance wishes to do anything, some diplomat gets up, interrupts him and throws a veto in his teeth.' And it is true that there was little in the international relations of Turkey—or, indeed, of anywhere in the Levant—which could be divided neatly and distinctly into its political, financial, and commercial elements. A political policy might damage a commercial interest; financial proposals might upset the political balance. It was difficult to move one way or the other without injuring some interest, and the result, as likely as not, was no movement at all.

The sociologist L. L. Bernard took Turkey as his sole illustration of financial imperialism in operation,[1] and the intricate relationship between politics and finance in the Near East has confused even those who are inclined to reject a purely economic interpretation of imperialism. Professor Thornton, for example, after mentioning the Administration of the Ottoman Public Debt, the Deutsche Bank, the Imperial Ottoman Bank, and the Turkish railways, concluded that: 'This example is perhaps the one that best illustrates the theory that a cohesive, single-minded *bourgeoisie*, motivated only by profit and careless of all other human values, possessed of the power to summon up all the resources of the State, set to work to expand the area of capitalism beyond anything it had previously known.'[2] Yet Professor Thornton would almost certainly agree that the part of the bourgeoisie in determining the policy of the Powers at Constantinople was slight in comparison with political rivalries. Sir Charles Webster described the relationship correctly when he argued, for the first half of the nineteenth century, that though the rivalry of the Western Powers for markets was one factor, it was a subordinate one—'Those in charge of policy

1. L. L. Bernard, *War and its Causes* (New York, 1944), pp. 371–2.
2. A. P. Thornton. *Doctrines of Imperialism* (New York, 1965), p. 103.

were more concerned with strategy and politics than with the economic consequences of their actions. The heart of the problem was the Straits . . .'.[3]

The security of the Straits was a late developer in British foreign policy; it was insignificant until the end of the eighteenth century. The appointment of Lord Elgin as ambassador on a special mission to the Porte in 1799 marked the recognition that the rôle of the Constantinople embassy was henceforward to be primarily political; and the distinction between political and commercial functions was confirmed when, in June 1804, H.M. Government informed the Levant Company that it had chosen Charles Arbuthnot as ambassador with exclusively political functions, and requested the Company to appoint a consul-general at Constantinople to look after its commercial affairs. The consular establishments were themselves removed from the control of the Company in 1825 in recognition of the difficulty of separating political consequences from trade, and the Company's monopoly was relinquished in May the same year.[4] Even before the crisis of 1833, H.M. Government had become aware of the commercial and strategic importance to British interests of upholding the Ottoman Empire. 'To Great Britain', Stratford Canning had written in his Memorandum of 19 December 1832, 'the fate of this Empire can never be indifferent. It would affect the interests of her Trade and East Indian Possessions, even if it were unconnected with the maintenance of her relative Power in Europe.'[5] The 1833 crisis awoke the Foreign Office to the serious and immediate danger to be expected from Russia, and began what Sir Louis Mallet has called 'the stupid and hideous dream of Anglo-Indian Chauvinism', the sustained nightmare of a Russian threat to India.

C. J. Lowe argued recently that Mediterranean problems, of which 'by far the most important' was the safeguarding of the Straits, determined British foreign policy until as late as 1896, and it was only then that Egypt replaced the Straits as the key

3. Webster, *Foreign Policy of Palmerston*, I, p. 85.
4. The last years of the Company are described by Alfred C. Wood, *A History of the Levant Company* (Oxford, 1935), ch. X.
5. The Memorandum on the Turco-Egyptian Question is printed in full in F. E. Bailey, *British Policy and the Turkish Reform Movement* (Cambridge, Mass., 1942), pp. 237–46.

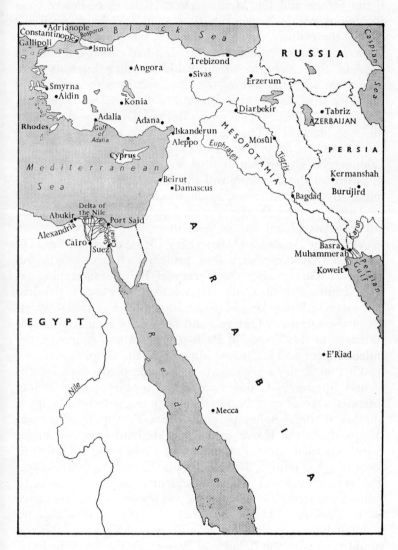

Map 1   The Near East

to British Mediterranean policy and the route to India.[6] But if the Straits and the Mediterranean Balance of Power were the major political preoccupations of the Embassy until the end of the century, what was the relative standing of British trade and finance? Stratford Canning had called attention in 1832 to the extent to which British trading interests were bound up with the fate of the Ottoman Empire, and it was certainly true that, in the first half of the nineteenth century, Britain was able to develop a substantial trade with Turkey and the Black Sea. The exceptionally liberal terms on which trade was conducted in Turkey under the Anglo-Turkish Commercial Convention of 1838 no doubt encouraged Britain to postpone the dissolution of the Empire for fear that trade might, by the transference of the whole course of the Danube to Austria or the Dardanelles and the Bosphorus to Russia, fall into less liberal hands. And in making this point in an article in the *Nineteenth Century* (May 1877), Stratford Canning observed that there were four principal elements in British policy in Turkey after the Treaty of Paris—communication with India, British trade requirements, the 'vast political interests which may be said to constitute us the natural supporters of the Ottoman Empire', and our treaty obligation under Article 7 of the Treaty of Paris to respect and guarantee the independence and territorial integrity of the Empire.

Whether Bailey's argument can be accepted—even for the second quarter of the nineteenth century—that trading interests were of *equal* importance to political factors, is quite another matter.[7] Bailey points out that Turkey, by 1850, was third only to the Hanse towns and Holland as an outlet for British manufacturers. But, of course, out of a total of only just short of £200 million for British imports and exports in 1850, Turkish imports and exports represented only £2,811,000. In spite of the Great Elchi's tendency to apostrophize Commerce as 'that source of blessings to our race, the bond of nations, and first-born of peace', it was unlikely that a trade of this size would rank with the Balance of Power and the Route to India as a determinant of British foreign policy. By the last decades

6. Lowe, *Salisbury and the Mediterranean*, p. 118.
7. Bailey, *Journal of Modern History*, XII, 455–6; Bailey himself recognizes the flaw in his argument in *British Policy and the Turkish Reform Movement*, p. 75.

of the century German competition was making it difficult even
to preserve the level of British exports, and the relative position
had deteriorated sharply: cotton held its ground but subsidiary
exports, such as British woollens and hardware, were forced out
of the Turkish market. French financiers had completely routed
the British at Constantinople.[8]

* * *

Any estimates, then, of the impact of British policy in Turkey
which are based on the size of trade and investment in the area
must be treated with some caution—the British commercial
and financial stake in Turkey was a significant, though far from
vital, element in British overseas commitments, and this is
precisely reflected in the part it was allowed to play in determining British policy.

When British statesmen and diplomatists urged the Porte to
accept loans, develop Turkish trade, open mines, construct an
enlarged system of communications, the object was not
primarily to develop markets for British trade and investment
but rather—as Lord Aberdeen instructed Canning when he
returned as Ambassador in 1842—'to impart stability to the
Sultan's Government by promoting judicious and well-
considered reforms'.[9] Canning had reported to Palmerston as
early as 1832 that the Turkish Empire was 'evidently hastening
to its dissolution', and that if dismemberment and the consequent prolonged disturbance of the peace in Europe were to
be avoided, the only chance (and 'a very precarious one at
best') was to promote development towards the civilization of
the West.[10] The encouragement of commercial and financial
reform as a basis for political stability remained one of the most
important objectives of British policy in Turkey until the last
decades of the century, but it was an ambiguous policy which
has encouraged the popular identification of commerce and
finance with Anglo-Turkish diplomacy.

The problem will be examined more closely below in the

8. The effects of German competition in trade and French competition in
finance is discussed by Harold S. W. Corrigan, 'British, French and German
Interests in Asiatic Turkey, 1881–1914', London thesis, 1954, pp. 20–30,
168–9.
9. Quoted in Stanley Lane-Poole, *The Life of the Rt. Hon. Stratford Canning*
(London, 1888), II, 79.
10. ibid., p. 78.

context of the Ottoman Debt and the Turkish Asiatic railways, but a point needs to be made in passing about the attitude of British diplomatists at Constantinople to the promotion of British finance. The scandalous condition of the consular service in the Levant, which Hornby and Layard have described so graphically and which continued for at least the first half of the nineteenth century, gave rise to some perfectly legitimate complaints.[11] But the frauds and extortions of the Levantine families who traditionally acted as British consuls are no guide to the conduct of British diplomatists. Lord Stratford's advice to Edmund Hornby (who had been appointed to Constantinople in 1855 to oversee the expenditure of the Guaranteed Loan) was simply to help the Ottomans in reducing corruption, and to obtain recognition, as far as possible, of the principle that 'Honesty is the best policy' and in the long run 'pays best'; 'No one will ever succeed with Eastern rulers or with their subjects unless he is as firm as a rock and as *just* and honest as a god.'[12] British Ambassadors at Constantinople, with the possible exception of Sir Henry Bulwer, took this advice to heart. Lord Stratford himself, alarmed for the progress of governmental and financial reform, 'looked coldly on the capitalists who crowded into Constantinople' during the Concession mania which seized Turkey and Turkish officials during the last years of his Embassy. Stratford's successor, Sir Henry Bulwer, who prided himself on his mastery of economics and his devotion to trade and finance, gave some encouragement to the concession hunters. None of their schemes met with financial success, and Hornby complained thirty years later that 'from the day I left Constantinople until I think I may say the present day [1894] the chief work of the "Corps Diplomatique" has been that of an attorney pressing the claims of his client on an insolvent and fraudulent debtor'.[13] But Hornby left Constantinople just before Lord Lyons took over the Embassy. 'I have done the business', Lyons told Hammond a couple of years later, 'in a different manner, and have deliberately foregone the use of many of the old methods of acquiring information and exercising influence. I have perhaps gone a

11. Hornby, *Autobiography*, ch. V; Layard, *Autobiography*, II, 25–26.
12. Hornby, *Autobiography*, p. 74.
13. ibid., p. 114.

little too far in this direction, but I thought it necessary to be strict, at all events at first, in keeping to the direct path.[14] Lord Newton, Lyons's biographer, was inclined to think that Lord Lyons, in his rejection of concession-hunting, had 'carried the principle of abstention to almost extravagant lengths'. Even Thomas Brassey, the famous railway contractor, when applying for support in obtaining a concession for the construction of a railway from Constantinople to Adrianople, was refused assistance. Lyons claimed that he was always being asked to support concessions, and that it was his practice to refer concession-hunters to the Foreign Office (without the authority of which he was unprepared to act in such matters)— 'the fact is that there is often much dirty work connected with the management of such matters at the Porte, and I wish to be clear of them'.[15]

Although, in response to increasing foreign diplomatic and financial competition, some modification of this attitude became necessary around the turn of the century, H.M. Government remained inhibited by the price which Adbul Hamid expected for Turkish concessions: unqualified acceptance of his régime, silence about the Armenian massacres, non-intervention in Macedonia, support and protection for Turkey in the Concert of Europe. No British Government, Sir Edward Grey claimed many years later, could pay this price:

Lord Salisbury could not have done it, if he would, and he made it evident, after the horrors of 1895, that he would not, if he could. . . . British representations about Armenian massacres made us hated, but not feared. . . . Public opinion in Britain demanded that we should make representations; we did so, to the cost of British material interests in Turkey. The irony of it all was that little or no good was done . . .[16]

And this was no mere apologia. Maurice de Bunsen, who was First Secretary at the Embassy at the time, described the cold audience which Sir Philip Currie received on his departure from Constantinople in 1898, and explained that while other diplomatists had grovelled before the Sultan in return for

14. Quoted by Kenneth Bourne, 'The Foreign Secretaryship of Lord Stanley, July 1866–December 1868', London thesis, 1955, pp. 19–20.
15. Newton, *Lord Lyons*, I, 175–6.
16. Grey, *Twenty-five Years*, I, 131–2.

railway and other concessions, we had made him feel that he was not yet forgiven for the 1895 massacres; 'Sir Philip', de Bunsen added, 'has been quite consistent with this policy, which is not a mean one.'[17] The constant pressure for reform in Macedonia weighed heavily against British commercial and financial enterprise in Turkey. In Sir Nicholas O'Connor's Annual Report for Turkey in 1907, the Ambassador pointed out that whatever criticisms might be made of German policy, at least it had had the positive results of securing the Baghdad Railway concession, the monopoly of munition supplies for the Turkish Army, and the privileged position which the Sultan was able to bestow on his German friend and patron with respect to all industrial and commercial concessions. Relations between Turkey and Britain, in contrast, so far as they depended on the Sultan, were little more than tolerable; H.M. Government's championship of the oppressed nationalities in Macedonia, Armenia and elsewhere was 'objectionable and even hateful'.[18]

It was not to be expected that the British trading and financial community in Turkey would accept without protest the sacrifice of their interests. The British Chamber of Commerce of Turkey provided a focus for an increasingly strident chorus of complaint and resentment against H.M. Government and the Embassy. J. W. Whittall, the President of the Chamber, questioned (in his 1891 Address) the extent to which H.M. Government was justified in withholding support for British capital in Turkey when other Powers were acting energetically on behalf of their own subjects:

Doubtless, the policy she follows is dignified, I might even say chivalrous, but, in these matter of fact days, as it certainly does not promote her interests, her motives are misunderstood. Certainly we Englishmen living in Turkey disapprove of such a policy of efface-ment, for we know that it diminishes our power for good, it prevents the proper expansion of our trade, and lowers our prestige amongst the races which surround us.[19]

17. Quoted by E. T. S. Dugdale, *Maurice de Bunsen* (London, 1934), p. 156. Sir Thomas Hohler, who was First Secretary in 1908, makes the same point in his memoirs: *Diplomatic Petrel* (London, 1942), p. 151.
18. *B.D.O.W.*,V,43.
19. Printed in the *Report of the British Chamber of Commerce of Turkey for 1890–91* (Constantinople, 1891), p. 25.

The Armenian massacres did nothing to improve the situation, and in 1897 Whittall made a strong plea for further government assistance to British trade and capital overseas. British trading interests, he observed, had suffered very serious losses from H.M. Government's past obstinacy in refusing to promote and protect British entrepreneurs to the extent that their foreign rivals were assisted by their governments. The *laissez-faire* traditions of his youth, Sir William added, and the confidence in British ability to withstand any foreign competition, were only just now beginning to be shaken; but in these days the most important requirement of all in maintaining or developing British trade was determined action by H.M. Government in its support.[20] In 1903 *The Economist* reported the Chamber of Commerce as still protesting strongly against the official policy and calling, in a number of resolutions, for more vigorous protection and promotion of British enterprise. A more vigorous official protection, the meeting had agreed unanimously, would undoubtedly remove the existing belief that British subjects need not apply for railway, mining or other concessions in Turkey, because justice would not be done to them. *The Economist*, however, took the traditional view that the question as to whether British diplomatic representatives should act practically as agents for obtaining trade concessions was a difficult one, and should not be answered without very full consideration.[21]

Whether the blame lay with the passivity of H.M. Government or, as Sir Edward Grey suspected, in part at least with the 'very poor set of financiers [who] have got commercial enterprise in Turkey into their hands', it was unfortunately true that, by the first decade of this century, France and Germany had gained an overwhelming financial position in Turkish loans and railways.[22] Grey described German policy in Turkey, perhaps a little unjustly, as appearing to have been

20. Presidential Address, *Report of the British Chamber of Commerce of Turkey for the Year 1897* (Constantinople, 1897), pp. 18–19, 23–24.
21. *The Economist*, 24 October 1903, 1798–9.
22. Mr. Block, the British Delegate on the Council of the Administration of the Ottoman Public Debt, communicated to the Embassy a long and interesting Memorandum on Franco-German Economic Penetration in Turkey, dated 18 June 1906: printed as Enclosure 1 in No. 147, *B.D.O.W.*, V, 175–80.

based upon 'a deliberate belief that moral scruples and altru-
istic motives do not count in international affairs'; and the
French attitude towards our cherished Macedonian reforms
—the British Chargé d'Affaires reported in 1906—was tersely
indicated by an expression which M. Constans, the French
Ambassador, was fond of using at the time—'*Je me f—de la
Macédoine!*'

Within the limits imposed by the priority which Britain gave
to Turkish reform (which, for example, effectively blocked
H.M. Government's support for Baron G. de Reuter's application at Constantinople for a Balkan railway concession),[23] the
Embassy attempted to secure fair treatment for British interests.
But it was no easy matter so long as Abdul Hamid remained
personally in control. As for trade, the Capitulations ensured
that Turkish import duties were restricted to 8 per cent. *ad
valorem* and that any extension could only follow negotiations
with, and concessions to, the Powers. Moreover, the Capitulatory Powers all enjoyed most-favoured-nation treatment, with
the result that any trading privileges open to one were automatically open to the others. But the fair treatment which
British trade undoubtedly enjoyed in this general sense did not
apply to the allocation of contracts and concessions, or to the
trade which these brought with them. In an effort, no doubt,
to meet British claims for fair treatment in an increasingly
bitter phase of international competition, H.M. Government
used its good offices to help secure a rifle contract from the
Porte for the Bolton Iron & Steel Company, and to assist
Kynochs (on the proviso that there were no rival *British*
tenders) to get a cartridge contract.[24]

Orders for war material, clearly, were not simply of commercial interest; contracts for warships carried with them the
probability of a request for training facilities in the navy of the
supplying nation, and the naval rivalry between Britain and
Germany in the decade before the First World War made it

23. Sir Edward Grey had told the Italian Chargé d'Affaires that 'to press for
railway concessions at a moment when Macedonian reforms were making no
progress would produce the very unfavourable impression that the Powers
were abandoning the reforms in order to pursue their own interests': No. 247,
B.D.O.W.,V,350.
24. Both incidents are reported in Corrigan, 'British, French and German
Interests in Asiatic Turkey', p. 38 and ns.

seem important to ensure that naval contracts should be placed, if not necessarily in the United Kingdom, at least any-where but Germany. But the Foreign Office admitted an obligation to assist British traders and manufacturers to meet manifestly unfair competition. When, in 1900, it was reported that a contract had been signed for the repair of eight Turkish ironclads at Genoa with armaments supplied by Messrs. Krupp, the British ambassador was authorized to express the hope that British firms might receive a 'fair share' in Turkish orders for war material.[25] Similarly, when the Italian Embassy, after a prolonged and vigorous campaign, was able to secure a Turkish Government order in 1907 for a cruiser from Ansaldos of Genoa, Sir Nicholas O'Conor reminded the Sultan of a promise he had made some years before to Armstrong's to allocate the next ship to them, and made it known that H.M. Government would expect compensation in one form or another.[26]

But to admit the need to secure fair treatment for British enterprise was not necessarily to abandon old standards altogether. O'Conor, who was perfectly aware of the financial difficulties of the Empire and who knew as well as anyone else in Constantinople that it was the destiny of the Turkish navy to lie rotting, unmanned and at anchor, in the Golden Horn or at the Dardanelles, did not feel himself able to meet the Ansaldos contract with pressure for a direct and immediate order to a British firm. 'I should be loth', he admitted, 'to make the commission of an act of folly by the Sultan an excuse for urging him to commit another.' And criticism of H.M. Government for failing to secure Turkish government contracts had been rebutted by Mr. Brodrick, the Under-Secretary of State for Foreign Affairs, some years before:

I confess that I think, on these questions, my hon. friend [Sir E. Ashmead Bartlett] is on rather dangerous ground in invoking continually the influence of Her Majesty's Ambassador. I would point out to him that the question of the contractors to whom a Government should give its contracts is really a question for that Government. Has it ever occurred to a foreign Government to ask my right hon. friend the First Lord of the Admiralty, if he gives a contract for a certain number of guns to one foreign contractor,

25. 84 *Parl.Deb.*4s.626–7 (21 June 1900).   26. *B.D.O.W.*,V,47.

that he should give a contract for an equal number to a contractor of their's? I think that beyond friendly representations it is impossible for Her Majesty's Government to go.[27]

'Friendly representations' were rather less than the diplomatic services available to foreign competitors. Lord Salisbury, when considering the case for supporting British concessionaires against German competition for a Smyrna electrification concession, felt it necessary to warn such applicants in general that H.M. Government was not prepared 'to proceed from words to blows', though he could see no harm in H.M. Ambassador 'putting such bad language as he has at his command against corresponding vituperation employed by the German Embassy'.[28]

The Young Turk Revolution (beginning in July 1908) gave H.M. Government new hope of restoring Britain's political and economic position at Constantinople. Only a few months before, Fitzmaurice, the Chief Dragoman at the Embassy and almost certainly the most knowledgeable of the Embassy staff, had complained bitterly, in a private letter to Mr. Tyrrell, of the 'equivocal, if not impossible' position in which British Ambassadors found themselves at the Porte; they were compelled 'to goad the Sultan with the pinpricks of reform proposals while being expected to score in the commercial line successes which are dependent on the Sultan's goodwill'.[29] But the overthrow of the old régime put the German nose out of joint. The British Ambassador, Sir Gerard Lowther, speculated delightedly on the treatment the German Ambassador, with all his friends locked up, might expect on his return, and wished that there were some similar possibility of 'getting rid of the Frenchman'.[30] Fitzmaurice's letter to Tyrrell of 25 August was a paean of triumph. He told Tyrrell that at last we had the ball at our feet, to the chagrin of the Germans. He had been pressing Sir William Willcock's ambitious schemes for the irrigation of Mesopotamia on the Minister of Public Works— 'One hopes fervently that our people will not lose the present

27. 87 *Parl.Deb.*4s.482–3 (2 August 1900).
28. Quoted in Corrigan, 'British, French and German Interests in Asiatic Turkey', p. 174.
29. No. 196, *B.D.O.W.*,V,247.
30. No. 206, ibid., 265.

golden opportunity after being out in the cold all these years. The iron is hot and we must get a few of them to strike. It may cool before long.'[31]

Fitzmaurice's hopes were not fulfilled. It proved impossible to work up enough interest among British capitalists. By no stretch of the imagination could it be said that the motive power behind British diplomacy was Capital pressing for an outlet. Turkey after 1908 was the classic example of diplomatists jockeying for a political position towards which, it was hoped, capital would provide the impetus. Sir Edward Grey was approached by the Turkish Chargé d'Affaires in London, on 11 September 1908, with a request from the new Turkish government for H.M. Government's assistance in inducing London bankers to come forward with proposals for a loan of a million Turkish pounds. He at once passed on the application to Messrs. Rothschild, who refused to enter into direct negotiations with the Porte on the grounds that the English public had abstained in recent years from buying Turkish securities and that an issue in London would stand the risk of failure. Grey then approached Messrs. Baring, but was informed by Lord Revelstoke that, in the present political condition of Turkey, the issue of a Turkish loan on the London market was an impossibility. He was compelled, therefore, to tell the Turkish Government that although H.M. Government was 'most anxious to attract British capital into Turkey for *bona fide* concessions and commercial enterprises, and . . . sincerely desirous that . . . the entry of British capital into Turkey should not be greatly delayed', there was no prospect of a London flotation at the present time. Grey offered the hollow consolation that the decision of the bankers was really in the best interests of Turkish credit, since no loan was better than the risk of a failure.[32]

Relations between H.M. Government and British financiers remained close. With the Imperial Ottoman Bank so clearly under French Government influence and the Deutsche Bank, with the assistance of the German Government, so closely devoted to the promotion of German interests, the British Government felt that equality of opportunity could never exist for British capital at Constantinople short of the creation of some comparable British financial institution. Consequently,

31. No. 210, ibid., 269.   32. No. 202, ibid., 261–2.

early in 1909 a British financial consortium, headed by Sir
Ernest Cassel, established the National Bank of Turkey. H.M.
Government's approval was given to the new enterprise, and Sir
Henry Babington-Smith, Secretary to the Post Office, accepted
the Presidency at the Government's special request.[33] But the
Bank itself was soon in difficulties. British capital still refused
to come forward in sufficient quantity. Sir Henry explained
to the Grand Vizier at the end of 1910—after warning him
that the Bank would not be able to continue operations in
Turkey unless the Turkish Government could put some business
in its way—that the absence of roads and railways in Turkey
made mining operations unremunerative, while the conditions
attached to concessions by the Public Works Department were
impossibly restrictive.[34]

The situation had changed very little by the eve of the First
World War. There was more than a little justice in the Finance
Minister's complaint to Sir Louis Mallet (the British Ambassador) in June 1914, that in marked contrast to the huge French
investment in Turkish loans and railways and the liberal spirit
of the French Government in its dealings with the Porte, H.M.
Government was asking for feeder lines for riverain navigation
while offering no prospect of construction. The Minister 'asked
for nothing better than British assistance, which was, however,
not forthcoming. His Majesty's Government merely wished to
earmark certain districts in which no one else was to build
railways, and of what good was that to Turkey?'[35]

The response of British capitalists was disappointing, but
H.M. Government did what it could to make sure that they
got their fair share of whatever was going. When Tewfik Pasha,
late in 1909, mentioned the possibility of raising a large loan
on the guarantee of additional customs revenues, Sir Edward
Grey warned him that, since the security offered (the customs
revenues) was largely contributed by British trade, at least one-
third of the loan should be offered for subscription in London
on terms equally favourable with those offered elsewhere.[36]

33. The formation of the Bank (and H.M. Government's part in it) is discussed briefly in Baster, *International Banks*, pp. 107–8; Ralph Hewins, *Mr.
Five per Cent* (London, 1957), p. 72.
34. Enclosure in No. 6, *B.D.O.W.*,X, Pt.II,15.
35. No. 252, ibid., 412.
36. Appendix VI, *B.D.O.W.*,VI,792.

Two years later, Sir Edward Grey and Sir Francis Bertie (the British Ambassador at Paris) were urging on the French Government the advantages of financial as well as political co-operation in Turkey in an effort to combat the predominance of Germany; such co-operation, however, would not serve any purpose unless the Imperial Ottoman Bank were prepared to relax its opposition and give equal opportunities to British capital and enterprise.[37]

By 1913 the Powers were thinking in terms of the ultimate dissolution of Turkey. France presented a substantial list of railway and port concessions as the price of her continued financial and fiscal assistance.[38] The Italian Government, anxious as ever for its place in the sun, felt that while it desired above all to see the integrity of Asiatic Turkey preserved, if Germany, France, and Russia all sought spheres of economic interest in Asia Minor, Italy should have her share too, and a claim was presented for a concession for a port at Adalia and other connected enterprises.[39]

Great Britain, with its eyes on Mesopotamia in any future formal or informal partition, made special claims to British control over the Mesopotamian oil and to concessions and contracts for British firms in the irrigation of Mesopotamia.[40] The aim, clearly, was only in part financial. Fair shares, in the event of political collapse, could only be secured by mapping-out a sphere of interest, but the strategic importance of Mesopotamian communications and of the supply of oil weighed more heavily with the Foreign Office.

Oil, particularly, preoccupied the officials. Since 1913, when a mission despatched on Winston Churchill's initiative had reported favourably on the Anglo-Persian fields as a source of fuel for the Royal Navy, H.M. Government had backed wholeheartedly the claims of the Anglo-Persian Oil Company in Persia and Mesopotamia. The principal object of H.M. Government in supporting the Anglo-Persian Oil Company's explorations in Mesopotamia—Mr. Parker explained to Herr von Kühlmann in August 1913—was:

37. Nos. 28, 31, *B.D.O.W.*, X,Pt.II,40,43.
38. M. Paul Cambon's Communication of 2 June 1913: No. 87, ibid., 134–5.
39. No. 157, ibid., 249–50.
40. Minute on No. 76, No. 96, ibid., 125, 153–4.

(a) to maintain the independence of the Anglo-Persian Oil Company as they [H.M. Government] were opposed to the creation of large trusts, (b) to secure satisfactory marketing arrangements, (c) to secure an abundant supply of oil at a reasonable price, and (d) to support the Anglo-Persian Oil Company in what they considered to be a just and well-established claim to the concession.[41]

Early in 1914, on the initiative and with the direct participation of Foreign Office officials, an agreement was accepted by which the Turkish Petroleum Company was reconstituted with 50 per cent. of the shares allotted to the D'Arcy group (the Anglo-Persian), 25 per cent. to the Anglo-Saxon Petroleum Company, and 25 per cent. to the Deutsche Bank. It was essentially a political initiative. Sir Robert Waley Cohen of the Anglo-Saxon group explained in a letter to *The Times* after the War that his Group did not believe in mixing politics with business; it led sometimes to corruption and always to inefficiency, and tended to convert commercial rivalries into national animosities:

Therefore we would have preferred to enter the Mesopotamian field, as we have every other oilfield in the world, by means of a free association with friends in a purely commercial enterprise, but in the circumstances we could only accede to the wishes of the British Government and join in the arrangement of the Turkish Petroleum Company.[42]

In further pursuit of a general political accord in Asiatic Turkey—which, unfortunately, was cut short immediately by the outbreak of the First World War—the British and German Governments agreed to exhange Notes on the date of the signature of the Anglo-German Convention (initialed 15 June 1914), by which both Governments undertook to use their good offices with the Turks to secure that 'the principle of open competition shall be upheld in regard to contracts or concessions for the future works of irrigation in Asiatic Turkey', but in

41. Minute on No. 140, ibid., 215.
42. *The Times*, 1 September 1921, 16e. The Agreement is reported in No. 214 and minutes, *B.D.O.W.*, X, Pt. II, 345–6: a good background article on H.M. Government's interest in Turkish oil both before and after the First World War is E. M. Earle, 'The Turkish Petroleum Company—a Study in Oleaginous Diplomacy', *Political Science Quarterly*, 39 (1924), 265–79.

which they agreed not to support the claims of their respective subjects in competition with certain existing proposals in Mesopotamia and the plain of Adana.[43]

* * *

In outline, then, H.M. Government's policy in Turkey until as late as 1896 had been to maintain the inviolability of the Straits, after which the political centre of gravity had shifted to Egypt. British political interest in Turkey for the period immediately prior to the First World War was part-and-parcel of the growing rivalry with Germany, with its focus on Asiatic Turkey rather than on the Straits. Trade and finance, though always important, took a back-seat when required to do so by broader national interests. Until the last decades of the nineteenth century British trade occupied an overwhelmingly superior position in the overseas trade of the Ottoman Empire, and apart from safeguarding Treaty and Capitulation rights and rejecting monopolies there was little that H.M. Government could have done for it—even if it had been permitted to do so by the *laissez-faire* tradition of the time. German competition in trade became serious later in the century. But far more serious was the competition in contracts and concessions, for which British traders and financiers were out-manoeuvred in part as a result of their own ineptitude, but in part also because of the reluctance of H.M. Government to join in concession-mongering or to abandon its damaging championship of the oppressed Balkan and Armenian minorities. The Young Turk Revolution of 1908 reopened the possibility of the recovery of British political influence at the Porte, and the interests of British finance were reconsidered both for their value as a political instrument and as a gesture of respect for the 'fair' conditions in trade and investment which the Foreign Office felt obliged to foster. The strategic need for oil, finally, entered as a clinching factor in the developing British claim for a sphere of interest in Mesopotamia, cut short in August 1914.

But there are two important areas of contact between H.M. Government and the financiers in Turkey which remain to be examined, and which deserve to be treated in isolation: the Ottoman Loans and the railways.

43. *B.D.O.W.*,X,Pt.II, 407–8.

The bondholders and their associated financiers have always, of course, occupied the unenviable position of arch-fiend in the demonology of economic imperialism. D. C. Blaisdell, to the indignation of Jacob Viner, described the Council of the Ottoman Public Debt as an 'instrument of imperialism', and presented his thesis as an essay in the 'technique of financial imperialism'.[44] Others have made the same assumption, and it is perfectly true that H.M. Government intervened to an exceptional degree in Turkey on behalf of the bondholders. It is also true, in spite of Viner's brave denials,[45] that there was a direct and close relationship between the Embassies at Constantinople and the European representatives on the Council of the Administration of the Ottoman Public Debt. Because of the uncomfortable political situation in and after the '90s, the contact between the British Ambassador and the representative of the British bondholders was perhaps less intimate than it was for the French and the Germans. But it was unlikely that the two should remain unknown to each other when the British representatives on the Debt Council included, at one time or another, Sir Edgar Vincent (private secretary to Lord Fitzmaurice, and later Financial Adviser in Egypt under Lord Cromer, Governor of the Imperial Ottoman Bank, a Member of Parliament and, as Lord D'Abernon, a distinguished British diplomatist), Sir Edward FitzGerald Law (previously Commercial Attaché at St. Petersburg, Commercial Secretary at Vienna, and resident Minister in Greece, and later Financial Member of the Council in India), Sir Henry Babington Smith (later Secretary to the British Post Office and President of the National Bank of Turkey), and Sir Adam Block (a former Chief Dragoman at the Embassy). Sir Edward Law's biographers make the revealing comment that his friendship with Sir Nicholas O'Conor (the British Ambassador) and Sir Hamilton Lang (President of the Imperial Ottoman Bank at Constantinople) enabled Law to form a link between high politics and finance, and as such 'to strengthen British influence at this somewhat critical period in the history of the Ottoman

44. D. C. Blaisdell, *European Financial Control in the Ottoman Empire* (New York, 1929).
45. Jacob Viner's review of Blaisdell's *European Financial Control in the Ottoman Empire: Journal of Political Economy*, 37 (1929), 746.

Empire'.[46] Indeed, Professor Thornton has gone so far as to claim that 'the modern age of economic imperialism' may be said to have begun when the European governments came to the support of their bondholders after the Turkish default of 1875.[47]

Professor Thornton was wrong, but why was he wrong? What was the explanation of this 'link between high politics and finance' which seems to fit at least one of the theories of imperialism so neatly?

The distinction which has to be made is between the guaranteed and the un-guaranteed Loans, and the motives which led H.M. Government to support the one and reject the others. The Loans of 1854, 1855, and 1862 all, in varying degrees, involved British Government responsibility. But the 1858 Loan and the 1871 Loan were conventional loans negotiated independently of H.M. Government and subject, therefore, to the policy of non-intervention expressed in Palmerston's famous Circular of 1848.[48]

Turkish loans had from an early date attracted the attention of both financiers and diplomatists. A group of English bankers approached Palmerston in 1840 with the proposal that H.M. Government should guarantee a Turkish loan negotiated on the security of the Customs at Constantinople, Salonika, and Smyrna. Palmerston refused, explaining that H.M. Government found it impossible to take any part or to give any security, direct or indirect, in such loans.[49] Political reasons, or rather the political stability which, he hoped, would follow reform at Constantinople, persuaded Stratford Canning to present the Sultan in August 1850 with a strongly-argued Memorandum in favour of a foreign loan; the discouraging reception which his proposal met with both in London and Constantinople forced him to drop the idea shortly afterwards.[50] Sir Henry Bulwer was constantly urging a guaranteed loan, applied and administered by Europeans, as the only means to save Turkey. But Dr. Bell points out that H.M. Government

46. Morison and Hutchinson, *Life of Sir Edward Law*, p. 239.
47. Thornton, *Doctrines of Imperialism*, p. 102.
48. Appendix II.
49. Quoted by Anderson, *Historical Journal*, VII, 47.
50. F. S. Rodkey, 'Ottoman concern about Western economic penetration in the Levant 1849–1856', *Journal of Modern History*, XXX (1958), 348, 352.

did not react favourably; 'anything savouring of economic imperialism or political control was out of the question'.[51]

The peculiarity of the 1854 Loan, which was later to be held to involve some degree of H.M. Government responsibility, was contained in the wording of the following paragraph in the Prospectus:

The undersigned [the promoters of the Loan] have the satisfaction to inform the public that they are authorized by the Earl of Clarendon, Her Majesty's Principal Secretary of State for Foreign Affairs, to state that this Loan is negotiated with the knowledge of the English Government; that Her Majesty's Government is satisfied that the Loan and the appropriation of the above-mentioned 30,000,000 piastres (£282,000 sterling) are duly authorized by the Sultan; and further, that the representatives of the Sublime Porte at Paris and London are empowered by virtue of the Imperial Firmans to ratify the contract for the Loan in the name of His Majesty the Sultan, and Lord Clarendon relies with confidence upon the Turkish Government fulfilling with good faith the engagements they entered into.[52]

There can be no doubt of the reluctance of the Cabinet to accept the implied responsibility in this paragraph, but a loan was essential to the finance of Turkey at a critical stage in the Crimean War. If it were to be raised on reasonable terms on the London market, there was no alternative to a Government statement of support; and there was the further risk of a unilateral guarantee by France with the object, Clarendon feared, of securing a lien on Egypt (the Tribute of which had been offered as a security for the Loan).[53] Clarendon fully realized the part which his certificate had had in the success of the loan—which was heavily over-subscribed—and the problem in future was not whether H.M. Government was, or was not, under a moral obligation to the bondholders of the 1854 Loan in the event of default, but the degree to which H.M. Government was obliged to intervene.

The decision of the Turkish Government in October 1875 to halve the interest on its debt over the next five years brought

51. K. Bell, 'The Constantinople Embassy of Sir Henry Bulwer, 1858–65', London thesis, 1961, p. 113.
52. Inclosure in No. 29, *Correspondence respecting the various Ottoman Loans*, P.P.1876(c.1424)LXXXIV.
53. Mrs. Anderson makes this point in her article, *Historical Journal*, VII, 51.

matters to a head. The Foreign Secretary (Derby) tried to maintain that Clarendon's undertaking, though going further in giving moral support to the Turkish Government than was altogether expedient, bound H.M. Government only to use such *moral* influence as it could bring to bear; 'anything in the nature of an official demand would be unadvisable and contrary to our policy'.[54] However, the pressure of public opinion, and in particular the support given on both sides of the House to Mr. Russell Gurney's Motion of 21 July 1876, compelled the Government to take more positive action. The Chancellor of the Exchequer (Sir Stafford Northcote) admitted during the Gurney debate that H.M. Government were 'not insensible to the gravity of the responsibility that rested upon them' with respect to the 1854 Loan,[55] and a Treasury letter to the Foreign Office the following October urged that the French Government, which was committed to the 1854 Loan by an identical formula, should be approached with a view to a joint official representation:

The justification of such a representation is to be found in the belief publicly expressed by the two Governments in 1854, that the Turkish Government would fulfil its promises, the object of that public expression of opinion being to assist an allied Power in procuring money for the prosecution of a war in which the two Powers were supporting it.

It would be necessary to state distinctly that Her Majesty's Government holds that the Loan of 1854 stands on a different footing from subsequent loans (the Guaranteed Loan excepted), that there is no necessity for the two Governments to interfere between the Porte and its ordinary creditors, and that their joint good offices should be confined to the loan which was introduced into the money market upon the recommendation of the Governments of England and France, with the view of obtaining money for the prosecution of a war in which England and France, equally with Turkey, were engaged.[56]

Joint action was agreed, and on 17 February 1877 an Anglo-French representation was delivered to the Porte on behalf of the 1854 bondholders.

54. No. 47, *Correspondence respecting the various Ottoman Loans*, P.P.1876(c.1424) LXXXIV.
55. 230 *Parl.Deb.*3s.1755.
56. No. 45, *Correspondence respecting the Ottoman Loans*, P.P.1877(c.1744)XCII.

The obligation of H.M. Government to secure the interests of the bondholders of the 1855 Guaranteed Loan, was, of course, unquestionable. The Loan of £5 million at the low interest rate of 4 per cent. was intended specifically to enable the Turkish Government 'to prosecute with vigour the war against Russia'. It was, in effect, a cheap way of giving a subsidy, and the Guarantee Convention bound H.M. Government to make up the interest in the event of a Turkish default. The undertaking was to prove a heavy burden to the English taxpayer, but it was indisputably the responsibility of the British Government, on whom the obligation to ensure Turkish probity rested. The Government felt obliged to see that the expenditure of the Loan was controlled, and Mr. Edmund Hornby and M. Cadrossi were sent out to Constantinople as Allied Commissioners to supervise its distribution. Hornby claimed later that, when all was said and done, not more than half a million was misapplied. He could not explain how this had happened, but he remembered one occasion on which he and Cadrossi, on inspecting and verifying the cash deposit at the Treasury, had found one bag which should have contained £20,000 in gold sovereigns full of copper coins—'Cadrossi nearly had a fit, and would then and there have strangled poor Kiani had I not interfered.'[57]

The last of the Turkish Loans to involve some form of H.M. Government responsibility was the Loan of 1862. After the total collapse of Turkish credit early in 1861, H.M. Government despatched two Treasury officials—Lord Hobart and Mr. Foster—to report on the financial situation. Their report, presented in December, was sufficiently favourable to persuade H.M. Government to give semi-official support to a loan designed to consolidate the floating debt and extinguish the *caimé* (paper money currently in circulation). The Prime Minister, Lord Palmerston, argued that financial reform must be the basis of all national strength; 'Until the finances of Turkey are placed in a healthy condition no other assistance that could be afforded her would be of any real or permanent value ... Nothing would more contribute to the permanent peace of Europe than the establishment of a strong, independent

57. Hornby, *Autobiography*, p. 77.

and well-administered Government in Turkey.'[58] At the request of the Turkish Government (which was anxious to secure as favourable terms as possible for the flotation), H.M. Government agreed to send Lord Hobart out on a further mission to make sure that the loan was not misappropriated. Furthermore, Lord Russell (the Foreign Secretary) consented to the insertion of a letter in the Prospectus in which the purpose of Lord Hobart's mission was explained. Russell added that 'Her Majesty's Government would take an interest in this operation from their feelings of friendship towards Turkey', and that 'the contractors of the Loan might see in such a mission a further security against the misapplication of the present loan, and the loss of credit which would ensue'.[59]

But an important distinction was drawn between H.M. Government's readiness to assist the Turkish Government with expert advice and any commitment which might seem to arise therefrom to the interests of the bondholders. Palmerston had explained in the Commons, 31 March 1862, that 'the British Government take upon themselves no responsibility whatever with regard to the payment of the interest of the loan',[60] and this was to form the basis of Foreign Office policy. Mr. Hammond, the Permanent Under-Secretary, reminded a bondholder representative in 1866 of Palmerston's statement and of his further observation that Lord Hobart's functions extended simply to seeing 'that the money raised is applied solely to the purpose for which it was raised'. Hammond concluded categorically that 'Her Majesty's Government continue to decline all responsibility with regard to the payment of the interest of the loan in question.'[61] The Foreign Office, which had, after all, some measure of responsibility for the successful *flotation* of the Loan, was prepared to advise the Porte on any number of occasions to observe its engagements, particularly with respect to the appointment of the bondholder Syndicate allowed for in the loan contract (which was to be charged with receiving directly the revenues assigned as

58. 166 *Parl.Deb.*3s.298–9 (31 March 1862).
59. Quoted in Borchard and Wynne, *State Insolvency and Foreign Bondholders*, II, 400.
60. 166 *Parl.Deb.*3s.296.
61. No. 16, *Correspondence respecting the Ottoman Loan of 1862*, P.P.1874(c.1077) LXXVI.

guarantees for the loan). But the intervention was covered by
the elastic term 'unofficial', and Lord Tenterden, while
assuring the bondholders as late as 1874 of H.M. Government's
readiness to continue pressing for the Syndicate, took the
opportunity to repeat that 'Her Majesty's Government can
acknowledge no responsibility on their part towards the bondholders nor any claim on their part for further interference on
their behalf'.[62]

The 1862 bondholders had at least some reason to claim
special attention from the Foreign Office; the 1858 and 1871
bondholders had no claim whatever. Neither for the 1858
Loan nor for the 1871 Loan was the approval of the Foreign
Office formally sought or obtained; the Loans were private
ventures which owed nothing to Government assistance or
inspiration. In both cases, therefore, H.M. Government held
to the principles of non-intervention expressed in the 1848
Circular. The Foreign Office steadfastly refused to intervene
officially on behalf of the 1858 bondholders,[63] and the last
word to the 1871 bondholders was said when the Treasury
informed Messrs. Palmer and Bouverie, in July 1877, that
though 'under the special circumstances of the case' H.M.
Government had consented to use its good offices on behalf of
the 1854 bondholders, 'Her Majesty's Government have no
privity with the Loan of 1871, and can offer no advice to those
who are interested in it.'[64]

Under analysis, then, the comparatively active record of the
Foreign Office on behalf of the Turkish bondholders falls very
much within the traditional pattern. For purely private loans,
to which only the Turkish Government and the bondholders
themselves were party, H.M. Government held to the principles
of 1848. Where Government responsibility was involved,
mildly in the case of the 1862 Loan, more so for the 1854 Loan,
and entirely so for the Guaranteed Loan of 1855, the Foreign

62. No. 136, ibid., This Blue Book and the *Further Correspondence* [P.P.1875
(c.1127, 1163, 1210, 1288)LXXXIII] contain a complete account of H.M.
Government's policy towards the 1862 bondholders.
63. The refusal of H.M. Government to support the 1858 bondholders is
illustrated in *Correspondence respecting the Ottoman Loan of 1858*, P.P.1874
(c.1077)LXXVI, and in *Further Correspondence*, P.P.1875(c.1210, 1288)
LXXXIII.
64. Inclosure in No. 17, *Further Correspondence respecting the Ottoman Loans*,
P.P.1878(c.2136)LXXXII.

Office was prepared to play a more or less active part. But—
and this is the essential point—Government responsibility was
involved in these loans purely for political reasons; in no sense
could it be said that the Government intervened as part of a
general policy of promoting British finance overseas. Nor had
its attitude anything to do with imperialism. Mrs. Anderson's
conclusion with respect to the 1855 Guaranteed Loan applies
equally to the Loans of 1854 and 1862. 'In giving her guarantee', Mrs. Anderson observed, '[Britain] bore witness not to
her faith in Turkish regeneration, still less to any lust for
imperialist penetration, but simply to the intensity of her
desire for victory against Russia.'[65]

The subsequent history of the Turkish Loans is less interesting,
and certainly of less concern to H.M. Government. Stratford
Canning, from his retirement, had urged on the Foreign
Office in 1874 the need to prevent Turkey recklessly dissipating
her resources and recreating the Eastern Question in a more
aggravated and perilous form in the ensuing financial collapse.
Canning emphasized, however, that the question of intervention was 'purely political'; 'our peculiar relations with Turkey
might indeed not improbably justify an exceptional interference
on behalf of our numerous bondholders; but that is not the
matter in hand'.[66] The Foreign Office, never inclined at the
best of times to undertake increased financial responsibilities
abroad, seems to have ignored Canning's advice. But the
Turkish default of 1875 put a different complexion on the
matter. The responsibility of the Guaranteeing Governments
was engaged, and their intervention thereafter was nothing
new, as Professor Thornton believes, but simply a fulfilment of
their obligations under guarantees undertaken twenty years
before. A Protocol (Protocol 18) was adopted at the Congress of
Berlin, 1878, which recommended the appointment of a
Financial Commission of specialists, named by their respective
governments; the Commission was to be charged with the
examination of the complaints of the bondholders and with the
formulation of proposals for their satisfaction, subject to the
needs and financial situation of Turkey. The Turkish Government, understandably anxious to avoid a financial Control

directed by the Powers, itself took the initiative, and invited the bondholders' delegates to Constantinople to negotiate an arrangement of the External Debt, '*sans aucune ingérence de la part des Puissances*'. The British Government was at first inclined to resent this independent action. The Ambassador's immediate reaction was to claim that the phrase referring to the interference of the Powers was a tacit protest against the Berlin Protocol; his advice was that the Powers should insist on adherence to the Protocol. Goschen explained himself more fully in a despatch a month later, 9 November 1880, in which he argued that the Protocol provided the opportunity for an International Financial Commission; experience in Egypt, he explained, had shown conclusively that the claims of public creditors provided a *locus standi* for a financial inquiry and even for financial reform which could be made use of most advantageously in the interest of the taxpayers and of the prosperity of the community generally:

The prospects for the public creditors of Turkey cannot, under any circumstances, be anything but gloomy, but the financial inquiry would have its use far beyond any slight satisfaction of the claims of the bondholders which might result from it. Financial reform ought in reality to precede almost any other reforms, and it is difficult even to see how the Turkish Empire can be held together without it.[67]

However, in London Granville felt less strongly about the whole affair, and when the French Government withdrew its support for an International Commission in favour of an independent arrangement by the bondholders, he allowed Goschen's financial inquiry to drop. Goschen himself left Constantinople in the summer of 1881, and his successor, the Earl of Dufferin, raised no objection to the agreement reached independently by the bondholders' representatives and the Turkish Government at the end of the year. By the Decree of Muharrem, an Administrative Council was established at Constantinople consisting of representatives of the British, Dutch, French, German, Austro-Hungarian, and Italian bondholders, who were appointed without the intervention of the Powers and charged with the supervision and receipt of the funds allocated to the service of the Debt.

67. No. 20, *Correspondence respecting the Financial Affairs of Turkey*, P.P.1882(c. 3197)LXXXI.

The Council's functions were enlarged subsequently to include the servicing of a number of further loans and railway kilometric guarantees, but the interest of H.M. Government in the Council's operations was slight, and grew slighter. A close personal contact often existed between the British bondholders' representatives and the Embassy, and the British Government naturally maintained its interest in the servicing of the Guaranteed Loan of 1855 (default on which had cost the Treasury nearly £225,000 by the time the Council was finally established). But the bondholders' representatives had no official *locus standi* with H.M. Government, and the declining interest of British investors in Turkey (which was so noticeable a feature of the later period) was an added disincentive to an active policy of intervention. Apart from the attempt in 1909 to ensure that new Turkish Loans should be made available at least in part to British investors, the attitude of the Foreign Office is exemplified by Salisbury's lighthearted comment in 1887 that the utmost H.M. Government could offer the Turkish bondholder in the circumstances was 'a tender, but perfectly platonic, expression of sympathy'.[68]

* * *

For reasons which, as will be seen, were largely political, H.M. Government could not afford quite such a platonic relationship with the Turkish Asiatic railways. Official demands for the participation of British capital in the Baghdad Railway, and Sir Edward Grey's charming remark to the Italian Ambassador in 1913 that the Smyrna-Aidin Railway 'was so to say our ewe lamb', seem to vindicate the claim that the Turkish Asiatic railways serve as an object lesson in economic imperialism.[69] Again there is an element of truth in this, and

68. Edwards, *Sir William White*, p. 245.
69. This viewpoint is less common now that so much research has been published on the Baghdad Railway: for example, Edward M. Earle, *Turkey, the Great Powers and the Baghdad Railway* (New York, 1923); William L. Langer, *The Diplomacy of Imperialism, 1890–1902* (New York, edn. 1951), ch. XIX ('The Baghdad Railway Project'); John B. Wolf, 'The Diplomatic History of the Baghdad Railroad', *University of Missouri Studies*, XI (1936); Maybelle K. Chapman, 'Great Britain and the Baghdad Railway, 1888–1914', *Smith College Studies in History*, XXXI (1948); Ravinder Kumar, 'The Records of the Government of India on the Berlin-Baghdad Railway Question', *Historical Journal*, V (1962), 70–79.

the Turks themselves might be excused for accepting it without reservation; but it all looks a little different if taken from the view-point of British officials.

Communications in Asiatic Turkey had always been of interest to the Foreign Office. Henry Layard—who had acted as Stratford Canning's confidential adviser at Constantinople, 1842–5—had been at pains to emphasize the future of the Tigris and the Euphrates as 'great military and trading highways'. Trade would be advantageous both to England and to Turkey, since the only way to settle and cultivate these wild and lawless areas was to provide a market for their produce, and this in turn could only be done by introducing foreign enterprise and capital into riverain navigation. Layard concluded that:

It was of no less importance to the political interests of England that, in the event of need, she should be able to send troops by water almost to the foot of the great chain of mountains which separates the high lands of Asia Minor and of Persia from Syria and the vast Mesopotamian plains.[70]

It was a similar line of reasoning which persuaded a Select Committee of the Commons to report, in 1872, in favour of a Government guarantee for the much-discussed Euphrates Valley Railway scheme. The Committee argued that the more speedy conveyance of mails, the existence under British control of an alternative and more rapid route for the movement of troops, and the great commercial benefits, both to Britain and India, which the opening of the route would confer, made a guarantee a worthwhile proposition for H.M. Government.[71] But whether or not, as Wilfrid Scawen Blunt claimed, it was *his* advice which was decisive in persuading Salisbury against the scheme,[72] the Committee's recommendations were never accepted by H.M. Government, and Salisbury was still speculating on the possibility of a British guaranteed railway to Baghdad in August 1878. He felt that a railway might lead to Turkish reforms—'we shall get the promise of the reforms which will not be kept; we shall set to work on the railway; we

70. Layard, *Autobiography*, pp. 71–72.
71. *Report from the Select Committee on the Euphrates Valley Railway*, P.P.1872 (c.322)IX.
72. Blunt, *Secret History*, p. 29.

shall get or claim the right to defend the railway; and then we shall carry out with a strong hand what had been promised'. But he was well aware of the difficulty of getting a guarantee accepted by Parliament, and he knew that everything was contingent on the railway becoming a reality. 'Can anything', he asked, 'be a reality in the hands of the Duke of Sutherland, and Sir Arnold Kemball, and a list of directors as long as my arm?'[73]

But no British Government could remain entirely indifferent to a system of communications which opened up the first stages of the overland route to India, and which promised to develop an area already of some importance to British trade. When Sir Charles Dilke, as Under-Secretary of State, was asked in the Commons (27 August 1880) for information on Government action in hand to promote railway enterprise in Asiatic Turkey, he replied that, while no action was proposed at present, the British Ambassador at Constantinople had been in the habit of giving such assistance as was consistent with his official position to *bona fide* schemes for that purpose in which British subjects were interested and for which there was a fair chance of realization.[74] It was true that the matter had not been overlooked at Constantinople, but problems existed which London businessmen found difficult to understand. Sir William White, who was perhaps the ablest of all British Ambassadors at the Porte, argued in a railway memorandum of 1887 that the railways in Asiatic Turkey were a subject of primary importance commercially, politically, and strategically, and on that account deserved all possible support. He added, however, that concessions, under whatever terms they were offered, could only be obtained in Turkey 'by the extensive use of baksheesh for the purpose of gaining the support of influential persons'; here, he felt, lay 'the chief and almost insurmountable impediment which militates against a British Embassy coming forward as the patron and active supporter of railway and other concessions in which money has to be spent in this way in the Ottoman Empire'.[75] White eventually allowed himself to be drawn into supporting an Anglo-German group in their bid for

73. Quoted by Cecil, *Life of Salisbury*, II, 306–7.
74. 256 *Parl.Deb.3s.359–60*.
75. Appendix IV of Smith, *The Embassy of Sir William White*, p. 166.

the Ismidt-Angora railway concession. The concession was granted, but Vincent Caillard, heading the British concession-aires, was unable to gain enough financial support in the City, and the concession became exclusively German. As White complained at the time, and as Sir Edward Grey was to complain again in 1908, it was impossible to interest first-rate London financial houses—disgusted as they were with the corruption and administrative inefficiency of the Porte—in larger-scale undertakings in Turkey.[76]

By default, then, railway enterprise in Asiatic Turkey (apart from some relatively minor lines) passed into the hands of the Germans. The Embassy did not abandon its pressure altogether, but it found itself unable to compete with the more urgent pressure applied by the German Government on behalf of its nationals.[77] Sir Edward Grey reported an extreme case in the early '90s. It was generally understood at Constantinople that diplomatic pressure was the rule, and the British Ambassador, with the approval of the Foreign Office, had undertaken to support the claims of British firms for railway concessions in Asia Minor. Quite suddenly, at the end of 1892 a sort of ulti-matum was delivered from Berlin requiring H.M. Government to abandon its support for competing British concessionaires: the price of continued diplomatic pressure would be the with-drawal of German support from the British administration in Egypt. Grey explained that H.M. Government had no choice except to withdraw; Britain could not face the reopening of the Egyptian Question without a single Great Power on her side.

As long as we assumed responsibility for the government of Egypt, the Capitulations were like a noose round our neck, which any Great Power, having rights under the Capitulations, could tighten at will. In this case the noose had been roughly jerked by Germany.[78]

The indifference of British entrepreneurs, the German ulti-matum, and the growing unpopularity of H.M. Ambassador's championship of minority rights, combined to put Britain out of the running for the new Baghdad Railway scheme. In any

76. Smith, *The Embassy of Sir William White*, pp. 115, 128.
77. The contrast between the methods used by both Embassies at this period emerges very clearly from Harold Nicolson, *Sir Arthur Nicolson, Bart., First Lord Carnock* (London, 1930), pp. 94–96.
78. Grey, *Twenty-five Years*, I, 9–11.

case, the British Government was at first inclined to regard a *German* undertaking of this kind with some favour; it would help to develop the Turkish interior by bringing trade, political stability, and, perhaps, reform, and it might act as a deterrent to further Russian encroachments in the area. But by the end of the '90s it was becoming clear that there were good political and commercial reasons for a British share in the line. *The Economist*, though unsympathetic about participation, reported in March 1900 that in the bustle of Constantinople, where Germans and Russians were jockeying for position on railway concessions, English capitalists and politicians were beginning to ask why we should not chime in and why H.M. Government was so indifferent to what promised to become the line of communication between Europe and Asia?[79]

The British Ambassador (Sir Nicholas O'Conor), worried at last at the prospect of an entirely non-British line with a *débouché* on the Persian Gulf, successfully communicated his anxiety to Lord Lansdowne, the Foreign Secretary. In a minute of April 1902 Lansdowne strongly urged British government participation in the railway, explaining how unfortunate it would be if such a railway were to be constructed without some British control. He agreed that it would be most unusual for the Government to invest public money in such a project, but felt that Government ownership of a certain number of shares seemed the only way of securing a voice in the control of the railway.[80] Investment of public money proved altogether too drastic a remedy to be acceptable to the Cabinet, but after some difficulty the Foreign Office was able to persuade a group of British capitalists (headed, at the request of the British Government, by Lord Revelstoke of Baring Bros.) to begin negotiations with the Germans. The approach could not have been worse-timed. The Germans were quite willing to negotiate, but there was powerful opposition from the British public, from the Government's own back-benchers, and even from the most influential member of the Cabinet, Joseph Chamberlain, whose views at the time were strongly anti-German. Germany's unpopular attitude to the Boer War had been compounded by her behaviour during the Anglo-German coercion of Venezuela

79. *The Economist*, 24 March 1900, 414.
80. Quoted in Lord Newton, *Lord Lansdowne* (London, 1929), p. 251.

in the winter of 1902–3; and the British press made some additional headway with the argument that British capital would
merely be strengthening Germany's political position in rivalry
with our own. Some opposition was to be expected from local
British interests in the area, notably Messrs. Lynch whose shipping business would be endangered by railway competition. But
there is no evidence that this weighed much one way or the
other with the British Government at the time,[81] the motives
of which were explained clearly enough by the Prime Minister
in his speech to the Commons of 8 April 1903. Defending the
Government's proposals against what he admitted to be the
strong counter-arguments of previous speakers, A. J. Balfour
pointed out that, whatever the British Government might be
able to do to delay construction, the railway would ultimately
be completed, with or without us. He claimed that there were
three points on which the House would have to make up its
mind; first, whether it was desirable that the shortest route to
India should be exclusively in the hands of German and
French capitalists; second, whether the Persian Gulf trade
terminus should or should not be in a territory, Kuwait, which
we had under our special protection; and third, whether we
should exclude ourselves from taking advantage of the very rich
country which was to be opened by the railway. He concluded
with the observation that on the whole it was in our interest in
this area that 'countries which certainly we cannot absorb
should not, on the other hand, be completely absorbed by
either one or two other Powers; and I should have thought that
this great international highway had better be in the hands of
three great countries than in those of two or one'.[82]

The uncertain tone in which Balfour had presented his
arguments made the withdrawal of H.M. Government's
support for British participation predictable. A fortnight later,
on 23 April, Balfour announced in answer to a Question in the
House that the Government had been unable to accept the
proposed international control as an adequate safeguard to
British interests, and could not, therefore, offer the assurances
on the Indian mails, the facilities at Kuwait, and appropriation

81. This conclusion has recently been confirmed in M. S. Anderson, *The
Eastern Question 1774–1923* (London, 1966), p. 265 n.
82. 120 *Parl.Deb.4s*.1372–4.

of the Turkish Customs revenue, in return for which British participation had been invited.[83]

Although, in 1903, the cause of those wishing—like Lansdowne—to participate in the Baghdad Railway was lost, the agitation for a reversal of this policy began almost at once. British merchants at Constantinople were worried that despite the terms of the concession (by which preferential rates were forbidden) German goods might still be conveyed to the new markets at specially favourable rates by arrangement between the German Levant Steamship Line and the Baghdad Railway Company.[84] The Foreign Office, in turn, was well aware of the long tradition of British trade in and with the Mesopotamian region (dating back to the foundation of the first English factory at Basra in the seventeenth century), and of the fact that the trade of Baghdad and Basra, which was predominantly in the hands of British and Indian merchants, was valued at £2,500,000 in 1903.[85] But the first interest of H.M. Government—concealed under a commercial veneer to avoid upsetting the Turks—was political. The Committee of Imperial Defence recorded the conclusion, at a meeting on 12 April 1905, that it was important that England should take a share in any extension of the Railway as far as the Persian Gulf 'with a view to insuring the effective neutralisation of the terminus'.[86] H.M. Government, as Lansdowne had declared emphatically in his statement of 5 May 1903, was not prepared to accept any radical disturbance of the *status quo* in the Gulf; and the British Government's position had been put very clearly in a confidential Memorandum prepared at the Foreign Office on 27 November 1906 for communication to M. Isvolski. The Memorandum declared that H.M. Government did not consider the Railway in its present stage to be of more than commercial importance, but that if that Railway were developed into a through line of communication between Europe and the Persian Gulf, it would raise political questions:

In these circumstances it would, H.M.G. consider, be desirable if an arrangement could be arrived at whereby Great Britain, Russia

83. 121 *Parl.Deb.4s.*222.
84. *The Economist*, 30 April 1904, 742.
85. Foreign Office Memorandum, June 1907: No. 250, *B.D.O.W.*,VI,356.
86. *B.D.O.W.*,VI,325 (editorial note).

and France, as well as Germany, might have an opportunity of participating in the undertaking.[87]

The Young Turk Revolution of 1908 provided the opportunity for renewed pressure for some form of British participation, but only if the railway were to be extended from Baghdad to the Persian Gulf. Sir Edward Grey's attitude was primarily defensive. He was not concerned with finding profitable outlets for British capital; as he told Sir Gerard Lowther in a private letter, 14 July 1909, he was much more anxious to secure British interests against damage by the construction of the Baghdad Railway than to obtain special advantages for Britain.[88] H.M. Government was aware of the difficulty of persuading British capitalists—short of a British government guarantee—to put their money either into a railway between Baghdad and the Persian Gulf or into one connecting Mesopotamia with the Mediterranean at Alexandretta by way of the Euphrates Valley and Aleppo. But the political importance of both routes was so great that in 1909 the Foreign Office seems to have accepted the expediency of a guarantee. On instructions from London, Sir Gerard Lowther called on the Grand Vizier in September and asked him whether the Turkish Government would be disposed to grant in principle a concession to a British syndicate to build two such lines. Lowther added that 'should such a concession be granted, a substantial syndicate would be forthcoming without delay to discuss details with the Ottoman Government'.[89]

Lowther's attempt to forestall the Germans seems to have come to nothing, and the impression that the Foreign Office papers give for the following years is one of a growing and resigned acceptance of German construction of the entire line as far as Basra, combined with a rear-guard action to protect what could be saved of the one-time trading and strategic paramountcy of Great Britain in the area. When Sir Gerard Lowther proposed, on 7 February 1911, to take joint action with the French in demanding a part in the completion of the line as far as Baghdad, Mr. Alwyn Parker (the Foreign Office Clerk most associated with the railway negotiations) minuted

87. No. 241, ibid., 350.   88. *B.D.O.W.*,VI,374.
89. No. 274, ibid., 376-7.

that the line was being built to Baghdad in pursuance of an international agreement concluded in 1903, and that we had 'no legal right whatsoever' to intervene or protest against the fulfilment of such an agreement; his immediate superior, Mr. R. P. Maxwell, added that 'our main interest lies in the Gulf section'.[90] It was not clear as yet whether the prolongation of the railway to the Gulf would be of commercial importance, and Foreign Office officials felt that any British syndicate which could be interested in the line would have to be assisted financially by the British Government. Sir Edward Grey, therefore, had no wish to press for the extension of the railway; his concern was to make sure that, if the railway *were* to be extended to touch the Gulf, it would (as he told M. Cambon, the French Ambassador) 'do so at a place and under conditions such that the present strategic position would not be prejudiced'.[91]

By 1912, when it became obvious that the Railway was planned to extend only as far as Basra (which was still some distance from the Gulf), Grey was prepared to drop the proposal for British participation in the financing or construction even of the Baghdad/Basra extension. 'We are now satisfied', he told the French and Russian Ambassadors on 21 May 1913, 'that, if the Railway does not go beyond Basra, we need not regard it as being prejudicial to British interests, and we need not oppose it'.[92] There were three conditions on which he continued to insist, and which formed the basis of the negotiations culminating in the Anglo-German Convention of June, 1914. The first was the maintenance of the *status quo* in the Persian Gulf; the second was the point which had been emphasized throughout, the need to protect British trade against differential treatment on the line; the third was the survival, relatively uninjured, of the two major British financial interests in the area, the Smyrna-Aidin Railway and British riverain navigation on the Tigris and Euphrates. The second and third conditions were covered in the 1914 Convention, and the first was met by Article 3 by which both Governments agreed that they would not support a branch from Basra to the Persian Gulf unless in complete mutual agreement. When the German Government, a few months before, had attempted to reopen

90. Minutes on No. 11, *B.D.O.W.*,X,Pt.II,21.
91. No. 24, ibid., 37.   92. No. 77, ibid., 126.

negotiations for German participation in any final extension of the railway from Basra to the Gulf, Mr. Alwyn Parker had pointed out in a private letter to his opposite number at the German Embassy, Herr von Kühlmann, that if any Article to this effect were inserted, it would be absolutely indispensable that British predominance should be secured *expressis verbis*:

if you desire the article for Parliamentary reasons in Germany, we desire this qualification added for similar reasons here; and no exchange of secret notes respecting the qualification would serve our purpose. For we must be able to satisfy Parliament that this extension will be as indisputably 'British' as the Baghdad Railway is indisputably 'German'.[93]

The Foreign Office attitude to the Baghdad Railway can be summed up, then, under two headings; the preservation of British political and strategic interests in the Persian Gulf, and the protection of the existing trading and financial interests of British subjects in Mesopotamia. In the event, the first motive played the larger part in determining policy, but the second was always borne in mind and the Anglo-German Convention did what it could to secure it.

As for the theory that the British Government was forced by London capitalists or local British interests into an active policy of securing new outlets for trade and finance in Mesopotamia, nothing could have been further from the truth. It was as much as the Government could do to protect the position which British trade had already obtained for itself, and it proved impossible, without guarantees, to interest British capital. The old accusation that Messrs. Lynch exercised a formidable influence on British Government policy in Mesopotamia keeps recurring,[94] but the truth of the relationship is far less exciting. British ships had been granted the right to navigate the Euphrates and Tigris by the Firmans of 1834 and 1841, and in 1862 the trading firm, Messrs. Lynch, had formed a company to run steamers on the rivers. The Company

93. No. 224, ibid., 356. The text of the Anglo-German Convention is printed as an Enclosure in No. 249, ibid., 398–402.
94. One of the more recent examples is to be found in Professor Zaki Saleh's absurd work, *Mesopotamia (Iraq) 1600–1914, a Study in British Foreign Affairs* (Baghdad, 1957), p. 191; but more respectable authorities have made the same assumption (for example: Moon, *Imperialism and World Politics*, p. 246).

received some support from the Government of India as a useful means of communication, and since it alone represented British interests on the Tigris and the Euphrates, H.M. Government felt an obligation to protect its existing rights. But the obligation was never felt to extend to protection irrespective of local Turkish interests; 'the object of means of communication', as Grey noted in 1909 in a minute on the Company's rights, 'is to develop a country not to block the development', and he went on to consider with complete equanimity the possibility of the Lynch concession being dropped altogether.[95] The proposed extension of the Baghdad Railway to Basra was likely to prove sharply competitive with British riverain navigation. The Foreign Office realized this, but it warned the German Government to treat anything Mr. H. F. B. Lynch said 'with great circumspection'. Lynch had no authority to negotiate with the Germans about the railway, and the solution favoured by the British Government was a joint Anglo-Turkish Company, with Lord Inchcape as the concessionaire. Again this was no case of pressure from London capitalists; quite the reverse. Lord Inchcape, who had been persuaded into taking on the enterprise by the Foreign Office, told Mr. Parker after a five-hour meeting with Hakki Pasha and British officials at the Foreign Office in December 1913 that 'he was very much disgusted with the whole matter, he could make more profit by bargaining in regard to a single ship to be built for British India than he would out of this concession in a whole year, and he had wasted so much time over the draft during the last six months that he had definitely decided to throw up the whole business if a settlement was not reached within ten days'.[96] The settlement *was* reached, but it derived from the anxiety of British and Turkish officials, and not at all from the commercial ambitions of the Peninsular and Oriental Steam Navigation Company.

*   *   *

Whether it was in trade, contracts, mining concessions or communications, the British Government in Turkey was prepared to protect but not to lead. It regarded its duty as fulfilled

95. Minute on No. 281, *B.D.O.W.*,VI,383-4.
96. Minute by Mr. Parker, 3 December 1913, on No. 183, *B.D.O.W.*,X, Pt.II,276.

if it could preserve fair and equal trading conditions, and even these might have to be sacrificed for political reasons in an area of strategic importance, or for humanitarian reasons in defence of Turkish minorities. The search for 'equal favour and open competition' drew H.M. Government into the international struggle for Turkish contracts and concessions, especially after the Young Turk Revolution of 1908. But this diplomatic activity was merely a realistic extension of an existing policy: a policy which had always included the obligation—subject only to the political security of the Empire and the official conception of international morality—to safeguard equality of opportunity for British trade and finance overseas.

It is, of course, true that an international crime can be committed as easily in the name of equality as it can in the interests of monopoly. The point is not to lay any special claims for the 'morality' of British policy in Turkey, but simply to explain the direction in which the general interests of British finance and trade influenced that policy, and the limits to the influence they were able to exert. The dangerous competitive conditions existing after the mid-'80s, and the growing diplomatic rivalry at the Porte for contracts, concessions and any kind of commercial or financial favour, certainly compelled H.M. Government to modify its *laissez-faire* tradition. But in Turkey, in contrast to what had become the case in some parts of contemporary Africa and the Far East, this modification never went so far as to suggest the need for a substantial change in British policy. It is clear that while H.M. Government remained conscious of its duty to protect British financial and commercial interests, the overriding considerations in forming British policy in Turkey were strategic, political, and humanitarian.

CHAPTER 3
PERSIA

THE GOVERNMENT of India, in a despatch dated September 1899, summarized Anglo-Indian interests in Persia under four headings: commercial, political, strategical, and telegraphic. The commercial interest was an annual trade of about £3½ million and a considerable investment of British capital. Political interest was originally almost exclusively Indian, but the widening circle of European politics and trade had included the future of Persia as part of the general Eastern Question. As for strategy, the Persian question was of such magnitude as to affect not merely the destinies of the British dominion of India but those of the entire Empire. And telegraphic communications through Persia were of interest and importance both to India and to the United Kingdom.[1]

The despatch, though it listed commerce and capital first, characteristically placed the main emphasis on political and strategic interests. But it was the confusion of commerce, finance, politics, and strategy which has led Professor Overstreet to describe the Anglo-Russian 'partition' of Persia as 'growing directly out of the interests or apparent interests of British and Russian investing groups';[2] Walter Lippmann to characterize the activities of Russian and British officials in Persia as 'one of the meanest policies of destruction in modern history';[3] and Dr. Brockway to subtitle his thesis on Iran and the West 'A case study in modern imperialism'.[4]

* * *

British policy in Persia at the beginning of the nineteenth century—as the Government of India despatch suggested—had been determined and developed by the British in India. When

1. *B.D.O.W.*,IV,366.
2. H. A. Overstreet, 'Foreign Investment Relations', *Proceedings of the Academy of Political Science*, VII (1917), 118.
3. Walter Lippmann, *The Stakes of Diplomacy* (New York, 1915), p. 79.
4. T. P. Brockway,'Iran and the West: a case study in modern imperialism', Yale thesis, 1937.

Canning decided in 1822 to transfer the responsibility for the
Persian Mission to India, he pointed out that 'the objectives of
the intercourse with Persia are principally, if not purely,
Asiatick' and that the Mission was established for objects in
which India was more intimately concerned.[5] The Tehran
Legation remained for some years under the jurisdiction of the
India Office, but it was felt at the time that the British Minister
would carry more weight at Tehran if he spoke for the British
Government rather than for the East India Company, and the
Legation was returned to the Foreign Office in 1835. Malmesbury took the opportunity of the dissolution of the Company to
re-transfer the Legation to the India Office in 1858, because,
he argued, Britain's interest in Persia was founded on the position Britain occupied in India, and 'almost every matter which
may come under discussion between this country and Persia
more or less concerns the British Government in India.'[6] But it
was an argument which could not stand up to the new political
situation in Europe. Whatever political interest the British
Government might have had in Persia at the beginning of the
nineteenth century had its origin in the French threat to India.
By the 1830's it was clear that the real threat was to be found
in a Russian hegemony in the Straits, from which it was a
short step to fears of Russian ambitions in India. Puryear claims
that when Britain broke off diplomatic relations with Persia in
June 1838, Palmerston was already aiming at an Anglo-Persian
treaty which would make Persia serve as a defensive barrier for
India.[7] Malmesbury felt that this problem could be met perfectly adequately by the India Office, but his successor, Lord John
Russell, found the arrangement unworkable; Persian affairs,
he explained, were now the concern of France, Russia, and
Turkey as well as ourselves and it was important that they
should be dealt with in the context of Eastern affairs as a whole.[8]
The Legation returned yet again to the Foreign Office in 1859,
but in recognition of the strong interest which the Government

5. Quoted by M. E. Yapp, 'The Control of the Persian Mission, 1822–1836',
University of Birmingham Historical Journal, VII (1959–60), 164–5.
6. No. 1, *Correspondence respecting the Transfer of the Persian Mission to the Foreign
Office*, P.P.1870(c.105)LXX.
7. Puryear, *International Economics and Diplomacy in the Near East*, p. 66.
8. Russell to Sir C. Wood, 31 October 1859: No. 3, *Correspondence respecting
the Transfer of the Persian Mission to the Foreign Office*, P.P.1870(c.105)LXX.

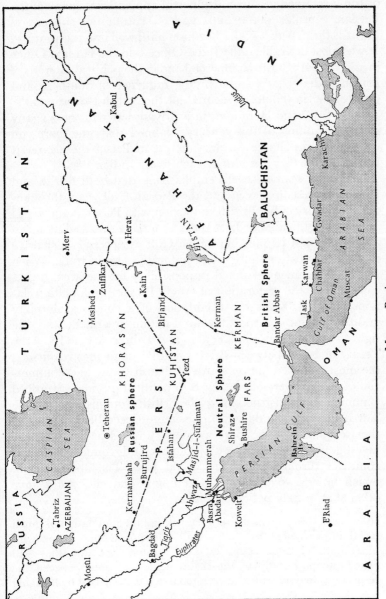

Map 2   Persia, 1914

of India retained in Persia, India still appointed to many of the Persian consular posts, and made a substantial subvention towards the expenses of the Legation until well into this century. It was most desirable—the India Office told the Foreign Office in 1887 —both in the commercial and in the political interests of British India that 'a commanding influence in Southern and Central Persia should be secured for the British Government',[9] and Lord George Hamilton, in a private letter to the Viceroy at the beginning of this century, claimed that 'the more you investigate the sources of our interest in Persia the clearer it becomes that they are almost exclusively Indian'.[10]

The point scarcely needs emphasizing that both British and Indian interests in Persia and the Persian Gulf were, throughout the history of the British connexion with Persia, commercial as well as political. The East India Company saw its diplomacy at Tehran and its policing of the Gulf as necessary defensive measures, but it was interested, naturally, also in trade. When H.M. Government assumed responsibility for the area, a precondition of the restoration of Anglo-Persian diplomatic relations after 1838 was the negotiation of a commercial treaty granting reciprocal most-favoured-nation treatment and the right to appoint consuls at Tehran and Tabriz. Article IX of the Treaty of Peace between Britain and Persia in 1857 reaffirmed the most-favoured-nation status of British trade, and commercial objectives were often tacked to political missions. Stratford Canning, in his instructions to the British Commissioner on the Turco-Persian Boundary Commission, 9 December 1848, asked the Commissioner to spare as much time as he could for the investigation of the natural products and commerce of the countries through which he would pass. The operations in which he was to take part, Canning explained, would have other than purely political results:

It is reasonable to expect that they will lay the foundation of much social improvement to be gradually developed among the wild inhabitants of those countries, at the same time that they will contribute powerfully to the maintenance of peace between the respective Governments. Nor is it too much to hope that by bringing

9. Quoted by Mahmood Ali Daud, 'British Relations with the Persian Gulf, 1890–1902', London thesis, 1957, p. 25.
10. Quoted in Greaves, *Persia and the Defence of India*, p. 42.

the local features and natural productions of a region hitherto little or at all frequented by intelligent travellers to the notice of the civilized world, your Commission may assist in extending the sphere of useful knowledge, and eventually in opening new channels of commercial intercourse.[11]

The opening of new areas to trade—in Persia as elsewhere in the world—was considered a legitimate function of H.M. Government. But the trade, once opened, was to be available on equal terms to all trading nations, and whatever restrictions were later to be applied to the allocation of loans or concessions in Persia, equal trading opportunities remained an axiom of British diplomacy. 'Diplomaticus' was speaking for British policy in general when he claimed (in an article on Persia in The *Asiatic Quarterly Review*) that 'English influence, wherever it is exerted, is in favour of free trade, and it asks for itself neither protection nor advantages which are not equally offered to all the world.' Although *other* countries, he continued, were becoming more Protectionist and seeking to exclude trading rivals from the new markets they acquired, this was not the case with Britain. With the closing of so many markets to British trade, with the increasing pressure of population, with our own colonies closing their doors to British emigration and raising protective tariffs against our manufactures, it was becoming of supreme importance to make sure that Britain secured a fair share of the new markets which were being opened in Asia and Africa, but 'we do not desire to exclude our rivals, and are content with obtaining such a position as to ensure our not being excluded by them'.[12]

Trade and politics, then, together formed the foundations of British interest in Persia, complicated in and after the 1890's by rivalry in international finance. The problem is to distinguish between the three as factors in British policy.

Persia was never the site of armed conflict between the Powers. In the later period of Nasr-ed-din's reign (that is, the last two decades of the century), what had once been a direct and open political rivalry between Russia and Britain was

11. Inclosure in No. 2, *Correspondence respecting the Demarcation of the Frontier between Turkey and Persia*, P.P.1865(3504)LVII.
12. Diplomaticus, 'The Imperial Bank of Persia', *Asiatic Quarterly Review* (October, 1889), 245.

translated into commercial and financial rather than military terms: the rivalry, so far as the governments were concerned, was still primarily political, but its aspect was now 'outwardly economic'.[13] Sir Edward Grey later acknowledged that Russian influence in Persia was more likely to have been the result of the momentum of Russia's own weight and the corresponding weakness of Persia than of a deliberate design to advance on the Indian frontier. But by the first decade of this century each new concession or extension of Russian influence increased British fears that at any time the Foreign Office might find itself confronted with a *fait accompli* in Persia, which British interests would require it to resist—a situation, as Grey said, which was 'very unpleasant to contemplate':

British policy in Persia was therefore constantly in opposition to Russia; it was not a forward policy pushed for the purpose of extending British territory or influence. Its object was to keep Persia as a buffer State and to maintain it as an independent country.[14]

In Persia, as in Turkey, the Foreign Office felt that the best chance of preserving independence lay in the improvement of Persian communications, the encouragement of international trade and commercial enterprise, and the creation of a Persian financial system. If this could be achieved, not only would the Persian State itself be strengthened, but an international vested interest would be created in the preservation of the *status quo*. In an effort to reduce tension and speed Persian development, Salisbury was even prepared to consider some form of unofficial agreement between Russia and Britain on the areas of Persia in which their major effort should lie. Britain, he told Morier at St. Petersburg, 21 February 1888, was interested above all in trade with the Southern provinces and in their communications with the Persian Gulf; Russia was naturally more concerned with promoting commerce over her frontier in the north. There was plenty of room for both without their rivalry degenerating into conflict, and the private enterprise of both would benefit by Persian progress and the development of her resources.[15] Sir

13. Sir Arnold T. Wilson, *The Persian Gulf* (London, 1928), pp. 257–8.
14. Grey, *Twenty-five Years*, I, 153–4.
15. Salisbury's despatch is paraphrased in A. P. Thornton's 'British Policy in Persia, 1858–1890 Pt. II,' *English Historical Review*, LXX (1955), 57–58.

Henry Drummond Wolff (the new British Minister at Tehran) emphasized still further the political advantages of concord in his 'very confidential' letter to his Russian colleague, Prince Dolgorouki, the following June. Wolff felt that by establishing Persian prosperity and developing her resources Britain and Russia would be able to interpose a neutral territory between their frontiers which would remove the present uncertainty and friction. A project on these lines would serve to complement the recent Russo-British arrangement regulating the Afghan frontier.[16]

Salisbury's appointment of Drummond Wolff, one of our most active and energetic diplomatists, reflected his anxiety about the rivalry with Russia and his belief in the need to promote the development of Persia as an independent, prosperous zone of neutrality between the Russian and Indian frontiers. Wolff's instructions were to establish 'the integrity of Persia, the development of its resources, and the maintenance of a strong, independent, and friendly Government',[17] and he interpreted these instructions as authorization to carry through Salisbury's proposal of a commercial entente with Russia and to give 'every encouragement' to European capitalists to establish themselves in Persia and develop its resources. The negotiations with the Russian Government failed, but Wolff was more fortunate elsewhere. He obtained an official Proclamation from the Shah on 25 May 1888 securing the property rights of Persian subjects; he achieved one of the most persistent of British diplomatic ambitions, the opening, on 30 October 1888, of the Karun River to navigation; and, on 30 January 1889, the concession of the Imperial Bank of Persia was signed, under his supervision, at Tehran. Until his health broke down in 1891, Wolff continued his efforts to convince the Shah of the need to employ foreign capital (not necessarily British) in developing the national resources, while at the same time he laboured to interest European capitalists in the possibilities which were opening out for them in Persia.

Dr. Brockway may, in part, be right in claiming that during the so-called 'Persian Bubble' of 1888–92 'the British Govern-

16. Sir Henry Drummond Wolff, *Rambling Recollections* (London, 1908), II, 347.
17. ibid., p. 337.

ment not only made no effort to check the debauch of ill-advised promotion but was itself in considerable part responsible for it'.[18] But Wolff's motives were not to reap profits for British finance but to attract foreign capital, of whatever nationality, as a vital contribution to increased Persian stability. British government support for the Imperial Bank of Persia's concession was founded on precisely the same reasoning. In general, H.M. Government avoided the implied responsibility of a Royal Charter, but a special exception was made in the case of the Imperial Bank. Lord Salisbury, arguing the case to the Treasury, pointed to the critical condition of Persia; if Persia's resources were not developed, he said, the decay would continue, and it would be only a matter of years before she would be absorbed by a powerful neighbour. If, however, she could increase her wealth and, above all, develop her communications, she could still avoid Russian subjugation. But present diplomatic conditions made it improbable that foreign capital would be employed in Persian railways. The only hope lay with native enterprises, 'nominally at least' supported by native capital, and the only possibility of capital accumulation in Persia lay through the medium of a successful banking system.[19]

The Imperial Bank never fulfilled these expectations, and Baster's conclusion that 'its moderate results in the commercial sense were in inverse relation to its effectiveness as a political weapon'[20] was unfortunately correct. But the British Government's motives in promoting the Bank and in recommending the grant of a Royal Charter (which had ensured that its issue was seven times oversubscribed) were not to ease the inflow of British capital, but to develop—in the face of a Russian veto on foreign railway construction in Persia—adequate native capital resources for railway construction within Persia itself.

The oversubscription of the Imperial Bank issue encouraged a number of other promotors to put forward proposals and to apply for concessions, but there is no evidence that Drummond Wolff went out of his way to support them. Brockway claims that it was Wolff who secured Major Talbot's concession of

18. T. P. Brockway, 'Britain and the Persian Bubble, 1888–92', *Journal of Modern History*, XIII (1941), 44.
19. Quoted in Greaves, *Persia and the Defence of India*, p. 176.
20. Baster, *The International Banks*, p. 125.

May 1890 for a fifty-year monopoly of the buying, selling, and manufacturing of Persian tobacco. The concession, which Talbot sold to the newly formed Imperial Tobacco Company of Persia, was for the establishment of a Tobacco Régie over the whole of Persia, staffed and run by the Company. The unpopularity of the Régie with the tobacco merchants and the Mollahs was such that it proved unworkable, and the concession was cancelled unilaterally by the Shah. The Talbot Tobacco Concession was one of the more scandalous concessions of the day, but there is no evidence to support the claim that the British Minister at Tehran had anything directly to do with it. He would certainly have known about Major Talbot's existence: Talbot's brother was a Major A. C. Talbot, an Indian political officer who, though not in Persia at the time, had long experience in the Persian Gulf and was later to serve as the Political Representative of the Indian Government in Persia; and the Talbots were related to Salisbury. Talbot must have had some contact, even if only social, with the Tehran Legation, and A. P. Thornton describes him, in fact, as a friend of Wolff. But Wolff denied having had anything to do with the actual concession; and his denial was twice repeated and confirmed by the Under-Secretary of State (Mr. Lowther) who explained quite categorically that the concession had been obtained from the Persian Government 'without the intervention of Her Majesty's Government, or their knowledge'.[21] Indeed, H.M. Government was instrumental in persuading the Company first to moderate its claims in Persia and then to relinquish the concession altogether; and such support as it gave to the Company's claims was granted *after* the cancellation, on the grounds that 'the concession was cancelled by the Shah for reasons not connected with any act or default of the Company, and under promise of compensation'.[22] Even *this* degree of support was bitterly criticized in the Commons. Mr. James Bryce pointed out that the Government's action seemed to be in contradiction to the sound principle of extreme caution laid down by Lord Granville in 1881 and Lord Rosebery in 1886 and followed subsequently

21. Greaves, *Persia and the Defence of India*, p. 183; 3 *Parl.Deb.4s.*1390–1 (26 April 1892), and 4 *Parl.Deb.4s.*1947 (26 May 1892).
22. Salisbury to Lascelles, 3 March 1892: No. 86, *Correspondence respecting the Persian Tobacco Concession*, P.P.1892(c.6707)LXXIX.

by both political parties.[23] Bryce's opposition to official concession-mongering was endorsed by the other speakers on the
Tobacco Monopoly, with only the Under-Secretary of State
defending the Government.

* * *

The failure of the Talbot Concession, the restriction on
foreign railway construction which followed a Russo-Persian
Agreement of 1887, the early difficulties of the Imperial Bank of
Persia, and the liquidation of the Persian Bank Mining Rights
Corporation in 1894, put Persian speculations out of the market
for at least a decade. In any case, British overseas investors had
burnt their fingers in the Baring Crisis at the beginning of the
'90s, and foreign speculative investment (apart from West
Australian and South African gold mines) was experiencing one
of its quieter phases. The Russian Legation, aided by the
proximity of Tehran to the Russian frontier and its distance
from the Gulf, came to exercise a commanding influence over
the Shah, and it was only with difficulty that the British
Government was able to maintain its position in the South.
Trade figures right up to the First World War show a steady
relative decline in the British share of Persian trade. Russia's
trade with Persia in 1898 was estimated at £1,788,500, British
and Indian combined at £1,379,000. By 1904, Russian trade
had reached £5½ million and, by 1914, £12 million; British
trade was £2½ million and £4½ million respectively.[24]

Britain kept her overwhelming superiority in the Gulf trade,
but her position in the interior of Persia, even in the South, was
increasingly threatened. Mr. Joseph Walton moved Amend-
ments to the Address both in 1902 and in 1903 in which he
called attention to the need for more government assistance in
the promotion of trade in Persia. Britain should, he said, join
with the Indian Government in guaranteeing loans for the
construction of roads from the Gulf to the interior of Persia to
facilitate British trade, 'in the same way that the Russian
Government have constructed three roads down from the north

23. 4 *Parl.Deb.4s.*1954-5.
24. These figures are derived from Gholam Reza Nikpay, 'The Political
Aspects of Foreign Oil Interests in Iran down to 1947', London thesis, 1956,
p. 141 n.

of Persia in the interests of Russian trade'. It was time to 'unite in urging a more vigorous and determined effort on the part of the Government to uphold British commercial interests in Persia and elsewhere'.[25] The British Consul for Seistan and Kain went so far as to recommend that some British firm of standing should be given a subsidy to trade on the eastern frontier; if some such arrangement could not be arrived at, British trade would not only be unable to regain its former position in the market, but would find it impossible to retain whatever share it could still command.

This, in view of Russia's extreme, and ever-increasing, commercial activity in both Khorasan and Seistan, and the close association which such commercial supremacy bears to political predominance, is a state of affairs which cannot but be regarded with anxiety.[26]

But there was little that the British Government could do, or felt able to do, directly for British trade, apart from securing fair treatment. The interest of the Tehran Legation was concentrated first on a petty war with the Russian Legation over Persian loans and then on the larger question of the development of Persian communications.

During the '90s the Russians had achieved a near monopoly of loans to the Persian Government, and, in doing so, had strengthened their political influence at Tehran still further. Sir Arthur Hardinge, the British Minister in Persia 1900–5, believed that the British influence could only be restored, and our position even maintained, *after* we had recovered our right to lend money to Persia—'once that is regained, everything else follows: as it is, we are ploughing the sands'. Persian Ministers, he claimed, understood only two things, force and money; with money one could do anything with them.[27] In the name, therefore, of the Imperial Bank of Persia—which, the Foreign Office explained to the Law Officers, was 'the only agency through which Her Majesty's Government can acquire the influence to be derived from placing the Persian Government under financial

25. 101 *Parl.Deb.4s.*586–7 (22 January 1902), and 118 *Parl.Deb.4s.*217–18 (18 February 1903).

26. Macpherson to the Secretary to the Government of India, 10 May 1904: P.R.O.,F.O/83/2152.

27. Hardinge to Lansdowne, 6 January 1902: quoted in Newton, *Lord Lansdowne*, p. 235.

obligations'[28]—the British Government and the Government of India made a series of loans to the Persian Government in 1903-4 and again in 1912-13. Sir Arthur Hardinge, at any rate, was convinced of their value. In a despatch to Lansdowne in June 1905, he noted with satisfaction that:

the advances which we have made and can continue in various ways to make to the Shah through his State Bank [the Imperial Bank of Persia] have broken the back of the financial monopoly and control with all its far reaching results, which Russia fancied her loan contracts had given her.[29]

Of course, the Imperial Bank gained by these transactions, but Persian loans were essentially inter-Government transactions which were intended to promote purely political objectives, and in which private capitalists were interested marginally if at all.

In contrast, H.M. Government's promotion of Persian communications had more of an eye for commercial advantage, though the objectives were still very largely political. The extension of British trade into the interior of Persia could only follow the development of an adequate system of communications. The position of Russia on Persia's northern frontier, so close to Tehran, gave her merchants a trading advantage in Persia's richest markets which British merchants found difficult to match. The opening of the Karun River to navigation had, therefore, both for trading and strategic reasons formed one of the principal objectives of British diplomacy in Persia, and the same arguments applied to railway construction from the Persian Gulf into the interior. At the same time, it was important to secure that, if and when Persian railways were built, their routes and tariff structure would give British and Indian trade equal advantages with the trade of all other interested nations.

These in themselves were strong arguments for a British interest in Persian railways, but even stronger were those which turned on political considerations. Throughout the Middle East, in Asiatic Turkey and in Persia, the main railway projects had fundamentally political objectives—'They are all "political" lines', Arnold Wilson wrote in 1911, 'not one of them will ever pay; whatever the promoters may say not one will be built

28. No. 19, *Reports by the Law Officers of the Crown, 1903*, F.O.,C.P.8168.
29. *B.D.O.W.*,IV,373.

without a guarantee. It is a diplomatic game in which Russia
and Germany are playing the leading part. . . .'[30] Britain was
concerned, above all, with safeguarding the strategic interests
of India, and these interests could best be served, it seemed,
either by the active policy of railway promotion which Salisbury
had adopted in and after 1886, or by its complete opposite, a
negative attitude to *any* railway construction in Persia.

Salisbury's argument was that the conversion of Persia into a
state of vassalage to Russia could be avoided only by making it
possible for British troops to be moved rapidly to within striking
distance of the Russo-Persian frontier region; there would be
advantages, too, in meeting Russian aggression against India
within a buffer region, rather than over the frontier of India
itself. However, as the political difficulties in Persian railway
construction increased, it became obvious that the first priority
was to prevent Russia from securing a special position in Persian
railway construction rather than to press for the right to build
railways ourselves. A certain amount of lip-service continued to
be paid to the interests of British trade and the development of
Persia, but it seemed to officials that the political consequences
of a clash between Russia and Britain in Persia outweighed either
our own commercial interests or the interests of the Persians
themselves. In consequence, apart from a small Russian line
from the frontier to Tabriz (begun in 1913), no railways were
constructed in Persia before the First World War.

To return for a moment to the situation in the 1880's, H.M.
Government had shown its interest in Persian railways when
first the Liberal and then the Conservative Administrations of
1885 had considered giving official support to an Anglo-
German company planned by Baron Reuter to work his concession. Bismark refused to co-operate and the scheme came to
nothing, although Salisbury was prepared even to consider the
'rather grave pledge' of an Anglo-German guarantee both of
the concession and of the integrity of Persia.[31] The following
year the Shah, to everyone's surprise, seemed to accept the need
for rail and road communication from the Persian Gulf. Dr.
Greaves reports that the new Persian initiative converted the

30. In a letter dated 7 February 1911: quoted in Sir Arnold Wilson, *S.W.
Persia, a Political Officer's Diary 1907–1914* (London, 1941), p. 137.
31. Greaves, *Persia and the Defence of India*, pp. 95–100.

Foreign Office into the headquarters of a series of Persian railway conferences attended by Foreign Office and India Office
officials and by two capitalists, Sir William Mackinnon and Sir
George Mackenzie (who had been invited to provide professional advice on the costing of the schemes and the estimation of
returns). It became clear almost at once that without some form
of Government guarantee British capitalists were not going to
risk their money in Persian railways. But the interest of H.M.
Government—Dr. Greaves points out—was not in possible
opportunities for British capital, but in the political and economic consequences which would follow from railway construction; and when the Shah, in a less confident mood, requested
that the railway should be constructed by a neutral Power such
as the United States, the Foreign Office made no objections,
welcoming U.S. participation since 'the great thing is to get
the Railway made'. Negotiations with U.S. capitalists failed,
and the British schemes themselves were abandoned, blocked by
the reluctance both of H.M. Government and of the Government of India to guarantee a rate of interest on Persian railway
capital. In any case, the Shah's secret agreement with Russia
of September 1887, by which he pledged himself not to give
foreign railway or river navigation concessions before consulting
the Tsar, made the London discussions purely academic.[32]

Persian railway construction was halted by the secret agreement for at least a couple of decades. Russia had no surplus
capital for railway development outside her own frontiers, and
native capital, in spite of the Imperial Bank of Persia, never
developed to the stage of financing major projects of this kind.
H.M. Government's interest in Persian railways continued, but
there was little that could be done under the Russian veto. The
Shah was persuaded to address a rescript to his Minister for
Foreign Affairs on 16 September 1888, by which he agreed to
give priority to the British Government over others in the construction of a Southern railway, and in which he gave a 'positive
assurance' that no railway concession would be granted to
foreigners in the South without consultation with the British
Government[33] (it was to this, presumably, that Lansdowne

32. The whole episode is discussed by Dr. Greaves in *Persia and the Defence of
India*, pp. 144 ff.
33. Reported in n.3 to No. 697, *B.D.O.W.*,X,Pt.I,671.

referred when he claimed British rights in railway construction
in Southern Persia in his important statement of 5 May 1903).[34]
But the Shah had merely given an assurance; he had not undertaken to give, nor did he give, any immediate concessions. In
1905 the Imperial Defence Committee was still urging H.M.
Government 'to maintain, and if possible to increase, our influence in Tehran, in order that we may be able to control railway
construction in Persia, which is by far the most important factor
in the strategic situation. . .'.[35]

*   *   *

Persia in the early 1900's was the scene of a sharp battle
between Russia and Britain for political hegemony at Tehran,
fought principally with economic weapons. Russia, on the
whole, had the upper hand, but H.M. Government, through
the medium of the Imperial Bank of Persia, had had some
success in breaking down Russia's financial monopoly, and
serious efforts were being made to stem the increasing disparity
between the Russian and British share of Persian external
trade. A Foreign Office Memorandum on British policy in
Persia, dated 31 October 1905, reported that:

We have sought to foster British trade and influence by every means
at our disposal. We have encouraged by moral and financial assistance such enterprises as the Bakhtiari road, uniting Ahwaz with
Ispahan, the navigation of the Karun, and the efforts of the Persian
Transport Company to improve communications in Central Persia.
We have given the Imperial Bank a full measure of support and
have assisted them to establish their agencies in provincial towns.
We have extended the network of our Indo-European telegraphic
system.

And the Memorandum concluded that other projects with
similar aims, such as the formation of a native force to police the
southern roads, were still under consideration.[36]
But few could doubt the risk which both countries were
running in promoting a rivalry of this kind. Russian advances
towards the Indian frontier—Sir Edward Grey remarked in his

34. 121 *Parl.Deb.4s.*1350.
35. Quoted in Foreign Office Memorandum of 31 October 1905: *B.D.O.W.*,
IV,371.
36. *B.D.O.W.*,IV,372.

memoirs—were 'the most sensitive and dangerous' sector in Anglo-Russian relations in the Near and Middle East, and within this area, 'Persia was the danger-point'. No subject, Grey complained, tried his patience more while at the Foreign Office than Persia.[37]

Salisbury had, of course, suggested an Anglo-Russian commercial entente in Persia as early as 1888. A decade later India put forward a more positive proposal. In a discussion of the alternative policies available for keeping Russian ambitions in Persia in check, the Government of India argued that one such policy would be an agreement on the lines of the Anglo-Russian Agreement recently concluded for China; in China the Agreement had been confined to a division of spheres of interest for railways, but there seemed no reason why such an agreement for Persia should not be equally extended to mines, roads, and other industrial or economic undertakings. Such understandings were of great value because, although they made no mention of political influence, 'yet in eastern countries commercial and industrial enterprises are the familiar agencies through which political influence is exercised by alien powers, and that influence is apt to follow in the wake of railways and trade'.[38]

The political situation in Europe in the first years of the century further stimulated the search for an Anglo-Russian compromise agreement on all major points of friction, and it was obvious that the agreement would have to go beyond that suggested by the Government of India to cover problems of politics as well as of finance. Russia's defeat by Japan and the resignation of Curzon had reduced tension in India, but, as Grey explained to Spring-Rice (the British Minister at Tehran), the existing policy of supporting Persia against Russian advances —the success of which in any case was in doubt—would create responsibilities which, sooner or later, might oblige us to come to the assistance of Persia by force.[39] Spring-Rice, understandably, regarded the proposed Agreement as a betrayal of the Persians, but Grey was not prepared to 'keep up a quarrel

37. Grey, *Twenty-five Years*, I, 152, 153, 169.
38. Government of India to the Secretary of State for India, 21 September 1899: *B.D.O.W.*,IV,361.
39. No. 421, *B.D.O.W.*,IV,471.

with Russia in order to curry favour with the Persians'.[40]

The Anglo-Russian Convention of 31 August 1907 divided Persia into three sectors—a Russian sphere of influence in the north, a British sphere in the south, and a neutral sector in between. It was intended almost exclusively as a political instrument, and its commercial and financial provisions were drafted with this in mind. At the insistence of H.M. Government, the Preamble observed that both countries sincerely desired the permanent establishment in Persia of equal conditions and opportunities for the trade and industry of all other nations. Trade was to be unaffected and was to continue to be conducted on equal terms in all parts of Persia. But both Russia and Britain bound themselves to abstain from seeking or maintaining within each other's spheres, on their own account or on behalf of their nationals, any concessions of a political or commercial character (defined as *telles que les concessions de chemins de fer, de banques, de télégraphes, de routes, de transport, d'assurance etc.*'); existing concessions in the Russian and British spheres were to be respected. It was, Grey claimed, a self-denying ordinance; there could be no question of the two Governments claiming the exclusive privilege of exploiting their spheres, and third parties were 'in no way excluded from seeking for concessions throughout Persia'.[41]

The Convention was severely criticized in Britain because it appeared to surrender British commerce and finance in Persia to political convenience, and Grey admitted as much when defending it in the Commons. The first point in the minds of the negotiators, he said, was not its commercial but its strategical importance; a different Agreement more favourable to British commerce might have opened up a new land door through Seistan for the Russian advance on India. The whole understanding of the Agreement, in any case, was that trade advantages were to be equal throughout Persia, and that there would be no differential advantages on trade routes in favour of the nationals of those holding the concessions.[42] Grey knew very well that perfect equality of trade was unlikely in the new

40. Minute on Spring-Rice's private letter of 26 April 1907: No. 412, ibid., 458.
41. The text of the Convention is printed as Appendix I, ibid., 618–19. Grey's optimistic interpretation is in No. 421. ibid., 471.
42. 184 *Parl.Deb.4s.*481–6 (17 February 1908).

Russian sphere. But he accepted the Foreign Office argument that British traders and entrepreneurs who, during a hundred years of commercial predominance in Southern Persia, had secured only a concession for the navigation of the Karun, the construction of a road from Ahwaz to Ispahan and Teheran, and some telegraph lines, would be no worse off than before; and he felt prepared to argue privately that, as anyone behind the scenes knew, 'what we have gained strategically is real, while the apparent sacrifices we have made commercially are not real'.[43]

The 1907 Convention successfully averted direct, armed conflict between the Powers, but it did little, in the long run, to solve the problem of the expansion of Russian influence in Persia. Sumner points out, with reason, that Russia 'rode roughshod over the formula [in the Convention's Preamble] of the integrity and independence of Persia'. The growing threat which Germany was presenting to British interests in Europe made H.M. Government willing, for the sake of preserving the Anglo-Russian entente, to withdraw step-by-step in face of further Russian encroachments in Persia. The Russians, Sumner claims, were well aware of this, and he quotes in support Sazonow's remark to the Russian Minister at Tehran (8 October 1910) that 'the English in pursuing aims of vital importance in Europe will abandon in case of necessity certain interests in Asia only in order to maintain the convention with us which is so important for them'.[44]

Moreover, although the Convention had, on the whole, meant what it said when it claimed to maintain an Open Door for international *trade* in Persia, the *financial* declarations were an empty formula designed specifically to appease the Germans and the French. Even before the Convention had been concluded, the British and Russian Governments had acted together in lending money to Persia and in pressing for payment on the coupons. Regarding themselves at the time as having the monopoly in Persian Government loans, they were not prepared to accept encroachments by capitalists from other nations. In

43. Private letter to Sir Arthur Nicolson, 24 February 1908: No. 550, *B.D.O.W.*,IV,616.
44. B. H. Sumner, 'Tsardom and Imperialism in the Far East and Middle East, 1880–1914', *Proceedings of the British Academy*, XXVII (1941), 64.

March 1907, for example, they requested the French Government to discourage French bankers from lending money to
Persia without their concurrence.[45] Similarly, with respect to
concessions, Sir Arthur Nicolson had proposed in his first draft
of the Convention that both Governments should agree to
prevent third Powers from obtaining concessions throughout
Persia. Grey had not accepted this drafting, since he felt satisfied with a declaration that Russia and Britain should abstain
from seeking influence in each other's sectors. But he was prepared to approach the Persian Government, after the Convention had been concluded, with the request for an undertaking
that Persia would not grant any concessions of a 'political'
character to a third Power in the British sector, while Russia
could do the same for hers.[46] Nicolson, meanwhile, had assured
the Russian Foreign Minister (M. Isvolsky), in reply to his
question on the reaction of the other Powers to encroachments
on the Open Door in Persia, that—

It was quite true that we should not admit that other Powers
should seek for concessions in our district, and he knew well that
concessions for railways and other enterprises in countries such as
Persia carried more with them than appeared on the surface. But
I did not think that it was desired to shut the door to legitimate
commerce, and in any case throughout the whole of the rest of
Persia the door would be sufficiently wide open to any concessions
and trade which other Powers might wish to promote.[47]

The final draft of the Convention declared an Open Door for
concessions in neutral Persia, but Russia and Britain agreed to
support subjects of third Powers in the other's sector.

The political reins were tightened still further in April 1910.
The British and Russian Representatives at Tehran presented
a joint note to the Persian Government in which they declared
that while the Powers had no intention of limiting the rights of
foreign nationals to undertake purely commercial enterprises in
Persia, they could not admit that concessions should be granted
to the nationals of other foreign Powers *'qui puissent porter
atteinte à leurs intérêts politiques ou stratégiques en Perse'*.[48]

45. Grey to Sir F. Bertie, 16 March 1907: No. 399, *B.D.O.W.*,IV,443.
46. Private letter to Nicolson, November 1906: No. 307, ibid., 414.
47. Nicolson to Grey, 4 November 1906: No. 367, ibid., 409.
48. Quoted in Mr. Parker's minute of 18 October 1910: *B.D.O.W.*, X,Pt.I,
551.

This was intended to apply throughout Persia, neutral or not, and the Persian Government naturally wanted to know what the phrase meant. In a further explanatory note of 20 May, political and strategic concessions were defined as those connected with communications, telegraphs or ports, before the granting of which the Persian Government was requested to enter into an exchange of views with the two Powers so that their political and strategic interests might be safeguarded.[49]

The position of H.M. Government was made plain in an interesting series of Foreign Office minutes on Goschen's telegram from Berlin, 10 April 1910. Mr Alwyn Parker suggested in the first minute that H.M. Government should inform the Persian Government that it would regard the granting of concessions to third Powers for railway construction in Persia as an unfriendly act, since such concessions could have a damaging effect on vital political and strategic interests. But Eyre Crowe, at that time Chief Clerk, argued that while we had certain vital political and strategic interests in Persia which we would defend, apart from these and from our obligations to Russia we had no desire to stand in Germany's way in Persia—'The Persian door is open. Let her walk in.' Sir Charles Hardinge, the Permanent Under-Secretary, concluded that the best course to follow was to inform the German Government, if it made any further reference to Persia, that Britain had always maintained an Open Door for commercial purposes, but that we would strenuously resist any encroachments by the Persians themselves or by foreign Powers on our political and strategic interests. Grey added a final minute to the effect that he agreed generally with the course suggested.[50]

H.M. Government's policy in Persia followed this pattern for the remaining years before the First World War. Russia's sphere was respected, and British concessionaires who applied for concessions which might infringe on that sphere were told to consult St. Petersburg. There was no absolute veto on foreign investment in Persia. In the case of the proposed Trans-Persian line, H.M. Government was prepared to accept international capital provided that the control of the section which passed through the British sphere was firmly in British hands.

49. Quoted in No. 112, *B.D.O.W.*,X,Pt.II,166.
50. Minutes on No. 343, *B.D.O.W.*,VI,452–4.

But, at the same time, neither the British nor the Russian Governments gave foreign capital a warm welcome, and the tendency was to apply for concessions as a means of forestalling the Germans rather than as a genuine prelude to exploitation. The result, as far as Persian railways were concerned, was a complete stalemate. Neither the British nor the Russian Governments were willing to give a guarantee except in a real emergency. Russia was short of capital for her own development, and H.M. Government—always unwilling to give guarantees for railway construction abroad—felt a first obligation to the Colonies or to projects which promised real benefit to British trade. The Foreign Office gave what assistance it could to British railway concessionaires—one of Arnold Wilson's functions as a political officer in South-West Persia was to accompany a survey party (sent out by the Persian Railway Syndicate Ltd.) along the alignment for a proposed railway from the Persian Gulf to Burujird—but this assistance always stopped short of a guarantee, and without a guarantee there was no hope of raising capital for Persian railway development on the London money market.

*   *   *

There was only one area in which H.M. Government was prepared to enter into a firm financial commitment in Persia other than in government-to-government loans, and that was in oil. The existence of large quantities of oil on the shores of the Persian Gulf had long been suspected, and Sir Henry Drummond Wolff's experience of Persia had convinced him that more oil was to be found in the Turco-Persian frontier region above the Gulf. It so happened that William Knox D'Arcy, an Australian who had made his fortune in gold mines, decided to take out a concession for oil exploration in Persia. He sent his secretary to Tehran in 1901 to negotiate a concession with the Persian Government, equipped both with the standard letter of introduction from the Foreign Office and with what was to count for much more—a letter of introduction from Wolff to Sir Arthur Hardinge, recommending Mr. Marriott to his good offices. Hardinge, who had only recently taken up his post in Persia and who was only too anxious to break the Russian monopoly of influence at Tehran, took the opportunity to urge the application on the Grand Vizier. The Russian Minister at Tehran could not read Persian, and the concession (in Persian, of course) which gave D'Arcy exploration rights over most of the country was rushed through before his Secretary and translator returned to the city.[51]

Hardinge, no doubt, saw the concession as an episode in the Anglo-Russian rivalry in Persia; it promised a substantial British investment at the peak of Russian influence, when Russia seemed to have achieved an almost unassailable position at Tehran. The initial support for the concession—and much of the support which it continued to get—formed part of this battle between the Tehran Legations. When Persia was 'partitioned' in 1907, the D'Arcy interests became even more important politically, since they formed the only considerable British enterprise in the 'neutral' zone.

But a new factor was emerging which was to be decisive in gaining British Government support. In 1898 an Admiralty Committee had been appointed by the First Lord, Lord Selborne, to consider fuel-oil supplies for the Royal Navy, and the Committee soon became aware of the need for an independent supply of fuel, both from the point of view of keeping down monopoly prices and of guaranteeing British control. A few years later, in 1903, it became known around the City that D'Arcy, disappointed by the results of his explorations in Persia and running out of capital for further exploration, was considering selling-out to a large foreign syndicate. The Admiralty regarded the concession as promising, and persuaded Lord Strathcona and the Burmah Oil Company to form an exploration company to continue working the concession; as Mr. Pretyman (a member of the Board of Admiralty in 1903) told the Commons in the Persian Oil Debate of June 1914, it was only due to the Company to explain that 'this enterprise originated at the request of the Admiralty, and not from a purely commercial purpose'.[52]

The Admiralty took little part in the London activities of the exploration company after 1903, but British officials in Persia and on the Persian Gulf were active in protecting the company's interests. Twenty troopers of the 18th Bengal Lancers, for

51. Sir Arthur Hardinge, *A Diplomatist in the East* (London, 1928), pp. 278–9.
52. 63 *H.C.Deb.*5s.1190 (17 June 1914).

example, were sent to Persia in 1907, ostensibly as a reinforce-
ment of the consular guard at Ahwaz but in fact to protect the
D'Arcy exploration team at their drilling site in the foothills of
South West Persia. And interest, of course, increased after the
team struck oil in large quantities at Masjid-i-Sulaiman on 26
May 1908; Sir Percy Cox, H.M. Resident and Consul at
Bushire, played a principal part in obtaining the Abadan
refinery site concession for the Syndicate in 1909.[53]

The relationship between the Company and British officials
had its inconveniences. Arnold Wilson, who had commanded
the detachment of Lancers, complained in a letter of March
1909 that his position was becoming that of an agent for the
Company, rather than its adviser. He added that—

The relations of the Consulate and the Oil Company's people grow
daily more difficult. . . . The position of a Company which is working
under a Concession from one Government (Persian) but depends on
the goodwill of a provincial administration (Arab and Bakhtiari)
and the military support of a third (British and Indian), with a
head office in Glasgow, dealing with the Foreign Office (in London)
and a Foreign Dept. (Simla) through local officers (in Persia) is not
easy.

But a year later Wilson claimed that whatever happened to all
the other matters he had dealt with in that part of the world, he
would always be proud of having helped the Oil Company to
start on sound lines. Its position, 120 miles inland with the long
pipe-line to Abadan, committed H.M. Government ultimately
to intervention if it were in danger of being destroyed—'But we
also have general strategic interests, due to our responsibilities
in India, and the oil fields give us a good *locus standi*.'[54]

By this time, however, oil supplies for the Royal Navy were
becoming a much more urgent issue. In 1913 the Admiralty
began negotiations for a forward contract with the Anglo-
Persian Oil Company for the supply of large quantities of
oil-fuel. The superiority of oil fuel to coal was already recognized for light cruisers and destroyers, and the five new battle-
ships under construction for the 1912–13 programme were
fitted experimentally as oil-burners. The Company, which was

53. Philip Graves, *Sir Percy Cox* (London, 1941), p. 125.
54. Wilson, *S.W. Persia*, pp. 84, 212.

short of working capital, asked for advance payment, and Winston Churchill sent out an Admiralty Commission of Experts that autumn to investigate Persian oil resources. The Commission's report was favourable, but it concluded that if H.M. Government were to provide some assistance in raising the additional capital needed by the Company adequately to develop the concession, then it would be advisable to insist on a Government voice in the direction of the Company's general policy.[55] It was on the basis of this report that H.M. Government bought a controlling interest in the Company early in 1914. Churchill defended the decision by the argument that H.M. Government needed to secure an adequate source of supply under British control and to break the stranglehold of the great Standard Oil and Shell Groups over production and prices; the Foreign Office, the Admiralty, and the Government of India had already for many years given what support they could to the independent British oil producers in Persia, above all to prevent them being 'swallowed up by the Shell or by any foreign or cosmopolitan companies'. Persia, he continued, was particularly suitable because it was the only place in the world which offered an immediate supply of oil with definite future prospects; because Britain already had a special position in the area; because transport in peace and war presented no serious problems; and because 'neither the native Government nor the native inhabitants are capable of pursuing a prolonged and formidable policy of hostility towards us'.[56]

* * *

Political and strategic motives played so obvious a part in determining British policy in Persia that it is easy enough to ignore trade altogether. Drummond Wolff's efforts, clearly,

55. Paras. 40–42, *Final Report of the Slade Commission*, bound with the *Agreement with the Anglo-Persian Oil Company, Ltd.*, P.P.1914(Cd.7419)LIV.

56. 63 *H.C.Deb.5s.*1133–45 (17 June 1914). The Admiralty's reasons for entering into the Agreement are set out in full in an Explanatory Memorandum of 20 May 1914. These are summarized in the categorical statement that—'The grounds on which His Majesty's Government arrived at their decision to enter into the Agreement with the Anglo-Persian Oil Company are purely naval, viz., the imperative need of direct control of a reasonable proportion of the supply of oil fuel required for naval purposes.' The Memorandum is bound with the *Agreement with the Anglo-Persian Oil Company Ltd.*, P.P.1914(Cd.7419)LIV. See also, in this connexion, M. Jack, 'The Purchase of the British Government's Share in the British Petroleum Co., 1912–1914'. *Past and Present* (1968).

had been directed at the development of Persia's resources as
the surest path to stability and continued independence. The
support given to railway schemes since the 1880's was similar
in purpose, with the added military incentive of speeding troop
movements in an area of prime strategic interest to the Government of India. The Imperial Bank of Persia, while a commercial
failure, was a successful political instrument in the hands of
H.M. Government. British trade in South West Persia was
stimulated by the agents of H.M. Government in order to
counter the Russian tendency to encroach on the neutral zone.
British concessionaires were supported so that they could add
strength to British political influence. The oil interests had
government backing not because they promised profits to the
British capitalists, but because they were operating in areas of
political interest to Britain and India, and because their oil was
vital to national security.

But in the midst of all this—unquestionably political as it
was—H.M. Government continued so far as it could to uphold
the interests of British trade, and to ensure at least a measure
of equality of opportunity for British finance. Even if, relatively
speaking, the British position in Persia's external trade took a
sharp downward turn in and after the last decade of the nineteenth century, Britain was able on the whole to maintain what
Lansdowne described in 1902 as that 'substantial and pre-
eminent mercantile position' in southern Persia which we had
developed over more than a century of trade. 'It may be stated
without exaggeration', Lansdowne continued, 'that the development of the whole southern trade of Persia is due to British
enterprise.'[57] When the Imperial Defence Committee claimed,
in March 1905, that it was essential to maintain the *status quo*
in Persia and to uphold, or even increase, our influence at
Tehran, it was taking into account the interests of British
commerce as well as strategy.[58] When Grey was considering, in
1911, the possible damage which might be done to British trade
by German railway construction in Persia, he observed that the
object of H.M. Government was, primarily, to retain our current position; German trade was guaranteed access to Tehran
by the Potsdam Agreement, and Britain 'must somehow be

57. *B.D.O.W.*,IV,369.
58. ibid., 372.

assured of equal advantages for British trade.'[59] It was a policy not of aggressive promotion but of a watchful insistence that British trading interests should not be under any unnecessary disadvantage. British trade in Southern Persia was suffering, in 1914, from the insecurity of the Persian trade routes. 'We have to see that affairs do not get so bad', Grey told the Commons in June, 'that British trade is entirely excluded from the South of Persia and is replaced by Russian trade coming in from the north. That I regard as our major interest and obligation in the matter.'[60]

The maintenance of British trade was always a factor in British policy in Persia; we sought no special treatment, but, in return, we were careful to detect and protest against any special treatment received by our trading rivals. But Britain was a great Empire as well as a trading nation, the share of Persia in her world trade was always small, and the political and strategic issues in Persia seemed, at the time, to be of crucial importance to British communications and the security of India. It was not, therefore, so surprising that when, as in the Anglo-Russian Convention of 1907, British political, financial and commercial interests seemed in conflict, it was commerce and finance which went to the wall.

The Persian Gulf

British policy in the Persian Gulf shares, of course, many of the features of policy in Persia itself. But the Persian Gulf was an area so closely under British control that the results of that policy were very much more favourable to British interests.

The East India Company had developed a connexion with the Gulf ports for trading purposes. But its first interest had been in the suppression of the piracy which endangered its Indian trade. The policing of waters so closely adjoining the British Empire in India continued to occupy the Royal Navy until late in the nineteenth century, but it was gradually over-laid by the more positive political threat first of Russian en-croachments in the area and then of what British officials took to be an urgent and deliberate effort by Germany to displace Britain in the Gulf.

59. Grey to Buchanan, 20 March 1911: No. 707, *B.D.O.W.*,X,Pt.I,684.
60. 63 *H.C.Deb.5s.*1182 (17 June 1914).

The separation of British trading and political interests in the Persian Gulf dated from the withdrawal of Consular permission to trade in the 1820's. Political officers, debarred from trading, had no further direct connexion with the East India Company's commercial activities in the ports, and British official interest and influence in the Gulf gradually became purely political in character.[61] There could be no doubt about the close and anxious watch which the Government of India kept on Gulf affairs, and although London was inclined from time to time to ridicule Indian anxieties, British statesmen and officials who went out to India were immediately converted to the Indian viewpoint. Curzon, always conscious of the political importance of Persia and the Gulf, became an hysterical opponent of Russian and German encroachments as Viceroy of India after 1898. Sir Charles Hardinge, who exchanged the Permanent Under-Secretaryship of the Foreign Office for the Viceroyalty in 1910, wrote privately to Sir Arthur Nicolson the following March to explain how important it was for Britain to strengthen her position as much as possible in the Persian Gulf, and to be very firm in declaring 'hands off' to the Turks and the Germans—'Strongly as I felt when in London on the question of the Persian Gulf, I feel infinitely more strongly out here and realize the intense importance of our predominance being maintained in those waters.'[62]

In the Gulf as in Persia itself, trade again took second place to politics. Admittedly, such foreign trade as existed in the Gulf remained very largely British until after the First World War. At the turn of the century (1901), £2,300,000 out of a total trade of £3,600,000 in the Gulf ports was British.[63] In 'the last fairly normal year', 1907–8, Bushire's total exports and imports totalled nearly £11,000,000, and the *foreign* trade of Bushire was still essentially British.[64] But these totals were not large in relation to Britain's world trade, and, in any case, until well into the first decade of this century H.M. Government took no steps to gain any preferential treatment for British trade

61. The point is made in Wilson, *Persian Gulf*, p. 261.
62. No. 25, *B.D.O.W.*,X,Pt.II,38.
63. Figures given by Lord Lansdowne in the House of Lords, 5 May 1903: 121 *Parl.Deb.4s.*1347.
64. Noted in the article printed in *The Times*, 20 July 1911, 5e (one of a series on the Persian Gulf by a Special Correspondent, June–July 1911).

in the Gulf. By the '90s the Germans were actively claiming a share of the Gulf's foreign trade. A German consulate was established at Bushire in November 1897, and efforts were made to strengthen the German trading position at Basra. But H.M. Government did not feel it to be a part of its function to shield British trade from all foreign competition, or to guarantee the continuance of its monopoly. Lord George Hamilton had explained to the Government of India in July 1900 that improved sea and land communications would inevitably bring a challenge to British trade, and that the British and Indian Governments would have to keep a careful watch over the situation to ensure that our interests and spheres of influence in Persia, so essential to India, were effectively safeguarded. But it could 'hardly be maintained that, in view of such a competition [in trade], civilized Powers can be permanently denied the benefit of access to the ports of Persia because their admission will infringe upon a monopoly which we have hitherto enjoyed'.[65]

H.M. Government's policy in the Persian Gulf, with respect both to trade and politics, was openly declared in two important public statements: in 1903 and in 1907. Lansdowne's Foreign Office Memorandum of 17 March 1902 had already made clear his position privately within British official circles; he claimed that Britain did not 'grudge a debouche for international commerce in the Gulf', but that the 'bed rock' of our policy was that no other Powers should secure a foothold on its shores for naval or military purposes.[66] On 5 May 1903 Lansdowne made an outspoken public statement to the same effect

65. Hamilton to the Government of India, 6 July 1900: No. 320, *B.D.O.W.*, IV,364.
66. Quoted by Kumar, *Historical Journal*, V, 72. Lansdowne's position had been anticipated by Curzon a decade earlier. Discussing British claims in the Persian Gulf in his *Persia and the Persian Question* (London, 1892), G. N. Curzon explained that Britain did not demand that the Gulf should become a *mare clausum* against foreign trade, but she did claim, 'in return for the sacrifices to which she has submitted, and the capital which she has sunk, and for the sake of the peace which she is here to guard, that no hostile political influence shall introduce its discordant features upon the scene . . . I should regard the concession of a port upon the Persian Gulf to Russia by any power as a deliberate insult to Great Britain, as a wanton rupture of the *status quo*, and as an intentional provocation to war; and I should impeach the British minister who was guilty of acquiescing in such a surrender, as a traitor to his country'. (Vol. II, 465)

in the Lords. British policy in the Persian Gulf, he declared, was directed in the first place to the protection and promotion of British trade in those waters, but these efforts were not, and should not be, 'directed towards the exclusion of the legitimate trade of other Powers'. Turning to politics, he declared 'without hesitation' that H.M. Government 'should regard the establishment of a naval base, or of a fortified port, in the Persian Gulf by any other Power as a very grave menace to British interests, and we should certainly resist it with all the means at our disposal'.[67] The Persian Gulf Declaration of August 1907, issued simultaneously with the Persian Convention between Russia and Britain, reaffirmed Lansdowne's statement of 1903, and added that 'His Majesty's Government will continue to direct all their efforts to the preservation of the *status quo* in the Gulf and the maintenance of British trade; in doing so, they have no desire to exclude the legitimate trade of any other Power.[68]

An Open Door for international trade in the Persian Gulf remained the declared policy of the British Government, but, as Lansdowne had told Lord Lamington at the time of his 1903 statement, it was impossible to dissociate commercial from political interests in the Gulf. British officials on the spot tended increasingly to regard any expansion of German trade as a political threat to be watched and counteracted if possible, and equality of trade became a victim of political rivalry. It has since become clear that British traders and officials grossly exaggerated the extent of the support which the German Government gave to its overseas trading interests. Whigham, writing of the Gulf at the turn of the century, pointed out that in fact British officials had more influence in such areas than all their foreign colleagues combined, and that the merchant who had complained most bitterly to him about the inactivity of his consul had been a German.[69] The point was confirmed by Herr Wönckhaus, head of the German firm regarded by British officials as the arch-agent of German political penetration in the Gulf. Wönckhaus, questioned on the point by

67. 121 *Parl.Deb.4s.*1348.
68. Published with the text of the Anglo-Russian Convention: P.P.1908 (Cd.3750)CXXV.
69. Whigham, *The Persian Problem*, p. 166.

Eugene Staley in the early '30s, explained that, suspicious though his trading and concession activities may have seemed to the English, they were nevertheless of a purely business character—

The German government not only did not support me or subsidize me, but even the legitimate assistance and protection which I might have expected was not always forthcoming. That diplomatic circles in Petersburg, London and Paris discussed my firm and said that the German government was following a far-sighted policy in the Persian Gulf was not my fault. I did nothing to deny these rumours; a contradiction from me would have changed no one's opinion, and anyway, the belief that my firm was backed by the government increased my credit and prestige in certain quarters.[70]

But it was impossible to conduct policy on purely rational lines. In London, Sir Charles Hardinge suspected the Germans of using the southern end of the Baghdad Railway and our vital interests in the Gulf as levers to force us into an understanding which would leave Germany 'practically mistress of the European continent';[71] and Sir Percy Cox, the British Political Resident at Bushire, saw 'his ambition of making the Gulf an exclusively British sea endangered by every shipload of barley and every ton of oxide exported by the Germans'.[72]

70. Quoted by Staley, *War and the Private Investor*, pp. 45–46.
71. Minute on a despatch from Sir Edward Goschen, 8 April 1910: No. 342, *B.D.O.W.*,VI,450.
72. Wassmuss to the Foreign Office at Berlin, 19 December 1913: quoted by Graves, *Sir Percy Cox*, pp. 173–4.

CHAPTER 4

AFRICA

FOR MOST of the nineteenth century little was expected from trade and finance in tropical and southern Africa. The Cape had been developed primarily as a staging post on the trade route to India and the Far East, and trading stations were opened on the West Coast; but neither the West Coast nor the Cape seemed to offer particularly encouraging prospects for trade, or promising openings for the investment of capital. Such prospects and openings as existed were concentrated in the relatively developed areas of the North—in Egypt, Tunisia, Morocco. And North Africa was interesting to the Powers not only for its trading and capital requirements, but for its place in the politics of the Mediterranean.

In both Tunis and Morocco during the second half of the nineteenth century a close relationship existed between foreign governments, finance, and trade. But as in the Mediterranean area generally, that relationship existed for political purposes, rather than economic. Leonard Woolf—writing before many of the official archives, French or British, had become available—described the situation in Tunis just before the French protectorate (May 1881) as created 'by the economic beliefs and desires of a small class of financiers and traders, and by the fact that the Governments of France, Italy, and Britain placed the power of the European State at the disposal of this class in furthering its aims'.[1] He took Tunis, in fact, as his principal example of the influence of finance on Government.

Woolf's conclusions were published in 1920, and they have been out-dated by more recent research. Eugene Staley, for example, using the French official documents, came to the conclusion that French investors and entrepreneurs in Tunis were acting rather as the instrument of French official policy than as its master, though in acting as an instrument they no doubt stimulated further advance. His investigation of the four affairs

---

1. Leonard Woolf, *Empire and Commerce in Africa: a study in Economic Imperialism* (London, 1920), p. 104.

which formed the main elements in the charge that the French
conquest had been undertaken for private economic ends, established—so Staley argued—that French Government support
for private profit-making was political in intention—'it seems
clear that the disputes over de Sancy's concession, the Tunis-La
Goletta railway, the Enfida, and the support of the Crédit
Foncier project were all incidents in a definite policy of political
penetration determined upon prior to the advent of these
particular interests'.[2]

The research of A. Raymond and Arthur Marsden leaves
little to be discovered on British official policy in Tunis.[3]
Richard Wood, who served as British Consul (and later as
Agent and Consul-General) from 1856 to 1879, shared Stratford
Canning's belief in the political importance of economic progress. He argued that if the political integrity and independence
of Tunis were to be preserved from French and Italian encroachment, the State must be strengthened; and the best way
to strengthen the State was to promote its economic interests.
On his own initiative, Wood undertook a campaign to encourage British capital to enter and develop Tunisia: he began
negotiations for a modern commercial treaty, he obtained concessions for railways, for gas works and even for the establishment of an issue bank. But almost immediately he came up
against the two obstacles with which any vigorous and ambitious official overseas was compelled to come to terms. The
first was the reluctance of the City to invest money in speculative enterprises in areas of political instability; the second, the
equal reluctance of H.M. Government both to become engaged
in private speculations and concession-mongering, and to
hazard our political relationship with another Power (France)
for the sake of private commercial or financial advantage.

2. Intervention in Tunis is discussed in Chapter 12 of Staley, *War and the
Private Investor*, pp. 327–52.
3. A. Raymond, 'Les tentatives anglaises de pénétration économique en
Tunisie (1856–1877)', *Revue Historique*, CCXIV (1955), 48–67; Arthur
Marsden, 'British Policy towards Tunis, 1875–1899', London thesis, 1963;
other useful studies are W. L. Langer, 'The European Powers and the French
Occupation of Tunis, 1878–81, I & II', *American Historical Review*, XXXI
(1925–6), Joan P. Schwitzer, 'The British Attitude towards French Colonisation', London thesis, 1954, and, for French colonialism in general, including Tunis, Henri Brunschwig, *Mythes et Réalités de l'Imperialisme Colonial
Français 1871–1914* (Paris, 1960).

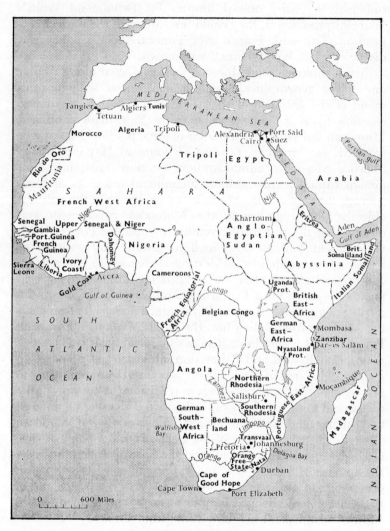

Map 3   Africa, 1914

Whereas in the case of Persia the political advantages which might be expected to result from economic progress seemed sufficient to justify official support for Drummond Wolff's financial promotions, they could not outweigh the danger of a head-on clash with France over Tunisia. Wood's policy was disowned, and Wood himself withdrawn.

British diplomacy in Morocco was conducted along similar lines.[4] The geographical situation of Morocco, with its command of the entrance to the Mediterranean and its Atlantic coastline fringing the Cape route to the East, made continued Moroccan independence a matter of some political importance to H.M. Government. Edward Drummond Hay's efforts to improve Moroccan administration, develop trade, introduce foreign capital, exploit Moroccan mineral resources and encourage the construction of roads and bridges, had the political objective of strengthening the Moroccan government and diminishing the risk of intervention by another Power. H.M. Government had no wish itself to assume any political or economic responsibilities in Morocco. It refused to guarantee a Moroccan Loan in 1861 and evaded the Moroccan Government's proposals for a British loan, railway concessions, and a territorial guarantee in 1902. But it aimed above all at preventing Morocco from falling into the hands of another European Power and at maintaining Tangier's neutrality. It was for this reason that Russell and Palmerston, although not prepared to guarantee a Loan in 1861, agreed to permit Drummond Hay to act as agent for the bondholders in receiving the customs duties earmarked to the servicing of the loan, in deducting the interest and sinking fund, and in returning the balance to the Moroccan Government; the purpose of the Loan, from the point of view of H.M. Government, was to meet the Spanish Indemnity after the Spanish Moroccan War and to bring to an end the Spanish occupation of Tetuan. British policy in Morocco by the end of the century had changed only in so far as the main threat to Moroccan independence now came from France.

*   *   *

4. This policy is described by F. R. Flournoy, *British Policy towards Morocco in the Age of Palmerston, 1830–1865* (London, 1935), and by A. J. P. Taylor, 'British Policy in Morocco, 1886–1902', *English Historical Review*, 66 (1951), 342–74.

H.M. Government's motives during the Partition of Africa have already been outlined most persuasively by Robinson and Gallagher in *Africa and the Victorians*. Selecting the nationalist crisis in Egypt as a starting point, they explain that, with the minor exceptions of Nyasaland and the lower Niger, the decisive factor in determining H.M. Government's occupation of African territory north of Rhodesia was the security of the routes to the East. Territorial claims by British statesmen in the '80s 'were not made for the sake of African empire or commerce as such'—

They were little more than by-products of an enforced search for better security in the Mediterranean and the East. It was not the pomps or profits of governing Africa which moved the ruling *élite*, but the cold rules for national safety handed on from Pitt, Palmerston and Disraeli.[5]

Conditions and motives were different in southern Africa, where the British Government, in its anxiety to preserve imperial influence, was drawn into an internal conflict between two groups of colonists. But both in the north and in the south the development of nationalism lay at the root of the political troubles of the period, to which British statesmen and officials— 'the official mind of imperialism'—reacted along the traditional lines of anxiety for the security of the Empire and the safeguarding of the routes to the East.

The Robinson and Gallagher thesis is in refreshing contrast both to the purely economic explanation of the Partition (dating from Hobson, and powerfully reinforced by Leonard Woolf's brilliant, if partisan, *Empire and Commerce in Africa*), and to the more recent interpretation of the Partition as an overseas expression of rivalries within the European Balance of Power. European rivalries, clearly, were a factor in the Partition. A. J. P. Taylor subtitled his *Germany's First Bid for Colonies, 1884–1885*, 'A Move in Bismarck's European Policy', and both Dr. Crowe and Professor Louis have emphasized the part played in British policy by the fear of France.[6] But the con-

5. Robinson and Gallagher, *Africa and the Victorians*, pp. 462–3.
6. S. E. Crowe, *The Berlin West African Conference, 1884–1885* (London, 1942), and Wm. Roger Louis, 'Sir Percy Anderson's Grand African Strategy, 1883–1896', *English Historical Review*, LXXXI (1966), 292–314.

tinuity of British policy in safeguarding the security of the Mediterranean and the East rings true as an explanation of the 'official mind' in Northern and Eastern Africa, and Professor Louis's work has, on the whole, provided an interesting confirmation of the main theme of *Africa and the Victorians*.[7]

From the point of view of the separation of commercial, financial and political strands in British foreign policy, one of the most satisfactory results of the new thinking on British policy in Africa has been the settlement, at least for the time being, of a persistent, nagging doubt as to the status of finance among the causes of the Boer War. Hobson, of course, described the Boer War as 'but the clearest and most dramatic instance of the operation of the world-wide forces of international finance'; Laski felt it to be, undeniably, 'simply a sordid struggle for the domination of [the] gold-mines'; and John Strachey enquired, as recently as 1959, whether there could really be any doubt that 'the simple issue on which the war was fought was whether or not independent Boer sovereignty was to be cleared out of the way of the British entrepreneurs and investors ... ?'[8] This was to be expected, but it is certainly more disturbing to find Eugene Staley (after rejecting investment as other than the tool of diplomacy in Tunis, Tripoli, the Yalu River, Persia, Manchuria, and elsewhere) including the Boer War among the rare examples of the investor directly promoting war for the sake of profits;[9] or to discover Professor Robbins (who, like Staley, saw finance as generally the *instrument* of official foreign policy) giving the Boer War as 'an excellent example of the way in which pressure from foreign investors can lead to international war'.[10] Even Professor Hugh Seton-Watson has questioned whether it can any longer be denied that the Boer War shared with the Russo-Japanese War 'the unenviable distinction of coming closest to the simple Marxist pattern of imperialist war'.[11]

7. For example, in the article cited immediately above and in 'The Anglo-Congolese Agreement of 1894 and the Cairo Corridor', *St. Antony's Papers*, 15 (1963), 81–100, and 'Great Britain and the African Peace Settlement of 1919', *American Historical Review*, LXXI (1966), 875–92.
8. Hobson, *Imperialism*, p. 359; Woolf (ed.), *Intelligent Man's Way to Prevent War*, p. 507; Strachey, *End of Empire*, p. 91.
9. Staley, *War and the Private Investor*, p. 359.
10. Lionel Robbins, *The Economic Causes of War* (London, 1939), p. 45.
11. Hugh Seton-Watson, *Neither War nor Peace* (London, 1960), pp. 310–11.

Robinson and Gallagher, however, claim that the motive which carried most weight with British statesmen was not the promotion of *local* economic interests—and these local interests were the only economic interests which stood to gain from war—but the importance which British statesmen attached to keeping South Africa within the Empire; if H.M. Government supported incidentally some sectors of the South African mining industry, or some trading and railway interests in the Cape and Rhodesia, it was because it had 'no other means of saving supremacy in South Africa'.[12] Milner's private correspondence certainly gives that impression. His interest was, above all, in the *survival* of the Empire and of the British race, and, as he told Miss Bertha Synge in the first days of the war, he felt himself sustained by his own belief 'in the soundness of the wholly misunderstood cause' in which Britain was fighting in South Africa—'It is a war of liberation—from the rule of the Mauser'. Describing the war again in March 1904, he wrote of it as 'the great struggle to keep this country within the limits of the British Empire' and explained that he had engaged in the struggle with all his might, because he was 'from head to foot one mass of glowing conviction in the rightness of our cause'.[13] In one of the more recent studies of the period, Professor Le May has felt able to discard the explanation of the Boer War as a capitalist conspiracy. The mines, he admitted, were clearly of international interest, but the mining magnates were not a united, homogeneous group, and, in the main, they would have preferred to stop short of a destructive war. Moreover, it was not they who could take such decisions, and Chamberlain and Milner, whose decision it was, 'were thinking not of goldfields but of the political supremacy of Britain in South Africa; and that supremacy, they had decided, was incompatible with the independence of Kruger's republic'.[14]

Whatever the results of H.M. Government's policy or the justification of its arguments (the 'Empire in danger', the threat to the Cape route to India, the 'legitimate' grievances

12. South Africa is discussed in Chapter XIV of Robinson and Gallagher, *Africa and the Victorians*.
13. Quoted in Edward Crankshaw, *The Forsaken Idea: a study of Viscount Milner* (London, 1952), pp. 100–1.
14. G. H. L. Le May, *British Supremacy in South Africa 1899–1907* (Oxford, 1965), pp. 29–30.

of the Uitlanders, the 'rule of the Mauser') it remains true that these were the factors, rather than the pressure from capitalists or the complaints of British investors, which brought British statesmen and officials finally to war.

*   *   *

There is, however, a danger that the new explanation of British official motives in Africa during the 'Age of Imperialism', while stressing, legitimately enough, such factors as the security of the routes to the East and of the Empire itself, will under-emphasize the part played in British policy by the need to protect the relative position of British trade in world markets. This need, which has already served as a constant, underlying theme in the description of British policy in Egypt, Turkey, and Persia, will be shown to have been of even greater importance in determining British policy in China and Latin America. Could it, then, have been so relatively unimportant in the Partition of Africa?

The Partition coincided with a period of depression in world trade and with a growing awareness in Britain both of rising competition in the new markets of the world and of the closure of some of the old markets under revived Protectionism. By the end of the '80s a temporary recovery was in progress, and officials, in any case, continued to be optimistic about the competitive power of British industry overseas. But it is difficult to ignore Joseph Chamberlain's outspoken concern for the creation of new markets or for the assurance that new markets, if opened by other trading Powers, would not be closed thereafter to British trade. Speaking in 1894, Chamberlain had singled out demand for more goods as essential to maintained employment. It was the duty of the Government, by creating new markets and effectively developing old, to give every inducement to demand, and it was for this reason that Chamberlain himself would not consider losing India or abandoning Egypt, and for this reason, too, that he had urged upon this and previous Governments 'the necessity for using every legitimate opportunity to extend our influence and control in that great African continent which is now being opened up to civilization and to commerce'.[15] Speaking as Colonial Secretary two years later, he told the Birmingham Chamber of Commerce that

15. Quoted in J. F. Horrabin, *How Empires Grow* (London, 1935), p. 6.

Britain alone offered an Open Door in the markets she had developed over the world. If we had stood aside in the Partition of Africa, 'the greater part of Africa would have been occupied by our commerical rivals, who would have proceeded to close this great commercial market to the British Empire'.[16]

Robinson and Gallagher have argued strongly that British aims in taking part in the Partition were 'essentially defensive and strategic'. The fact that British Governments were so slow to develop their territorial gains before 1900 showed 'the weakness of any commercial and imperial motives for claiming them'; the Partition was in advance of the trader—

So far from commercial expansion requiring the extension of territorial claims, it was the extension of territorial claims which in time required commercial expansion. The arguments of the so-called new imperialism were *ex post facto* justifications of advances, they were not the original reasons for making them.[17]

There is some truth in this, but it goes too far. Even in Egypt the protection of British trading interests, both on the Canal and in Egypt itself, had helped to persuade Gladstone to tolerate 'anarchy' no longer. In the controversy over the Congo in 1884–5, which is often taken (though not by Robinson and Gallagher) as marking the beginning of the 'Scramble' for Africa, the British Government's interest was above all to prevent France from closing the markets of the Congo region, presumptive or otherwise, to British trade. This was the principal motive for concluding the Anglo-Portuguese Treaty of 26 February 1884; and the anxiety to preserve international Free Trade in the Congo region formed the basis of British policy for the rest of that year and at the Berlin conference of 1884–5. And it is difficult to believe that commercial factors did not weigh heavily with H.M. Government elsewhere in Africa. Captain Lugard may have been using an *ex post facto* justification when he claimed in 1893 that British statesmen and traders urged expansion in East Africa as a stimulus to British trade and as an outlet for our manufactures. But was he so wrong in describing the scramble for Africa in general as being 'due to the growing commercial rivalry, which brought home

16. Quoted in Hancock, *Survey of British Commonwealth Affairs*, II, 82.
17. Robinson and Gallagher, *Africa and the Victorians*, p. 472.

to civilized nations the vital necessity for industrial enterprise and expansion'?[18] Was E. D. Morel really mistaken when he called commerce 'the *fons et origo* of our presence in West Africa'?[19] And was there not at least some truth in Sidney Olivier's conclusion, in 1906, that the recent partition of Africa had been undertaken 'in order to ensure that the markets of the several divisions should be kept open to the several Powers that appropriated them, or, in some cases, to guarantee the frontiers of previous acquisitions from molestation.'[20]

It was not the *expansion* of British trade that concerned the Foreign Office, so much as the obligation to ensure that British trade received at least equal treatment. It was up to British traders to make what they could of the new markets, and H.M. Government's obligation did not extend beyond ensuring that they had access to these markets and were not differentiated against. But even to obtain this much could involve the Foreign Office in protective annexations in West Africa, or in prolonged negotiations for a Free Trade area in Central Africa. The same argument applied to East Africa. When faced with the threat of a German confiscation of a stretch of African coast technically under the control of the Sultan of Zanzibar, Salisbury argued (in 1885) that a simple undertaking by the Sultan to levy a fixed 5 per cent. *ad valorem* duty equally on trade of any nationality would serve the German purpose far better than an annexation—

18. Quoted in Woolf, *Empire and Commerce in Africa*, p. 26.
19. E. D. Morel, *Affairs of West Africa* (London, 1902), p. 21. C. W. Newbury recently pointed to 'trade and revenue protection as a factor in explaining the origins of the "scramble" ', at least in so far as it concerned West Africa: 'The Partition of Africa: Victorians, Republicans, and the Partition of West Africa', *Journal of African History*, III (1962), 493–501.
20. Sidney Olivier, *White Capital and Coloured Labour* (London, 1906), p. 7. Jean Stengers, taking up Robinson and Gallagher's main point, has put forward an impressive counter-argument in favour of the thesis that the scramble for Africa had an economic as well as a political basis; it was, from the British point of view, a defensive reaction to the closing of African markets to British trade: 'The Partition of Africa: L'Impérialisme Colonial de la fin du XIXᵉ-Siècle; Mythe ou Réalité', *Journal of African History*, III (1962) 485–8, 491. The doubts felt about the general validity of the Robinson and Gallagher thesis have been summarized in three useful review articles: G. Shepperson, 'Africa, the Victorians and Imperialism', *Revue Belge de Philologie et d'Histoire*, 40 (1962), 1228–38; Eric Stokes, 'Imperialism and the Scramble for Africa: the new View', Historical Association of Rhodesia and Nyasaland, Local Series 10 (1963); and Ronald Hyam, 'The Partition of Africa', *Historical Journal*, vii (1964), 154–169.

This matter of equality is the only point in which the whole negotiation really touches Englishmen. The only issue to the discussion
which would be intolerable to us would be the possession of one or
two free ports by the Germans, and the rest of the coast in the hands
of Zanzibar, and a heavy tariff. This would, of course, make the
Germans the monopolists of the Big Lakes market.[21]

The point has been made, by Robinson and Gallagher
amongst others,[22] that the minimal economic value of the new
territories divided among the Powers during the Partition
shows how slight a part economics must have played in determining international policy. S. H. Frankel has argued that
economic development, apart from South Africa and some
of the West African colonies, did not really get under way
until the years immediately before the First World War. Even
as late as the mid-'30s the export trade of the new British
Colonies (in East Africa and the Sudan) was below that of the
Cape in 1875, and the same applied to the new territories taken
over by Germany and France.[23] Staley prints a chart showing
the geographical distribution of British foreign investments,
1913–14, which indicates that only 12·2 per cent. of these
investments were in Africa (including Egypt), of which 10 per
cent. were in South Africa.[24]

The point is well taken, but it was the fear of being excluded
from *prospective* as well as *existing* markets which prompted
H.M. Government's policy in West and Central Africa, and
nobody at the time could estimate precisely what these markets
might be worth in future. Officials were inclined to be pessimistic, traders optimistic, but no British Government could
afford to ignore altogether the claims of British trade. F. V.
Parsons has shown how H.M. Government was reluctantly
compelled to give some measure of support to the trading
claims of the North-West African Company against the Sultan
of Morocco. Drummond Hay had suggested that in return for
compensation the Company might agree to withdraw; the

21. Cecil, *Life of Salisbury*, III, 230.
22. For example, E. A. Benians in the *Cambridge History of the British Empire*
(Cambridge, 1959), III, p. 226; David Landes in *Journal of Economic History*,
21 (1961); F. Crouzet, 'Commerce et Empire: L'expérience britannique du
libre-échange à la première guerre mondiale', *Annales*, 19 (1964).
23. S. H. Frankel, *Capital Investment in Africa* (London, 1938), pp. 172–3.
24. Staley, *War and the Private Investor*, Chart IV.

Foreign Office could not agree, and the Parliamentary Under-Secretary (Lord Fitzmaurice) argued that 'it would bear the appearance of this country being a party to aiming a blow at British trade, the effect of which would be dangerous here'.[25] Even if there were good reasons to believe that an area would never prove of great advantage to British trade and investment, no political excuse could be given for not ensuring, within reason, that such British trade as existed (or might exist) would receive fair treatment. There is something in the argument, applied to international commercial diplomacy, that if you look after the pennies, the pounds will look after themselves.

Robinson and Gallagher's work on British government motives during the Partition of Africa makes it unnecessary to spend more time on the political factors which determined British annexations. The importance of British interests in India in the formulation of British policy in Uganda and the Upper Nile region is now undeniable, while British official policy in South Africa was as clearly the response to a nationalistic threat to continued Imperial supremacy. Nor do Robinson and Gallagher ignore commercial factors in describing British policy elsewhere in Africa, although they argue that commerce seldom led to direct annexation. What needs to be emphasized, however, is that the 'obsession with security' and 'fixation on safeguarding the routes to the East', which Robinson and Gallagher have rightly identified as recurrent features in the official attitude to British imperial expansion in Africa, applied almost as much to the safeguarding of the British position in world trade as they did to the physical maintenance of the Empire.

The importance of trade in British policy—which, in any case, applied very much more to the West and to the interior of Africa than it did to the East and North-East—can only be appreciated in the context of British policy elsewhere in the world. Depression and the return to Protection were closing the markets of Europe; British officials in the more distant markets of the Levant, the Far East, and Latin America were watching, with increasing alarm, the growth of foreign competition; the Royal Commission on the Depression of Trade and Industry was recommending a more positive Government

25. F. V. Parsons, 'The North-West African Company and the British Government, 1875–95', *Historical Journal*, I (1958), 143.

policy in the promotion of British trade; and Rosebery and Bryce at the Foreign Office had announced a new policy to meet the aggressive trade promotion of foreign governments overseas. Can it be doubted that this alarm and anxiety about the future of British trade—directly contemporary as it was with the Partition of Africa—had a significant part in determining the British reaction to European territorial annexations in Africa and to the probable erection of tariff barriers across the Continent? It may or may not have led straight to annexation: Earl Granville's reaction to the Manchester Chamber of Commerce's views on the Congo in 1884 was to ask whether we really intended 'to take possession of every navigable river all over the world, and every avenue of commerce, for fear somebody else should take possession of it?'[26] But it certainly sharpened British interest in what other Powers were proposing to do in Africa, and Granville, a few months later, found himself negotiating equal opportunities for British trade in the Congo region. The problem was obvious; Britain, no more than any other trading nation, could stand by while the markets of the world were closed to her trade. It was—as Jules Ferry had said in justification of French action in Tonkin—'a question of the future, fifty or a hundred years hence . . . of what will be the inheritance of our children, the bread of our labourers'.

26. 287 *Parl.Deb.*3s.1834 (9 May 1884).

CHAPTER 5

CHINA AND THE FAR EAST

THE SEPARATION of finance, trade, and politics in British policy in the Far East does not, on the whole, present such intractable problems as it does for Africa and the Levant. The influence of India was much less directly felt on British policy in China and Japan. Indian trade and revenue were affected by local restrictions, particularly on the opium trade; and, in the interests of untroubled government in India, it was desirable always to avoid a rebuff damaging to British prestige in the East. But the strategic factors which were so important in Persia, Egypt, and East Africa were insignificant in determining British policy at Peking or Tokyo. Even in those parts of the Far East where strategic and economic interests seem at first sight to go hand-in-hand, it takes little analysis to establish the priority of the one over the other. The annexation of Upper Burma in 1886 was, it is true, intended to forestall French traders and concessionaires, but it was not because Britain wanted the trade and concessions, but because officials in India feared that French traders would form the spearhead of further French political expansion from Indo-China. Similarly, when the Government of India sent Colonel Younghusband to Tibet in 1903, the object was to forestall Russian intrigues rather than to develop a trade with India. By Article IX of the Lhassa Convention, signed on 7 September 1904, the Tibetan Government undertook to make no grants or concessions for railways, roads, telegraphs, mining, or other rights to any foreign Power or the subject of any such Power without the previous consent of H.M. Government. But, as Lansdowne explained to the Russian Chargé d'Affaires, he understood the Article to be a self-denying ordinance which affected Britain as well as the other Powers—'We had no desire to annex Tibetan territory or to intervene in Tibetan affairs, or to have political representatives in the country, but it must be understood that other Powers were to be placed under a similar disability.'[1] The trade marts opened by the Convention on the Tibetan frontier were to be available on equal terms to all trade of whatever origin, and no effort was made to attract British capital. Indeed, by Article IV of the Anglo-Russian Convention of 31 August 1907, both Powers bound themselves not to seek or obtain, either on their own account or on behalf of their subjects, any railway, road, telegraph or mining concessions or other rights in Tibet.[2]

The balance between British commercial and political interests in South East Asia is nicely indicated in Lord Kimberley's instructions to Maurice de Bunsen (the new British Chargé d'Affaires in Siam), 27 October 1874. Kimberley pointed out that while Britain had no desire to interfere with Siam's authority over such of the Malay Peninsula as came under Siamese dominion, H.M. Government could not, 'from considerations of safety to their Indian and Colonial possessions', allow any other European Power to annex any part of that Peninsula or to secure concessions for a maritime canal, railways, or other important public works. Siam's independence was to be preserved as a buffer state between British and French possessions, and though it was to be remembered that British commercial interests in Siam were far greater than those of any other Power, and capable of extension, H.M. Government had 'no desire to obtain exclusive privileges to the detriment of other nations, but neither [could it] assent to such privileges being secured by others to the detriment of Great Britain'.[3]

In South East Asia, as elsewhere, British policy for trade was to secure a fair field and no favour. Where H.M. Government went beyond this in any respect, particularly in restricting international access to 'political concessions', the reasons were quite openly non-economic.

*   *   *

There can be no doubt, however, that trade was the focus of British policy in China and Japan, and that British expansion

1. Lansdowne to Sir C. Hardinge, 27 September 1904: No. 301, *B.D.O.W.*, IV,320.
2. Text of the Convention printed as Appendix I, ibid., 620.
3. Quoted in Dugdale, *Maurice de Bunsen*, pp. 117–18. The details of this policy are filled out in V. G. Kiernan's interesting article, 'The Kra Canal Projects of 1882–5: Anglo-French rivalry in Siam and Malaya', *History*, XLI (1957), 137–57.

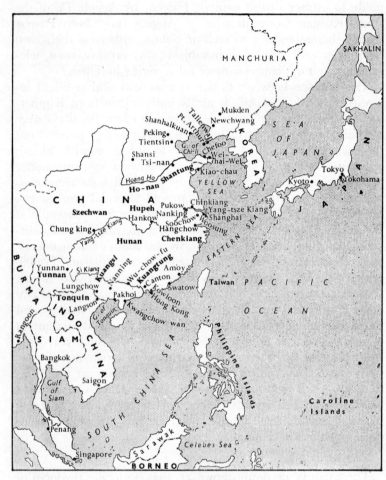

Map 4   The Far East

in the area, such as it was, was determined fundamentally by the interests of British trade and, later, of British finance. 'What British interests *are* at the present day,' Sir Rutherford Alcock wrote, early in the 1860's, 'and what the sole object of our policy, needs no explanation. Both should be, if they are not, patent to the world. Commerce is with us, in Siam, China, and Japan all equally (for with Cochin-China we have no relations yet) the one sole object.'[4]

The two Anglo-Chinese wars of 1839–42 and 1856–60 were fought not, as Strachey claims, 'primarily in order to prevent the Chinese Government from prohibiting the import of opium', but to open up the markets of China to world trade. Opium did not even figure in the Treaty of Nanking which ended the first of the so-called 'Opium Wars'. Although H.M. Government favoured legalization of the opium trade on 'practical' grounds, it made no demands on the Chinese Government in this respect, and the British negotiator, Sir Henry Pottinger, was instructed that H.M. Government had no right to make a demand—'The Chinese Government is fully entitled to prohibit the importation of opium if it pleases; and British subjects who engage in a contraband trade must take the consequences of doing so.'[5] The Treaty of Tientsin (26 June 1858), which followed the second Chinese war, was similarly intended to open up China. Lord Elgin's instructions were to negotiate a revision of the Chinese treaties so that facilities for trade might be improved and extended; but he was to bear in mind that, in opening the trade of China, 'Her Majesty's Government have no desire to obtain any exclusive advantages for British trade in China, but are only desirous to share with all other nations any benefits which they may acquire in the first instance specifically for British commerce.'[6]

To a Victorian, the ambition to open up China to trade was wholly admirable; even Cobden, the most violent of mid-century critics of British imperial expansion, supported the further opening of China, and felt that in a modern world of trade and investment China and Japan could not expect to

4. Sir Rutherford Alcock, *The Capital of the Tycoon: a narrative of a three years' residence in Japan* (London, 1863), II, 352.
5. Quoted in A. J. Sargent, *Anglo-Chinese Commerce and Diplomacy* (Oxford, 1907), p. 87.
6. ibid., p. 109.

continue to shut themselves up from the rest of the world.[7] Cobden, and probably the majority of officials at the time, resented the method rather than the motive; he described the India and China Association's memorial of January 1857 (which called for greater trading opportunities in China) as 'very like attempting to enter a house in the rear of a burglar and offering to transact business whilst some of its inmates are weltering in their blood and others still struggling with their assailants'.[8] Even Lord Elgin himself complained privately that 'nothing could be more contemptible than the origin of our existing quarrel. . . . That wretched question of the "Arrow" [was] a scandal to us.'[9]

The strong sense of the impropriety of the methods used in opening up China was, no doubt, a contributory factor in a growing distaste at Whitehall for the use of force. The creation in 1861 of the Tsungli Yamen (the Chinese Board of Foreign Affairs) was an additional reason for disapproving those local coercions which, in the absence of a central authority which could be held responsible for the actions of Chinese citizens, had proved only too frequent in the past. Sir Frederick Bruce, the first British Minister at Peking, circularized his consuls in September 1862 to warn them against calling for naval assistance unless the lives and property of British subjects were directly endangered.[10] And seven years later Clarendon told Rutherford Alcock that H.M. Government would 'visit with the severest condemnation acts of violence wantonly undertaken and carried out without [its] express sanction'.[11]

It was not always so easy for officials on the spot to avoid the use of force. They might be panicked into it, or they might genuinely consider that a small display of force at the right moment might be the only way to avoid a serious disaster. In a country like China, where rapid communication was almost impossible, where central authority was always weak, and where radical differences in religion and outlook made foreign-

---

7. Hobson, *Richard Cobden*, pp. 199, 355.
8. ibid., p. 199.
9. Quoted by Masataka Banno, *China and the West, 1858–1861* (Cambridge, Mass., 1964), p. 10.
10. S. T. Wang, *The Margary Affair and the Chefoo Agreement* (London, 1940), p. 2.
11. Sargent, *Anglo-Chinese Commerce and Diplomacy*, p. 181.

ers inevitably an object of suspicion, minor incidents were likely to get out of control; and no competent official could allow abstract principles to stand in the last event between him and his duty to ensure the safety of British lives and property. But the attitude of officials in London is suggested very clearly in Edmund Hammond's warning to Rutherford Alcock in 1864 against a planned international reprisal on Japan. The Permanent Under-Secretary explained how unpopular both with H.M. Government and with the country in general was the use of force in order to extend, or even to maintain, a trade; even if such measures were successful the morality of them was doubtful, and if, as was likely enough, they degenerated into a protracted warfare, 'the extent of the inconvenience they may entail is beyond calculation'.[12]

*   *   *

Subject to the flexibility to which British diplomatists in 'semi-civilized' countries felt themselves occasionally entitled (to the despair of the Foreign Office), there is no evidence that British officials went beyond the normal scope of their commercial functions before the early '80s. In the general interests of British trade, H.M. Representatives frequently urged the Chinese Government to relax its prohibitions, to rationalize its taxation system, and to consider opening up the interior to mining and railway concessions. But these were general objectives, not in any sense confined to the interests of individual British traders or concession hunters, and, indeed, designed altruistically to open the trade of China to the world. Nor was the opening of trade expected exclusively to benefit the foreign trade. International trade, in mid-Victorian England, had something of the character of a universal panacea; its expansion in the East could not fail to bring benefits to the world in general, including, of course, the East itself. 'In Japan, as in China', Sir Harry Parkes told the Select Committee of 1872, 'I do not myself recognise any very defined line between our political and our commercial interests; the two are so intimately woven together, that one often leads to the other; and it

12. Quoted in M. A. Anderson, 'Edmund Hammond, Permanent Under Secretary of State for Foreign Affairs, 1854–1873', London thesis, 1956, p. 169.

appeared to me that I could not better perform my duties than by making all reasonable effort in my power to persuade the Japanese to lay aside their peculiar martial characteristics, and become industrial and commercial instead.'[13]

Developments in contemporary China seemed as promising, and it was not unusual to find British officials defending the general interests of the trade of China against the particular interests of the resident British mercantile community. In a quarrel with the views of the Shanghai Chamber of Commerce, the Board of Trade found it impossible to forget the general rule that 'the interest of the Mercantile class engaged in the trade with Asiatic countries, is not of so permanent a character as in the trade with European and Anglo-Saxon communities— and that from this cause there arises a constant tendency to look rather to immediate than to prospective and permanent advantage'.[14]

The general objectives of British policy were summarized in Derby's despatch to Sir Thomas Wade in 1876 in which he pointed out that H.M. Government attached great importance to adequate and mutual diplomatic representation, to the proper protection of foreigners travelling in China, to the execution of treaty stipulations with respect to trade and other matters, and to the establishment of commercial relations between India and Western China.[15] Trade as between foreign merchants in China was to be free and equal, and the efforts of the Powers acting—after the Treaty of Tientsin—jointly in China were to be directed at securing the agreement of the Chinese Government to further openings for trade.

For capital as for trade, official support was confined to the creation of conditions in which investment in general might take place. Individual projects were not supported, and the Foreign Office showed itself much more reluctant to consider the claims for investment opportunities in China than it was to press for the general interests of British trade. In the hope of speeding the commercial development of China, the consular body at Shanghai in July 1863 backed an application by 27

13. Minutes of Evidence, *Report of the Select Committee on the Diplomatic and Consular Services*, P.P.1872(314)VII, Q.1135.
14. Board of Trade to Foreign Office, 17 February 1863: P.R.O.,B.T/1/559.
15. Quoted by Sargent, *Anglo-Chinese Commerce and Diplomacy*, p. 188.

foreign firms (mostly British) for a concession to construct a railway between Shanghai and Soochow, but the application was turned down outright by the Chinese Government.[16] Neither the subsequent Shanghai-Woosung railway nor Mr. Thomas Fergusson's Chefoo-Tsinanfu project were able to obtain the support of the British Legation at Peking, and a generally discouraging attitude was adopted by the Foreign Office to railway concessions in other parts of China.[17]

The attitude of H.M. Government to Chinese finance was equally uncompromising. No direct part was taken in Chinese Loans until the Guaranteed Loan of 1898, and Lord Granville made the official position clear in the case of an Eastern Telegraph loan to the Chinese Government. He applauded Sir Harry Parkes's refusal to take any part in loan negotiations between British subjects and the Chinese Government, and added that—

Her Majesty's Government are strongly of opinion that it is very undesirable that Her Majesty's Representatives abroad should, in any way, however remotely, be connected with these transactions, and I have accordingly to instruct you, should your assistance or co-operation be at any future time invoked, to state that the instructions which you have received preclude you from intervening in such matters.[18]

When, in the context of the assistance given by Sir Harry Parkes to the Hong Kong & Shanghai Bank in 1884, the Assistant Under-Secretary (Julian Pauncefote) argued that 'the peculiar state of things in China' created an exception to the general rule, the Chancellor of the Exchequer (Mr. Childers) replied that he did not feel that an exception should be made. If it were, and China defaulted, H.M. Government's interven-

16. Kent, *Railway Enterprise in China*, p. 2.
17. ibid.; and H. B. Morse and H. F. MacNair, *Far Eastern International Relations* (Cambridge, Mass., 1931), pp. 412–13; N. A. Pelcovits, *Old China Hands and the Foreign Office* (New York, 1948), p. 135.
18. Quoted by Chen, 'British Loans to China from 1860 to 1913', p. 63. Dr. Chen discusses H.M. Government's policy to Loans before the late '90s in pp. 55–66 of his thesis. His argument can be accepted only with some reservations, but at least he comes to the right conclusion: 'At any rate, our analysis proves the purely commercial nature of these early financial transactions towards which the British Foreign Office adopted a largely *laissez-faire* attitude.'

tion would be insisted on, and it would be impossible to refuse it.[19]

*   *   *

However, by the 1880's it was no longer so easy to maintain the old standards of *laissez-faire* diplomacy. Until now, Britain, as the major trading nation in China with something like 80 per cent. of China's total foreign trade, had upheld—and had been able to afford to uphold—a complete Open Door in the areas of China available to international trade. Moreover, it had been in Britain's interest to work for the continued territorial integrity of China; she already had the bulk of the trade, and partition could only mean the creation of national areas where the Open Door might no longer apply.

The Open Door and the territorial integrity of China remained, in the '80s and '90s, central to British policy in the Far East. But it was only in the '80s that a genuine threat to both came to form a permanent background to British diplomacy. British statesmen were aware of the growing importance of the Far East in international diplomacy. When Lord Salisbury was trying to persuade Sir William White to accept the Legation at Peking in September 1885, he reminded him of the 'extreme importance' which that mission was assuming— 'The Power that can establish the best footing in China will have the best part of the trade of the world'.[20] Sir William Morier, writing on the same subject a few days before, had given his opinion that, political complications being as they were, Peking, St. Petersburg and Constantinople were likely to be the three key posts in the future; China was 'just getting within touch of planetary influence—we ought to secure China'.[21] British businessmen were as conscious of the problems which Protection in old markets and industrial competition in old and new were creating for British trade. When Sir Lowthian Bell, President of the British Iron Trade Association, gave evidence before the Royal Commission on the Depression of Trade and Industry, 27 January 1886, he pointed to the differential duties and protective barriers which were being

19. Pelcovits, *Old China Hands*, pp. 137–8.
20. Quoted in Edwards, *Sir William White*, p. 11.
21. ibid., pp. 12–13.

raised against British trade in Spain; the most promising fields for future British enterprise were likely to be in newer and more distant markets, the Indian possessions, Australia, and now, China.[22] It was a point which Curzon himself was to emphasize some years later. British commercial supremacy, he argued, must be preserved not merely for the sake of our Empire but to feed our own people; it was 'only in the East, and especially in the Far East, that we may still hope to keep and create open markets for British manufacturers'.[23]

Of course, ideally the new competitive situation should have been met by more effort on the part of British traders and manufacturers themselves; and there is no doubt that the Foreign Office would infinitely have preferred to have seen free and open international competition, even if Britain were to lose some of her position in the Chinese markets. But *laissez-faire* and the Open Door could not be expected to survive unscathed the introduction of foreign diplomatic pressure on behalf of national trading interests and concession-hunters. Nor could they survive the new concept of limited national treaties with China. The gains achieved principally by Great Britain in opening China to trade had been made freely available to all nationalities. Yet the Franco-Chinese Treaty of Tientsin, June 1885, introduced the differential duties, the preferential treatment, and the national railway concessions which gave a death-blow to international equality. The French Government had initiated the policy of concession and counter-concession which, by the end of the century, had brought the economic partition of China.

It was impossible for H.M. Government to stand aside while foreign diplomatists put pressure on the Chinese Government, and while whole areas of the Empire were progressively debarred to British trade. The evidence for foreign diplomatic activity was overwhelming. Julian Pauncefote had minuted as early as 7 June 1884, in discussing the Chinese loan situation, that 'other foreign Rep[resentatives] do not keep within the limits observed by the British Minister, but actually negotiate Loans and Contracts for their nationals and bluster and

22. Minutes of Evidence, *Second Report of the Royal Commission on the Depression of Trade and Industry*, P.P.1886(c.4715)XXI, Q.3662.
23. G. N. Curzon, *Problems of the Far East* (London, 1894), p. 421.

machinate on their behalf and the complaint of the British community is that their efforts to compete are not supported'.[24]

The first positive action taken by H.M. Government was in response to evidence of German activity in Japan. Mr. Plunkett, the British Minister at Tokyo, reported on 17 June 1885 that Count Bismarck (Bismarck's son) had personally recommended the German firms Illies & Co. and Ahrens & Co. to the Japanese Government. The following day Plunkett added in a further despatch that he had reason to know that 'in compliance with instructions from Berlin, Count Doenhoff [the German Minister] is pushing German commercial interests here to an extent unusual in diplomacy, and which, of course, is directly hurtful to English commerce and influence'.[25] Lord Salisbury's reply marked the beginning of a new phase in British commercial diplomacy. He telegraphed on 2 August:

In cases where foreign Representatives interfere to the detriment of British commercial interests, you are at liberty to give the latter your support.[26]

The importance of Salisbury's instruction lay not in its immediate impact—it is doubtful whether Plunkett ever went beyond urgent remonstrances with the Japanese Government[27]—but in the discretion it gave to British diplomatists in future as to the degree of assistance they might give to British commercial interests. Henceforward, exceptional assistance was dependent in theory only on evidence of a similar degree of exceptional assistance by the diplomatists of rival trading Powers; in practice, the traditions of the British Foreign Service were too strong for pressure ever to be equally applied.

In China, foreign diplomatic pressure in 1885 was posing similar problems. H.M. Consul at Taiwan, for example, gave a lurid account in his despatch to Salisbury of 9 December of the activities of the United States Minister and his consuls in securing contracts for the construction of railways and other

24. Quoted by Pelcovits, *Old China Hands*, p. 138.
25. Nos. 1, 2, *Correspondence respecting British Trade and Commerce in China and other Foreign Countries, 1885–1886*, F.O.,C.P.5471.
26. No. 36, *Correspondence respecting the Question of Diplomatic and Consular Assistance to British Trade Abroad*, P.P.1886(c.4779)LX.
27. For example, No. 5, *Correspondence respecting British Trade and Commerce in China*, F.O.,C.P.5471; and No. 2, *Correspondence respecting British Trade and Commerce, 1887, Pt. II*, F.O.,C.P.5549.

public works by U.S. citizens. The German Minister, he added, was also hard at work in the same cause.[28] Meanwhile, public opinion had been aroused in London by an article in *The Times* in which the China Correspondent discussed the extent of foreign diplomatic pressure in the context of news of a proposed £35 million German loan to China. The Correspondent reminded readers of the long tradition of rigorous abstention from business transactions practised by British diplomatists and consuls in the East—'they have jealously confined themselves to what may not inaptly be described as keeping the ring'. Hitherto, with some notorious exceptions, other diplomatists had adopted the same attitude:

but quite lately bitter complaints have been publicly made, both in China and Japan, that German officials have recently adopted a wholly new method, and have made themselves the agents of their countrymen with native officials. In one part of the East the native authorities have expressed themselves as scandalized at the eagerness and zeal with which a prominent German official is touting for orders; but orders are given nevertheless.

The Correspondent concluded with some suggestions for reconsidering the scope of British diplomatic assistance, particularly in China.[29]

The Times' article had come at the right moment. The Great Depression was almost over, but conditions still seemed difficult, and the future position of Britain in world trade looked far from promising. The evidence produced before the Royal Commission on the Depression of Trade and Industry suggested the closure of European home markets, the rise of foreign competition in neutral markets—particularly the East, where British trade had had the field virtually to itself—and the current limitations of the Government assistance available to British business overseas. As evidence accumulated at the Foreign Office, through the press, privately, and in the despatches, something had to be done. Salisbury repeated his telegram of 2 August 1885 on 26 January, and a telegram and despatch to the same effect were sent to Mr. O'Conor at Peking. Lord Rosebery, on taking over the Foreign Office,

28. No. 18, *Correspondence respecting British Trade and Commerce in China*, F.O., C.P.5471.
29. *The Times*, 2 January 1886, 12a, b.

confirmed the instructions, 24 February, adding that any cases
of contracts or other concessions granted by the Chinese
Government to the subjects of Governments of foreign Powers
should be brought immediately to the notice of H.M. Government.[30] Three days later he wrote to his Parliamentary Under-
Secretary, Mr. Bryce, to ask him to examine 'the question of
how much further we can go in the direction of developing and
assisting commerce by means of diplomatic and consular
agency, without running the risk of possible connexion with
private firms or enterprise, and the consequent lowering of the
standard and repute of those services'.[31] It was from this
initiative that, after consultation with business interests at
home and diplomatists and consuls abroad, Mr. Bryce's
definitive Memorandum evolved—the Memorandum which
The Times described as an almost final expression of reasonable
opinion on this matter.[32] And it was in the Memorandum[33]
that the new commercial policy of the Foreign Office was
clearly defined; 'new', at least, in the sense that it recognized
officially the need for 'action (firm but cautious) by Diplomatists in remote countries in counteracting the pressure used by
the Representatives of other States to push the mercantile
interests of their countrymen'.

*   *   *

But it is often as important to note the qualifications to a
reform as it is to report the reform itself. Bryce himself had
felt that, with respect to loans, contracts, and concessions,
British diplomatists had erred on the safer side if they erred by
abstention. Moreover, both O'Conor at Peking and Plunkett at
Tokyo had reservations about the appropriate degree of
assistance to be given to British commerce in the East. O'Conor,
after describing early in February 1886 the scramble by the
German and United States Ministers for railway contracts and
concessions, concluded that British interests would be served
better by abstaining, especially just at that moment. He added,
two months later, that:

30. Nos. 36, 38, 39, *Correspondence respecting Diplomatic Assistance to British
Trade Abroad*, P.P.1886(c.4779)LX.
31. Rosebery to Bryce, 27 February 1886: P.R.O.,F.O./83/932.
32. *The Times*, 6 August 1886, 9d.
33. For text, see Appendix V.

It is one thing to interfere directly, or, so to speak, to tout for contracts for your own countrymen, and another to interfere to prevent as far as possible any unfair advantage being given to foreign subjects in consequence of official support, and I am confident that in abstaining from the one and in bearing the other constantly in mind, I shall meet with your Lordship's approval.[34]

Plunkett felt much the same. In a despatch from Tokyo of 8 April 1886, he referred to the dangers of the German diplomatic pressure, and argued that Britain's wisest course was to watch what other foreign diplomatists were doing 'but to be very chary in departing ourselves from the prudent line of conduct Her Majesty's Agents have hitherto been accustomed to consider it their duty to follow in regard to individual commercial speculations'.[35] Rosebery agreed, but reminded Plunkett of the instructions of 2 August 1885.

With attitudes as rigid as this, it was unlikely that the Bryce Memorandum, important though it was in marking a new departure in commercial diplomacy, would have much immediate effect in the Far East. Improving trading conditions in the late '80s had in any case removed the pressure to increase the pace of government activity on behalf of trade, and for a short period the commercial community seemed content with the progress they had achieved in 1885–6. The Government declined to accept Colonel Vincent's suggestion of a Select Committee on the subject. The Under-Secretary, James Lowther, replying to Vincent in a letter to *The Times*, 2 April 1892, reminded readers of Lord Salisbury's instructions of January 1886 to support British commercial interests 'where the interference of the representatives of foreign Powers is exercised to their detriment'. He added that he found it difficult to discover what other or further instructions could properly be given to British diplomatists:

In such matters, for example, as obtaining concessions it cannot be too steadfastly borne in mind that the very fact of official pressure being brought to bear in favour of one party must *ipso facto* exercise a

34. No. 52, *Correspondence respecting British Trade and Commerce in China* F.O.,C.P.5471.
35. No. 62, ibid., Plunkett's comments on the views of the London Chamber of Commerce are also instructive, especially since Rosebery agreed with them: Plunkett to Rosebery, 23 April 1886, No. 52, *Correspondence respecting Diplomatic Assistance to British Trade Abroad*, P.P.1886(c.4779)LX.

detrimental influence on the claims of all other competitors; and it would be obviously improper to impose on a British official, who before all things should be characterized by absolute impartiality, the invidious task of determining the respective merits of competing firms.[36]

The difficulty of assisting an individual merchant did not, however, preclude the Foreign Office from acting in China in the general interests of British trade. Any examples of foreign diplomatic pressure were vigorously protested, and the beginning of the policy of 'counter-concessions', adopted reluctantly after the Franco-Chinese Treaty of Tientsin, was marked by the conclusion of the Convention of 1886 (by which the Burmese frontier was defined, and promises exchanged to encourage the Burma-Yunnan trade). Counter-concessions remained the basis of active British diplomacy. When the Chinese, in response to the Franco-Chinese Convention of 1895, agreed to M. Gerard's concession for an extension of a railway from Langson in Indo-China over the frontier to Lungchow—the first railway concession given by China to a foreign company to construct a railway on Chinese territory—the British Government, as compensation for the violation of the Anglo-Chinese Convention of 1894, demanded and obtained the right to extend the Burma railway into Yunnan. France then proceeded to claim satisfaction, and China was compelled, in June 1897, to agree to further railway extensions, a French priority in the exploitation of mines in Kwangtung, Kwangsi and Yunnan, and the right to connect Indo-China to Yunnan by rail.

*   *   *

The complex story of the growth of European political interest in China during the '90s is already familiar, and it is unnecessary to repeat it here.[37] It might be argued that Russian political ambitions on the Pacific coast date, in any practical form, from the first work in 1891 on the trans-Siberian railway. The political interest of the Powers in

36. *The Times,* 9 April 1892, 6c.
37. The details are clearly set out in Philip Joseph, *Foreign Diplomacy in China, 1894-1900* (London, 1928), and in Langer, *Diplomacy of Imperialism.*

general seems to post-date the collapse of China in the Sino-. Japanese War. Dr. Joseph has explained that with

the Balkan scramble over and the partition of Africa nearly complete, the disclosure of China's weakness by Japan served as an invitation to the colonizing powers to stake their claims in China. Their relations with China, which until 1894 had been primarily commercial, now became predominantly political.

But he added that there was a distinction between the political demands and exactions of the Powers—'France and Russia were aggressive in their imperialism. Britain mainly sought to adjust the disturbed balance by compensatory gains.'[38]

Perhaps the most remarkable feature of the British attitude to China in the '90s was the prolonged failure to realize the political and commercial implications of what has been described as a shift of the focus of the Balance of Power to the Far East. Pelcovits claims that British mercantile opinion was not fully alerted until as late as 1897, when, for the first time, it became clear that the problem was no longer that of opening China equally to world trade, but of preventing the exclusion of British trade altogether from a China partitioned into self-sufficient European spheres of influence.[39] Curiously enough, Pelcovits seems to have overlooked altogether the events of 1885–6, when the change in H.M. Government's policy towards the promotion of trade and finance had turned on the fears, both of officials and traders, that unfair methods and foreign competition were severely encroaching on the British position in China. Curzon was certainly aware of a general anxiety among the British in the Far East at unfair foreign competition, government-aided, during the early '90s.[40] But it is true that an improvement in trading conditions since the mid '80s had tended to put foreign competition in the background again, and to restore belief in the truth of the Disraelian maxim that 'in Asia, there is room for us all'. The Foreign Office itself was almost as slow to realize that the 'commercial' activity of Russia, in particular, had a political importance.

38. Joseph, *Foreign Diplomacy in China*, pp. 62, 186–7.
39. Pelcovits, *Old China Hands*, pp. 206–7.
40. He had made this plain in his remarks to the Commons, when attacking the Government's passive attitude towards French activities in Siam: 27 *Parl.Deb.*4*s*.1349–50 (30 July 1894).

Salisbury, indeed, seems at first to have welcomed further Russian interest in China as a distraction from the Balkans, and said as much to the German Ambassador in October 1895.[41] When the Tsar visited Balmoral a year later, Salisbury took the opportunity to speak to him about conditions in the Far East. Instead of reproaching him with the steady increase of Russian political influence at Peking, Salisbury assured the Tsar that England had no desire to hinder the commercial and industrial development of Russia in that quarter 'because all that favoured industry created trade, and it was on our trade we lived'.[42] His attitude to commercial competition was as sanguine, and he told a deputation from the Associated Chambers of Commerce that if 'England, with all her traditions, with all her commercial machinery, with all her tremendous capital, with all her accumulated knowledge—if she cannot compete with Russia in the race for a market, we are, indeed, a degraded generation compared with what our fathers were'.[43] Even as late as March 1897 Salisbury had felt able to assure the Associated Chambers of Commerce that the lesson of history was that 'left alone, British industry, British enterprise, British resource is competent, and more than competent, to beat down every rivalry, under any circumstances, in any part of the globe, that might arise'.[44]

*   *   *

Other things being equal, Salisbury was probably right, but other things were not equal, and the competition which British merchants and contractors were facing in China was loaded against them. When British diplomacy was finally compelled, in 1898, to intervene decisively in the economic partition of China, there appear to have been two motives. The scene of rivalry and distrust in Anglo-Russian relations, as Professor Penson has remarked,[45] had shifted, moving east with Russian

41. A. W. Palmer, 'Lord Salisbury's Approach to Russia, 1898', *Oxford Slavonic Papers*, VI (1955), 103.
42. Salisbury to the Cabinet, 27 September 1896: quoted by L. K. Young, 'British Policy in China and the Boxer Rising, 1898–1902', Oxford thesis, 1960, p. 54.
43. Quoted, with approval, by *The Economist*, 20 June 1896, 794.
44. Langer, *Diplomacy of Imperialism*, p. 389.
45. L. M. Penson, 'The new course in British Foreign Policy, 1892–1902', *Transactions of the Royal Historical Society*, 4th ser. XXV (1943), 132.

expansion into Siberia and with the decline in the strength of the Chinese Empire. But, quite apart from that, the political influence of the Powers threatened the general interest of British trade (which any British Government was bound to defend, and on behalf of which H.M. Government had been pledged, since 1885, to intervene wherever foreign diplomatists were exercising undue influence on behalf of their own nationals). Considerations of the Balance of Power and national commercial interest were, in fact, interdependent; political power in the new context of international rivalry in China meant commercial advantage, and, similarly, commercial advantage was an element in the creation of political power. 1898 was the first international crisis of any importance to awake the Foreign Office to this politico-commercial equation —nowadays, unfortunately, a commonplace of world affairs.

The Foreign Office was alerted to the political dangers which faced Great Britain in China by two distinct events, occurring almost simultaneously—the German seizure of Kiao-chau, and the news of a further Russian Indemnity Loan. There is evidence that Germany had designs on a coaling station in the Far East from early in 1895, and that Russian assent was obtained for a German demand for Kiao-chau in August 1897; the murder of two German Catholic missionaries in South Shantung on 1 November 1897 was, of course, merely the pretext for occupation.[46] There is also evidence to suggest that the Russian decision to order a squadron to Port Arthur the following month was fully accepted by Germany, with whom Russia was to work 'hand-in-hand in the East', and that it resulted directly from the German occupation of Kiao-chau.[47] H.M. Government, which had known about German ambitions for a coaling station in the East for a couple of years, raised no objection to the German occupation so long as it resulted in no exclusive privileges for German subjects; equality of treatment had always been a central proposition in Anglo-Chinese diplomacy. Similarly, Britain had no objection to the Russian action in the Gulf of Pechili, provided that its aim was confined to securing an ice-free debouchment for the Trans-Siberian Railway.

Curzon alone among the Ministers was aware from the

46. *B.D.O.W.*,I,1(Ed. Note).   47. *B.D.O.W.*,I,3(Ed. Note),25.

beginning of the political implications; he even thought he saw the possibility of a war in the East, with Germany and Russia on one side and Japan and Britain on the other. In a Memorandum to Salisbury of 29 December he argued that the Russian and German position in the Gulf gave them command over the approaches to Peking and a consequent opportunity to exercise pressure on the Chinese Government—it was here that the British political position was most likely to suffer. Meeting with no response from the Cabinet, he argued again in a Cabinet Memorandum of 13 March that Britain would be wise to occupy Wei-hai-Wei. Retirement from north China would be fatal to our Far Eastern position, and decisive action was vital to retain whatever remained of our reduced influence in an area in which we had once been supreme.[48] Meanwhile, however, MacDonald had telegraphed from Peking, 7 March, the news that Russia had demanded the lease of Talienwan and Port Arthur, while the Sino-German Agreement on the cession of Kiao-chau and commercial concessions in Shantung had been signed two days before. Great Britain's political position was threatened, and H.M. Government was at last compelled to intervene. Salisbury, in a despatch to O'Conor (dated 28 March) which the Ambassador was instructed to read to the Russian Foreign Minister, set out the reasons which compelled Britain henceforward to treat the Chinese situation as directly involving the Balance of Power in the Far East. He explained that:

The commercial side . . . of the Russian policy in Manchuria . . . is in accord with the general views of Her Majesty's Government. Unfortunately, this cannot be said of the policy considered as a whole. The Russian Government have exacted from the Yamen not merely railway concessions through Manchuria and the lease of a commercial harbour at Talienwan; they have required also that the control of Port Arthur should be ceded to them for a like term of years under similar conditions. Now, Port Arthur is not a commercial harbour . . . (it) supplies a naval base, limited indeed in extent, but possessing great natural and artificial strength. And this, taken in connection with its strategic position, gives it an importance in the Gulf of Pechili and therefore at Peking. . . .

It is from this last point of view that the occupation of Port Arthur

48. Lord Ronaldshay, *The Life of Lord Curzon* (London, 1928), I, 277, 284.

chiefly concerns Her Majesty's Government. It is not because a position which can easily be made a naval arsenal of great strength has been acquired by Russia that they regret its occupation by that Power. It is because the possession, even if temporary, of this particular position, is likely to have political consequences at Peking of great international importance, and because the acquisition of a Chinese harbour notoriously useless for commercial purposes by a Foreign Power will be universally interpreted as indicating that the partition of China has begun. . . .[49]

In a sense Salisbury was right; the partial territorial disintegration of China had begun. In the name of the Balance of Power, Britain took up a lease of Wei-hai-Wei. France, shortly afterwards, leased Kwangchow Wan and claimed a special interest in the provinces of Kwangtung, Kwangsi, and Yunnan. And Britain immediately demanded, in recompense, the Hong Kong 'New Territories'.

Territorial disintegration brought with it elements of economic partition, but the main impetus towards the economic partition of China came from a different direction—the Indemnity Loan. The disastrous outcome of the Sino-Japanese War had left China with the need to raise—for indemnity and other purposes—an estimated £35 million. In 1895 the Russian Government provided a £16 million guaranteed loan, in return for which it obtained the right to establish the Russo-Chinese Bank (with wide financial and commercial powers in China) and permission to take the Trans-Siberian railway through Manchuria. To counteract this, Britain and Germany organized a joint £16 million loan in 1896 through a private Anglo-German Syndicate. But China needed a further loan, the conditions of which the Syndicate did not feel itself able to meet. On 22 December 1897, MacDonald cabled from Peking that he had heard that the Russian Government had offered a 4 per cent. Guaranteed Loan, the *quid pro quo* being the financing, construction, and control of all railways in Manchuria and North China, and a Russian successor to Sir Robert Hart as Inspector General of the Chinese Customs.[50] Salisbury's immediate reaction was to consider a counter-offer, either in

49. No. 41, *B.D.O.W.*,I,28.
50. The story of this and subsequent negotiations is told in J. A. C. Tilley's 'Memorandum respecting the Relations between Russia and Great Britain, 1892–1904', dated 14 January 1905, and printed in *B.D.O.W.*,I,1–3.

the form of a Guarantee or of a direct Government loan; 'if we can do nothing', he argued, 'the financial administration (of China) will fall into unfriendly hands to the detriment of our trade'.[51] Subject to Chinese acceptance of a formidable list of general concessions, H.M. Government offered on 8 January 1898 to provide a £12 million loan at 4 per cent. At the same time Salisbury, as a balm to Russian feelings and in order to reduce the international rivalry which threatened to lead to the partition of China, put out feelers for an Anglo-Russian entente. He suggested that a Russian sphere of influence should be accepted for the valley of the Hoang-Ho and territory to the north, while the Yang-tsze Valley should be under British influence. But his suggestions came to nothing, and their object was destroyed when, on 30 January, the Yamen informed H.M. Minister that China would borrow neither from Britain nor from Russia.

Here followed one of the least creditable episodes in the history of British diplomacy in China, but one, for all its unpleasantness, which established the basis of an official claim for British preponderance in the Yang-tsze Valley—the richest and most populous area of China. Salisbury's reaction to the news of the Chinese rejection was to insist, in the strongest terms, that British banks must have their share in any substitute loan negotiated by China with European financiers. Mac-Donald, meanwhile, was conducting a series of interviews with the Yamen 'for the purpose of extracting some concessions in return for the rejection of the offer of a guaranteed loan from Great Britain after it had in principle been accepted'. He told the Yamen, who could at first see no grounds for compensation, that H.M. Government had reluctantly agreed, at China's own request, to grant her a very exceptional favour, and that the Yamen could not expect us to accept with equanimity a brusque intimation that the Chinese Government had changed its mind—'Her Majesty's Government had a right to feel deeply affronted by what had occurred, and I would not be answerable for the consequences if they declined to make to Great Britain even such concessions as they had frequently admitted to be in China's best interests.' If, however, the concessions were granted, 'the rejection of our loan might be

51. Quoted by Palmer, *Oxford Slavonic Papers*, VI, 105.

forgiven'. Arguing on these lines MacDonald was able to secure the major conditions of the Loan itself without the need to raise a penny of Government money. The Chinese agreed to give an undertaking that the Inspector-Generalship of the Chinese Customs would remain in English hands so long as British trade was the most important in the Treaty Ports; they promised to open a port in Hunan within two years, and to open Chinese internal waterways to steam navigation; they gave a written guarantee against the alienation of the Yang-tsze region to a foreign Power.

The recognition by the Foreign Office of British interest in the integrity, above all, of the Yang-tsze Valley, brought H.M. Government irretrievably into Chinese affairs; and the political implications of a Russian advance on China from the North via Port Arthur and Manchuria, and a French advance via Indo-China from the South, meant some serious re-thinking on the eternal problem of the Balance of Power. British interests had always, until now, best been served by the Open Door for trade and the continued territorial integrity of China. But, as Professor Langer concluded:

The plain facts were that in 1898 China, unless she could rouse herself, was doomed. Her break-up and partition among the powers had begun. It was a calamity for the British, who could find not a single power to stand by them. So they jumped from the frying pan into the fire.[52]

* * *

In China, more than anywhere else, the political battle in 1898 was fought with economic weapons. For one reason or another, the expected total territorial partition of China never took place; the Balance of Power was decided by economic partition. In part for political reasons but above all for the security of her trade, Britain could not afford to allow her case to go by default. Curzon, again, was one of the first to see the new direction which British diplomacy should take. Writing to Salisbury on 11 April, after the British intention to take a lease of Wei-hai-Wei had been officially declared, he argued that:

... our next step in China should be to get some reliable syndicates to undertake the trunk lines N. and S. from the Yangtsze—N. towards Peking, S. towards Canton. People talk as if we could

52. Langer, *Diplomacy of Imperialism*, p. 480.

absorb, protect and administer the whole Yangtsze valley in the twinkling of an eye. I calculate that it contains over 150 million people, or two thirds of the whole population of China. Fifty years hence we shall not have done it, if we ever do. But I expect that railways are the best way of getting at the people and making your sphere of influence practical.[53]

Although Salisbury was far from ready, at this stage, to accept Curzon's suggestion, the basic argument—that the British political position in the Yang-tsze, if it were to be maintained at all, would have to be consolidated by the introduction of private capital—became, in time, a focal point in Anglo-Chinese diplomacy. The interests of the individual British concession hunter had very little, if anything, to do with it; indeed, concessions were obtained by MacDonald in rather greater numbers than British capitalists or concessionaires could cope with.[54] This was no case of British capitalists pressing for Government assistance in obtaining concessions for their private enrichment; the British Government was pressing concessions on an often reluctant City in the political interest of the Empire and in the general interest of British trade.

The first step taken by MacDonald in the battle for 'political' concessions was in answer to the French claims of April 1898. The Chinese Government had conceded the right to construct a railway to Yünnan-fu from the Tonquin frontier, and among Balfour's retaliatory demands (telegraphed to MacDonald on 13 April) was one for the grant of 'some railway concession'. MacDonald proceeded to claim, 'as a political concession', the right to construct a railway from Shanghai to Nanking on behalf of a British syndicate which had applied for his support earlier that month.[55] As the pressure increased among foreign diplomatists for Chinese railway concessions, H.M. Legation, under the energetic leadership of MacDonald, found itself drawn further into the struggle, reluctantly to begin with but with a certain competitive relish before very long.

Where no obvious political interest was involved, H.M.

53. Ronaldshay, *Lord Curzon*, I, 286.
54. See, for example, T. T. G. Mar, 'Anglo-Chinese Diplomacy, 1898–1911,' London thesis, 1929, pp. 152, 155–6, 166–7, and E-tu Zen Sun, *Chinese Railways and British Interests, 1898–1911* (New York, 1954), p. 44.
55. Nos. 5, 17, 21, 40, *Correspondence respecting the Affairs of China*, P.P.1899 (c.9131)CIX: Joseph, *Foreign Diplomacy in China*, p. 330.

Government was prepared to welcome further extensions of the Chinese railway system, whatever the nationality of the contractors and operators—'the more railways the better, from a commercial point of view' was Salisbury's reaction to the news of a possible French railway concession from Pakhoi to Nanning, *provided* that there was no danger of differential rates.[56] But 'political' railways presented a very different problem, and it was H.M. Government's serious objection to the Belgian Hankow-Peking concession which committed British diplomacy to an unprecedented degree of 'concession-mongering' in the Yang-tsze region, in which Britain, of course, claimed a special interest. A Belgian concession was itself a blow to this interest, but the news that the Russo-Chinese Bank was behind the Belgian Syndicate made the concession intolerable. In a telegram to MacDonald, 9 June 1898, Salisbury pointed out that:

A concession of this nature is no longer a commercial or industrial enterprise, and becomes a political movement against British interests in the region of the Yang-tsze.

You should inform the Tsung-li Yamen that Her Majesty's Government cannot possibly continue to co-operate in a friendly manner in matters of interest to China if, while preferential advantages are conceded to Russia in Manchuria and to Germany in Shantung, these or other foreign Powers should also be offered special openings or privileges in the region of the Yang-tsze. Satisfactory proposals will be forthcoming if the Chinese Government will invite the employment of British capital in the development of those provinces.[57]

The last sentence revealed the extent to which Salisbury was prepared to go to consolidate British gains in the Yang-tsze, and on 23 June he suggested to MacDonald, 'now that Kowloon and Wei-hai-Wei are arranged', the order in which other British projects should be pressed on the Yamen. Messrs. Jardine's Nanking–Shanghai railway was to be put first, followed by the Peking Syndicate's lines, the right of the Hong Kong/Shanghai Bank to finance the Newchwang line, and the opening of Nanning-fu.[58] MacDonald replied that he was

56. Salisbury to MacDonald, 25 May 1898: No. 137, *Correspondence respecting the Affairs of China*, P.P.1899(c.9131)CIX.
57. No. 175, ibid.
58. No. 202, ibid.

pressing all these, in addition to Mr. Pritchard-Morgan's scheme for a central mining administration in China, but he added that 'the relative urgency of each of these must be decided by circumstances'.[59] In spite of urgent British protests and the activity of the Legation, the Hankow-Peking concession was still in doubt. The China Association's letter to Salisbury of 8 July, for all its special pleading, summarizes the difficulties of the British position, both for businessmen and diplomatists. The Association argued that international rivalry in Far Eastern railway development was not purely financial—if it were, there might not be anything to worry about. The danger, in a politically helpless China, was that railways 'constructed by foreign states, under State auspices, with State aid' might become the basis of territorial claims. The Association, commenting on the particular case of the Hankow–Peking railway, argued with some justice that:

Commercial enterprise may be left to compete with commercial enterprise, private capital may be left to compete with private capital, but the operations of a great State bank [the Russo-Chinese Bank] cannot be rivalled by private finance either in regard to promptitude or daring. . . . State finance must be opposed by State finance, and the Association ventures to suggest that a great trunk line leading from North China into the heart of the Yang-tsze Valley is an enterprise too pregnant with political importance to be disregarded.[60]

Not without design, the Association had touched on the two factors which weighed most with the Foreign Office—the obligation to secure fair treatment for British commercial interests, and the danger to the political Balance of Power implied by foreign encroachments on the Yang-tsze. By the middle of July, the outlook was most depressing. Salisbury cabled despondently to MacDonald that the battle of concessions did not appear to be going well for Britain and that, with the mass of Chinese railways in foreign hands, we should concentrate on resisting the differential rates and privileges by which British trade might be strangled.[61] It was in this mood, depressed still further by news of Russian opposition to the Hong Kong & Shanghai Bank's loan concession for a railway from Shanhaikuan to Newchwang, that Salisbury

59. No. 205, ibid.   60. No. 214, ibid.   61. No. 232, ibid.

instructed MacDonald to inform the Chinese Government that H.M. Government would support it against 'any Power which commits an act of aggression on China by reason of China having granted to a British subject permission to make or support any railway or similar public work'.[62] MacDonald was less pessimistic, but even he was shaken by the news that, in spite of repeated assurances to the contrary and promises to consult before ratification, the contract for the Hankow–Peking line had been ratified on 12 August.

The Hankow–Peking ratification was decisive in bringing H.M. Government unreservedly into the race for railway concessions. MacDonald immediately advised London that heavy payment would have to be exacted for Chinese 'bad faith' if British opinion were to continue to bear any weight in Peking. As a punishment for bad faith rather than as compensatory concessions, MacDonald suggested that H.M. Government should insist that all the railways for which British syndicates were currently negotiating should be granted without delay on terms identical to those contained in the Hankow–Peking contract. Balfour accepted his suggestion for the Tientsin/ Chinkiang line, the Shanghai/Nanking line, and the lines in Honan and Shansi. Moreover, he authorized MacDonald, if the Chinese should show any signs of delay, to inform the Yamen that, unless they agreed at once, their breach of faith over the Peking–Hankow line would be regarded by H.M. Government as an act of deliberate hostility against Great Britain, and H.M. Government would act accordingly:

After consultation with the admiral, you may give them the number of days or hours you think proper within which to send their reply. The delay should not be of too long duration.[63]

A week later, MacDonald was instructed to inform the Chinese Government that, unless it complied immediately with these 'very moderate' terms, H.M. Government would require the concession of another line, and 'additional demands will be preferred as the result of further delay'.[64] Railway concessions, irrespective of merit, had become mere counters in a political game, and the Chinese Government wisely admitted total defeat. By the middle of September it had capitulated entirely,

62. No. 243, ibid.   63. No. 286, ibid.   64. No. 300, ibid.

denied all intention of disrespect to Britain, and agreed to the British demands.[65]

Political factors, clearly, were of importance in the 1898 'battle for concessions', although for British diplomacy the need to ensure fair treatment for the very considerable existing British trading interest was perhaps of even greater importance. As for the men on the spot, the tone of MacDonald's despatches suggests that he was carried away by the competitive atmosphere among the Legations in Peking. He did his job supremely well; as he boasted to Lord Charles Beresford in November 1898, 'not a single bona fide or approximately practical scheme which has been brought to this legation has failed to be put through, and the total mileage of British railway concessions gained by the end of the year was nearly twice that of our nearest rival [Russia]'.[66] But it is doubtful whether, once he realized the association of British political and commercial interests in the race for concessions, he ever took time to consider the precedents. British political interests were endangered, the whole position of British trade in China was threatened, and there was certainly no precedent which could over-rule both of these factors combined.

The tradition of non-intervention was too strong to permit a total abandonment of the old standards, however politically valuable diplomatic assistance to the individual concession-hunter or capitalist might be. The limits set to Government intervention, even where the strongest political reasons existed for permitting pressure with no holds barred, indicate the strength of the opposition to concession-mongering and loan promotion in the British Foreign Service, and suggest why it was that, where no urgent political reasons existed for change, British commercial diplomacy remained largely un-influenced by the new standards of Government trade promotion until after the First World War.

The basic attitude of British politicians and diplomatists to the promotion of trade and finance did not necessarily change, despite the excitement of 1898. A man like Curzon, who had dedicated his *Problems of the Far East* (London, 1894):

To those who believe that the British Empire is under Providence the greatest instrument for good that the world has seen, and who

65. No. 323, ibid.   66. No. 459 and enclosures, ibid.

hold, with the writer, that its work in the Far East is not yet accomplished

could accept a radical change in diplomatic methods as a means to a worthy end. The same, however, was not true of Salisbury. Only a few days after receiving the first news of the Hankow–Peking concession and after offering British capital to develop the Yang-tsze provinces, Salisbury assured a delegation from the Associated Chambers of Commerce, 14 June 1898, that Parliament would never consent to such a 'very grave departure from policy' as a British Government guarantee, financial support, or control of a Chinese railway—'the best way of obtaining the construction of railways in China is for independent English companies to produce the capital and ask for the concession'.[67] Even MacDonald, who had done more than anyone else to assist British concession-hunters in China, could explain to the China Association (at a dinner given in his honour in 1899) that:

British enterprise in China must be independent, individual and self-reliant. The moment it ceases to be this and leans too much on State assistance, it ceases to be enterprise, indeed I may say it ceases to be British.[68]

Both Salisbury and MacDonald were speaking from the stand-point of Government representatives, but there is no doubt that many in their audience of businessmen were in complete agreement.

* * *

An article in the *Edinburgh Review*, printed the year after the 'Battle for Concessions' and written, it seems, by St. John Brodrick (the Under-Secretary of State for Foreign Affairs), explained current and prospective policy with admirable clarity. Brodrick claimed that the days were over when British traders in China could be left to fight their battles for themselves, and when their only enemies were the Chinese preference for seclusion, and the corrupt bureaucracy. British enterprise had now to struggle with rivals 'to whom *laissez-faire* is an idle phrase', and who would accept any help in competition. British traders and entrepreneurs, no doubt, would have preferred to

67. Quoted by Pelcovits, *Old China Hands*, p. 235.
68. ibid., p. 257.

meet competition alone, had it not been for the unfair element introduced by foreign diplomatic participation. British policy for the immediate future should continue to be 'that of giving legitimate countenance and protection to our trading interests, and of seeing that our capital, if sent to China, incurs no undue risk'. Diplomacy must concentrate on protecting our treaty rights from infringement either by the Powers or by China herself; the published Blue Books had given the public some indication already of the diplomatic methods which the Foreign Office had been forced to adopt:

When we fence with Russia or France, China has to stand between the points of the foils. Each lunge is made, as it were, through the body of the Tsungli-Yamen.[69]

The period which follows, until 1914, is less interesting politically, since the rivalry between the Powers shifted back to Europe, the Mediterranean and Africa; but it left some fascinating problems for a student of the relationship between finance, trade and diplomacy. 1898 had established a pattern which proved irreversible; China was divided into spheres of 'interest'—Russian in the North, German in Shantung, British in the Yang-tsze Valley, and French in the South. While the door remained open, technically, for international trade throughout China, Chinese Loans and certain types of concessions, notably railways, were seen to have political implications which made free and open international competition impracticable.

The Powers were ready to subscribe to the United States' Open Door declaration in the autumn of 1899. Salisbury replied at once that British policy had always been to secure equal opportunities for the citizens of all nations in the trade of China, and that H.M. Government had no intention of departing from it.[70] When Mr. Choate, the U.S. Ambassador, asked him whether he would still be prepared to make the declaration if Russia refused to do so, Salisbury replied that he could see no reason not to, since 'the principles proclaimed in the Declaration were so exactly those on which Her Majesty's

69. Anon., 'The Problem of China', *Edinburgh Review*, (July, 1899), 244–66.
70. Salisbury to Mr. Joseph H. Choate, 29 September 1899: P.R.O.,F.O/ 405/90.

Government had habitually acted for many years'.[71] But the
point was that the Open Door was confined to trade; even the
British Government was compelled to acknowledge, after 1898,
that it no longer applied universally to finance. Mr. Chamberlain
had made the necessary distinction in a speech at the Royal
Exchange in Manchester, 16 November 1898. He explained
that H.M. Government had fought successfully for the principle
that no territorial acquisition by a foreign Power should alter
the existing position of an open door in the markets of China.
There had, it was true, been disputes about concessions, but
concessions stood on a very different footing from ordinary
trade; in railway finance, a requirement might be a mortgage
upon some territory—'This may have a political value and
involve political interests which take it altogether out of the
category of ordinary trade, and, therefore, the policy of the
open door must receive some modification if applied to the
question of concessions'. In theory, Chamberlain concluded,
there was still an Open Door for concessions in China—it was
open to anyone to request a concession from the Chinese
Government—but in practice the question of whether or not
the concession was obtained depended very largely on the
diplomatic pressure behind it.[72]

The restrictions on the Open Door in finance (and inevitably
also on the kind of trade which followed finance) became more
severe as international competition increased in China, and as
China itself lost its political stability. If Britain were to avoid
the physical partition of China—which would be politically
dangerous, and disastrous to the Open Door in trade—it was
important to limit as far as possible the points of friction
between the Powers. It was with this object that H.M. Government had accepted a 'modified' Open Door in Chinese finance
in 1898, and it was with the same object that H.M. Government
took the initiative, during the first decade of this century, in
reducing foreign competition over Chinese railway loans by
international agreement. But the central feature in the British
argument was the need for a mutually self-denying understanding between the Powers on the promotion of their citizens'
financial activities in alien spheres of interest. The need, in the

71. Salisbury to Lord Pauncefote, 19 December 1899: ibid.
72. As reported in *The Times*, 17 November 1898, 10c.

opinion of the Foreign Office, was aggravated by the breakdown in former restraints on foreign competition in China which followed the Chinese Revolution of 1911, and, more specifically, by the increased foreign interest in Chinese industrial opportunities which followed the successful conclusion of the Reorganization Loan of 1913. Unless the Powers were prepared to regulate the activities of their nationals—the Foreign Office told the French Government at the beginning of 1914—this new competition would spread indiscriminately throughout the industrial areas of China, with obvious risk to the continued good relations of the Powers. The Foreign Office memorandum (which was communicated in almost identical form to the German Government some months later) explained that H.M. Government was still, as always, 'entirely in favour of the policy of the open door in China and of equal opportunities for all', but that it felt that even among the most friendly Powers friction must arise unless this policy were 'by tacit arrangement interpreted in a spirit of accommodation to the known aspirations of the individual Powers to certain particular fields of industrial activity'. Britain had no desire to subscribe to 'the dangerous policy of defining spheres of influence', but H.M. Government could not fail to recognize that harmony between the Powers could only be maintained by each Power warning off its nationals from enterprises in areas in which other Powers, by long association, had acquired 'special interests'.[73] The occasion of this Memorandum was the recent conclusion of a loan by the Banque Industrièlle de Chine for the construction of harbour works at Pukow (which was in the heart of the British zone). The Foreign Office pointed out that it had recently declined to approve a British railway concession in Southern Yunnan (in the French zone), and asked that the French Government should be prepared to do the same for Pukow.

The division of China into areas of 'special interest' was, then, to some extent the responsibility of H.M. Government. But it is important to explain and emphasize the motive behind the division, and the limitations which were recognized

73. Memorandum communicated to the French Embassy, 1 January 1914: P.R.O.,F.O/405/90. The Memorandum to the German Government was communicated on 27 June 1914.

in applying it. The motive was quite clearly to avoid the political friction which would result from unbridled international competition. Such friction might have serious political consequences in Europe, but also it would end, most likely, in the physical partition of China, the erection of tariff barriers, and an end to the Open Door for trade. It was for these reasons alone that special privileges were given to British *finance* in the British zone in China; and even those privileges were bought at the price of exclusion from concessions in other parts of China and of agreed, limited shares in Chinese international loans. Nor was there to be a completely free hand for British finance in the Yang-tsze. Sir Edward Grey, in the context of a Japanese proposal for an industrial alliance in China to supplement the existing Anglo-Japanese political *entente*, reminded Sir J. Jordan, Minister at Peking, of the 'immense British interests' in the Yang-tsze region. British policy, he said, had been simply to safeguard these interests by maintaining control of the industrial situation (in particular, control of the lines of communication) and by preventing the challenging of our privileged position by the establishment of 'fresh foreign interests' in that region.[74] Jordan, however, telegraphed in reply that he understood 'fresh foreign interests' to apply to:

industrial interests of a political complexion only, such as railway, territorial, and perhaps mining concessions or loans involving control of important Government undertakings like China Merchants' Company, ironworks, docks, new ports etc., and not such industrial interests as *bona fide* participation in shipping, mining, or mills, in spite of specific allusion to latter in beginning of your telegram.

We were, Jordan pointed out, rigidly excluded only from *railway* construction in Manchuria, but Japanese and Russian railway policy operated there to our commercial disadvantage in a number of ways and warned us 'against treating railway concessions elsewhere as on the same footing as other industries'. He concluded that H.M. Government should give Japan clearly to understand that, apart from railways and such activities as were connected with them, 'we adhere alike in Manchuria and in the Yang-tsze Valley to the principle of equal economic oppor-

74. Grey to Jordan, 23 February 1914: P.R.O.,F.O/405/216.

tunities for all'.[75] Jordan's opinion was endorsed by Sir Edward Grey, and instructions to this effect were sent to Sir C. Greene, British Minister at Tokyo, the following day.[76]

The financial circumstances created by the First World War made it impossible to stick to the letter of this policy, but the general principle remained unchanged. When an American contracting firm, the Siems-Carey Company, was considering in 1917 the construction of a railway through the Province of Hupeh (in the Yang-tsze Valley), H.M. Government objected to the proposal. The State Department supported the right of the American company to proceed, but the Foreign Office explained that, much though it favoured the Open Door, the existence of special spheres of interest in China meant that British railway contractors were directly excluded from opportunities in China other than in the British sphere, and that it would be unjust to expose them to competition in the sole area within which they could operate; co-operation, however, between British and American capitalists might be considered, since the war was making overseas investment impossible for London.[77]

*   *   *

International loans, railways, and, to a more limited extent, mining enterprises in China were the areas in which British diplomacy worked most closely with finance in the period 1898–1914, a period which Overlach described as one of 'conquest by railroad and bank'.[78] It had been a firm tradition in British foreign policy not to favour one British interest over another: never to give exclusive support to individual interests, but only such support as could be of value to British trade and finance in general. In 1888, it may be remembered, Lord Rosebery had warned the Leeds Chamber of Commerce of the problems of supporting particular firms in the East. It was sound policy, he said, for British representatives to promote the claims of British commerce as a whole, but they would be put in a most invidious position if they were to make representations

75. Jordan to Grey, 27 February 1914: ibid.
76, Grey to Greene, 28 February 1914: ibid.
77. Williams, *Economic Foreign Policy of the United States*, pp. 42–43.
78. T. W. Overlach, *Foreign Financial Control in China* (New York, 1919), p. ii.

on behalf of particular firms, more especially if British firms were competing against each other for the same business and simultaneously claiming diplomatic support; moreover, there was always the possibility that a consul might become liable to charges of promoting his own commercial interests if he became too closely identified with one particular firm.[79]

The intense competition of 1898, and the serious threat to British political and trading interests which that competition implied, made it impossible to maintain this position. It was much more efficient, clearly, to press the interests of specific British financial groups than it was to crowd all British interests under the same diplomatic umbrella; and an additional stimulus derived from the fact that other Powers, with fewer existing interests to support in China, had even fewer scruples about putting their full support behind one particular financial group. The Banque de l'Indo-Chine, the Russo-Chinese Bank, and the Deutsche Asiatische Bank all had a direct connexion of one kind or another with their respective governments, and of the great foreign banks operating in the Far East at the beginning of 1898, the British banks were among the very few with no direct allegiance or formal government control. When in 1895 the Hong-Kong/Shanghai Bank took part in an Anglo-German financial combination to compete for the Second Indemnity Loan, it was in a business capacity and not as the nominee of the British Government; the British Legation approved of its action, but it never regarded itself as responsible for it.

There could be little doubt, however, of the full support which Sir Claude MacDonald was prepared to give to the Hong Kong and Shanghai Bank in 1898 (when it allied with the Deutsche Asiatische Bank in a loan to pay off the last Japanese indemnity), nor of the support which the Legation continued to give to the Bank, to the British and Chinese Corporation, and to Jardine, Matheson & Co. (acting as a group) in all requests for railway concessions over the next few years. The group, together with the Peking Syndicate's mining enterprises, tended to get what amounted to a monopoly of British diplomatic assistance. H.M. Government found no

79. Address to the Leeds Chamber of Commerce, 11 October 1888, printed in *Lord Rosebery's Speeches*, pp. 48–49.

pleasure in the monopoly, but it was difficult enough to attract British capital at all to China, and as difficult to ensure that applications for concessions were genuine and likely to be carried out once granted. China at the end of the century was a bright light against which all kinds of financial moths fluttered, and no diplomatic support could be wholly indiscriminate. Brodrick made this clear in March 1900, when he explained to the Commons that it was impossible to force every kind of concession from the Chinese Government:

They are concessions, let us remember, for mining, for railways, and for other advantages for which absolutely no payment is to be made in most cases—or at all events, no payment of which we are aware. Therefore we cannot, as a matter of right and justice, insist in every case where a British subject, sometimes without any serious capital at his back, comes forward and states that he desires to have the whole mining concessions throughout an entire province. That has been the case in some instances. We cannot in those cases declare to the Yamen that unless the concessions are granted we shall use force in order to compel them to do so.[80]

It was the need to attract responsible capitalists, and the difficulty of raising capital at a time when the City was distracted by events in South Africa, which, no doubt, persuaded H.M. Government to permit an official letter to be printed in the Prospectus of the Chinese Imperial Railway 5 per cent. Gold Loan (issued in 1899 by the Hong Kong and Shanghai Bank, for a total of £2,300,000). The letter declared that H.M. Government regarded as binding the Chinese promise not to alienate to any foreign Power lines named in the Contract for the Loan, and authorized the Bank to announce in the Prospectus that the Loan had been arranged 'with the full knowledge of Her Majesty's Government'. For similar reasons, a direct instruction seems to have been sent to Sir John Jordan at Peking to confine his support in railway concessions to the British and Chinese Corporation,[81] and the railway Agreements negotiated by the Corporation were formally registered at the Legation.[82]

80. 81 *Parl.Deb.4s.*883–4 (30 March 1900).
81. Referred to in Baron Erlanger's Memorandum to the Foreign Office of 4 June 1907: P.R.O.,F.O/405/180.
82. A selection of Chinese Railway Agreements is printed in Kent, *Railway Enterprise in China*, Appendices A–F.

The restriction of support in railway concessions to the British and Chinese Corporation became increasingly irksome to H.M. Government. By November 1898 (shortly before the Imperial decree which called a halt to further railway concessions), Sir Claude MacDonald had obtained concessions for 2,800 miles of line in China, compared with 1,530 obtained by the Russians and 720 by the Germans (the nearest rivals).[83] But when Kent was writing in 1907, only 94½ miles of British line and 588 miles of Anglo-Chinese line (counted as half that length in MacDonald's calculations) were in operation, with a further 300 miles of British line under construction; this was out of a total of 3,539 miles constructed and 1,285 under construction.[84] The policy of exclusive support was not yielding particularly rich dividends, and it was acting as a brake on the enterprise of other perfectly respectable British railway contractors, such as Messrs. Paulings and Messrs. Samuel & Co. When, in 1909, the Hong Kong and Shanghai Bank, together with its associates, was negotiating a general Agreement with French and German financial groups for equal participation in all loans and advances for railway purposes floated out of China by the Chinese Government, Sir Edward Grey felt compelled to point out to the Bank that although he would give its group exclusive support for the two lines now in question (the Hankow–Canton and Hankow–Szechuan Railways), he could not commit himself to support one particular firm for all future railway business in China, thereby debarring from the 'good offices' of H.M. Government other British firms of good standing who might wish to compete. Grey had already had to refuse support to Messrs. Samuel and Paulings, and he claimed that he would find it impossible to defend such a course with respect to future transactions. Grey closed the interview with the Bank's Manager (Charles Addis) by suggesting that British firms of financiers and contractors interested in the Far East should follow the French and German example and form a combination within which to share out business in the area.[85]

83. MacDonald to Lord Charles Beresford, 23 November 1898: Enclosure 1 in No. 459, *Correspondence respecting the Affairs of China*, P.P.1899(c.9131)CIX.
84. Kent, *Railway Enterprise in China*, pp. 182–3.
85. Grey to Jordan, 12 May 1909: P.R.O.,F.O/405/197.

Grey forwarded an account of this interview to Jordan at Peking for comment. Jordan endorsed Grey's opinion, and pointed to the invidious position in which he found himself, committed to the support of the Hong Kong and Shanghai Bank and under fire both from rival British groups (which accused him of using his position to further the interests of a particular set of British subjects to the exclusion of all others) and from the Chinese (who thought that they were being 'cornered' and forced into a relationship with one group of financiers when better terms could be obtained from another).[86] Grey replied that for future transactions H.M. Government should try to make it clear to the Chinese Government that they were at liberty to 'deal with the offers of all British firms of good standing on their own merits', provided that this was not going to result in a net loss to British enterprise in general.[87]

H.M. Government's aim was to ensure fair shares for British finance (for which a Combination would have provided the most sensible answer), and to reduce international friction by arranging parallel agreements sharing out the Chinese business between the Powers. The second objective could be achieved more readily than the first, since it proved impossible to bring the British capitalists together; but it could be achieved—in the absence of agreement between British capitalists—only by granting official support to the Hong Kong and Shanghai Banking Corporation. In 1908 the Hong Kong Bank, the Deutsche Asiatische Bank, and the Banque de l'Indo-Chine had agreed to act together in financing Chinese railways; U.S. bankers joined the Group in 1910, and it was this 'four-Power Consortium' which issued the Hukuang Railway Loan of June 1911.

Meanwhile, on the initiative of H.M. Government, the British and French Governments had exchanged Notes early in 1909 designed to restrain international competition in Chinese loans. 'A return to the system of active international competition for every loan which the Chinese may desire to issue'—the Foreign Office argued in a Memorandum communicated to M. Cambon in February 1909—'would be most unfortunate', since it would lead to misconception and competi-

86. Jordan to Grey, 23 June 1909: P.R.O.,F.O/405/198.
87. Grey to Jordan, 21 July 1909; ibid.

tion, resulting in turn in the Chinese obtaining cheap loans but with no effective guarantees.[88] The motive, naturally, was not to secure more profitable terms for British financiers, but to avoid the default and financial collapse which would follow an indiscriminate issue of Chinese Loans on inadequate securities; H.M. Government had too much experience of similar situations in the Near and Middle East to be prepared to see the same thing happen again under its eyes in the Far East. Of course, the Foreign Office was anxious to safeguard the interests of British financiers and the investing public, but, as Jacob Viner explained in this connexion, it was concerned not with the consequences of straightforward commercial competition for Chinese loan contracts, but with 'the results of competition by bankers who were acting as agents for their government, and who were not governed by strictly business considerations'.[89]

The problem of support for a particular British financial group came to a head in 1912. Yuan Shih-Kai, President of the Chinese Provisional Government formed after the collapse of the Empire, required immediate financial assistance; he therefore entered into negotiations with the Consortium for an interim loan, pending the negotiation of a large Reorganization Loan. But other groups in the City were also interested in Chinese finance; the Chinese Government's record in servicing its loans was remarkably good, and the issue of a large new loan offered a promising business proposition. An Anglo-Belgian Group, headed on the English side by Lord Balfour of Burleigh for the Eastern Bank (and including Schroders, E. D. Sassoon & Co. and Brown, Shipley & Co.), opened simultaneous negotiations, but H.M. Government, in return for the temporary support which the Consortium had given to Yuan Shih-Kai's government, regarded itself as committed to the Hong Kong & Shanghai Bank. The Foreign Office explained this position to the Hong Kong Bank in a letter of 14 March 1912; but it was careful to disclaim any intention of giving that Bank a monopoly of support in regard to any other loans to China, and reminded the Bank of Sir Edward Grey's proposal of a few days before that a British group should be formed on the lines of the French

88. Memorandum communicated 15 February 1909: ibid.
89. Viner, *Journal of Business of the University of Chicago*, I, 357–8.

and German groups, which would include the competing British houses and solve the problem of 'the obvious impossibility of granting exclusive Government support to one British bank'. The exclusive support promised to the Bank was to apply only to the temporary arrangements which had been made by the Consortium for financing the Chinese Provisional Government, and to the postponement of any competing loans which might conflict with the terms, or weaken the security, of the large Reorganization Loan which the Consortium was negotiating. The Bank was reminded, however, that Sir Edward Grey expected it in return for these assurances to arrange for the participation of competing British houses in the issue of the Reorganization Loan.[90]

In August 1912 the Foreign Office had news of two further loans which were being negotiated in London on behalf of the Chinese Government—a £10 million loan by the Crisp Syndicate, and a £10 million loan by the Chinese Engineering and Mining Co. Both proposers were informed that H.M. Government did not consider the Chinese Government free to borrow outside the Consortium until provision had been made for the repayment of the Consortium's advances. It was explained at the same time that 'as a matter of principle His Majesty's Government would never support a loan concluded without adequate guarantees for the control of the expenditure of the proceeds and without proper security'.[91] The Chinese Engineering and Mining Co. seems to have taken the hint, but Mr. Crisp, in defiance of H.M. Government's declared policy, went ahead with his loan, telling the Foreign Office that he knew that the issue would be a success and 'he did not see how His Majesty's Government could prevent the transaction from being carried through'. The Foreign Office acknowledged that they could not put pressure on the Syndicate interested in the Loan, but claimed that they could, and would if necessary, put considerable pressure on the Chinese Government.[92] Crisp still ignored the warning and concluded the loan with the Chinese Government; the first half was issued

90. No. 6, *Correspondence respecting Chinese Loan Negotiations*, P.P.1912–13(Cd. 6446)CXXI.
91. Grey to Jordan, 23 and 30 August 1912: Nos. 22, 24, ibid.
92. Grey to Jordan, 10 September 1912: No. 30, ibid.

in September 1912, but it was not well received and no second issue was made. The Foreign Office was able to persuade the Chinese Government to cancel the Crisp option on the Reorganization Loan, and the Consortium (from which the Americans had withdrawn) signed the contract for the £25 million Reorganization Loan in April 1913.

Several questions were asked in the House about the monopoly position enjoyed by the Hong Kong and Shanghai group with official support. In reply to Major Gastrell's enquiry, on 12 February 1913, Mr. Acland assured the House that H.M. Government's exclusive support was given pending only the successful negotiation and issue of the Reorganization Loan, after which it would not be continued.[93] Nor was exclusive support, even in this temporary phase, to apply to Central or Provincial Government industrial contracts, which were to be 'subject, as in the past, to open tender';[94] it extended merely to finance. And even in finance the pressure of the excluded financiers was so great that it proved impossible to maintain the Consortium's monopoly. The Sextuple Agreement of 1912 (between representatives of the British, French, German, Japanese, Russian and American groups) had covered industrial and railway loans, but the groups agreed, at an Intergroup Conference in Paris in September 1913, that the provisions of the Sextuple Agreement would no longer apply to these categories. The British Government—Balfour told the U.S. Ambassador several years later—were impelled at the time to accept this modification 'by the desire of the Japanese Government to resume their freedom in respect to industrial loans, and also by pressure from independent banking and other interests outside the British group which made it impossible for them to continue to recognize the British group in the consortium as alone entitled to their official support for the financing of industrial enterprises in China'.[95]

For a variety of motives, the principal of which was to bring to an end the spheres of special interest and re-create an international Open Door in Chinese finance, the U.S. Government

93. 48 *H.C.Deb*.5*s*.980.
94. 43 *H.C.Deb*.5*s*.1702–3 (11 November 1912).
95. Balfour to the U.S. Ambassador, 14 August 1918: No. 2, *Correspondence respecting the New Financial Consortium in China*, P.P.1921(Cmd.1214)XLII.

took the initiative in 1918 of proposing a new international consortium, consisting of all groups interested in Chinese finance in each of the main Powers. The groups were to be made as comprehensive as possible, were to act both with respect to administrative *and* industrial loans, and were to receive the exclusive support of their respective governments. H.M. Government was in favour of international co-operation, but Balfour felt that it would be difficult, in view of what had happened in 1913, to revive a monopoly in industrial loans.[96] As the negotiations developed, Lord Curzon (Balfour's successor at the Foreign Office) felt obliged—because of the dangerous financial situation in China, and the advantages which would be derived both for China and for foreign finance and trade from the proper control possible through an international consortium—to abandon H.M. Government's objections to an Agreement covering both administrative and industrial loans, and to authorize a British group to participate in the new consortium. But, in communicating this decision to the Hong Kong and Shanghai Bank, Curzon pointed out that exclusive Government support remained subject to certain conditions, the principal of which was that the existing Hong Kong and Shanghai Bank group should be enlarged 'in such a manner as to render it sufficiently representative of the financial houses of good standing interested in loans to China to prevent criticism on the ground of exclusiveness'. Industrial loans were to be included only on the understanding that H.M. Government's support was limited to the financial side of the loans, and that the industrial side—the contracts for the execution of works and the supply of materials—would be put to public tender.[97] The Bank pointed out in reply that this was the third time H.M. Government had requested an enlarged participation in the financing of Chinese Government Loans. The Bank, which had previously acted independently in this respect, had already found its share of the business reduced by two-thirds, and it refused to reduce it any further except to invite the participation of N. M. Rothschild and Sons ('as a representative financial house of standing') and of the British

96. ibid.
97. Foreign Office to Hong Kong and Shanghai Banking Corporation, 17 March 1919: No. 5, ibid.

Trade Corporation (which was an institution created and operating under Government auspices).[98]

It was this which proved the chief stumbling block. Neither the British nor the French Governments were prepared to give exclusive support to any particular group of financiers. As Curzon told the Hong Kong Bank, other than the existing members of the Bank's group (Baring Bros., the London County and Westminster Bank, Parr's Bank, Schroder's, and the Chartered Bank), Lloyd's Bank, Messrs. Brown, Shipley & Co., the Eastern Bank, Messrs. M. Samuel & Co., and Messrs. C. Birch, Crisp & Co. had all expressed a wish to participate in any group enjoying British Government support; the Midland Bank, Barclay's, and the National Provincial might also be included.[99]

But Curzon was under pressure from the United States; the situation in China, as always, was deteriorating; and a rapid agreement of some kind was necessary. There was some point in the Hong Kong Bank's argument that unrestricted participation, besides impairing the efficiency of the British group and reducing individual shares to insignificant proportions, would be difficult and invidious to apply; it was impracticable to include everyone, but complaints of partiality would be as loud whichever interest, in the end, were excluded. Curzon, who attached the 'highest importance' to British participation in the consortium, finally agreed to a compromise by which the Hong Kong Bank Group, extended as suggested by the Bank itself, would be accepted

as a representative national partner in the consortium, even without a guarantee of exclusive official support, it being of course understood that His Majesty's Government would continue, as hitherto, to afford to the group the fullest measure of support possible in all operations arising out of its connection with the consortium.[1]

The China Consortium Agreement, concluded on 15 October 1920 and approved by the British, American, French, and Japanese Governments, was obviously an object of intense suspicion and hostility in China itself.[2] A Foreign Office

98. Hong Kong and Shanghai Banking Corporation to the Foreign Office, 21 March 1919: No. 8, ibid.
99. Foreign Office to the Bank, 20 May 1919: No. 10, ibid.
1. Foreign Office to the Bank, 17 July 1919: No. 21, ibid.
2. Printed as No. 39, ibid.

Memorandum, surveying British policy in China a decade later (8 January 1930), felt that the Consortium was so unpopular that it was probably doing more harm than good; it might be more in the British general interest to return to a condition of free and open competition.[3]

*   *   *

The 1930 Memorandum summarized the principles of British policy in China:

We have no territorial or imperialistic aims. Our first concern is to maintain our position in the trade of China, which is largely bound up with the prosperity of Hong Kong and the fortunes of the Maritime Customs Administration, and to secure adequate protection for British lives, property and business enterprises. Our second concern is to maintain the principle of the 'open door' and equal opportunity for all and to see that China does not fall under the tutelage of any single Power. For these reasons we desire to see a united, well-ordered, prosperous and peaceful China, and it is our policy to endeavour to co-operate to that end with the other Great Powers concerned. These are the root principles underlying all our efforts in China.[4]

There could hardly have been a better statement of British official motives since 1834. Trade and its protection were the major, and, indeed for most of the time, almost the *sole* preoccupation of British policy. Back in 1864, Henry Layard, as Under-Secretary of State, had told the House that British policy in Japan and China 'was founded almost entirely upon our commercial interests' and that 'we were there because we wished to protect and extend our commerce'.[5] For a short time, in and around 1898, China became the centre of international political rivalry, but that rivalry had shifted back to the West by the beginning of the twentieth century.

In many respects, therefore, the history of the British in China provides the clearest illustration of the developing relationship between finance, trade, and British diplomacy under stress of increased foreign competition. The decision in

3. Printed in R. Butler and J. P. T. Bury (eds.), *Documents on British Foreign Policy 1919–1939* (London, 1960), 2nd ser. VIII, 26.
4. ibid. 4.
5. 174 *Parl.Deb.3s.*1101(15 April 1864).

1885—a crucial decision—to give diplomatic support to British commercial interests where foreign diplomatic representatives were interfering to their detriment, was based on experience in China and Japan. It was this experience, too, which had contributed to the revised formulation of British commercial diplomacy in Bryce's Memorandum of 1886. The British commercial position in the Far East was shaken by the impact of foreign competition. But it was not against genuine competition that British merchants felt able to complain, or against which the Foreign Office was prepared to act. Official intervention was intended to forestall, prevent, or remedy the closing of doors to trade and the unfair competition of differential rates and selective tariffs. At the height of the battle of concessions, when MacDonald in Peking had thrown most of his scruples to the winds and was brow-beating the Chinese Government into accepting his demands, he had still (as he told Salisbury in July 1898) 'consistently informed the Chinese Government that, as to differential rates and privileges [in railway concessions], we want none ourselves, and cannot admit that other nationalities have a claim to them'.[6]

The battle of concessions itself was a startling departure from precedent, but, in the political and economic condition of contemporary China, H.M. Government had no alternative except to participate. Britain still retained by far the largest share of China's external trade; it may not have been so important a trade as had been expected earlier in the century, but it was politically impossible for any British Government to permit it to be eliminated. A partition of China without British participation, or even a division into spheres of influence, could have had no other result than the decline and possible destruction of Britain's trading position. Britain, no more than Baron von Bülow, wanted a partition of China, formal or informal, but she had even more to lose if she held back—'The traveller cannot decide when the train is to start, but he can make sure not to miss it when it does. The devil takes the hindmost.'[7]

6. MacDonald to Salisbury, 23 July 1898: No. 245, *Correspondence respecting the Affairs of China*, P.P.1899(c.9131)CIX.
7. Baron von Bülow on the Partition of China, as quoted by Kent, *Railway Enterprise in China*, p. 142.

Once the battle of concessions was over, H.M. Government was left with the distasteful but, in the circumstances, inevitable legacy of exclusive support for the few substantial British enterprises in China. But the support which it gave was not intended to guarantee substantial profits on investment. Nor did it usually go further than the provision of opportunities for such investment. Much diplomatic effort, for example, went into Article IX of the Treaty of Shanghai (5 September 1902) by which the Chinese Government, recognizing the advantages of developing its mineral resources and the desirability of attracting foreign capital, undertook to bring out a completely revised and improved code of Mining Regulations. But, once this undertaking had been obtained, H.M. Government was unprepared to take any part either in raising the capital for mining enterprises, or in their management: 'You may take a horse to the water', said Lord Cranborne, 'but you cannot make him drink.' The result, as with the railway concessions, was that British capital simply failed to come forward.[8] While Earl Percy (Lord Cranborne's successor) complained bitterly in 1905 that British capitalists were not as ready as foreign capitalists to finance railway construction in China, he still maintained that the Foreign Office itself would take no part in raising the money; the limit of its functions was the application of pressure for valuable concessions, after which the rest must be left to private enterprise.[9]

If H.M. Government were to maintain (in the interests of British trade) its special position in the Yang-tsze Valley and prevent the encroachment of other Powers (and the possible subsequent closure of the Yang-tsze markets), it needed to develop the British sphere; and the only way by which the sphere could be developed was by concentrating official influence behind the few British capitalists who could be persuaded to take an interest in the area. As and when other City groups or British contracting firms began to take an interest themselves, the Foreign Office, though bound to some

8. The reasons for the failure of British mining concessions to pay dividends, or even to be developed at all, are explained by William F. Collins, *Mineral Enterprise in China* (London, 1918), pp. 55–77.

9. 151 *Parl.Deb.4s.*158 (3 August, 1905). Lord Cranborne's remark, in the context of a general complaint of British capital failing to come forward to develop Chinese concessions, is in 110 *Parl.Deb.4s.*739 (3 July, 1902).

extent by existing obligations, attempted to ensure that they received equal opportunities. But there was always a balance to be struck between the equitable and the practicable. When Yuan Shih-Kai's Provisional Government needed money in 1912, it needed it in a hurry, and H.M. Government thought it saw an opportunity to bring anarchy, at last, to an end. The obvious source for rapid financial support was the Consortium, already deeply involved in Chinese finance. And rapid support, given without what would normally be regarded as sufficient security (but with the full approval of the Powers), gave the Consortium in turn a reasonable claim for exclusive support pending the issue of the Reorganization Loan.

Underlying the whole of British policy in China was the need—either by maintaining the Open Door for trade, or by the prevention of anarchy—to ensure equal opportunities and fair treatment for British traders and capitalists in China. Conditions in China modified the actual *practice* of British diplomacy: 'it is clear', Consul Bourne once argued, 'that Englishmen in China cannot be confidently left to crytallize, as our fellow subjects in the colonies can be'.[10] But the general policy of a 'fair field and no favour' remained fundamentally unchanged; and it was this policy which was to end, inexorably, in British official participation in, and even promotion of, the economic partition of China.

10. *Report of the Mission to China of the Blackburn Chamber of Commerce, 1896–1897* (Blackburn, 1898), p. 146.

CHAPTER 6

LATIN AMERICA

LATIN AMERICA was one of the most important outlets for British trade and investment throughout the nineteenth century, and it maintained its relative importance until the Second World War. But at the same time, the Republics have attracted little attention among British historians.[1] The penalty of neglect has been an understandable confusion as to the part taken by Britain's very considerable economic interests in the formulation of British official policy.

The combination of substantial economic interests with frequent, if minor, naval coercions has laid H.M. Government open to the charge of economic imperialism in the Western hemisphere. Brailsford believed that it was 'the claims of various financial adventurers' which persuaded Britain and Germany to blockade Venezuela in 1902, while, in Latin America generally, 'the European financier goes forth equipped with resources taken from our stores on a career of conquest and exploitation, protected by our flag and backed by our prestige'.[2] Lenin wrote of 'semi-colonies' such as Persia, China and Turkey, and other 'dependent' countries such as those of South America, 'which formally are politically independent, but which are in fact enmeshed in the net of financial, and diplomatic dependence'; British finance capital dominated Argentina in particular, aided by 'its faithful "friend" diplomacy'.[3] Achille Viallate described how the Latin American Republics had often, in the nineteenth century, 'found them-

---

1. The only work of any importance to be published on the British connection (after the Emancipation period itself) is H. S. Ferns' *Britain and Argentina in the Nineteenth Century* (Oxford, 1960). Two American historians, J. F. Cady and A. K. Manchester, have contributed specialized studies of British policy—*Foreign Intervention in the River Plate* (Philadelphia, 1929) and *British Pre-eminence in Brazil* (Chapel Hill, 1933). Two useful works published within the last few years are A. P. Tischendorf, *Great Britain and Mexico in the era of Porfirio Díaz* (Durham, N.C., 1961) and David Joslin, *A Century of Banking in Latin America* (London, 1963)
2. Brailsford, *War of Steel and Gold*, pp. 54, 237.
3. Lenin, *Imperialism*, p. 78.

selves threatened by foreign intervention in behalf of creditors', and quoted Mexico in 1862 and Venezuela in 1902 as examples of forcible intervention by European Powers in the interests of their bondholders.[4] Lambert explained that, 'as a rule, European governments were interested in the Latin American states only when they defaulted on loans made by European capitalists'.[5] Fritz Sternberg classified Central and South America before the First World War as 'important components of the general pre-capitalist and semi-capitalist periphery of the European capitalist imperialist states', adding that 'in some cases Central and South American countries were so dependent on them as to be practically semi-colonies'.[6] More recently John Strachey could explain the embarrassing failure of British policy in Latin America to fit his rules only by the absurd argument that the two reasons why Britain never tried to annex parts of South America were, first, that South America was protected by the Monroe Doctrine, and second, that 'the types of governments which existed in South America ... were comparatively well suited to the interests of foreign investors':

Neither Egyptian chaos nor Boer intransigence menaced the interests of the (predominantly) British bondholders and entrepreneurs in South America. There were defaults, but there were no insuperable obstacles to successful investment such as existed in North and South Africa until the regions were annexed. There was no final necessity for whistling up the gunboats.[7]

These interpretations of British policy would be unimportant if any substantial study of the subject actually existed, or if serious historians were not inclined to accept them. D. W. Brogan, for example, when reviewing Strachey's *End of Empire*, regretted that Strachey had not discussed Latin America as an area of 'imperial aggression'; these 'weak, corrupt, ever-changing independent governments were obviously and conspicuously open to foreign pressure'[8]—a point which is valid enough, but which is likely to be misleading without an explanation of the nature of that pressure and its source.

4. Viallate, *Economic Imperialism*, pp. 61, 64–65.
5. R. S. Lambert, *Modern Imperialism* (London, 1928), p. 66.
6. Fritz Sternberg, *Capitalism and Socialism on Trial* (London, 1951), p. 236.
7. Strachey, *End of Empire*, p. 118.
8. *Encounter* (May, 1960), 77.

Herbert Feis, in his deservedly-praised *Europe: the World's Banker, 1870–1914*, refers to the Anglo-German coercion of Venezuela as 'the most startling' of British Government interventions to make Governments face old debts and claims—'the government had swung full circle; the whole force of the state had been put behind the foreign investor'.[9] Even Professor Ferns—who, of course, should have known better—felt able to argue that 'the pressure of the financial interests to use force in the collection of debts and other claims, which Salisbury had resisted during the Baring Crisis, was successful in 1902 in the case of Venezuela'.[10] A misunderstanding of the scope, nature, and degree of the assistance H.M. Government was prepared to give to British traders and investors lies at the heart of Gallagher and Robinson's interesting paper on 'The Imperialism of Free Trade', and, to some extent, invalidates the argument. It cannot reasonably be maintained, for example, that a policy of 'indirect political hegemony over new regions for the purposes of trade' was adopted by British diplomacy in Latin America after the 1820's, even if this were true—which is arguable—for the decade before. Gallagher and Robinson claim that a conscious and deliberate policy of expansion in the 'informal dependencies' was adopted by H.M. Government during the mid-Victorian age, a period in which 'the orthodox interpretation would have us believe . . . the political arm of expansion was dormant or even withered'. The Government's policy was to force an entry into Latin America, 'to encourage stable governments as good investment risks', and to coerce 'weaker or unsatisfactory states . . . into more cooperative attitudes'. Intervention declined as the stability of the main centres of British investment interest, Brazil and Argentina, increased. But 'British governments still intervened, when necessary, to protect British interests in the more backward

9. Feis, *Europe: The World's Banker*, pp. 108–9.
10. Ferns, *Britain and Argentina*, p. 486, though it might be a bit unfair to single this out. After all, such is the obscurity of Latin American affairs in general, and of Venezuelan affairs in particular, that both a former Historical Adviser to the Foreign Office and a former Permanent Under Secretary appear to believe that it was the bondholder grievance in Venezuela which was referred to arbitration at the Hague in 1903, whereas in fact, of course, it was nothing of the kind: Sir James Headlam-Morley, *Studies in Diplomatic History* (London, 1930), p. 16 n; Lord Strang, *Britain in World Affairs* (London, 1961), p. 233.

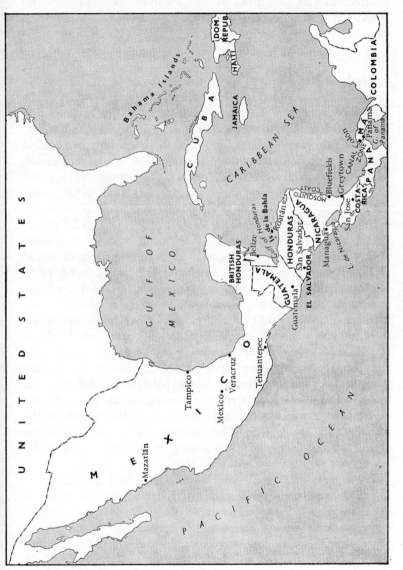

Map 5   Mexico and Central America

states; there was intervention on behalf of the bondholders in Guatemala and Colombia in the 'seventies, as in Mexico and Honduras between 1910 and 1914'.[11] The argument is unsound.

*   *   *

Trade and investment formed the basis of British interest in Latin America, and trade, together with the protection of the lives and property of British subjects, was the preoccupation of British diplomacy. But the claim that this had anything to do, except in the most indirect sense, with the political condition of Latin America after the Emancipation, is misconceived. Latin America, unlike China, never at any point reached the centre of the international political scene. Of the areas where questions need to be asked about the relationship of trade, finance and politics in British foreign policy—Egypt, Turkey, Persia, Africa, China—Latin America alone was unquestionably a-political. Not only was it so in the context of world affairs. British statesmen resolutely refused to intervene, or to become entangled, in the internal political affairs of the Continent. Castlereagh, after the disastrous episode of the British expeditions to Buenos Aires, drafted a Memorandum for the Cabinet in 1807 on future British policy in South America. He rejected altogether any prospect of territorial acquisition, any dream of exclusive British political influence, or any intention to intervene further in the political condition of the Spanish Colonies—'the particular interest which we should be understood alone to propose to ourselves [in the context of the war with Napoleon] should be the depriving our enemy of one of his chief resources, and the opening to our manufactures the markets of that great Continent'.[12]

The rejection of any territorial ambitions in Latin America; the resolve not to intervene in internal politics; the desire to open Latin American markets to British trade—these have been the guide-lines of British official policy ever since. *Equality* of treatment was all that was asked. Late in 1815, Castlereagh refused outright Spain's offer of special trading privileges in

11. John Gallagher and Ronald Robinson, *Economic History Review*, 2nd ser. VI (1953), 8–10.
12. Quoted in Ferns, *Britain and Argentina*, p. 48.

return for British mediation and active assistance with the rebellious colonies. He advised the Spanish Government that:

to command success the views of both nations ought to be liberal to South America and not invidious to other nations. A system of exclusive commercial advantage to the mediating Power would render her interposition odious and destroy all her just influence; you will perceive that the Prince Regent has never sought for any exclusive advantages. He has always recommended the commerce of South America to be opened to all nations upon moderate duties, with reasonable preference to Spain herself.[13]

Canning's policy for Latin America followed exactly these lines, though the political situation had developed to such an extent that a decision could no longer be avoided on Recognition. The Republics, by the beginning of the 1820's, had overcome all but the last vestiges of Spanish resistance. Out of respect for Spain and for the principle of monarchy, Britain delayed recognizing the *de facto* governments as long as she could. But the decision of our most dangerous trading rival on the Continent (the United States) to recognize in 1822, and the need for diplomatic protection for British lives and property during a boom period in British trading and investment interest in the new Republics, meant that recognition could not be postponed indefinitely. Canning gave these as his reasons, in fact, when recommending the recognition of Mexico in his Cabinet Memorandum of December 1824. The most important reason, he argued (possibly because he realized that it was the one likely to carry most weight with his aristocratic colleagues), was to check the ambitions and ascendancy of the United States. But there was the further point that more and more British capital was daily being sunk in mining and territorial enterprises in Mexico. This was money which would take time to mature, and during this time it was inevitable that troubles would arise which would require the diplomatic intervention of the British Government.[14]

13. Quoted in C. K. Webster, *The Foreign Policy of Castlereagh 1815–1822* (London, 1925), p. 409. A similar preference was acknowledged for Portuguese trade with Brazil in the Anglo-Brazilian Commercial Treaty of 1827 (Article XX).
14. Quoted by Harold Temperley, *The Foreign Policy of Canning, 1822–1827* (London, 1925), p. 553.

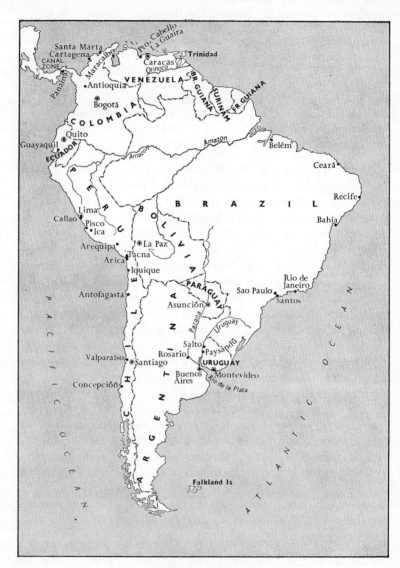

Map 6   South America

Recognition took the form of Commercial Treaties, negotiated on a standard pattern which secured a *locus standi* for British subjects and consular officials in the countries in which they operated, provided them with some protection against forced enlistment, inequitable taxation and interruption in the practice of their religion, and guaranteed most-favoured-nation treatment for their trade. The Latin American treaties were not, as Fay imagined, 'exceptionally favourable' to Britain.[15] They promised certain minimum standards of security without which foreigners were unlikely to wish to settle or invest in the Republics, and they guaranteed for trade, in either direction, as fair or as unfair treatment as that received by the best-situated foreign trade. They were not designed to secure any preference for British traders in Latin American markets, since the whole object of British policy was to open the markets of Latin America on equal terms to world trade.

To the extent that there were more British traders in Latin America than there were Latin American traders in Britain, it was true to begin with that the Treaties were often one-sided in effect, if not in intention. But to later generations the position could be reversed; Britain began to buy much more from the Argentine, for example, than the Argentine bought from us. It was true also that the Treaties, some of which were of unlimited duration, restricted the freedom of the Republics to alter their tariffs as between nations, but they were designed only to ensure equality of treatment for all foreigners, and the tariffs themselves were free to move vertically, if not horizontally. The notorious 1827 Anglo-Brazilian Commercial Treaty was the only Latin American Treaty to contain a provision setting a maximum tariff on imported British manufactures (of 15 per cent.). Article XIX, which contained this provision, was an inheritance from an earlier phase of Anglo-Portuguese diplomacy: it represented a departure from what had become the usual British practice; it was unpopular with Canning himself; and it was thoroughly damaging to native Brazilian manufactures. Beginning as a concession to extensive British trading interests in Brazil (which had enjoyed similar privileges while Brazil was still Portuguese, as a reward for the rescue of the Portuguese Court in 1808), Article XIX ended as a weapon in

15. E. A Benians (ed.), *The Cambridge History of the British Empire*, II, 398.

H.M. Government's attempt to enforce the abolition of the Brazilian slave trade. But it should be made clear that there was nothing in the Treaty to make this privilege exclusive to Britain; any other trading nation could negotiate a similar treaty provision or could, through the most-favoured-nation clause in its own treaty, claim identical treatment.[16]

* * *

Fair and equal treatment, not *favoured* treatment, was what British diplomacy aimed to achieve for British trade in Latin America; and this could and had to be achieved, *pace* Gallagher and Robinson, without intervention in the politics of the Republics. Canning—Temperley explains—was well aware that attempts to stabilize conditions in Latin America would only have resulted in that perpetual interference in their politics which he so detested. Canning hoped to promote political tranquillity by developing trade, 'but he always refused to sanction their loans or to give direct financial aid, for he knew that such financial methods would bring political complications in their train'; Hamilton, in fact, was disowned and recalled from his post in Mexico in 1824 for proposing a British guaranteed loan.[17]

With a brief and painful exception in the 1840's, this was the policy which was observed thereafter. H.M. Government was prepared to defend the general interests of British commerce and the particular interests of legitimately aggrieved British claimants, but it was *not* prepared to take the defence of general interests as far as intervention in the internal affairs of foreign states.

The Allied expedition to Mexico of 1861–2 is an instructive example. British claims against the Mexican Government for damages to the persons and property of British subjects had been accumulating over several decades of civil war. A conclusive Liberal victory at the end of 1860 seemed at last to provide an opportunity to press these claims. But Lord Russell's instructions to the new British Minister in March 1861 emphasized that H.M. Government's policy in Mexico was non-

16. The text of the Anglo-Brazilian Treaty is printed in *B.&F.S.P.*, 1826–1827, pp. 1008–25.
17. Temperley, *Foreign Policy of Canning*, pp. 185, 184 n.2.

intervention and the preservation of Mexican independence; Sir Charles Wyke was urged always to bear in mind that 'neither in Mexico nor in any part of the world do Her Majesty's Government seek any exclusive political influence, nor any commercial advantages which they are not ready to share with all the nations of the earth'.[18] Mexico, unfortunately, was in no position to meet the claims, and by September 1861 negotiations were proceeding at Paris, London and Madrid for combined action. It was already clear that France was not unprepared for active intervention in the internal politics of Mexico, and Russell warned Earl Cowley (the British Ambassador in Paris) that H.M. Government was on principle opposed to forcible interference in the internal affairs of an independent nation, believing that the institution of a capable Government in Mexico was 'more likely to follow a conduct studiously observant of the respect due to an independent nation, than to be the result of an attempt to improve by foreign force the domestic institutions of Mexico'.[19]

It was on this understanding that Sir Charles Wyke was instructed to be 'most careful to observe with strictness' Article II of the Convention of London (signed by the three Powers on 31 October 1861) by which, in the hope of restraining the French, it was provided that no influence was to be used in the internal affairs of Mexico calculated to prejudice the right of the Mexican nation freely to choose and establish its own form of Government.[20] When, in January 1862, Wyke and the British Commodore were unwise enough to put their names to a Proclamation to the Mexican people (which argued the 'higher interest' of the Allies—over and above the ordinary claims—in urging the formation of a firm and stable form of government), Russell strongly disapproved. He told the Admiralty that Sir Charles Wyke and Commodore Dunlop obviously believed that

the 'regeneration' of Mexico [was] the primary object to which the efforts of the Allied forces [were] to be directed, a belief wholly unwarranted by the terms of the Tripartite Convention, and by the instructions given to Her Majesty's servants for carrying them out. ... Commodore Dunlop must not suppose that Her Majesty's

18. No. 1, *Correspondence relative to the Affairs of Mexico*, P.P.1862(2915)LXIV.
19. No. 45, ibid.   20. No. 67, ibid.

Government have undertaken to inaugurate a new era or to attempt the regeneration of Mexico. The object of Her Majesty's Government is definite and is limited to the protection of British persons and British property.[21]

The mention of the Tripartite Convention in the Queen's Speech on 6 February 1862 brought fresh fears of territorial and political ambitions, and fresh affirmations of political disinterestedness from the Government. Ironically enough it was Disraeli—who in 1846 had urged the creation of a European Protectorate in Mexico[22]—who, sixteen years later, showed the greatest alarm at the prospect of Britain striking at the political independence which she herself, through Canning, had created, and playing a principal part in the reintroduction of monarchical rule at the point of the sword.[23] Russell himself felt nothing but apprehension at Archduke Charles's proposed candidature for the throne of Mexico. He told Lord Bloomfield, in a prophetic despatch, 13 February 1862, that if Charles were to accept the crown he would have to rely wholly on the support of the French troops; support for the monarchy would be long in arriving, and if foreign support were withdrawn, the Emperor might be driven out by the Republicans.[24]

The final break took place at the Allied Conference at Orizaba, 9 April. Relations had grown increasingly strained, particularly over the offensive attitude of the French to the Mexican Government and the harbouring of the leaders of the Church party in the French camp. The French Commissioner wanted to march on Mexico City, declaring his intention to discontinue negotiations with the Government of President Juarez. The British and Spanish Commissioners refused to agree, and shortly afterwards withdrew their remaining forces from Vera Cruz.

* * *

Non-intervention, illustrated so clearly by H.M. Government's withdrawal from Mexico in 1862, was to be the rule.

21. No. 47, *Correspondence relative to the Affairs of Mexico, Part II*, P.P.1862 (2990)LXIV.
22. 88 *Parl.Deb.3s.*992 (24 August 1846).
23. For these debates, see 165 *Parl.Deb.3s.*(6 February 1862).
24. No. 10, *Correspondence relative to the Affairs of Mexico, Pt. II*, P.P.1862(2990) LXIV.

Professor Ferns, for example, describes the agitation among British commercial circles for British government intervention in Chile and Argentina in the early '90s: Salisbury's reply, given in his speech at the Mansion House in July 1897, was that Britain should maintain Canning's policy of non-intervention in the internal affairs of the Republics:

> We have no intention of constituting ourselves a Providence in any South American quarrel. We have been pressed, earnestly pressed, to undertake the part of arbitrator, of compulsory arbitrator in quarrels in the west of South America. . . . We have been earnestly pressed, also . . . to undertake the regeneration of Argentine Finance. On neither of these subjects are Her Majesty's Government in the least degree disposed to encroach on the function of Providence.[25]

The same applied to revolutions, wars or blockades in which British interests were the third party, except in so far as British lives and property were in need of protection. When some officers and men from H.M.S. *Narcissus* were landed in February 1868, at the request of the Uruguayan Government, to protect the Customs House at Montevideo, Lord Stanley instructed Major Munro (the British Representative) that although it was difficult to lay down any rule for these cases, such proceedings amounted to direct interference in the internal affairs of a foreign country; they 'should only be resorted to under circumstances of the greatest urgency' for the protection of British lives and property, and, with respect to property, 'specifically, when the local authorities have applied for such assistance as being unable to ensure its safety'. The British admiral, Admiral Ramsay, subsequently instructed the Senior Officer in the River Plate 'on no account to interfere in the disputes of the contending parties'; his objectives were to be limited to the protection of the lives and properties of British subjects.[26] In spite of the urgent requests for protection and intervention on the occasion of the Chilean revolution of 1891—and British interests in Chilean trading, banking, railways, and nitrates were, at that time, very considerable indeed —the British admiral was under orders to confine his action

25. Ferns, *Britain and Argentina*, p. 465.
26. Scottish Record Office, Dalhousie Papers, 10/20b and 10/27.

strictly to the protection of those interests, and H.M. Minister in Chile was instructed to abstain from all expression of opinion.[27]

Wars between Latin American States were subject to the same general policy. Mediation was offered where possible (as it was, for example, between Buenos Aires and Brazil in the late '20s), but actual intervention was restricted to the protection of British lives and property. On the occasion of the Brazilian attack on Uruguay, Mr. Thornton (the British Minister at Buenos Aires) informed the Paraguayan Foreign Minister that he considered every nation to have 'an inherent right to insist upon satisfaction for injuries done to her subjects', even though it might result in war and temporary occupation of territory.[28] The Foreign Office preserved its complete neutrality both here and in the subsequent Paraguayan War. H.M. Government—Lord Stanley told Mr. Stuart in a despatch dated 7 July 1868—had no inducement to interfere in the war in Paraguay so far as British interests were concerned; its only interest was in the removal of the impediments placed by President Lopez on the retirement of British subjects trapped in Paraguay.[29]

Blockades, damaging as they often were to British commercial interests, were respected so long as they were effective. When Mr. Lettsom, the British Chargé d'Affaires at Montevideo, asked the Foreign Office how long the Brazilian blockade (1865) of the ports of Salto and Paysandú was to be observed in the absence of the military forces which were supposed to be acting in concert with the Brazilian navy, Russell instructed him to respect the blockade, irrespective of any military forces, so long as the naval force maintaining the blockade was fairly adequate for the purpose.[30] The Foreign Office's reply to a request in 1891 for official protection of the Glasgow steamer *Mount Tabor* on the coast of Chile was to telegraph:

27. No. 11, *Correspondence respecting the Revolution in Chile*, P.P.1892(c.6636) XCV.
28. No. 17, *Correspondence respecting Hostilities in the River Plate*, P.P.1865(3463) LVII.
29. No. 45, *Correspondence respecting Hostilities in the River Plate*, P.P.1867–68 (3984)LXXIII.
30. No. 43, *Correspondence respecting Hostilities in the River Plate*, P.P.1865(3463) LVII.

Commander of Her Majesty's ship *Champion* on coast of Chile, has reported that Chilean squadron blockades Valparaiso and Iquique. Assuming effective blockade to exist, escort through it cannot be given.[31]

Of course, on a number of occasions a measure of intervention to safeguard British subjects or their property had the result of favouring one or other of the contending factions in internal politics. In the Dominican Republic, for example, a revolution was in progress in 1904 against the government of Dr. Morales, which had already been the cause of trouble and damage to British subjects for several months. At one point it appeared as if fighting were about to take place in Puerto Plata, with inevitable damage to foreign property. Commander Dillingham (U.S.S. *Detroit*) and Commander C. Hope Robertson (H.M.S. *Pallas*) landed small detachments, placed a cordon of flags around the city, and notified the opposite sides that they would not allow fighting within that cordon. The battle finally took place outside the cordon, and the insurgents were defeated.[32]

But there was only one case of any importance—possibly only one case altogether—where H.M. Government broke with its tradition of deliberate non-intervention in the internal affairs of the Republics, and this was in the River Plate during the '40s.

James Murray, a Second Class Clerk at the Foreign Office, had drafted a *Memorandum on British Trade* in 1841 which, as Professor Ferns has said, 'contained the germs of all the mistakes of the succeeding years'. Murray stressed both the need for more markets, and the damaging effects on British trade of chronic anarchy in South America. British trade with Latin America was expanding, while our European trade was bound to contract as Europe itself became industrialized. Latin America's markets, however, were being wrecked by perpetual civil war, owing its origin 'mainly to the ambition or necessities of a few armed chiefs'. Intervention in the affairs of other states might generally be unwarrantable, but there was 'a point at which it may become to a certain degree justifiable, if not

31. No. 27, *Correspondence respecting the Revolution in Chile*, P.P.1892(c.6636) XCV.
32. The incident is described by Milton Offutt, *The Protection of Citizens Abroad by the Armed Forces of the United States* (Baltimore, 1928), pp. 99–100.

imperative, upon each state to look to such interference on account of self-interest, and as a means of self-preservation'.[33] Murray chose the protection of Montevideo against the Buenos Aires dictator, General Rosas, as a starting point for his 'Plan of Pacification'; but interesting though his Memorandum certainly is in the foretaste it gave of the Anglo-French intervention, there is no evidence that H.M. Government accepted more than some of the implications of Murray's arguments—if that much. Indeed, in 1843 Sir Robert Peel assured the Commons, on the subject of Rosas's attack on Montevideo, that, far from giving any promise of intervention,

he was prepared to say that the Government, deprecating those hostilities, and convinced that their only effect was to retard the growing prosperity of both countries, determined as they were to use all the influence they could command to put an end to them, and all their power to protect British subjects, could not encourage the hon. Member to hope that Britain would become a principal in the hostilities, or that British forces would be brought to bear on the issue of the contest.[34]

A year later British naval forces were bombarding Colonia, and Aberdeen, whose ignorance of Latin American affairs was rivalled—among British Foreign Secretaries—only by Malmesbury, had blundered into a costly and futile intervention. Defending himself in the Lords in February 1846, Aberdeen pointed out that Buenos Aires had refused British mediation in 1841 and 1842, and despite attacks from every quarter on H.M. Government's 'most culpable apathy and indifference to British commerce, and neglect of British interests', the Foreign Office had abstained from taking any action for a further two years. At length, after representations from every interest (including the Government of Brazil), Britain and France had decided to offer mediation a third time, and, if that were refused, to achieve peace by coercion. Aberdeen himself admitted that 'it required strong grounds to interfere with the free exercise of power by an independent state', even when employed by General Rosas 'in a manner so senseless and

33. 'Memorandum on British Trade', December 1841, quoted from at some length by V. G. Kiernan, 'Britain's First Contacts with Paraguay', *Atlante*, III (1955), 175–6.
34. 69 *Parl.Deb.*3s.1251 (2 June 1843).

barbarous'; but he seems to have believed that intervention, or rather enforced mediation, could alone secure the independence of Montevideo and the safeguarding of British trade.[35]

It is quite evident that Aberdeen drifted into the coercion entirely against his natural inclination. Professor Ferns could find no suggestion either in the official papers or in Aberdeen's own private papers that Britain intended to use force against the Argentine,[36] and force, when it came, was unpopular both with the British merchants at Buenos Aires and in Parliament. Palmerston, who replaced Aberdeen as Foreign Secretary in 1846, immediately recognized the futility of the blockade. He told the French Ambassador in London that he would gladly finish 'the bad business which [England and France] began together'. The blockade, he claimed, was piracy, and he was very glad that we were out of such a system.[37]

* * *

The Anglo-French blockade of the River Plate, feeble and uncertain as it was, is the only case which fits the Gallagher and Robinson theory of active intervention in Latin American politics in the interests of British trade and finance. The Foreign Office burnt its fingers so badly that it never tried the same policy again.

British intervention in mid-century Central America, which Robert Naylor claims to have been in the interest of local British trade,[38] was quite clearly nothing of the kind. Our trade with the Central American Republics was insignificant, and we had no substantial investments. The reasons for the interest of the Foreign Office in Central America until the conclusion of the Clayton-Bulwer Treaty of 1850 are obvious. Britain, with its West Indian colonies, the settlements at Belize (British Honduras) and British Guiana, and the Panama route to Australasia and to the trade of the West Coast of South America, had as much reason before the middle of the century

35. 83 *Parl.Deb.*3*s.*1158–9 (19 February 1846), also No. 1, *Instructions to Mr. Ouseley*, P.P.1846(683)LII.
36. Ferns, *Britain and Argentina*, p. 251.
37. Quoted in ibid., p. 279.
38. Robert A. Naylor, 'The British Role in Central America prior to the Clayton-Bulwer Treaty of 1850', *Hispanic American Historical Review*, 40 (1960), 361–82.

as the United States to regard the Caribbean as her own private lake. But as the West Indian sugar colonies went into decline, and as, after 1848, the United States actively developed the West Coast (for which, in the absence of trans-continental railways, the sea-route via the Isthmus was the obvious means of communication), it became apparent that, quite apart from the developing U.S. trade with the Caribbean, the balance of interest had shifted sharply in favour of the United States. The Clayton-Bulwer Treaty of 1850, for all its apparent equal partition of U.S. and British interest in Central America, was in fact the first stage in the British retreat from any form of political responsibility in the area. H.M. Government was interested solely in the provision of adequate interoceanic communication free to all comers on equal terms, and it was this equality of treatment that the Clayton-Bulwer Treaty was intended to ensure. Anxious though H.M. Government was to secure freedom and equality, once that had been achieved— Lord Clarendon explained in the '50s—British policy would be 'to interfere as little as possible in the internal affairs of Central America'.[39] Nor did it matter who made the railway or canal, whether the capital or contracting was British or of any other nationality. Malmesbury assured the U.S. Government in 1858 that he had no desire to obtain any advantages for British subjects by negotiation with the Governments of Central America which would not equally be shared with the citizens of any other state, and that 'so long as the transit communication across the Isthmus is promptly and effectively made, it is a matter of perfect indifference to Her Majesty's Government by what association of individuals that desirable object is accomplished.'[40]

Subject to a guarantee of free and equal treatment for British trade and communications generally, H.M. Government, after the mid '50s, would have been only too happy to have withdrawn altogether from Central American affairs, leaving them thankfully to 'policing' by the United States.

You ask me whether I would abandon Central America [Richard Cobden wrote to a friend in 1856]. There is not a man at head-

39. No. 20, *Correspondence respecting Central America, 1856–1860*, P.P.1860 (2748)LXVIII.
40. No. 127, ibid.

quarters who would not be glad if we had never set foot there, or who does not know that by one means or another we must abandon all claim to possession or protectorate, or ultimately be driven out with discredit. In *private*, all our leading public men hold but one language—that we have no interest in Central America, and the sooner we get rid of all connection with that region of earthquakes and volcanoes the better.[41]

The protectorate, to which Cobden referred, was the unfortunate obligation, inherited from the previous century, to uphold the interests of the Mosquito Indians. It was an obligation which the British Government found irksome, embarrassing, and increasingly disagreeable, and it was complicated by the settlement at Greytown (San Juan de Nicaragua)—within the territory claimed for Mosquito—of an armed and aggressive Anglo-American community violently opposed to incorporation in Nicaragua. The Foreign Office searched anxiously for some form of honourable settlement, and, after painful negotiations, Treaties were concluded with Honduras in 1859 and Nicaragua in 1860 by which the Mosquito territory, with some guarantees for its British and Indian inhabitants, was ceded to the Republics. With these Treaties went the last vestiges of direct British interest in the internal affairs of Latin America.

* * *

But a legend survives which, if only for its persistence, deserves attention, and that is that British diplomacy intervened in the internal politics of Mexico, 1913–14, under the influence of the Cowdray oil properties.[42]

Lord Cowdray, the famous British contractor, had undertaken a number of important engineering contracts in Mexico, of which the best known were the draining of the Valley of Mexico and the rehabilitation of the Tehuantepec Railway. His work had brought him into close touch with the dictator Porfirio Díaz, and when he became interested in Mexican oil, these contacts, to the disgust of rival American oil interests, were continued and strengthened. In May 1911 Porfirio Díaz

41. Quoted in Hobson, *Richard Cobden*, p. 153.
42. I must acknowledge with gratitude Dr. P. A. R. Calvert's comments and suggestions on the draft of the following pages on Mexico. His book, *The Mexican Revolution, 1910–1914: the Diplomacy of Anglo-American Conflict*, (Cambridge, 1968) supports the general argument below.

was overthrown. He was replaced by an idealistic but ineffect-
ual liberal, Francisco Madero, who was himself assassinated
early in 1913. The Presidency was seized by General Huerta,
whom H.M. Government recognized soon afterwards, and the
British example was followed by most of the other Powers. The
suspicion, loudly voiced in the U.S. press, was that Cowdray
was backing Huerta and that it was Cowdray's influence, as a
rich and powerful Liberal Member of Parliament, which had
persuaded the British Government to recognize Huerta so
rapidly.

Since then, the close relationship between Cowdray's
lieutenants in Mexico and the British Legation, and between
Cowdray himself in London and the Foreign Office, has been
very generally accepted. And its acceptance was much assisted
by the coincidence of Huerta's seizure of power with the
beginning of the Wilson Administration at Washington, since
Wilson, and more particularly his Secretary of State (Bryan),
had fought their election campaign—and won it—on the cry
of the dangerous ascendancy of Wall Street in American politics
during the Taft Administration. They found no difficulty in
identifying their favourite antagonist in the apparent obedience
of British policy in Mexico to the dictation of Cowdray's oil
interests, and the situation was not improved when Sir William
Tyrrell, Edward Grey's principal private secretary, allowed his
sense of humour to get the better of him in a conversation with
Secretary Bryan. Bryan, as usual, had accused the Cabinet of
being in the pay of the British oil interests. Tyrrell, who plainly
found Bryan ridiculous, answered that he was wrong, since
Cowdray was not rich enough—'Through a long experience
with corruption the Cabinet has grown so greedy that Cowdray
hasn't the money necessary to reach their price.' Bryan, of
course, took this seriously, and claimed triumphantly that
Tyrrell had admitted the charge; and Tyrrell, after listening
good-humouredly to further abuse of the Foreign Office and the
oil barons, left with the remark, as he bowed deferentially, 'You
have stripped me naked, Mr. Secretary, but I am unashamed.'[43]

43. Burton J. Hendrick, *The Life and Letters of Walter H. Page* (London, 1924),
pp. 202–3. Tyrrell's interview with President Wilson, however, was more
successful, and Dr. Calvert believes that the crisis in Anglo-American relations, which had reached a peak in late October, was largely resolved by
Tyrrell's visit to Washington.

It was certainly difficult, during those months, to take U.S. foreign policy seriously. Cowdray had a great deal of money invested in Mexican oil, and it was obvious that he would try to do what he could to make it safe from the revolutionaries. The British Government was bound, as far as possible, to protect British subjects and their property, but at the same time it had no wish in Mexico, or anywhere else on the Continent, to become involved in revolutionary politics. Thomas Hohler, who as First Secretary at the British Legation had every reason to know, described British recognition of Huerta as the result of H.M. Government's belief that 'he [Huerta] was the only man capable of reestablishing order, and if he failed, intervention by the U.S.A. or anarchy would be inevitable'. Hohler added that this was the view taken by all foreign diplomatists at the time, including the American Ambassador.[44]

Of course, the description of Sir Edward Grey as the tool of the oil barons is only slightly less absurd than that of the British Minister in Mexico—the eccentric Francis Stronge—as working hand-in-glove with Cowdray's lieutenants. Sir Edward Grey was perfectly aware of the situation in Mexico, and by the time Sir Lionel Carden took over, late in 1913, Grey was as unlikely to be persuaded one way or the other by Cowdray as he was to believe everything Carden told him about the Americans. The difficulty which Grey faced, and which President Wilson seemed incapable of facing himself, was that if Huerta were forced to leave there was no realistic alternative; Villa and Carranza were just as bad and the trouble would start all over again. But President Wilson, unfortunately, had chosen that particular moment to formulate a 'New Principle' in American foreign policy: the United States, instead of granting immediate recognition to *de facto* governments as it had until then, would refuse to recognize governments introduced by force. Furthermore, he explained earnestly that he was going to 'teach the South American Republics to elect good men', the first step in which was to get rid of Huerta. The American Ambassador in London reported the following conversation with Sir Edward Grey, in which Grey asked:

44. Hohler, *Diplomatic Petrel*, p. 185.

'Suppose you have to intervene, what then?'
'Make 'em vote and live by their decisions.'
'But suppose they will not so live?'
'We'll go in and make 'em vote again.'
'And keep this up 200 years?' asked he.
'Yes', said I. 'The United States will be here for two hundred years and it can continue to shoot men for that little space till they learn to vote and to rule themselves.'

The Ambassador added that he had never seen Grey laugh so heartily.[45]

When it came to the point, Grey—who was not in the least personally interested in Huerta—was not prepared to back either Carden or the oil interests. By the end of 1913, H.M. Government had withdrawn entirely; it was far more concerned with the maintenance of good relations with Washington than it was with the preservation of an obscure Mexican general. When Hohler took over from Carden at Mexico City in August 1914, he claimed that he put himself in the hands of the American Government:

After my unsuccessful attempt to induce Wilson to recognize Huerta [in 1913] I assented to whatever the U.S. chose to do, and while pointing out that their action was not in accord with what I myself believed right and prudent, I said I had no doubt they would protect us from any injury that might be incurred as a result of their action.[46]

The oil fields, meanwhile, had had rather less than their share of British Government protection. Dr. Hayes wrote to Cowdray from Tampico on 19 December 1913 that he was convinced that the Company had 'absolutely nothing to expect in the way of protection to its property from the American and British forces'.[47] Cowdray canvassed urgently in London for adequate protection, and Asquith finally felt obliged to do something. The British Ambassador saw President Wilson on 8 April 1914, and, acting 'quite beyond instructions', told him that H.M. Government 'could not remain indifferent' to the

45. Walter Page to President Wilson: quoted in Hendrick, *Life of Page*, p. 188.
46. Hohler, *Diplomatic Petrel*, p. 196.
47. Quoted in J. A. Spender, *Weetman Pearson, first Viscount Cowdray* (London, 1930), p. 198.

loss and damage caused to the wells, and might be forced by public opinion to instruct the British navy to act. By this time British policy in Mexico had swung into line with American, and the old objections no longer had any force. The Royal Navy, with American approval, was at last instructed to send up a protective force to the drilling areas.[48]

Altogether, there was little resemblance between what actually happened and the story which has since passed into folklore; Cowdray was no better treated than any other British subject, and as for intervention in Mexican politics, nothing could have been further from Sir Edward Grey's mind. The recognition of any government, of course, can be interpreted as intervention in the internal affairs of another nation, but it is a decision that has to be taken at some point—to withhold recognition is often as much of an intervention as to grant it. Huerta's government was definitely in control at Mexico City, and H.M. Government hoped that international recognition might at last give a Mexican Government a chance to bring the anarchy and disruption of contemporary Mexico under control.

In deference to President Wilson's wishes, Grey abandoned any attempt at conducting an independent British policy in Mexico. Far from intervening actively in Mexican politics, H.M. Government, after standing helplessly on the sidelines in 1913, left the field altogether. Its interest, as always, was in the security of British subjects and their property—an interest which was sharpened by the fact that the property in this case consisted largely of oil. But once the American Government had, by implication, accepted responsibility for maintaining order in Mexico, H.M. Government was only too happy to contract out. It was no more interested in the political 'regeneration' of Mexico in 1914 than it had been in 1861-2. The English— Walter Page complained to President Wilson, late in 1913— 'have a mania for order, sheer order for the sake of order; they can't see how anything can come in anyone's thought before order or how anything need come afterwards'.[49]

* * *

48. R. K. Middlemas, *The Master Builders* (London, 1963), p. 228.
49. Hendrick, *Life of Page*, p. 188.

If, then, the British Government was unprepared to intervene in Latin American politics in the interests of British trade and finance, what *was* it prepared to do? It did what it could, of course, to ensure that British trade received fair and equal treatment and that the persons and property of British subjects were adequately protected. The Commercial Treaties were the first and most important stage towards this, but there was the further obligation to ensure that the Treaties were observed and that a proper degree of support was given to the legitimate claims of British subjects for personal outrage or damage to property. It is the support of claims which has led to so much misunderstanding of the nature of British diplomacy in Latin America.

At least forty examples can be quoted for the period 1820–1914 of coercion and the landing of armed forces by Britain in Latin America; of these, ten were concerned with offences against national honour or dignity (primarily outrages against British consuls or the British flag, with the addition of unsettled claims), fourteen were to enforce the claims of British subjects for outrage and injury, twelve were to restore order and protect property, three were to safeguard nations under British protection, and one was to occupy an uninhabited Atlantic island as a telegraph station.[50] But the point is that these coercions were designed to secure redress for damages that had already taken place, or to ensure the security and fair treatment of existing trade. They were not intended to force British trade down Latin American throats, to promote the interests of British finance, or even to bring about any change in the form of government more favourable to British entrepreneurs.

In some of the more unstable Republics force might genuinely be the only means by which justice might be obtained; the law courts were only too often the tools of a corrupt Executive. A Foreign Office Memorandum of February 1896 claimed that it would be a complete waste of time to give an account of every occasion on which foreign governments had used threats of force or exceptional pressure in their dealings with the Govern-

50. The references to these coercions are given in D. C. M. Platt, 'British Capital, Commerce and Diplomacy in Latin America', Oxford thesis, 1962, pp. 28–30.

ment of Venezuela—'a very large proportion of the correspondence of Venezuela consists of reclamations and remonstrances,
and the facts . . . go to show that few acts of justice have been
obtained from that country by mere negotiation'.[51]

The vetting and presentation of claims formed a major, if not
the major, preoccupation of British diplomacy in Latin America,
whether at the Legations or at the Foreign Office itself.
Scarcely a day passed, Mr. Layard complained to the Commons
in 1863, when some such Latin American claim was not
received at the Foreign Office, and there was not a single
South American State against which there were no claims for
redress outstanding.[52] But non-intervention, Free Trade, and
laissez-faire left little for British representatives to do other
than improve their commercial intelligence. Foreign competition, German and American in particular, became a serious
problem in Latin American markets after the 1870's, but there
was no question of attempting to meet this competition by
diplomatic pressure. Curzon's solution for an area in which he
felt Britain to be losing most ground was to increase the supply
of 'precise and up-to-date information'; he suggested a Commercial Mission to study and report upon foreign competition and
the markets of Latin America, and his suggestion was taken up
by the Board of Trade in the Worthington Mission at the turn
of the century.[53] The de Bunsen Mission at the end of the First
World War and the D'Abernon Mission in 1929 had similar
objectives. It was only in the last of these Missions that the
principle of reciprocal trade agreements was introduced and
the gathering of information was replaced by a new era of
hard commercial bargaining.

As for finance, the motives which had persuaded the Foreign
Office to associate itself so closely, for example, with the Imperial
Bank of Persia, the Hong Kong and Shanghai Banking Corpora-
tion, or the Peking Syndicate simply did not apply to conditions
in Latin America. There was no political rivalry with a major
Power (as there was in Persia), and there was no danger of a

51. *Memorandum respecting the Internal Condition of Venezuela*, F.O.,C.P.6753.
52. 172 *Parl.Deb.*3s.898–9 (16 July 1863). Palmerston had much the same
complaint to make a decade earlier: 114 *Parl.Deb.*3s.278 (10 February 1851).
53. Curzon (as Under Secretary at the Foreign Office) to the Board of Trade,
21 January 1897: P.R.O.,B.T/13/29, file no. 12084.

physical partition and the consequent closing of markets to international trade (as there was in China). There was, in fact, no reason why the Foreign Office should feel obliged to depart from its preferred policy of non-intervention in the affairs of British financiers. *The Times*, in its 'South American Supplement' for October 1910, suggested that this might not always be the case, since although the Republics had so far been exempt from the influences of *welt-politik* and British capital had found a fair field of investment, 'all indications, here as elsewhere, point clearly to the increasing weight hereafter of the political factor in international finance and to the consequent necessity for so directing the uses of capital that its employment abroad shall be co-ordinated with, and beneficial to, our commercial and industrial purposes'.[54] But it was in advance of its time, and Sir Edward Grey, less than a month before the outbreak of the First World War, still felt able to dissociate H.M. Government entirely from the question of Brazilian loans. He did not deny—no doubt with Turkey, Persia, and China in mind—that there were some cases where loans had a political character and where financiers consulted the Foreign Office before an issue was made, but 'generally speaking, and especially in South America, these are things in which the Foreign Office do not interfere'.[55]

Similarly, there was no pressure on H.M. Government in Latin America to alter its traditional policy of non-intervention for contracts and concessions, and there were special reasons why it was particularly dangerous for diplomatists to become involved in financial promotions. These were set out clearly by Sir Edmund Monson in 1886 in his reply to a Foreign Office circular despatch. Monson, who as a former Minister at Montevideo and Buenos Aires (1879–84) had had some experience of Latin American conditions, explained that the standard of political and commercial morality in South America made it most undesirable for British diplomatists to depart from their traditional policy of abstention in matters of business:

In those countries every concession to foreign capitalists, foreign Companies, foreign syndicates, is made a matter of pecuniary

54. *The Times*, South American Supplement, 25 October 1910, 5a.
55. 64 *H.C.Deb.*5s.1448–9 (10 July 1914).

bargaining. All speculations and enterprises, railways, banks, harbour schemes, mines, land concessions, taken in hand by foreigners, depend for their preliminary success upon the readiness of the promoters to bribe the wire-pullers of the Government. Commercial houses seeking contracts or simply desirous of increasing their ordinary operations, are driven to have recourse to the same measures. Individuals or associations who have wrongs to redress or claims to assert can only hope to succeed by paying blackmail to officials; and when such cases are taken up and carried to a successful issue by Diplomatic Agents, the latter can never escape suspicion of having received a share of the plunder.

Indeed, no evidence has come to hand which indicates that British diplomatists, before 1914, took an active part in promoting the contracts and concessions of British subjects in Latin America. In the last decades before the World War, the pressure of foreign competition (aided occasionally by foreign diplomacy) might persuade British diplomatists to give what support they properly could to individual British interests, of sufficient respectability, engaged in the negotiation of substantial contracts. But that support always stopped short of preferential treatment, or of action which might prove detrimental to rival British interests in the area.[56]

* * *

But the main item in the popular indictment of British policy in Latin America still remains to be examined, and that is that it was a policy dictated and controlled by the bondholders.

There is no doubt about the size of the British stake in Latin American government bonds. In the first boom period before the crash of 1825 an enormously larger proportion of actual British investment went into bonds than into joint-stock enterprises; the figures for paid-up investment at the time of the crash were around £20 million and £3 million respectively. In the investment period before the renewed collapse of Latin American government finances in the early '70s, British investors still favoured government bonds, though they had begun, in the '60s, to show some interest in railways; in 1880, their nominal investment in bonds was over £123 million

56. The point is illustrated in a recent article: Peter A. R. Calvert, 'The Murray Contract: An Episode in International Finance and Diplomacy', *Pacific Historical Review*, XXXV (1966), 203–24.

compared with £56½ million in other enterprises. The effect of
the crash and of the alarming Report of the Select Committee
on Loans to Foreign States (which had concentrated its attention on the iniquities of Latin American loan flotations) was
to shift the main focus of interest to railways; but government
bonds, although relatively less important in 1913, still represented £316½ million out of a total of nearly £1,000 million of
nominal British capital invested in Latin America.[57]

Allusions to 'bondholder' interventions in Latin America are
so common that it would be impracticable to attempt an
answer to every charge. The charges are seldom documented,
and there is no consistency in classifying 'intervention': to one,
it is merely a word in the ear of a Minister; to another, 'official'
intervention cannot exist short of a bombardment. But if some
examples have to be given as a basis for deciding exactly how
much support H.M. Government was in fact prepared to give
to the Latin American bondholders, it seems sensible to take
the two most spectacular occasions on which bondholder and
British official policy appeared to coincide—in Mexico 1861–2
and Venezuela 1902–3—together with the less-known (but
equally instructive) history of the relationship between the
Foreign Office and the Peruvian bondholders during the last
three decades of the nineteenth century.

The Mexican intervention, it will be remembered, was an
attempt to compel the new Mexican Government to settle a
number of claims which had developed over decades of Civil
War. Some of these were for damages suffered by the bondholders or by their agents, and it has been assumed that the
main purpose of the expedition was to secure both payment of
existing bondholder debts and an undertaking to continue
servicing the Public Debt.

There were, however, two factors in the Mexican situation
which took it out of the normal run of bondholder grievances.
In the first place, the bondholders had claims for 'outrages' by
Mexican Government officials which were no more nor less
deserving of support than the claim of any British subject for

57. The figures are from C. K. Hobson, *The Export of Capital* (London, 1914),
pp. 100–105, and from J. Fred Rippy, *British Investments in Latin America,
1822–1949* (Minneapolis, 1959), pp. 20, 25, 68. Professor Rippy's estimates
must be treated with caution, but the order of magnitude is likely to be just
about right.

illegal damage to his property overseas. A *conducta* of silver, on its way from Guanaxuato and San Luis Potosí to Tampico for embarkation, had been seized by officers of the Constitutional Party acting under the orders of General Degollado, and an armed party had broken into the former British Legation at Mexico City (on the instructions of General Miramon and his Ministers), carrying off 660,000 dollars—the property of the British bondholders—placed under the security of the Minister's official seal. Nobody could have been more opposed on principle to government intervention on behalf of the bond-holders than Richard Cobden, yet even he, when he heard about these incidents, acknowledged that they altered his view of the right and duty of the Government to interfere—'If our bondholders have been robbed of money in transition by what is called a Government we certainly have a right to redress, if it can be had.'[58]

The other factor, which was perhaps of more interest to international lawyers than it was to the British or Mexican public, was that the Agreement entered into by Captain Dunlop (1859) with Juarez's Constitutional Government at Vera Cruz (for the assignment of a proportion of the port's Custom-house dues to the payment of the interest on the Doyle Convention bonds) included an undertaking to pay the amounts due to the *ordinary* bondholders.[59] Captain Dunlop was perfectly entitled to negotiate for payment on the Doyle Convention bonds (which were not bonds in the normal sense of voluntary investments for profit in foreign government loans, but government securities issued by the Mexican Government in settlement of previous 'outrage' claims). Whether Juarez was wise to agree to the further undertaking (to pay the ordinary bondholders) is another matter—no British Government would have compelled him to do so. But the fact was that the ad-mission of responsibility which Juarez had made in the Dunlop Convention converted the right of the bondholders into an international right founded on an agreement between two sovereign states. Under international law, by which H.M.

58. Letter to Henry Richard, 2 February 1862: quoted by Hobson, *Richard Cobden*, p. 302.
59. *Agreements entered into with the Constitutional Authorities at Vera Cruz by Captain Dunlop, R.N., and by Captain Aldham, R.N.*, P.P.1861(2816)LXV. The Aldham Convention of 1860 reaffirmed the Dunlop Convention.

Government's attitude to the protection of British subjects overseas was governed almost exclusively in the last century, the British Government was not only entitled to intervene in this case, but was actually under an obligation to do so.[60] The bondholder claims, therefore, were included among the others presented to the Mexican Government in 1862; but they were still regarded as being on a different plane from those of the ordinary claimants, and the bondholders' Debt was in fact specifically excluded from the functions of the Arbitration Tribunal provided for in the Agreement of 1884 (for the renewal of diplomatic relations).[61]

*   *   *

The authoritative intervention of the British Government on behalf of the Peruvian bondholders provides one of the most comprehensive case studies in existence of H.M. Government's attitude to bondholder claims. Herbert Feis cited the incident as an example of how British Government policy could fluctuate; he observed the shift from non-intervention in 1876 to intervention in 1879 (without discussing the reasons which prompted this change), and claimed that British official efforts ceased after 1879.[62] He was, however, arguing from insufficient information. There was no change of heart at the Foreign Office, merely a change in circumstances; and as for intervention ceasing, the only thing that ceased was the publication of Blue Books after 1882.

Official intervention on behalf of the Peruvian bondholders

60. The two factors governing H.M. Government's support of the bondholders in Mexico are explained in Russell's instructions to Sir Charles Wyke, 3 March 1861: No. 1, *Correspondence relative to the Affairs of Mexico*, P.P.1862(2915)LXIV; also in Mr. Layard's reply to the outspoken criticisms of Lord Montagu in the Commons: 168 *Parl.Deb.3s.*364–5 (15 July 1862). An interesting parallel case took place in Venezuela in 1867. H.M. Government was prepared to press diplomatically a bondholder claim based on the seizure of 18,443 dollars by the Venezuelan Government while in the hands of the bondholders' agents pending transfer to London. H.M. Government came very near to employing coercive measures to compel a settlement of this and other claims, but coercion was forestalled by an agreement establishing a Mixed Commission, 21 September 1868: F. Irving, 'Memorandum respecting British Claims on Venezuela,' 2 February 1867, bound in with P.R.O.,F.O/80/188.
61. Inclosures 1 and 2 in No. 16, *Papers respecting the Renewal of Diplomatic Relations with Mexico*, P.P.1884(c.4176)LXXXVII.
62. Feis, *Europe: The World's Banker*, pp. 106–7.

dated from the end of 1878, when the British Government proposed that the other creditor nations should join in a representation to the Peruvian Government.[63] The grounds for intervention were the misappropriation of securities specifically hypothecated to the bondholders—a misappropriation which Sir Julian Pauncefote characterized as a 'gross Public Fraud'. Similar cases had frequently formed the basis of official protests by the Foreign Office, and when Salisbury intervened in 1879 the intervention represented no change of policy, as Feis suggested, but merely a response to this new factor.

Intervention became even more necessary in and after 1883, when the Treaty of Peace between Chile and Peru (after Chile's victory in the War of the Pacific) included the cession of the Peruvian province of Tarapacá. No Treaty provision was made for the transfer, with that province, of a proportionate share of the Peruvian Debt, and although the Law Officers in London advised that in normal circumstances international law did not necessarily require such a transfer of obligation, a special circumstance existed in that the Peruvian bondholders had lent their money to the Republic on the specific security of the guano deposits, one of the most important of which was included in Tarapacá. The Law Officers felt that in these circumstances the bondholders had an equitable claim of a special character which might justly be urged on the consideration of the Chilean and Peruvian Governments;[64] and their Opinion remained the basis of British diplomatic policy throughout the protracted controversy which followed.

But it is important to realize that the British case was not founded primarily on the rights and wrongs of intervention for the Peruvian *bondholders*. Sir Julian Pauncefote's letter to Sir E. Reed, 8 April 1884, puts the case very clearly. Sir Julian pointed out that the British diplomatic protest was directed against the attempt of Chile to take over a portion of the Peruvian territory free of the charges and obligations to

---

63. For this proposal and its origins, see Sir Julian Pauncefote's Memorandum of 2 October 1878, and the draft circular to Foreign Governments of November 1878: P.R.O.,F.O/61/323.
64. Quoted in McNair, *International Law Opinions*, I, 170–1.

foreign creditors which had already been incurred by the Peruvian Government:

Her Majesty's Government are not pressing for the payment of claims or for the enforcement of the lien which the foreign creditors have on the territory in question. They are not, in fact, supporting the British bondholders and nitrate certificate-holders as such. They are maintaining a principle applicable to all cessions of territory, namely, that private rights within the ceded territory should be respected. . . . The fact that the British interests which are menaced are those of the bondholders does not affect the principle for which Her Majesty's Government contend.[65]

When Earl Granville approached the French Ambassador a few days later with a proposal for a joint diplomatic protest, he explained that H.M. Government was not departing from its traditional policy; it was not pressing for the payment of the bondholders or for any favour or even for the enforcement of their rights. But H.M. Government felt entitled to protest against the Articles of a Treaty that deprived British subjects of their property, and it particularly insisted that the cession of Tarapacá, freed from the specific lien on the guano deposits created by the Peruvian Government in favour of the bond-holders (which formed the main security of nearly £20 million of loan), was inequitable and constituted an act of spoliation.[66] Lord Fitzmaurice made the same point to the bondholders themselves when arguing that H.M. Government's action represented no departure from the principles set out in Palmerston's Circular of 1848. Although, he said, the British bondholders were not entitled to look to their government for assistance in obtaining payment of their claim, the Foreign Office felt that it would be failing in its duty if it did not protest against an action 'in violation of the principles of justice and of the practice of nations'.[67]

On these grounds, international protests were delivered to Chile by the creditor Powers in 1884, 1885, and 1889. But the

65. No. 139, *Further Correspondence respecting the Foreign Creditors of Peru, 1881–84*, F.O.,C.P.5046.
66. No. 144, ibid.
67. Lord Fitzmaurice to Mr. Williamson, M.P., 8 May 1884: No. 155, ibid. Palmerston's Circular on Loans to Foreign States is printed as Appendix II.

protests were limited to the questions arising out of the cession of Tarapacá, and the British Government consistently refused to intervene in the other grievances pressed on its attention by the Peruvian bondholders. Salisbury answered a long letter of protest from Sir H. Tyler, M.P., Chairman of the Peruvian Bondholders' Committee, with the remark that the letter appeared to renew the application frequently made for diplomatic support in pressing the claims of the Peruvian bondholders on the Peruvian government. Salisbury declared himself unprepared to depart from the principle of non-intervention laid down in Palmerston's 1848 Circular, to which frequent reference had been made in correspondence with the bondholders and in Parliament.[68]

Although the British Minister in Peru often used his 'good offices' on behalf of the bondholder claims, the Foreign Office continued to consider itself bound by the principle of non-intervention. The dispute dragged on almost interminably. In 1887 the London Peruvian Bondholders' Committee concluded an arrangement with the Peruvian Government with respect to one half of the Peruvian Debt, the other half being attributed to Chile as the result of her annexation of Tarapacá. Chile refused to acknowledge this solution, and it was not until January 1890 that a Protocol providing for the settlement of the bondholder claims was signed between Chile and Peru. The Chilean Revolution of 1891 (which brought the fall of President Balmaceda's Government) and continued opposition to a settlement from the French Government (which was still pressing the Dreyfus claims), meant further delays, and a final solution was postponed for at least another decade.

* * *

The Anglo-German coercion of Venezuela is the 'bondholder' intervention which has attracted most attention, and not only from those who have always accepted the identification of finance and diplomacy. Professor Robbins, for example, felt compelled to add Venezuela to the Boer War as the other British exception to the general rule of finance as the *instrument* of diplomacy; these were cases 'in which, whatever the penum-

68. No. 37, *Further Correspondence respecting the Claims of the Peruvian Bond-holders, 1885*, F.O.,C.P.5245.

bra of other factors, the leading role of investment seems reasonably well authenticated'.[69]

As in Mexico in the early '60s, the coercion of Venezuela was intended to force the settlement of an accumulation of claims. An ultimatum was delivered by the British and German Ministers at Caracas on 7 December 1902, after which a few gunboats (the Venezuelan fleet) were seized, two were sunk by the German Commodore, and a blockade was imposed on the Venezuelan coast. By the end of the month President Castro declared himself ready to give way to the Allied demands, and a representative was sent to Washington to negotiate with the Allies. Protocols were signed at Washington on 13 February 1903 by which the claims were to be submitted to mixed commissions sitting at Caracas; the question of whether the Allies' claims should receive preferential treatment in the final payment was put to the Permanent Tribunal at The Hague.[70]

Where do the bondholders come in? Venezuela was in default on her Public Debt, and the bondholders, as might be expected, were anxious to obtain Government assistance in reaching a settlement. But the existence of these bondholder aspirations simultaneously with the shipping outrage and property claims pressed by the Foreign Office was a coincidence which, if not unexpected at the time, played virtually no part in determining H.M. Government's policy or its decision to join Germany in a combined naval coercion.

Larcom's Memorandum on the existing causes of complaint against Venezuela, prepared on 20 July 1902 in answer to the growing feeling at the Foreign Office that coercion might be necessary, made no mention of the bondholders. The various shipping outrages were detailed, as were the grievances of the 30 per cent. preferential duty imposed by Venezuela against imports from Trinidad, the misbehaviour of the Venezuelan consul at Trinidad, and the substantial claims of the Railway

69. Robbins, *Economic Causes of War*, p. 45.
70. I have already discussed this episode at length in an article 'The Allied Coercion of Venezuela, 1902–3: a Reassessment', *Inter-American Economic Affairs*, 15 (1962), 3–28. By kind permission of the Editor, the paragraphs on the bondholders' part in the coercion are reprinted below. The article was based on the following volumes at the Public Record Office: F.O/80/425–98; F.O/199/157–73.

Companies. But the first appeal for assistance was not received from the bondholders until 23 September—that is, *after* the decision to intervene had already been taken.[71] A minute on the appeal, by the Hon. F. H. Villiers (the Assistant Under-Secretary responsible), set the tone of Foreign Office policy for the rest of the incident. Villiers felt that the Foreign Office would have to include the loan arrears in a general settlement, but that care should be taken, in acknowledging the appeal, to avoid giving an incorrect or exaggerated impression of the extent of possible intervention.

The bondholders again approached the Foreign Office on 9 October, forwarding the Bases of an Arrangement concluded with the Disconto Gesellschaft which offered a possible solution to the accumulation of arrears. But Clause XI of the Arrangement specified that the German and British Governments should take note of the new Contract with the Venezuelan Government and receive a formal undertaking from Venezuela that none of the revenues hypothecated to the bondholders would be alienated to any other purpose. The Foreign Office agreed that the Arrangement as a whole was a reasonable compromise, but refused as usual to consent to the possible future obligations implied by Clause XI. The Clause was accordingly withdrawn.

No more was heard of the bondholders until 8 November; the Memorandum of British grievances communicated to the German Ambassador by the Foreign Office at the end of October made no mention of bondholder claims. Villiers minuted, on the reverse of the Council of Foreign Bondholders' letter (8 November) accepting H.M. Government's modification of Clause XI, that he thought the best way of including the external debt in the general settlement would be by urging upon the Venezuelan Government the acceptance of the bond-holders' Agreement (to which the Foreign Office, now that the objectionable responsibility implied by Clause XI had been removed, could take no exception). The suggestion that the various claims should be formally ranked seems to have

71. An appeal for Foreign Office intervention had been received on 3 January 1902, but it was for intervention in the event of German bond-holders receiving preferential treatment (as the result of a projected German naval demonstration). The Foreign Office merely acknowledged the appeal, and the failure of the naval demonstration removed its purpose.

originated from the German Ambassador on 11 November, and it was at once adopted by the Foreign Office. A couple of days later Villiers produced a Memorandum in which the shipping claims and claims for illegal imprisonment or personal injury were to rank first, followed by claims for injury to British property; ranking third were the bondholders' claims. He added that the bondholders' claims could be put forward at the proper moment 'to make the Slate clean'.

Clearly, then, the Foreign Office was interested in the bond-holder settlement only as a convenient adjunct to a general solution of British claims. The position was confused by the publication (in one of the Blue Books) of Lansdowne's decision to press all categories of claims equally and without distinction on the Venezuelan Government. It has been argued that this decision implied a failure to acknowledge any legal or moral priority as between one claim and another; but it is perfectly obvious, from Lansdowne's despatch to Buchanan, 17 November, that it was merely a tactical device designed to prevent any diminution, by the grant of priority to one class of claims, of the chances of securing just reparation for the others. Lansdowne pointed out, indeed, that on learning that the Venezuelan Government was prepared to admit their liability on every count, H.M. Government would exact immediate payment only for the pressing claims in the first category, and would consent to the submission of the other claims to some form of arbitration. And the willingness to accept arbitration in all but the first rank claims was in fact reaffirmed in the ultimatum finally presented to the Venezuelan Government. H.M. Government's bondholder policy, as announced by Lansdowne to Buchanan on 17 November, remained confined to the application of pressure on Venezuela to accept an independent arrangement with the bondholders.

In the circumstances, it was hardly surprising that the Government, when accused of conducting a bondholder campaign, had no hesitation in denying it. Mr. Balfour, the Prime Minister, explained to the Commons on 15 December that he looked upon international action on behalf of the bond-holders with 'the gravest doubt and suspicion'—'The real crux of this difficulty had been the outrageous manner in which the Venezuelan Government, not once nor twice, but time after time, have invaded the rights of British seamen and British shipowners, have insulted our nationality, have treated English sailors and English captains as no nation in the world treats us'.[72] And, in reply to Mr. Keir Hardie's question on 17 December, Mr. Balfour repeated emphatically that the Venezuelan operation had not been undertaken to recover bondholder debts.[73]

The reaction of the British Cabinet to the Venezuelan wish for arbitration (communicated by the U.S. Chargé d'Affaires on 17 December) clearly indicated that the ranking of British claims was no mere formality. Lansdowne informed the British Ambassador in Germany that the Cabinet had agreed to arbitration subject to the following reservations: shipping claims were not to go to arbitration, and a liability was to be admitted in principle for claims resulting from injury to, or wrongful seizure of, property (the decisions of the Arbitrators being confined to whether the wrongful act took place, and, if so, to the assessment of adequate compensation). In cases other than the above, the Cabinet was ready to accept arbitration without any reserve. The conditions were very largely those later to be adopted in the Protocol of 13 February 1903. The Venezuelan Government agreed to the cash payment of £5,000 to meet first line claims (the shipping outrages, and the maltreatment and false imprisonment of British subjects). Second rank claims were to be governed by the conditions laid down by the Cabinet on 16 December. The bondholder claims, however, were to be settled independently between the bondholders themselves and the Venezuelan Government, the Venezuelan Government merely undertaking to enter into a fresh arrangement on their behalf.

The treatment of bondholder claims departed in no significant respect from the policy normally pursued by the Foreign Office. While there was still a prospect of all the claims (other than those in the first rank) being submitted to arbitration at The Hague—which would have been the case had no previous agreement been reached at Washington—the British Government was prepared to agree to the addition of a bondholder settlement to the general arbitration. In fact, of course, the Washington Protocols removed any need to apply to The

72. 116 *Parl.Deb.4s.*1273.   73. ibid., 1490–1.

Hague, except on the question of preferential treatment, and the Mixed Commissions were not felt to be a suitable forum for the discussion of the Venezuelan External Debt. H.M. Government's position was explained by Lord Lansdowne, in answer to serious criticisms in the Lords, 2 March 1903. He pointed out that the Foreign Office had

... throughout placed these bondholders' claims in a wholly different category from the shipping claims and the second-class claims. It seemed to us desirable that, if there was to be a settlement with the Venezuelan Government, that settlement should be of a general and comprehensive character; and we thought that it ought, if possible, to include some kind of arrangement with the bond-holders. But our proposals with regard to the bondholders never went further than this—we proposed that if there was an arbitration, the bondholders' claims should go to arbitration; and that if, on the contrary, there was a direct settlement by negotiation at Washington, then the Venezuelan Government should give us an undertaking that they would make a fresh arrangement with the bondholders. That was not an engagement of a dangerous or far-reaching character.[74]

Article VI of the Washington Protocol provided an under-taking by the Venezuelan Government that a fresh arrange-ment would be arrived at, and H.M. Government, in spite of the vehement protests of the bondholders, refused to accept any further responsibility. The Council of Foreign Bondholders was informed (13 March), in reply to its anxious enquiries, that an agreement having been obtained from the Venezuelan Government to satisfy the bondholder claims, the bondholders 'should now take such steps as may seem to them proper for rendering this undertaking effective'. A similar reply was returned to further requests for intervention in 1904, and the

---

74. 118 *Parl.Deb.*4*s*.1063. This was by no means a case of a public attitude struck for the benefit of posterity. Lansdowne, in an internal Foreign Office Memorandum dated 26 January 1903 (on the question of the inadequacy of the 30 per cent of customs duties at Puerto Cabello and La Guaira, offered by Mr. Bowen, to satisfy all international claims *and* those of the bondholders), observed that such an arrangement would not only delay a final reparation almost indefinitely but would 'at once place the claims of the bondholders, between which and the other claims we have throughout drawn a sharp distinction, upon the same line as the rest'. And Sir Michael Herbert was at once instructed to this effect.

Foreign Office refused even to advise as to the nature of the proceedings to be undertaken to hold the Venezuelan Government to the terms of Article VI.

On 11 January 1905 a provisional draft agreement was finally signed in Paris by representatives of the bondholders and of the Venezuelan Government. The Agreement was communicated to the Foreign Office on 25 January, when it was found to include several objectionable features. Article I created a new title for the reorganized Debt, which was to be known as the *Dette Diplomatique*; Article 23 provided for the servicing of the Debt through the British and German legations; and Article 41 insisted that, since the issue of the new Debt could not take place except by virtue of a diplomatic agreement, the contract should be formally communicated by the Venezuelan Government to the Governments of Great Britain and Germany. The Foreign Office was outraged. Villiers felt that it was 'quite unjustifiable' for the Council of Foreign Bondholders to include in the contract a provision involving a 'diplomatic arrangement' with a foreign Power, without the knowledge or sanction of the Secretary of State; while he was prepared to admit the possibility of interest being remitted by the Legations 'if it were made clear that this imposed no obligation, or financial responsibility, whatever upon H.M.G.', he thought that 'it would not be at all desirable, more especially in view of all that passed with regard to the Venezuelan bondholders, to accept . . . the risk of an implied obligation to intervene hereafter'. Lansdowne agreed, and the Treasury felt that even the remission of the service of the Debt would be understood to give an undesirable measure of official recognition to the new Contract. On 22 March an ungracious letter to this effect was sent to the Council of Foreign Bondholders which brought Lord Avebury (the Chairman), Sir Charles Fremantle and the Secretary hurrying to the House of Lords. They received little comfort from Lansdowne who pointed out that a formal diplomatic communication of the Contract, if it meant nothing, would be of no use to the bondholders, and if it implied British official recognition, would not be acceptable to H.M. Government; Foreign Office policy in regard to these matters was well understood, and H.M. Government had no intention of departing from it, especially in dealing with a government such as that of Venezuela for which H.M. Government could not accept 'even the faintest shadow of responsibility'.

The bondholders continued to argue their case, and the Foreign Office was obliged to prepare a long letter for the Council of Foreign Bondholders, 27 April, explaining in detail the fundamental distinction between the first and second rank claims, and the claims of the bondholders. Even in the case of claims arising from investments by private persons, such as the second rank claims of the British companies, the fact that the money had been advanced for the purpose of furthering enterprises of general utility over which the investor had some control entitled shareholders to claim compensation for damage or loss to their legitimately acquired property at the hands of the local government—'Such a claim stands on a very different footing to that of a person who has merely advanced money, at the high rate of interest which is usually the accompaniment of bad security, to meet the needs of a foreign Government, a form of investment which it has never been the policy of His Majesty's Government to encourage.'

Under constant pressure from Lord Avebury, the Foreign Office relented slightly and, with the consent of the Treasury (which agreed to waive its objection), agreed to authorize the British Legation at Caracas to receive the service of the Debt, on the clear understanding, however, that this would involve no obligation whatever beyond mere remittance of the funds. An amended Contract was signed by the bondholders on 7 June 1905 in which the objectionable Article 41 was removed, and instructions were sent to the British Chargé d'Affaires (20 June) to receive and remit the service of the Debt. The term 'Diplomatic Debt' remained unaltered since the Foreign Office felt unable to enforce its withdrawal, and the American Ambassador had to be assured that it implied no official part in the arrangement.

*　　*　　*

Bondholder grievances, whatever the provocation, never became a determining factor in British policy in Latin America. The tradition of *laissez-faire* and non-intervention was at its harshest when applied to the bondholders, and their complaint was not simply that they were normally unsuccessful in persuading the Foreign Office to take up their cause, but that even when they were entitled to official support they received less than their due.

But it is often argued that non-intervention in Latin America—whether for the bondholders, for the traders, or for the concession-mongers—owed nothing to *laissez-faire*, Free Trade and George Canning, and everything to the existence of the Monroe Doctrine; British financial, commercial, and political ambitions in Latin America were frustrated by the existence of a powerful and protective United States, and—but for the restraining hand of Washington—H.M. Government would have joined as eagerly in the political and economic partition of Latin America as she had in the spoliation of Africa, the Levant, and the Far East.[75]

It is certainly true that, once the Foreign Office had come to accept the natural hegemony of the United States both in the Caribbean and among the northern Republics of South America (as it did from just after the middle of the last century), British officials became even more reluctant to employ force in the redress of legitimate claims against Latin American governments than they were elsewhere in the world. Where possible, the British Government attempted to enlist U.S. support in any major coercive measure: against Mexico in 1861, against Chile and Peru in 1879, against Venezuela in 1886, and against Venezuela again in 1902. A genuine restraint was felt by officials. When Mr. Elliot prepared a Memorandum in 1881 on a proposal to stage a naval demonstration against Venezuela in support of British claims, he explained that though Venezuela was clearly in the wrong and the use of force amply justified, the proposed demonstration might be objected to on grounds of expediency; it might lead to 'complications with other creditor nations, especially the United States—always jealous of foreign nations across the Atlantic'.[76]

The Monroe Doctrine itself, however, had little effect one way or the other on British official policy in Latin America. The last thing H.M. Government wanted was to become

75. Most recently by Strachey, *End of Empire*, p. 118, but it was a popular position with an earlier generation of North American historians.
76. No. 3, *Further correspondence respecting the claims of British subjects on Venezuela*, F.O.,C.P.4934.

involved in Latin American politics or to annex Latin American territory. It suited Britain far better, as a great trading and investing nation, to maintain the independence and integrity of nations which offered promising openings for trade and finance; a Bourbon monarchy on the River Plate might well end in a special trading relationship with France and Spain and the exclusion of British enterprise. Some months before the Monroe Doctrine was actually formulated, Canning suggested a joint Anglo-American stand in support of the territorial integrity of the new Republics, and when President Monroe announced his doctrine to the world on 2 December 1823 he was reflecting an existing British policy as faithfully, for example, as was Secretary Hay in declaring the Open Door in China in 1899.

H.M. Government's attitude towards the Doctrine was guarded but in practice aquiescent. Lord Clarendon told the U.S. Minister in London (Mr. Buchanan), 2 May 1854, that the Doctrine could 'only be viewed as the dictum of the distinguished personage who delivered it'; it could not be admitted 'as an international axiom which ought to regulate the conduct of European States'.[77] But as and when Britain withdrew politically from the Caribbean—an abdication which was complete by 1860—there was no point in making an issue of an American political supremacy which was already a *fait accompli*. Malmesbury, as Foreign Secretary in 1858, seems to have been quite prepared to accept as 'probable and not at all dangerous to European interests' an ultimate U.S. annexation of Mexico, though he, like other British statesmen, could not accept such a thing as the 'so-called Monroe Doctrine'.[78] Salisbury, nearly forty years later, still refused to acknowledge that the Doctrine made any difference, but he was perfectly prepared to accept the natural hegemony of the United States in the Caribbean. 'Considering the position of Venezuela in the Caribbean Sea', he said in February 1896 in the context of the Venezuelan Boundary Dispute, 'it was not more unnatural that the United States should take an interest in it than

77. No. 3018, *Diplomatic Correspondence of the United States; Inter-American Affairs 1831–1860* (Washington, 1936), VII, 541.
78. Quoted in H. Hearder, 'The Foreign Policy of Lord Malmesbury, 1858–9', London thesis, 1954, pp. 60–61.

that we should feel an interest in Holland and Belgium'.[79]

The Monroe Doctrine, coinciding as it did with the traditional British policy inherited from Castlereagh and Canning, had no influence on British political ambitions. But neither was it any real restraint on British commercial and financial policy. The Doctrine applied, as late as the Roosevelt corollary of 1904–5, solely to the threat of political intervention or territorial annexation in the Western hemisphere; it was not intended to restrict coercions with limited objectives. Although the United States was prepared to go to some lengths to prevent a possible clash between European and Latin American Governments, she did not deny the right of European governments to enforce just claims. Under the shadow of the proposed Allied coercion of Mexico, the U.S. Government even considered a loan to Mexico in 1861 to dispense with the need for European intervention; but, at the same time, it did not question the 'undoubted right of the European Powers to decide for themselves the fact whether they have sustained grievances, and to resort to war with Mexico for the redress thereof'.[80] Similarly, although early in the '70s Secretary of State Fish had told the German Minister that 'if Germany or any other power had just cause of war against Venezuela, this Government could interpose no objection to her resorting thereto', ten years later, in order to forestall armed French intervention in Venezuela, the U.S. Government proposed to appoint an agent at Caracas to collect the sum due to the creditor nations, and to authorize this agent to take charge of the custom-house in event of prolonged default.[81] The American attitude was summarized by Mr. Seward when he told the American Minister at Santiago (2 June 1866) that the United States did not intervene in wars between European and American states 'if they are not pushed, like the French war in Mexico, to the political point'.[82]

The United States, therefore, had no objections to European

79. 37 *Parl.Deb.*4s.52 (11 February 1896). Salisbury's rejection of the Monroe Doctrine itself as conferring any special rights was conveyed in his reply to the Olney Note on the Venezuelan boundary: Salisbury to Pauncefote, 26 November 1895, printed as No. 15, *Correspondence respecting the Question of the Boundary of British Guiana*, P.P.1896(c.7926)XCVII.
80. No. 28 and Inclosure in No. 102, *Correspondence respecting the Affairs of Mexico*, P.P.1862(2915)LXIV.
81. Moore, *Digest of International Law*, VI, 531, 584–6.
82. ibid., 596.

intervention for the redress of torts, and indeed was prepared to accept even the landing of European troops and the seizure of custom-houses provided that there was no prospect of a permanent occupation.[83] Mr. Olney explained to Lord Salisbury in 1895 that the Monroe Doctrine 'does not establish any general Protectorate by the United States over American States. It does not relieve any American State from its obligations as fixed by international law, nor prevent any European Power directly interested from enforcing such obligations or from inflicting merited punishment for the breach of them.'[84] When, early in 1902, the European Powers presented a joint Note to the Guatemalan Government on the subject of default on the External Debt, Mr. John Hay told the U.S. Minister in Guatemala that no action was called for from the United States, 'inasmuch as it is within the right of the creditor nations to require payment of debts due to their nationals'.[85]

The new role of 'policing' power in the Caribbean, which President Roosevelt had assumed in 1904–5, was exactly what the Foreign Office wanted. Roosevelt realized that European financial intervention in Latin America could often involve the prolonged occupation of Latin American territory (in the form of European-administered custom-houses or permanent international Debt Commissions); if, in the interests of U.S. hegemony in the area, this were to be avoided, some substitute would have to be found for European Government coercions, since it would be inequitable to deny European creditors all possibility of redress. The only substitute which coincided with continued U.S. political authority was the acceptance of an obligation to keep Latin American States to their promises, and even, if necessary, to reorganize their finances. Since the British Government had no wish to undertake anything of the kind, nothing could have suited it better than Roosevelt's final decision to shoulder the burden himself; and the Roosevelt corol-

83. Roosevelt, surprisingly, was prepared to accept this as late as the end of 1905, even after declaring his own corollary to the Doctrine; this, at least, was what he told the French Ambassador on 14 December 1905 in the context of a proposed French coercion of Venezuela: Philip C. Jessup, *Elihu Root* (New York, 1938), I, 495–6.
84. No. 11, *Correspondence respecting the Question of the Boundary of British Guiana*, P.P.1896(c.7926)XCVII.
85. *Papers relating to the Foreign Relations of the United States* (Washington, 1902), p. 578.

lary, though it represented a formidable extension of the Monroe Doctrine, was a welcome excuse for the Foreign Office to contract-out of any further financial responsibilities in the area.

The idea, then, that the Monroe Doctrine controlled or even profoundly influenced British policy in Latin America, either in politics or in finance, is clearly absurd. Strachey used it to bridge an awkward gap between what he believed to be the sub-ordination of British diplomacy to finance elsewhere in the world, and the passive, non-interventionist policy which he ob-served in Latin America. But of course this explanation is beside the point. British Governments were simply not interested in Latin American territory and, in the absence of any political threat or any danger of a partition leading to the erection of tariff barriers, British diplomatists had no motive to intervene further than to protect the persons and property of British sub-jects.

* * *

It is difficult, no doubt, and dangerous, to generalize for a continent the size of Latin America, or for a period as long as that between 1815 and 1914. But the more British policy is studied, the more clear it becomes that that policy developed hardly at all from the time of Castlereagh to that of Sir Edward Grey. Once the Continent had been opened to world trade—a painless process compared with that in the Far East—the British Government was able to limit its functions to ensuring fair and equal treatment for British trade in Latin American markets, and adequate protection for the persons and property of British subjects. There was no reason to expand these func-tions, except in so far as to improve the facilities for commercial intelligence.

Foreign competition was fierce enough in and after the last decades of the nineteenth century, but it was not threatening in the same sense as it was in Africa and the Far East; there was no danger of a territorial partition of Latin America which might close whole areas of the continent to British trade. Foreign diplomatists might be prepared to press the interests of their subjects in Latin America much harder than the Foreign Office would press its own, but that was understandable when these countries were trying to gain a foothold in markets where British trade, with its great network of banks, agencies, import/export houses, was already so well established. The heavy British investment in Latin America by 1913—at nearly £1,000 million well over twice that of its nearest rival (France, with about £350 million)—was likely to give added advantage to British products, even though the loans or joint stock investments were never, in Latin America before 1914, tied to the purchase of British material. The commercial and financial advantages of British businessmen in Latin America until the First World War were such that the Foreign Office felt itself justified in following its traditional policy of *laissez-faire*; 'For herself,' Canning had written to the British Minister at Madrid in January 1824, 'Great Britain asks no exclusive privileges of trade, no invidious preference, but equal freedom of commerce for all'; and what was true of 1824 remained true in 1914.

Trade, in fact, was the beginning and end of British diplomacy in Latin America. Sir Edward Grey explained official policy, unaltered since the days of Castlereagh and Canning, in his address to the Dominion delegates to the Imperial Conference of 1911:

We have not the least idea [he said], and, indeed, we should be foolish if we had, of attempting to acquire fresh territory on the American Continent. . . . As long as it is the policy of the United States as I believe it will always be not to disturb existing British possessions, she may be perfectly certain we are ready at any time to give her any amount of assurance that we shall certainly not try to disturb, not only her possessions, but the possessions of other independent countries in Central and South America. In South America it is an instruction to all our Diplomatists that they are to regard their work there as not entailing upon them taking a hand in the politics of South America or acquiring political influence; they are to regard their work there as upholding our commercial interest and promoting British trade, in which, of course, I include the trade of the British Empire, and we have kept, and shall keep, carefully clear of all entanglements in the politics, which are often very complicated, of the Central and South American Republics with each other . . .[86]

86. Extract from Grey's 'strictly confidential' Address on the international situation, delivered at the special meeting of the Imperial Defence Committee of 26 May 1911 to which Dominion delegates to the Imperial Conference were invited. The Address is printed in full as Appendix V, *B.D.O.W.*, VI, 781–90.

CONCLUSION

THE POLICY of H.M. Government in the century before 1914 is simply stated: it was to maintain 'equal favour and open competition' for British finance and trade overseas. But there are questions still to be answered. How and where, for instance, did this policy react on political diplomacy, and to what extent can it be said to have moulded the total shape of British foreign policy?

Laissez-faire, Free Trade, social class, and the tradition of non-intervention combined to limit the degree to which British statesmen were prepared to support and promote international finance and trade. The prejudice against the 'pushing' of individual financial and trading interests remained strong until well into the twentieth century, but this did not preclude an urgent official interest in the general welfare of British commerce overseas. Lord Strang, a former Permanent Under-Secretary, recently reminded an audience that no British Foreign Secretary could ignore Britain's position as a 'small, densely populated island with wide overseas interests, inescapably dependent upon foreign trade for the maintenance of its high standard of living'.[1] And this was as plain to Victorian statesmen and officials as it is to statesmen and officials today.

The argument developed in Part III (during the studies of British finance, trade, and politics in joint operation) was intended to call attention to a relatively neglected concept of British foreign policy. The first interest of all countries, Sir Eyre Crowe had explained in his well-known 1907 Memorandum on British foreign policy, was 'the preservation of national independence ... [But] second only to the ideal of independence, nations have always cherished the right of free intercourse and trade in the world's markets'.[2] Crowe had isolated the two principal strands in British foreign policy for the century before 1914: Security and Trade. Security has received the close at-

1. Lord Strang, *The Diplomatic Career* (London, 1962), p. 121.
2. The Memorandum, dated 1 January, 1907, is printed as Appendix A, *B.D.O.W.*,III,397–420; the particular reference is to the top of p. 403.

354   *Finance, Trade, and British Foreign Policy*

tention of generations of diplomatic historians, but the effect
of Trade in determining policy is one of the least understood
areas of Victorian history. Could it be true that trade and
finance played no significant part in diplomatic decisions? The
evidence suggests the contrary. A close connexion existed
in British foreign policy between national security and the
maintenance of British trade, more particularly in and after the
last quarter of the nineteenth century.

*   *   *

What were the traditional elements in British political diplomacy? Most diplomatic historians have remarked on the extraordinary continuity of British foreign policy through the
nineteenth and early twentieth centuries. Crowe's 1907 Memorandum—Temperley and Penson point out—reproduced in the
main the ideas and assumptions accepted by British statesmen
since Pitt: 'The balance of power, the sanctity of treaties, the
danger of extending guarantees, the value of non-intervention,
the implications of what Castlereagh called "a System of
Government strongly popular and national in its character"
were understood by all.'[3] Until the first decade of the twentieth
century, independence and non-intervention formed the guide-
lines of a foreign policy which spanned party politics. It was often
difficult or even impossible to stand aloof, but the genuine
interest of H.M. Government, as Bismarck explained to Lord
Dufferin, was in maintaining the peace of Europe; she too, like
Germany, might be said to belong to the party of *les satisfaits*.[4]
Germany, of course, was to leave that party soon afterwards, but
Bismarck's description of British interest remained true not only
of British policy in Europe but of British policy throughout the
world. Ironically (in view of the enormous expansion of the
British Empire over the period) British Government policy was
fundamentally anti-expansionist. The obsession of British states-

3. Harold Temperley and Lillian M. Penson, *Foundations of British Foreign
Policy from Pitt (1792) to Salisbury (1902)* (London, 1938), p. xxvii.
4. December 1879 at Varzin, quoted in Harold Nicolson, *Helen's Tower*
(London, 1937), p. 175. It was an opinion echoed by Langer in the con-
clusion to his monumental *Diplomacy of Imperialism*, p. 789, and repeated by
G. P. Gooch as applied to the period after the Boer War, when Britain's 'sole
ambition . . . was to keep what she had got': *Recent Revelations of European
Diplomacy* (London, 1928), p. 175.

men and officials was with security—the safeguarding and maintenance of the *existing* Empire rather than its extension; and this obsession survived largely unmodified until the First World War.

It would be untrue to say that the early and mid-Victorians were universally opposed to *any* form of territorial expansion overseas. Most, if not all, Victorians believed in the universal benefit to be derived from the expansion of trade, and it was obvious that colonies would bring both demand for our goods and employment for our working class. But the colonies which the Philosophical Radicals supported,[5] and which the Gladstonian Liberals themselves were prepared to welcome, were the colonies of settlement—Australia, New Zealand, and Canada: 'white' colonies which were likely to provide markets and which might legitimately be expected, in time, to look after their own affairs. These were the colonies to which Gladstone referred in his Chester Address of 12 November 1855, when he claimed that colonies were desirable for the trade and employment they brought and the moral and social results which followed from a wise system of colonization—'if it please Providence to create openings for us upon the broad fields of distant continents, we should avail ourselves in reason and moderation of those openings to reproduce the copy of those laws and institutions, those habits and national characteristics, which have made England so famous as she is'. But in the same Address Gladstone had argued that the mere extension of territory could not be a legitimate object of ambition unless good use could be made of that territory.[6] And it did not follow that even proposals for settlement in vacant territories overseas suitable for colonization by northern Europeans would receive Government sanction. When Pakenham suggested that Britain should establish a colony in the still unsettled California, the Colonial Office replied that it was 'not anxious for the formation of new and distant Colonies, all of which involve heavy direct and still heavier indirect expenditure, besides multiplying

5. The Benthamite attitude to colonization is discussed by Bernard Semmel, 'The Philosophic Radicals and Colonialism', *Journal of Economic History*, XXI (1961), 513–25, and by Donald Winch, *Classical Political Economy and Colonies* (London, 1965).
6. Address printed in full in Paul Knaplund, *Gladstone and Britain's Imperial Policy* (London, 1927), pp. 185–227.

the liabilities of misunderstanding and collisions with Foreign Powers'.[7]

If even colonies of settlement could be resisted on political or financial grounds, tropical colonies ('exploitation' colonies) could expect a poor reception in Whitehall. Palmerston told the Belgians in 1837 that he himself was not among those who attached very great importance to colonies, being inclined on the contrary to believe that 'the value of Such Appendages is in general opinion Much over rated'.[8] Twenty years later he was resisting the burden of taking on the government of Egypt:

Let us try to improve all those countries by the general influence of our commerce, but let us abstain from a crusade of conquest which would call down upon us the condemnation of all other civilised nations.

Lord Cromer, who quoted this extract from a letter to Clarendon, added that 'the general aims of British policy in 1879 were much the same as they had been when Lord Palmerston wrote these lines'.[9]

The general aims were common to both political parties. The resistance of the Gladstonian Liberals to expansion and intervention is notorious; they felt that the needs of British trade were met by the expansion of Free Trade and the opening of world markets, that the Empire was large enough already, and that any further extension would dilute the effort which was needed to improve conditions at home. In the mid-'90s John Morley described 'all this empire building' as 'tainted with the spirit of the hunt for gold', and he together with the remainder of the Gladstonian Liberals remained loyally opposed to expansionism until well into the twentieth century. But Disraelian imperialism, although more colourful in the attitude it took to the existing Empire, was no more wedded to expansion. In the famous Crystal Palace speech of 24 June 1872, which (Schumpeter says) marked 'the birth of imperialism as the catch phrase of domestic policy', Disraeli spoke not of expanding the Empire

7. Quoted by E. D. Adams, 'English Interest in the Annexation of California', *American Historical Review*, XIV (1909), 747.
8. Quoted by Brison D. Gooch, 'Belgium and the prospective sale of Cuba in 1837', *Hispanic American Historical Review*, 39 (1959), 421.
9. Cromer, *Modern Egypt*, I, 92.

but of the need to uphold and maintain it and to protect it from disintegration.[10] And this, indeed, was the essence of British foreign and imperial policy. The *preservation* of the existing Empire was as much the policy of Gladstone as it was of Disraeli; he saw self-government simply as a means of maintaining imperial unity. When, in the early '70s, real strains began to be felt on the fabric of the Empire and disintegration threatened, Gladstone's followers rallied to the defence. 'Who talks now of casting off the colonies?', W. E. Forster asked in 1875, 'What more popular cry than the preservation of our colonial empire?'[11]

The outstanding feature of British foreign policy after 1870 was that it was perpetually on the defensive. Almost by accident we had built up a position across the world which put us ahead of other Powers, but which had also vastly increased our vulnerability. We had expanded—Lord Cromer explained—because, like Rome in the past and Russia in the present, we had been 'impelled onwards by the imperious and irresistible necessity of acquiring defensible frontiers'.[12] We had been engaged also in the settlement and development of the great 'white' colonies. We found ourselves, in and after the 1870's, presented with accumulating threats against our existing possessions from Powers like Germany which, having achieved unity and prosperity at home, felt the need for 'a place in the sun' overseas. We found also that our possessions began, as in Persia, Afghanistan and Tibet, to abut directly on those of a newly expanded Power (Russia). Robinson and Gallagher have explained for Africa and Mrs. Greaves for Persia how British policy turned on the security of the Empire and, above all, on the defence of India. The imperial expansion which occurred during this period and British policy in the Levant, Africa, and the Far East

---

10. The speech is printed in T. E. Kebbel (ed.), *Selected Speeches of the Late Earl of Beaconsfield* (London, 1882), II, pp. 523–35. Disraeli's opposition to expansionism is described by Stanley R. Stembridge, 'Disraeli and the Millstones', *Journal of British Studies*, V (1965), 135–8.

11. Quoted by J. E. Tyler, *The Struggle for Imperial Unity, 1868–1895* (London, 1938), p. 6.

12. Lord Cromer, *Ancient and Modern Imperialism* (London, 1909), pp. 19–20. John S. Galbraith has recently re-emphasized Cromer's point in his article, 'The "Turbulent Frontier" as a Factor in British Expansion', *Comparative Studies in Society and History*, II (1960), 150–68.

were designed to secure the Empire—they were defensive measures; attempts to preserve our position in the world, not to extend it.

To take the separate areas of international conflict in turn. In Turkey, British policy was hampered by our defence of the Armenians and by our championship of minority rights in Macedonia, and Sir William White used to say that the task of a British Ambassador was restricted to 'striving manfully to keep the boat of British prestige and interests from slipping downstream'. In Persia, as Sir Edward Grey explained in retrospect, British policy was 'not a forward policy pushed for the purpose of extending British territory or influence', but a policy intended to preserve Persia as an independent buffer state,[13] while for the Gulf Lord Curzon had declared in 1899 that Britain had no wish to disturb the political *status quo* 'as long as it can be maintained',[14] and this remained the basis of the Persian Gulf Declarations of 1903 and 1907. British officials moved into Africa—Robinson and Gallagher have pointed out—'not to build a new African empire, but to protect the old empire in India'.[15] British policy in China, said a Foreign Office Memorandum in 1930, 'can be stated in a very few words... We have no territorial or imperialistic aims.'[16] As for Latin America, Grey had assured the Dominion delegates in 1911 that Britain 'had not the least idea, and, indeed, we should be very foolish if we had, of attempting to acquire fresh territory on the American Continent'.[17] It was a mistake, Lord Milner explained, to think of Imperialism as 'principally concerned with extension of territory, with "painting the map red". There is quite enough painted red already.' And in his great speech at Manchester, 14 December 1906, when he described his 'Imperialist Creed', Milner observed that the 'maintenance and consolidation of what we call the British Empire should be the first and highest of all political objects for every subject of the Crown'; our ob-

13. Grey, *Twenty-five Years*, I, 154.
14. Curzon, 21 September 1899: quoted by Ward and Gooch, *Cambridge History of British Foreign Policy 1783–1919* (Cambridge, 1923), p. 319.
15. *Africa and the Victorians*, p. 464.
16. Memorandum dated 8 January 1930, printed in Butler and Bury, *Documents on British Foreign Policy*, 2nd ser. III, 4.
17. Confidential Address of 26 May 1911, printed as Appendix V, *B.D.O.W.*, VI, 786.

ject was not 'domination or aggrandisement' but 'consolidation and security'.[18]

British foreign policy over the decades which spanned the century was deeply concerned with the preservation of the imperial frontiers and lines of communication; it was a defensive policy which had remained defensive since the first threats were felt to Britain's world position in the '70s. Curzon observed in 1892 how Britain, in contrast to Russia, had already passed through the acquisitive stage of Empire, and having in her own time 'experienced its intoxicating fumes in all their intensity', had now emerged into the quieter atmosphere of the conservative stage. He was quite correct. Britain was indeed preoccupied with holding what she already had, and whatever she gained was demanded because it helped her to preserve the rest. She belonged to the party of *les satisfaits*, but she had to fight ever harder to stay with them, and she had by far the most to lose.

* * *

It should be remembered, however, that the threat which had put British foreign policy on the defensive since the 1870's was not only a threat to her physical possessions and frontiers: it was also a threat to her livelihood, her position in world trade and finance. And if Britain was generally on the defensive in foreign policy after 1870, was it not likely that a major element in determining this policy was the threat to our markets overseas?

During the first period—that is, the period which ended in the early '80s—H.M. Government's reaction to British trading

18. Lord Milner, *The Nation and the Empire* (London, 1913). The other great Imperial Pro-Consuls, Lord Cromer and Lord Curzon, felt much the same. Introducing a volume of Curzon's speeches, Cromer referred to 'the fallacy that every Imperialist agent is possessed with an insane desire to enlarge the area of territories painted red on the map of the world'. The point was driven home in the first of the speeches printed—an address given by Lord Curzon at a dinner given to Lord Milner, under the presidency of Mr. Chamberlain, on Empire Day, 1906. 'Believe me', Curzon had assured his audience, 'it is not those who know most of the Empire who make broad its phylacteries. It is not from their lips that you hear about painting the map of the world red. I doubt if in the mind of any of them—and there are many here tonight—expansion ever figures as an object of ambition, though it may sometime present itself to them, as it has often presented itself in the past, as an obligation of duty'. D. M. Chapman-Huston (ed.), *Subjects of the Day* (London, 1915), pp. xvi, 4.

and financial interests overseas was governed by the traditions of *laissez-faire*, Free Trade, and non-intervention in the internal affairs of sovereign states. The Government recognized its duty to open world markets to British trade and to protect legitimate trade in those markets once opened: British policy in China, Japan, and Latin America was wholly determined by this duty, and policy in the Levant and North Africa, if very much more closely tied to conventional political aims, depended to a lesser degree on an official engagement to smooth the way for British trade. The duties of British consuls in Asiatic Turkey or Persia were certainly political, but consuls were also expected often to act as pioneers of British trade, and a Political Convention negotiated in the Levant was followed by a Treaty of Commerce. The legitimate functions of government ended, however, with the opening of markets, the maintenance of Treaty rights, and the protection of British subjects. 'The modern application of the principles of political economy', said Cobden in 1858, 'has destroyed the motive of self-interest which formerly tempted us to wars of conquest', and Gladstone certainly held the same opinion. Trade could be conducted—after Adam Smith—without the physical possession of foreign territories. Protection, outmoded in political economy, was dead or dying. With the markets of the world freely open to international trade, what motive could there be for undertaking the expense and trouble of colonial administration? What reason could there be, likewise, to depart from the principle of non-intervention inherited from Castlereagh and Canning?

How accurate, then, would it be to include this period under the general description of the 'Imperialism of Free Trade'?[19] Gallagher and Robinson, who coined the phrase in challenging the traditional view of anti-imperialism in British policy before 1870, certainly did useful service in emphasizing the importance of trade in British foreign policy even during these years of *laissez-faire* and Free Trade; the opening of world markets and the protection of British subjects were major preoccupations of overseas policy in and after the 1820's, especially in Latin America and China. They were correct, too, in drawing attention to the reluctance of British statesmen and officials—even in

19. Gallagher and Robinson, 'The Imperialism of Free Trade', *Economic History Review*, 2nd ser. VI, 1–15.

the period of the so-called 'New Imperialism'—to undertake 'formal' control when 'informal' control would serve as well. But the 'Imperialism of Free Trade' was intended to cover a much wider area than this: Gallagher and Robinson have re-written the usual reading of mid-Victorian official policy ('trade not rule') into the new formula of 'trade with informal control if possible; trade with rule when necessary'; and it is this new formula which simply will not stand up to examination. Ingenious though the argument is, the Gallagher and Robinson thesis was founded neither on an understanding of the very real limitations set to the support which H.M. Government was prepared to give to trade and finance overseas, nor of the details of the areas to which British 'informal' control was claimed to apply. Non-intervention applied as often to 'informal' as to 'formal' control. It is not true, for example, that H.M. Government was prepared to exercise informal control in Latin America, whatever the provocation, and the examples quoted by Gallagher and Robinson go nowhere to prove their case. Nor could it be said that 'informal control' applied even to China; officials confined themselves to objectives (in opening China to world trade) well below the expectations of the merchants and financiers, and slight attempt was made to exercise control over the internal affairs of the Empire—beneficial though such control would undoubtedly have been to British trade. Any British Government welcomed the opening of further sectors of the world to trade and, within limits, did what it could to assist that opening. But even 'informal' control was the last thing that officials were likely to seek out. Intervention was occasionally forced on them, but the notion of a deliberate policy 'to establish and maintain British paramountcy' in the interests of British trade—the so-called 'Imperialism of Free Trade'—describes the *ad hoc* decisions of officials on the spot and the reluctance of Whitehall to break with *laissez-faire* and Free Trade no better than the contrary view that *laissez-faire* and Free Trade left no positive role to the Foreign Office whatever.

What it amounted to was that H.M. Government before the '80s undertook a strictly limited range of functions—the opening of markets, the protection of British interests under international law, the guarantee that, so far as possible, British trade would receive fair and equal—not favoured—treatment overseas.

Special conditions for British traders, diplomatic pressure for contracts and concessions, diplomatic support for general bond-holder claims, intervention in internal politics in the interests of British trade and finance, interference with the free play of the international money market—all these were denied; they were regarded as coming well outside the legitimate functions of government. Trade was an important factor in determining British policy in certain parts of the world, but the issues were simple. Britain's ascendancy as the workshop of the world was still virtually unchallenged. Universal Free Trade seemed at least a possibility before the early '70s, and there was no real pressure to depart from the basic principle of classical political economy—the free play of markets. H.M. Government used British diplomatists to open up the world to trade and to protect British interests overseas, but there was no question as yet in international trade, any more than there was in international politics, of a serious threat to Britain's position abroad. *Laissez-faire*, non-intervention, the rejection of control—formal or informal—still served as the common ground on which policy was determined.

*   *   *

The situation became markedly different in and after the '80s. Under pressure, British foreign policy shifted to the defensive. British interests had to be sustained and protected not only against threats to frontiers or imperial communications but also against exclusion from the markets on which we depended for our survival. The growing manufacturing industries in Continental Europe, in the United States, and later even in Japan, were genuinely competitive, and the Great Depression of the '70s and '80s badly frightened British exporters. The threat of foreign competition was less obvious in some years than in others, and the general optimism of officials as to British trading prospects in the twenty years before 1914 acted as a brake on too sharp an official reaction. But in and after the '80s there was no escape from competition in one part or another of the world at some point or other in time, whether in the developed markets themselves or in the newer, more competitive markets of the Levant, Africa, China, or Latin America. However disinclined by class or tradition, British officials were at last compelled to take trade seriously. 'I think the best way of putting it', said Sir Philip Currie (Permanent Under-Secretary of State) in 1889, 'is that an ambassador or minister's duty is to look after British interests, and our commercial interests are naturally the most important'.

The question is how and in what direction did British trade and finance affect British foreign policy after the mid-'80s? Was Leonard Woolf right in giving first place to trade as the motive for British imperialism? Or Hobson when he chose finance? Or Robinson and Gallagher, when they claimed that political security was the highest common factor in determining British policy during the scramble for Africa (and the highest by a handsome margin)? Or Fieldhouse, who described international politics after the early '80s as simply the reflection of new *diplomatic* pattern in Europe?

Laissez-faire, Free Trade, and the tradition of non-intervention still continued to act as a check on British Government promotion of trade and finance overseas. But the studies in Part III of the crisis points during the decades spanning the two centuries have shown the extent to which the general interest of British trade in fact reacted both on British *imperial policy* and on British *diplomacy* in what has been described as the 'informal empire' (the Levant, China, and Latin America). As might be expected, trade had little to do with foreign policy in the 'civilized' world (Europe and North America), but it could be the main element in determining the relationship of the Powers both among themselves and with the local inhabitants in the 'semi-civilized' and 'barbarous' remainder.

In reaction, no doubt, against the extreme positions taken by Hobson and Leonard Woolf, it has become fashionable over the last twenty or thirty years to downgrade the part played in British policy-making in the '80s by the need to forestall the exclusive partitioning of the remainder of the world by the Continental Powers. Yet Sir Charles Dilke, who (as a member of the Government for the first half of the decade and as a specialist in imperial affairs) had every reason to know, explained the position in his *Problems of Greater Britain*, published in 1890 during the white-heat of European imperialism. Dilke argued that until about 1884 H.M. Government had almost consistently refused offers of territory pressed upon it, and that this attitude had been shared by Palmerston, Disraeli, and Gladstone. But

a necessary change of policy followed on the discovery that Germany and France appeared to intend to lay hands between them upon almost all those territories in the globe which did not belong to the European races. The movement of Germany and France seemed to foreshadow the possibility of large markets being gradually closed to our trade by paper annexations, followed, certainly in the case of France, and probably in that of Germany, by the imposition of differential duties.[20]

Dilke was by no means alone. Sir Percy Anderson's attitude at the Foreign Office to the problem of the Congo, 1884–5, was determined by the fear that France would establish control and close the markets to British trade. And Salisbury, under whom the actual Partition of Africa very largely took place, had criticized Gladstone's opposition to territorial annexations—in a speech at Manchester (16 April 1884)—on the grounds that its effect had been to permit France and other Powers who practised a discriminatory tariff policy to monopolize the new markets in the undeveloped areas. A decade later, speaking in support of a forward policy in Uganda (for which he had a particularly soft spot), Salisbury explained to the Lords that—

It is our business in all these new countries to make smooth the paths for British commerce, British enterprise, the application of British capital, at a time when other paths, other outlets for the commercial energies of our race are being gradually closed by the commercial principles which are gaining more and more adhesion. Everywhere we see the advance of commerce checked by the enormous growth which the doctrines of Protection are obtaining. We see it with our three great commercial rivals, France, Germany, and America. The doctrines of Protection are stronger and stronger, and operate to the exclusion of British commerce wherever their power extends.[21]

Experience was to show that British fears in this respect were exaggerated, but they seemed real enough at the time, coinciding as they did with the anxieties created among British manufacturers by the Great Depression. It was not that H.M. Government had any wish to extend its responsibilities; Britain was

20. Sir Charles Wentworth Dilke, *Problems of Greater Britain* (London, 4th. revd. edition 1890), pp. 461–2.
21. 30 *Parl.Deb.4s.*698–9 (14 February 1895).

quite prepared to leave the Africans to themselves so long as the British Government preserved its unquestioned influence along the trading coast. But in the 1880's, once France and Germany had declared their intention to divide Africa, it was a case of the devil takes the hindmost. Joseph Chamberlain reminded the Birmingham Chamber of Commerce in November 1896 of a recent calculation that 2,600,000 square miles had been added to the Empire over the last few years. He was prepared to admit that, if other nations had stood aside, we might have been wiser to go more slowly, but what would have happened, he asked, if we had failed to act?

The greater part of Africa would have been occupied by our commercial rivals, who would have proceeded to close this great commercial market to the British Empire . . .

We, in our colonial policy, as fast as we acquire new territory and develop it, develop it as trustees of civilization for the commerce of the world. We offer in all these markets over which our flag flies the same field to foreigners that we offer to our subjects, and on the same terms. In that policy we stand alone.[22]

Robinson and Gallagher have shown that political reasons played a large part in determining British policy during the scramble for Africa, particularly in the North East and the South. This may have been so, but the rejection of trade as an important factor takes no account of contemporary trading rivalries and competition in, for example, the Far East or Latin America; nor does it allow for the re-thinking in London (1885–6) on the appropriate degree of official support for British trade and finance overseas; nor, indeed, for the genuinely economic rivalries in West Africa. What was true of North-East and South Africa was not true of many of the remaining areas of international competition. Anticipatory annexations for the safeguarding of markets played at least some part in the scramble for Africa. Similar arguments were influential in determining British claims to spheres of influence in Southern Persia, the Persian Gulf and in Mesopotamia; and they were probably decisive in creating the demand for a British sphere of 'interest' in the Yang-tsze Valley. '*Si vous n'étiez pas si acharnés protectionnistes*', Salisbury complained to the French

22. Speech of 15 November 1896, as quoted by Hancock, *Survey of British Commonwealth Affairs*, II, 82.

Ambassador in 1897, *'vous ne nous trouveriez pas si gourmands de territoires.'*[23]

The scramble for Africa and the spread of Protectionism posed one set of problems; yet another developed quite simply from the growth of international trading and financial competition overseas after the delayed industrialization of Continental Europe and North America. This was not a case merely of 'pegging-out claims for posterity' in markets (such as those over most of Africa) which were virtually undeveloped and of doubtful prospect. It was a direct attack on Britain's monopoly in some of her most important export markets.

European and North American competition was no new phenomenon. The United States had been regarded as a dangerous trading rival in Latin America during the 1820's, and Palmerston was certainly aware of European competition from a comparatively early date. He told Auckland in January 1841 that European manufactures were displacing ours in the markets of Europe, and that Britain must constantly be on the watch for new outlets in other parts of the world—'The world is large enough and the wants of the human race ample enough to afford a demand for all we can manufacture; but it is the business of the Government to open and to secure the roads for the merchant.'[24]

But the scale and intensity of foreign competition increased enormously during the last two decades of the century. British foreign policy in Latin America, in China (with a brief 'Balance of Power' interlude in 1898), and in the Levant (where it was more closely integrated with European political rivalries), became exclusively or very largely concerned with the defence and maintenance of British trade. Foreign diplomatic pressure, applied unsparingly on behalf of national trading and financial interests, made it impossible for H.M. Government to stand aside. In the 1880's diplomatic pressure was a relatively new phenomenon, and if the Foreign Office were to uphold its obligation to secure a 'fair field and no favour' for British trade, then new measures, unnecessary before, would have to be taken. H.M. Government did not aim to preserve the *relative* position of British trade—this would clearly have been impractic-

23. Quoted by Stengers, *Journal of African History*, III, 487.
24. Quoted by Webster, *Foreign Policy of Palmerston*, II, 750–1.

able when we had started with such an advantage—nor did it claim any exclusive advantages. 'Neither Crowe nor we who succeeded him,' said Lord Vansittart in his autobiography, 'ever gave to the Germans the least ground for thinking our antagonism due to commercial jealousy; it would have suited us well that Germany should develop *peacefully* and buy more. . . .' But the problem was that peaceful development seemed out of the question; and if H.M. Government were to maintain equality of opportunity—no more—for British trade and finance, the 'unfair' methods employed by foreign diplomatists would have to be met by diplomatic pressure, however reluctant, from the British Legation. 'Our first concern', the Foreign Office Memorandum on British Policy in China had said, 'is to *maintain* our position in the trade of China . . . Our second concern is to *maintain* the principle of the "open door" and equal opportunity for all and to see that China does not fall under the tutelage of any single Power.'

*   *   *

The continuity in British foreign policy between 1815 and 1914 extended beyond conventional political diplomacy; it lay in the division of British policy into two main strands—the maintenance of national security, and the creation and preservation of fair and equal opportunities for British trade in the markets of the world. National security was always the prime function of foreign policy, but access to markets and fair treatment in those markets was, for Britain especially, an interest only just subordinate—and closely related—to the safeguarding of our national and Imperial frontiers.

The temptation must be to devalue trade as a factor in British foreign policy simply because the range of action permitted to the Government by *laissez-faire* and Free Trade was sharply defined and limited. But a restricted role did not absolve H.M. Government from the responsibility to obtain 'a fair field and no favour' for British trade and finance overseas, and this responsibility, while never particularly onerous for the mid-Victorians, became increasingly so for their successors.

In trade as in politics H.M. Government was on the defensive after the mid-'80s. 'Fair and equal' treatment for British trade and finance served as a principal element in Anglo-German relations in Asiatic Turkey and in China, in Anglo-American relations in Latin America and the Far East, and even in Anglo-French relations in the Levant, China, and South East Asia. It was both the defence of Imperial frontiers and communications *and* the defence of British trade which compelled H.M. Government to take a share in those Partitions, 'protective' or 'anticipatory' annexations, spheres of 'interest' or 'influence', which disfigured and undermined international relations in the quarter-century before 1914.

APPENDIXES

APPENDIX I

GOVERNMENT MACHINERY
FOR OVERSEAS TRADE

Laissez-faire and Free Trade left little scope for the development of an elaborate official organization for the promotion of overseas trade before the First World War. Yet there were certain services, notably in the provision of commercial intelligence and the negotiation of commercial treaties, which required government machinery, and these services tended to broaden their scope both as British trade expanded and as increased foreign competition put pressure on the more extreme interpretations of *laissez-faire*.

1. *London*

Such commercial services as were provided by H.M. Government in London before the 1860's came almost exclusively from the Board of Trade. It was not until 1865 that the Foreign Office felt the need to create a department specifically charged with commercial affairs (which had been handled by the regional divisions), and in practice the Foreign Office acted scarcely more than as a post office for the Board of Trade. Commercial reports from British legations and consulates overseas, together with notices of any change in commercial relations, were forwarded to the Board of Trade; if the Board felt that any action should follow from these reports, it briefed the Foreign Office, and instructions were sent back overseas; if the Foreign Office received any representations from trade associations or individuals on matters of trade, it normally referred them at once to the Board of Trade for comment.[1] The relationship was one well-suited to the Foreign Office. Tedious and degrading matters of commerce could be delegated with a clear conscience, and aristocratic officials could return to the politi-

1. The distribution of functions between the Board of Trade and the Foreign Office is described in Earl Russell's Circular of 19 April 1864, printed as Appendix 5, *Report from the Select Committee on Trade with Foreign Nations*, P.P.1864(493)VII. Two valuable sources for the overseas trade functions of the Board of Trade during the nineteenth century are: 'The Board of Trade: Its Origins, Authority and Jurisdiction', P.R.O., Round Room, Press Mark 15/99 AA; Hubert Llewellyn Smith, *The Board of Trade* (London, 1928), pp. 56 ff. For the earlier period, the best authority is Lucy Brown, *The Board of Trade and the Free-Trade Movement 1830-42* (Oxford, 1958).

cal problems which they felt more appropriate to their rank. Nor did this really cease to be the case—for all the reforms undertaken after 1864—until as recently as the early 1930's. David Kelly reports that when he was working in the American Department in the 1920's, the usual minute on any commercial or financial problem was 'Query Board of Trade/Treasury, what answer?', after which one turned to the next file and waited patiently for instructions from the experts.[2]

The Board of Trade, in contrast, became particularly active in overseas commercial policy after the arrival of Huskisson as its President in 1823. Under a succession of Free Trade Ministers— Huskisson himself, Poulett Thomson, Gladstone—the Board acted as the focus of that great tariff reform movement which culminated in the arrival, effectively, of Free Trade in 1846. Free Trade was the Board's great achievement, but it also had three main functions in relation to overseas trade. First, although the Foreign Office Treaty Department was technically responsible, the main preparation and drafting of the many commercial treaties negotiated over this period were undertaken at the Board of Trade. Then, the Board advised the Foreign Office on commercial questions generally, and particularly on those which arose out of treaties with foreign states. Finally, it undertook the collection and revision of statistics relating to trade, and the digestion and abstraction of national statistics in general.

The division of functions between the Foreign Office and the Board of Trade was never satisfactory—there is no reason to suppose, in fact, that the problem of an appropriate division of responsibility for overseas trade between the principal Trade Department and the Foreign Office has yet been solved. After 1846, the Board of Trade lost much of its early importance. It was natural that responsibility for the remaining tariffs, now levied for revenue rather than protective purposes, should pass from the Board of Trade to the Treasury, and Llewellyn Smith explains that without these tariff negotiations, the Board lost its chief contact with commercial and industrial opinions and conditions. He adds that the Board, deprived of any direct communication with H.M. Representatives abroad, became increasingly diffident about offering sound and useful advice on commercial questions to the other Departments of State. When Mr. Cardwell became President in 1853, 'he was very largely absorbed by the urgent problems of merchant shipping and railways. . . . Commercial policy under free trade conditions seemed to him so simple a matter that there was no reason why the Foreign Office should consult the Board of

2. Sir David Kelly, *The Ruling Few* (London, 1952), p. 207.

Trade thereon, or why an important branch of the Board of Trade should be occupied with the subject'.[3]

The Anglo-French Commercial Treaty of 1860, and the series of Cobdenite negotiations which followed, gave new life to the Commercial Department of the Board of Trade. Under the direction of Louis Mallet, the Department became the headquarters for the new treaty negotiations. But the revival of reciprocity treaties proved only temporary; and the confusion of commercial functions between the Board of Trade and the Foreign Office was actually increased as a result of the recommendation of a Select Committee appointed in 1864 to resolve the problem.

The Select Committee on Trade with Foreign Nations concerned itself (in response to complaints from the Chambers of Commerce about the delays and inefficiencies of dual responsibility) with the question of a division or reallocation of duties. The Chambers of Commerce wanted to see *one* Department, firmly charged with the protection of British commercial interests abroad. They were not particularly concerned whether the Department came under the Foreign Office or the Board of Trade, but there was a feeling that the problem of the traditional distaste for commercial questions shown by Foreign Office clerks and British diplomatists might be solved by the establishment of a department *within* the Foreign Office which would handle commercial affairs. At present, it was argued, it was too obvious that political questions had the priority, that nobody at the Foreign Office appreciated an enthusiastic performance of commercial duties, and that British diplomatists tended therefore to regard commercial questions as of decidedly secondary importance.[4] The Committee, unfortunately, after taking a great deal of evidence from the Chambers of Commerce, the Foreign Office and the Board of Trade, recommended a compromise that did more harm than good. While it correctly stressed the need for greater importance and prestige to be given to the Board of Trade, with a seat in the Cabinet for its President, it failed altogether to separate the overseas trade functions of the Board and the Foreign Office, and, indeed, emphasized the duality by recommending the formation of the nucleus of a Commercial Department at the Foreign Office to act as a point of liaison with the Board of Trade. What this meant in practice was that when, in response to

3. Llewellyn Smith, *The Board of Trade*, pp. 58–59.
4. For example, Jacob Behrens's evidence and the tone of the questions put to him by Mr. Charles Turner and Sir Minto Farquhar; Minutes of Evidence, *Report of the Select Committee on Trade with Foreign Nations*, P.P.1864(493) VII, QQ.651–4, 657–8.

this recommendation, a commercial branch was established at the Foreign Office in January 1865 (amalgamating with the consular branch into the Commercial and Consular Division in 1866), there were two Commercial Departments to which merchants might go, neither of which, under Free Trade and *laissez-faire,* had much of a job to do, and one of which (in the Foreign Office)—in fact, if not in name—was merely a transmitter of information and opinions to and from the Board of Trade.

The strong opposition of Edmund Hammond (the Permanent Under Secretary of State) to the formation of a commercial division meant that, when he was overruled, the new Commercial Department at the Foreign Office began its life under a cloud from which it never really emerged. At the Board of Trade, the Austrian Commercial Treaty of 1865 and the 1868 Zollverein Treaty kept the Commercial Department busy, but the return of a Liberal administration in 1868 (with an orthodox Free Trader, Lowe, as Chancellor of the Exchequer) reversed the trend, and tariff negotiations were again classed as economic heresy. The prospect of returning to the positive policy urged by Mallet and the Cobdenites vanished with the Protectionist reaction in Europe which followed the Franco-Prussian War. Louis Mallet, fretting away the years in the Board of Trade with no effective responsibilities now that even the Department's advisory functions with the Treasury and the Colonial Office had largely disappeared, could see 'nothing but weakness and inefficiency' in the remaining advisory relationship with the Foreign Office—'Power separated from knowledge, action uninspired by interest, interest chilled and suspended by inaction, divided responsibility, want of unity and continuity, circumlocution, delay and feebleness.'[5]

Louis Mallet and his friend and ally, Sir Robert Morier, recognized the problem and had the answer. Morier, writing to Mallet from Darmstadt in 1869, pointed to the administrative disaster which dualism ('I will not call it an antagonism') imposed; the solution, he argued, was to unite the overseas commercial functions of the Board of Trade and the Foreign Office into one strong commercial department at the Foreign Office, with the Foreign Minister solely responsible before Parliament and the country for the commercial policy of the Empire.[6] Mallet himself agreed. He advised his Minister that his own Department at the Board of Trade should be wound-up, and that its functions should be transferred to the Foreign Office. The Foreign Office, he said, must

5. Quoted by Bernard Mallet, *Sir Louis Mallet,* p. 98.
6. Quoted by Wemyss, *Sir Robert Morier,* II, 134.

increasingly turn its attention to problems of overseas trade, and the importance of a new Commercial Department (with undivided responsibilities) might well be enough to attract the younger talent from within the Foreign Office and overcome its traditional distaste for commercial questions.

Mallet's advice was accepted. The Commercial Department of the Board of Trade was disbanded, its advisory functions with respect to commercial treaties tariffs were transferred to a newly-created (1872) Commercial Department at the Foreign Office, and its remaining functions were reallocated to the other Departments within the Board of Trade.[7] But a fundamental error wrecked the whole reform. As a result, according to Mallet's biographer, of 'official etiquette and the hostility of the Chancellor of the Exchequer to the treaty policy', Sir Louis Mallet (to the disgust of Sir Robert Morier, and probably of Mallet himself) was not appointed Head of the new Commercial Department at the Foreign Office, but diverted to a seat on the India Council. The one man with the knowledge and enthusiasm to build an effective Commercial Department in the hostile air of the Foreign Office was removed; 'coma', Algernon Cecil reported, 'presently attacked the new Department; and, in the end, the old dualism was revived'.[8]

Farrer, the Permanent Secretary of the Board of Trade, put his finger on the trouble at the Foreign Office in a Memorandum of 29 January 1880; he argued that the new arrangement had not worked out simply because the Commercial Department had not been given enough status or importance within the Office, and attention had been diverted elsewhere. In an Appendix to his Memorandum he showed that in fact the Foreign Office had again become dependent on the Board of Trade for commercial and statistical information, consulting the Board with great frequency on matters ranging from the Colorado beetle to the negotiation of the French and Servian Commercial Treaties.[9] The situation was officially recognised in 1882, when the Board's Statistical and Commercial Department again became the official adviser of the Foreign Office on matters of commercial policy. The revived relationship was explained by Mr. C. M. Kennedy, the Senior Clerk of the Foreign Office Commercial Department, in his evidence before the Ridley Commission in November 1889. He was asked how, exactly, the two Departments shared-out their overseas trade functions. His reply was that in the case, for example, of the nego-

7. P.R.O.,B.T/13/5, file no. 1772.
8. Ward and Gooch, *Cambridge History of British Foreign Policy*, p. 608.
9. P.R.O.,B.T/13/12, file no. 4909.

tiation of commercial treaties, the actual initiative in drafting the treaties and consulting the interested parties was taken by the Foreign Office, after which the completed draft was referred to the Board of Trade for its observations; in the 'old days'—that is, before 1872—the Board of Trade undertook the consultations, and simply advised the Foreign Office what was to be done, 'which the Foreign Office did ministerially at the instance of the Board of Trade'.[10]

The Ridley Commission took the optimistic view that the division between intelligence and advisory services (provided by the Board of Trade) and the executive functions (exercised by the Foreign Office) could hardly be improved on, and Sir Hubert Llewellyn Smith argued many years later that this division was in fact the only possible solution and had always been 'the accepted position among those who best understood the intricacies of inter-depart-mental relations, except possibly for a few years following 1871'. But this was not an opinion shared either by a number of officials or by the commercial community. A Confidential Memorandum in the Board of Trade, dated 27 July 1903, argued that more direct responsibility might be passed to the Board for Consular instructions and the editing of Consular reports; and two former Foreign Service officials—Algernon Cecil and George Young—strongly opposed the existing division of responsibility in their critical accounts of general Foreign Office administration, published shortly after the First World War.[11] Commercial opinion, which was always inclined to press for a single Ministry of Commerce on the Continental model, felt seriously aggrieved by the Government's refusal to create a single commercial authority. Mr. Brocklehurst, an M.P. and the head of a large silk manufacturing firm at Macclesfield, complained to the Royal Commission on the Depression of Trade and Industry (1886) about his experience when accompanying deputations on subjects connected with the foreign tariff; they were 'bandied about from one department to another', and could never get to anybody who could give them any definite information.[12] When Mr. Joseph Walton (a constant spokesman for the commercial interest) was moving a resolution in 1903 calling for the reorganization of the Consular Service, he observed that the functions of the Board of

10. Minutes of Evidence, *Report of the Royal Commission on Civil Establishments*, P.P.1890(c.6172)XXVII, QQ.26,829–31.
11. 'The Board of Trade: Its Constitution and Development', Appendix A of the 1914 Memorandum: P.R.O., Round Room, Press Mark 15/99 AA; Ward and Gooch, *Cambridge History of British Foreign Policy*, pp. 623–4; George Young, *Diplomacy Old and New* (London, 1921), pp. 35–36.
12. Minutes of Evidence, *Second Report of the Royal Commission on the Depression of Trade and Industry*, P.P.1886(c.4715)XXI, QQ.7233–5.

Trade, the Foreign Office and the Commercial Intelligence Branch were all overlapping; 'we want the whole thing reorganized; one authority constituted on lines to the interest of British commerce, and not a divided responsibility as at present'.[13]

The Cabinet's decision *not* to proceed with the recommendations of the Jersey Committee in favour of the creation of a Minister of Commerce prompted a storm of protests and resolutions from Chambers of Commerce all over the United Kingdom, and one of the points to be raised most frequently was the damage to commercial interests caused by the lack of co-ordination in commercial functions between the various Government Departments.[14] But some of the criticisms were met automatically by the remarkable expansion of Government functions in overseas trade during the last decades of the century, in which both Commercial Departments shared.

At the Foreign Office, although commercial questions relating to Africa and Eastern Asia continued to be handled in their respective political departments (because commercial questions in those areas, as Sir Henry Bergne told the Select Committee on Steamship Subsidies in 1901, were 'so mixed up with political questions'), the new institutions of Commercial Attachés and Commercial Agents placed a great deal of additional responsibility on the Commercial Department. By 1914, by which time the Department had become known as the Commercial and Sanitary Department, it had absorbed an enormous range of miscellaneous duties, from the 'defence and support of British commercial interests' to 'questions relating to the protection in foreign countries of wild birds and their plumage'.[15]

Over the same period, the Board of Trade had greatly extended its commercial intelligence service. One of the more positive results of the general anxiety in 1886 over foreign competition and increased government assistance to trade had been the *Board of Trade Journal*; published monthly at first and weekly after 1900, it brought up-to-date information to British merchants and manufacturers in a form far more assimilable than the old Blue Books. Furthermore, a Trade and Treaties Committee, established early

13. *Official Report of the Fifth Congress of the Chambers of Commerce of the Empire* (Montreal, 1903), p. 37.
14. P.R.O.,B.T/13/28, file no. 13581.
15. A list of the subjects dealt with by the Commercial Department was given to the Royal Commission on the Civil Service by Mr. Algernon Law, Controller of Commercial and Consular Affairs: Minutes of Evidence, *Fifth Report of the Royal Commission on the Civil Service*, P.P.1914–16 (Cd.7749) XI, Q.37,339.

in the '90s under the chairmanship of Mr. Mundella (the Liberal President of the Board of Trade), prepared a series of reports on tariffs and commercial relations with foreign nations which whetted the public appetite, helped to create a strong demand for improved commercial intelligence services, and no doubt stimulated both Mr. Chamberlain's famous enquiry on foreign competition in the colonies, and the appointment, in 1897, of a Departmental Committee by the Board of Trade to investigate the provision of commercial intelligence.

As a direct result of the Departmental Committee's report, published in July 1898, a Commercial Intelligence Branch was formed within the Commercial Department of the Board of Trade, which opened enquiry offices in Parliament Street in October 1899. The main function of the Branch—under the supervision of an Advisory Committee on Commercial Intelligence, appointed by the President of the Board of Trade in May 1900—was to answer commercial enquiries. But it also undertook the initiation of commercial missions overseas, the editing of the *Board of Trade Journal*, the preparation of an index to the Consular trade reports, and, after 1907, the commercial editing of the Consular reports themselves before publication by the Foreign Office. In 1903 the Branch accepted responsibility for the imperial commercial intelligence services administered by the Imperial Institute at South Kensington, while the Board of Trade took over the management of the Institute. Two further organizational reforms were the creation of a new Exhibitions Branch at the Board of Trade in 1907 (as a result of the report of a departmental committee on British participation in International Exhibitions) with the task of organizing, managing, and winding-up the British Section in any future international exhibition in which H.M. Government chose to take part, and the development (following the Imperial Conference of 1907) of a system of Trade Commissioners to provide official representation for British commerce in the Dominions.

The First World War, while it caused a revulsion against state control among some commercial men, encouraged others to look to the State for further assistance. The relatively prosperous condition of British trade during the first decade of this century had lessened the pressure for active government assistance, but conditions just before the War had deteriorated and it was difficult to gloss-over the strong competition which Britain might expect to face in world markets once peace was restored. When Lord Robert Cecil, the Assistant Secretary of State for Foreign Affairs, spoke at the Supply Debate of 31 July 1918, he pointed out that all three previous speakers on the proposed Foreign Service reforms had agreed on one general observation, that the functions of diplomacy ought to be extended. This, he claimed, was 'obviously true'. It was no longer possible for diplomacy to confine its attention to international politics; politics and trade, diplomacy and commerce were closely intertwined, and Cecil believed that it was 'absolutely true that any attempt to draw a dividing line and say that commercial interests stop here and diplomatic interests begin would be absolutely impossible and fraught with disaster both to commercial interests and to diplomacy.'[16]

Meanwhile, in 1917 an attempt had been made to solve the problem of the division of functions between the Board of Trade and the Foreign Office by the creation of a compromise department— the Department of Overseas Trade—with a Minister responsible both to the Foreign Secretary and to the President of the Board of Trade, and a Comptroller General appointed by both senior Ministers in collaboration. It had seemed illogical to separate overseas trade from the Board of Trade, which alone was equipped to act as a British Ministry of Commerce. But the commercial community itself, as represented by the Association of Chambers of Commerce and the Federation of British Industries, had objected to the removal of Foreign Office responsibility for trade, since, it argued, this would result in the firm separation of politics and commerce in British diplomacy at a time when so much of trade abroad could no longer be separated from diplomatic pressure. The Cave Committee, appointed to examine the question of government machinery for dealing with trade and commerce, reported in 1919 in favour of continuing the Department of Overseas Trade, recommending that the two principal Departments and their sub-Department should continue to work in the closest association with each other, and that the Consular and Commercial Departments of the Foreign Office should be transferred to the Department of Overseas Trade. The Commercial Diplomatic Service, formed the same year, was also placed under the direction of the new Department.

The result, unfortunately, was confusion worse confounded. Sir William Clark, the permanent head of the Department of Overseas Trade, was optimistic enough to write (in the first issue of the *Journal of Public Administration*) as if the problem of duality had been solved. The advantage of the twin control exercised over the new Department, he felt, was that 'such duality of control as remains is concentrated, so to speak, on the heads of the depart-

16. 109 *H.C.Deb.5s.*568–9.

ment: so far as the overseas services are concerned, unity of control and unified direction of their work is secured through their being now administered by a single department of the Government; while the commercial community has now a single department to which to apply when they require information or help'.[17] But the commercial community was more inclined to see it as yet another bureaucratic barrier to direct access to the seat of power, and the result was certainly to fulfil just those anxieties which had led businessmen to oppose the transfer of overseas trade functions to the Board of Trade—that is, to divorce the Foreign Office itself from commerce. The Committee on Industry and Trade, though recommending in 1929 the continuance of the existing machinery, was aware of this problem, and observed that the present advantages brought by a specialized commercial diplomatic service might be 'dearly bought' in the long run if the end result was to diminish the interest of Heads of Mission in commercial matters.[18] The end result was exactly that.

The Department of Overseas Trade was a compromise which had a chance of working only if the Department's officers had been able to command any prestige in the Foreign Service (instead of being 'secretly regarded', as Sir David Kelly once said, as a 'regrettable innovation'), if the commercial community had been prepared to make use of its services, and if—and this was perhaps the greatest stumbling block of all—the Department had been able to survive the wave of economy in government expenditure which swept through Whitehall in and after the early '20s. As it was, after what has been described as a 'somewhat shadowy' existence in the '20s and '30s, the Department of Overseas Trade lost the Consular Service and the Commercial Diplomatic Service to the new Foreign Service by the Eden reforms of 1943, and was finally absorbed into the Board of Trade in 1946. Responsibility for overseas trade services, today greatly increased in comparison with those existing even a couple of decades ago, has reverted to the Foreign Office

17. Sir William Clark, 'Government and the Promotion of Trade', *Journal of Public Administration*, I (1923), 31. A more common opinion within the Service at the time (and one which proved more reliable over the years) was expressed by H. Montagu Villiers (Consular Service) in his book *Charms of the Consular Career* (London, 1925). Villiers described the Department of Overseas Trade as 'that mongrel product of Board of Trade and Foreign Office interdepartmental squabbles—a Department well conceived but rendered sterile in spite of the self-sacrificing and heartbreaking efforts of its original organisers, as they themselves will be the first to admit' (p. 153).
18. *Final Report of the Committee on Industry and Trade*, P.P.1929(Cmd.3282) VII, Sect.III(3).

and the Board of Trade, with the Trade Commissioner Services (Dominion and Colonial) administered by the Board of Trade, and the Consular and Commercial Diplomatic Services forming part of the general Foreign Service under the administration of the Foreign Secretary. At home, the Export Promotion Department of the Board of Trade succeeded in 1946 to the functions of the Department of Overseas Trade, in turn to be merged three years later with the Commercial Relations and Treaties Department into a new Commercial Relations and Exports Department. The Export Services Branch of the Board of Trade is now responsible for most of the trade promotional functions of H.M. Government overseas, aided by a number of Export Councils for each of the main trading areas jointly sponsored by government and industry; and commercial intelligence remains very largely the province of the Overseas Divisions of the Board of Trade.

2. *Overseas*

H.M. Government's commercial organization overseas, of course, developed simultaneously with the organization in London. By 1914 it consisted of the Consular Service, a number of Commercial Attachés, and the 'Commercial Secretaries'.

In a general sense diplomatists, and more particularly consuls, had long been instructed to give protection and assistance to British trade overseas. Eighteenth century diplomatists were directed, on taking up an appointment, to 'protect and countenance' trade, applying themselves by all proper means to making the commerce of British subjects 'as free and as beneficial to them as possible'. They were not, however, to interpose in 'frivolous and ill founded' matters.[19] This, in general, remained the basis of diplomatic instructions. The sign-manual instructions to all Victorian Heads of Mission urged them to make 'the commercial interests of Great Britain an object of [their] constant attention'.[20]

Consuls, necessarily, were given more detailed instructions. The Patent of Appointment (1814) of Henry Chamberlain, H.M. Consul-General in the Brazils, gave him

full power and authority to govern our said merchants, subjects, masters of ships, mariners and people within the dominions and limits aforesaid, and to counsel and assist them, their agents, factors and servants in any just and lawful occasions, wherein they may have need of his counsel and

19. D. B. Horn, *The British Diplomatic Service, 1689-1789* (Oxford, 1961), p. 252.
20. Appendix (A), *Correspondence respecting Assistance to British Trade Abroad*, P.P.1886(c.4779)LX.

direction, as well as in furthering their trade and commerce in those parts, as by way of interposition to compound decide and make up all contentions and strifes that shall happen to arise amongst them, and may be conveniently ordered without any further proceedings at law; and if any damage shall happen to be done to any of our subjects in those parts, to endeavour to cause reparation to be made by complaint to our good brother the Prince Regent of Portugal.[21]

The Consular Instructions, issued and circularized in 1833, advised the Consul to bear in mind that it was 'his principal duty to protect and promote the lawful trade and trading interests of Great Britain by every fair and proper means'. He was urged to take special notice of customs regulations, both of the country in which he lived and of the United Kingdom, so that he might caution British subjects against violation of the law. It was his duty to advise and assist British subjects as best he could, and to quieten their differences whether between themselves or with the local inhabitants. He was to uphold their rightful interests and the privileges secured to them by treaty, but he was to be careful at all times 'to conduct himself with mildness and moderation in all his transactions with the public authorities; and he will not upon any account urge claims, on behalf of His Majesty's subjects, to which they are not justly and fairly entitled'.[22] The substance of these instructions remained unaltered in 1914.

All British diplomatists might expect at some point or another to act on behalf of British trade, but the two groups more specifically charged with commercial functions were the Consuls and the Commercial Attachés. The Commercial Secretaries, an innovation of the turn of the century, never took an important part in trade promotion; with the occasional exception, they were officers of the general diplomatic service who, in return for a special allowance, were expected to interrupt their political work for a few years in order to make themselves thoroughly acquainted with the commerce of their regions. Lacking any permanent interest in trade, they tended to regard their service as a vexatious break in their careers to be conducted without serious mistakes, if possible, but also without enthusiasm.

* * *

It was the Consular Service with which the commercial community had most contact, and reforms and abuses within that

21. Return No. 4, *Accounts relating to Consulage and Contribution in the Brazils*, P.P.1822(465.604)XX.
22. Appendix No. 1, *Report of the Select Committee on Consular Establishment*, P.P.1835(499)VI.

service had an immediate effect on British trade overseas. Consular reform was a gradual and long-term process. Sir John Tilley claimed that the Consular 'Service' was not created until the adoption of the recommendations of the Departmental Committee of 1903.[23] And it was certainly true that the elements which go to creating a Service—a rational system of recruitment, salaries, ranking and promotion—were non-existent for most, if not all, of the nineteenth century.

It is, of course, necessary to realize that there was no one Consular Service in the last century, appointed for a single purpose and supplied with identical instructions. The Victorian Consular Service consisted of the General Service, the Far Eastern Service (China, and later Japan, Siam, and Korea), and the Levant Service— though the Levant Service was not formally separated from the General Service until the Currie reform of 1877. The absence of security for important British trading interests had obliged the Levant and East India Companies to establish their own services of officials with wide judicial and political powers over their countrymen. The Levant Service was inherited by the British Government in 1825 and the Far Eastern Service in 1834 (when the East India Company's monopoly of trade with China expired). In both cases the judicial powers remained, and they continued in existence in China and Turkey, though not in Japan or Siam, until the twentieth century. The Far Eastern Service developed at once into a 'close' service, specially recruited with its own system of promotion and payment and its own code of instructions. The Levant Service, once reconstituted in 1877, quickly adopted the high standards of organization and service of its Eastern counterpart. By 1914 it was generally understood that the two Services stood on a higher level than the General Service, both in intellect and in performance.

Before 1825 the great majority of British consuls abroad were merchants, remunerated by fees levied on the tonnage of British ships and the value of their cargoes. The size of fees, especially when combined with salaries, created marked resentment among the commercial community. The British Consul-General at Rio, for example, enjoyed an income averaging £9,000 per annum, and the

23. Tilley and Gaselee, *The Foreign Office*, p. 246. Parts of the following section on the Consular Service have already appeared in an article published by the *Economic History Review*, and I would like to acknowledge with gratitude the Editors' permission to reproduce them. The article was: D. C. M. Platt, 'The Role of the British Consular Service in Overseas Trade, 1825–1914', *Economic History Review*, 2nd ser. XV (1963), 494–512.

British merchants trading to Rio complained to the Commons with some justice that:

It generally happened that an enormous salary made a gentleman superior to the duties of his office; and therefore it was not wonderful that Mr. Chamberlayne, the present consul, neglected everything which he was paid for attending to; and, in fact, rather prejudiced the British interest, than did anything to advance or facilitate it.[24]

Canning's Consular Act of 1825 was intended to remedy this and similar grievances. All consular fees on tonnage and cargoes were abolished, the right to levy fees of any kind was narrowly restricted, and a scale of fees was prescribed. The Act attempted to create a salaried service, and a policy was formulated of restricting consuls from engaging in trade. It was determined, in fact, that 'British consuls should not be in any way concerned directly or indirectly in commercial pursuits'. But nothing was done to alter the organization or recruitment of the Service, and when, in 1832, consular salaries were substantially reduced as part of a general government retrenchment, the 1826 principle was reversed, and denial of permission to trade became the exception rather than the rule.[25] Even after the strong opinions expressed on the subject of trading consuls before the Select Committee on Consular Establishments of 1835, the prohibition was not revived. Indeed the Committee's report approved the relaxation of the rule, recommending that no fixed rule should be laid down on the subject;[26] it was determined to reduce government expenditure on the Consular Service, or at least, by applying the money saved to raising salaries at the more important posts, to avoid any increase in the total budget.

No reform resulted from the recommendations of the 1835 Committee, and the recommendations of the Select Committee of 1858, important as they were, were as barren of result. But the Select Committee on the Diplomatic and Consular Services of 1870–2 adopted the principal recommendations of the Committee of 1858. The Consular Service was to be divided into 'salaried' and 'unsalaried' classes; salaried consuls were to be restricted from trading and all fees were to go to the Exchequer; unsalaried consuls were to be allowed to retain fees for office expenses; young men

24. 6 *Parl.Deb.2s.*1468 (22 April 1822).
25. Memorandum dated 16 August 1838, *List of Her Majesty's Consuls Abroad: Distinguishing those who are restricted from trading, and those who are not*, P.P.1839(158)XLVI.
26. *Report of the Select Committee on Consular Establishment*, P.P.1835(499) VI.

were to be introduced into the Service as subordinate or probationary officers.[27] The recommendation on fixed salaries and the payment of fees into the Exchequer had, in fact, been in operation at least as early as 1859, when Mr. Laing, Secretary to the Treasury, explained that though it was impossible at once entirely to abolish the system of consular fees and to substitute fixed salaries, new appointments were made only on condition that the fees should be paid into the Consolidated Fund (the officer appointed being given a fixed salary).[28] Shortly after the presentation of the 1872 Report, reforms were introduced into the Consular Service which embodied the majority of its recommendations, and, in 1877, consuls *de carrière* were formally debarred from trading.

The Consular Service remained organizationally unaffected by the pressure in 1886 for increased Government support for overseas trade. The Ridley Commission (the Royal Commission on Civil Establishments) examined the Service and reported in 1890, but its recommendations were intended to improve the attractions and efficiency of the Service as a career and effected no fundamental changes in its character. Universal entrance examinations, experience in the Commercial Department of the Foreign Office or in the Board of Trade before appointment, grading of Consuls and Vice-Consuls into classes with increased salaries, and more frequent honorary distinctions for meritorious services, were scarcely, in the absence of any particular pressure, epoch-making proposals, and their effect was equally unpretentious.

The Walrond Committee (the Departmental Committee of 1903) had a profoundly greater influence. Its Report explained that the existing General Consular Service was recruited solely by the nomination of the Secretary of State, and that there was no definite prospect of promotion. It recommended, therefore, that admission to the Service should be by limited competition (the age of admission to be between 22 and 27, preference to be given to men with commercial experience, and an official nomination still to be a precondition of acceptance as a candidate); that successful candidates should spend a training period in the Commercial Intelligence Branch of the Board of Trade; that the China, Japan, and Siam Consular Services should be recruited on the same system of limited competition, and that the Siam Consular Service be amalgamated into the General Service; that salaries should be rationalized and

27. *Report of the Select Committee on the Diplomatic and Consular Services* P.P.1872 (314)VII.
28. 155 *Parl.Deb.*3s.533 (28 July 1859); the procedure was confirmed by Lord John Russell, 164 *Parl.Deb.*3s.1077 (18 July 1861).

allowances given for expensive districts; and that periodical inspections should be made of all Consulates and Vice-Consulates.[29] Nearly all the recommendations were adopted, but it was found in practice that it was not feasible to give preference to men of commercial experience in competition with other candidates. Sir John Tilley (the Committee's Secretary) was later to remark on the difficulty of obtaining men with four or five years of experience in business, who were then prepared to transfer from more lucrative openings in London to many years of provincial exile in government service; nor were many young men ready to wait so long before beginning their professional careers. He added that although the Committee's recommendation remained in force until after the Great War, he could not recollect that any candidates came forward with commercial experience.[30]

The reaction of British commerce to the 1903 Report was generally favourable. Mr. Musgrave, the Secretary of the London Chamber of Commerce, agreed (1914) that the considerable improvement he had noticed in the Consular Service dated from the Departmental Report. He added that 'As an ideal or as a programme of what would be desirable to be attained, this report is admirable from the point of view of the commercial community'.[31] The basis of a true service had been prepared, and the Departmental Committee of 1912 went some way towards refining the details. Its recommendations were directed mainly at making a consular career more attractive to young men; they included higher salaries, more discretion to remove inefficient senior officials barring the way to promotion, an increase in clerical staff, better training for newly joined vice-consuls, more generous treatment in matters of leave and conditions of service, and the institution of a regular system of consular inspection.[32] These proposals were adopted, and the Royal Commission on the Civil Service (1914) settled some of the remaining controversial issues. It advised the appropriation of all fees (consuls were still allowed to retain a portion of fees for special services outside office hours), the abandonment of the 1903 suggestion of recruiting 'experienced business men', and recruitment in future from secondary schools for the Levant and General Services, and from universities for the Far Eastern. Preference was

---

29. *Report of the Departmental Committee on the Consular Service*, P.P.1903(Cd. 1634)LV.
30. Sir John Tilley, *London to Tokyo* (London, 1942), pp. 39–40.
31. Minutes of Evidence, *Fifth Report of the Royal Commission on the Civil Service*, P.P.1914–16(Cd.7749)XI, QQ.38,878–9.
32. *Report of the Departmental Committee of 1912*, F.O.,C.P.10129.

to be given to British subjects in the appointment of unpaid consular officers; all unpaid officers were to be directly supervised by
salaried consular officers of a higher rank; and both the existing
system of Consular Inspection and the practice of employing at
political posts Consular Officers with diplomatic rank were to be
extended. The recommendations recall a number of the more
prominent issues of the nineteenth century, and the most persistent
of all—that of trading consuls—reached its final solution. The
Commission, making a virtue of necessity, concluded that 'the
appointment of whole-time salaried officers to unimportant posts
is not only unnecessary and extravagant, but . . . would prove
actually prejudicial to the efficiency of the officers in question'.[33]

Reform of the Service along the lines suggested by the Royal
Commission was, of course, delayed by the outbreak of war. Yet a
great deal had been done since 1825 to produce a Service more
capable of performing the immense variety of functions thrust upon
it. When a Board of Trade Committee could describe the Consular
Service, as late as 1917, as 'hampered by low salaries, poor prospects,
lack of funds for expenditure, and, so far as we can judge, largely
cold-shouldered by the Ambassador',[34] it would be incautious to
overestimate the effect of reform. But it can safely be said that the
Consular Service in 1914, if not as yet entirely efficient, made an
appreciable contribution to the promotion of British commerce
overseas, whereas the Consular Service of 1825 was hardly more
than an overseas extension of the native British system of taxation
and registration.

* * *

The system of 'commercial attachés' was a response to the need
for a more general representation of British commercial interests
overseas, detached from the routine and detail which formed so
large a part of consular duties. The first experimental appointment
was that of J. A. Crowe as commercial attaché at Paris in 1880.
Sir Joseph Crowe was a man of exceptional ability, and he did as
much as any man could have done in his situation. But the terms
of his appointment and of those of his successors show the odds
against which they were working. Attachés were instructed to avail
themselves of all sources of commercial information; to pay particular
attention to the preparation of Annual and Special Reports;

33. *Fifth Report of the Royal Commission on the Civil Service*, P.P.1914–16(Cd.
7748)XI.
34. *Report of the Departmental Committee appointed by the Board of Trade to consider the position of the Engineering Trades after the War*, P.P.1918(Cd.9073)XIII.

to watch all tariff questions, and report alterations; to follow the proceedings of Legislatures, of Chambers of Commerce, and of any commercial associations which had reference to affairs of a commercial or industrial character; to give advice and assistance to British consuls within their areas on all commercial matters, and also to British Chambers of Commerce, merchants, manufacturers and shippers; to prepare reports on, in addition to commercial matters, a number of related subjects—concessions, labour questions, sanitary questions, trade marks and patents, road and rail transport and routes, technical education, bounties and subsidies, improvements in industrial methods and machinery, and the state and prospects of agriculture; to assist British subjects in the settlement of customs claims; and, finally, to hold a watching brief over commercial questions affecting India and the Colonies.[35] Moreover, this formidable range of duties applied to impracticably large areas. J. A. Crowe was at first responsible for the whole of Europe. By the first years of this century there were commercial attachés at Paris, Berlin, Madrid, Constantinople, Vienna, Peking, and Yokohama. But the areas were still large, and the Commercial attaché at Berlin, for example, was expected to include the commercial affairs of Denmark, Holland, Sweden, and Norway within his responsibilities.

The problem, naturally, was money, and the Foreign Office itself was aware of the system's deficiencies. St. John Brodrick, Under-Secretary of State, prepared a Memorandum at the turn of the century which expressed his fear that however useful commercial attachés might be for routine work, little practical result had emerged from their efforts in pushing British trade. He suggested that the fault in the system lay in the over-large areas, the location of the attachés in the national capitals (that is, often at some distance from commercial centres), and their recruitment from among the diplomatic rather than the 'bagman' class.[36]

Further criticisms were presented in a report on the system of commercial attachés prepared by Eldon Gorst and Llewellyn Smith in 1906. The report claimed that the commercial attachés had become too closely associated with the Missions (with the result that they merely took over the Missions' commercial duties); that they had no opportunity or time to study national commercial centres;

35. These functions are listed in a memorandum on the scope of duties assigned to commercial attachés attached to the despatch appointing J. W. Jamieson as the new British commercial attaché in China, 17 October 1889: P.R.O.,F.O/83/1846.
36. Memorandum dated 28 July 1899: P.R.O.,F.O/83/1784.

and that the rest of the Mission staff were in no position to gain acquaintance with commercial work ('though this work must necessarily become one of their chief preoccupations when they rise to the charge of a Mission'); long and continuous residence abroad meant that commercial attachés had no opportunity of studying manufacturing conditions and needs at home, and were soon out-of-touch with British commercial development. Gorst and Smith suggested that commercial attachés in Europe should have their headquarters in London and divide their time between special investigations abroad, work in the Board of Trade or in the Commercial Department at the Foreign Office, and visits to manufacturing districts in the United Kingdom. Commercial attachés at more distant posts should continue to have their headquarters on the spot, but should be relieved of day-to-day commercial work at the Embassies, required to move about freely in their districts, and expected to pay periodical visits to government commercial departments and the commercial centres at home. The current commercial business of the Diplomatic Missions should be put in charge of a specially selected member of the diplomatic staff.[37]

The recommendations of the Gorst report were accepted by the Foreign Office, but they were without significant effect. The suggestion that commercial attachés should have their headquarters in London proved in practice unworkable and was soon abandoned; while the appointment of Commercial Secretaries at the Missions (to which a brief reference has already been made), though relieving the commercial attachés of some routine business, put that business into the hands of inexperienced, and too often incompetent, junior diplomatists.

*   *   *

The Gorst Report had also concerned itself with the experimental system of Commercial Agents. By the last quarter of the nineteenth century a need was beginning to be recognized for an official who would act, in range of duties, somewhere between a commercial attaché and a consul. A commercial attaché was expected to deal with commerce only in a very broad sense—his duties were of too wide a nature to permit detailed assistance to individual firms. The consul, on the other hand, was occupied to a great extent with non-commercial activities—he, too, had little time to devote to the interests of individual firms, and his official position debarred him from taking an active part in the 'pushing' of British trade. Consular

37. *Report by Sir Eldon Gorst and Mr. Llewellyn Smith on the System of British Commercial Attachés and Commercial Agents*, P.P.1907(Cd.3610)LXXXVII.

duties were never intended to include a general agency for British commerce, even if the commercial community thought otherwise. 'Judging by the letters and circulars a Consul receives during a year', the British consul at Calais complained in 1896, 'he is evidently supposed by many British firms to be their lawful medium for promoting the sale of their goods; however able and willing a Consul may be to supply such information as he properly can as to the trade requirements of his districts, it is impossible for him to act as a general agent for British firms.'[38] Mr. Bryce made the same point at the debate on the Foreign Office vote, 3 July 1902. He deprecated the policy of making British consular officers trade agents; they should certainly watch trade and prepare efficient reports, but they would be less effective in the performance of their obligatory functions if they were to combine them with the functions of trade agents.[39]

The first suggestions to meet this problem were those put to the Royal Commission on the Depression of Trade and Industry in 1886. It was proposed that trading commissioners should be appointed and paid by the commercial bodies in the United Kingdom, who would have the 'countenance and assistance' of the Government but for whom the Government would not be responsible: the usual arguments against permitting consuls to push trade would not apply to privately appointed agents.[40] The suggestion was taken a step further by a former Consul-General for Korea (W. G. Aston) who proposed, in a memorandum addressed to the Under-Secretary (1897), that these commercially-appointed, traveling commissioners should be formally recognized by H.M. Government by means of a notification of their appointment in the *Gazette*, and should be provided with a special passport recommending them particularly to H.M. representatives abroad.[41] But, of course, it was not easy for British business to co-operate sufficiently to maintain a system of overseas commissioners on its own. The returns were too speculative and long term, and the sharing-out of costs and the distribution of services between competing firms created almost insuperable difficulties.

In 1899, on the initiative of St. John Brodrick, H.M. Government

38. Appendix, *Opinions of H.M. Diplomatic and Consular Officers on British Trade Methods*, P.P.1899(c.9078)XCVI.
39. 110 *Parl.Deb.4s.*728.
40. For example, the Chairman's remarks in Minutes of Evidence, *Second Report of the Royal Commission on the Depression of Trade and Industry* P.P.1886 (c.4715)XXI, QQ.5300-1.
41. Appendix No. 17, *Report from the Departmental Committee on Commercial Intelligence*, P.P.1898(c.8963)XXXIII.

decided to appoint Commercial Agents of its own in certain countries, with the duty of watching and reporting on the commerce,
industries, and products of special districts, and answering inquiries
from Chambers of Commerce and individual firms on payment of a
fee. The relation between the functions of the new Commercial
Agents and the existing Consular Service naturally caused some
confusion. An attempt was made to clarify the position in a Memorandum prepared by the Foreign Office for Consul Wyndham of
Chicago, who had written privately to Mr. Cockerell (of the Commercial Department) to enquire whether the functions of the newly-
appointed commercial agent would not overlap his own. The
Memorandum pointed out in reply that:

British Commercial Agents are appointed by and are under the control of the
Secretary of State. Their duties will be to report on special branches of trade
and to answer such inquiries as may be addressed to them by British
Chambers of Commerce, firms and individuals. Their work will therefore
be entirely supplementary to the business carried on and to the reports
required to be furnished by Consular Officers.
They will receive their instructions from the Embassy, or Legation as the
case may be, and will be independent of the Consulates. Consular Officers
should on their application give them all the assistance in their power.[42]

This was not, in fact, a complete answer to Consul Wyndham's
question. The ludicrous sum of £20 collected in fees by the Commercial Agents in all areas (i.e. Chicago, Moscow, Zurich, and
Central America) for the first year of the system's operation,
indicated that the commercial community was understandably
reluctant to pay money for information which it could receive
free from similar enquiries addressed to the consuls direct. Sir Harry
Bergne (Head of the Commercial Department) remarked sourly
that—'So far as assistance to trade goes, the amount of fees shows
that these appointments are practically useless—as I always thought
they would be.'[43] But the Foreign Office was careful to point out to
the Treasury, when applying for an extension of the scheme and for
the abolition of the system of fees, that the services of the Commercial Agents could not be estimated solely on receipts; the
numerous and valuable commercial reports submitted must also
be taken into account.[44]
The failure of the system of Commercial Agents resulted essen-

42. Minute attached to Mr. Wyndham's letter of 3 May 1900: P.R.O.,F.O/
83/1784.
43. Minute on a despatch from Lord Pauncefote dated 15 January 1901:
P.R.O.,F.O/83/1881.
44. F.O. to Treasury, 29 May 1901: ibid.

tially from the ignorance and apathy of the British merchants themselves. When Mr. Seymour Bell, the British Commercial Agent in the United States, wrote to the Birmingham Chamber of Commerce announcing his intention to be in Birmingham in January 1902 to answer any questions on business with America, the Chamber wrote back to the Board of Trade to ask whether he held any official position. Yet all the Chambers of Commerce had been officially notified of the appointments when they were first made, and, as Bergne said, it was 'beyond belief' that an important Chamber like Birmingham should not have been fully informed of Bell's position and of his functions. The remainder of Mr. Bell's tour confirmed the general ignorance; the Secretaries of the Liverpool and Belfast Chambers of Commerce had apparently never heard of Commercial Agents.[45] And worse than ignorance was indifference. Mr. Henry Cooke, the British Commercial Agent in Russia, excused himself (before his exploratory mission to Siberia) from yet another trip around the British Chambers of Commerce:

I know now more about Chambers of Commerce than I did, and they chiefly consist of a Secretary. At important places like Manchester and Blackburn, though my visit was advertised locally beforehand, the attendance not counting Secretary and Vice-President or other official presiding, was 0, 3 and 2 respectively. At Manchester the President shook hands with me on being introduced in the Secretary's office, 'Ah, yes, Commercial Agent, goodbye, no time to attend meetings' and hurried away. . . .[46]

The practical value of the appointments (to which Vladivostock was later added) is difficult to gauge. By 1902 the agents were all answering a large number of enquiries and had presented reports of varying quality and value. The only Agent whose work received unqualified praise at the Foreign Office was Mr. Cooke, but even he, when reporting on the results of his work, frankly admitted that 'in the sense that the Commercial Agent can serve to increase trade, the post cannot answer the expectations formed'. He added that Commercial Agents were of more service in assisting individuals to increase their trade than they were in bringing about any general extension of commercial intercourse.[47] And assistance to individuals—Sir Harry Bergne was quick to notice—was not in the general tradition of the British Foreign Service. In a minute dated 1 February 1900 he expressed his opinion that it should not be the

45. Bell to Sir Henry Bergne, 9 January 1902: ibid.
46. Henry Cooke to Mr. Graham, 16 February 1903: P.R.O.,F.O/83/2100.
47. Report attached to Sir Charles Scott's despatch of 4 September 1902: P.R.O.,F.O/83/1881.

care of the Government, via the Commercial Agents, to assist the commercial public in the actual conduct of business:

Better results would, I believe, follow from appointing more Comml. Attachés to H.M. Embassies and Legations—as specialists to do the work that more properly concerns Govt.—viz obtaining information etc. for general public use, instead of helping individuals to any great extent.[48]

Commercial Agents did not survive for long. Permission was obtained to extend the system to 1907, but the Treasury was unwilling to sanction a further extension without positive proof of good results. The Gorst Report of 1906 recommended that the Commercial Agencies should be discontinued and their functions assigned to members of the Consular Service. The recommendation was adopted without delay.

* * *

The First World War was as influential overseas as it was at home in speeding the reform of government services to trade. As a result of the recommendations of a committee on which business interests were represented, the Commercial Attaché Service was increased in April 1918 from ten posts to twenty-eight. The following year a major reform took place in the whole system of overseas commercial representation. The Commercial Attaché Service was disbanded and a Commercial Diplomatic Service created under the direction of the Department of Overseas Trade. The new Service, which began with forty-four officers (but which was later reduced in number as a result of the government economies of the early '20s), consisted of Commercial Counsellors in the highest grade and Commercial Secretaries in the three lower grades. They were independently recruited, mainly from the Consular Service or from business, and their duties at the Missions to which they were attached resembled those of the former Commercial Attaché Service, except that they were expected to take over the commercial duties of the Mission and were responsible for supervising and co-ordinating the commercial work of the Consuls within their districts.

The new Service had its points. Even as truncated by Government economies it was still much more widely distributed than the pre-war Commercial Attaché Service, and the annual reports which its officers were obliged to prepare on the commercial, economic, and financial conditions of the countries in which they were stationed were useful to journalists, if never much valued or appreciated by

48. Bound mistakenly with Mowatt's letter to Gosselin, 15 July 1901: ibid.

the commercial community. But certain factors had been over-looked in the original proposals for the Commercial Diplomatic Service which were seriously to detract from its prestige and utility.

One of the main preoccupations of the more alert Foreign Office officials since at least the 1870's had been the need to break down that traditional snobbery and prejudice against commercial affairs which stood in the way of an active commercial diplomacy. The experiment of the Commercial Secretaries was only a late continuation of an effort to interest British diplomatists in commercial affairs dating back at least as far as Lord Clarendon's instructions of 1857. But the 1919 reform reintroduced that sharp break between political and commercial services which had already had so damaging an effect on British trade overseas. The new Commercial Diplomatic Service assumed complete responsibility for commercial business at each Mission to which its officers were appointed. The Commercial Counsellor or Secretary tended to have his own offices—often at some distance from the Legation—with his own subordinate staff. Members of the Commercial Diplomatic Service, though technically diplomatists and regarded as members of the diplomatic corps in the capitals in which they served, ranked 'with but after officers of the similar grade in the Diplomatic Service proper'; their conditions of service were on a consular model; they were '*of*, rather than *in*, the Diplomatic Service'. W. J. Glenny, from whose paper (read before the Institute of Public Administration in 1924)[49] these remarks are taken, drew no conclusions from the distinction, but the conclusions were fairly evident for members of both the Diplomatic Service 'proper' and the Commercial Diplomatic Service. Commerce had again been placed on a lower level than politics. In spite of all the protestations in 1919, politics in some way were more respectable than trade, and British diplomatists could thankfully pass the commercial file to the inferior Service to which it properly belonged. The Diplomatic Service, Harold Nicolson wrote, 'warmly welcomed' the new Commercial Service 'as ridding them of an embarrassing and sometimes uncongenial task to which they knew themselves unfitted'.[50] But this was just what it should never have done. The social stigma attached to commerce was still almost as painful as that experienced by Crowe in Paris in the early '80s. When Valentine Lawford went to Paris half a century later (1937) as a young Third Secretary in the general Diplomatic Service, he tells how he had to make a round

49. W. J. Glenny, 'The Trade Commissioner and Commercial Diplomatic Services', *Journal of Public Administration*, II (1924), 284–5.
50. Nicolson, *Diplomacy*, p. 166.

of calls on the various departments at the Embassy. After he had made most of his calls, 'there was the commercial department to be placated'—

Not that I had as yet consciously done anything to offend its members. It was not what I had done, but who I was. And who they were. Whether I liked it or not, I was a junior Secretary in the Diplomatic Service; and they, who in those far-off days never quite belonged to the Diplomatic Service, were occupationally aggrieved, resenting, as well they might in the twentieth century, the traditionally assumed superiority, intellectual as well as social, of young men engaged on what was regarded as political work over far older colleagues whose activities were connected, alas, with trade.[51]

There was still a long way to go before trade could become—as the Plowden Report insisted in 1963—'a first charge on the resources of the overseas Services'.

The main purpose of the Eden reforms of 1943 was to upgrade the status and performance of British commercial services overseas. Mr. Richard Law, who (as Under-Secretary of State) introduced the reforms to the Commons in March of that year, pointed to the great change that had come about in foreign affairs as a result of the modern fusion of politics and economics. 'The day has quite clearly gone for ever', he claimed, 'when the diplomat can concern himself solely with those fascinating questions of high policy and leave the bread and butter questions to more vulgar minds'; our whole existence would depend on our ability to revive our export trade after the war, and the Foreign Service would have to do all it could to revive, develop, and increase that trade.[52] By an Order in Council of 20 May 1943, the Diplomatic Service, the Commercial Diplomatic Service, and the Consular Service were amalgamated, and Mr. Eden insisted, in the White Paper which set out the reforms, that all officers in the new combined Service would be called upon to serve in commercial and consular as well as political capacities. The effect of the combined Service, he believed, would be to 'broaden the training (in its fullest sense) by combining knowledge of economic, industrial and shipping affairs with practical experience of dealing with the public and the Press and with the wider appreciation of international relations which is the field of diplomacy'. Provision was also to be made for training new diplomatists in economic and commercial affairs, and this training, together with the experience which they would normally receive in

51. Valentine Lawford, *Bound for Diplomacy*, (London, 1963), p. 298.
52. 387 *H.C.Deb.5s.*1361–2 (18 March 1943).

commercial diplomatic and consular as well as diplomatic posts, should ensure that all members of the new 'Foreign Service' possessed at least a general knowledge and understanding of ordinary economics and commercial practice'.[53]

In principle the amalgamation of the Services was excellent; in practice it fell short of expectations. Harold Nicolson foresaw this at the time. He told the Commons in the 1943 debate that functions would still have to be differentiated in the combined Service, and that this might again lead to a man feeling himself classed as a consular or commercial type, with all the plums of the Service going to the diplomatic type.[54] Snobbery remained, and a *Manchester Guardian* enquiry into the Foreign Service in the autumn of 1955 reported that most Foreign Service officers still regarded economic or commercial posts as 'less elevated than a political one'—'Officially, the Foreign Office is at war with this snobbery; but it still exists and is a stultifying thing'.[55]

But a more effective barrier to a general rise in the status of commercial work has been the continued caste system in government service, expressed in the Foreign Service by the division of officers into Branch A and Branch B. Since 1943 commercial or consular posts have often been staffed by Branch B officers. This is, of course, only an inevitable reflection of the minor importance of many posts which would have made any other staffing policy irrational and wasteful. But while the caste system exists—and (as the *Manchester Guardian* pointed out) 'in posts abroad, wives of Branch A officers sometimes find an excessive amount of time on their hands in which to point out their differences in status from wives of Branch B officers'[56]—some of the mud slung at Branch B is bound to stick to commerce. There is no easy solution to this problem; it may lie only with an elimination of the distinction between Branch A and Branch B, and the creation of one broad ladder for promotion. If the minor commercial and consular posts were regarded not as lower-grade posts but as appointments to be held at an earlier stage in promotion up a common ladder, then it is possible that size of post rather than nature of employment might come to be the means of measuring progress in the diplomatic profession.

*　　*　　*

The up-grading of commercial work in government service, both at home and overseas (but more particularly overseas), was

53. *Proposals for the Reform of the Foreign Service*, P.P.1942–43(Cmd.6420)XI.
54. 387 *H.C.Deb.*5s.1393 (18 March 1943).
55. *Manchester Guardian*, 26 October 1955.
56. ibid., 28 October 1955.

a painfully slow process, and few would claim that it is complete even today. Time and again thinking men have pointed to the absurdity of a social distinction between politics and commerce in a nation which lives by trade. Conditions, no doubt, keep improving. But can all be well when the Plowden Committee felt it necessary, as recently as the end of 1963, to lay stress on the relative importance of commercial work overseas? The Committee claimed that it could not 'emphasize too strongly the importance of the commercial work of the new Diplomatic Service'—

The country cannot afford to entrust commercial work to any but the best. The custom is growing of ensuring that promising officers get experience of commercial work in the early and formative states of their careers. This custom should become the rule. We look forward to the day, in the not too distant future, when every Ambassador and High Commissioner will have served in a commercial capacity and have acquired at first hand a detailed knowledge of export promotion and what it entails. Each Ambassador and High Commissioner must regard commercial work as a prime function of his Mission and its subordinate posts.[57]

57. *Report of the Committee on Representational Services Overseas*, P.P.1964(Cmnd. 2276), para. 255.

APPENDIX II

Circular addressed by Viscount Palmerston to Her Majesty's Representatives in Foreign States, respecting the Debts due by Foreign States to British Subjects:

Foreign Office, January 1848

Her Majesty's Government have frequently had occasion to instruct Her Majesty's Representatives in various foreign States to make earnest and friendly, but not authoritative, representations in support of the unsatisfied claims of British subjects who are holders of public bonds and money securities of those States.

As some misconception appears to exist in some of those States with regard to the just right of Her Majesty's Government to interfere authoritatively, if it should think fit to do so, in support of those claims, I have to inform you, as the Representative of Her Majesty in one of the States against which British subjects have such claims, that it is for the British Government entirely a question of discretion and by no means a question of international right, whether they should or should not make this matter the subject of diplomatic negotiation. If the question is to be considered simply in its bearing upon international right, there can be no doubt whatever of the perfect right which the Government of every country possesses to take up, as a matter of diplomatic negotiation, any well-founded complaint which any of its subjects may prefer against the Government of another country, or any wrong which from such foreign Government those subjects may have sustained; and if the Government of one country is entitled to demand redress for any one individual among its subjects who may have a just but unsatisfied pecuniary claim upon the Government of another country, the right so to require redress cannot be diminished merely because the extent of the wrong is increased, and because, instead of there being one individual claiming a comparatively small sum, there are a great number of individuals to whom a very large amount is due.

It is therefore simply a question of discretion with the British Government whether this matter should or should not be taken up by diplomatic negotiation, and the decision of that question of discretion turns entirely upon British and domestic considerations.

It has hitherto been thought by the successive Governments of Great Britain undesirable that British subjects should invest their capital in loans to foreign Governments instead of employing it in profitable undertakings at home, and with a view to discourage hazardous loans to foreign Governments who may be either unable or unwilling to pay the stipulated interest thereupon, the British Government has hitherto thought it the best policy to abstain from taking up as international questions, the complaints made by British subjects against foreign Governments which have failed to make good their engagements in regard to such pecuniary transactions.

For the British Government has considered that the losses of imprudent men who have placed mistaken confidence in the good faith of foreign Governments would prove a salutary warning to others, and would prevent any other Foreign Loans from being raised in Great Britain except by Governments of known good faith and of ascertained solvency. But nevertheless, it might happen that the loss occasioned to British subjects by the non-payment of interest upon Loans made by them to Foreign Governments might become so great that it would be too high a price for the nation to pay for such a warning as to the future, and in such a state of things it might become the duty of the British Government to make these matters the subject of diplomatic negotiation.

In any conversation which you may hereafter hold with the——Ministers upon this subject, you will not fail to communicate to them the views which Her Majesty's Government entertain thereupon, as set forth in this despatch.

I am, &c.
(Signed) PALMERSTON

Printed as P.P.1849(1049),LVI.

APPENDIX III

Mr. Hammond to Mr. Hyde Clarke:

Foreign Office, April 26, 1871.

Sir,

I AM directed by Earl Granville to acknowledge the receipt of your letter of the 12th instant on the subject of the views entertained by the Council of Foreign Bondholders, as expressed by Mr. Gerstenberg and Mr. Eastwick on the occasion of their interview with his Lordship on the 29th ultimo.

In alluding in your letter to the observations made by Earl Granville to those gentlemen, I am desired to point out that you omit all reference to his Lordship's remarks with regard to the principles which had been acted upon by successive Secretaries of State, with reference to the undesirability of Her Majesty's Government encouraging hazardous loans to foreign countries, or of their giving such transactions an impetus, such as would be afforded if it were understood that the repayment of loans, made probably at a high rate, would be enforced by the power of Great Britain.

In order, therefore, to prevent any misapprehension as to the amount of support which Her Majesty's Government are prepared to afford to British holders of foreign bonds, Earl Granville is desirous that the Council of Foreign Bondholders should clearly understand that his Lordship in no way departs from the views and principles entertained and frequently laid down by his predecessors.

The policy of Her Majesty's Government with regard to the general question of the assistance to be given to foreign bondholders who fail to obtain their rights, has always been, and will continue to be, limited to unofficial support and friendly remonstrance with such foreign States as from time to time fail to meet their obligations.

Her Majesty's Government are in no way party to private loan transactions with foreign States. Contracts of this nature rest only between the Power borrowing and the capitalists who enter into them as speculative enterprises, and who are content to undertake extraordinary risks in the hope of large contingent profits. Further, it is scarcely necessary to point out the endless troubles which certainly would arise if the active intervention of England were exerted to redress the grievances of bondholders. Independently of the expense which would necessarily be incurred, and the risk of international complications, forcible measures, if adopted towards small States, which for the most part are the ones complained of, would subject this country to grievous imputations. For such and other obvious reasons, Her Majesty's Government have determined, as a matter of wise policy, to abstain from taking up, as international questions, the complaints of British subjects against foreign States which fail to make good their engagements in regard to such pecuniary transactions, or to interpose, except by good offices, between bondholders and the States by which they may be wronged.

Her Majesty's Government will, however, be at all times ready to give their unofficial support to bondholders in the prosecution of their claims against defaulting States, and such parties may always count upon the moral influence of this country being exerted, though unofficially, on their behalf; but the parties must not expect that forcible measures, such as reprisals, and still less any of a more decidedly warlike character, will ever be resorted to by Her Majesty's Government in support of their claims.

Her Majesty's Government will not lose sight of the specific claim of the Venezuelan bondholders for the 18,000 dollars which is alluded to in your letter, and which stands on a different footing from the general claims of the bondholders; but they must remain free to decide as to the manner in which, and the time when, that claim, as well as the claims of other of Her Majesty's subjects, shall be pressed upon the Republic.

In accordance with your request I inclose a letter of introduction for Mr. Gerstenberg to Her Majesty's Ambassador at Vienna, who is directed to afford him such unofficial assistance as his Excellency properly can, during Mr. Gerstenberg's residence at Vienna.

I am, &c.
(Signed) E. HAMMOND

Printed as No. 61, *Correspondence on the Ottoman Loans of 1858 and 1862*, P.P.1874(c. 1077),LXXVI.

APPENDIX IV

Earl Granville's Circular of 8 March 1881:

It has been the general rule of this Department that the Secretary of State should decline to give letters of introduction or recommendation to Her Majesty's Diplomatic or Consular Agents abroad in favour of gentlemen proceeding to foreign countries for the purpose of promoting any specific commercial or industrial undertaking, or of obtaining Concessions from a foreign Government. The reasons for this rule are obvious. It is generally impossible for the Secretary of State to form a correct judgment as to the soundness or practicability of such undertaking; he cannot be well acquainted with the nature or merits of rival enterprises, and in the possible case of several British subjects of equal respectability being competitors for the same Concession, he might be placed in an embarrassing position if one or more had not received the facilities which had been afforded to the other.

The strict and universal application of this rule is, however, difficult.

It is not always possible to decline altogether to British subjects of good standing and respectability the introduction which is necessary to show that they are persons of consideration, and to enable them to obtain access to the authorities before whom their proposals are to be laid. It may also occasionally happen that the bearer of a formal letter of introduction granted in the belief that it is desired for social purposes only may endeavour to turn it to account for purposes of business.

I think it desirable, therefore, in order to guard against the risk of misunderstanding, to state that letters of introduction must not under any circumstances be construed as committing the Home Government to the promoting of any particular enterprise, but only as intended to insure for the bearer that he should meet with such a reception as a traveller of respectability is entitled to.

Printed in Appendix A, *Correspondence respecting Diplomatic Assistance to British Trade Abroad, Part I*, P.P.1886(c.4779)LX.

APPENDIX V

Extract from a Memorandum by Mr. James Bryce (Under-Secretary of State for Foreign Affairs) respecting the question of Diplomatic and Consular Assistance to British Trade Abroad, Foreign Office, 17 July 1886.

The impression that British trade suffers through insufficient action being taken on its behalf by Her Majesty's Diplomatic and Consular officers has been so frequently conveyed, both in Parliament and in the press, that the grounds for it deserve to be carefully examined, and a respectful consideration given to the suggestions offered by merchants and manufacturers for directing and enabling these officials to render more active help to interests admittedly vital to our prosperity. I must, however, begin by observing that, after reading many communications from mercantile persons and bodies, listening to many speeches, and conversing with many persons of ability and experience in commercial questions, I cannot discover that any want of efficiency is chargeable on the Diplomatic and Consular Services as a whole. They seem, in the great majority of instances, to have carried out the instructions given them by the Foreign Office with energy and tact, and their unfailing courtesy is admitted even by those who allege that their zeal lags behind their discretion.

The communications received by the Foreign Office on this subject include both complaints and suggestions. I will take the former first. They are reducible to two:

1. It is said that the traditions of the Foreign Office and of the Diplomatic Service are unfriendly or, at least, indifferent, to the promotion of commercial interests; that there exists a certain disposition to snub British traders, and to leave them without the countenance and support to which they are entitled.

A charge of this kind is so vague that it can only be tested by instances. The few instances that have been cited do not bear it out. Whatever may have been the case in time past when rich men often entered the Diplomatic Service as an excuse for fashionable idleness, there seems to be at present a full appreciation on the part of the Diplomatic and Consular Services of the extreme importance of our foreign trade to the general well-being and prosperity, as well as to the political influence, of this country. The duty now imposed on Secretaries of Legation and Consuls of preparing annual Commercial Reports reminds the members of both Services of the value which this Office sets upon their functions in regard to trade, just as the creation and constant activity of a Commercial Department within the Foreign Office testify to the anxiety of successive Secretaries and Under-Secretaries of State, as well as of the permanent Staff, to provide for the prompt and efficient handling of questions of this nature.

Sometimes it may happen that a Consul does not identify himself so fully with a merchant's projects as the merchant expects, or is not found able to supply all the information which his travelling fellow-countrymen desire. It must, however, be remembered that the Consul, living on the spot, sees difficulties which the visitor ignores, that in many foreign countries information is hard to procure, that a British Consul at a busy post is a hard-worked man, and that he is obliged to exercise much caution in espousing and aiding the schemes of persons whose commercial standing at home is imperfectly known to him.

Cases are of course put forward in which the Diplomatists or Consuls of other States have successfully pushed the interests of their countrymen. But those who dwell on these cases in Parliament or in the press omit to notice either the cases in which British subjects have been similarly helped, or those, not rare, in which foreigners have suffered from the obtrusive attitude or grasping intrigues of Diplomatists purporting to act on their behalf. There are countries in which the commercial interests of a European nation have suffered from the excessive energy of its Consular Agents, an energy which has aroused the suspicion and alarm of the native authorities.

I may also remark that the countries in which British traders have been most largely supplanted by other foreigners are not those from which complaints of the interference of foreign Governments to help their subjects are most frequently received. There are, for instance, parts of Central and South America where we appear to have lost ground, but where our rivals are not believed to owe their success to any official action on their behalf.

One specific complaint, however, needs further notice. It is alleged that in some of the more remote and less developed countries such as those of the East and in the Republics of Central and South America, British subjects who seek to obtain contracts or concessions from the Government of the country suffer from the reluctance of British Representatives to push their claims, while the subjects of some other State benefit by the constant pressure which the Envoys of their Governments exert.

Even admitting this to be the case—though there seems to be some exaggeration in the statements made as to the action of these

Envoys, and still more in the estimate of the results attained thereby
—it must be asked whether Her Majesty's Representatives ought to
be instructed to follow such an example. Pressure upon such foreign
Governments as those referred to usually means pressure upon some
particular official who has the contract to give away. It is apt to be
accompanied and softened by corruption, in the form either of a
bribe or of some service to be rendered or commission paid to this
official, inconsistent with the duty which he owes to his own Government. A Diplomatic Representative joining in or even conniving
at such inducements runs a double risk, that of lowering the dignity
and character of his own country, and that of soiling his own
personal reputation. People begin to hint that he is himself to share
the expected gains, and as he cannot tell the whole truth, he is
obliged to remain under imputations which go far to destroy his
influence and usefulness.

These dangers are especially visible in the case of loans at high
rates of interest which the subjects of civilized States sometimes seek
to press on Eastern Governments. Besides the political mischief
which is apt to flow from such usurious transactions (of which there
has been ample evidence in recent years), they confer no benefit on
either the commerce or manufactures of the country to which the
lender belongs, and are therefore no proper objects of the benevolent
intervention of his Government.

Moreover, he who forces a contract upon a foreign State makes
his own Government to some extent responsible for the honesty
and business capacity of the contractor—things which he may not
be able to guarantee. In getting the better of competitors from other
countries he rouses jealousies and creates grounds of quarrel
between his own and other European Governments; and in identifying himself with the contractor he disposes the latter to believe
that he may rely on the power of his Government to compel the
payment of such debts as the foreign State may incur under the
contract. Bearing all this in mind, I believe that if our Diplomatists
have erred in this matter by abstention, they have erred on the
safer side. Cases may of course occur where another European
Government seeks to use its political influence to obtain exceptional
advantages for its subjects from an Eastern State. In such cases it
is no more than right that our Envoys should remonstrate, and
insist on an equally favourable hearing for British subjects as for
other foreigners; but this, I believe, is the regular practice of Her
Majesty's Agents, and has been repeatedly approved by the Foreign
Office.

2. The other complaint is that the information regarding com-

mercial matters which is transmitted from abroad is not of the right kind, comes too late, and is not published in an accessible and attractive form.

There may be some foundation for this complaint. But it must be remembered that few of Her Majesty's Representatives can be expected to possess special competence for reporting on technical questions relating to particular branches of industry. No person can enlighten British manufacturers on such special matters unless he has himself a practical knowledge of them, and has kept that practical knowledge up to the level of to-day's requirements. Taking the Secretaries' and Consular Reports as a whole, they are equal in quality and superior in quantity to those prepared by the foreign Representatives of any other European country, or of the United States, and as good as can be looked for from persons few of whom possess special knowledge.

The suggestions made for the better promotion of British trade abroad by means of Her Majesty's Representatives are as follows; I give not only those addressed to the Foreign Office by its correspondents, but such also of those made in Parliament or the press as have come to my knowledge:

1. The publication of a weekly commercial paper—somewhat analogous to the French *Moniteur Officiel du Commerce*—setting forth Tariff changes, movements in foreign markets, foreign commercial legislation, port and harbour regulations, &c.

2. The establishment of an office in London—like the French *Bureau de Commerce*—where Tariffs, Circulars, items of commercial news, &c., can be referred to by the public, who may inspect and copy.

3. That sample and specimen rooms should be attached to the principal Consulates abroad, where various classes of British manufactured goods would be on view, and that the expense of maintaining such rooms should be met by fees to be fixed by an Order in Council.

4. That Commercial Museums and Exhibitions of manufactured goods be established in well-chosen manufacturing centres, and that floating Museums or Exhibitions should be sent to various ports with samples of British goods.

5. That foreign Tariff changes and projected changes should be made known more rapidly than heretofore.

6. That Her Majesty's Diplomatic and Consular Officers abroad should use their best efforts to place British subjects on a not less favourable footing than foreigners in search of Concessions or other commercial enterprises.

7. That any such undertakings should be at once reported home by Her Majesty's Representatives.

8. That Consuls be chosen from men possessing commercial qualifications and technical knowledge.

9. That the names and addresses of Consuls abroad, and their office hours, should be made public.

10. That Trade Reports should appear at fixed and stated intervals; that more details respecting wages, hours of labour, cost of living, &c., should be put in them.

11. That copies of these Reports should at once be sent to trade journals. That samples of manufactured goods and of agricultural products be sent home with them.

12. That changes in the classification of goods for Tariff purposes be noted, and the decisions of Commercial Tribunals.

13. That more Commercial Attachés be appointed to Embassies and Legations.

14. That Consuls should assist in recovering debts, and recommend trustworthy lawyers and accountants.

15. That Consuls should report what means other countries adopt to push their trade.

16. That naval officers should write Trade Reports.

17. That Consuls, when at home on leave, should visit commercial centres, and acquire technical knowledge.

18. That they should answer inquiries regarding the stability of foreign business houses, and how far credit may safely be given them.

19. That Commercial Clerks (or *Chanceliers*) should be appointed to all Consulates.

20. That a Department be constructed in the Foreign Office specially charged with the prompt collection, publication, and diffusion of important information concerning commercial and industrial affairs.

21. That the Foreign Office should send abroad advertisements, commercial newspapers, etc., to Consuls to distribute or show.

22. That every Consulate should keep a registry of persons who are willing to act as Agents abroad for British traders.

23. That Her Majesty's Consuls should act as quasi Public Prosecutors in cases of trade-mark or patent infringements, &c.

24. That native Agents be more employed by merchants in China and elsewhere than at present.

25. That the Commercial Department of the Foreign Office be 'assisted by a Council of Advice, which should be drafted from the representative ranks of Chambers of Commerce, and that it should

be assimilated with a kindred Department of the Colonial Office and India Office'.

26. That Consuls should be placed in direct communication with Chambers of Commerce.

27. That Consuls should cultivate a 'closer personal touch' with traders in their district.

28. That Consuls be allowed to buy and charge for such statistical information as they may be unable to procure otherwise, or not till too late a date.

Instead of examining in detail these suggestions, some of which are obviously useful, others obviously inapplicable, while many of them are acted on already, I shall state what seem to be the functions which the Foreign Office may properly instruct its Agents abroad to discharge, and what kind of action, both at home and abroad, the Foreign Office and its Agents may take without substantially increasing the present expenditure on the Diplomatic and Consular Services. Some of the forms of action suggested would require a very considerable increase, but it is evidently the duty of the Foreign Office to await in such a manner the expression of the wish of Parliament.

These functions and forms of action fall under two heads: those which relate to the conduct of Her Majesty's Representatives in foreign countries for the promotion of British trade there, and those which relate to the action, both of them and of the Foreign Office, in the collection, transmission, and diffusion at home of information serviceable to the industrial and commercial classes of this country.

It must be remembered that most of what is in the following remarks described as desirable had been and is now done by the Commercial Department of the Foreign Office or by Her Majesty's Agents abroad under their instructions. There are very few possible lines of action which the Commercial Department has not already opened up, so that further progress must be chiefly in improving some details, and in the maintenance of an unflagging interest and activity in commercial matters among those who serve the country.

I. *As to the action in foreign countries of Her Majesty's Representatives*

1. Her Majesty's Representatives and Consuls ought to be at all times ready to afford orally, or by letter, the best information they possess, to those British subjects who may apply for it, regarding the state of business in their respective districts, the openings for trade which exist, the new undertakings projected, the new industries started, the new lines of communication which are being opened,

and (where they are in a position and feel at liberty to do so) the respectability of foreign commercial houses. Obviously, they can only speak to the best of their knowledge, information, and belief. They cannot be expected to incur expense and neglect their other duties for the purpose of procuring information for a private person, and if they venture to speak at all regarding the character of the firms as to which they may be questioned, they will have to speak guardedly, warning the questioner that they give no guarantee.

2. They ought to be prepared to introduce to persons or firms or Government officials in the districts where they reside such British subjects as come properly recommended. Here, too, there is much room for discretion as to the extent to which they may go in recommending a British merchant or his agent to a foreigner. In some cases they will merely state that he is a British subject who has brought a letter from some person of respectability, or from the Foreign Office, as the case may be. Very rarely would it be expedient that they should make themselves responsible for any person not travelling on an official mission.

3. They may properly recommend to British subjects having legal business competent and trustworthy legal advisers and accountants, and render to British litigants such advice and help as their own experience may show to be useful. In many countries the difficulty of knowing the law of the country, and of ascertaining how far it is fairly administered in cases where foreigners are concerned, is a serious hindrance to traders who may not be established there, but do their business through the post or by local agents. A Consul cannot be expected to become a debt collector, but he may sometimes be able to keep or to help a British merchant out of a peculiarly annoying source of loss.

4. They may intercede on behalf of British ships which have un-intentionally infringed Quarantine or Customs Regulations, and endeavour to obtain either exemption from any oppressive for-mality, or the remission of a fine imposed when there was no wrong-ful purpose on the part of the captain or freighter. Services of this kind are rendered every day, and are so much a matter of course that the commercial public at home hardly realize how essential they are, and how much of a Consul's time they occupy in busy ports.

5. It has been suggested that Consuls might regularly (as some now do occasionally) distribute the circulars of British trading firms, or might undertake the control of a showroom, to be placed at or near the Consulate, in which British goods could be displayed. Apart from the additional labour which this would impose on a

Consul, to the disadvantage of his other duties, it must be observed that this would turn him into a sort of commercial agent, a character scarcely compatible with his position as representing a great State, and that it would be hard for him to show equal zeal in pushing the interests of the various firms who would seek to use him. Most of the commercial authorities whose opinion I have asked disapprove of the proposal.

6. The case of British subjects seeking to obtain contracts or concessions from foreign Governments presents special difficulties (averted to above). It will of course be the duty of Her Majesty's Representative to secure a fair hearing and full consideration for his countrymen, and to see that competitors belonging to other countries gain no advantage by the influence of their Envoys. When exceptional pressure is being used by these Envoys, it may be necessary for him to exert similar pressure, and to remind the Government of the country where he resides that the British Government will regard exceptional favour shown to the subjects of other Powers as being a departure, amounting to a mark of unfriendliness to itself, from the safe rule of equal favour and open competition.

Such pressure, however, if justified by the circumstances of the case, would have to be employed under several conditions, viz.:

That no preference should be sought for one of two or more British competitors *inter se*.

That no use of questionable means (*e.g.*, by the offering of benefits to the Minister controlling the contract) should be connived at.

That, in the absence of special instructions from home, no guarantee should be given, nor the faith of Her Majesty's Government in any way pledged, on behalf of a person seeking a contract.

That, in the absence of such special instructions, no such action should be taken as would lay Her Majesty's Government under an obligation in respect of the favour shown to the British subject.

II. *As to the obtaining and publishing of intelligence from abroad*

[*Here follow a number of criticisms of the existing Government commercial intelligence services, together with detailed recommendations for their improvement.*]

III. *Miscellaneous Suggestions*

It remains to advert to some other suggestions which have been made for increasing the commercial utility of our Services.

One is, the establishment of Commercial Museums, a matter discussed in an interesting Memorandum by Mr. Kennedy, and

Mr. Bateman of the Board of Trade, on the similar institutions in France, as also in a Report recently received from Mr. Crowe at Paris, which will shortly be published. English commercial opinion is not quite unanimous on this subject. Most of our authorities conceive that such Museums would be useful, but remark that they ought to be planted, not in the capital, but in such centres of industry as Manchester, Leeds, Sheffield, Birmingham, Nottingham, Glasgow, Dundee. Others observe that although collections of foreign patterns would help to show the tastes and tendencies in matters of design and colour of consumers in foreign markets, British novelties would be less easy to procure, because manufacturers are jealous of letting their patterns come to the knowledge of their rivals. Nor is it clear that the State should bear the expense of such Museums. They seem rather an enterprise proper to be undertaken by the Chamber of Commerce of a great town, or by an Association of such Chambers; although no doubt Consuls ought to be encouraged or required to supply materials by sending home patterns and inventions as well as samples of foreign produce suitable for such a collection.

Much matter of interest to British traders is annually published in the official Reports of the leading European States and of the United States. The suggestion that extracts from these Reports should be collected and officially published here is a good one, but one which it does not seem the special province of the Foreign Office to carry out, although, of course, it is through our Diplomatic Agents that these documents might be most readily procured.

Still more weight has been laid upon the suggestion that there should be added to the Diplomatic Service a new class of persons specially trained for and charged with the duty of promoting British commercial interests. It was even proposed in the House of Commons last session that a Commercial Attaché should be appointed at every foreign capital where Her Majesty is represented. Not to speak of the expense which this would involve, it may be doubted whether a Commercial Attaché would at most capitals find enough work to occupy him, or whether, by any exertions he might put forth, he could render much further help to British manufacturers and merchants than they now obtain through the press and private channels of information. His presence would be an excuse for the neglect of commercial affairs by the rest of the Embassy; there would be little promotion for him; nor would it be easy to secure, except by a large salary, capable men for a post so much out of the line of the regular service. Only a person of large commercial knowledge, judgement, and experience would be worth having, and such a person would be almost certain to prefer a private commercial career to the prospect which this special branch of diplomacy would hold out. If such a class of officials are needed, it is not necessarily in capitals that they would be most serviceable; but the view that they are generally needed seems anyhow to rest on a wholly exaggerated estimate of the services which Diplomatic Representatives can render to private traders.

More may be hoped from stimulating the interest of our present Diplomatic and Consular officers in commercial affairs, and from giving them both a stronger motive and better facilities for activity in this department of their duties. There will always be among our Diplomatists some men with a special turn for mastering commercial subjects. Such men might be encouraged to prosecute inquiries into these subjects, and be selected by preference for posts where proficiency in them was likely to be valuable. As regards the Consular branch, even if it be not turned into a regular Service similar to the Diplomatic, a question too large to be discussed here, something more than has yet been attempted might be done to develop its aptitudes in this direction. Special regard might be had, in the appointment of Consuls, to their capacity for commercial work. Opportunities might be given to Consuls of obtaining the sort of knowledge which would help them, as, for instance by extending their acquaintance with mercantile law and the methods of commerce, or by visiting some of the chief seats of British manufacturing industry. Promotion to a higher post might be influenced by the tact and zeal a Consul had shown in helping English trade, and by the mastery of commercial questions displayed in his Reports. He should be encouraged to communicate more frequently with the Foreign Office on these topics, and similarly the Commercial Department of the Office might become to a larger extent than at present the means of conveying to our Representatives the wishes and inquiries of the mercantile community at home. It is not easy to specify the precise forms which this kind of intercommunication would take, nor would it be prudent to anticipate large new results from it; all I suggest is that more might be done than is now done to focus by means of the Foreign Office, the ideas and desires of those who in England are employed in foreign trade, and to radiate, so to speak, these ideas from home over all those places wherein help is sought or whence information is required.

It does not, however, follow that the notion which lies at the bottom of the proposal to appoint Commercial Attachés is an unfruitful one. We, in England, have much to learn from other countries, not only as respects the methods by which they conduct their industries and their commerce, but also as regards their legislation, the condition of the masses of their people, the various means by which they deal with those social and educational problems which confront all great modern States. Any one who has been accustomed to travel on the continent of Europe or in North America is daily struck by the number of points in which the experience of other countries throws light on our difficulties—sometimes in the way of suggestion, sometimes in that of warning—and is led to desire that a more constant and systematic means existed than we now possess of obtaining and rendering available, for the benefit of Britain and her Colonies, the results of that experience. Of late years much has been done to procure such data, both by sending out occasional Commissioners to inquire on specific subjects, and by requiring special Reports from Her Majesty's Representatives in foreign countries. We have a Commercial Attaché at Paris, whose Reports on trade and industrial questions are excellent, and who should be frequently instructed to report on these questions as arise in different parts of France. But our Diplomatic Representatives (even supposing that they could quit their posts to travel when required) are not always qualified by their knowledge, by their literary skill, or by the possession of a keenly observant mind, to obtain the right sort of information, or to present it in an effective form. There would be ample occupation for two or three men of exceptional aptitude in going from place to place to report upon subjects belonging to what may be called the realm of economic and social progress. One might be kept busy in the United States, where the diversity of laws and the continual development of new branches of industry furnishes an almost boundless field for instructive inquiry; two more in the continent of Europe, with most of whose States we have frequent negotiations on commercial questions, in which a knowledge of their commercial condition becomes important. Although commerce and manufactures would afford the most frequent occasions for Reports, one might suggest a great number of other topics to which the inquiries of such roving Commissioners might be from time to time directed.

[*A list follows.*]

Summary of Results

I may conclude by recapitulating briefly the conclusions to which the communications received by the Foreign Office and the foregoing examination of their contents seem to point.

The Foreign Office may seek to continue to be itself useful, and to utilize the services of those who act under its instructions abroad in the following directions:

Increased activity by Diplomatists and Consuls in affording information and help to Englishmen seeking to do business abroad.

Action (firm but cautious) by Diplomatists in remote countries in counteracting the pressure used by the Representatives of other States to push the mercantile interests of their countrymen.

More precise definition of respective duties of Diplomatists and Consuls in procuring information.

Prompter transmission of current commercial news from abroad.

More regular transmission of annual Reports.

Better arrangement and prompter publication of Reports.

Publication in a special journal of current commercial foreign news.

Sending home of samples of goods and of foreign products for exhibition in Commercial Museums (when established) or otherwise.

Greater encouragement to members of Diplomatic and Consular Services to master commercial questions, and better facilities therefor.

Appointment of two or three qualified persons to be sent abroad to report upon commercial and industrial questions of immediate interest.

I conceive that Circulars may properly be issued to Her Majesty's Diplomatic Representatives and Consuls, conveying to them the substance of the suggestions with regard to their duties, and impressing upon them the value attached by the Foreign Office to the rendering by them of all such services as they properly can render to British commerce, assuring them also that the Foreign Office itself will not cease to guide and assist all their efforts in this direction, by turning to the most prompt and efficient account such materials as they can supply, and rendering itself a more and more perfect channel of communication between them and the commercial community at home.

Considering that in most of the specific directions above indicated something is being done already, and in several nearly as much as can be done, the above suggestions may appear disappointing to persons who have been expecting great results from State action in the promotion of our foreign trade. That those who are suffering from the existing depression should look wistfully to Government for help is not surprising. Under the changed condition of the world, with telegraphs and lines of steamers everywhere, with some large markets closed by protective Tariffs, with native dealers supplanting the old system under which British mercantile houses did business through their branches abroad, the competition to which our commerce is exposed is far more severe than at any previous time. We must face this, perceiving that it was impossible under these changed conditions to retain the sort of monopoly which we practically enjoyed in many parts of the globe, and comforting ourselves with the knowledge that we are still far ahead of any other people.

But we must also admit that if our rivals have in some directions gained on us, this has been partly due to our own shortcomings. As we have neglected the technical training of our artizans, so we have done little to prepare by an appropriate education our young men for the career of commerce. There is no denying that the youths who go from Germany or Belgium to push their fortunes abroad in trade go better equipped than are our own in knowledge of languages and of the methods of business. They are willing to live more plainly than Englishmen will do, to work for smaller profits, to allow themselves fewer amusements. If they have less dash and enterprise than our countrymen, they have a steady tenacity and habits of systematic application not less valuable in the long run. They are more alive to the results attainable by attention to minutiæ, and perhaps more keenly watchful of all such new facilities as the progress of science affords. Some of these disadvantages we may remove when once their existence has been realized; and it is rather by their removal than by any action on the part of Government that the maintenance of our commercial supremacy must be sought. The fabric of British trade was built up by the energy and self-reliance of individual men; it is the same qualities, supplemented by the knowledge and the training which have now become necessary, that are needed to maintain it.

Not the less, however, is it the clear and constant duty of the Government which holds in its hands the threads of a vast organization stretching over the world to do all that it legitimately can to further the interests of our commerce.

This is not likely to be forgotten by the Foreign Office, which has the best reason to know how wide is the range of our commercial relations, and how much strength and influence they give us. Manufacturing industry at home and commerce abroad are, and seem likely long to remain, the chief sources of our prosperity; the chief means by which this little country holds her splendid place in the world and has become the most potent of its civilizing forces.

Printed as No. 1, *Correspondence respecting Diplomatic Assistance to British Trade Abroad, Pt. II.* P.P.1886(c.4779–1)LX.

APPENDIX VI

Extract from the Report of the Foreign Office Committee (Sir Eyre Crowe's Committee), 10 August 1916:

GENERAL PRINCIPLES

The objects and functions of any Government organization to promote and assist British trade in foreign countries are—

(1) To collect, co-ordinate, and present all information relating to the trade, industries, and shipping of those countries in such a way as to—

    (i) enable the Government to form a correct appreciation of the general commercial relations between the British Empire and the several foreign countries from the point of view of British commercial interests;

    (ii) afford advice to the Government on questions arising in connection with the negotiation of commercial treaties and tariffs, based on a comprehensive knowledge of the commercial geography, history, legislation, and actual conditions of the foreign countries concerned;

    (iii) enable the Government to furnish to British traders reliable information as to—

        (a) local laws, rules, regulations, and trade customs;

        (b) existing or potential markets for British exports;

        (c) supplies needed by, or useful to, British industries, which are or may be produced in the countries concerned;

        (d) openings for British capital in developing the natural resources and general commercial prosperity of such countries;

        (e) suitable agents for British firms in foreign countries.

(2) To facilitate the efforts of British traders to get into touch with the mercantile and industrial community in foreign countries as well as with the national or local authorities where necessary;

(3) To enable the Government to promote, and if necessary assist in negotiating through its agents abroad, commercial or industrial concessions to British subjects, where such concessions are of sufficient importance to call for Government intervention;

(4) To afford, within the limits of diplomatic or consular action, assistance in composing or smoothing over any difficulties that

may arise between British subjects in the exercise of their trade or legitimate commercial activity, and foreign government or local authorities.*

Paragraph 1 of the Report, printed in full as an Appendix to *Memorandum by the Board of Trade and the Foreign Office with respect to the Future Organisation of Commercial Intelligence.* P.P.1917–18 (Cd.8715)XXIX.

* It is not the function of Government agents in foreign countries to take any part in the actual carrying-on of a trader's private business; to assume responsibility for individual commercial transactions; to collect private debts; interfere in ordinary trade disputes; or intervene in private litigation on behalf of British claimants, save in exceptional cases and on the express authority of the Secretary of State.

SELECT BIBLIOGRAPHY

A. MS. SOURCES AND PRINTED DOCUMENTS:

Foreign Office and Board of Trade archives (including the *Law Officers' Reports*) at the Public Record Office, London. Foreign Office *Confidential Print* at the Foreign Office Library, London. Printed *Parliamentary Papers, Parliamentary Debates, British and Foreign State Papers, British Documents on the Origins of the World War*.

B. BOOKS, ARTICLES, AND THESES:

This subject is one for which there are no well-defined boundaries. I have, therefore, confined myself to listing below the books and articles cited in the footnotes, together with a few additional works which seemed to me to contribute something to the subject. The editions are those cited in the footnotes.

ADAMS, E. D., 'English Interest in the Annexation of California', *American Historical Review*, XIV (1909).

ADAMS, H. C., 'International Supervision over Foreign Investments', *American Economic Review*, Supplement (March, 1920).

ALCOCK, Sir Rutherford, *The Capital of the Tycoon: a Narrative of Three Years' Residence in Japan*, 2 vols. (Longmans & Co., London, 1863).

ANDERSON, M. A., 'Edmund Hammond, Permanent Under Secretary of State for Foreign Affairs, 1854–1873', London thesis, 1956.

ANDERSON, M. S., *The Eastern Question 1774–1923* (Macmillan, London, 1966).

ANDERSON, Olive, 'Great Britain and the Beginnings of the Ottoman Public Debt, 1854–55', *Historical Journal*, VII (1964).

— *A Liberal State at War* (Macmillan, London, 1966).

ANGELL, James W., *Financial Foreign Policy of the United States* (Council on Foreign Relations, New York, 1933).

ANON., 'The Problem of China', *Edinburgh Review* (July, 1899).

ANON., 'The Consular Service and its Wrongs', *Quarterly Review* (April, 1903).

ARMITAGE-SMITH, G., *The Free-trade Movement and its Results* (Blackie & Son, London, 1898).

ASQUITH, H. H., *Trade and the Empire* (Methuen & Co., London, 1903).

BADEN-POWELL, George, *State Aid and State Interference* (Chapman & Hall, London, 1882).

BAGEHOT, Walter, *Biographical Studies* (Longmans, Green & Co., London, 1881).

BAILEY, F. E., *British Policy and the Turkish Reform Movement* (Harvard University Press, Cambridge, Mass., 1942).

— 'The Economics of British Foreign Policy, 1825–50', *Journal of Modern History*, XII (1940).

BAKELESS, John, *The Economic Causes of Modern War; a study of the period 1878–1918* (Moffat, Yard & Co., New York, 1921).

BANNO, Masataka, *China and the West, 1858–1861* (Harvard University Press, Cambridge, Mass., 1964).

BASTER, A. S. J., *The International Banks* (P. S. King & Son, London, 1935).

BEASLEY, W. G., 'Lord Malmesbury's Foreign Office Circular of 8 March, 1858', *Bulletin of the Institute of Historical Research*, 23 (1950).

— *Great Britain and the opening of Japan, 1834–1858* (Luzac & Co., London, 1951).

BELL, Herbert C. F., *Lord Palmerston*, 2 vols. (Longmans & Co., London, 1936).

BELL, K., 'The Constantinople Embassy of Sir Henry Bulwer, 1858–65', London thesis, 1961.

BENIANS, E. A., BUTLER, Sir James, and CARRINGTON, C. E. (eds.), *The Cambridge History of the British Empire*, 8 vols. (C.U.P., Cambridge, 1929–63).

BERNARD, L. L., *War and its Causes* (H. Holt & Co., New York, 1944).

BINDOFF, S. T., 'The Unreformed Diplomatic Service, 1812–60', *Transactions of the Royal Historical Society*, 4th ser. XVIII (1935).

BLAISDELL, D. C., *European Financial Control in the Ottoman Empire* (Columbia University Press, New York, 1929).

BLAKE, Robert, *Disraeli* (Eyre & Spottiswoode, London, 1966).

BLAUG, Mark, 'Economic Imperialism Revisited', *Yale Review*, L (1961).

BLUNT, Wilfrid Scawen, *Secret History of the English Occupation of Egypt* (Chiswick Press, London, 1907).

BODELSEN, C. A., *Studies in Mid-Victorian Imperialism* (Gyldendalske Boghandel, Copenhagen, 1924).

BOLITHO, Hector, *Lord Inchcape* (John Murray, London, 1936).

BONN, M. J., *The Crumbling of Empire: The Disintegration of World Economy* (G. Allen & Unwin, London, 1938).

BORCHARD, Edwin M., *The Diplomatic Protection of Citizens Abroad; or, The Law of International Claims* (The Banks Law Publishing Co., New York, edn. 1928).

— and WYNNE, William H., *State Insolvency and Foreign Bondholders*, 2 vols. (Yale University Press, New Haven, 1951).

BOURNE, Kenneth, 'The Foreign Secretaryship of Lord Stanley, July 1866–December 1868', London thesis, 1955.

BRAILSFORD, H. N., *The War of Steel and Gold* (G. Bell & Sons, London, 1914).

BREBNER, J. Bartlet, 'Laissez Faire and State Intervention in Nineteenth Century Britain', *Journal of Economic History*, Supplement VIII (1948).

BRIGGS, Herbert W., *The Law of Nations* (Appleton-Century-Crofts, New York, 2nd edn. 1952).

BROCKWAY, T. P., 'Britain and the Persian Bubble, 1888–92', *Journal of Modern History*, XIII (1941).

— 'Iran and the West: a case study in modern imperialism', Yale thesis, 1937.

BROWN, Benjamin H., *The Tariff Reform Movement in Great Britain, 1881–1895* (Columbia University Press, New York, 1943).

BROWN, L. M., 'The Board of Trade and the Tariff Problem, 1840–1842', *English Historical Review*, LXVIII (1953).

— *The Board of Trade and the Free-Trade Movement 1830–42* (Clarendon Press, Oxford, 1958).

BRUNSCHWIG, Henri, *Mythes et Réalités de l'Impérialisme Colonial Français 1871–1914* (Librairie Armand Colin, Paris, 1960).

BUCKLE, G. E., see MONYPENNY, W. F., and BUCKLE, G. E.

BUKHARIN, Nikolai, *Imperialism and World Economy* (International Publishers, New York, 1929).

BUTLER, Sir James, see BENIANS, E. A., BUTLER, Sir James and CARRINGTON, C. E.

CADY, J. F., *Foreign Intervention in the Rio de la Plata, 1835–50* (University of Pennsylvania Press, Philadelphia, 1929).

CALVERT, Peter A. R., 'The Murray Contract: An Episode in International Finance and Diplomacy', *Pacific Historical Review*, XXXV (1966).

CAMPBELL, A. E., 'Great Britain and the United States in the Far East, 1895–1903', *Historical Journal*, I (1958).

CAMPBELL, Sir Gerald, *Of True Experience* (Hutchinson & Co., London, 1949).

CARRINGTON, C. E., *The British Overseas* (C.U.P., Cambridge, 1950).

— see BENIANS, E. A., BUTLER, Sir James, and CARRINGTON, C. E.,

CECIL, Lady Gwendolen, *Life of Robert, Marquis of Salisbury*, 4 vols. (Hodder & Stoughton, London, 1921–32).

CHAPMAN, Maybelle K., 'Great Britain and the Bagdad Railway, 1888–1914', *Smith College Studies in History*, XXXI (1948).

CHEN, Chung-Sien, 'British Loans to China from 1860 to 1913, with special reference to the period 1894–1913', London thesis, 1940.

CHILDERS, Spencer, *The Life and Correspondence of the Rt. Hon. Hugh C. E. Childers*, 2 vols. (John Murray, London, 1901).

CLARK, J. Reuben, Jr., 'Foreign Bondholders in the United States', *American Journal of International Law*, 32 (1938).

— 'Collecting on Defaulted Foreign Dollar Bonds', *American Journal of International Law*, 34 (1940).

CLARK, Sir William, 'Government and the Promotion of Trade', *Journal of Public Administration*, I (1923).

COLBERT, Evelyn Speyer, *Retaliation in International Law* (King's Crown Press, New York, 1948).

COLLINS, William F., *Mineral Enterprise in China* (William Heinemann, London, 1918).

COOKE, Sidney Russell, see DAVENPORT, E. H., and COOKE, Sidney Russell.

CORRIGAN, Harold S. W., 'British, French and German Interests in Asiatic Turkey, 1881–1914', London thesis, 1954.

COSTIN, W. C., *Great Britain and China, 1833–1860* (Clarendon Press, Oxford, 1937).

CRANKSHAW, Edward, *The Forsaken Idea: a Study of Viscount Milner* (Longmans, Green & Co., London, 1952).

CROMER, Lord, *Modern Egypt*, 2 vols. (Macmillan & Co., London, 1908).
— *Ancient and Modern Imperialism* (John Murray, London, 1910).
CROUZET, F., 'Commerce et empire: L'expérience britannique du libre-échange à la première guerre mondiale', *Annales*, 19 (1964).
CROWE, S. E., *The Berlin West African Conference, 1884–1885* (Longmans, Green & Co., London, 1942).
CULBERTSON, W. S., *Commercial Policy in War Time and After* (D. Appleton & Co., New York, 1919).
— *International Economic Policies, a survey of the Economics of Diplomacy* (D. Appleton & Co., New York, 1925).
CURZON, G. N., *Persia and the Persian Question*, 2 vols. (Longmans, Green & Co., London, 1892).
— *Problems of the Far East* (Longmans, Green & Co., London, 1894).
— 'The True Imperialism', *Nineteenth Century* (January, 1908).
DAHL, V. C., 'Business influence in the Anglo-Mexican Reconciliation of 1884', *Inter-American Economic Affairs*, XV (1961–2).
DAUD, Mahmood Ali, 'British Relations with the Persian Gulf, 1890–1902', London thesis, 1957.
DAVENPORT, E. H., and COOKE, Sidney Russell, *The Oil Trusts and Anglo-American Relations* (Macmillan & Co., London, 1923).
DAWSON, W. H., *Richard Cobden and Foreign Policy* (George Allen & Unwin, London, 1926).
DELAISI, Francis, *Political Myths and Economic Realities* (Noel Douglas, London, 1927).
DILKE, Charles W., *Greater Britain*, 2 vols. (Macmillan & Co., London, 1868).
— *Problems of Greater Britain* (Macmillan & Co., London, 4th edn. revd. 1890).
'DIPLOMATICUS', 'The Imperial Bank of Persia', *Asiatic Quarterly Review* (October 1889).
DONALDSON, John, *International Economic Relations: a Treatise on World Economy and World Politics* (Longmans, Green & Co., New York, 1928).
DRUMMOND WOLFF, Sir Henry, *Rambling Recollections*, 2 vols. (Macmillan & Co., London, 1908).
DUGDALE, E. T. S., *Maurice de Bunsen* (John Murray, London, 1934).
DUNHAM, A. L., *The Anglo-French Treaty of Commerce of 1860 and the Progress of the Industrial Revolution in France* (University of Michigan Press, Ann Arbor, 1930).
DUNN, F. S., *The Protection of Nationals* (Johns Hopkins Press, Baltimore, 1932).
EAGLETON, Clyde, *The Responsibility of States in International Law* (New York University Press, New York, 1928).
EARLE, Edward M., *Turkey, the Great Powers and the Bagdad Railway* (The Macmillan Co., New York, 1923).
— 'The Turkish Petroleum Company—a Study in Oleaginous Diplomacy', *Political Science Quarterly*, 39 (1924).

EDWARDS, G. W., 'American Policy with Reference to Foreign Investments', *American Economic Review*, Supplement (1924).

— 'Government Control of Foreign Investments', *American Economic Review*, XVIII (1928).

EDWARDS, H. Sutherland, *Sir William White, his Life and Correspondence* (John Murray, London, 1902).

ELLIOT, Hon. Arthur D., *Life of Lord Goschen, 1831–1907*, 2 vols. (Longmans & Co., London, 1911).

FABER, Richard, *The Vision and the Need; late Victorian Imperialist Aims* (Faber, London, 1966).

FACHIRI, A. P., 'Expropriation and International Law', *British Year Book of International Law*, VI (1925).

FAIRBANK, John King, *Trade and Diplomacy on the China Coast, 1842–1854* (Harvard University Press, Cambridge, Mass., 1964).

FARRER, Lord, *Free Trade versus Fair Trade* (Cobden Club, London, 1882).

— *The State in its Relation to Trade* (Macmillan & Co., London, edn. 1902).

FEIS, Herbert, *Europe; the World's Banker, 1870–1914* (Yale University Press, New Haven, 1930).

FERNS, H. S., *Britain and Argentina in the Nineteenth Century* (Clarendon Press, Oxford, 1960).

FIELDHOUSE, D. K., ' "Imperialism"; An Historiographical Revision', *Economic History Review*, 2nd ser. XIV (1961).

— *The Colonial Empires: a comparative survey from the Eighteenth Century* (Weidenfeld & Nicolson, London, 1966).

FITZMAURICE, Lord, *Life of Earl Granville*, 2 vols. (Longmans & Co., London, 1905).

FLOURNOY, F. R., *British Policy towards Morocco in the Age of Palmerston, 1830–1865* (P. S. King & Son, London, 1935).

FRANKEL, S. H., *Capital Investment in Africa* (O.U.P., London, 1938).

FRASER, Herbert F., *Foreign Trade and World Politics* (A. A. Knopf, New York, 1926).

FRECHTLING, L. E., 'The Reuter Concession in Persia', *Asiatic Review*, XXXIV (1938).

FREEMAN, Alwyn V., *The International Responsibility of States for Denial of Justice* (Longmans & Co., London, 1938).

FREEMAN, Joseph, see NEARING, Scott, and FREEMAN, Joseph.

FREYCINET, C. de, *La Question d'Egypte* (Calmann-Lévy, Paris, 1905).

FRIEDMAN, S., *Expropriation in International Law* (Stevens & Sons, London, 1953).

FUCHS, C. J., *The Trade Policy of Great Britain and her Colonies since 1860* (Macmillan & Co., London, 1905).

GALBRAITH, J. S., 'The "Turbulent Frontier" as a Factor in British Expansion', *Comparative Studies in Society and History*, II (1960).

— 'Myths of the "Little England" Era', *American Historical Review*, LXVII (1961).

GALLAGHER, J. and ROBINSON, R., 'The Imperialism of Free Trade', *Economic History Review*, 2nd ser. VI (1953).

— see ROBINSON, R. and GALLAGHER, J.

GARDINER, A. G., *The Life of Sir William Harcourt*, 2 vols. (Constable & Co., London, 1923).

GARVIN, J. L., *The Life of Joseph Chamberlain*, 4 vols. (Macmillan & Co., London, 1931–4).

GASELEE, Stephen, see TILLEY, Sir John, and GASELEE, Stephen.

GASTRELL, W. H. S., *Our Trade in the World in Relation to Foreign Competition, 1885 to 1895* (Chapman & Hall, London, 1897).

GILLE, Bertrand, 'Finance Internationale et Trusts', *Revue Historique*, 227 (1962).

GLADSTONE, W. E., 'Aggression in Egypt and Freedom in the East' *Nineteenth Century*, II (1877).

GLENNY, W. J., 'The Trade Commissioner and Commercial Diplomatic Services', *Journal of Public Administration*, II (July, 1924).

GOOCH, Brison D., 'Belgium and the Prospective Sale of Cuba in 1837', *Hispanic American Historical Review*, 39 (1959).

GOOCH, G. P., *Recent Revelations of European Diplomacy* (Longmans & Co., London, 1928).

— see WARD, A. W. and GOOCH, G. P.

GOSSES, F., *The Management of British Foreign Policy before the First World War* (A. W. Sijthoff's Uitgeversmaatschappij, Leiden, 1948).

GRAMPP, William D., *The Manchester School of Economics* (Stanford University Press, Stanford, 1960).

GRAVES, Philip, *Sir Percy Cox* (Hutchinson & Co., London, 1941).

GREAVES, R. L., *Persia and the Defence of India, 1884–1892* (Athlone Press, London, 1959).

GREENBERG, Michael, *British Trade and the Opening of China, 1800–1842* (C.U.P., Cambridge, 1951).

GREENVILLE, J. A. S., *Lord Salisbury and Foreign Policy. The Close of the Nineteenth Century* (Athlone Press, London, 1964).

GREY OF FALLODON, Viscount, *Twenty-five Years, 1892–1916*, 2 vols. (Hodder & Stoughton, London, 1925).

GUYOT, Yves, 'The Amount, Direction and Nature of French Investments', *Annals of the American Academy of Political and Social Science*, LXVIII (1916).

GWATKIN, F. T. Ashton, *The British Foreign Service* (Syracuse University Press, Syracuse, N.Y., 1951).

GWYNN, Stephen, and TUCKWELL, Gertrude M., *The Life of the Rt. Hon. Sir Charles W. Dilke*, 2 vols. (John Murray, London, 1917)

HALE, Oron J., *Publicity and Diplomacy, with special reference to England and Germany, 1890–1914* (D. Appleton-Century Co., New York, 1940).

HALL, S., 'Sir Edward Hertslet and his Work as Librarian and Keeper of the Papers of the Foreign Office from 1857 to 1896', London thesis, 1958.

HALLGARTEN, G. W. F., *Imperialismus vor 1914* (C. H. Beck, Munich, 1951).

HALPÉRIN, Vladimir, *Lord Milner and the Empire: the evolution of British Imperialism* (Odhams Press, London, 1952).

HAMILTON, Lord Frederic, *The Vanished Pomps of Yesterday* (Hodder & Stoughton, London, 7th edn. n.d.).

HAMMOND, Richard J., 'Economic Imperialism: Sidelights on a Stereotype', *Journal of Economic History*, XXI (1961).

HANCOCK, W. K., *Survey of British Commonwealth Affairs: Problems of Economic Policy, 1918–39* (O.U.P., London, 1940–2).

HARDINGE OF PENSHURST, Lord, *Old Diplomacy* (John Murray, London, 1947).

HARDINGE, Sir Arthur, *A Diplomatist in the East* (Jonathan Cape, London, 1928).

HARGREAVES, J. D., 'Lord Salisbury, British Isolation and the Yangtsze, June–September, 1900', *Bulletin of the Institute of Historical Research*, XXX (1957)

HARRIS, N. D., *Europe and Africa* (Houghton Mifflin Co., Boston, 1927).

HARVARD LAW SCHOOL, 'Draft Convention and Comments on Responsibility of States for Injuries to Aliens', *American Journal of International Law*, 23 (Special Supplement, April 1929).

HAWTREY, R. G., *Economic Aspects of Sovereignty* (Longmans & Co., London, 1930).

HEADLAM-MORLEY, Sir James, *Studies in Diplomatic History* (Methuen & Co., London, 1930).

HEARDER, H., 'The Foreign Policy of Lord Malmesbury, 1858–1860', London thesis, 1954.

HENDERSON, W. O., 'British economic activity in the German Colonies, 1884–1914', *Economic History Review*, XV (1945).

— 'German Economic Penetration in the Middle East, 1870–1914', *Economic History Review*, XVIII (1948).

HENDRICK, Burton J., *The Life and Letters of Walter H. Page* (William Heinemann, London, 1924).

HERTSLET, Edward, *Recollections of the Old Foreign Office* (John Murray, London, 1901).

HEWINS, Ralph, *Mr. Five per Cent* (Hutchinson, London, 1957).

HINDMARSH, Albert E., 'Self-Help in time of Peace', *American Journal of International Law*, 26 (1932).

HIRST, F. W., *From Adam Smith to Philip Snowden: A History of Free Trade in Great Britain* (T. Fisher Unwin, London, 1925).

— *Gladstone as Financier and Economist* (Ernest Benn, London, 1931).

HOBSON, C. K., *The Export of Capital* (Constable, London, 1914).

HOBSON, J. A., 'The Economic Taproot of Imperialism', *Contemporary Review* (August 1902).

— *Imperialism, a Study* (Allen & Unwin, London, edn. 1954).

— *Richard Cobden, the International Man* (T. Fisher Unwin, London, 1918).

HOFFMAN, Ross J. S., *Great Britain and the German Trade Rivalry, 1875–1914* (University of Pennsylvania Press, Philadelphia, 1933).

HOHLER, Sir Thomas, *Diplomatic Petrel* (John Murray, London, 1942).

HORN, D. B., *The British Diplomatic Service, 1689–1789* (Clarendon Press, Oxford, 1961).

HORNBY, Sir Edmund, *An Autobiography* (Constable & Co., London, 1929).

HORNBECK, Stanley K., 'Trade, Concessions, Investments Conflict and Policy in the Far East', *Proceedings of the Academy of Political Science*, VII (1917).

HORRABIN, J. F., *How Empires Grow* (N.C.L.C. Publishing Society, London, 1935).

HOSKINS, H. L., *British Routes to India* (Longmans, Green & Co., New York, 1928).

HOWE, Frederic C., 'Dollar Diplomacy and Financial Imperialism under the Wilson Administration', *Annals of the American Academy of Political and Social Science*, LXVIII (1916).

HUTCHINSON, G. T., see MORISON, Theodore and HUTCHINSON, G. T.

HYDE, F. E., *Mr. Gladstone at the Board of Trade* (Cobden-Sanderson, London, 1934).

ILIASU, A., 'The role of Free Trade Treaties in British Foreign Policy, 1859–1871', London thesis, 1965.

IMBERT, Henri, *Les Emprunts d'Etats Etrangers* (A. Leclerc, Paris, 1905).

IMLAH, Albert H., *Economic Elements in the Pax Britannica* (Harvard University Press, Cambridge, Mass., 1958).

JENKS, L. H., *The Migration of British Capital to 1875* (Jonathan Cape, London, edn. 1938).

JONES, L. E., *Georgian Afternoon* (Hart-Davis, London, 1958).

JOSEPH, Philip, *Foreign Diplomacy in China, 1894–1900* (G. Allen & Unwin, London, 1928).

JOSLIN, David, *A Century of Banking in Latin America* (O.U.P., London, 1963).

KEBBEL, T. E., (ed.), *Selected Speeches of the late Earl of Beaconsfield*, 2 vols (Longmans, Green & Co., London, 1882).

KELLY, Sir David, *The Ruling Few* (Hollis & Carter, London, 1952).

KENNEDY, A. L., *Salisbury 1830–1903* (John Murray, London, 1953).

KENT, P. H., *Railway Enterprise in China* (Edward Arnold, London, 1907).

KEYNES, J. M., *The End of Laissez-Faire* (L. & V. Woolf, London, 1926).

KIERNAN, V. G., 'Britain's First Contacts with Paraguay', *Atlante*, III (1955).

— 'The Kra Canal Projects of 1882–5: Anglo-French rivalry in Siam and Malaya', *History*, XLI (1957).

KNAPLUND, Paul, *Gladstone and Britain's Imperial Policy* (G. Allen & Unwin, London, 1927).

— *Gladstone's Foreign Policy* (Harper & Bros., New York, 1935).

KNIGHTBRIDGE, A. A. H., 'Gladstone and the Invasion of Egypt in 1882', Oxford thesis, 1960.

KOEBNER, R., 'The Concept of Economic Imperialism', *Economic History Review*, 2nd ser. II (1949).

— 'The Emergence of the Concept of Imperialism', *Cambridge Journal*, V (1952).

— and SCHMIDT, H., *Imperialism* (C.U.P., Cambridge, 1964).

KUMAR, Ravinder, 'The Records of the Government of India on the Berlin–Baghdad Railway Question'. *Historical Journal*, V (1962).

LAMBERT, R. S. *Modern Imperialism* (Longmans & Co., London, 1928).

LANDES, David S., *Bankers and Pashas* (Heinemann, London, 1958).

— 'Some thoughts on the Nature of Economic Imperialism', *Journal of Economic History*, XXI (1961).

LANE-POOLE, Stanley, *The Life of the Rt. Hon. Stratford Canning*, 2 vols. (Longmans & Co., London, 1888).

LANGER, W. L., 'The European Powers and the French Occupation of Tunis, 1878–81, Pts. I & II', *American Historical Review*, XXXI (1925-1926).

— 'A Critique of Imperialism', *Foreign Affairs*, 24 (1935).

— *The Diplomacy of Imperialism, 1890–1902* (Knopf, New York, 2nd edn. 1951).

LAVES, Walter H. C., 'German Governmental Influence on Foreign Investments, 1871–1915', *Political Science Quarterly*, 43 (1928).

LAWFORD, Valentine, *Bound for Diplomacy* (John Murray, London, 1963).

LAYARD, Sir A. Henry, *Autobiography and Letters*, 2 vols. (John Murray, London, 1903).

LE MAY, G. H. L., *British Supremacy in South Africa 1899–1907* (Clarendon Press, Oxford, 1965).

LENIN, V. I., *Imperialism, the Highest Stage of Capitalism* (Lawrence, London, 2nd edn. 1934).

LEVI, Leone, *History of British Commerce and of the Economic Progress of the British Nation 1763–1870* (John Murray, London, 1872).

LINGELBACH, A. L., 'Huskisson and the Board of Trade', *American Historical Review*, XLIII (1938).

LIPPMANN, Walter, *The Stakes of Diplomacy* (H. Holt & Co., New York, 1915).

LIVERMORE, Seward W., 'Battleship Diplomacy in South America: 1905–1925', *Journal of Modern History*, XVI (1944).

LOUIS, Wm. Roger, 'The Anglo-Congolese Agreement of 1894 and the Cairo Corridor', *St. Antony's Papers*, 15 (1963).

— 'Sir Percy Anderson's Grand African Strategy, 1883–1896', *English Historical Review*, LXXXI (1966).

LOWE, C. J., *Salisbury and the Mediterranean 1886–1896* (Routledge, London, 1965).

LUXEMBURG, Rosa, *The Accumulation of Capital* (Routledge, London, edn. 1963).

MACDONAGH, O., 'The Anti-Imperialism of Free Trade', *Economic History Review*, 2nd ser. XIV (1962).

McGRANE, Reginald C., 'Some Aspects of American State Debts in the Forties', *American Historical Review*, XXXVIII (1933).

MacNAIR, H. F., see MORSE, H. B., and MacNAIR, H. F.

McNAIR, Lord, (ed.), *International Law Opinions*, 3 vols. (C.U.P. Cambridge, 1956).

MALET, Sir Edward, *Egypt 1879–1883* (London, 1909).

MALLET, Bernard, *Sir Louis Mallet* (James Nisbet & Co., London, 1905).

MANCHESTER, A. K., *British Pre-Eminence in Brazil* (University of North Carolina Press, Chapel Hill, 1933).

MAR, T. T. G., 'Anglo-Chinese Diplomacy, 1898–1911', London thesis, 1929.

MARLOWE, John, *Anglo-Egyptian Relations, 1800–1953* (Cresset Press, London, 1954).

MARSDEN, Arthur, 'British Policy towards Tunis, 1875–1899', London thesis, 1963.

MARVIN, C., *Our Public Offices* (S. Tinsley & Co., London, 1879).

MAXWELL, Sir Herbert, *The Life and Letters of George William Frederick, Fourth Earl of Clarendon*, 2 vols. (Edward Arnold, London, 1913).

MIDDLEMAS, R. K., *The Master Builders* (Hutchinson, London, 1963).

MILLER, William, *Travels and Politics in the Near East* (T. F. Unwin, London, 1898).

MILNER, Alfred, *England in Egypt* (Edward Arnold, London, edn. 1894).

— *The Nation and the Empire* (Constable & Co., London, 1913).

MONGER, George, *The End of Isolation: British Foreign Policy, 1900–1907* (Nelson, Edinburgh, 1963).

MONYPENNY, W. F., and BUCKLE, G. E., *The Life of Benjamin Disraeli, Earl of Beaconsfield*, 6 vols. (John Murray, London, 1910–1920).

MOORE, J. B., *A Digest of International Law*, 8 vols. (Washington Government Printing Office, Washington, 1906).

MOREL, E. D., *Affairs of West Africa* (William Heinemann, London, 1902).

MORISON, Theodore, and HUTCHINSON, G. T., *The Life of Sir Edward Fitz-Gerald Law* (William Blackwood & Sons, Edinburgh, 1911).

MORLEY, John, *The Life of Richard Cobden*, 2 vols. (Chapman & Hall, London, 1881).

— *The Life of William Ewart Gladstone* (Macmillan, London, edn. 1911).

MORSE, H. B., and MACNAIR, H. F., *Far Eastern International Relations* (Houghton Mifflin Co., Boston, 1931).

MOWAT, R. B., *The Life of Lord Pauncefote* (Constable & Co., London, 1929).

MURTI, B. S. N., 'Anglo-French Relations with Siam, 1876–1904', London thesis, 1952.

MUSTAFA, Ahmed Abdel-Rehim, 'The Domestic and Foreign Affairs of Egypt from 1876 to 1882', London thesis, 1955.

NAYLOR, Robert A., 'The British Role in Central America prior to the Clayton-Bulwer Treaty of 1850', *Hispanic American Historical Review*, 40 (1960).

NEARING, Scott, and FREEMAN, Joseph, *Dollar Diplomacy—a study in American Imperialism* (B. W. Huebsch & The Viking Press, New York, 1926).

NEARING, Scott, *The Twilight of Empire; an economic interpretation of Imperialist Cycles* (The Vanguard Press, New York, 1930).

NEISSER, H., 'Economic imperialism reconsidered', *Social Research*, 27 (1960).

NETTLES, H. E., 'The Drago Doctrine in International Law and Politics', *Hispanic American Historical Review*, VIII (1928).

NEWBURY, C. W., 'The Partition of Africa; Victorians, Republicans, and the Partition of West Africa', *Journal of African History*, III (1962).

NEWTON, Lord, *Lord Lyons, a Record of British Diplomacy* (Edward Arnold, London, 1913).

— *Lord Lansdowne* (Macmillan & Co., London, 1929).

NICOLSON, Harold, *Sir Arthur Nicolson, Bart., First Lord Carnock* (Constable & Co., London, 1930).

— *Helen's Tower* (Constable & Co., London, 1937).

—*Diplomacy* (O.U.P., London, 2nd edn. 1950).

NICOLSON, Nigel, (ed.), *Harold Nicolson, Diaries and Letters 1930–1939* (Collins, London, 1966).

NIGHTINGALE, Robert, 'The Personnel of the British Foreign Office and Diplomatic Service, 1851–1929' *The Realist* (December, 1929).

NIKPAY, Gholam Reza, 'The Political Aspects of Foreign Oil Interests in Iran down to 1947', London thesis, 1956.

O'CONNELL, D. P., 'Economic Concessions in the Law of State Succession', *British Year Book of International Law*, XXVII (1950).

OFFUTT, Milton, *The Protection of Citizens Abroad by the Armed Forces of the United States* (Johns Hopkins Press, Baltimore, 1928).

OLIVIER, Sidney, *White Capital and Coloured Labour* (Independent Labour Party, London, 1906).

OVERLACH, T. W., *Foreign Financial Control in China* (The Macmillan Co., New York, 1919).

OVERSTREET, H. A., 'Foreign Investment Relations', *Proceedings of the Academy of Political Science*, VII (1917).

PALMER, A. W., 'Lord Salisbury's Approach to Russia, 1898', *Oxford Slavonic Papers*, VI (1955).

PAPADOPOULOS, G. S., 'Lord Salisbury and the Projected Anglo-German Alliance of 1898', *Bulletin of the Institute of Historical Research*, XXVI (1953).

PARES, Richard, 'The Economic Factors in the History of the Empire', *Economic History Review*, VII (1936–7).

PARSONS, F. V., 'The North-West African Company and the British Government, 1875–95', *Historical Journal*, I (1958).

PAVLOVITCH, Michel, *The Foundations of Imperialist Policy* (The Labour Publishing Co., London, 1922).

PEARS, Sir Edwin, *Forty Years in Constantinople* (Herbert Jenkins, London, 1916).

PELCOVITS, N. A., *Old China Hands and the Foreign Office* (King's Crown Press, New York, 1948).

PENSON, L. M., 'The Principles and Methods of Lord Salisbury's Foreign Policy', *Cambridge Historical Journal*, II (1935).

— 'The New Course in British Foreign Policy, 1892–1902', *Transactions of the Royal Historical Society*, 4th ser. XXV (1943).

— see TEMPERLEY, Harold, and PENSON, Lillian M.

PHILIPS, C. H., 'The East India interest and the British Government, 1784–1883', London thesis, 1938.

PLATT, D. C. M., 'The Allied Coercion of Venezuela, 1902–3: a Reassessment', *Inter-American Economic Affairs*, 15 (1962).
— 'The Role of the British Consular Service in Overseas Trade, 1825–1915', *Economic History Review*, 2nd ser. XV (1963).
— 'The Imperialism of Free Trade: Some Reservations', *Economic History Review*, 2nd ser. XXI (1968).
— 'Economic Factors in British Policy during the "New Imperialism",' *Past and Present* (1968).
PROUTY, Roger, *The Transformation of the Board of Trade, 1830–1855* (Heinemann, London, 1957).
PURYEAR, Vernon J., *International Economics and Diplomacy in the Near East: a Study of British commercial Policy in the Levant 1834–1853* (Stanford University Press, Stanford, 1935).
RANDOLPH, Bessie C., 'Foreign Bondholders and the Repudiated Debts of the Southern States', *American Journal of International Law*, 25 (1931).
RAYMOND, A., 'Les tentatives anglaises de pénétration économique en Tunisie (1856–1877)', *Revue Historique*, CCXIV (1955).
REMER, C. F., *Foreign Investments in China* (The Macmillan Co., New York, 1933).
RIPPY, J. Fred, *British Investments in Latin America, 1822–1949* (University of Minnesota Press, Minneapolis, 1959).
ROBBINS, Lionel, *The Economic Causes of War* (Jonathan Cape, London, 1939).
ROBERTS, George E., 'Property Rights and Trade Rivalries as Factors in International Complications', *Proceedings of the Academy of Political Science*, VII (1917).
ROBINSON, R., and GALLAGHER, J., *Africa and the Victorians, the official mind of Imperialism* (Macmillan, London, 1961).
— see GALLAGHER, J., and ROBINSON, R.
ROBSON, Maureen M., 'Liberals and "vital interests"; the Debate on International Arbitration, 1815–72', *Bulletin of the Institute of Historical Research*, XXXII (1959).
RODD, Sir Rennell, *Diplomacy* (Ernest Benn, London, 1929).
RODKEY, F. S., 'Palmerston and the Rejuvenation of Turkey, 1830–41', *Journal of Modern History*, I (1929).
— 'The Attempts of Briggs and Co. to Guide British Policy in the Levant in the Interest of Mehemet Ali Pasha, 1821–41', *Journal of Modern History*, V (1933).
— 'Ottoman concern about Western economic penetration in the Levant, 1849–1856', *Journal of Modern History*, XXX (1958).
RONALDSHAY, Lord, *The Life of Lord Curzon*, 3 vols. (Ernest Benn, London, 1928).
ROOT, J. W., *The Trade Relations of the British Empire* (J. W. Root, Liverpool 1903).
ROSEBERY, Lord, *Lord Rosebery's Speeches, 1874–1896* (N. Beeman, London, 1896).

ROTH, Andreas H., *The Minimum Standard of International Law Applied to Aliens* (A. W. Sijthoff's Uitgeversmaatschappij, Leiden, 1949).

ROTHSTEIN, Theodore, *Egypt's Ruin. A Financial and Administrative Record* (A. C. Fifield, London, 1910).

SANDERSON, G. N., *England, Europe and the Upper Nile 1882–1899* (Edinburgh University Press, Edinburgh, 1965).

SARGENT, A. J., *Anglo-Chinese Commerce and Diplomacy* (Clarendon Press, Oxford, 1907)

SATOW, Sir Ernest, *A Guide to Diplomatic Practice* (Longmans, Green & Co., London, 4th edn. 1957).

SAUL, S. B., 'The Economic Significance of "Constructive Imperialism" ', *Journal of Economic History*, XVII (1957).

SCHATZ, S. R., 'Economic Imperialism Again', *Social Research*, 28 (1961).

SCHMIDT, H., see KOEBNER, R. and SCHMIDT, H.

SCHUMAN, Frederick L., *War and Diplomacy in the French Republic* (McGraw-Hill, New York, 1931).

SCHUYLER, R. L., 'The Climax of Anti-Imperialism in England', *Political Science Quarterly*, XXXVI (1921).

— *The Fall of the Old Colonial System: A Study in British Free Trade, 1770–1870* (O.U.P., New York, 1945).

SCHWARZENBERGER, Georg, 'The Most-Favoured-Nation Standard in British State Practice', *British Year Book of International Law*, XXII (1945).

— 'The Protection of Human Rights in British State Practice', *Current Legal Problems*, I (1948).

— 'The Protection of British Property Abroad', *Current Legal Problems*, V (1952).

SCHWITZER, Joan P., 'The British Attitude towards French Colonisation', London thesis, 1954.

SEELEY, J. R., *The Expansion of England* (Macmillan & Co., London, 1883).

SEMMEL, B., *Imperialism and Social Reform* (Allen, London, 1960).

— 'The Philosophic Radicals and Colonialism', *Journal of Economic History*, XXI (1961).

SETON-WATSON, Hugh, *Neither War nor Peace* (Methuen, London, 1960).

SHEA, Donald R., *The Calvo Clause, a problem of Inter-American and International Law and Diplomacy* (University of Minnesota Press, Minneapolis, 1955).

SHEPPERSON, G., 'Africa, the Victorians and Imperialism', *Revue Belge de Philologie et d'Histoire*, XL (1962).

SMITH, Colin L., *The Embassy of Sir William White at Constantinople, 1886–1891* (O.U.P., London, 1957).

SMITH, Sir Hubert Llewellyn, *The Board of Trade* (G. Putnam, London, 1928).

SONTAG, Raymond J., *Germany and England 1848–1894* (D. Appleton-Century Co., New York, 1938).

SPENDER, J. A., *Weetman Pearson, first Viscount Cowdray* (Cassell, London, 1930).

STALEY, Eugene, *War and the Private Investor* (Doubleday, Doran & Co., New York, 1935).

STEINER, Zara, 'The Last Years of the Old Foreign Office 1898–1905', *Historical Journal*, VI (1963).

STEMBRIDGE, Stanley R., 'Disraeli and the Millstones', *Journal of British Studies*, V (1965).

STENGERS, Jean, 'The Partition of Africa: L'Impérialisme Colonial de la fin du XIXᵉ Siècle: Mythe ou Realité', *Journal of African History*, III (1962).

STERNBERG, Fritz, *Capitalism and Socialism on Trial* (Victor Gollancz, London, 1951).

STEWART-SMITH, D. G., *The Handmaidens of Diplomacy* (Monday Club, London, 1964).

STOKES, Eric, 'Great Britain and Africa; the myth of imperialism', *History Today*, 10 (1960).

— *Imperialism and the Scramble for Africa: the new view* (Local Series No. 10, Historical Association of Rhodesia and Nyasaland, 1963).

STRACHEY, John, *The End of Empire* (Victor Gollancz, London, 1959).

STRANG, Lord, *Home and Abroad* (Deutsch, London, 1956).

— *The Foreign Office* (Allen, London, 1956).

— *Britain in World Affairs* (Deutsch, London, 1961).

— *The Diplomatic Career* (Deutsch, London, 1962).

STRATFORD DE REDCLIFFE, Viscount, *The Eastern Question* (John Murray, London, 1881).

STRAUSS, William J., *Joseph Chamberlain and the Theory of Imperialism* (American Council on Public Affairs, Washington, 1942).

STRUPP, Karl, 'L'Intervention en Matière Financière', Academie de Droit International, *Recueil des Cours*, 8 (1925).

SUMNER, B. H., 'Tsardom and Imperialism in the Far East and Middle East, 1880–1914', *Proceedings of the British Academy*, XXVII (1941).

SUN, E-Tu Zen, *Chinese Railways and British Interests, 1898–1911* (King's Crown Press, New York, 1954).

SWEEZY, Paul M., *The Theory of Capitalist Development* (Dennis Dobson, London, 1946).

— *The Present as History* (Monthly Review Press, New York, 1953).

TAYLOR, A. J. P., *Germany's first bid for colonies, 1884–1885* (Macmillan & Co., London, 1938).

— 'British Policy in Morocco, 1886–1902', *English Historical Review*, 66 (July, 1951).

TEMPERLEY, Harold, *The Foreign Policy of Canning, 1822–1827* (G. Bell & Sons, London, 1925).

— 'Lord Granville's Unpublished Memorandum on Foreign Policy, 1852', *Cambridge Historical Journal*, II (1928).

— 'British policy towards Parliamentary Rule and Constitutionalism in Turkey (1830–1914)', *Cambridge Historical Journal*, IV (1933).

— and PENSON, Lillian M., *Foundations of British Foreign Policy from Pitt (1792) to Salisbury (1902)* (C.U.P., Cambridge, 1938).

THOMPSON, Sir Geoffrey, *Front-Line Diplomat* (Hutchinson, London, 1959).

THORNTON, A. P., 'British Policy in Persia, 1858–90, Parts I and II', *English Historical Review*, LXIX, LXX (1954–5).

— *The Imperial Idea and its Enemies* (Macmillan, London, 1959).

— *Doctrines of Imperialism* (Wiley, New York, 1965).

TILLEY, Sir John and GASELEE, Stephen, *The Foreign Office* (G. P. Putnam & Sons, London, 1933).

TILLEY, Sir John, *London to Tokyo* (Hutchinson & Co., London, 1942).

TISCHENDORF, Alfred P., 'The British Foreign Office and the Renewal of Anglo-Mexican Diplomatic Relations, 1867–1884', *Inter-American Economic Affairs*, XI (1957).

— 'The Loss of British Commercial Pre-eminence in Mexico, 1876–1911', *Inter-American Economic Affairs*, XI (1957).

— *Great Britain and Mexico in the era of Porfirio Díaz* (Duke University Press, Durham, N.C., 1961).

TREVELYAN, G. M., *The Life of John Bright* (Constable & Co., London, 1913).

— *Grey of Fallodon* (Longmans & Co., London, 1937).

TUCKWELL, Gertrude M., see GWYNN, Stephen and TUCKWELL, Gertrude M.

TURLINGTON, Edgar, *Mexico and Her Foreign Creditors* (Columbia University Press, New York, 1930).

TYLER, J. E., *The Struggle for Imperial Unity, 1868–1895* (Longmans & Co., London, 1938).

VANSITTART, Lord, *The Mist Procession* (Hutchinson, London, 1958).

VIALLATE, Achille, *Economic Imperialism and International Relations during the last fifty years* (The Macmillan Co., New York, 1923).

VILLIERS, H. Montagu, *Charms of the Consular Career* (Hutchinson, London, 1925).

VINER, Jacob, 'Political Aspects of International Finance, Parts I and II', *Journal of Business of the University of Chicago*, I (April and July, 1928).

— 'International Finance and Balance of Power Diplomacy, 1880–1914', *South Western Political and Social Science Quarterly*, IX (1929).

VYSE, Griffin W., *Egypt: Political, Financial and Strategical* (Allen & Co., London, 1882).

WANG, S. T., *The Margary Affair and the Chefoo Agreement* (O.U.P., London, 1940).

WARD, A. W., and GOOCH, G. P., (eds.), *The Cambridge History of British Foreign Policy, 1783–1919*, 3 vols. (C.U.P., Cambridge, 1922–3).

WARD, John M., *British Policy in the South Pacific 1786–1893* (Australasian Publishing Co., Sydney, 1948).

WATERFIELD, Gordon, *Layard of Nineveh* (John Murray, London, 1963).

WEBSTER, C. K., *The Foreign Policy of Castlereagh 1815–1822* (G. Bell & Sons, London, 1925).

— *The Foreign Policy of Palmerston, 1830–1841*, 2 vols. (G. Bell & Sons, London, 1951).

— *The Art and Practice of Diplomacy* (Chatto, London, 1961).

WEMYSS, Rosslyn, *Memoirs and Letters of the Rt. Hon. Sir Robert Morier*, 2 vols. (Edward Arnold, London, 1911).

WHARTON, Francis, *A Digest of the International Law of the United States*, 3 vols. (Govt. Printing Office, Washington, 1886).

WHIGHAM, H. J., *The Persian Problem* (Isbister & Co., London, 1903).

WILLIAMS, Benjamin H., *Economic Foreign Policy of the United States* (McGraw-Hill, New York, 1929).

WILLIAMS, Sir John Fischer, 'International Law and the Property of Aliens', *British Year Book of International Law*, IX (1928).

WILSON, Sir Arnold T., *The Persian Gulf* (Clarendon Press, Oxford, 1928).

— *Mesopotamia 1917–1920: a Clash of Loyalties* (O.U.P., London, 1931).

— *S.W. Persia, a Political Officer's Diary 1907–1914* (O.U.P., London, 1941).

WILSON, F. M. Huntington, 'The Relation of Government to Foreign Investment', *Annals of the American Academy of Political and Social Science*, 68 (1916).

WINCH, Donald, *Classical Political Economy and Colonies* (Bell, London, 1965).

WINKLER, Max, *Foreign Bonds, an Autopsy* (Roland Swain Co., Philadelphia, 1933).

WINSLOW, Earle, 'Marxian, Liberal and Sociological Theories of Imperialism', *Journal of Political Economy*, XXXIX (1931).

WOLF, John B., 'The Diplomatic History of the Baghdad Railroad', *University of Missouri Studies*, XI (1936).

WOOD, Alfred C., *A History of the Levant Company* (O.U.P., London, 1935).

WOOLF, Leonard, *Empire and Commerce in Africa: a study in Economic Imperialism* (George Allen & Unwin, London, 1920).

— *Economic Imperialism* (Harcourt, Brace & Howe, New York, 1920).

— *Imperialism and Civilization* (L. and V. Woolf, London, 1928).

— (ed.), *The Intelligent Man's Way to Prevent War* (Victor Gollancz, London, 1933).

WORTLEY, B. A., 'The Mexican Oil Dispute 1938–1946', *Transactions of the Grotius Society*, 43 (1957).

— *Expropriation in Public International Law* (C.U.P., Cambridge, 1959).

WYNNE, William H., see BORCHARD, Edwin, and WYNNE, William H.

YAPP, M. E., 'The Control of the Persian Mission, 1822–1836', *University of Birmingham Historical Journal*, VII (1959–1960).

YOUNG, George, *Diplomacy Old and New* (The Swarthmore Press Ltd., London, 1921).

YOUNG, L. K., 'British policy in China and the Boxer Rising, 1898–1902', Oxford thesis, 1960.

ZEBEL, Sydney H., 'Fair Trade: an English Reaction to the Breakdown of the Cobden Treaty System', *Journal of Modern History*, XII (1940).

INDEX

Aberdeen, Lord, and the bondholders, 35, 44n., 46n.; and Russia in Turkey, 93

Accountants, recommendation of, 120, 407, 409

Acland, F. D., 301

Addis, Sir Charles, 100, 297

Admiralty, and shipping subsidies, 146; and Persian oil, 240–2

Africa, markets in, 223, 256–61; British policy in, 249–61, 357, 358, 362, 363–6; Germany in, 258–9; France in, 249–52, 257, 259, 261; Foreign Office and commercial affairs in, 377

Africa and the Victorians, 253, 254

Agents, consuls as, 43–46, 131–5, 141, 166, 252, 346, 389–90, 409–10; diplomatists as, 60, 61, 141; recommendation of, 119–20, 407, 416; Commercial Agents, 389–93

Alcock, Sir Rutherford, on British policy in the Far East, 265

Alexandria, bombardment of, 165, 172, 175; riot in, 175, 176

America, Central, consuls as bond-holder agents in, 43–44, 45; Federal Debt of, 47–48; debt-collecting in, 138; British policy in, 323–5, 352

America, Latin, diplomatic postings in, xxi; H.M.G. and loans to, 13, 20, 316; British banks in, 33; H.M.G. and the bondholders in, 34, 35, 37n., 333–46; commercial treaties with, 86, 91–92, 315–16; Canning on equality of trade in, 90; debt-collecting in, 138; British policy in, 308–52, 360–8 *pass.*; foreign coercion of, 308–12, 316–18, 321–3, 339–40, 349–51; oil and politics in, 325–9; Monroe Doctrine and, 346–51

America, North, *see* United States of America

Anderson, M. S., 212n.

Anderson, Olive, 16n., 200n., 205

Anderson, Sir Percy, on promotion of individual interests, 99; and the Congo, 364

Anglo-Costa Rican Bank, 134

Anglo-Iranian Oil Co., cancellation of contract of, 69n.; nationalization of Persian interests of, 71n.; H.M.G.

and (in Mesopotamia), 195–7; H.M.G. and (in Persia), 240–2

Anglo-Saxon Petroleum Co., and Mesopotamian oil, 196; and Persian oil, 242

Antioquia Railway, claim of, 66n., 70

Arabi Pasha, and British intervention in Egypt, 173–9 *pass.*

Arbitration Agreements, 126

Arbuthnot, Charles, 182

Argentina, H.M.G. and forcible intervention in, xiv, 319, 321–3; railways buy British in, 29; H.M.G. and bondholders of, 35, 39n., 46n., 47n., 52; contract claim against, 66n.; discriminatory taxation in, 94; consul as railway chairman in, 134; and Free Trade propaganda, 143; debt-collecting in, 310; British mediation in, 320

Armenian massacres, and British policy, 187, 188, 189

Armitage-Smith, G., on state inter-ference, xxxv

Armstrong, naval contract for, 191

Asquith, H. H., on Free Trade, 97–98; on foreign competition, 107; on sugar bounties, 146; and Lord Cowdray, 328–9

Aston, W. G., and trade commissioners, 390

Austria, H.M.G. and loan to, 19, 152; and Egypt, 32, 160, 164, 167, 169; and credit information, 121; and sugar bounties, 145; and Turkey, 184

Avebury, Lord, 345–6

Backhouse, J., 127

Baden-Powell, George, on state interference, xxxiv–xxxv

Bagehot, Walter, on Clarendon, xiv–xv; on aristocrats in diplomacy, xxvii

Baghdad Railway, and the French Government, 8; and differential rates, 95; and German diplomacy, 188; and H.M.G., 207–17

Bailey, F. E., 184

Bakeless, J., 155

Balfour, A. J., on the Baghdad Railway, 212; and Chinese railway concessions, 284, 287; and Chinese

Balfour A. J., *continued*
loans, 302; and the Venezuelan
bondholders, 342–3
Balfour, Gerald, on *laissez-faire*, 102
Balta Liman Convention (1838), 86,
90, 184
Bankers, attitude of diplomatists to,
xviii; and relationship with H.M.G.,
23–33, 73–77; consuls as agents of,
134, 135; approached by Grey on
Turkish Loan, 193–4; persuaded by
Lansdowne to negotiate on
Baghdad Railway, 211–12; supported
in Persia, 225–6, 229–30; negotiated
with on Chinese loans, 269–70,
294–304. *See also* Imperial Bank of
Persia, Hong Kong & Shanghai
Bank, National Bank of Turkey
Banque de l'Indo-Chine, 295, 298
Banque Industrielle de Chine, 292
Barclay's Bank, 303
Baring Bros., and Evelyn Baring, 5;
and Gladstone, 74; and Turkish
loan, 193; and Chinese loans, 303;
Crisis, 228, 310
Baring, Evelyn, and Baring Bros., 5;
as bondholder representative in
Egypt, 160; appointed as Controller,
169; on evacuation of Egypt, 178.
See also Cromer
Bartlett, Sir E. Ashmead, 191
Baster, A. S. J., 32–33, 226
Bathurst, E., 127, 129
Baumann, Bentley M., on consular
attitude to trade, xxiii
Beaconsfield, Earl of, see Disraeli
Belfast Chamber of Commerce, 392
Belgium, and Chinese finance, 25,
285, 299–300; and commercial
information, 113, 121
Bell, Sir Hugh, objects to tied loans,
22
Bell, K., 199–200
Bell, Sir Lowthian, on future of
British trade, 270–1
Bentinck, Lord George, 36
Bergne, Sir Henry, on recommendation
of agents, 119; on credit information,
122; on consular reports, 124–5;
on debt-collecting, 137; on Africa
at Foreign Office, 377; on Commer-
cial Agents, 391; on diplomatic
assistance to individuals, 393
Berlin, Congress of, and the
bondholders, 47, 48; and British
intervention in Egypt, 165
Bernard, L. L., 181
Bertie, Sir Francis, on the French
Government and the Bourse, 8
Birch, Crisp & Co., Messrs., 300–1, 303

Birmingham Chamber of Commerce,
and Commercial Agents, 392
Bismark, Herbert, and commercial
promotions in Japan, 272
Bismark, Otto von, and the
Rothschilds, 167; on British
interests overseas, 354
Blackburn Chamber of Commerce, on
state intervention, xxxv; and
Commercial Agents, 392
Blaisdell, D. C., 198
Blanco, Guzman, 92
Blignières, M. de, 160, 166, 169
Block, Sir Adam, 198
Blunt, W. S., on aristocratic
pretensions in the Foreign Office,
xxvi; and the Egyptian bondholders,
154, 159; on Suez and the Cave
Mission, 157; and the deposition of
the Khedive, 167; and anarchy in
Egypt, 172; on the bombardment
of Alexandria, 175; on the
Euphrates Valley Railway, 208
Board of Trade, duty to public and
trade, xix; and Free Trade, xix,
xxxvii–xxxix, 102, 372; and *laissez-
faire*, xxx–xxxiv; and sugar
bounties, 102–3; on foreign
competition, 104–8; and
commercial information, 108–26
pass.; on debt-collecting, 138; and
Free Trade propaganda, 143–4; on
character of traders in the East,
268; commercial services provided
by, 371–81
Board of Trade Journal, 111–12, 118, 377
Boer War, 254–6
Bolivia, severance of diplomatic
relations with, 65
Bolton Iron & Steel Co., 190
Bondholders, and H.M.G., 34–53,
400–1, 405; consuls as agents for,
43–46, 135, 166, 252, 346; and
British policy in Egypt, 154–80
pass.; and H.M.G. in Turkey,
198–207, 400–1; and H.M.G. in
Morocco, 252; and H.M.G. in
Latin America, 308–12, 333–46,
400–1; Palmerston's 1848 Circular,
398–9; Granville and, 400–1
Bondholders, Council of the
Corporation of Foreign, and
H.M.G., 10, 11; origin of, 51
Booker, W. L., on commercial
information, 115
Booth, James, on H.M.G. and trade,
xix
Borchard, E. M., 20–21, 66
Bounties, H.M.G. and, 93–95, 102–3,
145–6

Bourke, R., on Chinese loans, 18; on Turkish bondholders, 37n.; on letters of introduction to bondholder agents, 42n.

Bourne, F. S. A., on concessions in Formosa, 60–61; on diplomatic support for Bss. in China, 307

Bourse, French Government and, 7–8

Bowring, E. A., on Free Trade and *laissez-faire*, xxxvii

Boyle, Sir Courtenay, on foreign competition, 106–8; on State intervention, 106–7, 108

Brackenbury, George, on concessions, 56

Bradbury, Lord, on state interference, xxxii–xxxiii

Brailsford, H. N., 5, 10, 308

Brassey, Thomas, and Turkish concession, 187

Brazil, diplomatic posting to, xxi; loans to, 19–20, 332; contract claims against, 67, 68; cancellation of concession by, 69; value of letter of introduction to, 127; H.M.G. and intervention in, 310–11; British Commercial Treaty with, 313n., 315–16; British mediation in, 320; and intervention in the River Plate, 320, 322

Brebner, J. Bartlett, xxxiii

Bright, John, on aristocratic diplomatists, xxv; and Egypt, 174, 176

British and Chinese Corporation, negotiates 'tied' loan, 21, 28; and H.M.G., 31–33, 294–304 *pass.*

British Iron Trade Association, and diplomatic pressure in China, 58–59

British Trade Corporation, and Chinese loans, 302–3

Brocklehurst, W. C., on F.O. and Board of Trade, 376

Brockway, T. P., 219, 225–6, 226–7

Broderick, John, on 'touting' for trade, 133

Brodrick, St. John, on concessions, 62–63, 296; on recommendation of agents, 119; on contracts, 191–2; on British policy in China, 289–90; and Commercial Attachés, 388; and Commercial Agents, 390–1

Brown, Shipley & Co., and Chinese loans, 299–304

Bruce, Sir Frederick, on use of force in China, 266

Bryan, William Jennings, and British oil interests in Mexico, 326

Bryce, James, on Foreign Service

attitude to commerce, xxiv; on bondholders, 38–39; on contracts and concessions, 56–57, 59, 60, 61; and foreign competition, 82; on promotion of individual interests, 97, 99, 141; on consular reports, 116; on recommendation of lawyers, 120; on credit information, 121; on introductions, 131; on debt-collecting, 139; and British interests in China, 274; Memorandum by, 275–6, 403–15; on Consuls as trade agents, 390

Buchanan, and concessions in China, 62

Buenos Ayres Great Southern Railway Co., 134

Bülow, Baron von, on the Partition of China, 305

Bulwer, Sir Henry Lytton, on trade and finance, xvi; on debt-collecting, 137; and Turkish concessions, 186; and Turkish loans, 199

Bunch, Robert, on 'Convention' bondholders, 52–53; on Anglo-Venezuelan Commercial Treaty, 92

Burgin, E. L., on commercial information, 148

Burma, nationalization of property by, 71n.; annexation of Upper Burma, 262

Burma/Yunnan Railway, H.M.G. and, 14, 276

Burmah Oil Co., 204

Caillard, Vincent, 210

Caisse de la Dette Publique (Egypt), 160

California, proposal for British colonization of, 355–6

Campbell, Sir Gerald, on status of Consuls, xxii

Canals, in Malay peninsula, 263; in Central America, 324

Canning, George, on guaranteed loans, 13; on the bondholders, 34–35; on equality in world trade, 90; on Persia, 220; on Latin America, 313, 316, 348, 352; and reform of Consular Service, 384

Canning, Sir Stratford (Viscount Stratford de Redcliffe), on trade, xvi; and Layard, xxvi; and Ottoman Bank, 32; and British policy in Turkey, 93, 182, 184, 185, 205, 250; on honesty in diplomacy, 186; and loan to Turkey, 199; and extension of trade, 222–3

Canton/Kowloon Railway, 'tied' loan for, 21

Capitulations, in Turkey, 90–91, 190; and debt-collecting, 136–7; and intervention in Egypt, 162, 164, 165, 210. *See also* Exterritoriality

Carden, Sir Lionel, and the Guatemalan bondholders, 47; in Mexico, 327, 328

Cardwell, E., and Turkish loan, 16; and Board of Trade, 372–3

Cartwright, W. C., on debt-collecting, 138

Cassell, Sir Ernest, and National Bank of Turkey, 194

Castlereagh, Lord, and the French *rentes*, 48; and British policy in Latin America, 312–13, 351, 352

Cave, Stephen, mission to Egypt of, 157–8

Cave Committee, 379

Ceará Water Co., contract claim by, 68

Cecil, Algernon, on Foreign Service recruitment, xxviii–xxix; on F.O. and Board of Trade, 375, 376

Cecil, Lord Robert, on trade in diplomacy, 96, 378–9

Chamber of Commerce Journal, on *laissez-faire*, xxxiii

Chamberlain, Henry, 381–2, 383–4

Chamberlain, Joseph, on commerce and government departments, xv–xvi; and tariffs, xxxviii, 107; and Rhodes, 5; on foreign competition, 105; on government intervention, 105; Circular despatch, 105–6; and intervention in Egypt, 175, 176; on evacuation of Egypt, 179; and Baghdad Railway, 211–12; and Partition of Africa, 255, 256–7, 365; on the Open Door in China, 291

Chambers of Commerce, overseas, xvii, 126, 188–9, 268; on state interference, xxxv–xxxvii; and diplomatic assistance, 57, 58, 82, 141; and commercial information, 112, 113–14, 118, 120–1, 123–4, 148; on F.O. and Board of Trade, 373, 376–7, 379; and Commercial Agents, 392

Charles, Archduke, and the throne of Mexico, 318

Chartered Bank, 303

Chatfield, Frederick, and the bondholders, 41, 43, 48n.

Chérif Pasha, 166–7

Chevalier, Michel, and the Anglo-French Commercial Treaty, 87–88

Childers, Hugh C. E., on foreign loans, 17, 269–70; and Egypt, 174

Chile, loan issue to, 12; H.M.G. and bondholders in, 47, 48, 337–9; expropriation of Nitrate Railways by, 70; H.M.G. and intervention in, 319, 320, 321, 347

China, H.M.G. and loans to, 14–15, 17–18, 19, 34, *269–70*, 271–2, *281–3*, 290, 293, *294–304*, 306–7; tied loans in, 21–22; railways in, 21, 31, 58–9, 62, 100, 105, 267, 268–9, 274, 276, 280, *283–9*, 290, 291, 292, *294–8*, 301, 306; H.M.G. and British financiers in, 25, 30–33, 100, 269–70, *294–304*; British policy in, 32–33, *262–307*, 358–68 *pass.*; diplomatists as only link with government in, 43; *Times* and trade promotion in, 57–58; German diplomatic pressure in, 57–59; U.S. diplomatic pressure in, 59; H.M.G. and concessions in, 58–60, 61, 62, 64, 65, *283–9*, 291–8, H.M.G. and opening of, 85, 86; Commercial Treaties with, 86; France and preferential treatment in, 95; H.M.G.'s opposition to differential rates and privileges in, 95; Consular Service in, 104, 115–16, 383, 385, 386; letters of introduction in, 127, 128; the Partition of, 276–83; the 'Battle of Concessions' in, *283–9*; spheres of interest in, 289–94; international finance in, 294–304; commercial attaché in, 387–8

China Association, and expansion of trade, 266; on state-aided foreign competition, 286, 289

Chinese Engineering and Mining Co., and Chinese loan, 300

Chinese Imperial Railway, H.M.G. and, 5on., 296

Chinese Reorganization Loan, 299–301, 307

Churchill, Winston, on influence of capital, 3; on Free Trade, 107–8; and Persian oil, 241–2

Civil Establishments, Royal Commission on (Ridley Commission), on promotion of individual interests, 97, 99–100; on F.O. and Board of Trade, 376; on reform of Consular Service, 385

Civil Service, Royal Commission on (Macdonnell Commission), and social composition of Diplomatic Service, xvii–xviii, xxviii; on concessions, 65; on promotion of individual interests, 65, 96, 97; and consular reports, 125; and introductions, 131; on consuls as agents,

132; on reform of Consular Service, 386–7

Clarendon, Lord, interest in commerce, xiv; on guaranteed loans, 15; on commercial information, 109–10; on introductions, 128; on British interest in Turkey and Egypt, 156; recommends Turkish loan, 200–201; on use of force in China, 266; on British policy in Central America, 324; on the Monroe Doctrine, 348

Clark, Sir William, on the Dept. of Overseas Trade, 379–80

Clayton-Bulwer Treaty (1850), and British policy in Central America, 323–5

Clipperton, Charles, on 'touting' for for trade, 135–6

Cobden, Richard, and Anglo-French Commercial Treaty, xxv, 87–88; on opening of China and Japan to trade, 85, 265–6; and Free Trade propaganda, 143–4; on H.M.G. in Central America, 324–5; and the Mexican bondholders, 335; on imperial expansion, 360

Cobden Club, xxxviii; 104

Cockerell, S. P., on consular reports, 125

Cohen, Sir Robert Waley, on politics and business, 196

Colombia (New Granada), H.M.G. and bondholders in, 35, 47, 312; consuls as agents in, 43, 44n., 134; contract claims against, 67n.; expropriation of property by, 66n., 70; and wish to terminate Commercial Treaty, 91

Colonial Office, on letters of introduction, 129; and proposed colony in California, 355–6

Colonial preference, Giffen on, 103; and West Indian sugar, 102–3, 145; Chamberlain and Asquith on, 107

Colonies, foreign competition in, 105–106

Colvin, Auckland, 169, 173

Commerce, attitude of politicians to, xiii–xvi, 404; attitude of officials to, xvi–xxv *pass.*, 394–7, 403–4

Commercial Agents, low status of, xxi–xxii; and recommendation of agencies, 119–20; and credit information, 122–3; and debt-collecting, 137–8; and Commercial Department, 377; history of, 389–93

Commercial Attachés, and Romanian loan, xviii; low status of, xxi–xxiii; and 'touting' for trade, 133; and

Commercial Department, 377; history of, 381, 382, 387–9, 393; Bryce on, 407, 411–12

Commercial Department (Foreign Office), functions of, 97, 374, 375–6, 377; treatment of consular reports by, 124; formation of, 373–4, 404; relationship with the Board of Trade, 374–9; Bryce on, 412

Commercial Diplomatic Service, history of, 379–81, 393–5

Commercial Information, *see* Information

Commercial Intelligence, Advisory Committee on, 112–113; 378

Commercial Intelligence, Departmental Committee on (1898), formation and recommendations of, 112, 378; on credit information, 122; on consuls as agents, 132

Commercial Intelligence Branch (Board of Trade), Chamberlain and, 105; formation and duties, 112–13, 123, 378

Commercial Intelligence Committee, Sub-Committee of, on 'tied' loans, 22

Commercial Secretaries, 381, 382, 389, 394

Commercial travellers, diplomatists and, xviii

Commercial Treaties, H.M.G. and, 85–92, 147; with Turkey, 86, 90, 184; with Persia, 220, 222; with China, 265; with Latin America, 315–6; drafting and negotiation of, 372, 373, 375–6

Concessions, H.M.G. and, xviii, 25–27, *54–72*, 404–5, 406, 410, 414, 416; in Persia, 56–7, 63–4, 65, 69n., *224–8*, 233, *235–40*, 243; in China, 58–60, 61, 62, 64, 65, 267, 268–9, 274–6, 282–3, *283–9*, 290, *295–8*, 305; in Turkey, 61–63, 65, 186–7, 189, 190, 192, 193, 195, 196–7, 209–10, 214, 217–18; Granville on, 129–30, 402; consular instructions on, 130; *The Economist* on, 189; distinction between 'political' and ordinary, 235, 237–8, 293–4; in Tunis, 249–52; in Morocco, 252; in Tibet and S.E. Asia, 262–3; and Open Door in China, 291–4; in Latin America, 332–3. *See also* Reuter Concession, Talbot Concession, Railways, Loans

Confiscation (of foreign property), 70–71

Congo, British policy in, 257, 261, 364

Constans, Jean E., on the Macedonian Reforms, 190

Consular Establishment, Select Committee on (1835), recommendations, 384

Consular Instructions, on commercial information, 114; on credit information,123; on agencies, 134; on debt recovery, 139; on trade, 381–2

Consular Service, low status of, xxi–xxiii, 396–7; deficiencies of, xxii; transfer to Diplomatic Service, xxv–xxvi; Chambers of Commerce on, xxxvi; duties in China of, 104; and commercial information, 108–26 *pass.*; and introductions, 130–1; and 'touting' for trade, 131–6; and agencies held by, 133–5; and debt-collecting, 136–9; and the Levant Co., 182; organization of, 374, 376, 378, 379, 380, 381, *382*–7, 395; and Commercial Agents, 389–91; and the Bryce Memorandum, 403–15 *pass.*

Consular Service, Departmental Committee on (Walrond Committee, 1903), and commercial information, 117, 125; and reform of Consular Service, 385–6

Consular Service, Departmental Committee on (1912), recommendations of, 386

Consular Service and Appointments, Select Committee on (1858), recommendations, 384–5

Contracts, H.M.G. and, *54*–72, 404–5, 410, 414; information on, 112; in Turkey, 190–2, 196–7, 217–18; in China, 271–3, 274–6, 301–2; in Latin America, 332–3

Control, International Financial, in Greece, 12, 47; in Portugal, 17; in Egypt, 163–79 *pass.*; in Turkey, 205–7

Convention bondholders, as distinguished from ordinary bondholders, 52–53, 335–6

Cooke, Henry, and credit information, 122; and debt-collecting, 137–8; and British Chambers of Commerce, 392; on Commercial Agents, 392

Copyrights, 126

Corbett, Mr., and bondholder agency, 44, 45

Costa Rica, diplomatist as bondholder agent in, 43–44, 45; consul as bank cashier in, 134

Cotton, xviii, xxxix n., 156–7, 185

Countervailing duties, and H.M.G., 145–6, 147

Cowdray, Lord, and H.M.G. in Mexico, 325–9

Cowper, Consul, 134

Cox, Sir Percy, and Persian oil, 241; and German trade in the Persian Gulf, 248

Cranborne, Lord, on 'touting' for trade, 132–3; on debt-collecting, 137–8; on 'new departure' in commercial diplomacy, 142

Crawford, Earl of, and government control over capital issues, 11

Crawfurd, Oswald, on Consular reports, 116

Crédit Foncier, and French Government, 30; in Tunis, 250

Credit information, H.M.G. and, 120–3, 407, 408–9

Crimean War, and Turkish loans, 200–5

Crisp Syndicate, and Chinese loans, 18, 300–1, 303

Cromer, Lord, on origin of Egyptian Question, 157; on contrast between British and French policy in Egypt, 160–1, 356; on H.M.G. and bondholders, 165; on Egypt in 1882, 174, 175; and imperial expansion, 357, 359n. *See also* Baring, Evelyn

Crowe, Sir Eyre, on Consular Service, 123; on German competition, 238, 367; on British foreign policy, 353, 354; on government assistance to trade overseas, 416–7

Crowe, J. A., on low status of commercial diplomacy, xxii–xxiii, 152; on concessions, 55; and duties as commercial attaché, 387–8

Culbertson, W. S., 10, 155

Currie, Bertram Wodehouse, and Gladstone, 74

Currie, Sir Philip, on diplomatists and trade, 61n., 363; on consuls as agents, 132

Curzon, Lord, on limits to government intervention, 76, 83; on effect of Free Trade on diplomacy, 145; and the Persian Gulf, 245, 246n., 358; on markets in the East, 271; on unfair competition in the East, 277; on the German and Russian threat in China, 283–4; on British imperialism in the Far East, 288–9; and Chinese loans, 302–3; on foreign competition in Latin America, 331; on imperial expansion, 359

Czechoslovakia, nationalization of property by, 71n.

D'Abernon, Lord (Sir Edgar Vincent), and Ottoman Public Debt, 198; Mission to Latin America of, 331

Dahl, Victor, 52n.

Daïra debt, 166

D'Arcy, William Knox, and Mesopotamian oil, 196; and Persian oil,
239–41

Debts, officials and collection of
trading debts, xxiii, xxxvi, *136–9*,
405, 407, 409, 417n.; at
Constantinople, 136–7, 186. *See
also* Bondholders (for national
debts)

de Bunsen, Maurice, on British
policy in Turkey, 187–8; Mission to
Latin America, 331

Delagoa Bay Railway, cancellation of
concession of, 40n., 69, 70–71

Depression, effects on British policy of,
81–82, 362–3, 364, 414–5, (in
Africa) 256, 260–1, (in China)
273–4; and European Commercial
Treaties, 88–90

Depression of Trade and Industry,
Royal Commission on, on German
competition, 81–82; on promotion
of individual interests, 97; on
consuls as agents for particular
firms, 132; on trade commissioners,
390

Derby, Earl of (Lord Stanley), on
H.M.G. and bondholders, 37n.;
on British policy in Egypt, 158,
163–4; on Turkish loans, 201; on
British policy in China, 268; and
intervention in the River Plate,
319, 320

Dering, Sir Herbert, on bankers, xviii

Deutsche Asiatische Bank, 30, 295,
298

Deutsche Bank, and Ottoman Bank,
8; and Turkey, 31, 181, 193

Díaz, Porfirio, and Lord Cowdray,
325–6

Differentials, as grounds for intervention on behalf of the bondholders,
39–40, 46; H.M.G. and (in overseas
trade), 93–95; and Baghdad
Railway, 213–17; in Persia, 230,
235, 243–4; in Africa, 258–9; in
Spain, 270–1; in China, 271, 285,
286, 305; in Latin America, 312–13

Dilke, Sir Charles, attitude in Foreign
Office to appointment of, xxvi;
on policy in Egypt, 173, 174, 175–6,
177; and Turkish railways, 209;
and imperial expansion, 364

Diplomatic and Consular Services,
Select Committee on (1870–2), and
consuls as agents, 133; and debt-
collecting, 137; and reform of
Consular Service, 384–5

'Diplomaticus', on British policy in
Persia, 223; on Free Trade and
Protection, 223

Diplomatists, attitude to trade and
finance, xvi–xxv, 403–4;
aristocratic recruitment of, xxv–xxx;
instructions as to trade, 381;
attitude to commercial diplomacy,
394–5, 396–7

Disconto Gesellschaft, and the
Venezuelan bondholders, 341

Discrimination, *see* Differentials

Disraeli, Benjamin, on reform of
Consular Service, xxi; on importance of commerce, xxi; on Control
in Turkey, 15–16; Egyptian policy
of, 156, 170–1; and Egyptian
bondholders, 167; on intervention
in Mexico, 318; and imperialism,
277, 356–7

Dodson, Sir J., on contract claims,
66n., 67

Dominican Republic, H.M.G. and
bondholders in, 33n.; landing of
detachment in, 321

Dom Pedro I Railway, cancellation of
concession of, 69

Dufferin and Ava, Marquis of, and
Whitaker Wright, 74; and Turkish
Debt, 206

Dunlop, Hamilton, on state intervention, xxxv

Dunlop, Commodore Hugh, and British
policy in Mexico, 317–18; and the
Dunlop Convention, 335–6

Eastern Bank, and Chinese loans,
299–304

East India Co., and diplomatists'
attitude to trade, xxiv–xxv; and
Tehran Legation, 220; and Persian
Gulf, 222, 244, 245; and the
Consular Service, 383

Economic Causes of War, 74

Economist, on *Board of Trade Journal*,
112; on concessions, 189; on
Baghdad Railway, 211

Ecuador, H.M.G. and bondholders
in, 47

Eden, Anthony, and Foreign Service
reform (1943), 380, 395–6

Edinburgh Review, 289–90

Edward VII, 5

Egypt, guaranteed loans to, 16–17;
bankers and foreign governments
in, 32; H.M.G. and bondholders in,
34, 49, 154–80 *pass.*; nationalization
of Suez Canal by, 71n.; monopolies
in, 93; and compensation to shareholders, 94; British policy in,

Egypt, *continued*
    154–80, 182–4, 256, 257, 356;
    French policy in, 154–180 *pass.*;
    Austria in, 160, 164, 167, 169;
    Italy in, 160, 169; Germany in,
    164, 167, 169; in German diplomacy,
    210; and Partition of Africa, 253
*Egypt's Ruin: a Financial and Administra-
    tive Record*, 154, 159
Elgin, 7th. Earl of, mission to Porte, 182
Elgin, 8th. Earl of, and British policy
    in China, 265; on the 'Arrow' War,
    266
Elliot, Arthur D., 159–60
Elliot, H. C., on U.S. reaction to
    coercion of Venezuela, 347
Empire and Commerce in Africa, 253
Engineering Trades, Departmental
    Committee on (1917), on diplo-
    matists' attitude to trade, xxiv; on
    Consular Service, 387
Euphrates Valley Railway, 13, 208
Europe, finance and trade in British
    policy in, 151–2
Exhibitions (International), 126,
    378
Expropriation (of foreign property),
    70–71
Exterritoriality, and collection of debts,
    136; and consular duties, 383.
    See also Capitulations

Fair Trade, demand for, 83–84
Farrer, Lord, and state intervention,
    xxx–xxxi; and Free Trade, xxxviii;
    on the bondholders, 52; and sugar
    bounties, 102, 145; on F.O. and
    Board of Trade, 375
Fay, C. R., 315
Federation of British Industries, on
    officials as salesmen, 136; and
    commercial information, 148; on
    F.O. and Board of Trade, 379
Feis, Herbert, 310, 336, 337
Ferns, H. S., 310, 319, 323
Fieldhouse, D. K., 363
Finance and Industry, Committee on
    (1931), on state planning, xxxii;
    Bradbury's Memorandum of
    Dissent, xxxii; on 'tied' loans, 23;
    on contrast between British and
    European banking, 23–24;
    on survival of *laissez-faire*,
    142
Fishery agreements, 126
Fitzmaurice, Lord Edmond, and Rio
    legation, xxi; on H.M.G. and
    Egyptian finance, 178; on N.W.
    African Co., 259–60; and the
    Peruvian bondholders, 338

Fitzmaurice, G. H., 192, 193
Force, use of, 85, 266–7
Foreign Office, duty to trade of, xix;
    status of commercial work in,
    xxi; attitude to trade in, xxiv, 396;
    aristocratic composition of, xxvi–xxx;
    commercial services of, 371–81
Foreign Office, Departmental
    Committee on (1916), on concessions,
    65; on promotion of individual
    interests, 97; on commercial
    information, 123; extract from
    Report of, 416–17
Forman, Buxton, and *laissez-faire*,
    xxxii n.
Formosa, concessions in, 60
Forster, W. E., and the colonies,
    357
Foster, Mr., and financial report on
    Turkey, 202
France, control over capital exports,
    7–8; and Ottoman Bank, 8; and
    Greek finance, 12; and Brazilian
    loan, 19–20; bankers and investors
    in, 23–25; and capitalist combination
    in China, 25; British bondholders
    in, 36n., 46n., 48–49; and Peruvian
    bondholders, 49–50, 338–9; Anglo-
    French Commercial Treaties,
    86–90; compensation for shareholders
    obtained by, 94; preferential treat-
    ment in China for, 95; trade and
    foreign policy in, 101; competition
    of, 104–8; commercial information
    provided by, 113; and shipping
    subsidies, 146; Egyptian policy of,
    154–80 *pass.*; and the Egyptian
    bondholders, 160–1; finance of,
    in Turkey, 185, 189, 194; and the
    Macedonian reforms, 190; and
    concessions in Turkey, 195; and
    Turkish loans, 200–1; and Persia,
    220, 236, 237; and Tunis, 249–52;
    and Africa, 257, 259, 261; and
    Upper Burma, 262; and Partition
    of China, 271, 276, 277, 281, 283,
    290; and Chinese finance, 292, 295,
    297, 298, 301, 303; and coercion
    of Mexico, 316–18; and coercion
    of Venezuela, 349, 350n.; Latin
    American investment of, 352;
    tariffs as a factor in British
    imperial expansion, 363–6; trade
    and finance of, in Anglo-French
    relations, 367–8
Frankel, S. H., 259
Free Trade, attitude of politicians
    and officials to, xxxvii–xxxix, 104–8,
    372; H.M.G. and, 181; attack on,
    83–84; Anglo-French Commercial

Treaty and, 86–90; effect of, on commercial and financial policy, 142–7, 353, 360–2, 363, 367; propaganda for, 143; as a factor in British imperialism, 147

Free Trade Congress, International, 107

Free Trade versus Fair Trade, xxxviii

Fremantle, Sir Charles, 345–6

Freycinet, C. de, on France, Britain, and the bondholders, 161; and bombardment of Alexandria, 175; on Gladstone and Egypt, 180

Fuchs, C. J., on Fair Trade, 84

Gallagher, J., on British policy in Africa, 253–60 *pass.*, 357, 358, 363, 365; on H.M.G. and Latin America, 310–12, 316, 323; and the 'Imperialism of Free Trade', 360–2

Gambetta, Léon, 174

Gastrell, W. H. S., on state intervention, xxxi; on commercial information, 123–4

George V, 5

Germany, control over capital exports from, 7–8; and Brazilian loan, 19; and tied loans, 21; bankers, industrialists, and investors in, 23–25, 28; and capitalist combinations in China, 25; and Egypt, 32, 164, 167, 169; diplomatic pressure in China and Japan of, 57–59; competition of, 81, 104–8, 367; evasion of m-f-n clause by, 93; and the 'German system' of diplomacy, xxxvii, 96–97, 99; trade and foreign policy in, 101; commercial information supplied by, 113, 115–16; and sugar bounties, 145; and shipping subsidies, 146; and trade in Turkey, 184–5; Turkish policy of 188, 189–90; and Turkish contracts and concessions, 191, 192; and Young Turks, 192–3; and Convention with H.M.G. on Asiatic Turkey, 196–7, 215; and Turkish railways, 209–17 *pass.*; and Persian railways, 230–1; and Persian concessions, 236–9; and Persian trade, 243–4; and the Persian Gulf, 244–8; in Africa, 258–9; and Chinese and Japanese contracts and concessions, 272–3, 274–5, 292; and Partition of China, 279–83, 290, 305; and banks in China, 295, 297, 301; and coercion of Venezuela, 308, 339–40, 349; and the Venezuelan bondholders, 341, 345; and British foreign policy, 357–8,

367–8; tariffs and competition of, as factors in British imperial expansion, 363–7

Giffen, Sir Robert, on government intervention, xxxii n., 102–4; and Free Trade, xxxviii; on foreign competition, 107; on sugar bounties 145

Gladstone, W. E., on tariffs, xxxviii, 145; on guaranteed loans, 15; friendship with Currie, 74; as agent of bankers, 74; on Anglo-French Commercial Treaty, 87–89; on reciprocal trade agreements, 90, 144; on treaties in perpetuity, 91; the Egyptian bondholders and, 154, 156; Egyptian policy of, 170–80 *pass.*; and imperial expansion, 261, 355, 356–7, 360; and the Board of Trade, 372

Glasgow Chamber of Commerce, on state intervention, xxxv; and diplomatic assistance, 58; on commercial information, 114

Globe, 12

Gordon, Lucie Duff, 113

Gorst, Sir Eldon, report on Commercial Attachés by, 388–9, 393

Goschen, George, and Messrs. Frühling and Goschen, 5, 155, 158–9; on H.M.G. and the bondholders, 51–52; and the Egyptian bondholders, 158–60; on the Turkish Debt, 206

Gosselin, Sir M., on credit information, 121

Goulburn, Henry, on H.M.G. and the bondholders, 35

Granville, Lord, on H.M.G.'s duty to trade, xv; on loan policy in China, 17, 269; and the bondholders, 38, 400–1; and concessions, 56; on promotion of individual interests, 97; on letters of introduction, 130–1, 400–1; on consular agencies, 133–4; and British policy in Egypt, 173, 174, 176; on Turkish Debt, 206; on trade and annexation in Africa, 261; on the Peruvian bondholders, 338

Greaves, R. L., 231–2, 357

Greece, financial intervention in, 12; H.M.G. and bondholders in, 47; appropriation of property by, 71n.

Greenhill, Thomas, contract claim by, 68n.

Grey, Sir Edward, on H.M.G. and loan issues, 19–20, 152; and lack of contact with financial houses, 23; on difficulty of interesting British

Grey, Sir Edward, *continued*
capital in Persia and Turkey, 27, 210; and concessions in Turkey, 61, 62, 65; and concessions in China, 65, 293–4; on policy in Persia, 65, 358; on Turkish contract claim, 68n.; on H.M.G. and concessions, 73; on support of individual firms, 100; on policy in Turkey, 187; and Turkish loans, 193, 194–5; and Baghdad railway, 207, 214–17; and German pressure in Turkey, 210; and the Lynch concession, 217; on Russia in Persia, 224, 233–5; on the Anglo-Russian Convention (1907), 234–7; on Germany in Persia, 238, 243–4; on trade with Persia, 243–4; and Chinese railways, 297–8; and financial monopoly in China, 297–301; and British policy in Mexico, 326–9; and Brazilian loan, 332; on British policy in Latin America, 352

Guatemala, contract claim against, 34n.; H.M.G. and bondholders in, 47, 50, 312

Gurney, Russell, 201

Haidan Pasha/Ismid Railway, contract claim by, 68n.

Hallgarten, G. W. F., 5, 155

Hamid, Sultan Abdul, 187, 188, 190, 191

Hamilton, Mr., and guaranteed loan to Mexico, 316

Hamilton, Lord Frederic, on aristocrats in diplomacy, xxvii

Hamilton, Lord George, on Persia and India, 222, 246

Hammond, Edmund, on H.M.G. and bondholders, 37–38; on introductions, 128; on Turkish 1862 loan, 203; on the use of force in Japan, 267; and the Commercial Department, 374

Hankow/Canton Railway, 297

Hankow/Szechuan Railway, 297

Harbours, in Persia, 64, 238; contract claim in Guatemala, 68n.; in China, 292, 293; in Latin America, 333

Harcourt, Sir William, on evacuation of Egypt, 178, 179

Harding, J. D., on the bondholders, 37, 46, 47n.; on a contract claim, 68n.

Hardinge, Sir Arthur, on diplomatists and trade, xvii; on Persian loans, 229–30; and the D'Arcy concession, 239–40

Hardinge, Sir Charles, on concessions

in Persia, 63–64; on Open Door in Persia, 238; and the Persian Gulf, 245, 248

Hardware, xviii, 105, 185

Harris, Alexander, 105

Harris, N. D., 155

Harrowby, Earl of, on commercial depression, 82

Hart, Sir Robert, 281, 283

Hartington, Lord, and intervention in Egypt, 175; on evacuation of Egypt, 179

Hay, Edward Drummond, and British policy in Morocco, 252; and N.W. African Co., 259–60

Hay, John, and European coercion of Guatemala, 350

Helm, Elijah, on consular reports, 113

Henwood, W. J., 127

Hertslet, Sir Ernest, on discriminatory taxation, 94

Hirst, Francis, on commerce and the Foreign Office, xviii; on the Civil Service and Free Trade, xxxviii–xxxix; on Chamberlain and Rhodes, 5

Hobart, Lord, and the Imperial Ottoman Bank, 32; and Turkish loans, 202–3

Hobson, C. K., 10

Hobson, J. A., 5, 153; on the bondholders in politics, 34; on finance and British imperialism, 76–77, 363; on British policy in Africa, 253, 254

Hohler, Sir Thomas, on British policy in Turkey, 188n.; and British policy in Mexico, 327, 328

Holt, R. D., on promotion of individual interests, 96–97

Honduras, H.M.G. and the bondholders in, 49, 312; and the Mosquito Indians, 325

Hong Kong, 'New Territories', lease of, 281

Hong Kong & Shanghai Bank, and 'tied' loans, 21–22, 28; and relationship with H.M.G., 30–33, 100, 269–70, *294–304*, 331; and Newchwang line, 285, 286

Hornby, Sir Edmund, on contracts and concessions, 54–55; on Levant Consular Service, 186; on debt-collecting, 186; on misappropriation of Turkish 1855 loan, 202

Howe, Frederic C., 154–5

Huerta, Victoriano, and H.M.G., 325–9

Hughes, Mr., and the opening of Paraguay, 128–9

Hukuang Railway, 1911 loan, 21, 28, 298
Hume, James Deacon, and Free Trade, xxxviii
Hunter, W. A., 57
Huskisson, William, and tariffs, xxxviii, 86, 372
Hutchinson, Consul, 134

Iddesleigh, Earl of, and the Peruvian bondholders, 49–50
Imlah, Albert H., 3
Imperial Bank of Persia, rationale of British support for, 26, 225–6, 233, 243, 331; as agent of H.M.G., 30–31, 229–30
Imperial Brazilian Mining Corporation, 127
Imperial Defence, Committee of, and the Baghdad Railway, 213; on Persian railways, 233; and Persia, 243
Imperial National Bank of Turkey, 31–32
Imperial Ottoman Bank, 181, 198; and French Government, 8, 31, 193, 195
Inchcape, Lord, on state interference, xxxvii; and navigation of Tigris and Euphrates, 217
India, and 'tied' loans, 29; and British diplomacy, 32, 256; British banks in, 33; and sugar bounties, 145; importance of Turkey to, 182–4; and communications in Asiatic Turkey, 208–9, 211–17; and interest in Persia, 219–44 *pass.*; and interest in Persian Gulf, 244–8; and British policy in Africa, 253–6, 260; and British policy in the Far East, 262–3, 271; and communications with China, 268. *See also* Suez Canal
Industrial property conventions, 126
Industry and Trade, Committee on, on manufacturers and tariffs, xxxix n.; on direction of capital, 11; on commercial information, 114; on shipping subsidies, 146; on retaliation, 146; on most-favoured-nation clause, 147n.; on the Commercial Diplomatic Service, 380
Information (commercial), H.M.G. and, 106–7, *108–26*, 140, 148, 151, 404–16 *pass.*; in Latin America, 331; Board of Trade and improved service of, 377–8, 381; and Commercial Attachés, 387–8; and Commercial Agents, 389–93; and the

Commercial Diplomatic Service, 393–4. *See also* Credit information
Insurance, Uruguayan State Monopoly of, 70; Italian State Monopoly of, 70; consuls as agents for, 134–5
Introduction, letters of, and bondholder agents, 42, 401; and businessmen, 126–31; Granville's Circular on, 402; Bryce on, 409; Crowe on, 416
Iron and Steel Trades, Departmental Committee on, and 'tied' loans, 22
Iron Trade Association (British), 270–1
Irrigation, in Persia, 64; in Turkey, 192–3, 196–7
Ismail, Khedive, 94; spendthrift administration of, 157; and Cave Mission, 157–8; and Goschen's Mission, 160; debt to H.M.G. of, 163; and the Commission of Inquiry, 164, 165, 166; *coup d'état* by, 166–7; abdication of, 167–8
Ismidt/Angora railway, 210
Italy, confiscation claim against, 70; and Egypt, 160, 169; Turkish warship contract for, 191; and Turkish concessions, 195; and Tunis, 249–52

Japan, and capitalist combinations in China, 25; German pressure in, 59, 272–3; commercial treaty with, 86; British policy in, 263–4, 304, 360; opening of Japan to trade, 265–6, 267–8; use of force in, 267; and Manchurian concessions, 293–4; and loans to China, 301, 303; Consular Service in, 383, 385, 386; Commercial Attaché in, 388
Jardine, Matheson & Co., and H.M.G., 285, 294–304 *pass.*
Jardine, Sir Robert, and diplomatic support in China, 59
Jenner, Herbert, on contract claims, 67
Jersey Committee, 377
Joel, Lewis, on consuls as agents, 131–2
Jones, Sir Lawrence, xviii
Jordan, Sir John, and capitalist combinations in China, 25; on enterprises reserved to Bss. in China, 64, 293–4; and monopoly finance in China, 298
Joseph, Philip, 277

Karun River, opening to navigation of, 225, 230, 233

Keay, Seymour, 57
Kelly, Sir David, 372, 380
Kennedy, C. M., on F.O. and Board of Trade, 375–6
Keynes, J. M., xxx, xxxiv
Kiao-chau, seizure of, 279, 280
Kimberley, Lord, on British policy in Malay Peninsula, 263
Knox, Philander C., 10
Kwangchow Wan, lease of, 281
Kynochs, and Turkish cartridge contract, 190

Labouchere, Henry, and Free Trade, xxxviii
Labouchere, H., and the Talbot concession, 57
Laing, S., on consular fees, 385
Laissez-faire, attitude of H.M.G. to, xxx–xxxiv, 102–3, 415; economists and, xxxiii–xxxv; commercial men and, xxxv–xxxvii, 102; industry, the banks and, 24; government control of capital and, 28; and the bondholders, 51–52; and contracts and concessions, 54, 73; trade, H.M.G. and, 81, 353; effect of Depression on, 81–84; commercial diplomacy and, 102, 108; effect of foreign competition on, 141–2; survival of, 142; effect on policy in 'civilized' areas of, 151–2; in Turkey, 189; in China, 269n., 270–1, 278, 289–90; in Latin America, 346–7, 352; and British foreign policy, 360–2, 363, 367
Lambert, R. S., 5, 309
Land, in Greece, 71n.; in Latin America, 313, 333
Lang, Sir Hamilton, 198
Langer, W. L., 283
Lansdowne, Lord, on guaranteed loan to China, 15; and the bondholders, 50, 342–6; on debt-collecting, 138; on the Baghdad Railway, 211–12; on Persian trade, 243; on British policy in the Persian Gulf, 246–7
Larcom, Arthur, and Honduras bondholders, 49n.; on grievances against Venezuela, 340–1
Laski, Harold, 155, 254
Law, Algernon, on promotion of individual interests, 100n.; on commercial information, 117; on debt-collecting, 138
Law, Sir Edward Fitzgerald, and diplomatists' attitude to trade, xxiii–xxiv; and Greek finance, 12; and Turkish finance, 198

Law, Richard, on Foreign Service and trade, 395
Lawford, Valentine, on Commercial Diplomatic Service, 394–5
Lawson, H. L. W., 99
Lawyers, recommendation of, 120, 407, 409
Layard, Sir Henry, 74; on diplomatists' contempt for trade, xxvi–xxvii; and the Raikes charges, 75; on distinction between general and individual interests, 96; on commercial information, 115; on communications in Asiatic Turkey, 208; on British policy in China and Japan, 304; and claims against Latin American governments, 331
Lee, Sir Henry Austin, on diplomatists and trade, xvii; on 'touting' for trade, 133
Le May, G. H. L., 255
Lenin, V. I., 3, 5, 23–24, 30, 308
Levant Company, and Consular Service, xxiv–xxv, 383; end of monopoly, 182
Levi, Leone, on *laissez-faire*, xxxiv
Lindsay, Kenneth, on recruitment to Foreign Service, xxix
Lippmann, Walter, 219
Liquidation, Commission of (Egypt), formation of, 169; Salisbury on, 169–70; Malet and, 173
Liquidation, Law of, and British policy, 170; Gladstone and, 177
Lister, Sir V., on recommendation of lawyers, 120
Littlejohn, Robert, claim of, 139
Liverpool Chamber of Commerce, 392
Lloyd, Thomas, 127
Lloyds Bank, 303
Lloyd's (Insurance), consuls as agents for, 133–5
Loans, H.M.G. and, xviii, 7–33 *pass.*, 404–5; French, German and U.S. government control over, 7–9; consuls as agents for, 43–46, 135, 166, 252, 346; Turkish loans, 193, 194–5, *197–207*, 400–1; ;Persian loans, 229–30; Chinese loans, *269–70*, 271–2, *281–3*, 290, 293, *294–304*, 306–7; Latin American loans, 316, 331–2, 352, 400–1; Palmerston's 1848 Cicular on, 398–9
Loans (guaranteed), Palmerston and, 11; in Greece, 12; H.M.G. and, 13–17, 40; in Egypt, 179; in Turkey 199–207; in Morocco, 252; in China, 281–2; in Latin America, 316

Loans (tied), Committee on Industry and Trade on, 11; H.M.G. and, 21–23; City financiers and, 27–28; effect of rejection of, 28–29; in Latin America, 332, 352

Loans to Foreign States, Select Committee on, effect of Report, 334

London Chamber of Commerce, and foreign diplomatic pressure, 58; and contracts and concessions overseas, 72

London County and Westminster Bank, 303

Louis, Wm. R., 253–4

Lowe, C. J., 182, 184

Lowe, R., and commercial treaties, 89, 374

Lowther, Sir Gerard, and the Germans in Turkey, 192; and Turkish railways, 214

Lowther, James, and Talbot Concession, 57, 227; on concessions, 275–6

Lugard, F. J. D., on Scramble for Africa, 257–8

Luxemburg, Rosa, 154

Lynch, Messrs., 212, 215, 216–17

Lyons, Lord, and the Anglo-French Commercial Treaty, 88–89; and Egypt, 163; and concession-hunters at Constantinople, 186–7

MacDonald, Sir Claude, and the 'Battle of Concessions' in China, 61, 284–9, 297; on differential rates and privileges, 95; and the Indemnity Loan, 280, 281–3; and banking interests in China, 295–6

Macdonnell, Lord, on 'touting' for trade, 135

Macdonnell Commission, *see* Civil Service, Royal Commission on

Macedonian reforms, effect on British policy, 187, 188, 190n.; France and, 190

MacGregor, John, and Free Trade, xxxviii

Mackenzie, Sir George, 14, 232

Mackinnon, Sir William, 14, 232

McLaren, C. B. B., 18

Malay Peninsula, British policy in, 263

Malet, Sir Edward, and British policy in Egypt, 170–1, 172–4

Mallet, Sir Louis, and Free Trade, xxxviii; and the Commercial Treaties, 89, 373, 374; on Free Trade propaganda, 143; on Russian threat to India, 182; and the Commercial Department (Board of Trade), 374–5

Malmesbury, Lord, on the government's duty to trade, xv; on contract claims, 68n.; on equal opportunities in world trade, 86; and the Tehran Legation, 220; and British policy in Central America, 324; on U.S., Mexico, and the Monroe Doctrine, 348

Manchester Chamber of Commerce, on state intervention, xxxv–xxxvi; on commercial information, 112, 113; and the Congo, 261; and Commercial Agents, 392

Manchuria, 254; concessions in, 293–4

Mangles, Mr., contract claim by, 67

Maxwell, R. P., on Baghdad Railway, 215

Melville, E. H., and credit information, 122; and debt-collecting, 138

Mesopotamia, irrigation schemes in, 192–3, 195, 196–7; oil in, 195–7; British interests in, 216

Meugens, Consul, 134

Mexico, xiv; H.M.G. and bondholders in, 35, 52, 312, 334–6; bondholder agencies in, 45; contract claim against, 66n.; H.M.G. and oil in, 69, 71, 325–9; value of letter of introduction in, 127; Allied coercion of (1861–2), 309, 316–18, 347, 349; recognition of, 313; guaranteed loan to, 316; Malmesbury and U.S. annexation of, 348

Michell, John, on contracts and concessions, 56; on introductions, 130–1

Michell, Thomas, on contracts and concessions, 55; on introductions,130

Midland Bank, 303

Military Equipment Stores and Tortoise Tents Co., contract claim, 66n.

Milligan, Mr., and recommendation of agents, 119–20

Mills, in China, 64

Milner, Lord, on British policy in Egypt, 180; and the Boer War, 255; on imperial expansion, 358–9

Minas Central Railway Co., cancellation of concession of, 69n.

Mines, in China, 31, 62–63, 64, 267, 276, 286, 293, 295, 296, 306; in Latin America, 69, 127, 313, 319–20, 333; consuls as agents for, 135; in Turkey, 185, 189, 194, 217; in Persia, 234; in Morocco, 252; in Tibet, 262–3

Modern Egypt, 157, 165

Monopolies, in Britain, 23; and H.M.G. in Persia, 30–31; and

Monopolies, *continued*
 H.M.G. in Turkey, 31–32, 63; and
 H.M.G. in China, 31–33, 63,
 294–304; H.M.G.'s opposition to,
 93–95
Monroe Doctrine, and influence on
 British policy, 309, 347–51
Monson, Sir Edmund, on contracts
 and concessions, 55, 332–3
Montgomery, Nicod & Co., contract
 claim by, 66n.
Moon, P. T., 155
Morel, E. D., on Britain and West
 Africa, 258
Morgan, J. P. & Co., xviii
Morier, Sir Robert, on diplomatists
 and trade, xvi–xvii; on Rio legation,
 xxi; on promotion of individual
 interests, 55; on the Cobdenite
 commercial treaties, 144; on import-
 ance of China, 270; and F.O. and
 Board of Trade, 374–5
Morley, John, on imperial expansion,
 356
Morning Chronicle, 12
Morocco and German bankers, 7–8;
 H.M.G. and loans to, 14–15, 17,
 252; diplomatist as bondholder
 agent in, 44; commercial treaty
 with, 86; British policy in, 252;
 and N.W. African Co., 259–60
Morton, A. C., 57
Mosquito Indians, British protectorate
 of, 325
Most-favoured-nation clause, in
 Commercial Treaties, 86–92, 94;
 effects of, 147; in Latin American
 treaties, 315–16
Muharrem, Decree of, 206
Mundella, A. J., on government
 assistance to trade, 141; and Trade
 and Treaties Committee, 377–8
Munitions, xviii, 5; contract claim in
 Argentina, 27n.; and China,
 58–59; expropriation claim in
 Uruguay, 139; and Turkish
 contracts, 188, 190–1
Murray, James, on British policy
 in Latin America, 321–2
Museums (commercial), 126; 410–11
Musgrave, C. E., on contracts and
 concessions, 72n.; and consular
 reform, 386
Mustafa, A. A., 155–6

Nanking, Treaty of (1842), and
 opening of China, 86; and the
 opium trade, 265
Napoleon III, and the Anglo-French
 Commercial Treaty, 88

National Bank of Turkey, and
 H.M.G., 31–33; formation of,
 193–4; difficulties of, 194
National Provincial Bank, 303
Naval contracts, 190–1
Navigation Laws, 103
Naylor, Robert, 323
Netherlands, and Mexican contracts
 and concessions, 69
New Granada, *see* Colombia
Newton, Lord, 187
Nicaragua, H.M.G. and bondholders
 in, 47, 48n.; and Mosquito Indians,
 325
Nicolson, Sir Arthur, on guaranteed
 railways, 14; on concessions in
 Persia, 63–64, 237
Nicolson, Sir Harold, on diplomatists
 and bankers, xviii; on diplomatists'
 distaste for commerce, xxiv–xxv;
 on the Commercial Diplomatic
 Service, 394; on the Eden reforms,
 396
Nightingale, Robert, on aristocrats in
 diplomacy, xxvi
Nineteenth Century, 171, 184
Nitrate Railways, expropriation of, 70
Nitrates, in Chile, 70, 319–20; and
 the Peruvian bondholders, 45,
 337–9
Northcote, Sir Stafford, on British
 policy in Egypt, 159, 165, 168–9,
 170; on Turkish loans, 201
North-West African Co., and H.M.G.,
 259–60
Nubar Pasha, 166

O'Conor, Sir Nicholas, on difficulty
 of interesting capitalists in Turkey,
 26; on consuls and trade in China,
 104; on British policy in Turkey,
 188; on naval contracts in Turkey,
 191; and Sir Edward Law and the
 Ottoman Debt, 198–9; on the
 Baghdad Railway, 211; and
 financial diplomacy in China, 273,
 274–5
Oil, H.M.G. and (in Mexico), 69,
 71, 325–9; (in Mesopotamia)
 195–7; (in Persia) 69n., 71n.,
 239–42, 243
Olivier, Sidney, on partition of Africa,
 258
Olney, Richard, and the Monroe
 Doctrine, 350
Open Door, H.M.G. and, xviii, 85;
 and Commercial Treaties, 90–92;
 in Persia, 223, 237–8; in the
 Persian Gulf, 247–8; in Africa,
 256–7; in Tibet; 262–3 in S.E. Asia,

263; in China, 265, 267, 268, 270–1, 283, *290–5*, 304–7; in Latin America, 312–13, 315, 352
Opium, and India, 262; and H.M.G. in China, 262, 265
Orinoco Railway Co., cancellation of concession, 68
O'Shea, Mr., contract claim by, 67n.
Ottoman Public Debt, Administration of, 181; 198; 205–7
Overseas Trade, Department of, history of, 379–81; and Commercial Diplomatic Service, 393
Overstreet, H. A., 219

Page, Walter H., and U.S. policy in Mexico, 327–8; and H.M.G. in Mexico, 329
Palmerston, Lord, on British commercial interests, xiv; on H.M.G. and overseas loans, 11; warns Uruguayan investors, 12; refuses guaranteed loan to Turkey, 16, 199; on H.M.G. and the bondholders, 35–37, 48, 49, 398–9; and bondholder agencies, 44n.; on government and the merchant, 85; refuses to teminate Venezuelan Treaty, 91; on letters of introduction, 127–8; urges Free Trade on Buenos Aires, 143; on Turkish finance, 202–3; and Persia, 220; and Moroccan 1861 Loan, 252; on British intervention in the River Plate, 323; and colonial expansion, 356; and British policy in Egypt, 356
Panama, H.M.G. and the bondholders, 48
Paraguay, contract claims against, 68n.; H.M.G. and war in, 320
Parish, Frank, 134
Parker, Alwyn, on difficulty of interesting capital in Persia, 27; on Mesopotamian oil, 195–6; on Baghdad Railway, 215, 216; on Persian railway concessions, 238
Parkes, Sir Harry, and Eastern Telegraph loan, 43, 269; and policy in Japan, 267–8; and Hong Kong & Shanghai Bank, 269
Parr's Bank, 303
Parsons, F. V., 259–60
Patents, 126
Paulings, Messrs., and Chinese railway contracts, 297
Pauncefote, Sir Julian, on assistance to financiers in China, 17, 269; on foreign loans and contracts in China, 271–2; and the Peruvian bondholders, 337–8

Peel, Sir Robert, on British intervention in the River Plate, 322
Peking/Hankow railway, and H.M.G., 285–7
Peking Syndicate, and H.M.G., 31–33, 285, 294–6, 331
Pelcovits, N. A., 277
Peninsular & Oriental Steam Navigation Company, 217
Percy, Earl, on State credit for private undertakings overseas, 13; and Chinese railway concessions, 306
Persia, railways in, 14, 230–3, 238–9; difficulty of interesting capital in, 26–27; British policy in, 32–33, *219–44*, 357–68 *pass.*; H.M.G. and Reuter Concession for, 56; Commons and Talbot Concession for, 56–57; H.M.G. and Talbot Concession for, 57, 226–8; H.M.G. and concessions in, 63–64, 65, 225–8, 235–9; H.M.G. and oil in, 69n., 71n., 239–42, 243; commercial treaty with, 86; Russian policy in, 220–44 *pass.*; British and Russian trade in, 228–9; France and, 220, 236, 237; loans in, 229–30, 236–7; Germany and, 230–1, 236–9, 243–4; Anglo-Russian Convention (1907) for, 234–7, 244
Persian Bank Mining Rights Corporation, 228
Persian Gulf, British policy in, 101, 244–8, 358, 365; and Baghdad Railway, 211–17; communications from, 230, 231; Russia and, 244–7; Germany and, 244–8; foreign trade in, 245–6
Persian Railway Syndicate Ltd., 239
Persian Transport Company, 233
Peru, H.M.G. and bondholders in, 37n., 39, 42n., 44n., 47, 48, 49–50, *336–9*; consul as agent in, 134; coercion of, 347
Phillimore, Sir Robert, on contract claims, 67
Phillips, Samuel, and Co., contract claim by, 68n.
Philosophical Radicals, and colonial expansion, 355
Piraeus and Larissa Railway, contract claim by, 68n.
Plowden Committee, *see* Representational Services Overseas, Committee on
Plunkett, F., and German diplomatic pressure in Japan, 59, 272, 274–5
Plymouth, Earl of, on Mexican oil expropriation, 71
Port Arthur, lease of, 279, 280–1

Porter, George Richardson, and Free Trade, xxxviii
Portugal, Control in, 17; H.M.G. and bondholders in, 46n., 50; and Delagoa Bay Railway, 40n., 69, 70–71; contract claim against, 67n.; confiscation of property by, 71n.; Congo Treaty (1884) and, 257; and H.M.G. in Brazil, 313n., 315
Post Office, consuls as agents for, 133–5; and mail subsidies, 146
Pottinger, Sir Henry, 265
Pretyman, E. G., and Persian oil, 240
Primrose, Sir Henry, on consuls as commercial travellers, 135–6
Problems of the Far East, 288
Protection, British attitude to, xxxvii–xxxix, 360; renewed demand for, 83–84; Commercial Treaties and, 91–92; and colonial preference, 103; and sugar bounties, 145–6; and shipping subsidies, 146; and effect on policy in Africa, 256–61; diversion of British trade by, 220–1; as a factor in imperial expansion, 363–6
Prussian State Bank, 30
Puerto Rico, consul as agent in, 134
Punchard & Co., Messrs., contract claim by, 66n.

Railways, in Persia, 18, 26–27, 63–4, 226, 228, *230–3*, 234, 239, 243; in China, 21, 31, 58–9, 62, 100, 105, 267, 268–9, 274, 276, 280, *283–9*, 290, 291, 292, *294–8*, 301, 306; in Turkey, 26, 61–62, 68n., 94–95, 181, 187, 189, 190, 194, *207–17*; in Latin America, 29, 47, 66n., 67n., 69n., 70–71, 134, 319–20, 324, 333, 334, 340–1; in Africa, 40n., 69, 70–71, 255; in Eastern Europe, 55; in Tunisia, 250–1; in Morocco, 252; in Tibet and S.E. Asia, 262–3
Railways (guaranteed), H.M.G. and, 13–14; in Persia, 26–27, 231, 232, 239; in Turkey, 208–9
Rawson, R. W., and Free Trade, xxxviii, xxxix
Reciprocity of Duties Act, 86
Rees, J. D., 19
Representational Services Overseas, Committee on (Plowden Committee, 1963), on recruitment to Foreign Service, xxix—xxx; on commercial information, 125–6; on priority of commercial work, 395, 397
Reuter, Baron, 13, 231

Reuter Concession, H.M.G. and, 56, 231
Revelstoke, Lord, and Turkish Loan, 193; and Baghdad Railway, 211
Revenue duties, 146–7
Rhodes, Cecil, and Chamberlain, 5; and the Rothschilds, 5
Ricardo, J. L., and Turkish loan, 16
Ridley Commission, *see* Civil Establishments, Royal Commission on
River Plate, British intervention in, 319, 321–3
Roads, in Persia, 64, 228–9, 231, 233, 235, 236; in Morocco, 252; in Tibet, 262–3
Robbins, Lionel, 74, 254, 339–40
Robinson, R., on British policy in Africa, 253–60 pass., 357, 358, 363, 365; on H.M.G. and Latin America, 310–12, 316, 323; and the 'Imperialism of Free Trade', 360–2
Rodd, Sir Rennell, on concessions, 73
Rollit, Sir Albert, 83
Romania, xviii
Roosevelt, Theodore, and Monroe Doctrine, 349, 350–1
Root, J. W., on state interference, xxxv
Rosebery, Lord, and Rothschilds, 5; and bondholders, 38–39; and British interests in China, 59, 273–4, 275, 294–5; reacts to Depression, 82; on promotion of individual interests, 98–99; on *Board of Trade Journal*, 111–12; and Commercial Intelligence Committee, 112; on commercial information, 117–18; on credit information, 121
Rothschilds, and Rosebery, 5; and Rhodes, 5; and Gladstone, 74; and Egypt, 155, 166, 167; and Bismarck, 167; and Turkish loan, 193; and Chinese loans, 302–3
Rothstein, Theodore, 154, 159
Rowsell, Mr., and Daïra lands, 166
Royal Mail Steam Packet Co., consuls as agents of, 134–5
Russell, Lord John, on commercial information, 110; and Turkish 1862 Loan, 203; and Persia, 220; and Moroccan 1861 Loan, 252; and coercion of Mexico, 316–18; on consular fees, 385n.
Russell, Lord Odo, xx
Russia, and Greek finance, 12; and the Money Market, 14, 18; confiscation of property in, 71; and trading privileges in Turkey, 93; letter of introduction in, 128; debt-collecting in, 137–8; finance, trade,

and British policy in, 151–2; and the Straits, 181–2, 184, 220; threat to India of, 182; and policy in Persia, 220–44 *pass.*; trade in Persia of, 228–9; and the Persian Gulf, 244–7; and Tibet, 262–3; and Partition of China, 276–90 *pass.*; and Chinese finance, 293–4, 295, 301; and British foreign policy, 357–8

Russian State Bank, 30

Russo-Chinese Bank, and Russian Government, 281, 295; and the Hankow/Peking railway, 285, 286

Rylands, P., on debt-collecting, 137

Saigon, Treaty of (1874), 95

Salisbury, Lord, on guaranteed railways in China, 14; on International Control in Portugal, 17; on H.M.G.'s control over investment, 18–19; on British capital and Turkey, 26; on bankers' pressure in diplomacy, 32; and the bondholders, 39; and foreign diplomatic pressure in China, 59; on remonstrances against tariffs, 144; and Rothschilds in Egypt, 166; and Egyptian bondholders, 167; on policy in Egypt, 168, 169–70, 170–1, 179; and policy in Turkey, 187; on Turkish bondholders, 207; on guaranteed railway to Baghdad, 208–9; suggests partition of Persia (1888), 224; on policy in Persia, 225; supports Imperial Bank of Persia, 226; on Persian railways, 231; on Partition of Africa, 258–9, 364; on importance of China, 270; and commercial diplomacy in China, 272, 273; on Russia in China, 278, 280–1; and the Chinese Indemnity Loan, 281–2; on Chinese railways, 289; and the Open Door in China, 290–1; on non-intervention in Latin America, 319; and the Peruvian bondholders, 337, 339; and the Monroe Doctrine, 348–9; and Protection as a motive for imperial expansion, 364, 365–6

Samuel & Co., Messrs., and Chinese railway contracts, 297

Sanderson, Sir J. H., on credit information, 122

Sassoon, E. D., & Co., and Chinese loans, 299–300

Satow, Harold, on 'touting' for trade, 133

Schroders, and Chinese loans, 299–304

Schutze, Mr., 128

Schwabe, E. Salis, 128

Secret History of the English Occupation of Egypt, 154

Selborne, 1st. Earl of, 178

Selborne, 2nd. Earl of, 240

Seligman, Messrs., and Persian loans, 31

Seton-Watson, Hugh, 254

Seward, Wm. H., and European coercion in Latin America, 349

Seymour, Sir Beauchamp, 175

Shanghai Chamber of Commerce, 268

Shanghai/Nanking Railway, 284, 285, 287

Shantung, and Germany, 21

Shantung Agreement, 21

Shaw-Lefevre, Sir John, and Free Trade, xxxviii

Shepard, Clarence, 129

Shipping, in China, 64, 293; subsidies, 103–4, 146; competitiveness of British, 107; consuls as agents for, 133–4; and the Suez Canal, 156–7, 172; in Asiatic Turkey, 212, 215, 216–17; in Persia, 225, 230, 232, 233, 236; in the Persian Gulf, 244–8 *pass.*; and claims against Venezuela, 340–3 *pass.*; consular duties towards, 409. *See also* Steamship Subsidies, Select Committee on

Shipping and Shipbuilding, Departmental Committee on (1918), on government intervention, xxxii

Siam, British policy in, 263, 264, 277n.; Consular Service in, 383, 385

Sicilies, Two, Kingdom of, contract claim against, 66n., 67n., 70

Sinclair, L., on foreign competition, 141

Smith, Adam, on the functions of the State, xxxiii–xxxiv; and national security, 103–4

Smith, Sir Henry Babington, and the National Bank of Turkey, 194; and the Ottoman Debt, 198

Smith, Sir Hubert Llewellyn, on commercial information, 117; on F.O. and Board of Trade, 372–3, 376; on Commercial Attachés, 388–9

Smyrna/Aidin Railway, 207, 215

Société Agricole et Industrielle d'Egypte, 94

Souvazoglu, Theodore, 127

Spain, H.M.G. and bondholders in, 35, 36, 37n., 49; contract claim against, 67n.; and British policy in Morocco, 252; and trading privileges in Latin America, 312–13; and coercion of Mexico, 316–18

Spring-Rice, Sir Cecil, on the Anglo-Russian Convention (Persia), 234-5

Stacey, Vice-Consul, 134

Staley, Eugene, 5, 28, 249-50, 254, 259

Standard Oil, 242

Stanley, G. E., on concessions, 55

Stanley, Lord, *see* Derby, Earl of

State Aid and State Interference, xxxiv

State in its Relation to Trade, The, xxx, 103

Stationery Office, Controller of, on under-use of government statistics, 111

Status information, *see* Credit information

Steamship Subsidies, Select Committee on (1901-2), 103, 145, 146; on State interference, xxxii, xxxvi; on official optimism, 107; and consular reports, 124

Sternberg, Fritz, 309

Stewart-Smith, D. G., 97

Strachey, John, and the bondholders, 51; on British policy in Egypt, 154, 157, 179-80; on the Boer War, 254; on the Anglo-Chinese Wars, 265; and H.M.G. in Latin America, 309; on the Monroe Doctrine, 309, 347, 351

Straits, The, and international interest in Turkey, 181-4, 197

Strang, Lord, 310n., 353

Strathcona, Lord, 240

Stronge, Francis, and Cowdray in Mexico, 327

Suez Canal, importance of, 156-7; H.M.G. and, 163, 176, 179-80; Disraeli and, 171n.; Gladstone and, 172, 179; Dilke and, 175-6; and British policy in Africa, 253-6, 260

Sugar Bounties, Board of Trade and, 102-3; Brussels Sugar Convention and, 145-6. *See also* Bounties

Sumner, B. H., 236

Survey of Export Trade Facilities, on officials as salesmen, 136

Sweezy, Paul, M., 5

Taft, Wm. H., and overseas investment, 8-9, 326

Talbot Concession, Commons and, 56-57, 61; H.M.G. and, 57, 226-8

Tarapacá, and the Peruvian Debt, 48, 337-9

Tariffs, Britain and, xxxvii-xxxix, 223; Cobdenite Treaties and, 144; objections to retaliation against, 144-7

Taylor, A. J. P., 253

Tel el Kebir, 165, 177

Telegraphs, in China, 43, 269; in Persia, 64, 219, 233, 236, 238; and commercial information, 147, 148; in Tibet, 262-3; in Latin America, 330

Tenterden, Lord, on contract claims, 68; on Turkish 1862 Loan, 204

Tewfik, Khedive, 167

Thiers, Adolphe, and the Anglo-French Commercial Treaty, 88-89

Thomson, Charles E. Poulett, and Free Trade, xxxviii, 372; on commercial information, 109

Thornton, A. P., 181, 199, 205

Thornton, Sir Edward, and Argentine railways, 134; and war in the River Plate, 320

Tibet, and H.M.G., 262-3

Tientsin, Treaty of (1858), 86

Tientsin, Treaty of (1885), 95, 265, 268; and Partition of China, 271, 276

Tientsin/Chinkiang Railway, 287

Tilley, Sir John, on the F.O. and trade, xix; on the Consular Service, 383, 386

Times, on diplomatists' contempt for trade, xxi, xxiii; on commercial diplomacy in the Far East, 57, 273; on Bryce's Memorandum, 274; on 'tied' loans in Latin America, 332

Tobacco, and the Talbot Concession, 226-8

Trade, and distinction between respectable and other traders, xix, 333, 402; distinction between individual and general interests, xix-xx, xxxvi-xxxvii, 54, *95-101*, 135, 141, 268, 294, 392-3; distinction between assistance to in civilized and semi-civilized nations, 55-6, 58, 151-3, 267, 363; 'touting' for, by consuls, 132-6; optimism as to competitiveness of British, 104-8

Trade, Select Committee on Foreign, on *laissez-faire*, xxx

Trade and Treaties Committee, and commercial intelligence, 377-8

Trade Commissioners, 278, 381

Trade with Foreign Nations, Select Committee on, and F.O. and Board of Trade, 373-4

Trans-Persian Railway, H.M.G. and, 18, 238

Trans-Siberian Railway, 276, 279, 280, 281

Index

Index

Treasury, on guaranteed railways, 13; and control over foreign issues, 20–22; and Egypt, 158, 163; on Turkish 1854 Loan, 201; on the Venezuelan bondholders' Agreement, 345, 346

Trevelyan, Sir G., 57

Tripoli, 254

Tunis/La Goletta Railway, 250

Tunisia, difficulty of interesting capitalists in, 26; British policy in, 249–52

Turkey, and French capital, 8; and railways, 13, 26, 61–62, 181, 187, 189, 190, 194, *207–17*; guaranteed loans to, 15–16, 199–207; and Turkish loans, 19, 193, 194–5, *197–207*, 400–1; difficulty of interesting capitalists in, 26, 193–4, 210; British policy in, 32–33, *181–218*, 358–68 *pass.*; H.M.G. and bondholders in, 34, 37n., 39–40, 47, *197–207*, 400–1; concessions in, 61–63, 65, 186–97 *pass.*, 209–10, 214, 217–18; contract claims against, 68n.; commercial treaties with, 86, 90, 93; Capitulations and tariffs in, 90–91; monopolies in, 93; 'touting' for trade in, 133; debt-collecting in, 136–7, 186; and Egypt, 156, 167–8, 177; German trade in, 184–5; French finance in, 185, 189, 195; German policy in, 188, 189–90; French policy in, 190; contracts in, 190–2, 196–7, 217–18; Consular Service in, 186, 383, 386

Turkish Petroleum Company, 196

Twiss, Sir Travers, on contract claims, 67n.

Tyrrell, Sir William, on F.O. and loan flotations, 19; on H.M.G. and oil in Mexico, 326

Uitlanders, 255–6

United States of America, control over capital exports from, 8–9; H.M.G. and State bondholders in, 42; and Chinese contracts and concessions, 59, 272–3, 274; and H.M.G. in Mexico, 69, 325–9; trade and foreign policy in, 101; competition of, 104–8, 313, 366; and commercial information, 113, 406; and credit information, 121–2; and defence of citizens abroad, 137; influence of finance and trade on British policy in, 151–2; and Open Door in China, 290–4; and bankers in China, 298, 301; and the Chinese Loan Consortium, 301–4; and

the Monroe Doctrine, 309, 347–51; and H.M.G. in Central America, 323–5; and the coercion of Venezuela (1902–3), 340, 343, 344, 346; and influence on British foreign policy, 364–8 *pass.*

Uruguay, confiscation claim against, 70; debt-collecting in, 139; H.M.G. and intervention in, 319, 320, 321–3

Vansittart, Lord, on priorities in F.O., xx; on diplomatic posts in Latin America, xxi; on German commercial competition, 367

Venezuela, H.M.G. and the bondholders in, 37, 39, 40, 46, 47, 50, 52–53, 336n., *339–46*, 400–1; contract claim against, 67n.; cancellation of concessions by, 68; H.M.G. refuses to terminate treaty with, 91–92; and Allied coercion of (1902–3), 308, 309, 339–40; foreign coercion of, 330–31, 347, 349; Boundary Dispute of, 348–9

Venezuela-Panama Gold Mine Co., cancellation of concession of, 68

Viallate, Achille, 10, 308–9

Villiers, F. H., on the Venezuelan bondholders, 341, 342, 345

Villiers, H. Montagu, on the Dept. of Overseas Trade, 380n.

Vincent, Sir Edgar (Lord D'Abernon), and Ottoman Public Debt, 198; Mission to Latin America of, 331

Viner, Jacob, 10, 30, 198, 299

Vivian, C., introduces Goschen to Khedive, 160; urges intervention in Egypt, 162–3

Waddington, W., on Anglo-French cooperation in Egypt, 163

Wallas, Graham, on consuls as commercial travellers, 135

Walpole, Sir Spencer, and *laissez-faire*, xxxi in.

Walrond Committee, see Consular Service, Departmental Committee on (1903)

Walton, Joseph, on Consular Service, 113; on British policy in Persia, 228–9; on F.O. and Board of Trade, 376–7

Ward, William, on consuls as agents, 132

Waring Bros., Messrs., contract claim by, 67

Waterway treaties, 126

Watherston, Edward J., on commercial information, 111

Webster, Sir Charles, 181–2
Wei-hai-Wei, lease of, 280, 281
West Indies, and sugar bounties, 102–3; value of letter of introduction in, 127; and British policy in Central America, 323–4
Whigham, H. J., on British capital in Persia, 26; on German competition in the Persian Gulf, 247
White, Sir William, and Rio Legation, xxi; on promotion from Consular to Diplomatic Service, xxv–xxvi; and Turkish railways, 209–10; on British policy in Turkey, 358
Whitley, E., on commercial depression, 82
Whittall, J. W., on British policy in Turkey, 188–9
Willcocks, Sir William, and irrigation scheme in Mesopotamia, 192
Wilson, Sir Arnold, and Persian railways, 230–1, 239; on H.M.G. and Persian oil, 241
Wilson, Belford H., 41
Wilson, Sir Charles Rivers, 164, 166, 169
Wilson, Huntingdon, and control over U.S. investment, 9
Wilson, Woodrow, and overseas investment, 9; and policy in Mexico, 326–9
Winterbotham, A. B., 57

Winterton, Earl, on 'tied' loans, 29
Wolff, Sir Henry Drummond, 74, 252; and British policy in Persia, 225, 242–3; and the Talbot concession, 227; and the D'Arcy concession, 239
Wolseley, Sir Garnet, 165, 177
Wönckhaus, Herr, on Germany in the Persian Gulf, 247–8
Wood, Richard, and failure to interest capitalists in Tunisia, 26; and British policy in Tunis, 250–2
Woolf, Leonard, 5, 249, 253, 363
Worthington Mission, 331
Wright, Mr., contract claim against Kingdom of the Two Sicilies by, 66n., 67n.
Wright, Whitaker, 74
Wyke, Sir Charles, and British policy in Mexico, 316–18

Yalu River, 254
Yang-tsze Valley, as the British sphere, 282, 283, 306; development of, 283–9; concessions in, 291–4
Young, George, on F.O. and Board of Trade, 376
Young Turk Revolution, effect on British interests, 26, 192–7, 214
Younghusband, Francis, and Tibet, 262